Lecture Notes in Computer Scien

Commenced Publication in 1973
Founding and Former Series Editors:
Gerhard Goos, Juris Hartmanis, and Jan van Leeuwen

Klaus Miesenberger Arthur Karshmer
Petr Penaz Wolfgang Zagler (Eds.)

Computers Helping People with Special Needs

13th International Conference, ICCHP 2012
Linz, Austria, July 11-13, 2012
Proceedings, Part I

 Springer

Volume Editors

Klaus Miesenberger
Universität Linz, Institut Integriert Studieren
Altenbergerstraße 69, 4040 Linz, Austria
E-mail: klaus.miesenberger@jku.at

Arthur Karshmer
University of San Francisco
2130 Fulton St., San Francisco, CA 94117, USA
E-mail: arthur@lakeland.usf.edu

Petr Penaz
Masaryk University, Support Centre for Students with Special Needs
Botanická 68A, 602 00 Brno, Czech Republic
E-mail: penaz@fi.muni.cz

Wolfgang Zagler
Vienna University of Technology, Institute "Integriert Studieren"
Favoritenstr. 11/029, 1040 Vienna, Austria
E-mail: zw@fortec.tuwien.ac.at

ISSN 0302-9743   e-ISSN 1611-3349
ISBN 978-3-642-31521-3   e-ISBN 978-3-642-31522-0
DOI 10.1007/978-3-642-31522-0
Springer Heidelberg Dordrecht London New York

Library of Congress Control Number: 2012940983

CR Subject Classification (1998): K.4.2, H.5.2-3, H.5, H.4, K.3, H.3, J.3

LNCS Sublibrary: SL 3 – Information Systems and Application, incl. Internet/Web
and HCI

Typesetting: Camera-ready by author, data conversion by Scientific Publishing Services, Chennai, India

Printed on acid-free paper

Springer is part of Springer Science+Business Media (www.springer.com)

Preface

Welcome to the ICCHP 2012 Proceedings

The information society is moving towards eAccessibility and eInclusion around the world, facilitated by better and user-friendlier assistive technologies. Research and development are important drivers in moving the sector forward and also in implementing accessibility as a key feature of today's mainstream systems and services. Evidence of this trend can be seen in new

July 11-13, 2012
Pre-conference July 9-10

International Conference on Computers
Helping People with Special Needs
Johannes Kepler University Linz

free and commercial products, such as screenreader software, working seamlessly on all up-to-date smartphones, pads and tablets.

ICCHP is proud of being an active force in this process since the 1980s. Scientific conferences, besides showcasing the newest ideas and developments, facilitate exchange and cooperation. They are indispensable ingredients of innovation and progress.

This year, as in the past, we are proud to welcome more than 500 participants from over 50 countries from around the world; 112 experts selected 147 full and 42 short papers out of 364 abstracts submitted to ICCHP. They form the core of the program of ICCHP 2012. Each paper was reviewed by three expert reviewers and every submission was then further evaluated in a meeting of the international Program Committee. The acceptance ratio of about 50% of the submissions demonstrates our strict pursuit of scientific quality both of the program and in particular of the proceedings in your hands.

The concept of organizing "Special Thematic Sessions" helped to structure the proceedings and program. The process supports focusing on selected topics of high interest in the field as well as bringing new and interesting topics to the attention of the research community. This approach makes the 13th edition of ICCHP proceedings a valued and interesting contribution to the state of the art and a reference in our domain of study.

ICCHP, for the first time, features and includes the conference "Universal Learning Design (ULD)." This part of the ICCHP program invites experienced practitioners and users to present their ideas, problems, experiences and concepts in an open forum, allowing us to learn from and advance our work based on experience and best practice. Most of these contributions are of a practical nature and are therefore included in a special publication of the ULD hosting partner Masaryk University Brno, Czech Republic. We recommend referring to them when reading these proceedings. With ULD, ICCHP will advance more rapidly towards a platform facilitating the exchange and cooperation of a diverse set of stakeholders allowing deeper and more sustainable impact.

ULD complements ICCHP very well. Together with the "Young Researchers Consortium", the "Summer University on Math, Science and Statistics for Blind and Partially Sighted Students", the finals of the international coding event "SS12 – Project:Possibility", intensive workshops, meetings and an exhibition including presentations and demonstrations of major software and assistive technology producers and vendors, ICCHP will once again be the international meeting place and center of advanced information exchange.

ICCHP 2012 is held under the auspices of Dr. Heinz Fischer, President of the Federal Republic of Austria, an honorable Committee of Honor and under the patronage of the United Nations Educational, Scientific and Cultural Organization (UNESCO), and of the European Disability Forum (EDF).

We thank the Austrian Computer Society for announcing and sponsoring the ICCHP Roland Wagner Award, endowed in 2001 in honor of Roland Wagner, the founder of ICCHP.

Former Award Winners:

- Award 5: Handed over at ICCHP 2010 in Vienna to:
    - Harry Murphy - Founder, Former Director and Member of Advisory Board of the Centre on Disabilities, USA
    - Joachim Klaus - Founder, Former Director of the Study Centre for the Visually Impaired at Karlsruhe Institute of Technology (SZS - KIT), Germany
- Award 4: George Kersher, Daisy Consortium, ICCHP 2008 in Linz
- *Special Award 2006:* Roland Traunmüller, University of Linz
- Award 3: Larry Scadden, National Science Foundation, ICCHP 2006 in Linz
- Award 2: Paul Blenkhorn, University of Manchester, ICCHP 2004 in Paris
- *Special Award 2003:* A Min Tjoa, Vienna University of Technology
- Award 1: WAI-W3C, ICCHP 2002 in Linz
- Award 0: Prof. Roland Wagner on the occasion of his 50th birthday, 2001

Once again we thank everyone for helping with putting ICCHP in place and thereby supporting the AT field and a better quality of life for people with disabilities.

Special thanks go to all our sponsors and supporters.

July 2012

Klaus Miesenberger
Arthur Karshmer
Petr Penaz
Wolfgang Zagler

Organization

ICCHP 2012 General Chair

A. Karshmer	University of San Francisco, USA

Program Board

D. Burger	INSERM, France
J. Klaus	Karlsruhe Institute of Technology (KIT), Germany
H. Murphy	California State University, Northridge, USA
M. Suzuki	Kyushu University, Japan
A.M. Tjoa	Vienna University of Technology, Austria
R. Wagner	University of Linz, Austria

Program and Publishing Chairs

K. Miesenberger	University of Linz, Austria
W. Zagler	Vienna University of Technology, Austria
P. Penaz	Masaryk University Brno, Czech Republic

Young Researchers Consortium Chairs

D. Archambault	Université Paris 8, France
D. Fels	Ryerson University, Canada
D. Fitzpatrick	Dublin City University, Ireland
M. Kobayashi	Tsukuba College of Technology, Japan
M. Morandell	AIT Austrian Institute of Technology GmbH, Austria
E. Pontelli	New Mexico State University, USA
S. Trewin	IBM, USA
G. Weber	Technische Universität Dresden, Germany

Workshop Program Chair

F. Pühretmair	KI-I, Austria

Program Committee

J. Abascal	Euskal Herriko Unibertsitatea, Spain
C. Abbott	King's College London, UK
S. Abou-Zahra	W3C Web Accessibility Initiative (WAI), Austria
A. Abu-Ali	Philadelphia University, Jordan
I. Abu Doush	Yarmouk University, Jordan
R. Andrich	Polo Tecnologico Fondazione Don Carlo Gnocchi Onlus, Italy
A. Arató	KFKI-RMKI, Hungary
P. Arató	TU Budapest, Hungary
L. Azevedo	Instituto Superior Tecnico, Portugal
M. Batusic	University of Linz, Austria
C. Bernareggi	Università degli Studi di Milano, Italy
I. Bosse	Technische Universität Dortmund, Germany
H.-H. Bothe	Hochschule für Technik und Wirtschaft Berlin, Germany
J. Bu	Zhejiang University, China
C. Bühler	TU Dortmund University, FTB, Germany
J. Coughlan	Smith-Kettlewell Eye Research Institute, USA
G. Craddock	Centre for Excellence in Universal Design, Ireland
D. Crombie	Utrecht School of the Arts, The Netherlands
H. Cui	China Disabled Persons' Federation, China
M. Cummins Prager	California State University Northridge, USA
A. Darvishy	Zurich University for Applied Sciences, Switzerland
J. Darzentas	University of the Aegean, Greece
M. Debeljak	University of Ljubljana, Slovenia
F. DeRuyter	Duke University Medical Centre, USA
R. Diaz del Campo	Antarq Tecnosoluciones, Mexico
A.D.N. Edwards	University of York, UK
P.L. Emiliani	Institute of Applied Physics "Nello Carrara", Italy
J. Engelen	Katholieke Universiteit Leuven, Belgium
G. Evreinov	University of Tampere, Finland
Ch. Galinski	InfoTerm, Austria
J. Gardner	Oregon State University, USA
G.-J. Gelderblom	Zuyd University, The Netherlands
V. Hanson	University of Dundee, UK
S. Harper	University of Manchester, UK
A. Holzinger	Medical University of Graz, Austria
E.-J. Hoogerwerf	AIAS Bologna, Italy
T. Inoue	The National Rehabilitation Center for Persons with Disabilities, Japan

M. Jemni	University of Tunis, Tunisia
L. Kalinnikova	Pomor State University, Russia
A. Koronios	University of South Australia, Australia
G. Kouroupetroglou	University of Athens, Greece
W. Kremser	OCG, HSM, Austria
V. Lauruska	Siauliai University, Lithuania
D. Leahy	Trinity College Dublin, Ireland
A. Leblois	G3ict, USA
M. Magnussen	Stockholm University, Sweden
R. Manduchi	University of California at Santa Cruz, USA
K. Matausch	KI-I, Austria
N.-E. Mathiassen	Danish Centre for Assistive Technology, Denmark
Ch. Mayer	Austrian Institute of Technology, Austria
E. Mendelova	Comenius University of Bratislava, Slovak Republic
Y. Mohamad	Fraunhofer Institute for Applied Information Technology, Germany
H. Neveryd	Lund University, Sweden
L. Normie	GeronTech - The Israeli Center for Assistive Technology & Aging, Israel
G. Nussbaum	KI-I, Austria
T. Ono	Tsukuba University of Technology, Japan
M. Paciello	The Paciello Group, USA
P. Panek	Vienna University of Technology, Austria
P. Penaz	University of Brno, Czech Republic
H. Petrie	University of York, UK
A. Petz	University of Linz, Austria
G. Quirchmayr	University of Vienna, Austria
R. Raisamo	University of Tampere, Finland
D. Rice	National Disability Authority, Ireland
A. Salminen	KELA, Finland
C. Sik Lányi	University of Pannonia, Hungary
D. Simsik	University of Kosice, Slovak Republic
D. Sloan	University of Dundee, UK
M. Snaprud	University of Agder, Norway
C. Stephanidis	University of Crete, FORTH-ICS, Greece
R. Stiefelhagen	Karlsruhe Institute of Technology, Germany
B. Stoeger	University of Linz, Austria
Ch. Strauss	University of Vienna, Austria
O. Suweda	The Hyogo Institute of Assistive Technology, Japan
Y. Takahashi	Toyo University, Japan
M. Tauber	University of Paderborn, Germany
R. Traunmüller	University of Linz, Austria
P. Trehin	World Autism Organisation, France

J. Treviranus	University of Toronto, Canada
E. Vlachogiannis	Fraunhofer Institute for Applied Information Technology, Germany
C.A. Velasco	Fraunhofer Institute for Applied Information Technology, Germany
N. Vigouroux	IRIT Toulouse, France
K. Votis	CERTH/ITI, Greece
G. Wagner	Upper Austria University of Applied Sciences, Austria
H. Weber	ITA, University of Kaiserslautern, Germany
J. Weisman	Rehab Technology Service, USA
W. Wöß	University of Linz, Austria

Organising Committee

Austrian Computer Society (OCG), Masaryk University (MU),
Johannes Kepler University of Linz (JKU)

Bieber, R. (OCG, CEO)
Damm, Ch. (MU)
Feichtenschlager, P. (JKU)
Göbl, R. (OCG, President)
Heumader, P. (JKU)
Kremser, W. (OCG, Working Group ICT with/for People with Disabilities)
Miesenberger, K. (JKU)
Ossmann, R. (JKU)
Penaz, P. (MU)
Petz, A. (JKU)
Pölzer, S. (JKU)
Schult, Ch. (JKU)
Wagner, R. (JKU)
Zylinski, I. (JKU)

Table of Contents – Part I

ULD - Universal Learning Design

Towards a Visual Speech Learning System for the Deaf by Matching
Dynamic Lip Shapes 1
  Shizhi Chen, D. Michael Quintian, and Yingli Tian

Teaching Support Software for Hearing Impaired Students Who Study
Computer Operation SynchroniZed Key Points Indication Tool:
SZKIT 10
  Makoto Kobayashi, Takuya Suzuki, and Daisuke Wakatsuki

The Hybrid Book - One Document for All in the Latest Development ... 18
  Petr Hladík and Tomáš Gůra

Dealing with Changes in Supporting Students with Disabilities in
Higher Education 25
  Andrea Petz and Klaus Miesenberger

Putting the Disabled Student in Charge: User Focused Technology in Education

Putting the Disabled Student in Charge: Introduction to the Special
Thematic Session 33
  Lisa Featherstone and Simon Ball

Biblus – A Digital Library to Support Integration of Visually Impaired
in Mainstream Education 36
  Lars Ballieu Christensen and Tanja Stevns

Alternative Approaches to Alternative Formats – Changing
Expectations by Challenging Myths 43
  Alistair McNaught and Lisa Featherstone

Access Toolkit for Education 51
  Mike Wald, E.A. Draffan, Russell Newman, Sebastian Skuse, and
  Chris Phethean

Community-Based Participatory Approach: Students as Partners in
Educational Accessible Technology Research 59
  Poorna Kushalnagar, Benjamin Williams, and Raja S. Kushalnagar

Applying New Interaction Paradigms to the Education of Children
with Special Educational Needs 65
    *Paloma Cantón, Ángel L. González, Gonzalo Mariscal, and
    Carlos Ruiz*

InStep: A Video Database Assessment Tool 73
    Fern Faux, David Finch, and Lisa Featherstone

SCRIBE: A Model for Implementing Robobraille in a Higher Education
Institution 77
    Lars Ballieu Christensen, Sean J. Keegan, and Tanja Stevns

Identifying Barriers to Collaborative Learning for the Blind 84
    Wiebke Köhlmann

Deaf and Hearing Students' Eye Gaze Collaboration 92
    Raja S. Kushalnagar, Poorna Kushalnagar, and Jeffrey B. Pelz

The Musibraille Project – Enabling the Inclusion of Blind Students in
Music Courses 100
    José Antonio Borges and Dolores Tomé

Important New Enhancements to Inclusive Learning Using Recorded
Lectures 108
    Mike Wald

Development of New Auditory Testing Media with Invisible
2-Dimensional Codes for Test-Takers with Print Disabilities 116
    *Mamoru Fujiyoshi, Akio Fujiyoshi, Akiko Ohsawa,
    Toshiaki Aomatsu, and Haruhiko Sawazaki*

Access to Mathematics and Science

More Accessible Math: The LEAN Math Notation 124
    John Gardner and Courtney Christensen

Accessible Authoring Tool for DAISY Ranging from Mathematics to
Others 130
    Katsuhito Yamaguchi and Masakazu Suzuki

Blind Friendly LaTeX: An Option for Adapting Electronic Documents
Containing Mathematical Text 138
    Wanda Gonzúrová and Pavel Hrabák

A System for Matching Mathematical Formulas Spoken during a
Lecture with Those Displayed on the Screen for Use in Remote
Transcription 142
    *Yoshinori Takeuchi, Hironori Kawaguchi, Noboru Ohnishi,
    Daisuke Wakatsuki, and Hiroki Minagawa*

Supporting Braille Learning and Uses by Adapting Transcription to
User's Needs 150
Bruno Mascret, Alain Mille, and Vivien Guillet

A Non-visual Electronic Workspace for Learning Algebra.............. 158
Nancy Alajarmeh and Enrico Pontelli

Interaction Design for the Resolution of Linear Equations in a
Multimodal Interface 166
Silvia Fajardo-Flores and Dominique Archambault

Development of Software for Automatic Creation of Embossed
Graphs: Comparison of Non-visual Data Presentation Methods and
Development Up-to-date 174
Tetsuya Watanabe, Toshimitsu Yamaguchi, and Masaki Nakagawa

Expression Rules of Directed Graphs for Non-visual Communication.... 182
Ryoji Fukuda

How to Make Unified Modeling Language Diagrams Accessible for
Blind Students 186
Karin Müller

AutOMathic Blocks Usability Testing Phase One 191
Yonatan Breiter, Arthur Karshmer, and Judith Karshmer

MathInBraille Online Converter 196
*Klaus Miesenberger, Mario Batusic, Peter Heumader, and
Bernhard Stöger*

The Effects of Teaching Mathematics to Students with Disabilities
Using Multimedia Computer-Assisted Instruction Coupled with ARCS
Model 204
Chen-Tang Hou and Chu-Lung Wu

Policy and Service Provision

Information Needs Related to ICT-Based Assistive Solutions 207
Renzo Andrich, Valerio Gower, and Sabrina Vincenti

The European Assistive Technology Information Portal (EASTIN):
Improving Usability through Language Technologies 215
*Valerio Gower, Renzo Andrich, Andrea Agnoletto,
Petra Winkelmann, Thomas Lyhne, Roberts Rozis, and
Gregor Thurmair*

Use of Assistive Technology in Workplaces of Employees with Physical
and Cognitive Disabilities 223
Kirsi Jääskeläinen and Nina Nevala

Multimodal Guidance System for Improving Manual Skills in Disabled
People   227
  Mario Covarrubias, Elia Gatti, Alessandro Mansutti,
  Monica Bordegoni, and Umberto Cugini

Identifying Barriers to Accessibility in Qatar   235
  Erik Zetterström

NCBI and Digital Literacy: A Case Study   243
  Denise Leahy and Stuart Lawler

CDI - Creative Design for Inclusion

A User-Friendly Virtual Guide for Post-Rehabilitation Support
Following Stroke   251
  Sascha Sommer, Matthias Bartels, Martina Frießem, and
  Joachim Zülch

Musicking Tangibles for Empowerment   254
  Birgitta Cappelen and Anders-Petter Andersson

RHYME: Musicking for All   262
  Harald Holone and Jo Herstad

Enhancing Audio Description: A Value Added Approach   270
  Jack Sade, Komal Naz, and Malgorzata Plaza

Triple Helix – In Action?   278
  Niels Henrik Helms and Susanne Tellerup

Virtual User Models for Designing and Using Inclusive Products

Virtual User Models for Designing and Using of Inclusive Products:
Introduction to the Special Thematic Session   284
  Yehya Mohamad, Manfred Dangelmaier, Matthias Peissner,
  Pradipta Biswas, and Carlos A. Velasco

Creative Design for Inclusion Using Virtual User Models   288
  Markus Modzelewski, Michael Lawo, Pierre Kirisci,
  Joshue O. Connor, Antoinette Fennell, Yehya Mohamad,
  Svetlana Matiouk, Markus Valle-Klann, and Haluk Gökmen

A Methodology for Generating Virtual User Models of Elderly and
Disabled for the Accessibility Assessment of New Products   295
  Nikolaos Kaklanis, Konstantinos Moustakas, and Dimitrios Tzovaras

VERITAS Approach for Parameterization of Psychological and
Behavioral Models 303
*Ana María Navarro, Juan Bautista Mocholí, and
Juan Carlos Naranjo*

Integration of a Regular Application into a User Interface Adaptation
Engine in the MyUI Project 311
*Alejandro García, Jesús Sánchez, Víctor Sánchez, and
José Alberto Hernández*

Using Annotated Task Models for Accessibility Evaluation 315
Ivo Malý, Jiří Bittner, and Pavel Slavík

Web Accessibility in Advanced Technologies

Web Accessibility in Advanced Technologies: Introduction to the
Special Thematic Session 323
Shadi Abou-Zahra, Konstantinos Votis, and Karel Van Isacker

The eAccess+ Network: Enhancing the Take-Up of eAccessibility in
Europe 325
*Klaus Miesenberger, Eric Velleman, David Crombie, Helen Petrie,
Jenny S. Darzentas, and Carlos A. Velasco*

A Method for Generating CSS to Improve Web Accessibility for Old
Users 329
Jesia Zakraoui and Wolfgang Zagler

Implementing Web Accessibility: The MIPAW Approach 337
*Jean-Pierre Villain, Olivier Nourry, Dominique Burger, and
Denis Boulay*

Accessibility of Dynamic Adaptive Web TV Applications 343
Daniel Costa, Nádia Fernandes, Carlos Duarte, and Luís Carriço

Ontology Based Middleware for Ranking and Retrieving Information
on Locations Adapted for People with Special Needs 351
Kevin Alonso, Naiara Aginako, Javier Lozano, and Igor G. Olaizola

Automatic Color Improvement of Web Pages with Time Limited
Operators 355
Sébastien Aupetit, Alina Mereuţă, and Mohamed Slimane

Improving Web Accessibility for Dichromat Users through Contrast
Preservation 363
Alina Mereuţă, Sébastien Aupetit, and Mohamed Slimane

Sociological Issues of Inclusive Web Design: The German Web 2.0
Accessibility Survey 371
  Michael Pieper

Online Shopping Involving Consumers with Visual Impairments –
A Qualitative Study 378
  Elisabeth Fuchs and Christine Strauss

Website Accessibility Metrics

Website Accessibility Metrics: Introduction to the Special Thematic
Session 386
  Shadi Abou-Zahra

Integrating Manual and Automatic Evaluations to Measure Accessibility
Barriers 388
  *Paola Salomoni, Silvia Mirri, Ludovico A. Muratori, and
  Matteo Battistelli*

Assessing the Effort of Repairing the Accessibility of Web Sites 396
  Nádia Fernandes and Luís Carriço

Lexical Quality as a Measure for Textual Web Accessibility 404
  Luz Rello and Ricardo Baeza-Yates

Accessibility Testing of a Healthy Lifestyles Social Network 409
  Cecília Sík Lányi, Eszter Nagy, and Gergely Sik

Following the WCAG 2.0 Techniques: Experiences from Designing a
WCAG 2.0 Checking Tool 417
  *Annika Nietzio, Mandana Eibegger, Morten Goodwin, and
  Mikael Snaprud*

Entertainment Software Accessibility

Entertainment Software Accessibility: Introduction to the Special
Thematic Session 425
  Dominique Archambault and Roland Ossmann

Assessment of Universal Design Principles for Analyzing Computer
Games' Accessibility 428
  Moyen Mohammad Mustaquim

One Way of Bringing Final Year Computer Science Student World to
the World of Children with Cerebral Palsy: A Case Study 436
  *Isabel M. Gómez, Rafael Cabrera, Juan Ojeda, Pablo García,
  Alberto J. Molina, Octavio Rivera, and A. Mariano Esteban*

Making the PlayStation 3 Accessible with AsTeRICS 443
Roland Ossmann, David Thaller, Gerhard Nussbaum,
Christoph Veigl, and Christoph Weiß

Creating an Entertaining and Informative Music Visualization 451
Michael Pouris and Deborah I. Fels

Music at Your Fingertips: Stimulating Braille Reading by Association
with Sound.. 459
Felix Grützmacher

Improving Game Accessibility with Vibrotactile-Enhanced Hearing
Instruments 463
Bernd Tessendorf, Peter Derleth, Manuela Feilner, Daniel Roggen,
Thomas Stiefmeier, and Gerhard Tröster

An OCR-Enabled Digital Comic Books Viewer 471
Christophe Ponsard, Ravi Ramdoyal, and Daniel Dziamski

Spe-Ler: Serious Gaming for Youngsters with Intellectual Disabilities ... 479
Joan De Boeck, Jo Daems, and Jan Dekelver

Document and Media Accessibility

An Accessibility Checker for LibreOffice and OpenOffice.org Writer..... 484
Christophe Strobbe, Bert Frees, and Jan Engelen

Visualization of Non-verbal Expressions in Voice for Hearing Impaired:
Ambient Font and Onomatopoeic Subsystem 492
Hidetaka Nambo, Shuichi Seto, Hiroshi Arai, Kimikazu Sugimori,
Yuko Shimomura, and Hiroyuki Kawabe

XML-Based Formats and Tools to Produce Braille Documents 500
Alex Bernier and Dominique Burger

Japanese Text Presentation System for Pupils with Reading Difficulties:
Evaluation in Presentation Styles and Character Sets Changes without
Reading Difficulties 507
Shinjiro Murayama and Kyota Aoki

Development of a DAISY Player That Utilizes a Braille Display for
Document Structure Presentation and Navigation 515
Kazunori Minatani

Acce-Play: Accessibility in Cinemas 523
Alexandre Paz, Mari Luz Guenaga, and Andoni Eguíluz

Automatic Simplification of Spanish Text for e-Accessibility 527
Stefan Bott and Horacio Saggion

Can Computer Representations of Music Enhance Enjoyment for
Individuals Who Are Hard of Hearing? 535
  David Fourney

Assistive Photography 543
  Luděk Bártek and Ondřej Lapáček

The LIA Project – Libri Italiani Accessibili 550
  Cristina Mussinelli

Inclusion by Accessible Social Media

Inclusion by Accessible Social Media: Introduction to the Special
Thematic Session 554
  Harald Holone

The Use of Multimedia to Rehabilitate Students and Release Talents ... 557
  Luciana Maria Depieri Branco Freire

Use of Social Media by People with Visual Impairments: Usage Levels,
Attitudes and Barriers 565
  Kristin Skeide Fuglerud, Ingvar Tjøstheim,
  Birkir Rúnar Gunnarsson, and Morten Tollefsen

User Testing of Social Media – Methodological Considerations 573
  Oystein Dale, Therese Drivenes, Morten Tollefsen, and
  Arthur Reinertsen

Designing User Interfaces for Social Media Driven Digital Preservation
and Information Retrieval 581
  Dimitris Spiliotopoulos, Efstratios Tzoannos, Pepi Stavropoulou,
  Georgios Kouroupetroglou, and Alexandros Pino

PDF/UA – A New Era for Document Accessibility. Understanding, Managing and Implementing the ISO Standard PDF/UA (Universal Accessibility)

PDF/UA – A New Era for Document Accessibility. Understanding,
Managing and Implementing the ISO Standard PDF/UA (Universal
Accessibility): Introduction to the Special Thematic Session 585
  Olaf Drümmer and Markus Erle

PDF/UA (ISO 14289-1) – Applying WCAG 2.0 Principles to the World
of PDF Documents 587
  Olaf Drümmer

Mainstreaming the Creation of Accessible PDF Documents by a
Rule-Based Transformation from Word to PDF 595
  Roberto Bianchetti, Markus Erle, and Samuel Hofer

Developing Text Customisation Functionality Requirements of PDF
Reader and Other User Agents 602
    Shawn Lawton Henry

Using Layout Applications for Creation of Accessible PDF: Technical
and Mental Obstacles When Creating PDF/UA from Adobe Indesign
CS 5.5... 610
    Olaf Drümmer

Validity and Semantics – 2 Essential Parts of a Backbone for an
Automated PDF/UA Compliance Check for PDF Documents.......... 617
    Markus Erle and Samuel Hofer

Two Software Plugins for the Creation of Fully Accessible PDF
Documents Based on a Flexible Software Architecture 621
    Alireza Darvishy, Thomas Leemann, and Hans-Peter Hutter

Human – Computer Interaction and Usability for Elderly (HCI4AGING)

Privacy Preserving Automatic Fall Detection for Elderly Using RGBD
Cameras 625
    Chenyang Zhang, Yingli Tian, and Elizabeth Capezuti

The Proof of Concept of a Shadow Robotic System for Independent
Living at Home 634
    *Lucia Pigini, David Facal, Alvaro Garcia, Michael Burmester, and
    Renzo Andrich*

Task Complexity and User Model Attributes: An Analysis of User
Model Attributes for Elderly Drivers 642
    Thomas Grill, Sebastian Osswald, and Manfred Tscheligi

AALuis, a User Interface Layer That Brings Device Independence to
Users of AAL Systems 650
    *Christopher Mayer, Martin Morandell, Matthias Gira,
    Kai Hackbarth, Martin Petzold, and Sascha Fagel*

Comparison between Single-touch and Multi-touch Interaction for
Older People 658
    Guillaume Lepicard and Nadine Vigouroux

Online Social Networks and Older People 666
    Guillermo Prieto and Denise Leahy

"Break the Bricks" Serious Game for Stroke Patients................. 673
    Tamás Dömők, Veronika Szűcs, Erika László, and Cecília Sík Lányi

Development of a Broadcast Sound Receiver for Elderly Persons   681
*Tomoyasu Komori, Atsushi Imai, Nobumasa Seiyama, Reiko Takou,
Tohru Takagi, and Yasuhiro Oikawa*

Complexity versus Page Hierarchy of a GUI for Elderly Homecare
Applications.   689
*Mustafa Torun, Tim van Kasteren, Ozlem Durmaz Incel, and
Cem Ersoy*

Benefits and Hurdles for Older Adults in Intergenerational Online
Interactions   697
*Verena Fuchsberger, Wolfgang Sellner, Christiane Moser, and
Manfred Tscheligi*

kommTUi: Designing Communication for Elderly   705
Wolfgang Spreicer, Lisa Ehrenstrasser, and Hilda Tellioğlu

Reducing the Entry Threshold of AAL Systems: Preliminary Results
from *Casa Vecchia*   709
*Gerhard Leitner, Anton Josef Fercher, Alexander Felfernig, and
Martin Hitz*

Author Index   717

Table of Contents – Part II

Portable and Mobile Systems in Assistive Technology

A Multimodal Approach to Accessible Web Content on Smartphones . . .   1
   Lars Emil Knudsen and Harald Holone

Mobile Vision as Assistive Technology for the Blind: An Experimental
Study   9
   Roberto Manduchi

Camera-Based Signage Detection and Recognition for Blind Persons   17
   Shuihua Wang and Yingli Tian

The Crosswatch Traffic Intersection Analyzer: A Roadmap for the
Future   25
   James M. Coughlan and Huiying Shen

GPS and Inertial Measurement Unit (IMU) as a Navigation System for
the Visually Impaired   29
   Jesus Zegarra and René Farcy

Visual Nouns for Indoor/Outdoor Navigation   33
   Edgardo Molina, Zhigang Zhu, and Yingli Tian

Towards a Real-Time System for Finding and Reading Signs for
Visually Impaired Users   41
   Huiying Shen and James M. Coughlan

User Requirements for Camera-Based Mobile Applications on Touch
Screen Devices for Blind People   48
   Yoonjung Choi and Ki-Hyung Hong

A Route Planner Interpretation Service for Hard of Hearing People   52
   Mehrez Boulares and Mohamed Jemni

Translating Floor Plans into Directions   59
   Martin Spindler, Michael Weber, Denise Prescher, Mei Miao,
   Gerhard Weber, and Georgios Ioannidis

Harnessing Wireless Technologies for Campus Navigation by Blind
Students and Visitors   67
   Tracey J. Mehigan and Ian Pitt

Eyesight Sharing in Blind Grocery Shopping: Remote P2P Caregiving
through Cloud Computing   75
*Vladimir Kulyukin, Tanwir Zaman, Abhishek Andhavarapu, and
Aliasgar Kutiyanawala*

Assessment Test Framework for Collecting and Evaluating Fall-Related
Data Using Mobile Devices   83
*Stefan Almer, Josef Kolbitsch, Johannes Oberzaucher, and
Martin Ebner*

NAVCOM – WLAN Communication between Public Transport Vehicles
and Smart Phones to Support Visually Impaired and Blind People   91
Werner Bischof, Elmar Krajnc, Markus Dornhofer, and Michael Ulm

Mobile-Type Remote Captioning System for Deaf or Hard-of-Hearing
People and the Experience of Remote Supports after the Great East
Japan Earthquake   99
*Shigeki Miyoshi, Sumihiro Kawano, Mayumi Shirasawa,
Kyoko Isoda, Michiko Hasuike, Masayuki Kobayashi, and
Midori Umehara*

Handheld "App" Offering Visual Support to Students with Autism
Spectrum Disorders (ASDs)   105
Bogdan Zamfir, Robert Tedesco, and Brian Reichow

Cloud-Based Assistive Speech-Transcription Services   113
Zdenek Bumbalek, Jan Zelenka, and Lukas Kencl

Developing a Voice User Interface with Improved Usability for People
with Dysarthria   117
*Yumi Hwang, Daejin Shin, Chang-Yeal Yang, Seung-Yeun Lee,
Jin Kim, Byunggoo Kong, Jio Chung, Sunhee Kim, and
Minhwa Chung*

Wearable Range-Vibrotactile Field: Design and Evaluation   125
Frank G. Palmer, Zhigang Zhu, and Tony Ro

System Supporting Speech Perception in Special Educational Needs
Schoolchildren   133
*Adam Kupryjanow, Piotr Suchomski, Piotr Odya, and
Andrzej Czyzewski*

Designing a Mobile Application to Record ABA Data   137
*Silvia Artoni, Maria Claudia Buzzi, Marina Buzzi, Claudia Fenili,
Barbara Leporini, Simona Mencarini, and Caterina Senette*

Assistive Technology, HCI and Rehabilitation

Creating Personas with Disabilities 145
  Trenton Schulz and Kristin Skeide Fuglerud

Eye Controlled Human Computer Interaction for Severely Motor
Disabled Children: Two Clinical Case Studies......................... 153
  Mojca Debeljak, Julija Ocepek, and Anton Zupan

Gravity Controls for Windows 157
  Peter Heumader, Klaus Miesenberger, and Gerhard Nussbaum

Addressing Accessibility Challenges of People with Motor Disabilities
by Means of AsTeRICS: A Step by Step Definition of Technical
Requirements.. 164
  Alvaro García-Soler, Unai Diaz-Orueta, Roland Ossmann,
  Gerhard Nussbaum, Christoph Veigl, Chris Weiss, and Karol Pecyna

Indoor and Outdoor Mobility for an Intelligent Autonomous
Wheelchair.. 172
  C.T. Lin, Craig Euler, Po-Jen Wang, and Ara Mekhtarian

Comparing the Accuracy of a P300 Speller for People with Major
Physical Disability 180
  Alexander Lechner, Rupert Ortner, Fabio Aloise, Robert Prückl,
  Francesca Schettini, Veronika Putz, Josef Scharinger, Eloy Opisso,
  Ursula Costa, Josep Medina, and Christoph Guger

Application of Robot Suit HAL to Gait Rehabilitation of Stroke
Patients: A Case Study 184
  Kanako Yamawaki, Ryohei Ariyasu, Shigeki Kubota,
  Hiroaki Kawamoto, Yoshio Nakata, Kiyotaka Kamibayashi,
  Yoshiyuki Sankai, Kiyoshi Eguchi, and Naoyuki Ochiai

Sign 2.0: ICT for Sign Language Users: Information Sharing, Interoperability, User-Centered Design and Collaboration

Sign 2.0: ICT for Sign Language Users: Information Sharing,
Interoperability, User-Centered Design and Collaboration: Introduction
to the Special Thematic Session................................... 188
  Liesbeth Pyfers

Toward Developing a Very Big Sign Language Parallel Corpus 192
  Achraf Othman, Zouhour Tmar, and Mohamed Jemni

Czech Sign Language – Czech Dictionary and Thesaurus On-Line 200
  Jan Fikejs and Tomáš Sklenák

The Dicta-Sign Wiki: Enabling Web Communication for the Deaf 205
Eleni Efthimiou, Stavroula-Evita Fotinea, Thomas Hanke,
John Glauert, Richard Bowden, Annelies Braffort,
Christophe Collet, Petros Maragos, and François Lefebvre-Albaret

Sign Language Multimedia Based Interaction for Aurally Handicapped
People 213
Matjaž Debevc, Ines Kožuh, Primož Kosec, Milan Rotovnik, and
Andreas Holzinger

Meeting Support System for the Person with Hearing Impairment
Using Tablet Devices and Speech Recognition 221
Makoto Kobayashi, Hiroki Minagawa, Tomoyuki Nishioka, and
Shigeki Miyoshi

Dubbing of Videos for Deaf People – A Sign Language Approach 225
Franz Niederl, Petra Bußwald, Georg Tschare, Jürgen Hackl, and
Josef Philipp

Towards a 3D Signing Avatar from SignWriting Notation 229
Yosra Bouzid, Maher Jbali, Oussama El Ghoul, and Mohamed Jemni

Sign Language Computer-Aided Education: Exploiting GSL Resources
and Technologies for Web Deaf Communication 237
Stavroula-Evita Fotinea, Eleni Efthimiou, and
Athanasia-Lida Dimou

SignMedia: Interactive English Learning Resource for Deaf Sign
Language Users Working in the Media Industry 245
Luzia Gansinger

SignAssess – Online Sign Language Training Assignments via the
Browser, Desktop and Mobile 253
Christopher John

Computer-Assisted Augmentative and Alternative Communication (CA-AAC)

Towards General Cross-Platform CCF Based Multi-modal Language
Support 261
Mats Lundälv and Sandra Derbring

Developing an Augmentative Mobile Communication System 269
Juan Bautista Montalvá Colomer,
María Fernanda Cabrera-Umpiérrez, Silvia de los Ríos Pérez,
Miguel Páramo del Castrillo, and
María Teresa Arredondo Waldmeyer

The Korean Web-Based AAC Board Making System 275
  Saerom Choi, Heeyeon Lee, and Ki-Hyung Hong

SymbolChat: Picture-Based Communication Platform for Users with
Intellectual Disabilities 279
  *Tuuli Keskinen, Tomi Heimonen, Markku Turunen,
  Juha-Pekka Rajaniemi, and Sami Kauppinen*

Developing AAC Message Generating Training System Based on Core
Vocabulary Approach.. 287
  *Ming-Chung Chen, Cheng-Chien Chen, Chien-Chuan Ko,
  Hwa-Pey Wang, and Shao-Wun Chen*

New Features in the VoxAid Communication Aid for Speech Impaired
People 295
  Bálint Tóth, Péter Nagy, and Géza Németh

AAC Vocabulary Standardisation and Harmonisation: The CCF and
BCI Experiences 303
  Mats Lundälv and Sandra Derbring

Speaking and Understanding Morse Language, Speech Technology and
Autism 311
  András Arató, Norbert Markus, and Zoltan Juhasz

Reverse-Engineering Scanning Keyboards 315
  Foad Hamidi and Melanie Baljko

A Communication System on Smart Phones and Tablets for Non-verbal
Children with Autism 323
  Harini Sampath, Bipin Indurkhya, and Jayanthi Sivaswamy

Assessment of Biosignals for Managing a Virtual Keyboard 331
  Manuel Merino, Isabel Gómez, Alberto J. Molina, and Kevin Guzman

Applying the Principles of Experience-Dependent Neural Plasticity:
Building Up Language Abilities with ELA®-Computerized Language
Modules 338
  *Jacqueline Stark, Christiane Pons, Ronald Bruckner, Beate Fessl,
  Rebecca Janker, Verena Leitner, Karin Mittermann, and
  Michaela Rausch*

Assistive Technology: Writing Tool to Support Students with Learning
Disabilities 346
  Onintra Poobrasert and Alongkorn Wongteeratana

Communication Access for a Student with Multiple Disabilities:
An Interdisciplinary Collaborative Approach 353
  Frances Layman, Cathryn Crowle, and John Ravenscroft

Easy to Web between Science of Education, Information Design and (Speech) Technology

Multimedia Advocacy: A New Way of Self Expression and
Communication for People with Intellectual Disabilities 361
  Gosia Kwiatkowska, Thomas Tröbinger, Karl Bäck, and
  Peter Williams

How Long Is a Short Sentence? – A Linguistic Approach to Definition
and Validation of Rules for Easy-to-Read Material 369
  Annika Nietzio, Birgit Scheer, and Christian Bühler

CAPKOM – Innovative Graphical User Interface Supporting People
with Cognitive Disabilities 377
  Andrea Petz, Nicoleta Radu, and Markus Lassnig

Smart and Assistive Environments: Ambient Assisted Living (AAL)

A Real-Time Sound Recognition System in an Assisted Environment ... 385
  Héctor Lozano, Inmaculada Hernáez, Javier Camarena,
  Ibai Díez, and Eva Navas

Gestures Used by Intelligent Wheelchair Users 392
  Dimitra Anastasiou and Christoph Stahl

Augmented Reality Based Environment Design Support System for
Home Renovation 399
  Yoshiyuki Takahashi and Hiroko Mizumura

Fall Detection on Embedded Platform Using Kinect and Wireless
Accelerometer 407
  Michal Kepski and Bogdan Kwolek

Controlled Natural Language Sentence Building as a Model for
Designing User Interfaces for Rule Editing in Assisted Living
Systems – A User Study 415
  Henrike Gappa, Gaby Nordbrock, Yehya Mohamad,
  Jaroslav Pullmann, and Carlos A. Velasco

MonAMI Platform in Elderly Household Environment: Architecture,
Installation, Implementation, Trials and Results 419
  Dušan Šimšík, Alena Galajdová, Daniel Siman, Juraj Bujňák,
  Marianna Andrášová, and Marek Novák

Text Entry for Accessible Computing

Modeling Text Input for Single-Switch Scanning 423
I. Scott MacKenzie

DualScribe: A Keyboard Replacement for Those with Friedreich's
Ataxia and Related Diseases...................................... 431
Torsten Felzer, I. Scott MacKenzie, and Stephan Rinderknecht

Easier Mobile Phone Input Using the JusFone Keyboard 439
Oystein Dale and Trenton Schulz

Automatic Assessment of Dysarthric Speech Intelligibility Based on
Selected Phonetic Quality Features 447
Myung Jong Kim and Hoirin Kim

Adaptation of AAC to the Context Communication: A Real
Improvement for the User Illustration through the VITIPI Word
Completion 451
*Philippe Boissière, Nadine Vigouroux, Mustapha Mojahid, and
Frédéric Vella*

Tackling the Acceptability of Freely Optimized Keyboard Layout 459
Bruno Merlin, Mathieu Raynal, and Heleno Fülber

Measuring Performance of a Predictive Keyboard Operated by
Humming 467
Ondřej Poláček, Adam J. Sporka, and Zdeněk Míkovec

Dysarthric Speech Recognition Error Correction Using Weighted Finite
State Transducers Based on Context–Dependent Pronunciation
Variation 475
Woo Kyeong Seong, Ji Hun Park, and Hong Kook Kim

Text Entry Competency for Students with Learning Disabilities in
Grade 5 to 6 483
Ting-Fang Wu and Ming-Chung Chen

Tactile Graphics and Models for Blind People and Recognition of Shapes by Touch

Vision SenS 490
*Berenice Machuca Bautista, José Alfredo Padilla Medina, and
Francisco Javier Sánchez Marín*

Computer-Aided Design of Tactile Models: Taxonomy and Case
Studies 497
*Andreas Reichinger, Moritz Neumüller, Florian Rist,
Stefan Maierhofer, and Werner Purgathofer*

Three-Dimensional Model Fabricated by Layered Manufacturing for
Visually Handicapped Persons to Trace Heart Shape 505
    Kenji Yamazawa, Yoshinori Teshima, Yasunari Watanabe,
    Yuji Ikegami, Mamoru Fujiyoshi, Susumu Oouchi, and
    Takeshi Kaneko

Viable Haptic UML for Blind People 509
    Claudia Loitsch and Gerhard Weber

Non-visual Presentation of Graphs Using the Novint Falcon 517
    Reham Alabbadi, Peter Blanchfield, and Maria Petridou

Mobility for Blind and Partially Sighted People

Towards a Geographic Information System Facilitating Navigation of
Visually Impaired Users 521
    Slim Kammoun, Marc J.-M. Macé, Bernard Oriola, and
    Christophe Jouffrais

Combination of Map-Supported Particle Filters with Activity
Recognition for Blind Navigation................................. 529
    Bernhard Schmitz, Attila Györkös, and Thomas Ertl

AccessibleMap: Web-Based City Maps for Blind and Visually
Impaired 536
    Klaus Höckner, Daniele Marano, Julia Neuschmid,
    Manfred Schrenk, and Wolfgang Wasserburger

Design and User Satisfaction of Interactive Maps for Visually Impaired
People 544
    Anke Brock, Philippe Truillet, Bernard Oriola, Delphine Picard, and
    Christophe Jouffrais

A Mobile Application Concept to Encourage Independent Mobility for
Blind and Visually Impaired Students 552
    Jukka Liimatainen, Markku Häkkinen, Tuula Nousiainen,
    Marja Kankaanranta, and Pekka Neittaanmäki

Do-It-Yourself Object Identification Using Augmented Reality for
Visually Impaired People 560
    Atheer S. Al-Khalifa and Hend S. Al-Khalifa

An Assistive Vision System for the Blind That Helps Find Lost
Things 566
    Boris Schauerte, Manel Martinez, Angela Constantinescu, and
    Rainer Stiefelhagen

Designing a Virtual Environment to Evaluate Multimodal Sensors for
Assisting the Visually Impaired 573
    Wai L. Khoo, Eric L. Seidel, and Zhigang Zhu

A Segmentation-Based Stereovision Approach for Assisting Visually
Impaired People 581
    Hao Tang and Zhigang Zhu

KinDectect: Kinect Detecting Objects 588
    Atif Khan, Febin Moideen, Juan Lopez, Wai L. Khoo, and
    Zhigang Zhu

A System Helping the Blind to Get Merchandise Information 596
    Nobuhito Tanaka, Yasunori Doi, Tetsuya Matsumoto,
    Yoshinori Takeuchi, Hiroaki Kudo, and Noboru Ohnishi

Human-Computer Interaction for Blind and Partially Sighted People

Accessibility for the Blind on an Open-Source Mobile Platform: MObile
Slate Talker (MOST) for Android 599
    Norbert Markus, Szabolcs Malik, Zoltan Juhasz, and András Arató

Accessibility of Android-Based Mobile Devices: A Prototype to
Investigate Interaction with Blind Users 607
    Sarah Chiti and Barbara Leporini

TypeInBraille: Quick Eyes-Free Typing on Smartphones 615
    Sergio Mascetti, Cristian Bernareggi, and Matteo Belotti

Real-Time Display Recognition System for Visually Impaired 623
    Irati Rasines, Pedro Iriondo, and Ibai Díez

A Non-visual Interface for Tasks Requiring Rapid Recognition and
Response: An RC Helicopter Control System for Blind People 630
    Kazunori Minatani and Tetsuya Watanabe

Reaching to Sound Accuracy in the Peri-personal Space of Blind and
Sighted Humans 636
    Marc J.-M. Macé, Florian Dramas, and Christophe Jouffrais

Hapto-acoustic Scene Representation 644
    Sebastian Ritterbusch, Angela Constantinescu, and Volker Koch

Efficient Access to PC Applications by Using a Braille Display with
Active Tactile Control (ATC)...................................... 651
    Siegfried Kipke

Applications of Optically Actuated Haptic Elements................... 659
    Branislav Mamojka and Peter Teplický

Trackable Interactive Multimodal Manipulatives: Towards a Tangible
User Environment for the Blind..................................... 664
    Muhanad S. Manshad, Enrico Pontelli, and Shakir J. Manshad

Introduction of New Body-Braille Devices and Applications 672
    *Satoshi Ohtsuka, Nobuyuki Sasaki, Sadao Hasegawa, and
    Tetsumi Harakawa*

Author Index... 677

Towards a Visual Speech Learning System for the Deaf by Matching Dynamic Lip Shapes

Shizhi Chen, D. Michael Quintian, and Yingli Tian

Department of Electrical Engineering
The City College, City University of New York,
160 Convent Ave., New York, NY 10031
{schen21,dquinti00,ytian}@ccny.cuny.edu

Abstract. In this paper we propose a visual-based speech learning framework to assist deaf persons by comparing the lip movements between a student and an E-tutor in an intelligent tutoring system. The framework utilizes lip reading technologies to determine if a student learns the correct pronunciation. Different from conventional speech recognition systems, which usually recognize a speaker's utterance, our speech learning framework focuses on recognizing whether a student pronounces are correct according to an instructor's utterance by using visual information. We propose a method by extracting dynamic shape difference features (DSDF) based on lip shapes to recognize the pronunciation difference. The preliminary experimental results demonstrate the robustness and effectiveness of our approach on a database we collected, which contains multiple persons speaking a small number of selected words.

Keywords: Lip Reading, Speech Learning, Dynamic Shape Difference Features, Deaf people.

1   Introduction

About 35 million Americans today are deaf or hard of hearing. Approximately 12 out of every 1,000 individuals with hearing impairment are under 18 years of age, based on the most recently available data from the National Center for Health Statistics (NCHS). Recent research has demonstrated that even mild hearing losses can create significant challenges for children as they develop skills to interact with the world [5], [7].

The loss of auditory feedback poses significant difficulties on the speech learning for the deaf people, since it is difficult for them to know immediately if they speak correctly [1], [10], [12]. Some researchers propose to use animations as feedback according to audio signals [6], [11]. The animations can be helpful for the deaf people to know if they speak correctly. However, such animation does not provide feedback on how to correct their speech and how the incorrect speech different from that of the instructor.

On the other hand, visual cue often provides complementary information for speech recognition [8], [9], [15]. Figure 1 shows a lip movement in a video sequence

K. Miesenberger et al. (Eds.): ICCHP 2012, Part I, LNCS 7382, pp. 1–9, 2012.

when speaking word "apple". It is easier for a deaf person to visualize the difference between the incorrect and the correct utterances by simply looking at the lip movements.

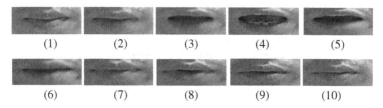

(1)   (2)   (3)   (4)   (5)

(6)   (7)   (8)   (9)   (10)

Fig. 1. Sample lip movements of a video sequence when speaking word "apple"

Potamianos et al. [9] have shown a significant improvement of speech recognition through both audio and visual modalities as compared to the approach of audio modality only. Matthews et al. combined lip contour and lip appearance information to recognize isolated letters A-Z [8]. Then the authors employ Hidden Markov models (HMM) as the classifier to model the temporal dynamics of a speech. The authors demonstrated the effectiveness of the speech recognition based on only visual modality. The visual based speech recognition becomes particularly useful in the noisy environment, in which audio signal is significantly degraded.

Zhou [15] recently captures temporal dynamics of a speech by extending Local Binary Pattern (LBP) to a temporal domain [14], which is also visual based speech recognition. Ten phrases are used for their speech recognition experiments. The experimental results also show a promising performance of visual based speech recognition.

Fig. 2. The basic hardware configuration of the proposed interactive intelligent tutoring system, which includes a computer (desktop or laptop), a web camera with auto focus (face to the user), and a microphone

Inspired by these advances on speech recognition, we propose a visual-based speech learning framework to aid deaf people. As shown in Figure 2, the system configuration is set up as an E-Tutoring system. A deaf student in front of a computer learns speech by following an E-tutor. A web camera is used to capture the student's face and lip movement. The video of the student is then processed in real-time by comparing the student's lip movements with those from the pre-recorded tutor. Interactive feedback is provided to students through easily understandable visual displays.

Different from the visual based speech recognition, which usually recognizes a few words, a practical speech learning system usually needs to handle much larger vocabulary. It would be extremely difficult to design a speech learning system if we have to recognize every single utterance between a student and an instructor. Hence, we propose a new framework by extracting dynamic shape difference features (DSDF) to directly measure the visual difference of lip shapes between two speakers, i.e., the student and the instructor. Therefore, we can reduce a multi-class recognition problem in a speech learning system to a binary class recognition problem, i.e., recognizing whether the student pronounce correctly according to the instructor's utterance. Our preliminary experiments have shown encouraging results of this approach.

2   Visual Based Speech Learning Method

2.1   Overview

Figure 3 shows an overview of our speech learning framework. First, the lip movements of both student and E-tutor are tracked by an Active Shape Model (ASM) [4, 13]. Then we align the lip shapes to remove the head movements while speaking, i.e., translation, and rotation. In this step we also remove the lip shape variance caused by different subjects. Due to the time resolution difference when speaking a word, we perform temporal normalization over the extracted lip shapes in a video sequence, so that both student and instructor can have same speaking speed. The resulted features are defined as dynamic shape features.

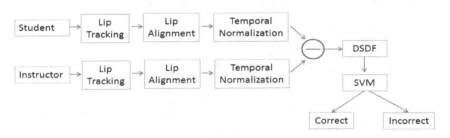

Fig. 3. Overview of our proposed visual speech learning framework

Finally we calculate the difference of the dynamic shape features between the student and the instructor, i.e., dynamic shape difference features (DSDF), as the input to a Support Vector Machine (SVM) based classifier. The SVM classifier then automatically determines if the lip movements of the student correctly follow the lip movements of the instructor based on the visual difference of lip shapes between the student and the instructor.

2.2   Lip Tracking

We employ Active Shape Model (ASM) [4], [13] to track lip movements. ASM is a shape-constrained iteratively fitting method, which utilizes prior knowledge of lip shapes in training images. The shape is simply the x and y coordinates of all landmark points on a lip after appropriate alignments, which is shown in Eq. (1).

$$\mathbf{X}_i = [x_1, y_1, x_2, y_2, \ldots x_j, y_j, \ldots x_n, y_n] \tag{1}$$

where n is the number of landmark points labeled for a lip. In our experiments, we choose 19 landmark points, including both outer contour and inner contour of a lip. For the simplicity, we use the built-in ASM model, which is trained using the 68 landmark points of the whole face including the 19 lip points [13]. Figure 4 shows a lip tracking example in a video sequence using the ASM model.

Fig. 4. An example of lip tracking in a video sequence by employing Active Shape. Model (ASM)

2.3   Lip Alignment

In order to remove the effects of head movements and rotations during the speech, we perform an alignment procedure. The alignment procedure calculates the angle formed by the line connecting both lip corners and x axis. Then we rotate the shape by the calculated angle so that the left lip corner and the right lip corner have the same y coordinate value. The mean x and y values are removed. The entire shape is then ad-justed vertically to align the two lip corners on the x axis.

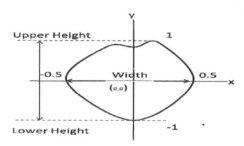

Fig. 5. Typical neutral lip shape after the alignment and the normalization with the upper height, lower height, and width of the lip shape on the neutral frame

Different subjects have different neutral lip shapes. To eliminate these subject de-pendent shape variations, we perform a normalization using the upper lip height, the lower lip height, and the width of the neutral lip shape for each subject. The neutral frame in our database is simply the first frame in the video sequence. Figure 5 shows a typically aligned and normalized lip shape on the neutral frame without the landmark points. The normalized lip shapes in a video sequence represent how the lip shape deforms from the neutral shape during the speech.

From the experiments, we find that the performance is usually improved by adding the upper height, the lower height, and the width of each frame's lip shape to the normalized shape vector as described in last paragraph. Finally, we perform the *L2* normalization on the resulted feature vector in each frame.

2.4   Temporal Normalization

The time usually varies for different subjects even when they speak same words. In order to handle this time resolution difference, we temporally normalize the video sequence to a fixed number of frames by linearly interpolating each frame's feature vector along the temporal direction [2 - 3]. We choose 30 as the number of temporally normalized frames in a video sequence.

Each frame's shape feature vector has the feature dimension of 41, i.e., 2*19+3. Therefore, a video sequence is represented by the concatenated frame feature vector with the total dimension of 1230, i.e., 41*30. The concatenated feature vector of a video sequence is defined as dynamic shapes.

2.5   Dynamic Shape Difference Features (DSDF)

By taking the difference of the dynamic shapes between the instructor and the student, we form the dynamic shape difference features (DSDF). The DSDF features directly measure the pronunciation difference of the two speakers, regardless the words spoken.

Here, we do not recognize the words spoken by the instructor and the student individually to determine if the student speaks same word as the instructor, since this approach can quickly become too complicated to recognize every word accurately as the number of words increase in the speech learning system. By employing the DSDF feature to recognize the similarity between the utterances directly, our system is not limited to the number of words or utterances spoken, which is desirable for any practical speech learning system.

2.6   Support Vector Machine Classifier

Finally, we employ a support vector machine (SVM) with RBF kernel as the classifier. The DSDF feature calculated from the instructor and the student is the input feature vector. The output of the classifier is to determine if the student correctly follows the instructor's utterance regardless words they speak.

3   Experimental Results

3.1   Database

We have recorded a database to study the effectiveness and robustness of the proposed speech learning framework. Nine words were chosen such that some words are unique, and some words are similar to each other. The selected words are "apple", "cruise", "find", "hello", "music", "open", "search", "vision", and "window".

In our database, each word is spoken ten times by each subject. There are four subjects in the dataset. The video is captured at frontal face by a web-camera with the entire head of the subject within the image frame, in order to ensure the face has enough resolution. The speaker begins a word with a neutral expression, says the word, and then returns to the neutral expression. Each of the chosen words takes an average of one second to complete. Depending on the speaker, some words take up to two seconds to complete.

All the videos have a spatial resolution of 640x480 pixels, with a frame rate of 30 frames per second. The videos are edited such that the first and last few frames (about 3-5) contain a neutral expression. The average video sequence is between 20 to 40 frames long. Figure 6 shows a sample video sequence of a subject speaking the word "apple".

Fig. 6. A sample video sequence of speaking the word "apple"

3.2   Subject Dependent Results

We evaluate the speech learning framework by pairing up two persons from the database. If the selected two persons speak same word, then we know that one speaker has correctly followed the other speaker. Otherwise, one speaker has incorrectly followed the other speaker. Hence we have the ground truth, whether one speaker correctly follows the other speaker, by simply checking the words they speak. That is, if they speak same word, the ground truth is "correct". Otherwise, the sample consisting of the pair of speech has the label of "incorrect".

Each word is spoken 10 times by each subject, and there are 9 words in our database. Therefore, we have 900 possible pairs of utterances which speak the same word for each selected pair of subjects, i.e., we have 900 "correct" samples. Similarly, for each pair of subjects, there are 7200 possible pairs of utterance which speak different words, i.e., there are 7200 "incorrect" samples. We choose 900 out of the 7200 "incorrect" samples, so that the number of "incorrect" samples from every combination of different words is approximately equal. Then we divide the 900 "correct" samples and the 900 "incorrect" samples to the training and testing sets by the ratio of 9 to 1.

Our speakers include one American male (M), one Chinese male (S), one Chinese female (X), and one American female (K). The capital letter is an identifier for the person. We adopt precision and recall as our evaluation metrics, which are defined in Eqs. (2) and (3).

$$Recall = \frac{TP}{TP+FN} \tag{2}$$

$$Precision = \frac{TP}{TP+FP} \tag{3}$$

where TP is the number of "correct" samples which are also predicted correctly. FP is the number of "incorrect" samples which are misclassified as "correct" samples. FN is the number of "correct" samples which are misclassified as "incorrect" samples.

Table 1(a) shows the average precision and the average recall over all words for each selected pair of speakers. That is to train and test the proposed speech learning framework by the same pair of subjects. Table 1(b) shows the detailed recall over the individual words for the corresponding pair of subjects. These results indicate the robustness of the proposed speech learning system.

There are some variations among different pair of speakers on the precision and recall. One explanation for this variation is the fact that different people say the same word differently. When collecting the database, we have observed some speakers open their mouse slightly prior to saying a word.

Table 1. (a) average precision and average recall over all words for each selected pair of speakers; (b) recall over the individual words for each selected pair of speakers

	Precision	Recall		Apple	Cruise	Find	Hello	Music	Open	Search	Vision	Window
M-S	95.2%	87.8%	M-S	70%	100%	90%	70%	100%	70%	90%	100%	100%
M-K	100.0%	97.8%	M-K	80%	100%	100%	100%	100%	100%	100%	100%	100%
M-X	98.9%	96.7%	M-X	80%	100%	90%	100%	100%	100%	100%	100%	100%
S-K	96.5%	91.1%	S-K	30%	100%	100%	100%	100%	100%	100%	90%	100%
S-X	100.0%	92.2%	S-X	70%	100%	80%	100%	100%	80%	100%	100%	100%
K-X	100.0%	92.2%	K-X	80%	100%	100%	90%	60%	100%	100%	100%	100%

              (a)   (b)

3.3   Subject Independent Results

In order to evaluate the proposed speech learning framework for the subject independent case, we group all "correct" and "incorrect" samples from every pair of speakers as shown in Table 1. Then we just train a single model to recognize if one speaker correctly follows another speaker. The precision and the recall shown in Table 2 demonstrate that the proposed framework is also effective for subject independent case.

Table 2. (a) Average precision and average recall over all words when grouping every pair of speakers in Table 1; (b) detailed recall of (a) over the individual words

Precision	Recall		Apple	Cruise	Find	Hello	Music	Open	Search	Vision	Window
98.7%	95.9%		81.7%	96.7%	100.0%	95.0%	95.0%	96.7%	100.0%	98.3%	100.0%

(a)   (b)

4   Conclusion

We have proposed a framework to help deaf people learn speech by visually comparing the lip movements of a student and an instructor. The framework utilizes lip reading technologies to determine if the student correctly follows the instructor in pronunciation of a word. Furthermore, our proposed framework is very practical by employing the dynamic shape difference feature (DSDF), which can avoid the large vocabulary problem in traditional speech recognition systems. The preliminary experimental results indicate that our proposed speech learning framework is robust in both subject dependent and subject independent cases. More extensive experiments and user interface study including the system test by deaf people will be conducted in future. A larger database with more subjects and more words will also be collected in order to train a model which can be robust in the practical application.

Acknowledgments. This work was supported in part by NSF grant IIS-0957016 and DHS Summer Research Team Program for Minority Serving Institutions Follow-on Award. Shizhi Chen is funded by NOAA CREST Grant NA11SEC4810004.

References

1. Awad, S.: The Application of Digital Speech Processing to Stuttering Therapy. IEEE Instrumentation and Measurement (1997)
2. Chen, S., Tian, Y., Liu, Q., Metaxas, D.: Segment and Recognize Expression Phase by Fusion of Motion Area and Neutral Divergence Features. In: IEEE Int'l Conf. on Automatic Face and Gesture Recognition, AFGR (2011)
3. Chen, S., Tian, Y., Liu, Q., Metaxas, D.: Recognizing Expressions from Face and Body Gesture by Temporal Normalized Motion and Appearance Features. In: IEEE Int'l Conf. Computer Vision and Pattern Recognition Workshop for Human Communicative Behavior Analysis, CVPR4HB (2011)
4. Cootes, T., Taylor, C., Cooper, D., Graham, J.: Active Shape Models – Their Training and Application. Computer Vision and Image Understanding (1995)
5. Hailpern, J., Karahalios, K., DeThorne, L., Halle, J.: Encouraging Speech and Vocalization in Children with Autistic Spectrum Disorder. In: Workshop on Technology in Mental Health, CHI 2008 (2008)
6. Lavagetto, F.: Converting speech into lip movements: a multimedia telephone for hard of hearing people. IEEE Transactions on Rehabilitation Engineering 3(1), 90–102 (1995)

 7. Marschark, M., Sapere, P., Convertino, C., Mayer, C., Wauters, L., Sarchet, T.: Are deaf students' reading challenges really about reading? American Annals of the Deaf 154(4), 357-176 (2009)
 8. Matthews, I., Cootes, T., Bangham, J., Cox, S., Harvey, R.: Extraction of visual features for lipreading. TPAMI 24(2), 198–213 (2002)
 9. Potamianos, G., Neti, C., Gravier, G., Garg, A., Senior, A.: Recent Advances in the Automatic Recognition of Audio-Visual Speech. Proceedings of the IEEE 91(9), 1306–1326 (2003)
10. Rahman, M., Ferdous, S., Ahmed, S.: Increasing Intelligibility in the Speech of the Autistic Children by an Interactive Computer Game. In: IEEE International Symposium on Multimedia (2010)
11. Riella, R., Linarth, A., Lippmann, L., Nohama, P.: Computerized System to Aid Deaf Children in Speech Learning. In: IEEE EMBS International Conference (2001)
12. Schipor, O., Pentiuc, S., Schipor, M.: Towards a Multimodal Emotion Recognition Framework to Be Integrated in a Computer Based Speech Therapy System. In: IEEE Conference on Speech Technology and Human Computer Dialogue, SpeD (2011)
13. Wei, Y.: Research on Facial Expression Recognition and Synthesis, Master Thesis (2009), Software available at http://code.google.com/p/asmlibrary
14. Zhao, G., Barnard, M., Pietikainen, M.: Lipreading with local spatialtemporal descriptors. TMM 11(7), 1254–1265 (2009)
15. Zhou, Z., Zhao, G., Pietikainen, M.: Toward a Practical Lipreading System. In: CVPR (2011)

Teaching Support Software for Hearing Impaired Students Who Study Computer Operation

SynchroniZed Key Points Indication Tool: SZKIT

Makoto Kobayashi[1], Takuya Suzuki[2], and Daisuke Wakatsuki[2]

[1] Faculty of Health Science, Tsukuba University of Technology, Japan
koba@cs.k.tsukuba-tech.ac.jp
[2] Faculty of Industrial Technology, Tsukuba University of Technology, Japan
{suzukit,waka}@a.tsukuba-tech.ac.jp

Abstract. Teaching support software for the hearing impaired students who study computer operation was developed. It is named as SZKIT. The software shows icons of modifier keys when the teacher presses modifier keys and shows mouse icon when he/she clicks a mouse button. These icons appear near the mouse cursor. By this function, a difference between simple dragging and dragging with modifier key can be distinguishable. For the hearing impaired students, it is difficult to distinguish such differences without voice information, because the motions of the mouse cursor on the screen are almost same. Also SZKIT can show instruction texts under the mouse cursor. The timing of changing the texts is controlled by a hot key, keeping the focus on the main application software. From the results of questionnaire to the hearing impaired students, it is clear that SZKIT is useful to learn computer operation.

Keywords: hearing impaired student, learning computer operation, modifier keys.

1 Introduction

Our university is a special one which admits only visually impaired or hearing impaired students. The division for the hearing impaired students has two departments. One of them is the department of industrial information, and the other one is the department of synthetic design. Both departments have several lectures concerned with computer operations. In these lectures, our teaching staffs are struggling every day to teach how to operate the computer using sign language, power point materials, video resources, et cetera. Addition to the lectures of basic computer operation, the curriculum of the department of synthetic design contains lectures to study software for design, such as "Adobe Photoshop" or "Illustrator." Fig.1 shows a scene of a lecture in which the staff shows how to use the designing software to our hearing impaired students. Such kind of software requires a variety of combine operations with mouse and modifier keys like dragging object with pressing Alt key. Therefor students have to understand these combined operations and remember them

K. Miesenberger et al. (Eds.): ICCHP 2012, Part I, LNCS 7382, pp. 10–17, 2012.

to gain a skill of using the software. However, teaching how to use such combination to the hearing impaired students is really difficult because there is no sign on the screen when the action of key pressing or mouse clicking starts. The main problem is that the students can't read the instruction text (or the sign language) and the mouse cursor movement at the same time when they watch the screen which reflects the teaching staff's operation. Even the difference between drugging and simply clicking two points is hard to distinguish for them.

Fig. 1. A scene of lecture in which a teaching staff shows how to use software

Fig. 2 shows an example of that situation. Each figure indicates operations with Adobe Illustrator respectively. The left one is only drugging an object to move right-downward without pressing any keys. The middle one shows an operation of copying the object, which is drugging with pressing Alt key. The right one shows an operation of copying the object to strictly obliquely downward (45 degree,) which is drugging with pressing Shift key After Alt key. As these figures shows, the difference among them is really slight, only the difference of mouse cursor's shape and the object positions. In ordinary lecture to students who can hear, they can understand the difference and its timing of key pressing because they can listen to the instruction via voice from the teaching staff during the real time operation at the same time. However, it is easy to imagine how great difficulty the hearing impaired students have, to recognize it only with visual information.

Of course, using video materials or having precise instruction is available when hearing impaired students learn such kind of things [1-2] and our teaching staffs utilized these education materials. Speech recognition system [3] or subscribing service is also available to support hearing impaired students. However, it seems they can't solve the problems of teaching computer operation because the instructing text information of these systems is not in the same place and not in the same time to the operation. Remote subscribing service is very convenient in these days though, in usual case its text information is slightly delayed and its display area is separated to the area of the computer operation. The delay and separation between the text information and the real time computer operation makes the students confuse, especially in the complex operation with complex combination mentioned above.

Besides such background, one of the authors was just against this problem in his lecture class. And then, he thought up an idea to solve it.

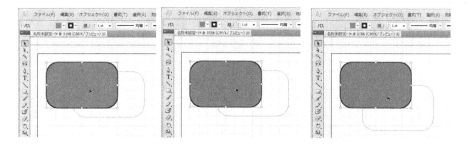

Fig. 2. Examples of mouse and keyboard operation using Adobe Illustrator

2   Basic Idea of SZKIT

The idea is really simple, which is showing icons of mouse clicks and pressed modifier keys and showing instruction text in real time aside of the mouse cursor. We started to discuss new supporting software based on this idea. The most important point is that the positions of each indicating components placed around the mouse cursor, not far from it. Because the hearing impaired students can't pay attention to the separated area at the same time. At first, we surveyed software which displays mouse clicking and pressing modifier keys. "Target [4]" is software which displays an action of mouse clicking. However, it is not appropriate because it hides background application software with large mark. "osdHotkey [5]"is a software which can display modifier key and mouse action, but unfortunately, the display area of them is fixed position with a window, not followed by the mouse cursor. After all, we decided to develop an original software tool and named it as "SynchroniZed Key points Indication Tool: SZKIT."

Fig. 3. An overview of proposed software tool, SZKIT

Fig. 3 shows an overview of SZKIT. To clear its function, the upper figure shows most of components. It consists of icons and the instruction text area. These icons are, mouse click (left, right) and modifier key (Shift, Control, and Alt) and normal key which appears in case of pressing a combination key. Each icon is hiding under normal condition and appears only when the user clicks mouse button or presses these modifier keys. After displaying, these icons gradually disappear taking approximately one second to impress to the students what kind of modifier key was pressed. On the other hand, the instruction text area is displayed all the time basically. But when the instruction text area isn't needed, it can be hided arbitrarily by pressing Windows key + Ctrl key. To re-display this text area, press Windows key + Shift key.

Other lower figures in Fig. 3 are examples of displaying these icons and instruction text area. The first example shows "Shift Key + Left Click" without instruction text area. The next figure is an example of "Ctrl Key + Right Click" with the texts. The difference of right click and left click is not only the shape of the icon but also its color. Left click button is green and right one is orange. The last example is "Ctrl Key + Alt Key + A." without mouse clicking. As shown in the last example, every combination key with modifier keys is displayed.

Fig.4 is a screen shot which shows operation of Adobe Illustrator with SZKIT. The operation is same as the second example in Fig. 2, drugging with Alt key. It is clear what kind of operation is done.

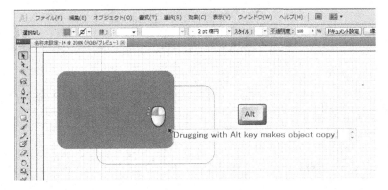

Fig. 4. A screen shot which shows operation of Adobe Illustrator with SZKIT

3   Function of Showing Instruction Texts

In this section, functions of showing instruction texts are explained. Basically, the instruction texts have a role to tell each steps of operation of the targeted software. To realize it, the series of texts should be prepared in advance and it will be changes sequentially in appropriate timing. To make it easy for teaching staffs, we designed SZKIT as to load series of texts at once and show each text blocks which is separated a brank line. It means that the works teaching staff has to do is preparing an instruction text file and input a brank line between each text blocks.

Then, these text blocks have to be changed in appropriate timing during the lecture such as subtitles in the movie film. To implement this changing function, SZKIT accepts triggered event like key action which causes forwarding or rewinding the text blocks. Actually we were annoyed by this point because SZKIT runs simultaneously to the targeted software and the focus of the operating system should be keep on the targeted software, not on SZKIT. It means that the key action to control SZKIT should not be the same as any operation of the other software. In usual, designing software has so many combination keys and it is difficult to find a combination which no software use. We had an idea of using gamepad to control SZKIT, however, it is better without special input devices. After several discussions, we finally decided that SZKIT uses key hooking of space bar. As shown in Fig. 5, "Space bar + S" causes forwarding and "Space bar + W" causes rewinding the instruction text block. Addition to that key assignment, "Space bar + number" is implemented for changing the series of text files which file name starts with numbers. Space bar works normally when the operator doesn't press any key after pressing space bar, this key hooking doesn't disturb normal operation of space bar.

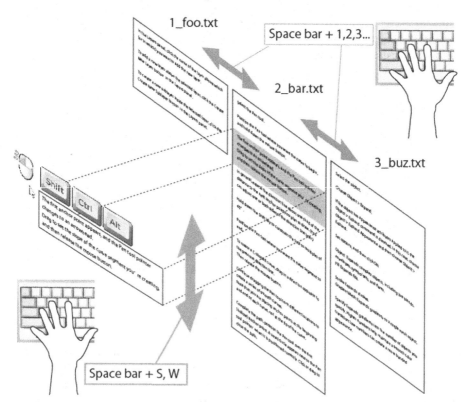

Fig. 5. Key assignment of changing instruction text blocks

Using this key assignment, teaching staff can change the instruction text block in appropriate timing without being out of focus on the targeted software. He can also show to hearing impaired students mouse click and modifier key operations without any special actions as a matter of course.

In addition, it is possible to edit the instruction text blocks after pressing "Windows + Shift Key" which means focusing on SZKIT. The edited instruction text is automatically saved when SZKIT exits. With help of this function, the teaching staff can brush up his instruction text after the lecture.

4   Estimation by Hearing Impaired Students

In the autumn semester of 2011, one of the authors uses SZKIT in his lecture after checking the plan by Ethical Review Board of our university. It was fifteen weeks lecture for teaching Adobe Illustrator. All students who participate in this lecture are hearing impaired, including severe one and the number of the students is fifteen. Then, we conducted simple questionnaire consists of two section to these students at the end of the semester. Unfortunately the number of valid responses is fourteen, because one of the students seems to misunderstand the questions and did not answer the most of questions. The questions of the first part are as follows:

- Do you think the function of showing modifier keys is useful for learning computer operation?
- Do you think the function of showing mouse click icon is useful for learning operation and learning a timing of clicking the mouse?
- Do you think the function of showing instruction texts is useful for leaning computer operation?

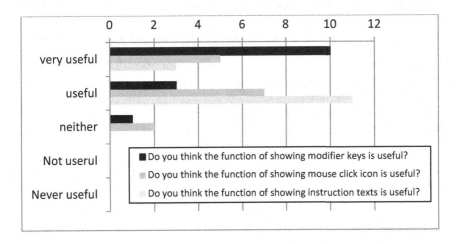

Fig. 6. Number of students answering the questionnaire after the lecture

The results of the first part of the questionnaire are shown in Fig.6. This can tell us most of students feel SZKIT is useful, especially showing modifier key is important rather than the instruction texts. We think the reason is that showing icons of modifier keys and mouse click are the first experience for them. On the other hand, text information is not so new for them because we usually use speech to text service in several lectures.

The second part of the questionnaire is conducted with forms of free comments. The questions are as follows:

- SZKIT shows icons and texts around of mouse cursor. What do you think about it? Please write any advantage or disadvantage of it, compare with a situation that these components are aligned separately to the mouse cursor.
- When do you feel SZKIT is useful? What is the situation you feel SZKIT is useful? Please write down it with its reasons.

The answers of the first question of the second part have same tendency. Most of students wrote more or less similar answer like as follows.

- "I think it is good because we don't have to transfer our gaze."
- "If the instruction text is placed far from the mouse cursor, I cannot follow the operation, the timing of clicking mouse button or hitting keys I have to do will be delayed."
- "I can really understand what operation is going on, because these icons are aside of the mouse cursor."

These comments are thought as an advantage of SZKIT. On the contrary, we acquired several feedback comments to improve SZKIT.

- "It is better to increase little bit the distance between icons and mouse cursor."
- "The modifier key icons disappear soon. I need more time to understand what the key is."
- "Sometimes the instruction text area covered objects which I would like to see."

From these comments, SZKIT should equip some adjustment function for distance between icons and mouse cursor, for delay time to disappear icons, for the space of the instruction text in the future.

Addition to these students answer, we would like to remark a comment from the teaching staff himself.

- "I feel surely that the students understand the designing software well compare with last lecture without SZKIT. The tangible effect is that there is less questions about operations from students and less miss operations. "

5   Conclusion

To solve the problems of teaching computer operation to hearing impaired students, we developed a support software tool which displays mouse clicking and modifier keys and instruction texts. With this software, instruction texts and its operation is clearly display on the screen. Moreover, it is easy to make e-learning contents only recording the operation, because all required information is automatically mix into the screen.

We think SZKIT is not only for the hearing impaired students, but also for elderly person or novice person when they learn computer operations.

References

1. Cruse, E.: Using educational video in the classroom: Theory, research and practice, http://www.libraryvideo.com/articles/article26.asp
2. Debevc, M., Peljhan, Z.: The role of video technology in on-line lectures for the deaf. Disability and Rehabilitation 26(17), 1048–1059 (2004)
3. Wald, M.: Captioning for Deaf and Hard of Hearing People by Editing Automatic Speech Recognition in Real Time. In: Miesenberger, K., Klaus, J., Zagler, W., Karshmer, A.I. (eds.) ICCHP 2006. LNCS, vol. 4061, pp. 683–690. Springer, Heidelberg (2006)
4. Target, http://download.cnet.com/Target/3000-2075_4-10915620.html
5. osdHotkey, http://www.romeosa.com/osdHotkey/help.html

The Hybrid Book – One Document
for All in the Latest Development

Petr Hladík and Tomáš Gůra

Support Center for Students with Special Needs
Masaryk University, Brno, The Czech Republic
hladik@teiresias.muni.cz,
tomas.gura@mail.muni.cz
http://teiresias.muni.cz,
http://teiresias.muni.cz/hybridbook

Abstract. The term "Hybrid Book" stands for a digital document with a synchronized multimedia content. In the narrower sense, the Hybrid Book is a name of a technology used at Masaryk University for creation of study materials for users with a variety of information channel impairments: the blind, the deaf, dyslectics, and others. A document in this format can include a digital text, an audio recording of a text read by a human voice, and a video recording of a translation of a text into a sign language. These records are shown simultaneously by the given software application when browsing documents. A user can navigate in documents using a variety of specific navigation functions. The Hybrid Book does not only compensate for an information channel; for example, it can also be used as a unique system for creation of foreign language textbooks.

Keywords: (e)Accessibility, Assistive Technology, Design for All, eLearning and Universal Learning Design.

1   Introduction

We have been continuously developing the Hybrid Book at Masaryk University for more than ten years [1]. We understand the term "Hybrid Book" as a digital document, which includes at least two parallel records of an identical content – typically, text and audio – with a possibility to browse both records at the same time or alternately. The aim of such document is primarily to provide access to the given content for readers with a limited perception of some of the information channels (for example, the blind, the deaf, dyslectics, and others) and to present information to them with the help of complementing records in the least possibly distorted form.

Viewed thus, the Hybrid Book is primarily a digital publication type. As such it may consist of a variety of recording formats, which are ordered according to given rules. It this broadest sense, it is not a specific digital format. At Masaryk alone, three version of the Hybrid Book are currently in use. This overview focuses on the latest

K. Miesenberger et al. (Eds.): ICCHP 2012, Part I, LNCS 7382, pp. 18–24, 2012.
© Springer-Verlag Berlin Heidelberg 2012

version, the third generation of the Hybrid Book, which we will refer to as the Hybrid Book 3.0.

2   Hybrid Book 3.0

2.1   What Is the Hybrid Book 3.0

Unlike the previous version and some of its competing systems, the Hybrid Book 3.0 excels mainly in its full multimedia equipment. A document in this format may include a digital text, an audio recording, and a video recording. It enables a synchronized "playback" of these records and a hierarchical navigation in their contents.

We have laid emphasis on several requirements during the development of the format: firstly, on the requirement of a low-cost preparation, which term does not primarily refer to financial costs, but rather aims at minimal allocation of labor force and also a possible use of already existing texts and multimedia documents when compiling a hybrid book. This lead to the idea of "external storage of synchronization data", which means that besides the document content as such, there will be created data structures that describe what the document consists of and how its components are interconnected.

After several attempts to use an existing technology for this purpose (such as the format SMIL, for example) which did not lead to promising results, we decided to develop the record of synchronization data on our own. Based on XML, we created a simple, manually editable record for publication and synchronization data.

2.2   Reading a Hybrid Book

As we decided to develop our own presentation format for the Hybrid Book, we are naturally also forced to offer tools for its decoding – tools for reading and browsing documents created in this format. Development of these software programs is carried out together with the development of the format itself. Each version of the Hybrid Book has its document reader.

Hybrid Book Reader [2]. The Web application "Hybrid Book Reader" is a practical means of hybrid document browsing. As of now, all possibilities that the Hybrid Book Format offers are not yet integrated, but its functionality is continuously expanded. Its current version supports the essential Hybrid Book functions:

- simultaneous playback of all table of contents records,
- synchronized navigation,
- navigation in the document hierarchical structure,
- switching between individual records,
- currently read passage display.

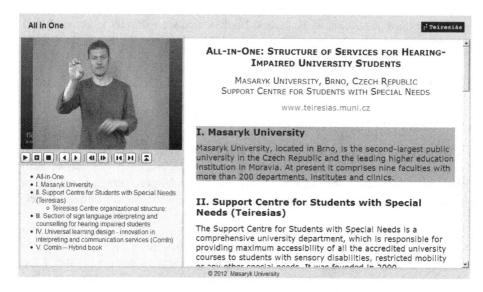

Fig. 1. Hybrid Book Reader

There are various ways of reading a Hybrid Book:

- following a continuously moving synchronized content,
- playback of individual passages,
- following a selected recording only,
- navigation in reading by phrases, headlines (including their level in the document outline).

Supported media:

- text in HTML format,
- video in MPEG-4 and FLV formats,
- audio in MP3, WAV, and FLV formats.

Document browsing functions:

- begin continuous simultaneous playback,
- play the selected passage only,
- skip to the next phrase,
- skip to the previous phrase,
- skip to the next headline,
- skip to the previous headline,
- skip to the next headline of the same level,
- skip to the previous headline of the same level,
- skip to one level above.

The Hybrid Book Reader enables the user interface adjustment according to the document content and according to the user's needs. For example, if a document only includes a text and audio, the video player automatically hides when the document is open.

A user can use simple controls to change positions of objects on the screen, hide or show objects according to their temporary needs, and it is also possible to change the color scheme and text size.

2.3   Creating a Hybrid Book

Just as the person reading a Hybrid Book needs the reader application, a creator needs a tool for a convenient creation of the Hybrid Book content. It has been mentioned above that the content itself (text and multimedia) basically remains in the form which is commonly used for other applications – thus it seems reasonable to leave creators with the liberty to use editing tools of their preference.

For these reasons, we do not pay much attention to developing tools for Hybrid Book content editing, but we focus primarily on tools enabling synchronization (and compiling) of already existing contents.

Hybrid Book Creator. The tool Hybrid Book Creator can be used for synchronization of various types of digital documents when creating a Hybrid Book. This tool was designed specifically for designing the document structure and subesquent synchronization of selected types of digital data.

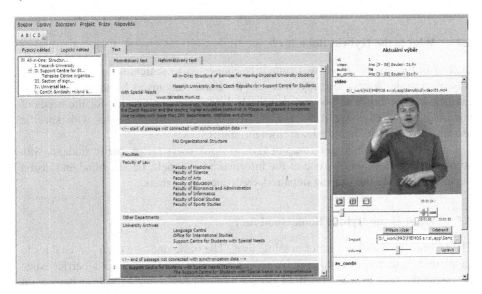

Fig. 2. Hybrid Book Creator

The application works primarily with a text in the HTML format, which it uses for marking the Hybrid Book structure and preparing a script for an audio/video studio creating the multimedia content. Naturally, it is also possible to attach already existing multimedia files and use an integrated editor to mark synchronization units in them.

The program creates a valid code of the Hybrid Book 3.0 and distributes it together with the document content to a selected storage. It includes a lot of automatic functions such as document content arrangement and existing multimedia data attachment.

The Hybrid Book Creator is also a universal application that also offers to import data from older Hybrid Book versions and the Daisy DTB format. It also allows publication of existing documents in these formats.

Alternative Uses. The code of the Hybrid Book has been designed so that it is transparent, comprehensible and "human-friendly". Although the use of automatic tools for document creation is the simplest way, the form of the record does not hinder a manual creation and editing of documents. The main aim is not as much to make manual editing possible; it is to make integration of the Hybrid Book format into other applications as simple as possible. For example, it is very simple to use this format to add sound to specific parts of web pages, or supplement them with a translation into or a commentary in a sign language.

This is a way to produce "miniature" Hybrid Books as alternative elements granting access to information on web pages to users with impairment. It is possible to manually create documents which include few synchronization units in a relatively short time.

2.4   Who Is the Hybrid Book for?

Interest in the Hybrid Book was primarily connected to searching for an alternative way of granting access to study materials for blind students at Masaryk University. Further practice however showed that the Hybrid Book can provide for the needs of not only the blind – we registered positive feedback from readers with specific learning disorders such as dyslexia from the start.

Currently, the main target group of Hybrid Book users are primarily students with an impaired perception of some of the information channels, i.e. the blind and vision impaired, the deaf and hearing impaired, dyslectics, and others.

2.5   What Is the Hybrid Book Good for?

The Hybrid Book offers a lot of possible uses. The basic ones are clear – it enables to supplement a text with an alternative record for users who encounter a barrier when accessing the text. The Hybrid Book does not only assist to get over these barriers: it can also be a unique tool for foreign language teaching (both spoken and sign languages) as proves the popularity of an English textbook published in this format at Masaryk years ago. A possibility to engage native speakers' services for creation of a content of such textbook is an obvious benefit for the user.

Besides teaching languages, the Hybrid Book aspires to reach completely different areas, too. As mentioned above, it is quite simple to use it to add an alternative content to a web page, and to supplement some of the parts of a web page with a spoken interpretation or a translation into a sign language. The use of the Hybrid Book 3.0 for these purposes is currently in the testing stage, which currently consists of specialized attempts to show whether the Hybrid Book 3.0 is really suitable for this. If our assumptions are confirmed, we could develop a framework for web page creators facilitating the integration of hybrid documents or Hybrid Book functions into web pages and applications.

2.6 Competing Applications

Creators of the Hybrid Book 3.0 began to work with a similar resolution as the one that preceded the birth of the first generation of the Hybrid Book: to create a system which will primarily supplement what is missing elsewhere. The Hybrid Book has been compared to its immediate competitor Daisy DTB [3] at Masaryk since the beginning of its development. The first two generations of the Hybrid Book are comparable to Daisy DTB, although the second generation of the Hybrid Book was already primarily intended for distribution in the World Wide Web environment; however, such a comparison is only hardly possible with the third generation. For one thing, the system now includes an element that Daisy does not take into account – video recordings; for another, the philosophy of the system itself has changed: it has been said that the Hybrid Book pushes the way of document creation from simple interpretation of a given text in the same language more towards a translation of the text into another language, or towards supplementing the pristine content with alternatives allowing to specify the presented information.

In the area of providing access to documents for the blind and vision impaired, the Hybrid Book compares well to Daisy DTB as concerns the user. As concerns creation, the Hybrid Book does not yet have such support. Technically, however, the Hybrid Book has an advantage in its code, which is transparent, logical and simply manually editable. Moreover, the code is designed so that it allows simple addition of new functionalities, such as new multimedia document and text formats. The code is not yet standardized, which can be viewed as its shortcoming, of course – on the other hand, SMIL – the language used by Daisy DTB – is the W3C standard but it lacks general support and is not widespread[d]. This language was also considered as the language of the Hybrid Book, but its complicated code and practically zero web support diverted the developers' interest towards a simple XML encoding[e].

The Hybrid Book 3.0 has been seen as a suitable format for the Internet environment from the beginning. Shortcomings in the possibilities to distribute Hybrid Books on hard media – still heavily requested mainly by the blind – will be gradually recompensed. Presently, the only Hybrid Book reader is a web application, which needs a web server to run; and, this does not help distribution on hard media much. The development team at Masaryk has already designed client applications able to run without the web environment. Their implementation is planned for the near future.

3   Future Prospects and the Conclusion

The Hybrid Book 3.0 is a young document format built on years of experience and verified basis. Its program code enables simple integration into other systems and introduction of new functionalities. Presently, software tools for document creation and reading in this format are available. These tools as well as the format itself are under constant development and testing. A lot of theoretical and practical attempts to integrate the technology into various systems, mainly web applications, are done.

We believe that the Hybrid Book is a sufficiently specific format not to remain unnoticed by professionals and users in the area of the creation of documents with synchronized contents as well as web and local software applications developers. By all means, the primary aim of the Hybrid Book development team is to provide its users with the easiest possible access to undistorted information presented by the author of the studied work.

References

1. Teiresias Centre, http://teiresias.muni.cz/?chapter=7-4&lang=en
2. Hybrid Book Reader, http://teiresias.muni.cz/hybridbook
3. Daisy Consortium, http://www.daisy.org

Dealing with Changes in Supporting Students with Disabilities in Higher Education

Andrea Petz and Klaus Miesenberger

Institute Integriert Studieren, Johannes Kepler University of Linz, Linz, Austria
{andrea.petz,klaus.miesenberger}@jku.at

Abstract. This paper discusses necessary changes and adaptations faced in supporting students with disabilities at Linz University within the last 20 years and the methodology used compared to other support schemes around Europe. The research is based on findings from the study "Social Situation of People with Disabilities in Austria", the only formal Austrian study also dealing with disability and higher education (as information on a possible "disability" is numbered among "highly sensitive personal data" and therefore not formally surveyed during enrollment), findings from an own survey collecting information from support structures for students with disabilities at Universities in Europe and experiences from supporting students with most diverse (dis-)abilities, skills and knowledge.

Keywords: Counseling, Support, Disability, Students, University, Higher Education, Social Inclusion.

1   Idea

Following a study on the "Social situation of People with Disabilities in Austria" carried out by the Austrian government (Federal Ministry of Labor, Social Affairs and Consumer Protection) within the framework of the annual "European Union Statistics on Income and Living Conditions" (EU-SILC) survey ([2], panel size 15.000 persons in 6000 households), 18% of all Austrian citizens without a formal recognized disability end their education after compulsory education (9 years of school). Within the group of people with disabilities, a significantly higher amount of persons (46%) end their educational path after compulsory school.

The "Matura", the formal certificate that entitles people in Austria to enter Higher Education (e.g. university or university of applied science) is reached by 30% of all Austrians without a formally stated disability and by 11% out of the group of people with disabilities. As information on disability is subject to special data security regulations, this information is not asked when people enroll for Higher Education. There are of course numbers given by disability support structures (installed at most Austrian Higher Education institutions) but it is up to the individual with a disability or chronic illness to get in touch with these structures and "re-appear on the screen". Therefore, there are no formal surveyed numbers on people with disabilities studying

K. Miesenberger et al. (Eds.): ICCHP 2012, Part I, LNCS 7382, pp. 25–32, 2012.

and/or finishing their studies and reaching a career different from "traditional" jobs but numbers given by disability support services throughout Austria are, again, far smaller than the number within the group of people without a disability. Out of own experiences, this group is further diminishing during their time in Higher Education until successfully entering the first labor market at a position corresponding to personal abilities, knowledge, skills and competences.

Many issues are to be sorted out before, during and after Higher Education – issues resulting from specific needs that might arise from a disability or chronic illness, issues connected to a specific study scheme, connected to Assistive Technologies (AT) and Information and Communication Technologies (ICT) in use… but first and foremost issues that should be part of a most flexible, interactive and reliable support framework in order to create possibilities and facilitate pathways [8].

2   State of the Art and Necessary Steps Beyond Seen from Austrian Perspective

In 1991, the institute Integriert Studieren at Linz University was founded as "Endeavour Informatics for the Blind", the first formal Austrian offer for students with disabilities, following experiences and expertise of a similar scheme at Karlsruhe Institute of Technology [7]. The 2 supported students already worked with Braille Displays and PCs (MS DOS™) and were supplied with study literature in accessible formats. [6]

In these first years, blind and partially sighted people from all over Austria came (or, more precise, 'had to come') to Linz and wanted to study computer science – even if this field of study was not the optimal for them. Today, the institute works as function unit in supporting the university board in various issues connected to "disability" at Linz University reaching from counseling administrative staff and lecturers in disability issues over teaching and research to the traditional service provision for our students.

Table 1. Distribution of disability forms amongst the institute's students population (N=60, 3 characterized their situation as "combined disability" - only the most influencing was counted)

Form of Disability	Numbers
Blind / Partially sighted	24
Motor / Manipulation	14
SPLD	4
Psychological constraints	2
Deaf / Hard of Hearing	3
Chronic Disease	2
Speech / Language	1
"Not to be published"	10
Total	**60**

To get an overview, table 1 shows the distribution of disability forms on the institute's student population in 2012.

There are 3 people out of these 60 individuals characterizing their constraints as "multiple disability / combination of different disabilities" where only the most influencing was counted.

Since 1991, as described above, a continuous and ongoing change has taken place, caused by:

- The rapid progress in ICT / AT facilitating more and more ways of transport and representation of knowledge and information, facilitating the inclusion of more and more people with most diverse forms and combinations of disabilities into secondary education that led to
- "New" forms of disabilities entering University. Connected to this,
- The numbers of people with disabilities entering University rose and of course that led to
- Additional fields of Study and universities our students with disabilities are interested in, resulting in changes in:
  - Work and workflows
  - Services provided
  - Tasks fulfilled and
  - Funding needed

This paper discusses the changes faced in supporting students with disabilities at Linz University and the methodology used compared to other support schemes around Europe presented within the EU wide "Higher Education Accessibility Guide" (HEAG) installed by the European Agency for Development in Special Needs Education. As the (online) survey amongst 100 support structures from Austria, Belgium, Croatia, Czech Republic, Denmark, Estonia, Finland, France, Germany, Greece, Iceland, Latvia, Lithuania, Luxembourg, Malta, the Netherlands, Romania, Sweden and UK that we designed to collect further information is running in the moment, only first results are available for this paper and stable results for the presentation in July. Feedback from more than half of the structures asked (from Austria, Czech Republic, Sweden and Germany) shows that the institute's working group "social inclusion" and its service offer follows a quite different approach, therefore it will be described on the following pages in more depth.

3   Methodologies Used to Comply with the Changes Faced in Daily Work

As described above, the most influencing changes resulted in necessary adaptations in the following areas:

- Work and workflows
- Services provided

- Tasks fulfilled and
- Funding needed, primarily for personal assistance, e.g. sign language interpretation

New technical / technological developments helped in solving some of the issues, other requirements had to be tackled by changes and adaptations in the basic organizational structure of the support scheme or adjustments in the provision with accessible study materials / study literature had to be evolved from 1:1 or face to face personal assistant settings to a user-centered, self administering and transferable (i.e. independent from University, field of study, disability form and number of students supported), highly available web based toolset, an experience also reported by some of the answering institutions from our survey [1].

The core idea in short words is to provide a web based tool / literature database where the students enter the study materials they need. If available, the students may download the adapted materials directly, otherwise a standardized workflow is triggered. This workflow reaches from putting a query to publishers in order to get the texts needed in digital formats over the adaptation process until the provision of the ready materials – based on "open document" files – easily convertible to diverse formats: "simple .doc / .html" over .xhtml to .mp3 and finally also Daisy versions.

4   R&D Work and Results

Within the first years of supporting blind and partially sighted students at Linz University, the provision with study materials / study literature and accessible working environments were at focus.

With the rising number of (prospective) students there was a need to expand and transfer the service scheme to other experts, supportive structures, universities, forms of disabilities and fields of study. Simultaneously, the administrative effort and the support expenses (in terms of time) for this process had to be reduced but in the same time tailored to the individual needs and nevertheless made efficient, manageable and affordable.

Another issue was the experience that the dropout rate of students with disabilities was – even with the best adapted study materials and technical / technological framework – reasonably higher than in the "mainstream population". Evaluations showed that - in most cases - there was a lack of:

- Social skills
  - Necessary to build up personal relationships and communicate own needs resulting from the disability and getting part of / build up supportive peer groups that are crucial in order to succeed at University, as "lone fighters" are always at the risk of failure caused by the far higher effort in studying and getting further
- Communicative skills
  - Strongly connected to the social skills needed for studying effectively – but in most cases not learned during (even integrative) first / secondary education

- Sound knowledge of studying at university level, planned fields of study and necessary ICT / AT skills
  - It is necessary to get in touch with prospective students as early as possible in order to counsel them in using ICT / AT efficiently and work with them on finding and choosing a study field corresponding to their skills, competences and interests;

That finally, amongst other issues (health related, related to financial issues or other influencing factors), led to the observed reasonably higher dropout rate.

Therefore, an additional service, the working group "social inclusion" was installed, responsible for supporting the students in this additional issues as well as doing research on the topic.

The following scheme was developed in order to complement the already implemented institute's technical / technological support:

Fig. 1. Support pyramid for students with disabilities at Linz University showing that most support is needed when starting or even before starting Higher Education

This model acts already before the formal start at university by contributing to activities like the "International Camp on Communication and Computers" [4] and provides interested young people as well as experts in the field with information and strategies on the efficient use of ICT / AT as well as informing them on studying and possible support structures available.

Before starting at university, there is also an orientation phase where the prospective students get to know the university, the campus, the people involved in supporting them and the support offers in terms of what the institute does and what is left to the individual. In this initial phase, it is necessary to get to know the structures and procedures the prospective students used to take part in classroom education, write exams, learn to check what means and support activities are best apted for the individual. It would be highly beneficial to get in touch with the High School teachers to discuss these issues also on a professional level (not to talk about a formal case management approach) but in most cases this contact is not possible so the first findings are based on remarks given by the prospective student.

This first interview is a guided interview following a checklist comprising all possible aspects and issues (e.g. financial, housing and transport or other mobility issues, differences between high school and university, possible study courses and interests, necessary steps to be taken,...) that leads to a "To-Do-List" for both, the student and the supporter and a first overview on needed support (digital format used, PC usage, AT usage, mobility training needed, help with further administrative steps,...) that will be improved and changed within the first weeks / months of study or lateron as this first file is used for the whole stay at Linz University and checked at least once a year for possible improvements.

If needed (and wanted), the institute connects the prospective students with different experts, from low vision or mobility trainers over AT providers to the psychological counseling services on site.

Furthermore the prospective students are put in touch as early as possible with the study course (e.g. by visiting lectures as guest and getting in touch with universitary teaching and all of its differences to High School education for the first time) and students out of the institute´s population [5]. Those students already study the course the prospective students are interested in and are able to give both, information, tips and tricks and an inside view as well as a first contact point, someone they already know for future questions and activities.

This "tandem" or "peer support" approach is highly effective and enriches similar offers provided for all students by the Linz University Students Union. It is important that the peers involved show a high level of stability, social skills and commitment. There is no formal additional training for them as this support – as well as what is done in meetings, how often the persons meet and how and where they do it – is totally user driven in order not to endanger this unique informal setting by "over – institutionalizing" it. In case of problems or questions that need other structures to jump in, the peers and mentees are asked to get in touch with the institute.

Of course this approach is depending on the number of students supported and the number of study courses present within the population and it might take some time to match the "right peer" for every new student, but this approach underpins the necessity to "know the people" that are supported and to check if they are able and willing to take over this or another future role within the institute what asks for an intensive contact between supporter and student – an investment of time that pays off in any case as students in most cases benefit from this setting and are keen in giving back their experiences and getting in touch with other people. The amount of time and contact needed gets smaller with the progresses the students make in their career at university. During their studies, a variety of offers (besides the "traditional" provision of accessible study materials) is provided.

The offers range from a representative of the supported student body, incoming/outgoing evaluation, team / students meetings, development dialogues, (inclusive) social events like cooking together, over organized excursions and events to specific trainings like "Body language, mimics and gestures / communicating disability", "assessment centre training", "presentation skills" and individualized mobility training.

Another important part of our activities concentrates on the provision of possibilities to test oneself within scientific / professional settings (projects and internships in connection to projects carried out at the institute or with partnering institutions like employment services), that often already opens important doors to a later professional entry and a mentoring program (planned for next summer term) to get professional feedback from outside university.

Before leaving University, the activities concentrate on the successful career entry and a smooth transition into the labor market. Co-operation with firms, partners and employment services gives the necessary basis.

All the described activities for students (except for the first guided interview where we get in touch with the student and set up a draft framework for support) are offers. Few students prefer to organize most of their study courses completely on their own and drop in or email from time to time to inform us on new activities / developments or that business is as usual and ok. Also these short contacts are as well important to stay in touch and keep connected to the institute what facilitates stability as well as flexibility and leads to a stronger cohesion and a smaller risk of dropping out. 1.5 full time equivalents were allocated for supporting those 60 students, all interested prospective students and fulfilling the other tasks above by order of the university administration / management that enriched the traditional service. Additionally to this highly individual counseling and support scheme, the institute appointed for the winter term ("semester") 2011/2012:

- 8 contract workers for the (accessible) digital adaptation of 85 books / handouts
- 8 contract workers for assistance during 65 exams (e.g. writing assistance),

what leads to expenditures of around

- 360 hours for the adaptation of study materials and
- 102 hours for exam assistance.

These conjoint activities will possibly lead to a better ratio in students with disabilities finishing their studies and successfully entering the first labor market as well as reduce the risk of dropping out to personal factors (that are in equal measure relevant to people without a formal recognized disability) like health related issues, financial issues etc., a fact that has to be evaluated and monitored formally during the next years as the first students that entered this new scheme are now preparing to finish their studies.

5   Impact on and Contributions to the Field

In designing the support structure as flexible, expandable and transferable as possible, the impact on the quality of support provided at university level can be estimated as high. Together with keeping the administrative scheme as efficient, user-centered and accessible as possible, more time and resources can be put in necessary activities in the field of social inclusion what leads to a smaller dropout rate and a complete package of support provided.

6   Conclusion and Planned Activities

The scheme of service provision for students with disabilities and chronic illness at Linz University is rather open, flexible and expandable to different needs, disabilities, AT and ICT used and fields of study. This leads to a higher number of students that can be served and therefore get the possibility to study and choose an educational path and a career corresponding to their personal skills, competences and interests.

During the next year(s), new activities like preparatory language courses for deaf students in order to enable them to write essays, mentoring or peer group counseling / learning support groups ("Tandem Learning") have to be implemented and the scheme has to be evaluated and benchmarked with other support structures (partially concentrating on a single form of disability or just dealing with the provision of accessible study literature / accessible study materials) in terms of resources needed, "output" of students, contentment of students and university partners involved.

References

1. Bernareggi, C., Hengstberger, B., Brigatti, V.: Transnational Support to Visually Impaired in Scientific University Courses. In: Miesenberger, K., Klaus, J., Zagler, W., Karshmer, A.I. (eds.) ICCHP 2008. LNCS, vol. 5105, pp. 946–952. Springer, Heidelberg (2008)
2. EU-silc survey, http://epp.eurostat.ec.europa.eu/portal/page/portal/microdata/eu_silc (last lookup in January 2012)
3. HEAG, Higher Education Accessibility Guide, http://www.european-agency.org/agency-projects/heag (last lookup in January 2012)
4. ICC, International Camp on Communication and Computers, http://www.icc-camp.info (last lookup in January 2012)
5. Katoh, H., Pauly, M., Hara, S., Nagaoka, H., Miesenberger, K.: Learning from Each Other: Comparing the Service Provision for Blind and Visually-Impaired Students in Post-secondary Education in Japan and Europe. In: Miesenberger, K., Klaus, J., Zagler, W. (eds.) ICCHP 2002. LNCS, vol. 2398, pp. 753–775. Springer, Heidelberg (2002)
6. Petz, A., Miesenberger, K., Stöger, B.: Developing Academic Skills among Print Disabled Students: IT Based Austrian-Wide Network for Service Provision. In: Miesenberger, K., Klaus, J., Zagler, W. (eds.) ICCHP 2002. LNCS, vol. 2398, pp. 739–746. Springer, Heidelberg (2002)
7. SZS, "Study Center for Visually Impaired Students" at Karlsruhe Institute of Technology, http://www.szs.uni-karlsruhe.de/ (last lookup in January 2012)
8. Weiermair-Märki, C., Unterfrauner, E.: Institutional Conditions for the Implementation of Accessible Lifelong Learning (ALL) Based on the EU4ALL Approach. In: Miesenberger, K., Klaus, J., Zagler, W., Karshmer, A. (eds.) ICCHP 2010. LNCS, vol. 6179, pp. 492–494. Springer, Heidelberg (2010)

Putting the Disabled Student in Charge: Introduction to the Special Thematic Session

Lisa Featherstone and Simon Ball

JISC TechDis
{lisa,simon}@techdis.ac.uk

Abstract. Students with disabilities or impairments have often been passive recipients of 'inclusive practice' or 'assistive technology'. The Special Thematic Session (STS) on Putting the Disabled Student in Charge focusses on topics that have a direct impact upon the education of disabled students and covers all aspects of disabled students' education, from the development of resources to full participation in lectures and collaborative work and the provision of alternative formats.

1   Introduction

Students with disabilities or impairments have often been passive recipients of 'inclusive practice' or 'assistive technology'. Technological developments are enabling the much more **active participation and influence of disabled students** upon their own education.

With an increasingly diverse student body taking part in further and higher education, the need for education to respond quickly and flexibly to a variety of needs is becoming more urgent. Many developments in enhancing the **accessibility or inclusivity of teaching and learning through technology** are now taking place.

Some of these developments are cohort-specific, such as tools to aid learners with specific impairments or learning disabilities. Others are more generally inclusive, such as the creation of accessible learning platforms or the inclusive use of technologies in the classroom or fieldwork. However, many barriers remain, and we wish to address these in this Special Thematic Session. The topics that could be covered under this STS are many and varied, but the key factor linking them is that they have a **direct impact upon the education of disabled students**, enabling those students to have a greater degree of control over their own education and destiny.

2   Areas Covered by This STS

Involving disabled students in the development of accessible technology is essential if they are to be active participants in their learning. **Kushalnagar** stresses the importance of this and suggests a methodology for doing so effectively. **Martinez, Lucas et al** acknowledge the difficulties faced by children, particularly those with particular needs, using a traditional mouse and keyboard to interact with a computer.

K. Miesenberger et al. (Eds.): ICCHP 2012, Part I, LNCS 7382, pp. 33–35, 2012.

They explore the possibilities presented by touch- and gesture-based inter-faces, and the possible need for a standard set of gestures. Synote is a system offering easier access, searching and management of lecture recordings developed by **Wald** and the team at the University of Southampton. Recently the system has been further developed to include conversion for narrated PowerPoint files, a tool for crowdsourcing corrections of speech recognition errors and a mobile speech recording app to provide and record real-time captions.

There are particular difficulties faced by deaf students in lectures. Sign language interpreters are usually provided, but this creates a conflict for deaf students between two simultaneously presented sources of visual information (the lectures slides and the interpreter). By comparing the eye gaze patterns of both deaf and hearing students during lectures, **Kushalnagar** was able to provide a visual cue for deaf learners, alerting them of the need to switch their attention from one to the other. A survey by **Khölmann** measured the use of collaborative e-learning environments by visually impaired students, which are often not accessible for this group. Participation by visually impaired students is also the focus of **Borges** and **Tomé** who look specifically at music education. Their Musibraille project provides free software for teaching and editing musical notation in Braille, create an online library of Braille music and provide training for music teachers. The Access Toolkit developed by **Wald** et al aims to increase participation by students with a range of disabilities. The toolkit comprises three tools: Web2Access, a website which rates Web 2.0 services on accessibility; an accessible menu for pen drives, allowing users to easily access their portable software; and a web toolbar offering a range of functions to make web pages more accessible.

Assessment is an area that can be particularly problematic for disabled students, particularly those with profound and complex needs. **Faux** et al describe the development of InStep, a video assessment database tool that allows the measurement of progress over time in areas that are not covered by traditional assessments. In Japan, a national test is part of the admissions process for universities, but there is no audio version of the test available for print impaired students. **Fujiyoshi** et al designed a system to provide two audio versions using invisible barcodes to encode an audio version of the question. These barcodes were printed on to either the full exam paper or a version containing just the document structure. The barcodes could be read by scanning pens, which then played the audio to the student enabling them to access the test.

For many print impaired students, access to textbooks in alternative formats is an area in which they rely heavily on outside help and it can be a time-consuming process. **McNaught** and **Featherstone** argue that there is too great an emphasis on disability support staff for this service, where perhaps library staff have the greatest expertise, and also that dyslexic students are often poorly served. In Denmark, **Christensen** and **Stevns'** Biblus project provides a digital library solution which acts as a repositorfor existing alternative formats and uses the RoboBraille service to create new alternative format versions of texts. A similar project at Stanford

University by **Christensen**, **Keegan** and **Stevns**, uses a customized version of RoboBraille which empowers students to create their own alternative format versions of texts.

3   Conclusion

Disabled students need to be actively involved in their own education, fully participating alongside their peers and able to access the resources they need when they need them. Each of the tools and technologies described in this STS is designed to either improve the general accessibility of a subject area, examine current teaching practices or give students direct access to the resources they need; putting them firmly back in charge.

Biblus – A Digital Library to Support Integration of Visually Impaired in Mainstream Education

Lars Ballieu Christensen and Tanja Stevns

Synscenter Refsnæs and Sensus ApS,
Torvet 3-5, 2.tv.,
DK-3400 Hillerød, Denmark
{lbc,tanja}@robobraille.org

Abstract. This paper presents the background, status, challenges and planned future directions of the Danish Biblus project which aims creating a digital library solution to be used to support the integration of visually impaired pupils and students in the mainstream educational system. As a supplement to the RoboBraille alternative media conversion system as well as a stand-alone repository for copyrighted educational material in alternate formats, Biblus was created to allow students, teachers, visual impairment professionals and relatives to access digital versions of educational material. Subject to proper access rights, material can either be delivered directly to the user in the formats stored in the library or indirectly via RoboBraille as mp3 files, Daisy full text/full audio, e-books or Braille books. Future versions of Biblus will be available in multiple languages and include digital rights management as well as support for decentralised contribution of material.

Keywords: Digital library, inclusion, integration, mainstreaming, educational material, alternative media, Braille transcription, Daisy, mp3, e-book, blind, partially sighted, visually impaired, dyslexic, dyslexia.

1   Introduction

In the Danish educational system, most pupils and students with special needs are integrated in the mainstream system. Of the approx. 2,000 blind and partially sighted pupils in the Danish basic educational system (Danish: Folkeskolen), less than 100 pupils attend special school, bringing the integration ratio well above 98 per cent. In high school and beyond, the integration ratio is even higher. Although the support structure is somewhat different for pupils and students with a reading impairment, the model is similar: The vast majority of children with dyslexia are expected to attend mainstream school, although they may be taught in special reading classes whilst in the basic educational system.

A key barrier to the successful integration of pupils and students with special needs is the availability of educational material in suitable formats. In accordance with section 17 of the Danish Copyright Law, material can be produced in alternative formats for people who are incapable of using printed material. However, although

K. Miesenberger et al. (Eds.): ICCHP 2012, Part I, LNCS 7382, pp. 36–42, 2012.

almost all material is prepared and published electronically, Danish publishers seem somewhat reluctant to make these electronic copies available for alternative media production. As a consequence, printed books may need to be cut up, scanned and the formatting reapplied before they can be made available to the visually and reading impaired [4], [5].

Visually impaired pupils in the basic educational system are supported by Synscenter Refsnæs, the National Centre for Visually Impaired Children and Youth, who operates an efficient alternate media production unit. Its materials, however, have until recently not been available in a searchable format, nor have teachers, pupils, visual impairment (VI) professionals or relatives been able to download such material.

Nota, the national Danish library for the print disabled, does offer a digital library in the form of E17 (www.e17.dk). This library system, however, primarily includes material found in ordinary public libraries, hence lacking educational material. Although international solutions such as Bookshare were considered, an internal survey conducted in the spring of 2011 of existing digital library solutions that might be used, revealed no suitable candidates. As a result, it was decided to create a free digital library solution.

The project has received financial support from the Danish Agency for Culture.

2   The Proposed Solution

Consulting teachers, parents, VI professionals and alternative media professionals throughout Denmark as well as partners in selected European countries, a list of requirements to the system was developed. In brief, the solution needed to be able to manage users, titles, digital assets, access rights and various means of delivery mechanisms.

Users: Because the contents of the digital library system largely consist of copyrighted material, user management had to be based on those accommodated in the Danish copyright legislation. Consequently, all external access rights have to be linked to the primary user. In Biblus, a primary user is defined as a person with a visual impairment and all other external access from teachers, relatives and VI professionals has to be linked to users in the primary user category. In addition to these groups, the system had to accommodate alternative media professionals, systems administrators and guest users.

Titles: Titles constitute representations of printed material; a title consists of meta data such as an ISBN number, an author, a book title as well as information about the publisher, publication year, language, edition, possible translator and similar. To ensure accurateness and limit the resources required to register existing material, the digital library system should be integrated with the official Danish library database, danbib, through its Z39.50-based interface [6]. In addition to published material, the digital library system should be able to manage unpublished material such as lecture notes and PowerPoint presentations.

Digital Assets: A fancy name for alternate versions of printed books or other material. The digital library solution should be able to contain one or more digital versions of the printed books in alternative formats such as plain text documents in text, Microsoft Word and ODT, audio books and audio pictures in mp3-format, structured talking audio books in Daisy format, image and pdf files with large-print versions, movies and more. As some alternative versions of titles – such as math books – consist of a combination of electronic files and tactile material, the digital library system should also be able to manage the administration and shipment of tangible assets.

Access Rights: Although the vast majority of the contents of the digital library is expected to consist of copyrighted material, the library should also be capable of handling unrestricted material. As such, the solution should implement a hierarchy of access rights ranging from guest rights (can only access unrestricted material and search the index), via teachers/VI professionals/relatives (must be linked to a primary user; can access all material) to primary users (can access all material). Furthermore, the solution should be able to manage alternative media professionals (can add titles and digital assets) and administrators (can manage users).

Delivery Mechanisms: Once the user has identified a digital asset and subject to adequate access rights, the solution should make it possible to deliver this directly to the user by email or via a download link, or indirectly via the RoboBraille document conversion system.

To ensure that the digital library can be accessed by all types of users and to accommodate a future decentralised upload model, the solution should be web-based, comply with the W3C web accessibility guidelines [7] and work across all major architectures, operating systems and browsers. It should furthermore be possible to localise the solution to other languages and to support different copyright regimes.

3   Biblus Implementation

Based on the requirements listed, the Biblus digital library was successfully implemented during the second half of 2011. The solution was implemented as a web application in a Microsoft Windows environment using Active Server Pages, .NET 4.0 and SQL Server. Figure 1 below illustrates the relationship between titles and alternatives in Biblus:

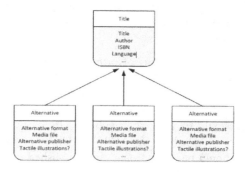

Fig. 1. The relationship between titles and alternatives in Biblus

The user interface adapts to the rights of authenticated users, making it usable for library consumers (primary users, professionals, relatives), as well as producers (alternative media professionals) and administrators.

Table 1 below summarises how different users may access the digital library:

Table 1. Functionality by user category

	Search/ Retrieve	Order	Manage titles	Reports	Manage users	Manage system
Administrators	✓		✓	✓	✓	✓
Producers	✓		✓	✓		
Primary users	✓	✓				
VI professionals	✓ *	✓				
Relatives	✓ *	✓				
Guests	✓ **	✓				

*   Must be associated with a primary user
**   Can only retrieve non-restricted material

The primary user must exist in the digital library before associated VI professionals and relatives can be created. Similarly, once a primary user is deleted, the access privileges of associated users are revoked. Access to the digital library is typically granted for a period of one year, but access privileges can be revoked at any time in case of misuse of the system or other circumstances.

Library consumers may search the digital library using simple as well as advanced search functions. Once a particular title has been located, the user can review available alternatives and order an electronic copy. Biblus supports two direct delivery methods and one indirect: Smaller files can be delivered directly through email whereas larger files need to be retrieved via download. The user may also use the download option in case of local limitations in his or her email system. Alternatively, the user can select to have documents delivered through RoboBraille [1 - 3], thus expanding the available formats beyond what is actually stored in the library. As an example, a user may locate an rtf version of a particular book and decide to have it converted by RoboBraille to a full-text/full-audio project, an mp3 file, an electronic Braille book or an e-book in EPUB format before it is actually delivered to the user. In cases where a piece of education material is not available in alternative format, users can place a request and be notified when it becomes available. Biblus can furthermore manage tactile illustrations and other tangible assets, informing the system administrator in cases where the user requests copies of these to be sent by ordinary mail.

Alternative media producers and administrators may create new titles and upload available alternatives of these titles to Biblus. Rather than having to type substantial amounts of meta data, available meta data may be retrieved through Z39.50 from the official Danish library database danbib by merely supplying the ISBN number of the title. In addition to standard meta data, producers and administrators can add specific information on the alternative media format such as Braille math in LaTeX, standard text with page markers for Braille, scanned document without OCR or plain text.

Likewise, it is possible to add information on the readability, suitable age groups and subject matter for the material. Figure 2 below shows the main interface of the Biblus digital library when logged in as an administrator:

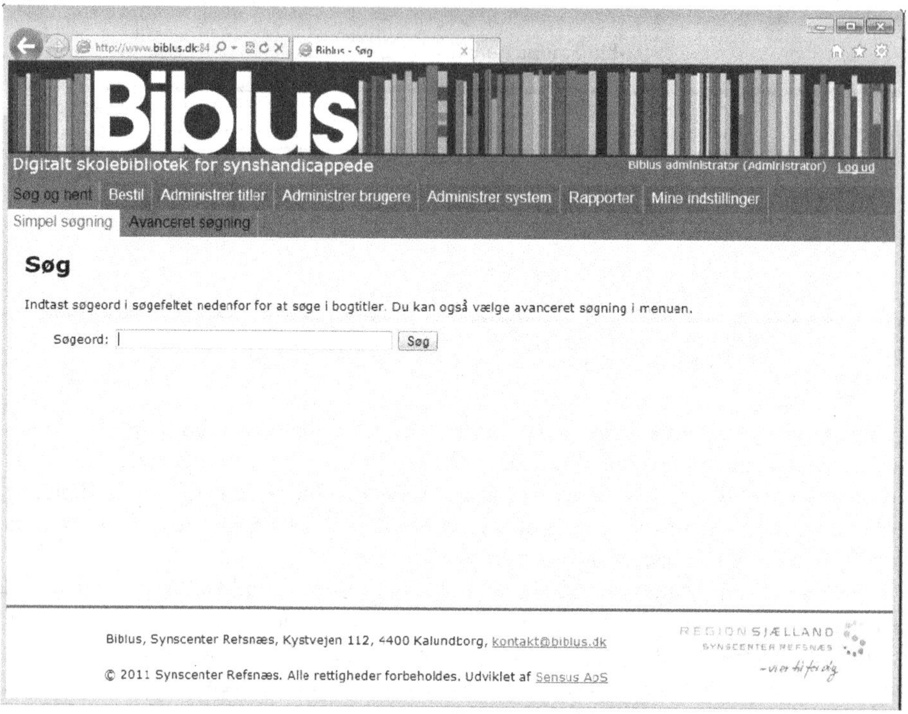

Fig. 2. The main Biblus interface when logged in as an administrator. The menus include Search and Retrieve, Order, Title administration, User administration, System administration, Reports and Personal settings. The user can furthermore switch between simple and advanced search.

To prevent abuse and copyright infringement, all activities are logged and material is made available to users with strict stipulations on acceptable use: Primary users may only use the material for their own, individual purposes. Teachers, professionals and relatives may on only use the material for their registered primary user. And producers and administrators may only use the material as part of their administration of Biblus.

4   Preliminary Results

Access to a searchable index of educational material in alternative media and the ability to download copies has long been on top of the requirement lists amongst teachers, VI professionals and parents. Although Biblus is still running in trial mode and is being populated with titles and alternatives, the digital library is expected to have a significant impact on the successful integration of visually impaired pupils and students through the Danish educational system. Not only will teachers be able to search and retrieve material when they prepare for class in order to find titles that are available in both print and suitable alternatives. VI professionals such as consultants and psychologists may search the index and propose suitable titles to parents and teachers, and parents and grandparents may retrieve material to study with their children and grandchildren.

During 2012, Biblus will be promoted to schools and other educational institutions, amongst VI professionals and through parents associations. Furthermore, the service will be localised to Polish, Hungarian, Bulgarian and Romanian and offered to similar groups in Poland, Hungary, Bulgaria, Romania and Moldova as part of RoboBraille-projects in those countries. Once the solution is operational, Synscenter Refsnæs will collect and publish information on its use and impact on a regular basis.

5   Conclusions and Future Activities

Creating a digital library for alternative media is a non-trivial activity with many caveats. As Synscenter Refsnæs has the intention of extending the Biblus user community to include different types of users as well as users outside of Denmark, the issue of copyrights is bound to become a challenge, not least the ability of the system to accommodate different copyright regimes.

Over the course of the coming years, Synscenter Refsnæs anticipates the following activities:

New Languages, New Countries: As a natural companion of RoboBraille, Biblus will become part of national RoboBraille implementation projects. Currently planned activities include a generic, English-language version as well as versions in East and Central Europe.

New user groups: Although the current version of Biblus has been created with the blind and partially sighted in mind, alternative media may also benefit the dyslexic, people with learning difficulties, people with poor reading skills and others. Subject to the provisions in the copyright legislation across Europe and elsewhere, Synscenter Refsnæs intends to target such groups as well.

Digital Rights Management (DRM): The current version of Biblus relies on access rights for protection. As the solution is offered to more users and user groups, a DRM mechanism is likely to be needed to digitally "watermark" media files in the library as well as the ability to supply material in accordance with different DRM implementations.

Decentralised Contribution: All material in the current version of Biblus is supplied by Synscenter Refsnæs and associated alternative media producers. Future versions will include the ability for decentralised contributions by teachers, relatives and volunteers to upload material. In order to facilitate such contributions, a quality management workflow must be added.

Integration with other Library Databases: As Biblus is introduced in other countries, the need arise for integration with other databases of library meta data. These include databases such as Google Books, Amazon and the US Library of Congress, and well as national databases.

Material Production Workflow: At present, the workflows in Biblus mainly support the needs of the library consumers, who can search and download material, and order material not already in the digital library system. To support the use of Biblus as a protected internal repository of alternative media as well as the process of receiving orders and converting material into alternative formats, a workflow component will be added to Biblus.

References

1. Christensen, L.B.: RoboBraille – Automated Braille Translation by Means of an E-Mail Robot. In: Miesenberger, K., Klaus, J., Zagler, W., Karshmer, A.I. (eds.) ICCHP 2006. LNCS, vol. 4061, pp. 1102–1109. Springer, Heidelberg (2006)
2. Christensen, L.B.: RoboBraille – Braille Unlimited. In: The Educator, ICEVI 2009, vol. XXI(2), pp. 32–37 (2009)
3. Christensen, L.B.: Multilingual Two-Way Braille Translation. In: Klaus, J., et al. (eds.) Interdisciplinary Aspects on Computers Helping People with Special Needs, Österreichische Computer Gesellschaft/R. Oldenbourg Wien München (1996)
4. Christensen, L.B.: The Importance of Information Technology for Visually Impaired Children and Youngsters and the Expectations for Future Development. In: Proceedings of the ICEVI European Conference (2000)
5. Bengtsson, S., et al.: Blinde børn – Integration eller isolation. SFI (2010)
6. Larsen, K.: Bibliotek.dk: opening the Danish union catalogue to the public. Interlending & Document Supply 35(4), 205–210 (2010)
7. Web Content Accessibility Guidelines 2.0, W3C (2008)

Alternative Approaches to Alternative Formats – Changing Expectations by Challenging Myths

Alistair McNaught and Lisa Featherstone

JISC TechDis
{alistair,lisa}@techdis.ac.uk

Abstract. Traditional textbooks can be difficult for print impaired learners to access. Every organisation has its own approach to providing alternative formats but there are common myths that need to be dispelled: the myth of responsibility, that alternative formats should be provided by disability support staff; the myth of specialism, that disabled students should be dealt with by a small team of specialist staff; and the myth that e-books are automatically accessible. This paper suggests a move beyond alternative formats to looking at alternative approaches to meeting the needs of print impaired students.

Keywords: e-books, alternative formats, dyslexia, libraries.

1 Overview

As students move through the education system, the role of the text book becomes increasingly important. However, a significant minority of *print impaired* people struggle to take the meaning from a traditional hard copy textbook for a number of reasons. Although every institution has its own approach to meeting the needs of disabled learners, many of these approaches share similarities: it is not unusual for them to be:

- Inefficient – taking significant staff or student time in manual scanning of text and OCR proofing.
- Expensive – where staff are paid to do the scanning the cost either comes from internal budgets or in some cases is charged to the Disabled Student's Allowance.
- Discriminatory – owing to the high cost of this process the service is offered mainly to blind students with dyslexic students hugely under-represented.

This paper suggests that some of the assumptions that underpin the provision of alternative formats are wrong and that we need to move beyond alternative *formats* to looking at alternative *approaches*. There are a number of myths surrounding the provision of alternative formats which need to be challenged. Each of these myths persists because, like all myths, they contain a grain of truth. However, they also contain significant falsehoods that not only undermine effective provision for disabled learners but also hamper good practices that would benefit all learners.

K. Miesenberger et al. (Eds.): ICCHP 2012, Part I, LNCS 7382, pp. 43–50, 2012.
© Springer-Verlag Berlin Heidelberg 2012

2   The Myth of Responsibility

2.1   Further / Vocational Education (FE)

Meeting the needs of disabled learners is too often the responsibility of one small part of an organisation. Whilst the expertise of such a group is valuable, they cannot form the whole solution. Library and information professionals have huge expertise in sourcing content in a variety of formats. The evidence we have collected shows these services are being wastefully under-employed. In July 2010 JISC TechDis conducted an online survey of over 100 further education library services. The survey was distributed via:

- Online library communities supported by 13 JISC Regional Support Centres. [1]
- Library specialists who had taken part in JISC TechDis focus groups on accessible library practice.
- Library groups with special interest / experience in disability issues – for example the Open Rose group [2] and the CLAUD library group [3].

The survey sought to discover librarian experience in contacting publishers for electronic copies of textbooks. The results showed that the vast majority of library staff had never contacted a publisher for an electronic format.

In 2009/10 just over 12% of the 4,635,500 learners participating in further education in the UK declared a Learning Difficulty, Disability or health problem [4]. Centralised data on the disability demographics of learners in further education is not readily available but the equivalent data for higher education is available [REF[. Dyslexia accounts for around 50% of disabilities declared. Visual impairment is around 2.5% of the total and motor/mobility difficulties similar. The figures for FE are assumed to be similar. Statistically we should expect alternative format requests for dyslexic learners to far outstrip those of other disabled learners but in reality the minority of visually impaired users were far more likely to have been served than the much bigger number of dyslexic learners. Most surprising of all, the majority of library services had never sought a publisher for a textbook in electronic format for ANY disabled learner.

Respondents who had never obtained a textbook in alternative format were asked to select from a range of reasons. Multiple responses were permitted but a single one was chosen by a large majority of respondents - "We were never asked" came top (84 respondents) followed by "We don't know how" (17) and "We have never offered that service" (14).

2.2   Higher Education (HE)

The figures in higher education would be expected to be far better because:

- Textbooks play a larger part in course delivery, and
- The disabled student allowance for HE students helps to formalise the support offered.

However, a follow-up survey in 2011 (http://www.surveymonkey.com/s/libaccess) showed a large range of experience and practice. 27 organisations responded, including those from large, small, academic and vocational HE institutions.

The results in Figure 3 show some library services are active in obtaining textbooks in electronic format but the modal value of 5 to 15 library requests included several organisations with 10,000 to 14,000 full-time undergraduates. Statistically [5], some 6% of those students would be disabled and half the disabilities declared would be dyslexia, giving 300 – 420 dyslexic students who could benefit from text books in electronic format. Yet only 5 – 15 publisher requests are being made per year. And who are requests made for? On a simple three-point scale respondents were asked whether particular disability requests were made often, sometimes or rarely/never. The summary figures for all 27 institutions are shown in figure 4.

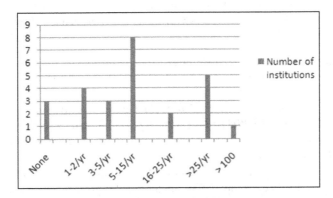

Fig. 1. Alternative format requests per year by higher education libraries show a very wide spread from zero to more than 100 per year. The modal value is 5-15 per year.

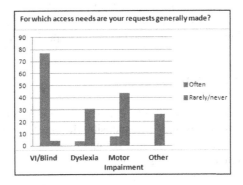

Fig. 2. Percentage of HE institutions surveyed that "often" or "rarely" obtain textbooks from publishers for learners with disabilities

The myth that alternative formats are the responsibility of a disability support team means that a highly efficient route to meeting learner needs (via library/publisher liaison) is vastly underused by most organisations.

Comments in the survey and conversations with heads of library services strongly suggest that many organisations take a specialist approach to providing textbooks in alternative format. Books are being scanned in-house by specialist teams. This process has the advantage of being independent of publisher response rates (although the same survey showed that the majority of publishers were rated by libraries as 'responsive'). There are however significant disadvantages:

- It is an expensive and time-consuming process.
- This cost is sometimes recouped from the learners Disabled Student Allowance - a morally questionable approach considering some publishers would provide a PDF of the textbook for free if the library already held a copy.
- It is not scalable to meet the needs of the large number of dyslexic learners in an organisation and as a result dyslexic learners are not being offered alternative formats.

Students with specific learning difficulties already form the majority of students declaring disability and the trend is upward. Recent discussion on the dis-forum JISCmail list quoted the following figures:

"78% of all disabled students at SGUL (St George's University of London) in 2010-11 had an SpLD...[Sheffield University] report that their percentage of disabled students on medical courses has risen from around 6% from 2008-9 to 10% in 2010-11. Prior to this, the percentage had been much the same for several years." [6]

In a recent conversation with a member of the disability team in a large university the author was told "we cannot offer an alternative format service for dyslexic students because we would be overwhelmed by the work involved in scanning". And this is the myth that needs tackling; it is perfectly possible to offer an efficient, cost effective alternative format service for dyslexic learners without manually scanning books. Such a service, however, moves the responsibility from a specialist disability team to a wider team that includes librarians and subject tutors. Tackling the myth of responsibility requires that we also look at the myth of specialism.

3   The Myth of Specialism

The JISC TechDis model of accessibility maturity [7] places different organisations along the spectrum according to who is responsible for meeting the needs of disabled learners. The more that responsibility is distributed and owned by different roles in the organisation the higher their "accessibility maturity".

The myth of specialism - that seeks to meet the needs of disabled learners with a small team of disability specialists - is an immature approach at the 'Specialism' stage. Being at the Specialism stage of the model has detrimental impacts on both learners and organisations. For the learner it encourages an unhelpful dependency and adds to the 'sense of differentness'. For the organisation it propagates an approach to accessibility that is based on retrospective fixes rather than proactive improvements. The problem lies not with the concept of specialism itself but with the myth that only one set of specialisms contribute to the solution – those of the disability support team.

As e-resources become part of the mainstream fabric we need teaching staff and support staff to make a shift away from a print paradigm towards a knowledge paradigm. Currently, tutors teach in the way they always taught and disability support staff pick up any issues that result; tutors specialise in subject content but disability staff specialise in making content accessible to disabled learners. In a world where subject content resides only in books this is not unreasonable but when excellent subject content exists in iTunesU, GoogleVideo, podcasts, specialist blogs etc then the tutor's knowledge of the subject can be expected to extend also to different formats. Providing learners with a range of content types and formats is the responsibility of the tutor as much as the disability specialist.

In reality a wide range of solutions are usually available for accessing the same knowledge and the 'scan from hardcopy' option should be the last solution tried rather than the first. The diagram below (figure 5) illustrates some of the key pathways that are potentially available to learners and those who support them. Critical to this approach is the idea that the tutor and the librarian are both empowered to be part of the solution alongside the disability support team.

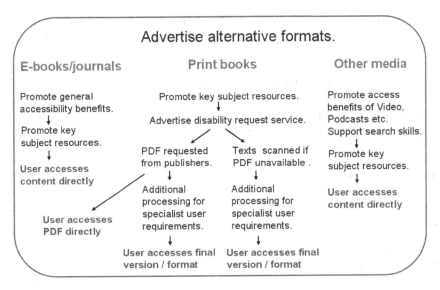

Fig. 3. By proactively promoting a range of alternative formats, more learners can have their needs met and more staff become involved in the delivery

For different learners, different solutions will prove to be optimal and draw on the expertise of different staff. Library staff can promote the accessibility features of their e-book platforms and ensure teaching staff are aware of subject related titles. Teaching staff can promote alternatives to the reading list – such as a "listening list" or a "watching list". Such approaches not only provide better services for disabled learners but they also provide support for:

- Students who are disabled but choose not to disclose it,
- Students who are disabled but not funded for support (e.g. international students),
- Students with disabilities that are undiagnosed (e.g. specific learning difficulties)
- Other learners who have strongly preferred learning styles.

It is important to recognise that many alternative formats will have partial accessibility – they will add significant value to some learners but pose barriers to others. A podcast without a transcript is an example of a partially accessible resource, adding significant value to one kind of access need (eg dyslexia) but creating barriers for another (for example hearing impaired). It is important that accessibility policies are not so rigid that they ban the use of partially accessible resources such as these. Value is most easily added through a rich range of resources from which tutors and learners can pick and mix.

4   The Myth of Accessible e-Books

Even resources which are "born digital" and have a high degree of accessibility – like some e-book platforms - can create very different user experiences. Research by Muir et al (2009) [8] timed a diverse learner group representing a range of disabilities to find out how long they took to access different functions in an e-book. In one test the dyslexic learner took nearly 30 times longer than a non-dyslexic peer whilst a blind user was unable to complete the task at all. These findings are very similar to those of JISC TechDis where research by disabled users from the Shaw Trust counted the number of actions required to perform a set task on different e-book platforms [9]. Two things in particular stood out from the JISC TechDis research:

- The variation in accessibility between different platforms. The worst platforms were wholly inaccessible to screenreader users but the best were usable by a wide range of disabilities.
- The absence of positive accessibility guidance. Even where good accessibility options existed, no platform had accessibility guidance built into their system.

No single technology yet offers a panacea for accessibility but e-books are an exciting development for accessible alternative formats. With properly implemented standards the shift to XML publisher workflows, ePUB3 and HTML5 gives us reason for optimism that a mainstream resource might be capable of meeting a wide range of accessibility needs. Accessibility awareness among publishers is growing - the accessibility seminar was oversubscribed at both the 2010 and 2011 London Bookfairs and the WIPO/EDiTEUR Enabling Technologies Framework [10] provides, for the first time ever, an industry sponsored exploration of accessible workflows and role based accessibility recommendations – an approach that is definitely at the *Mature* end of the model in figure 4. The Publishers Association/Right to Read Alliance joint statements on Text To Speech and Accessibility and eBooks (http://tinyurl.com/jtdr2rpa) [11] were symbolic of a joint quest for maximum accessibility – the flip side of which is maximum market. In Italy the publishers are spearheading the LIA project [12] to make books accessible at source while in the UK the RNIB [13] provides a range of free advice and guidance for publishers and JISC TechDis has been involved in embedding accessibility into the national occupational standards for publishers [14].

Technically it is not difficult to make e-books and e-book platforms accessible to a wide range of disabled users and their assistive technologies. The question for publishers is likely to be "do the customers demand it?". This is where the "Ownership and Partnership" stages of the accessibility maturity model are critical. If library procurement policies insist on high levels of accessibility then suppliers of e-books and e-book platforms have a real incentive to invest in increasing accessibility.

5   Conclusions

For a variety of reasons, disabled learners in further and higher education tend to have their alternative format needs met by labour intensive processes. In many cases the approach is for disability support staff to correct a problem created by a narrow and outdated approach to content provision. This article recognises that alternative format needs can be - and should be - met in a variety of ways, many of which are mainstream alternatives that would add value to a wide range of learners. The role of librarians in sourcing digital formats directly from publishers is often underestimated and so is the role of the tutor in recognising and signposting alternative resources.

There will always be a need for specialist skills in creating alternative formats – especially in relation to maths, science and engineering for screenreader users but these form a small proportion of print impaired learners. Organisations can better serve all their learners by:

- Recognising a spectrum of different approaches,
- Involving library staff in alternative format suggestions,
- Embedding accessibility in procurement policies,
- Involving teaching staff in being part of the solution.

The days of scanning books might be numbered but whether they are or not, the opportunities afforded by creative approaches to sourcing alternative formats must not be missed.

References

1. JISC Regional Support Centres, http://www.jiscrsc.ac.uk
2. The Open Rose Group, http://www.shef.ac.uk/library/services/openrose
3. CLAUD library group, https://wiki.brookes.ac.uk/display/CLAUD/Home;jsessionid=13C1CCA0DE0D4E20F0966A8E68618024
4. Quarterly Statistical First Release – The Data Service (March 31, 2011)

5. Higher Education Statistics Agency, http://www.hesa.ac.uk/dox/dataTables/studentsAndQualifiers/download/disab0910.xls?v=1.0

6. Slorach, R.: Disability Adviser. St George's University of London. Dis-forum (January 27, 2012)

7. JISC TechDis model of accessibility maturity, http://www.jisctechdis.ac.uk/techdis/keyinitiatives/supportingthesectors/higher_education/technological_maturity

8. Muir, L., Veale, T., Nichol, A.: Like an open book? Accessibility of e-book content for academic study in a diverse student population. Library and Information Research 33(105) (2009)

9. JISC TechDis. Towards Accessible e-book platforms - JISC TechDis (2010), http://www.jisctechdis.ac.uk/techdis/resources/detail/goingdigital/Towards_Accessible_e-Book_Platforms_Research

10. Enabling Technologies Framework – WIPO/EDiTEUR, http://www.jisctechdis.ac.uk/techdis/links/detail/editeur_Technologies_Framework

11. Publishers Association/Right to Read Alliance joint statement on Text To Speech, http://www.publishers.org.uk/index.php?option=com_content&view=article&id=1550:publisher-recommendation-on-text-to-speech&catid=503:pa-press-releases-and-comments&Itemid=1618, The statement on Accessibility and eBooks can be found at, http://www.publishers.org.uk/index.php?option=com_content&view=article&id=2207:joint-statement-on-accessibility-a-e-books&catid=536:joint-statement-on-accessibility-and-e-books&Itemid=1655

12. Associazone Italiana Editori - LIA project, http://www.jisctechdis.ac.uk/techdis/links/detail/PLS_lia_project

13. RNIB Publisher Advice Centre, http://www.jisctechdis.ac.uk/techdis/links/detail/RNIB_publishing_industry

14. Skillset consultation on national occupational standards for the publishing industry, http://www.jisctechdis.ac.uk/techdis/news/detail/2011/skillset

Access Toolkit for Education

Mike Wald, E.A. Draffan, Russell Newman, Sebastian Skuse,
and Chris Phethean

ECS, University of Southampton, UK
M.Wald@soton.ac.uk

Abstract. This paper describes three tools that have been developed to help overcome accessibility, usability and productivity issues identified by disabled students. The Web2Access website allows users to test any Web 2.0 site or software application against a series of checks linked to the WCAG 2.0 and other guidelines. The Access Tools accessible menu helps with navigation to portable pen drive applications that can assist with accessibility, productivity and leisure activities when on the move. The accessible Toolbar provides support for the majority of browsers and accessible websites through magnification, spellchecking, text to speech readout, dictionary definitions and referencing modification of text, page style, colour and layout.

Keywords: accessibility, tool, learning.

1 Introduction

The Access Technologies Team[1] at the University of Southampton School of Electronics and Computer Science (ECS) has developed a series of tools funded by the University and JISC TechDis[2] to help overcome accessibility, usability and productivity issues identified by disabled students. One of the points that arose out of the JISC funded LexDis[3] project [1] was the degree to which students were able to use their assistive technologies with Web 2.0 type services such as Facebook, blogs and wikis. It was found that those who did not need access tools, such as screen readers or keyboard only access, did not necessarily use their text to speech or spell checking software in these situations. There were also many students who did not have these technologies but still wanted to check their spelling and to change the look of the web pages they were reading. There were also those who wanted to access the web when using computers other than their own and they needed some form of support. One further issue that also arose was the general inaccessibility of some of the Web 2.0 sites. It was therefore decided that a more comprehensive approach was needed which is described further in this paper. Working through the issues discussed, a chart of document types was produced (table 1) to enable the team to make the pen

---

[1] http://access.ecs.soton.ac.uk
[2] http://www.jisctechdis.ac.uk
[3] http://www.lexdis.org

K. Miesenberger et al. (Eds.): ICCHP 2012, Part I, LNCS 7382, pp. 51–58, 2012.
© Springer-Verlag Berlin Heidelberg 2012

drive application choices and add to the JISC TechDis Accessibility Essentials Guides[4], which cover the creation of accessible Word, Adobe PDF and PowerPoint documents for on-line use.

The tools have been beta tested by ECS MSc students as part of their coursework and assessment for a module on assistive technologies and universal design.

Table 1. Chart of document types

Document Type	
Adobe PDF	Mind Mapping
Animation/video/simulation	Presentation
Audio	Project Management
Computer Aided Design	Qualitative data analysis
Database	References
Desktop Publishing	Spreadsheet
eBook/eText	Statistics
Graphics	Web pages
Maths/Science	Word processor

2   Web2Access

Web2Access allows users to test any Web 2.0 site or software application against a series of checks[5] linked to the WCAG 2.0[6] and other guidelines[7,8,9]. A summary of these is given in table 2 and table 3. Results can be viewed for each site (see Fig. 2.) or for a particular disability (see Fig. 3). Over 150 Web 2.0 services have already been checked that will hopefully help users make suitable choices whether for personal use or for a teaching and learning environment. A wizard offers a step by step walk through with links to the techniques used for others to independently conduct tests (see Fig. 1.). Web2Access allows students, teachers and course developers to check the accessibility and usability of websites and applications they will be expected or required to use during their studies.

---

[4] http://www.jisctechdis.ac.uk/accessibilityessentials
[5] http://www.web2access.org.uk/test
[6] http://www.w3.org/TR/WCAG20/
[7] http://www.universaldesign.ie/useandapply/ict/itaccessibility guidelines/applicationsoftware/guidelines/
[8] http://www.03.ibm.com/able/guidelines/software/ accesssoftware.html
[9] http://www.itic.org/resources/voluntary-product-accessibility-template-vpat/#1194.21

Fig. 1. Web2Access Interface reviewers screen

Table 2. Web 2.0 Service Tests

Login, Signup and Other Forms Accessible : *registering with a service or site, then returning to sign-in and work with forms.*
Image ALT Attributes: *A text alternative enables a screen reader user to hear about the image*
Link Target Definitions: *Link text needs to be understandable without a surrounding sentence or button.*
Frame Titles and Layout: *So screen reader users know where they are in the page*
Removal of Stylesheet: *to check how a site looks without style sheets*
Audio/Video Features: *text transcripts, captioning, and sign language can be helpful for deafness*
Video/animations - audio descriptions: *for scenes with no descriptive dialogue is essential.*
Appropriate use of Tables: *The order of content within the table and the use of row and column headers is important.*
Tab Orderings Correct and Logical: *in the same way that a page would linearise without any structural elements*
Page Functionality with Keyboard
Accessibility of Text Editors: *when using a keyboard or screen reader.*
Appropriate Feedback with Forms: *with no time restrictions and clear methods for pausing items or returning to a page to correct an error.*
Contrast and Colour Check: *Symbols and other items should not be provided in various colours without there also being other obvious differences to help those with colour deficiencies (colour blindness).*
Page Integrity when Zooming: *Zooming can improve readability but there are times when it also affects the layout of websites.*
Text size, style, blinking elements and Readability: *blinking at a certain rate can cause seizures and text needs to be understandable for all users*

Table 3. Application Tests

Built in accessibility checks: *using built-in system assistive technologies or accessibility options*
Application works with External Assistive Technologies: *additional screen reader, alternative input device and magnification should be able to work with all elements*
Text or other alternatives for image elements.: *It is important to ensure that colour alone is not used and text it easy to read.*
Keyboard / Alternative input with focus: *Fields, dialog boxes and focal points should all be reached in as logical a manner as possible so that the screen reader, keyboard and switch user can reach all the features in the application.*
Labels for objects, fields or controls : *Labels are linked to controls, objects, icons, and images so that screen reader users are aware of these elements within the application.*
Audio alerts have visual cues: *plus ability to use sounds sentries or show sounds. Audio options have volume control.*
Alternatives for Video / Animation: *such as transcripts or captions for those with hearing impairments. For visual impairments where there are long scenes with no descriptive dialogue.*
Media events offer user control: *such as video or animation playing, audio and blinking /flashing notification events with no part of the screen flashing between 2Hz and 55/60Hz.*
Textual Information for screen reader: *so user can hear when the action and changes are made within an application or when a dialog box appears on the screen.*
Keyboard shortcut keys offered: *where a program has its own access keys or shortcuts they must be clearly stated.*
Save user preferences for style and zoom: *For those with visual impairment and visual stress it may be important to be able to adapt the view of the application and content.*
Timed events can be altered: *so the user can work at their own speed.*
Change colours and contrast: *to support those who find the default settings unhelpful.*
Uniform and standardised presentation: Consistency of navigation and task procedures is important.
Documentation: *All instructions and help files should be clear, easy to read and available in accessible electronic format.*

Results for VoiceThread ®

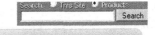

Web 2.0 Service Test Average: 44% Updated 10 August 2009

Description
Users upload images which become simple slideshows called Threads. Users can comment on 'Threads' by recording their voice and/or doodling on the image. When the comment is played back, the doodle is drawn as it was by the user, showing the creation. Users can also comment with text and video.

Accessibility Testing Results
This site is mainly made using Flash and keyboard access has been compromised. The player is only usable with a keyboard in certain browsers such as Internet Explorer. It is impossible to change the text or contrast levels and user control is minimal, although the text size is good and feedback when uploading files is good. This service offers scope for adding audio descriptions and captions but its format means that using it with a screen reader is impossible.

#	Test	Score	Summary
1	Login, Signup and Other Forms Accessible		All forms are within a Flash component, and therefore cannot be accessed with a keyboard.
2	Image ALT Attributes		The site is built using Flash, which cannot offer text alternatives for images.
3	Link Target Definitions		Every button is within the Flash component, which cannot provide titles or meaning for a screenreader.
4	Frame Titles and Layout		No frames or iframes, which can be disorientating for screen-readers, are used in the design.
5	Removal of Stylesheet		The page is still understandable and functional when it is viewed as a linear document, with no styles.
6	Audio/Video Features		It is a shame that the interface is not keyboard or screenreader accessible as it is possible to join in with the conversation in many different ways.

Fig. 2. Web2Access site results screen

3   Access Tools

There are many portable pen drive applications that can help with accessibility, productivity and leisure activities when on the move[10] but these can be rendered virtually useless without an accessible pen drive menu. An accessible menu (see Fig. 4.) has therefore been developed to help with navigation to these applications. The settings allow for colour and font changes, large text and keyboard access. This pen drive has been developed for staff to check the accessibility and usability of websites and applications but should also be useful for students. A series of simple guides has also been made available that complement the JISC TechDis Accessibility Essentials. The tools that have been used to test the Web 2.0 services and applications have been added to the Access Tools download page along with a page of instructions.

---

[10] http://access.ecs.soton.ac.uk/projects/access-tools

Blind and Severe Visual Impairments

Screen reading for all aspects of computer use may be the main access technology used, and it is important to remember navigational control may be by the keyboard rather than the mouse. Alternative information is required where multimedia, such as images, animation or videos are offered. Links to other areas need to have good labels and make sense when divorced from their web page. Layout, tables and forms also need to remain readable when the framework for the website is removed such as a style sheet. Further advice from RNIB.

Relevant Tests

- Accessibility of Text Editors
- Appropriate Feedback with Forms
- Appropriate use of Tables
- Audio/Video Features
- Frame Titles and Layout
- Image ALT Attributes
- Link Target Definitions
- Login, Signup and Other Forms Accessible
- Page Functionality with Keyboard
- Removal of Stylesheet
- Tab Orderings Correct and Logical
- Video/animations - audio descriptions

Score	Product
100%	Access Menu
100%	Blogdigger
97%	Accessible Twitter
97%	Connotea
97%	LinkedIn
95%	Microsoft Office Outlook
95%	Twitter
84%	delicious
92%	EtherPad
92%	tumblr

Fig. 3. Web2Access disability results screen

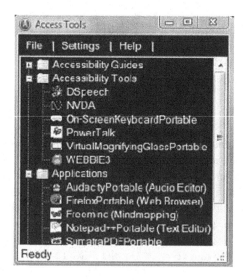

Fig. 4. Access Tools

4   Web 'ToolBar'

Although most browsers offer ways to change the look and feel of websites whether through colour or text changes and the use of add-ons such as text to speech, these only work within that particular browser. It was felt that it would be useful to have a 'toolbar' that would work with all browsers and with the majority of accessible web-sites. ATBar[11] (see Fig. 5.) can be simply run from your favourites/bookmarks and allows for text resizing, colour changes and text to speech. It can also be used with forms to check spelling and meanings of words. There is a tool for grabbing a web page's information such as the author, date and URL which may be handy when capturing sites for referencing and many other ideas have come up in discussion with those testing the toolbar. A button also allows users to report inaccessible websites to Fix the Web[12] whose volunteers take these issues forward with website owners. The Toolbar is available under the BSD Open Source license. Users are free to copy, re-distribute and study it as long as they leave the BSD license including original attribu-tion intact. Modifications and derived works can be distributed under the terms of the BSD. An Arabic version of the toolbar funded by MADA centre[13] and ATkit, a toolkit with which people can build their own version of ATbar customising it with the ac-cessibility features that they want are currently under development and will be able to be demonstrated at ICCHP 2012.

Table 4. ToolBar with explanation of icons and functions

Poor standards of web accessibility mean many disabled people are excluded from using big parts of the internet. Fix the Web is offering a solution! Disabled people report problems in under a minute. Volunteers take these issues forward with website owners.

Select the Magnifier buttons to increase or decrease the size of text. If text resizing makes the site unreadable you may wish to use your browser zoom feature to increase both the image and the text sizes.

Select the Font button to choose a different type of font for the text and increase line spacing.

Select the Spell Checker button **while writing in a plain text form**. Suggestions are shown below the text-area after a pause. Disable the checker by selecting the button once more. Note that this may not work with rich-text editors that already have spell checkers.

Select the Dictionary button **after highlighting a word** in the web page and a definition from Wiktionary will appear.

Select the text-to-speech button and choose whether you want the whole page read out loud, or just the highlighted text. You can highlight a portion of text before selecting the Text-to-Speech button to have only that text read out. Wait for that section to finish before highlighting a new section of text. Note that large pages, such as Facebook pages, may require you to select smaller portions of text at a time.

---

[11] http://access.ecs.soton.ac.uk/ToolBar/
[12] http://www.fixtheweb.net/
[13] http://mada.org.qa/

Table 4. (*continued*)

Select the References button and JISC TechDis Toolbar will scan the page for referencing information - it will collect as much as it can linked to authorship, dates, title of the page, name of the website and the URL. Once you have selected the green tick you can highlight the text and copy it into any notepad or word processor.

Select the Styles button to alter the colour of the JISC TechDis Toolbar, change the web page colours - background, text and links or choose pre-made page styles. Some web page colour changes also impact on the toolbar.

Select help to gain access to instructions for use.

Select the return menu if you wish to restore the webpage to its original style.

Select close to exit JISC TechDis Toolbar.

5   Conclusion

This paper has described three tools that have been developed to help overcome accessibility, usability and productivity issues identified by disabled students. The Web2Access website allows users to test any Web 2.0 site or software application against a series of checks linked to the WCAG 2.0 and other guidelines. The Access Tools accessible menu helps with navigation to portable pen drive applications that can help with accessibility, productivity and leisure activities when on the move. The accessible toolbar provides for the majority of browsers and accessible websites support through magnification, text and page style, colour and layout modification, spellchecking, text to speech readout, dictionary definitions and referencing. The tools have been beta tested by MSc students as part of their course and assessment for a module on assistive technologies and universal design.

Reference

1. Wald, M., Draffan, E.A., Seale, J.: Disabled Learners' Experiences of E-learning. Jl. of Educational Multimedia and Hypermedia 18(3), 341–361 (2009)

Community-Based Participatory Approach: Students as Partners in Educational Accessible Technology Research

Poorna Kushalnagar[1], Benjamin Williams[2], and Raja S. Kushalnagar[3]

[1] Chester F. Carlson Center for Imaging Science, Rochester Institute of Technology, NY
poorna.kushalnagar@mail.rit.edu
[2] College of Engineering, Texas Tech University, TX
benjamin.l.williams@ttu.edu
[3] National Technical Institute for the Deaf, Rochester Institute of Technology, NY
rskics@rit.edu

Abstract. This paper discusses the critical role of bringing together students with disabilities as research partners using principles of community-based participatory research (CBPR). Most accessible technology research approaches include the target population as end-users, not as community partners. This paper describes how CBPR can enhance designs and increase likelihood of effective and efficiency of end-user designs or prototypes that impact students in education. We conclude with a discussion on how to empower students as research partners using CBPR principles.

Keywords: Accessible Technology Research, Design and Evaluation, Students with Disabilities, Participatory Research.

1 Introduction

User-centered design is driven by the needs and input from end-users [1]. This approach of emphasizing end-user involvement throughout the design process takes into account the good practices in the process of designing products. This process includes using an iterative and several multiple criteria design. The process also emphasizes the need for evaluating the different design criteria and ease of use. It also discusses using the evaluation results to make appropriate trade-offs between the design criteria and ease of use. Most accessible devices are developed for a relatively small number of users, sometimes even for a single person. In some cases, accessible devices can result in broad dissemination and high usage. As people age and experience changes in physical or sensory functioning, there is a greater need and motivation for wheelchair or hearing aid usage. When the accessible device is evaluated by a small number of users, this frequently results in unorthodox approach to end-user design from development to distribution. For example, in the higher education system, accessible products are often supplied directly to the disability office, not to the student (end-user).

K. Miesenberger et al. (Eds.): ICCHP 2012, Part I, LNCS 7382, pp. 59–64, 2012.

The traditional design would focus only on the disability office, not the student. For example, the disability services office might limit focus to their needs. The disability office may want to ensure the laptop is on all day is available to the students. As a result, the disability office might specify a large, heavy laptop that has a long life, but not easily carried around. To reduce the risk of an injury, the disability office may also be required to include a wheeled carrier. However, this would not have been the preferred option for students (end-users). If the designer had included students as partners in the development of the captioning laptop device, the student would have expressed concerns about the weight of the device at the outset. The student-partner may suggest a light laptop with a solid drive in order to quickly start up, has a reasonably long life, and is easy to carry out without needing a wheeled carrier. The disability office could have then specified light laptops with an auxiliary battery that would meet both their own needs and the student's need. This solution would be a better fit for both than the original heavy laptop with wheeled carrier.

A highly cited user-centered design process [2] and [3] focuses on four key points: Early identification of users' task preferences; application of users' knowledge to design; repeated evaluation of early prototypes by users; and iterative design toward final prototype.

The above gold standard for user-centered design fails to consider the value of including users in the initial stage of development of the research idea, design, and evaluation of the product. To address this issue, we provide a brief introduction in the next section on the concept of community-based participatory research approach that serves as a viable model for empowering students as partners in user-focused design.

2   Community-Based Participatory Research

Community-based participatory research (CBPR) [4] is traditionally applied in health disparities research, where the community members of a population being studied are invited to collaborate with the investigators. CBPR is a process of systematic inquiry and its principles encourage more equitable collaboration, enhance the contributions of community partners and participants, improve health, and ensure cultural sensitivity [5]. Given that a large number of students with disabilities being studied for accessible technology research purposes, their perspectives and participation as partners in research are paramount to effective, low-cost design or improvement to existing technology products. The reason for this requirement is due to the diversity of disabilities among the students and the unique perspectives of disabled students that are easily overlooked by researchers.

3   Improved Approach

There are many advantages discussed in the CBPR literature. CBPR improves the application and use of the research data by having student partners involved. It connects student partners with varied experiences and skills in addressing barriers in the classroom, enhances quality and validity of accessible technology research by including local knowledge of the students with disabilities, and increases the likelihood of their student community overcoming distrust of researchers. Once trust is obtained, each student has a story to tell about his or her experience in the mainstream classroom. Their stories often vary, but share a common theme: educational disparity in the mainstream classroom is apparent.

The deaf population is a heterogeneous group comprised of individuals from diverse educational and communication backgrounds [6]. Some use exclusively sign language or speech, while others use a combination of both sign and speech in daily communication. Some come from specialized schools for the deaf, where full access to information is available. Others come from either inclusive mainstream schools, where they received little or no classroom accommodations, or from mainstream schools that provide deaf program and/or services. Appreciating the education-related quality of life in its diverse patterns of a mainstream student community is necessary for the planning, implementing, and delivery of appropriate accessible technology; and to assist in eliminating disparities in education. Therefore, it is important to look at the contextual characteristics such as communication, classroom space, accessibility and barriers as well as neurological differences that influence educational outcomes among students who have disabilities. Paying attention to the students' diverse needs will also assist in ensuring the accuracy of the design or development trajectory of an accessible technology that has strong potential in eliminating educational disparities in the classroom.

4   Methodology

The researchers involved in this study are deaf and use a combination of sign language and speech to communicate. All have extensive experience in the mainstream classroom and are intimately aware of the barriers that deaf students experience. We define student partners as those who contribute to the majority of the project development, whereas student participants are considered end-users.

Collaborative researcher-student discussion was used to make decisions on designing accessible research that is compatible with the specific desires and beliefs of the deaf college student population. We first started with finding deaf student representatives from a 4-year university. Through this student-researcher partnership, we initiated dialogues on how to improve classroom accessibility. We then identified community resources to carry out the research aim to recruit student users and obtained approval from the institutional review board.

Snowball sampling and purposive sampling were used to recruit student participants from both 2-year colleges and 4-year universities to evaluate the technology. The inclusion criteria for both of these sampling these users:

1. Present with severe to profound hearing loss;
2. Utilize classroom accommodation such as captioning, interpreting and/or note-taking;
3. Be 18 years of age or older and
4. Agree and provide consent.

Mixed quantitative-qualitative method was used to gather information on perceived benefits of the technology in question. Prior to write-up, results were shared and discussed with the student-partners from the community.

To assess specific and contextual characteristics, we included self-report questionnaires for communication preferences, neurological differences (i.e. history of attention or learning difficulties), and qualitative interviews for experiences with accessibility and barriers. For purpose of this paper, qualitative reports are used to summarize students' perspectives on accessible technology research in education.

5   Results

Student representatives who participated as partners in research reported feeling more responsible for future deaf student community. They expressed that they had some ideas of what needed to be done to improve deaf students' learning experience in the classroom. However, they stated that in order to carry out those ideas they preferred to have a knowledgeable and experienced researcher on the team. Student representatives also noted the importance and benefits of having a researcher with additional knowledge of the Deaf culture and its values, because it improves the transition of needs and suggestions.

Having a presence in the Deaf community and being involved helped the researchers cultivate the trust of the deaf student members. This presence and involvement in the deaf student community also contributed to the increase of word-by-mouth recruitment through leading student-partners and members who participated in the study.

One of the lessons learned from the student-researcher partnership was the need to include a broader diversity of deaf student-partner representatives to assist with the design and development prior to recruitment of research participants. Perspectives and experiences of deaf student-partner representatives from 4-year universities do not necessarily generalize to those of deaf students who attend 2-year colleges. Another lesson learned from relying on relatively homogeneous group as in the case of representatives from 4-year universities is that the snowballing recruitment resulted in a greater homogeneity among a particular student group who shared similar educational background. A very large sample will be required to increase the heterogeneity of student end-users who evaluate the prototype or product for usability and perceived benefits.

6   Conclusion: Application of CBPR in Accessible Technology Research

We propose CBPR approach as a viable method to increase collaboration with student participants in accessible technology research. Application of CBPR in research requires student community assessment of their priorities and needs as well as inclusion of a wide spectrum of target students with disabilities. Student community assessments provide information relevant to the community of students with disabilities. Examples of such information include the prevalence of classroom-related barriers and current practices used to reduce these barriers.

A recent accessible technology application that involved partial use of the CBPR approach was the installation of Interactive Video Classroom equipment, geared towards deaf students, to address the barrier of viewing the professor during lectures. Traditionally the solution has been to assign front row seating to deaf students but occasionally becomes a challenge due to the layout of the area and the number of deaf students. A component of CBPR approach involved the students into the design of the IVC equipment to address the barrier. As a result, the barriers encountered by the deaf students were addressed and furthermore, similar barriers faced by non-disabled students were also resolved. These student partners reportedly felt empowered in their contribution to the design and solution of the problem. A modified CBPR model has been developed for purpose of conducting accessible technology research involving student partnership as shown in Figure 1.

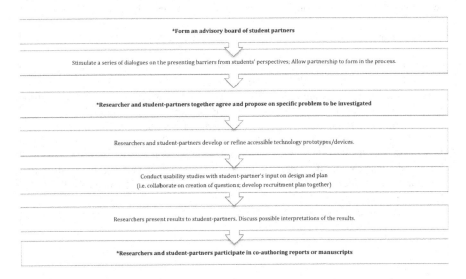

Fig. 1. Modified CBPR as applied to accessible technology research in education. (*bold indicates new addition to existing approach in accessible technology research).

7   Implications of CBPR in Accessible Technology Research

By using CBPR, researchers can improve efficiency of identifying and categorizing barriers. This is due to becoming increasingly aware of the system in which the students are exposed. When these situations are viewed as a system, no matter how different the students, as they are subjected to the same barriers inside the system, they tend to produce similar results [7]. CBPR methodology enables us to gain an understanding beyond the limited "problem-solution" process of user-centered design and to consider the effects of accessible technology on the barriers inside the system for a larger diversity of students. This enables researchers and student-partners to practically remove the barrier rather than settling on a temporary shortcut. With this insight, researchers have the ability to change that system and improve the outcome for the students. The students themselves gain awareness on how to improve the system through their participation and by observing the results of the accessible technology.

Acknowledgements. The authors extend their heart-felt appreciation to those student partners and participants for starting the initiative toward student community engagement in research partnership.

References

1. Abras, C., Maloney-Krichmar, D., Preece, J.: User-Centered Design. In: Bainbridge, W. (ed.) Encyclopedia of Human-Computer Interaction, Sage Publications, Thousand Oaks (2004)
2. den Buurman, R.: User-centred design of smart products. Ergonomics 40(10), 1159–1169 (1997)
3. Gould, J.D., Lewis, C.: Designing for usability: key principles and what designers think. Communications ACM 28, 300–311 (1985)
4. Israel, B.A., Eng, E., Schultz, A.J., Parker, E.A. (eds.): Methods in Community-Based Participatory Research for Health. Jossey-Bass Publishers, San Francisco (2005)
5. Wallerstein, N., Duran, B.: Using Community-Based Participatory Research to Address Health Disparities. Health Promotion Practice 7(3), 312–323 (2006)
6. Marschark, M., Spencer, P.E.: What we know, what we don't know, and what we should know. In: Marschark, M., Spencer, P.E. (eds.) Oxford Handbook of Deaf Studies, Language, and Education, 2nd edn., vol. 1, pp. 511–516. Oxford University Press, New York (2011)
7. Senge, P.M.: The Fifth Discipline: The Art and Practice of the Learning Organization. Currency Doubleday, New York (1990)

Applying New Interaction Paradigms to the Education of Children with Special Educational Needs

Paloma Cantón[3], Ángel L. González[1], Gonzalo Mariscal[2], and Carlos Ruiz[2]

[1] School of Computing, Technical University of Madrid, Boadilla del Monte, Madrid, Spain
agonzalez@fi.upm.es
[2] GI-CETTICO, Technical University of Madrid, Boadilla del Monte, Madrid, Spain
{gmariscal,cruiz}@cettico.fi.upm.es
[3] Consejería de Educación de la Comunidad de Madrid
pcanton@educa.madrid.org

Abstract. The proliferation of new devices over the last decade has introduced new ways of interaction such us tactile (iPhone [1]) or touchless gesture (Kinect [2]) user interfaces. This opens up new opportunities for the education of children with special needs. However, it also raises new issues. On the one hand, children have to be able to manage different technologies, some of which do not enable natural ways of interaction. On the other hand, software developers have to design applications compatible with many different platforms. This paper offers a state-of-the-art discussion about how new interaction paradigms are being applied in the field of education. As a preliminary conclusion, we have detected the need for a standard on gesture-based interfaces. With this in mind, we propose a roadmap setting out the essential steps to be followed in order to define this standard based on natural hand movements.

Keywords: SEN, Education, Touch, Touchless, Gesture, User Interface, Kinect, Interaction Paradigms.

1 Introduction

Computing has been successfully applied to education over the last few decades [3] [4]. This idea can be extended to education for children with special educational needs (SEN) [5]. However, interaction has been a barrier to applying computing to education for some student profiles. The use of the mouse or keyboard to control software does not come as naturally to younger learners as it does to adults. If the user is a motor impaired child, interaction becomes an accessibility issue.

Human computer interaction (HCI) research is a fast evolving field. These advances have been driven by improvements in user interface (UI) design and the definition of new forms of interaction. Interaction must be supported by devices that enable users to interact more naturally and communicate directly with the computer. Lately, the proliferation of tactile devices and the definition of new ways of interaction based on touchless gesture UIs, such us Kinect [6], are laying the

K. Miesenberger et al. (Eds.): ICCHP 2012, Part I, LNCS 7382, pp. 65–72, 2012.

groundwork for gesture-based interaction with machines. These interaction mechanisms appear a priori to be more natural than their conventional counterparts.

Up to now, however, no gesture-based interface standard has been defined. It can be confusing for users if different applications use different gestures and actions to enable the same kind of interaction. Users are likely to find applications based on standard gestures easier to use. This calls for the definition of a standard.

But, like many innovative technologies in the past, touch and touchless gesture UI technologies are raising optimistic expectations about how they could change education and have started to be applied in the field of education [7]. Two mistakes have been made over and over again every time a new technology has been introduced into education in the last forty years: over-generalization and over-expectation [7]. Delivering a technology does not by itself turn students into smart, motivated knowledge producers. The technology has to be contextualized, set against educational goals, and fitted into broader processes of learning. Therefore, the new ways of interacting with machines must be analysed in order to define the best way to apply interaction depending on the context. This analysis should be the starting point for introducing new interaction technologies into the education system.

New HCI technologies, such as gesture UIs, are even more important in teaching children with SEN. They, especially, could benefit from the improved accessibility to education offered by these technologies, which could break down some of the barriers still existing today. But before they do, rigorous research should be conducted in order to determine the contexts in which gesture UIs are more likely to be applied with success. As a result, guidelines should be defined for developing and implementing these new interaction techniques in the learning process of children with SEN.

This paper offers a state-of-the-art discussion about how new interaction paradigms are being applied in the field of education. This discussion will be the groundwork for examining the issues that we are likely to come across when teaching children with SEN supported by new interaction devices. Finally, we will describe a roadmap setting out the essential steps for successfully developing teaching tools for children with SEN based on the use of the new interaction paradigms.

2   State of the Art

In recent years, many of the new devices that have come onto the market have changed the face of human-machine interaction. Clear examples are products commercialized by companies such as Nintendo (Wii and DS), Apple (iPad and iPhone) or Microsoft (Surface and Kinect). In this section, we will look at new approaches in this field and their educational applications.

First of all, let us define some terms that will be used in this paper:

- A **gesture** is movement of part of one's body (e.g. finger, hand, head) that a software application interprets as an action.
- **Touch:** act of bringing a part of one's body (e.g. hand) into contact with an interaction component (e.g. tactile screen). The tactile device may be activated by one touch or several touches (**multi-touch**).

- **Touchless gesture UI:** UI based on contactless gestures (e.g. Kinect).
- **Touch gesture:** contact gesture on a tactile device (e.g. pinching to zoom).

2.1   Standards

We think that standards play an important role in providing a reference for developing accessible systems, especially at the present time when individual companies are going their own separate ways and commercializing devices using different forms of interaction. Standards are necessary to guarantee that we are sure to find the best way of interaction with different devices and electronic systems, depending on the time, environment and user profile.

To the best of our knowledge, the most related standard in this field is ISO/IEC 14754 [8]. ISO/IEC 14754 defines a set of basic gesture commands and feedback for pen interfaces. The gestures include select, delete, insert space, split line, move, copy, cut, paste, scroll and undo. However, ISO members recognize the importance and need for a standard on gesture-based interfaces, and members of Joint Technical Committee 1/Sub Committee 35/ Working Group 1 are working on defining a gesture-based interface standard.

2.2   Multi-touch Gesture and Touchless Gesture UIs

Not long ago Apple revolutionized the field of mobile devices by providing support for user interaction via gestures and actions. Apple introduced two concepts [9]: touches and gestures. Touches are important for keeping track of how many fingers are on the screen, where they are and what they are doing. Gestures are important for determining what users are doing with their two fingers on the screen, that is, pinching, pushing or rotating.

To do this, Apple developed Cocoa [1]. Cocoa is a native object-oriented application programming interface (API) for the Mac OS X operating system and iOS. The Cocoa Touch layer defines the basic application infrastructure and support for key technologies such as touch-based input for gesture recognition (e.g. swipes, pinches). Developers can define their own custom gesture recognizers based on the following standard gestures: tapping (any number of taps), pinching in and out (for zooming), panning or dragging, swiping (in any direction), rotating (moving fingers in opposite directions), and tapping and holding.

Microsoft has developed a similar effort for interacting with Microsoft software using gestures (from Windows to Kinect) [2]. Kinect is to officially interact with Windows and will support better skeletal tracking and improved speech recognition.

2.3   Gesture-Based Screen Reader

The iOS 5 system includes innovative tactile device assistive and accessibility technology. Apple developed the first gesture-based screen reader.

In response to a single tap on the screen, for instance, the screen reader will read what the user's finger is touching, whereas two taps activate the selected control.

Additionally, users can adjust controls by moving their finger up or down. To move through different controls, all users have to do is just touch the screen and move their finger left or right (panning). This way they will move from one object to another on the screen. The screen reader also provides a control called rotor. This control is useful for changing the way users move from one object to another on the screen. Note, finally, that iOS 5 provides accessibility features not only for sight-impaired people but also for users with other types of disability.

The a priori weakness of this solution is that, for the time being at least, it is only applicable to iOS systems. Also, it would be worthwhile evaluating whether these are the best gestures and settings for devices to be used by children with SEN.

2.4   New Interaction Paradigms in Education

Multi-touch desks [10] or interactive tabletops [7] are tools that help children in the learning process. They are good tools for empowering general competences, such as collaboration and group work.

An interactive tabletop is a computer interface that, as its name indicates, resembles a table: it is usually a horizontal (sometimes oblique) surface and is usually large enough to enable several users to interact simultaneously. User inputs are captured from the position of their fingers and dedicated objects using a wide variety of techniques. The system output is displayed on the tabletop surface.

3   Advantages and Disadvantages

The generalization of new ways of interacting with computers (touch and touchless gesture interfaces, interactive tabletops, ubiquitous devices, tangible UIs, etc.) bids us consider introducing this kind of tools in the classroom to support the learning process. In regard to HCI for education, however, it is more important to examine the roles of pervasive UIs in broader and real-world contexts, especially in classrooms, rather than just in lab settings [11].

Gesture-based interaction furthers the use of both touch and touchless devices for many kinds of applications in education. It can be especially useful for teaching motor impaired students with upper limb impairment unable to make independent finger movements to type, hold, move, or click the mouse, etc. These users are capable of making gestures that can, thanks to gesture-based interaction, be interpreted as specific interaction commands. Note, however, that the gesture recognition algorithms used in interaction devices are based on natural hand movements [12]. Therefore, we expect it to be necessary to (a) define new gestures, which will then have to be (b) carefully tested with real users and, finally, (c) standardized whenever possible.

People with cognitive difficulties, such as children with learning disabilities or developmental disabilities, find it hard to learn to use a mouse. To do this, they have to understand that the same object has more than one function, e.g. left-button click to select, double-click to run, drag and drop, etc. People find these functions easier to understand using hand or body part gestural interaction, as they use their body in the same way as in other everyday situations, i.e. using a hand gesture to point out something, ask for something or pick up something.

To sum up, using body parts (arms, hands, face, head, etc.) instead of external devices (mouse or keyboard, etc.) to interact with computers can improve the use of interactive systems. Like many other advances in the HCI field, its introduction and adoption will be an obstacle course. Most of the hurdles stem from the choice of vocabulary used to define well-known gestures. This does not take into account the diversity of potential users.

Table 1 below summarizes the commonly accepted gestures together with the associated action and users for which these gestures can pose a problem. This table will be extended as the research and standardization process advances.

Table 1. Some gestures and related constraints

Gesture	Associated action	Required ability	User constraints
One/two finger taps (tapping)	Execute	Tap surface with finger/hand sequentially twice with pause between taps	Motor impairment Small children Severe cognitive impairment
Side-to-side slide finger movement (panning	Page up, page down	Rapidly move fingers over surface	Severe mental disorder Small children Motor impairment
Pinching movement (pinching)	Zoom out	Move two fingers toward each other	Severe mental disorder Small children Motor impairment
Circular movement (rotating)	Turn objects	Touch the surface with two fingers and move one finger around the other in a circle	Severe mental disorder Motor impairment
Movement of outstretched hand from one side to another around an axis (wave)	Greet. Start up Kinect	Move hand from side to side from wrist or elbow	Severe mental disorder Motor impairment
Positioning of outstretched arm at a 45° angle with respect to vertical body axis (hover)	Guide/Pause Kinect	Keep outstretched arm in a raised and rather unstable and artificial position	Severe mental disorder Motor impairment
Short, rapid and sudden sideways movement of the hand (swipe)	Scroll Kinect	Move hand rapidly and precisely within a small space	Severe mental disorder Motor impairment
Movement of two fingers to form a circle (rotate)	Move to next semantic item iOS VoiceOver	Simultaneously move two fingers, thumb and forefinger, clockwise or anticlockwise around a central pivot	Motor impairment.
Up and down stroking movement of one or two fingers (scroll)	Move to next control iOS Voice Over	Move one or more fingers up and down	Motor impairment
Combination of a drag and up, down or side-to-side movement	Drag, move objects	Two-movement sequence.	Severe mental disorder Motor impairment
Movements of several body parts at once	Game-specific activities	General dynamic coordination	Severe mental disorder Motor impairment

4   Standardization Procedures

We consider it to be necessary to run several studies in order to determine how suitable different gestures and devices are for use with children with SEN. The results of such studies could be useful for compiling a gesture vocabulary suited for the special needs of each user type for later standardization.

To do this, we design a framework (Fig. 1) to be used to collect data. These data will be the basis for the process of selection and later standardization. Also, the devised framework could be useful for developing final systems that are capable of recommending the best gestures depending on user characteristics.

One of the characteristics of the proposed framework is composed of an interaction vocabulary specifying the different actions that a device can be used to perform, their associated gestures, manipulations and interactions and their purposes. The system will be composed of a module (interaction broker) that will select the best vocabulary depending on the user profile, the available devices and the application requirements.

In the early phases of the study, the interaction broker module will be very simple, and selection will be based on the preliminary hypotheses stated by the accessibility experts (Table 1). Interaction data will be collected from test applications. These data will be evaluated and used to refine the interaction vocabulary database. The interaction broker module will also be improved by defining new interaction vocabulary selection processes for use in an application.

This vocabulary, plus the context in which it was applied (user profile, application domain, operating system, etc.) and the resulting suitability measures, and success and error rates, will provide an important groundwork for standardizing gestures and determining their fitness in different contexts.

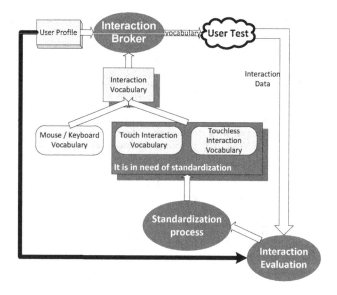

Fig. 1. Proposed architecture

5   Conclusions

New ways of interaction like tactile screens or touchless gesture UIs are becoming popular in personal devices such as smart phones, PCs or video consoles. In order to determine if the new interaction paradigms are suitable for use in education, and particularly for teaching children with SEN, we propose a roadmap with stages that must be carefully negotiated before we can answer this question.

First of all, the new devices should be tested in the classroom by students working on regular teaching activities. These tests will provide valuable feedback about how to apply these interaction paradigms and some guidelines for developing educational tools for classroom use.

For a full and fair assessment, educational UI technologies should be evaluated against learning outcomes bearing in mind the classroom experience. Based on the results of the classroom experience, it will be necessary to define which gestures are best for each and every action (interaction command) and profile. This should be a flexible set of associations where one set of gestures may turn out to mean the same action, whereas similar gestures may mean different actions.

This catalogue of gestures and actions will determine how humans interact with machines. It will be very important for the educational developer community to take into account this catalogue when they start to develop software tools adapted to a wide range of profiles.

This research should provide useful information for establishing standards related to gesture-based interfaces. First, it will help developers to adapt systems to different user profiles. Second, it will help to standardize gestures that make users feel more comfortable when interacting with machines.

References

1. Apple Inc.: Cocoa Touch Layer, https://developer.apple.com/ library/ios/#documentation/Miscellaneous/Conceptual/ iPhoneOSTechOverview/iPhoneOSTechnologies/iPhoneOSTechnologi es.html#//apple_ref/doc/uid/TP40007898-CH3-SW1
2. Microsoft. Windows Touch Gestures Overview, http://msdn.microsoft.com/ en-us/library/windows/desktop/dd940543%28v=vs.85%29.aspx
3. Bruckman, A., Bandlow, A.: Human-computer interaction for kids. In: The Human-Computer Interaction Handbook, pp. 428–440. L. Erlbaum Associates Inc., Hillsdale (2003)
4. Tse, E., Schöning, J., Rogers, Y., Shen, C., Morrison, G.: Next generation of HCI and education: workshop on UI technologies and educational pedagogy. In: Proceedings of the 28th of the International Conference Extended Abstracts on Human Factors in Computing Systems (CHI EA 2010), pp. 4509–4512. ACM, New York (2010)
5. Burgstahler, S.: Computing Services for Disabled Students in Institutions of Higher Education. Ph.D. Dissertation, University of Washington (1992)

6. Grandhi, S.A., Joue, G., Mittelberg, I.: Understanding naturalness and intuitiveness in gesture production: insights for touchless gestural interfaces. In: Proceedings of the 2011 Annual Conference on Human Factors in Computing Systems, pp. 821–824. ACM, New York (2011)
7. Dillenbourg, P., Evans, M.: Interactive tabletops in education. Int. J. Comput.-Support Collab. Learn. 6(4), 491–514 (2011)
8. International Standards Organization, ISO/IEC 14754 Pen-based interfaces - Common gestures for text editing with pen-based systems (1999)
9. SitePen Inc.: Touching and Gesturing on the iPhone, http://www.sitepen.com/blog/2008/07/10/touching-and-gesturing-on-the-iphone/
10. Rothman, W.: Education's Many Problems Solved With Multitouch Desks, http://gizmodo.com/5051486/educations-many-problems-solved-with-multitouch-desks
11. Do-Lenh, S., Jermann, P., Arn, C., Zufferey, G., Dillenbourg, P.: Classroom-experience evaluation: Evaluating pervasive technologies in a classroom setting. In: Child Computer Interaction: Workshop on UI Technologies and Their Impact on Educational Pedagogy, the ACM International Conference on Human Factors in Computing Systems, CHI 2011 (2011)
12. Yuan, Y., Liu, Y., Barner, K.: Tactile gesture recognition for people with disabilities. In: ICASSP 2005 (2005)

InStep: A Video Database Assessment Tool

Fern Faux[1], David Finch[1], and Lisa Featherstone[2]

[1] National Star College
{dfinch,ffaux}@natstar.ac.uk
[2] JISC TechDis
lisa@techdis.ac.uk

Abstract. InStep is an Open Source video database assessment tool designed to provide reliable assessment for students with LLDD in areas not covered by traditional measures. Videos of students undertaking specific activities are shown side-by-side so that changes in development over time can be seen. InStep has been trialled to measure how well teachiers can take suitable videos, the reliability of the assessments and whether learners and their parents could recognise progress using the tool.

Keywords: Assessment, LLDD.

1 Introduction

InStep is an Open Source tool combining an assessment continuum with a video database. It was conceived as a tool to provide reliable assessment measures for non-accredited learning for learners with learning difficulties and/or disabilities (LLDD), with an emphasis on learners being supported to recognise and record their own progress and achievement (RARPA) [1].

InStep is a plug-in that takes videos from a learner's e-portfolio, in this case a specialist e-portfolio called InFolio [2]. It consists of three screen interfaces:

1. An assessment screen on which the uploaded video is titled by activity and tagged. Assessment judgments are recorded and the context in which the video was taken is then added.
2. A database storing labelled and assessed videos for each learner, together with a search function.
3. An interface allowing the user to search and select two videos from the database to compare. Observations of the comparison can be recorded in a notes field and retrieved when the two videos are recalled again.

2 The State of the Art

Traditional assessment methods rarely acknowledge the progress made by learners with LLDD [3]. It is essential to develop additional forms of assessment which

K. Miesenberger et al. (Eds.): ICCHP 2012, Part I, LNCS 7382, pp. 73–76, 2012.

capture the achievements and attainments of such learners with authenticity, fairness and validity.

3   The Methodology

81 videos of 20 learners with profound and multiple disabilities and associated learning difficulties were taken by 11 teachers, assessed and uploaded into InStep. The videos focussed on less tangible outcomes such an improved interaction, social confidence or communication fluency. A moderation session was held to analyse the accuracy of assessments of individual videos against the assessment continuum.

The research team developed a video assessment guide giving guidance on how to capture clear and authentic video. A questionnaire completed by all teachers measured their level of confidence in the use of video assessment and InStep, and also asked about their perceptions of the finished video quality and its use for assessment purposes. InStep was used in two formal learner progress reviews, and feedback from those attending the reviews was captured and analysed.

In accordance with British Education Research Association (BERA)'s Revised Ethical Guidelines for Educational Research (2004), consent forms for the use of video were issued to teachers and learners for completion.

4   The Research and Development

The InStep assessment continuum was developed with cognisance of the achievement continuum of the Oxford Cambridge and RSA Examinations (OCR) [4] where which aims to reflect what the learner **has** achieved; InStep's assessment continuum, however, recognises the **continuous** developmental process over six defined stages; notice, respond, engage, can do, improve and skilled. Initial ideas were developed using Bloom's (1956) [5] domains of learning. The domains were combined a second level of assessment added. Within each stage there are three developmental levels; for example, within the 'notice' stage a learner can travel through 'aware', 'alert' and 'watches' as their interaction level increases. This enables judgments to be made more consistently.

There are seven components the teacher has to complete in order to upload an assessed video: a video no longer than 50 seconds; a description of the activity; the date on which the activity took place; the stage in which it was assessed; the level at which it was assessed; Tags (to enable searching) and a notes field for contextual information.

The video clips are shown side by side so that small differences in development can be seen. The assessments quantify the progress students make over time.

The research trial explored the level to which participant teachers would be able to take quality, reliable video footage; the extent that participant teachers could make assessment judgments using the assessment continuum and the extent that participant students and stakeholders could use comparisons of two videos to identify their own progress.

5   The Outcomes and Impact

Care needs to be taken with the reliability of assessments performed against video clips and the assessment of 'soft skills' will always be subjective. Standardisation is met through regular moderation meetings. During the trial testing the assessment judgments showed little deviation amongst the stages on the continuum. There was, however, some shift recorded in the levels within specific stages. This was deemed acceptable as it is likely to be reduced the more practiced teachers become in making judgments using the continuum.

Although video assessment was new to participant teachers, the format of the assessment structure itself was similar to that already in use and supported the existing assessment strategy in that it evidenced statements made about learner progression. Teachers indicated a noticeable impact on students in their improved confidence, social dialogue, social skills and communication responsiveness.

"Evidencing progression was good for teachers and students to see, and it then gave clear indications for development and the best way forward."

Where the assessment continuum was used in student progress reviews, it more clearly demonstrated student progress and parental responses were positive:

During my son's review we were able to share videos of new skills and activities. The improvements were clear by comparing previous footage with new ... and so the needs and skills are far more powerfully highlighted in this visual method. I was very happy to see my son so happily engaged and learning new skills. He too loves to watch it back and is a great discussion point for him.

Previously there were few ways in which these developmental changes in confidence, assertiveness and self-assurance could be measured, yet they are key to students' understanding of the progress they are making, particularly when students themselves are engaged in making such assessments. Using this technology in formal progress reviews gives students the opportunities to present their in a tangible and measurable way. Teachers also see the ability to demonstrate student developmental progress to parents and external bodies as a significant benefit, particularly in being able to measure progress that was deemed un-measurable.

6   Conclusion

This research set out to address three questions:

How well would teachers be able to capture video of students to use for assessment purposes?

Initially some teachers had difficulty in capturing the required steps of progress in 50 seconds, or editing quality, reliable video footage. However, all commented that as the project proceeded they learned how to limit their filming to that which was immediately relevant and pertinent. The support guide to filming and editing provided good guidance and it is intended to incorporate this guide into a help screen.

How well could reliable and valid judgments be made against these videos?

From the trial group it was evident that reliable and consistent assessments could be made on the assessment continuum. Knowledge of the student is an important factor in being able to make a reliable judgment - those teachers who made judgments about students with whom they were unfamiliar had the greatest shift in assessment judgment.

How well would learners and their parents be able to recognise progress and achievement through viewing the assessment comparisons?

In the formal progress reviews where InStep was used to illustrate developmental progress, both parents and other stakeholders commented favourably on the benefits of seeing comparisons of developmental changes. Learners in the trial group to a small extent were able to recognise the activities they were involved in from the videos recorded. However, they have significant cognitive difficulties and recognising progress from the videos taken was not apparent.

7   Future Work

Training packages are being developed to ensure that participants are should be supported to take quality video, edit, name and save it to InStep independently. InStep needs to be trialled by a broader range of users, contexts and with other providers. Interestingly, the only area where teachers did not see progress in students was in their physical development – this is currently being considered in the extended pilot group, which now includes practitioners from the areas of nursing and physiotherapy.

References

1. Recognising and Recording Progress and Achievement,
   http://www.niace.org.uk/current-work/rarpa
2. In-Folio, http://www.in-folio.org.uk/where.php
3. DfES. Person-centred approaches and adults with learning difficulties (2006),
   http://archive.excellencegateway.org.uk/pdf/
   Person-centredapproachesandadultswithlearningdifficulties.pdf
4. Oxford Cambridge and RSA Examinations assessment grid,
   http://www.ocr.org.uk/download/kd/
   ocr_5two77three_kd_qcf_rec_docs.pdf
5. Bloom, B.S. (ed.): Taxonomy of Educational Objectives, the classification of educational goals – Handbook I: Cognitive Domain. McKay, New York (1956)

SCRIBE: A Model for Implementing Robobraille in a Higher Education Institution

Lars Ballieu Christensen[1], Sean J. Keegan[2], and Tanja Stevns[1]

[1] Synscenter Refsnæs and Sensus ApS,
Torvet 3-5, 2.tv.,
DK-3400 Hillerød, Denmark
{tanja,lbc}@robobraille.org
[2] Office of Accessible Education/Schwab Learning Center
Stanford University
563 Salvatierra Walk, Stanford, California 94305, USA
skeegan@stanford.edu

Abstract. The provision of alternate formats for students with print-based disabilities can be challenging. Producing educational material in alternate formats is often time consuming, expensive and requires special knowledge and training of staff. Therefore, in most settings, students are dependent on others, such as disability service personnel or external producers, to obtain their academic materials in their preferred accessible format. Even with these resources available, students may still encounter delays in receiving their alternate formats in a timely manner. For example, a student receiving an inaccessible version of a hand-out or other academic content from a professor on a Friday afternoon may be required to wait until the next business week to receive an accessible version of the document as most institutions or external providers do not run their alternate format production centres seven days per week, year-round. The RoboBraille service offers fully automated conversion of text into a number of alternate formats allowing the individual student to be independent. This paper describes how the RoboBraille Service was turned into a self-service solution for students at Stanford University, called the Stanford Converter into Braille and E-Text – or SCRIBE. The overall purpose of SCRIBE is to encourage students to become self-sufficient by simplifying the production of accessible formats.

Keywords: Alternate formats, accessibility, self-sufficiency, conversion, educational material, print-based disability, Braille, MP3, DAISY, e-books, student independence.

1 Introduction

The provision of alternate formats for students with print-based disabilities is a standard practice at nearly all higher-education institutions. Disability services offices often develop policies and procedures for their alternate format programmes as well as invest in computers, software applications, and staff training to assist in the

K. Miesenberger et al. (Eds.): ICCHP 2012, Part I, LNCS 7382, pp. 77–83, 2012.

document conversion process. Despite such support, for students requesting their academic materials in alternate formats, obtaining accessible versions in a timely manner and in the format preferred by the student can be challenging. Additionally, a student may wish to use different document formats depending on the nature of the academic material and their preferred assistive technology or mobile device. As students change the manner in which they interact with their academic information, it is necessary for institutions to consider alternative options to successfully meet student needs.

Disability services offices often manage an alternate format production facility at the institution focusing on the conversion of academic materials for students with print-based disabilities into a variety of document formats, including Braille, e-text, tactile graphics, and large-print. Additionally, campus computer labs may include several computers with various software-based assistive technologies and alternate format applications allowing students to interact with their academic materials at these locations. Even with these resources available, students may still encounter delays to receiving their alternate formats in a timely manner. For example, a student who receives an inaccessible version of a hand-out or other academic content from a professor on a Friday afternoon may have to wait until the next week to receive an accessible version of the document as most institutions do not run their alternate format production centres seven days per week all year long. And while campus computer labs may offer software applications to assist with alternate format creation, such applications generally require training and familiarity in order to produce a usable version by the student.

With these challenges in mind, in 2011 the Office of Accessible Education/Schwab Learning Center at Stanford University implemented a pilot project to develop a simple web-based, document conversion system supporting the production of accessible formats for students with print-based disabilities as well as the conversion capabilities to document formats for emerging mobile devices. The system was based on RoboBraille [1 - 3] and the objective was to create an online solution to promote student independence while delivering alternative media accurately, timely and in student-preferred formats.

2   RoboBraille

RoboBraille is a web and email based service capable of automatically transforming documents into a variety of alternative formats for the visually and reading impaired such as Braille, structured audio books in Daisy format, plain mp3 files, e-books and more. RoboBraille can furthermore convert otherwise inaccessible documents such as scanned images and image-pdf files into more accessible formats. RoboBraille is available free of charge to all non-commercial users and users need not register in order to use the service. RoboBraille supports the Braille codes and contraction regimes of many national Braille systems and includes audio support for many European languages as well as for many other languages such as Arabic, American English and Latin American Spanish.

Originally a Danish service developed jointly the National Danish Centre for Visually Impaired Children and Youth and Sensus ApS, a research-based private consultancy company, RoboBraille has been validated throughout Europe with financial support from the European Commission in order to verify its technical, commercial and cultural viability. Building on the European results and supported by public and private donations, the RoboBraille team is currently engaged in several international projects aimed at improving the service in terms of quality and functionality, and expanding its geographical coverage. The objective is to create an unlimited supply of accessible material to anyone, anywhere with a need.

Combining commercial text-to-speech, text-to-Braille and OCR software and open source Daisy authoring and e-book conversion, RoboBraille currently serves some 1-2,000 daily user requests from all over the world.

3   The SCRIBE System

In order to be able to offer educational material in alternate formats 24/7 and to support students being independent, the Office of Accessible Education/Schwab Learning Center at Stanford University implemented a customised version of the RoboBraille Service during the fall of 2011. Built upon the RoboBraille engine, SCRIBE is a customised implementation intended to improve the availability of alternate formats to students with print-based disabilities. Figure 1 below shows the main user interface of the SCRIBE system [6]:

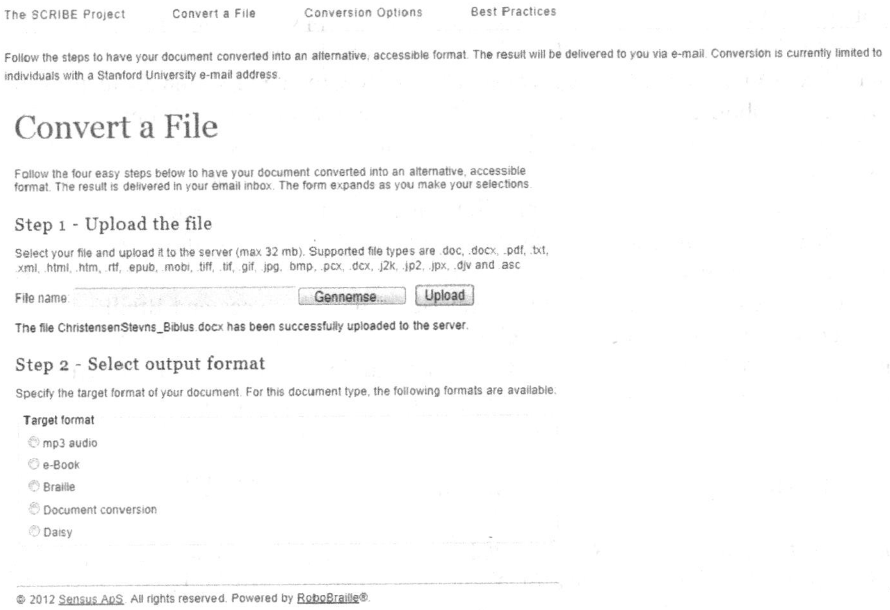

The SCRIBE Project   Convert a File   Conversion Options   Best Practices

Follow the steps to have your document converted into an alternative, accessible format. The result will be delivered to you via e-mail. Conversion is currently limited to individuals with a Stanford University e-mail address.

Convert a File

Follow the four easy steps below to have your document converted into an alternative, accessible format. The result is delivered in your email inbox. The form expands as you make your selections.

Step 1 - Upload the file

Select your file and upload it to the server (max 32 mb). Supported file types are .doc, .docx, .pdf, .txt, .xml, .html, .htm, .rtf, .epub, .mobi, .tiff, .tif, .gif, .jpg, .bmp, .pcx, .dcx, .j2k, .jp2, .jpx, .djv and .asc

File name: [Gennemse]   [Upload]

The file ChristensenStevns_Biblus.docx has been successfully uploaded to the server.

Step 2 - Select output format

Specify the target format of your document. For this document type, the following formats are available.

Target format
- mp3 audio
- e-Book
- Braille
- Document conversion
- Daisy

Fig. 1. The SCRIBE user interface showing the first two (of four) steps of converting documents into alternative media

Through an accessible web-based interface, a student can upload a file for conversion into different alternate formats. Depending on the original file type, a student may select from a variety of output formats, including mp3 audio, e-book, Braille, full-text/full audio Daisy or document conversion. Image-based files, such as image-only PDF documents, JPEG, or TIFF, undergo a separate optical character recognition (OCR) process to convert the document from an image format into a text-based version.

Once converted, the final document is sent to the student via email making it simple to deliver the accessible file to computers, tablets and smartphones. No training or familiarisation on the use of the OCR software is required from the student and the system is available outside of normal business hours.

SCRIBE is implemented as a customised version of RoboBraille. As such, a set of RoboBraille agents have been set up to manage the conversion of documents into alternative media. The RoboBraille agents have been configured with Microsoft Office 2007 for document conversion, Sensus Braille 4 for Braille transcription [4], Calibre e-book management for e-book conversion, Daisy Pipeline for Daisy conversion and three NeoSpeech voices for audio support. A designated agent handles all OCR conversions using ABBYY FineReader 10 Corporate Edition. In addition to the RoboBraille and OCR agents, the SCRIBE system is composed of a web server (Microsoft IIS 7.5), a mail server (hMailServer) and an ftp server (Argosoft FTP). All agents are running 32-bit Microsoft Windows 7 and hosted in a virtual environment using WMWare ESXi. At this time, access to the system is currently limited to members of the Stanford community with a valid institutional email account.

A number of additional functionalities were added to the core RoboBraille engine to satisfy the functional requirements of the project: Support for the American Braille code and US Braille paper formats had to be implemented; the university furthermore required a web interface to the service as opposed to the traditional email-based interface to RoboBraille. Finally, the SCRIBE system had to support conversion into the most popular e-book formats. Likewise, some components were removed from RoboBraille as part of the customisation. These mainly include the multilingual aspects of the service such as the multilingual user interface, the range of available TTS voices and the support for multiple Braille codes and contraction regimes. As a consequence, the SCRIBE user interface is only available in American English, the TTS voices have been limited to three American English voices and Braille support has been reduced to Grade 1 and Grade 2 in the North American Braille code. Furthermore, ABBYY FineReader Corporate Edition is utilised in SCRIBE as opposed to ABBYY Recognition Server 3.0 currently used in RoboBraille.

4   Advantages and Results of Implementing SCRIBE

Following the launch of SCRIBE in 2011, students have the options of requesting alternative media from the Office of Accessible Education or use the SCRIBE self-service platform. SCRIBE is not limited to students with print-based disabilities but is available to the entire Stanford community. Usage figures from the initial four months of operation suggest that students find the document conversion and mp3 conversion features of SCRIBE especially useful. Table 1 below summarises the usage split between the different services offered by SCRIBE during the period November 2011 to February 2012:

Table 1. Usage split by SCRIBE function. November 2011 – February 2012

SCRIBE function	Percentage	
Document conversion	**58%**	
Mp3 conversion	**34%**	
- of which NeoSpeech Julie		30%
- of which NeoSpeech Paul		3%
- of which NeoSpeech Kate		1%
E-book conversion	**6%**	
- of which Mobi Pocket		3%
- of which ePub		3%
Braille	**2%**	
Daisy	-	
Administrative	**2%**	

The self-service approach of SCRIBE appears to offer a number of technological and service-related advantages as well as advantages of a more principle nature. Based on experienced from early stage use of the SCRIBE system, advantages in the areas of scalability, availability and flexibility, privacy and extended support have been derived.

Scalability: The SCRIBE system is unique in its approach to providing multiple conversion system in an efficient and effective manner. Converting text files into mp3 audio using computerised text-to-speech as well as performing OCR functions can require significant CPU processing requirements. Such computational processing generally requires a mid- or high-level computer to perform these tasks efficiently. Purchasing multiple physical machines can be costly, both in terms of hardware and the requisite office space. Rather than multiple physical computers, the SCRIBE system is built upon multiple virtual machines with each virtual system hosting a "conversion agent" to process files. As the OCR and the creation of audio files from text-to-speech programs can increase CPU requirements, the advantage of the virtual machine model is that additional computing and CPU resources can be directed to the appropriate virtual machine as needed.

Additionally, the existence of multiple virtual machines ensures that during periods of high usage there are several "conversion agents" available to process files into the desired output formats. A virtual machine model also has the advantage of decreasing the overall footprint required for numerous physical computers and releasing office space for other production needs. In order to expand upon text-to-speech, OCR, or document conversions capabilities within the SCRIBE system, system administrators can easily clone more virtual machines with the requisite appropriate software licenses to support any increased demand rather than purchase and deploy additional hardware solutions.

Availability and Flexibility: Rather than wait for a document to be processed into an accessible format by the alternate format production office, there is now an institutional model demonstrating a new concept in the acquisition of accessible formats by students with print-based disabilities. The SCRIBE is system is available 24/4 and students can request as many different alternative formats as they wish. Similarly, students can convert extracurricular material and other material not necessarily offered by the alternate format production office. As students begin using various assistive technologies, mobile devices, and document formats, it is necessary for institutions to consider new methods to meet the unique academic needs of this student population. Alternate format production offices will remain a key component in producing accessible formats for students at higher education institutions; however, a web-based alternative, such as the SCRIBE system, may provide a simple and efficient platform for meeting student alternate format demands.

Privacy: By relying on alternate format production offices to convert material into alternative formats, students loose the privacy granted everyone else. By offering a self-service solution such as SCRIBE, students can maintain their privacy of what they are reading.

Extended Support: While alternate format production offices may be available to students at academic institutions, this is not necessary the case when students graduate and find a job. However, the need to convert material into alternative formats is likely to remain amongst print-impaired graduates. By offering a self-service solution such as SCRIBE, academic institutions are capable of extending the service they offer to students beyond the period when the students are enrolled at the institutions.

5   Conclusions and Future Activities

In 2011, the SCRIBE system was successfully implemented as a pilot project at Stanford University and a phase 2 has been planned for 2012. Although usage figures are still low compared to RoboBraille, the number of SCRIBE users and user requests submitted to SCRIBE is increasing monthly. Print-impaired students as well as other students, faculty and others within the Stanford community now have access to a self-service solution capable of automatically converting a wide range of document types into alternative media.

Based on the experienced from the implementation and initial period of use, the following conclusions can be made:

Technical Challenges: During the implementation, a number of technical challenges were experienced. Some were overcome during the project whereas others were postponed to subsequent phases of the project. Several virtualisation platforms were tested during the project before settling on VMware, as this supported sound-card emulation for the text-to-speech conversions. For OCR production, ABBYY FineReader 10 Corporate Edition was implemented as a (somewhat stable) "waterfall" conversion model, where the input file is passed from one conversion "hotfolder" to the next as each output format is created. Subsequent investigations have identified the possibility to move away from a "waterfall" model with ABBYY

Finereader while still creating the necessary output formats. Amongst challenges that were postponed is the implementation of support for conversion of Microsoft Word documents containing math formula into full-text/full audio Math Daisy projects. The project furthermore experienced license restrictions regarding the use of TTS voices. Because of these restrictions, SCRIBE currently only supports American English and the audio service is only available on one of the three RoboBraille agents in operation.

Ideas for Improvements: Obviously, the project spawned a number of ideas for improvements to the system. Amongst these are support for conversion of Microsoft Word and PowerPoint documents into tagged and accessible PDF, conversion of Microsoft PowerPoint into alternative formats, auto-editing of scanned documents for features such as headings and optional hyphens prior to conversion, and improved system monitoring. These features are expected to be included during phase 2 of the SCRIBE project and will subsequently be rolled into RoboBraille thereby making the improvements available for a larger educational and public community.

Spreading Interest: The potential of SCRIBE as a means for self-sufficiency and independence amongst print-disabled students is demonstrating the capacity to implement a localized version of the RoboBraille platform, and other academic institutions are currently considering how they may implement versions of the system on their own.

The perspectives in using the RoboBraille Service a customised, self-service solution are numerous. Because of the simplicity of the user interface in combination with the multiple conversion possibilities, a solution similar to SCRIBE is well suited for number of educational institutions, such as schools, colleges and universities. The web interface can be customised to fit the exact needs of the individual setting in terms of style and colour, name, user management, conversion possibilities and languages. This allows the students to be self-sufficient when it comes to simple conversion whilst retaining their privacy. The diversity in output formats accommodates a number of different modern platforms, e.g. tablets and mobile devices and puts the student in charge of managing his or her own alternate format production.

References

1. Christensen, L.B.: RoboBraille – Automated Braille Translation by Means of an E-Mail Robot. In: Miesenberger, K., Klaus, J., Zagler, W., Karshmer, A.I. (eds.) ICCHP 2006. LNCS, vol. 4061, pp. 1102–1109. Springer, Heidelberg (2006)
2. Christensen, L.B.: RoboBraille – Braille Unlimited. In: The Educator, ICEVI 2009, vol. XXI(2), pp. 32–37 (2009)
3. Christensen, L.B.: The RoboBraille Service, http://www.robobraille.org (retrieved)
4. Christensen, L.B.: Multilingual Two-Way Braille Translation. In: Klaus, J., et al. (eds.) Interdisciplinary Aspects on Computers Helping People with Special Needs, Österreichische Computer Gesellschaft/R. Oldenbourg Wien München (1996)
5. Web Content Accessibility Guidelines 2.0, W3C (2008)
6. Keegan, S.: The SCRIBE Project, http://scribe.stanford.edu/ (retrieved)

Identifying Barriers to Collaborative Learning for the Blind

Wiebke Köhlmann

Universität Potsdam, Institut für Informatik
August-Bebel-Straße 89, 14482 Potsdam, Germany
koehlmann@cs.uni-potsdam.de

Abstract. Digital materials can help blind and visually impaired students to participate in e-learning and collaborative settings. The use of multimedia content enhances the learning experience of sighted students, but new barriers arise for the visually impaired. This paper describes surveys on e-learning and collaborative settings, defines existing barriers and presents a survey on the use of computer usage, e-learning and collaborative learning amongst 42 blind and visually impaired users in educational and professional life.

Keywords: Collaborative learning, CSCL, virtual classroom, e-learning, accessibility, visually impaired, survey.

1 Introduction

Blind and visually impaired individuals[1] usually access information via screen reading software and Braille displays (see [10]). In an educational context, analogue learning materials, panel paintings, location related problems etc. can pose great barriers to these students.

The use of the Internet and of digital material, e.g. in an e-learning context, serves as a supplement to attendance learning. The availability of digital material facilitates access to information, and online lectures spare students travelling and orientation issues. Additionally, the student can choose his/her own learning speed and can cooperate with other students.

The use of multimedia learning content increases (e. g. in form of graphics, videos, films and animation) to enhance the learning experience. But unfortunately, in order to make this primary visual content accessible to visually impaired students, supplemental effort of the authors is required. In addition to existent problems with the learning content, restraints concerning the use of the learning software can also occur, e. g. in terms of noticing changes of dynamic content or gaining an overview of complex structures.

Regarding e. g. a synchronous collaborative learning environment with functionality comprising a dynamic whiteboard, text chat, audio conference, video, participants' list and file transfer (see Fig. 1), multiple barriers arise for visually impaired participants. These comprise:

---

[1] In the following by "visually impaired" we include blind and visually impaired persons.

K. Miesenberger et al. (Eds.): ICCHP 2012, Part I, LNCS 7382, pp. 84–91, 2012.

- Resolution and orientation: Applications for collaborative communication are complex due to their various functions and require a high resolution. As assistive devices for the visually impaired usually only provide one line of text, the amount of information perceived at a time is very low. Additionally, spatial relations between application elements are hard to recognize because of this linear information. Thus orientation can be difficult.
- Semantics: Visually impaired persons have to recognize the context between different media elements such as chat, whiteboard and audio.
- Synchronicity: Using synchronous communication, many activities take place in parallel. Non-disabled participants register changes immediately due to a general visual overview. Since visually impaired register only few details at a time, the recognition of changes and correlations between elements can cause difficulties.
- Social presence: The problem of a lack of social presence using web-based communication exists for all users, as communication interaction is best perceived in face-to-face situations. But the advantage of non-disabled participants is that they can use video to e. g. perceive gestures and facial expressions.

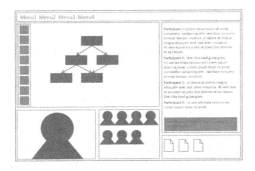

Fig. 1. Schematic drawing of a virtual classroom. Elements (from top left to bottom right: ...): menu bar, whiteboard with toolbar, chat, video, participants, file transfer.

The paper discusses current research in the field of collaborative learning among visually impaired students and presents a survey on the present usage of e-learning and collaborative learning among visually impaired. The paper concludes with a discussion whether the survey verifies previous assumptions concerning the barriers to collaborative learning.

2   Related Work

Surveys conducted on the accessibility of e-learning and collaborative learning tools for visually impaired can be essentially divided into surveys looking at asynchronous functions of Learning Management Systems (LMS) and synchronous communication with collaborative communication tools.

Power et al. [7] analysed three LMS in terms of general usability and the accessibility of forums for visually impaired users. All LMS showed accessibility problems which could be resolved by adequate authoring. Synchronous communication functionality was not analysed. Bühler et al. [1] analysed five open source LMS in terms of login, start and content page, navigation, forum, chat and mail functionality using the German BITV[2] and different adapted concepts dividing the LMS into "inherent courseware features", "designer controlled utilities and functions" and "communication components". Buzzi et al. [2] describe problem fields of LMS and define general guidelines for the access to information. But these only address the possibility to access all information with assistive devices. Aspects such as semantics, structural information or an adaption of presentation according to the user's needs are not sufficiently addressed.

Slavin [9] summarizes over 70 surveys on collaborative learning which show that it can support, among others, academic achievement, intergroup relations and self-esteem. Visually impaired persons should also be able to use collaborative learning methods equally. But according to McGookin et al. [6] and Winberg et al. [12] the special needs of visually impaired concerning computer supported collaborative work (CSCW) have not yet been analysed sufficiently.

Many surveys on collaborative learning look at situations with only two collaborators and special support for the visual impaired participant (see e. g. [3], [5], [8] and [11]). There are only few surveys regarding general learning situations using synchronous distance communication tools such as a virtual classroom in which a visually impaired participates. In such situations, direct help of other participants can not be expected.

Generally, in virtual classrooms, textual content can be accessed easily, whereas graphical content can cause problems. Freire et al. [4] present a survey on an accessible whiteboard in a virtual classroom setting. A real life person works as a translator and describes the presented content in a textual form almost in real time. The use of a translator seems to be a good approach, but the time delay between presentation and translation of the content and the time-consuming preparation for the teacher and the translator before the lessons still cause problems.

IMS Guidelines[3] describe common problems with synchronous communication and give advice how to avoid them, although it is questionable if the provision of alternative descriptions for visual elements is practical in a synchronous setting without additional manpower like in [4].

3   Survey

The objective of our survey was to find out to what extent and for what purpose visually impaired persons use (electronically supported) collaboration and

---

[2] The German "Barrierefreie Informationstechnik-Verordnung" (BITV) defines guidelines for accessible information technology, http://www.einfach-fuer-alle.de/artikel/bitv/

[3] IMS Guidelines:http://www.imsproject.org/accessibility/accessiblevers/sec7.html

e-learning in educational and also professional settings and to prove assumed barriers occurring in synchronous collaborative settings (see section 1). The main research questions were:

1. Which problems occur when visually impaired use (synchronous) e-learning and participate in synchronous collaborative situations?
2. In which context are collaborative situations used (number of (blind, seeing) participants, purpose, assistive devices used etc.)?
3. How many visually impaired persons already use collaborative learning and with which tools?

The following describes the design of the survey, the sampling methods and teh results.

3.1 Survey Design

The survey consisted of six sections divided into several pages besides of the welcome and final pages:

- *General information*: age, sex, visual impairment, education etc.
- *Braille*: Braille knowledge, use of Braille displays, use of tactile graphics etc.
- *Computer knowledge*: use of computers and software, assistive devices etc.
- *E-learning*: experience with e-learning, e-learning tools, barriers etc.
- *Collaboration*: experience with collaboration, fields of use, software etc.
- *Final questions*: problems concerning e-learning and collaboration etc.

The questions posed depended on the answers of the participants. Certain answers to key questions resulted in skipping other questions related to this topic (see Fig. 2). For instance there were no more questions posed concerning Braille if the participant did not know it and the questionnaire continued with the next section: computer knowledge.

3.2 Sample

The target group of the survey was visually impaired people from any fields of work. Most representative results were expected from participants in the field of education because of the high probability of the use of cooperative learning and e-learning. As lifelong learning gains in importance, all ages were included.

The duration of the survey amounted to 17 weeks in the autumn of the year 2011 during which 222 page views were registered. Thereof 97 persons exited the survey on the welcome page and 83 participants did not complete the survey. The number of completed questionnaires counts 42, whereof 19 persons were male and 23 female. Half of the participants has residual vision.

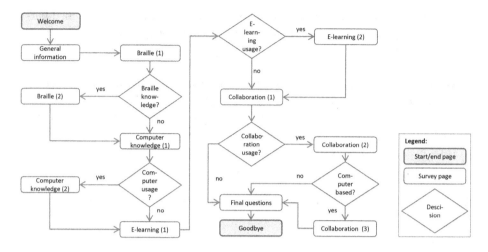

Fig. 2. Flow chart of survey design

3.3   Method

In order to reach as many subjects as possible, the survey was conducted online and via telephone. Beforehand, the survey was tested in terms of content, logic and functionality by the author and a blind person.

The online survey tool "oFb"[4] was chosen because of its special screen reader mode. The survey was distributed via e-mail, which was sent to schools for visually impaired, associations for visually impaired and individuals all over Germany with the request to forward the information. Several subjects used the possibility to send problems and suggestions via e-mail which could mostly be solved quickly. A total of three surveys were completed via telephone.

4   Results

The survey showed a broad use of e-learning applications in education and professional life, whereas collaboration is mostly used in face-to-face situations with sighted people. In the following, the results are presented in detail.

4.1   Computer Usage

The survey showed that all participants use a computer, whereof 83 % do so several times a day (see Fig. 3, left). The most frequently used applications are e-mail programs, Microsoft Internet Explorer and Microsoft Word (see Fig. 4, left). Looking at assistive devices, 81 % use screen reader software, 57 % a Braille display and 19 % speech recognition (see Fig. 3, right).

---

[4] oFb (onlineFragebogen), https://www.soscisurvey.de

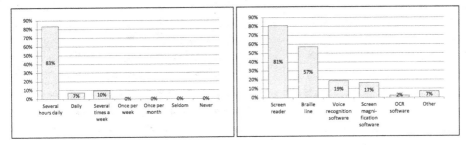

Fig. 3. Left: How often do you use a computer? Right: Which assistive devices do you use? (Multiple answers possible.)

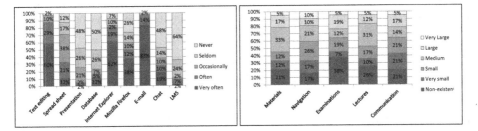

Fig. 4. Left: Which programmes do you work with? Right: How do you rate the barriers of these aspects concerning education?

4.2   E-Learning

Looking at education, barriers concerning different areas such as learning material, navigation, assessments, courses (writing on the board, speed etc.) and communication with teachers and students were perceived differently by the participants. The largest barrier seems to be the navigation (see Fig. 4, right).

38 % use e-learning in their (continuing) education, whereof the online learning materials are used the most, followed by LMS (see Fig. 5, left). Collaborative software is only used by 12 % of the e-learning users. E-mail and online learning material are the most and the least used functionalities for e-learning activities are shared desktop, live presentations and whiteboard (see Fig. 5, right).

4.3   Collaboration

95 % of the participants collaborate with fellow students, colleagues and friends. Regarding the collaborating persons, collaboration most often takes place with sighted people (see Fig. 6, left). A collaboration with sighted and more than one visually impaired person takes place only very rarely. 70 % state, they use collaboration for private, 65 % for professional and only 43 % for educational purposes.

Only 23 % of the participants who collaborate have taken part in computer-supported collaborative situations. The purpose of the collaboration was mostly

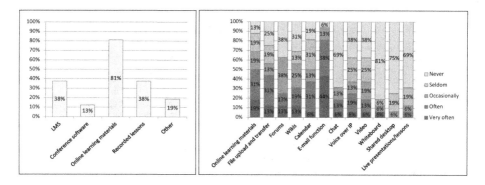

Fig. 5. Left: Which e-learning tools have you already used? (Multiple answers possible.) Right: Which functionality do you use of these e-learning tools and how often?

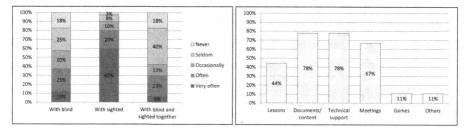

Fig. 6. Left: How often and with whom do you cooperate? Right: For what purpose do you use computer based cooperation? (Multiple answers possible.)

document editing (78 %), technical support (78 %) and meetings (67 %). The use for courses was only named by 44 % (see Fig. 6, right).

5   Conclusion and Outlook

Most e-learning experiences named by the participants of this survey are based on asynchronous learning materials and learning organisation with the help of LMS. Collaboration is mostly used in face-to-face situations and online-based computer supported collaboration with more than one blind participant is rare. Unfortunately, the data of the survey do not allow us to draw a conclusion whether this is due to inaccessible software or to rare use of collaborative tools in educational settings.

Overall this survey shows that collaborative communication tools are not commonly used by visually impaired students. In fact, face-to-face collaboration and traditional learning settings still seem to be predominant. Because of the little experience with collaborative learning of the target group, the barriers assumed (see section 1) could not be affirmed, but can nevertheless serve as a basis for future research and alternative concepts.

Thus, future research will focus on the accessibility of collaborative tools for educational purposes and methods how to adapt content, especially graphical information and on testing alternative concepts aimed at minimizing the assumed barriers such as orientation, semantics, synchronicity and social presence.

Acknowledgements. I thank all participants of this survey and Oliver Nadig for his valuable advice concerning content and format of the survey.

References

1. Bühler, C., Fisseler, B., Schaten, M.: Lessons to be learned - implementing real-life accessibility features in faculty's e-learning initiative. In: Lingnau, A., Martens, A., Weicht, M. (eds.) Workshop-Proceedings Informatik, Franzbecker, Hildesheim (2009)
2. Buzzi, M.C., Buzzi, M., Leporini, B.: Accessing e-Learning Systems Via Screen Reader: An Example. In: Jacko, J.A. (ed.) HCII 2009. LNCS, vol. 5613, pp. 21–30. Springer, Heidelberg (2009)
3. Crossan, A., Brewster, S.: Micole - inclusive interaction for data creation, visualization and collaboration. In: Hands on Haptics Workshop, CHI 2005 (2005)
4. Freire, A., Linhalis, F., Bianchini, S., Fortes, R., Pimentel, M.: Revealing the whiteboard to blind students: An inclusive approach to provide mediation in synchronous e-learning activities. Computers & Education 54, 866–876 (2010)
5. Kuber, R., Yu, W., McAllister, G.: A Non-visual Approach to Improving Collaboration Between Blind and Sighted Internet Users. In: Stephanidis, C. (ed.) HCI 2007. LNCS, vol. 4556, pp. 913–922. Springer, Heidelberg (2007)
6. McGookin, D., Brewster, S.: An initial investigation into non-visual computer supported collaboration. In: CHI 2007: CHI 2007 Extended Abstracts on Human Factors in Computing Systems, pp. 2573–2578. ACM, New York (2007)
7. Power, C., Petrie, H., Sakharov, V., Swallow, D.: Virtual Learning Environments: Another Barrier to Blended and E-Learning. In: Miesenberger, K., Klaus, J., Zagler, W., Karshmer, A.I. (eds.) ICCHP 2010. LNCS, vol. 6179, pp. 519–526. Springer, Heidelberg (2010)
8. Sallnäs, E.-L., Bjerstedt-Blom, K., Winberg, F., Eklundh, K.S.: Navigation and Control in Haptic Applications Shared by Blind and Sighted Users. In: McGookin, D., Brewster, S. (eds.) HAID 2006. LNCS, vol. 4129, pp. 68–80. Springer, Heidelberg (2006)
9. Slavin, E.R.: A practical guide to cooperative learning. Allyn and Bacon, Boston (1994)
10. Völkel, T., Weber, G., Baumann, U.: Tactile Graphics Revised: The Novel BrailleDis 9000 Pin-Matrix Device with Multitouch Input. In: Miesenberger, K., Klaus, J., Zagler, W., Karshmer, A.I. (eds.) ICCHP 2008. LNCS, vol. 5105, pp. 835–842. Springer, Heidelberg (2008)
11. Winberg, F.: Supporting Cross-Modal Collaboration: Adding a Social Dimension to Accessibility. In: McGookin, D., Brewster, S. (eds.) HAID 2006. LNCS, vol. 4129, pp. 102–110. Springer, Heidelberg (2006)
12. Winberg, F., Bowers, J.: Assembling the senses: Towards the design of cooperative interfaces for visually impaired users. In: CSCW 2004: Proceedings of the 2004 ACM Conference on Computer Supported Cooperative Work, pp. 332–341. ACM, New York (2004)

Deaf and Hearing Students' Eye Gaze Collaboration

Raja S. Kushalnagar[1], Poorna Kushalnagar[2], and Jeffrey B. Pelz[2]

[1] National Technical Institute for the Deaf
[2] Chester F. Carlson Center for Imaging Science
Rochester Institute of Technology, Rochester, NY 14623
{rskics,pxk6223,jbppph}@rit.edu
http://www.ntid.rit.edu/avd

Abstract. In mainstreamed lectures, deaf students face decision-making challenges in shifting attention from looking at the visual representation of the lecture audio, i.e., sign language interpreter or captions. They also face challenges in looking at the simultaneous lecture visual source, i.e., slides, whiteboard or demonstration. To reduce the decision-making challenge for deaf student subjects, we analyze the efficacy of using hearing students' eye gaze and target as reference cues in lectures. When deaf students view the same lectures with reference cues, they show less delay in switching to the active visual information source and report high satisfaction with the reference cues. The students who liked the cued notifications were more likely to demonstrate reduction in delay time associated with shifting visual attention.

Keywords: deaf, hearing, attention switching, cues.

1   Introduction

Most deaf and hard of hearing students do not hear or understand the lecture audio. They obtain access to the audio through legally mandated service providers that transform the audio to a visual information source. For example, sign language interpreters translate the spoken audio to visual sign language; similarly, captioners transform the spoken audio to visual text in real-time. However, there are two major issues with these accommodations. First, there is a delay of about a few seconds, as the service provider has to listen, understand and rapidly present the information to the student. Second, and more importantly, deaf students find it difficult to manage multiple classroom visuals, especially with visual accommodations such as sign language interpreters or real-time captioners. Consequently students can easily miss information because they can only attend to one of these visuals. Unlike hearing students, deaf students do not pick up the lecturer's auditory cues that hint at the switch from one visual to another. A mechanism is sorely needed for these deaf students to easily manage learning focus in the classroom, by enabling them to select and focus on visuals within their view. We show that for deaf and hard of hearing students, presenting visual cues over a video recording of a lecture can positively affect cognitive load and enable students to feel more comfortable about their visual attention management.

K. Miesenberger et al. (Eds.): ICCHP 2012, Part I, LNCS 7382, pp. 92–99, 2012.
© Springer-Verlag Berlin Heidelberg 2012

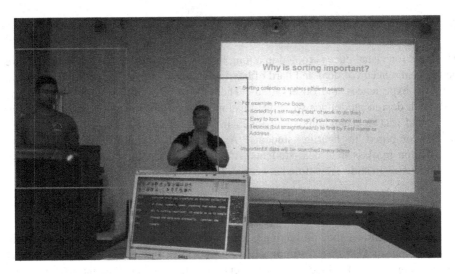

Fig. 1. A typical lecture with a sign language interpreter and captioner; each simultaneous visual source is outlined in red

The provision of the visual accommodation creates one more visual source that is simultaneously presented with the main lecture visual, such as the slides as shown in Figure 1. The deaf student is forced to choose and switch between the visual representation of the audio and the active lecture visual source. In addition to the simultaneously presented visual accommodation, students have to deal with multiple classroom visuals. Presenters often combine visual and verbal materials and repeat key terms to reinforce class visuals to enhance student engagement and learning. While this teaching approach is effective and beneficial for hearing students, this teaching approach is not effective for deaf students [7], as deaf students use their attentional resources to switch between focusing on the interpreter and slides. The student is expending significant effort in focusing on the interpreter or slides, while monitoring for changes in the periphery and making decisions on whether to shift attention between the interpreter and slides. This effort is for naught when the student discovers that the information in the periphery was irrelevant, causing missed information on the student's part. If students attempt to monitor changes or switch often, this leads to mental fatigue among deaf students. Conversely, if students focus exclusively on the interpreter or captions, they cannot see the visuals and do not connect the verbal materials with the visuals, which leads to less understanding. The main contribution of this article is the idea of using visual cues aid deaf students better manage their visual attention and thereby reducing their cognitive demands. This article analyzes the role of reference cues in reducing deaf students' delay associated with shifting attention from one source to another source. It quantifies the benefit of using hearing students' visual gaze as a visual reference cues for deaf students.

2   Related Work

The basis for visual cues is rooted in a long history of cognitive psychology, literature on the visual needs of deaf and hard of hearing students in learning environments, and our own experiences and observations. The following outlines this prior work and ends with design guidelines we have developed based on this work. Marschark et al [8], found that deaf students spent much less time watching course materials, e.g., slides, compared to hearing students. As a result, hearing students gain more information in class than deaf students. Appropriate reference cues can help remedy the imbalance in slide view time between deaf and hearing participants.

2.1   Visual Cues

Research has shown that presenting a cue is less disruptive to slower, cognitively demanding tasks than faster, stimulus driven tasks [12]. For deaf students, researchers have shown that deaf subjects have different, enhanced visual strategies that could be incorporated into cues for more efficient attention prompting, also they respond faster than hearing subjects to targets flashed on the periphery [6]. We analyze the effectiveness of collaborative gaze cue as a technique to increase deaf students' attention management and information acquisition.

3   Pilot Study

We used a SensoMotoric Instruments (SMI) eye-tracking machine that was attached to a 22" LCD monitor. The instrument tracks and records the subject's eye movements relative to objects displayed and viewed on the screen using low-intensity infra-red light reflected off the pupils.

To generate video with cues, we recruited a hearing student to view a lecture video, and captured their eye tracking data. Next, we created a circle cue that was a simple average of this eye-gaze data to create a visual reference cue that would be usable by deaf subjects. For the first iteration, we averaged the gaze location over the immediate past 2 seconds and drew a 100 pixel diameter circle centered on the averaged eye gaze location. We then asked students to view a simulated lecture without cues and with visual cues. We drew the circle and overlaid this on the video.

We recruited four deaf and four hearing student participants to watch a mainstream video lecture in front of an eye-tracking machine. For the video lecture recording, we recorded a professor and professional sign language interpreter. We divided the lecture into two segments of four and a half minutes each so that showing a visual cue could be compared against not showing any cue and displayed the lecture in a balanced, repeated measures design. We also included a short instruction video that enabled users to get comfortable with the system. We divided the lecture view into three regions of interest (ROIs): the lecturer, interpreter, and slides.

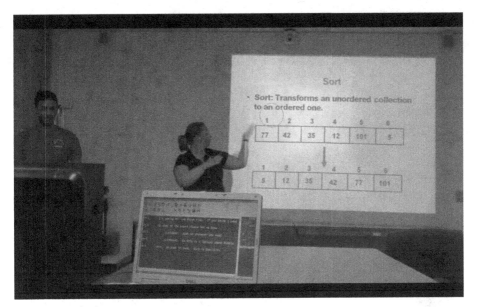

Fig. 2. The circle gaze cue is on the interpreter, and the hearing circle gaze is on the slide

3.1   Pilot Study Findings

When students watched the video without any cues, hearing students spent 74% of the time looking at the instructor or around the instructor, 19% on the slides, and 4% on the lecturer. The deaf students spent much less time on the slides or teacher. Overall, deaf students looked at the instructor 10% of the time and on the slides 14% of the time, as compared to 16% and 22% reported by Marschark et al [9], and 12% and 18% reported by Cavender et al [2]. They mostly watched the interpreter and only occasionally looked the slides. Indeed, most never looked at the teacher after their first introduction. Qualitatively, the deaf students had difficulty in noticing changes on the screen that were outside the current focus of attention, due to interpreter delay as shown in Figure 2. They showed greater delay compared with hearing students in noticing changes outside their viewing focus. This delay was likely due to a combination of cognitive demands that the deaf student experiences: first, to actively attend to the interpreter, and second, to process information that is being relayed through the interpreter and third, to understand the lecture content.

When deaf students watched the cued video, they looked at the instructor 8% of the time and on the slides 16% of the time, which was a small improvement over watching video without cues. Many students felt distracted by the rapid movement of the circle cue, and had a hard time in reorienting to the relevant visual when using the circle cue. However, the students were excited about the potential improvements of using visual cues. For example, they suggested the cues could vanish when they moved away from the slides.

Fig. 3. Visual differences between hearing and deaf student gazes due to delay in noticing changes by the deaf student with the new reference cue

Similarly, they wanted to turn on and off the cues if they become visually distracting. Their qualitative comments suggested that a cue would have to be large enough to be visible with peripheral vision, yet subtle enough to not interfere with the visual source as shown in Figure 3. Viewing the visual representations of lecture audio can be a very immersive, intense focus for students, especially when conveying emphasis or inflections. However, this intensity can trap the student's attention. There is evidence that as visual information increases in the fovea, "tunnel vision" is induced which reduces sensitivity to the changes occurring within the periphery [1], [11]. Our study supports this phenomenon. That is, the focused attention on interpreters appeared to induce tunnel vision [3] as shown in Figure 1 above, which shows the hearing student has switched to the slide, while the deaf student is still looking at the interpreter.

4   Main Study

Based on the findings and feedback from the pilot study, we decided to look at related HCI search cue literature in order to effectively redesign the reference cues. We then ran a study using the redesigned reference cue in the lecture video with more deaf students.

4.1   Reference Cue Redesign

Spotlight cues are effective and have had a long history that predates computing. Spotlights have a long tradition in the theatre and cinema in drawing attention of the audience as well as evoking emotional responses. In computer applications, the spotlight metaphor has been widely used [4]. In this line, Hoffman, et al [3] suggest that easy to find cues should be visually sparse, i.e., combine curved frames that use color to visually pop-out. created a more usable visual cue based on the spotlight theory based on the literature review above [3]. To generate a large, slow moving visual spotlight cue, we calculated a probability map of the hearing students' gaze location over the past 2 seconds. Then to create a spotlight like cue, we overlaid this map onto the lecture video with a 90% transparency so as not to block the visuals underneath it.

4.2   Study

Eight deaf students were recruited to watch videos with the reference cue overlays. The students ranged in age from 18-24 (5 male, 3 female). They were asked to use the reference cues as an aid to shift attention from the interpreter to the active source (e.g. slides). The same procedure from the pilot study was repeated. We then analyzed the total duration within each region of interest, i.e., the distribution of total gaze duration in the instructor, interpreter, and slides regions of interest.

4.3   Findings

On average, students looked at the slides 31% of the time, and at the interpreter 64% of the time. There was an inverse correlation between the time spent on the interpreter and time spent on slides. The students preferred a large and slow moving visual cue over no cue or small and quickly moving cue that would guide them towards the slides rather than having to switch attention and eye focus onto the slides. In general, their comments revealed that they were not distracted by the large and colorful cue that they viewed. Their gaze duration on the instructor appeared to be unchanged at less than a second as compared with the pilot study.

5   Conclusion

The reference cues appear to have a beneficial effect on relieving the effort involved in decision-making related to shifting and re-focusing attention on an active source. One participant commented, "The cues significantly reduced my worry that I would miss new slides". Deaf students viewed information sources with greater focus than hearing students. The study shows that eye-tracking reference cues help subjects better distribute their visual attention. Many subjects commented that they did not realize the extent of their "tunnel vision" in locking in on interpreters or captions. They expressed interest in distributing their focus more evenly between classroom information sources.

Fig. 4. Collaborative eye-gaze cues enable both the hearing and deaf students to focus on the slides simultaneously

They became more aware of information source shifts as shown in Figure 4. The students reported that they realized that in mainstream lectures, they were constantly guessing on whether to shift attention away from the interpreter to the slides. Based on this study, the eye-tracking data showed that students often guessed wrong, and discovered only after shifting attention that the information in the periphery was irrelevant. Presenting a visual cue based on the gaze of a hearing student helps reduce the deaf student's higher-order attention resources that are spent on decision making rather than actually learning the material.

6   Conclusions and Future Work

Qualitative review of the student's eye-gaze replay with un-cued video showed that the visual and cognitive resources required in following the interpreter or captioner appeared to induce tunnel vision. This made it difficult for students to notice changes in other information sources. However, simply presenting the actual eye-tracking center of focus was not enough as students were overwhelmed by quick moving eye-gaze of the hearing student. Instead, displaying the hearing student's eye gaze as a slow moving and averaged heat map appeared to yield the highest preference ratings. Furthermore, the use of cues resulted in a more balanced distribution between focus on the visual representation of audio and other classroom visual information sources.

Acknowledgements. This work was supported in part by the NTID Innovation Grant and RIT Boot Camp Grant awarded to Raja S. Kushalnagar. The authors thank Erica Israel and Gianni Manganelli for their assistance with running the eye tracking experiments.

References

1. Apfelbaum, H., Pelah, A., Peli, E.: Heading assessment by "tunnel vision" patients and control subjects standing or walking in a virtual reality environment. ACM Transactions on Applied Perception 4(1), 8 (2007)
2. Cavender, A.C., Bigham, J.P., Ladner, R.E.: ClassInFocus. In: Proceedings of the 11th International ACM SIGACCESS Conference on Computers and Accessibility, ASSETS 2009, pp. 67–74. ACM Press (2009)
3. Hoffmann, R., Baudisch, P., Weld, D.S.: Evaluating visual cues for window switching on large screens. In: Proceeding of the Twenty-Sixth Annual CHI Conference on Human Factors in Computing Systems, CHI 2008, pp. 929–939 (2008)
4. Khan, A., Matejka, J., Fitzmaurice, G., Kurtenbach, G.: Spotlight. In: Proceedings of the SIGCHI Conference on Human Factors in Computing Systems, CHI 2005, pp. 791–799. ACM Press (2005)
5. Kushalnagar, R.S., Cavender, A.C., Pâris, J.-F.: Multiple view perspectives. In: Proceedings of the 12th International ACM SIGACCESS Conference on Computers and Accessibility, ASSETS 2010, pp. 123–130. ACM Press (2010)
6. Marschark, M., Hauser, P.H.: Visual Attention in Deaf Children and Adults. In: Deaf Cognition: Foundation and Outcomes, p. 328 (2008)
7. Marschark, M., Pelz, J.B., Convertino, C., Sapere, P., Arndt, M.E., Seewagen, R.: Classroom Interpreting and Visual Information Processing in Mainstream Education for Deaf Students: Live or Memorex(R)? American Educational Research Journal 42(4), 727–761 (2005)
8. Marschark, M., Sapere, P., Convertino, C., Pelz, J.: Learning via direct and mediated instruction by deaf students. Journal of Deaf Studies and Deaf Education 13(4), 546–561 (2008)
9. Marschark, M., Sapere, P., Convertino, C., Seewagen, R.: Access to postsecondary education through sign language interpreting. Journal of Deaf Studies and Deaf Education 10(1), 38–50 (2005)
10. Peli, E.: Vision multiplexing: an engineering approach to vision rehabilitation device development. Optometry & Vision Science 78(5), 304–315 (2001)
11. Peli, E.: Vision multiplexing: an optical engineering concept for low-vision aids. In: Proceedings of SPIE, p. 66670C. SPIE (2007)
12. Salvucci, D.D., Taatgen, N.A., Borst, J.P.: Toward a unified theory of the multitasking continuum. In: Proceedings of the 27th International Conference on Human Factors in Computing Systems, CHI 2009, pp. 1819–1828. ACM Press (2009)
13. Williams, L.J.: Tunnel vision induced by a foveal load manipulation. Human Factors 27(2), 221–227 (1985)

The Musibraille Project – Enabling the Inclusion of Blind Students in Music Courses

José Antonio Borges[1] and Dolores Tomé[2]

[1] Instituto Tércio Pacitti, Universidade Federal do Rio de Janeiro, Brazil
antonio2@nce.ufrj.br
[2] Universidade de Brasília, Brazil
dolorestome@terra.com.br

Abstract. The Musibraille Project was created to address the difficulties to include blind students in music courses in Brazil. The strategy of this project involves the development of powerful software for Braille music edition, building of an online library of Braille music and the application of intensive courses on music transcription, both for blind and non-blind people. This project is producing an extraordinary effect on revitalizing Braille Music in this country, with hundred of teachers and students already trained.

Keywords: Assistive technology, Education of blind, Braille Music.

1 Inclusion of Visually Disabled Students in Brazil: New Challenges for Music Teaching

In Brazil, the inclusion of visually impaired students in conventional classrooms is recent [1]. However, within certain limits, the use of computers and adaptive technologies, some of them created especially for use in the Brazilian context, associated with the specific training of teachers, enabled to overcome many difficulties in teaching, especially those associated with reading and writing in a common context. We highlight here the DOSVOX system [2], used extensively in this country, which offers good support for the disciplines where the production and consumption of alphabetic writing is enough, but offers little support for disciplines with strong emphasis on mathematical representations and almost nothing related to music teaching.

In this context, a simplistic alternative would be the use of Braille Music by the students with visual impairments inside the classroom. This technique was developed from 1829 by Louis Braille, who adapted the technique he developed to transcribe texts, to write music. Through this technique a musical text of any complexity can be transcribed to a tactile format, using an encoding with 6 points similar to Braille marking, easily learned by a visually impaired person [3]. However, generally speaking, teachers and other students have absolutely no knowledge about this technique.

K. Miesenberger et al. (Eds.): ICCHP 2012, Part I, LNCS 7382, pp. 100–107, 2012.

It is important to note that many programs exist to support Braille transcription of music scores[1], which make use the following means (not necessarily all): direct typing in Braille, typing in a Midi Keyboard in real time and automatic transcription of digital music formats, in particular Music XML and MIDI. However, in addition of being too expensive for a broad use (as in the case of teaching in elementary public schools) they have not been created with an inclusive perspective. The interface for these programs is either intended for operation by a sighted person that produces the transcription for consume by blind people, or is made solely in Braille, isolating the seer colleague.

In addition to this, it is very difficult to obtain Braille Music scores in Brazil [4]. There are few places with trained personal to do transcriptions, and if a person wishes to obtain a single work not yet transcribed, he may have to spend hundreds of dollars, either in the import process, or to pay the price charged by a specialized institution to transcribe it.

Today, almost all the Music teachers in the public schools are seers and have no knowledge of Braille, and their refusal to teach to blind students is very common, as they think that is impossible for them to teach the contents of sheet music effectively. In addition, it is also very difficult to include blind musicians in regular music schools. There are several good blind musicians in Brazil, but almost all musicians have no classical training, and a big amount is not able to read Braille, even in its literary format.

2   The Musibraille Project

The Musibraille Project [5] aims to create conditions that make possible the music learning for people with visual impairments, equivalent to those of sighted peers. The strategy of this project is based on:

- Creating free software for teaching and editing Braille Music, also able to perform automated mid-sized transcripts.
- Creating and publishing an Internet Online Library, containing the major works of music education and including an extensive set of Brazilian music.
- Training for music teachers and art educators nationwide.

The heart of the project is the Musibraille software (fig. 1) that is distributed free of charge as part of a kit that contains instructional material on CD and in Braille. The software is designed to be operated by both blind and sighted people and embeds a voice synthesizer and a small screen reader to be independent of other products, increasing the possibilities of its use.

---

[1]   Tocatta and GoodFeel in U.S, DaCapo in Germany and Braille Music Editor (BME) in Latin America, are the more well known programs to transcribe Braille Music. In Brazil, this transcription is almost always done textually, via a free Text to Braille editor-translator (Braille Fácil) – but this system doesn't produce any sound feedback.

Fig. 1. Musibraille Splash Screen and Logo

3   The Musibraille Software

In Musibraille (Fig. 2) music information can be simultaneously displayed in Braille and in conventional musical notation, listened as musical sounds and translated to speech synthesis. During the creation and edition many operations can be performed, promoting insertion, deletion, modification and movement of musical symbols, operations that are somewhat similar to the functions offered by a conventional text editor.

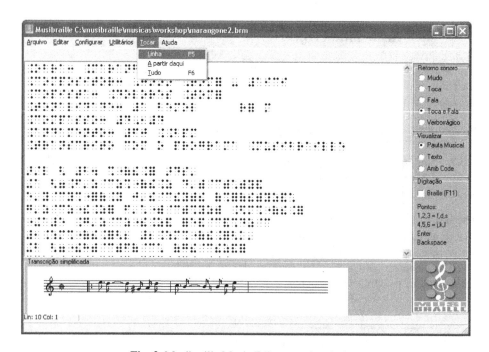

Fig. 2. Musibraille Music Editor – main window

Concurrently with entering music – which includes typing directly in Braille - some consistency tests are performed, ensuring a reliable transcription. When typing you can hear the musical notes created or even name the pictures created in the Braille score. This probable overload of sound feedback can be lowered by choosing some "economic styles" of sound return.

The software also provides an interactive dictionary of music symbols (Fig. 3) and some functions to help exploring Braille symbols. Thus, a seer or a novice teacher can use the software to learn Braille Music interactively. It's even possible to produce a complete score directly clicking on the desired symbols in the dictionary. A virtual music keyboard (Fig. 4) can optionally be simulated on the screen, allowing easier input for people that are not familiar with Braille notation.

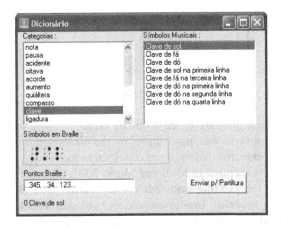

Fig. 3. Braille Music online dictionary

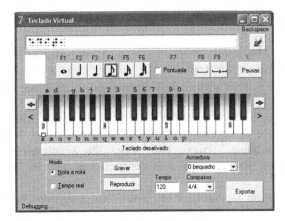

Fig. 4. Virtual Keyboard for music entry in the Musibraille Program

The accepted file formats were chosen to allow exchanges with various programs, both for input and for processing data Braille to other systems. Input can be done by alphanumeric keypad, Simulated Braille keyboard for Midi files or printing standard Braille (BRL) or Music XML.

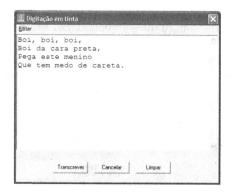

Fig. 5. Text to Braille editor-converter

Texts (lyrics for example) are typed normally on a specialized text editor (Fig. 5) that automatically converts and paste them to the Braille music score. It's also possible to get an inverse translation of a text written in the score.

The output can be generated in Midi and Music XML in music sheet or in Braille printer, or targeted for printing with Microsoft Word. The Braille text can be produced in various types of Braille embossers, and can also be transcribed into conventional musical notation, possibly in large printing for consume by partially sighted people.

4   Socio-Technical Characteristics of the Musibraille Program

The design of the Musibraille program had a strong pedagogical orientation that allows the dissemination of Braille music culture in a country with continental dimensions like Brazil, associated to the characteristics of its music teachers [6]. Thus it becomes possible for a non blind musician (a teacher, probably), without previous literacy in Braille, to be able to read and write Braille music with minimal human guidance. It's also easy to create interesting strategies to teach the basic music concepts (notes, durations, tempo, etc.) using the simultaneous feedback that Musibraille produces: sound, notes with conventional notation and Braille Music symbols.

The program also has facilities for self-assessment and online help with examples that could be copied to the software and experimented. The training also can be done either in conventional classrooms or distance learning. Being easy to use and focused on learning is one of its greatest strengths, and what make it different from similar systems.

The quality of the feedback is important: each musical symbol entered can be displayed in real time together with:

— the voice synthesis of the symbol name;
— the associated musical sound;
— the graphical representation.

This feedback must also be very precise to enable that Braille generation is done safely, even in situations in which the coding becomes ambiguous (as in Braille, depending on the context, the symbols may have different meanings).

A lot of schools where the software is installed have equipment with several years of use. To be disseminated to all schools, the software must keep the computational complexity under control, being able to offer a good performance even on very modest computers.

An innovative characteristic of the software is the inclusion of some features designed to give full access to the blind user, in particular a built-in speech synthesizer and a small built-in screen reader.[2] The reason for these inclusions is the fact that not all schools have this kind of pre-installed facilities. Thus, having our software installed on a particular computer means that, within certain limits, a reasonable (and free) screen reader will also be available to any user. We must also emphasize that our screen reader was specifically built to adapt well to the characteristics of Braille music editing feedback. In the classes we have conducted, the feedback of this screen reader is superior in quality and accuracy, when compared to the feedback of some professional screen readers.

The program was compiled with Borland Delphi 6/7, and was built with 45 modules, that represent circa 12000 lines of code. The source code is available free of charge for academic institutions directly from the authors. The software is free and downloadable directly from the Musibraille Project's homepage.[3]

5   The Musibraille Online Library

There are two main ideas behind the creation of this library:

1. Generate and make available on Internet a fair amount of educational music scores and texts related to music education, so that a blind student can have immediate access to them, making easier its interaction with teachers in conventional schools of music.

---

[2] The LianeTTS voice synthesizer, distributed together with Musibraille, is unique to Portuguese. However, Musibraille is capable of producing speech synthesis using any SAPI 5 synthesizer, and therefore it is normally easy to use Musibraille's screen reader with other languages. It is also important to mention that the screen reader is aimed to be used in the Microsoft Windows environment only, and that when Musibraille is run in other environments, it becomes not operational.

[3] http://www.musibraille.com.br

2. Provide a set of Brazilian music in various styles and origins that could be consumed by blind people all over the world (which of course includes Brazilian musicians).

This library contains Braille music, ready to edit and print. The musical texts are available in a form that is suitable to the Musibraille program, but being computationally represented directly in the American Braille Code, can be easily read by other systems (which include direct printing to the main Braille printers). Almost all texts are copyright free or have permission to copy (with a few exceptions, accessed through passwords).

To date, the Musibraille Library has a collection of 600 scores, almost all transcribed by us or one of our students. The collection includes mainly basic classical material (in particular studies for instruments), many Brazilian folk songs, and some non-classical music from Brazil and other countries. It also includes many scores of João Tomé, an important blind Brazilian composer (patron of the library).

6   Evaluation of the Project

The project has been implemented in eight Brazilian states, and more than 500 people have been trained, including teachers and students, both seers and blind in inclusive classrooms, somewhat provoking the revitalization of Braille Music in Brazil. The ease of learning and speed of transcription allowed each student in each course of two days, to generate around five musical transcriptions, which is a very positive result for people without prior knowledge of Braille Music. The transcripts could be automatically published on our public digital library, from the software itself.

The evaluation of this project shown:

- Much improved educational prospects in basic education courses, enabling the integration of blind and seer children in classes of musical initiation.
- Increase the quality and quantity of sheet music available for conventional musical education for blind people.
- Better education training of classical musicians.
- Integration of blind and non-blind musicians, mediated by this software.

This project has the support of many entities, mainly the Instituto Tércio Pacitti of the Federal University of Rio de Janeiro, the University of Brasilia, the State Secretariat of Culture of the Federal District, the Federal District Government, the Ministry of Culture and the Federal Government. The main funds have been obtained from Petrobras through the resources of the Rouanet Law.[4]

---

[4] Thanks to Natalia Luna for carefully reviewing the English language of this text.

References

1. Kaiado, K., Laplaine, A.: The Inclusive Education program: the right to diversity – an analysis from the point of view of administrators of a hub municipality. Educação e Pesquisa 35(2) (2009)
2. Borges, J.A.: Do Braille ao Dosvox – diferenças nas vidas dos cegos brasileiros[5] PhD in Computer Engineering Thesis (in Portuguese). COPPE/UFRJ, Rio de Janeiro, Brazil (2009), http://teses2.ufrj.br/Teses/COPPE_D/ JoseAntonioDosSantosBorges.pdf
3. Marsan, C.: Louis Braille: A Brief Overview. Association Valentin Haüy, Paris (2009)
4. Bonilha, F.: Leitura musical na ponta dos dedos: caminhos e desafios do ensino de musicografia Braille na perspectiva de alunos e professores[6]. Master in Music Thesis (in Portuguese). Universidade de Campinas, Brazil (2006)
5. Tomé, D., Borges, J.A.: The Musibraille Project - World Congress Braille21 - Innovations in Braille in the 21st Century, Leipzig, German (2011)
6. Mateiro, T.: Education of music teachers: A study of the Brazilian higher education programs. International Journal of Music Education 29(1), 45–71 (2011)

---

[5] Translation: From Braille to Dosvox – differences in the lives of Brazilian blind people.
[6] Translation: Reading music at your fingertips: challenges and ways of teaching Braille music in the perspective of students and teachers.

Important New Enhancements to Inclusive Learning Using Recorded Lectures

Mike Wald

ECS, University of Southampton, Southampton, UK
m.wald@soton.ac.uk

Abstract. This paper explains three new important enhancements to Synote, the freely available, award winning, open source, web based application that makes web hosted recordings easier to access, search, manage, and exploit for learners, teachers and other users. The facility to convert and import narrated PowerPoint PPTX files means that teachers can capture and caption their lectures without requiring institution-wide expensive lecture capture or captioning systems. Crowdsourcing correction of speech recognition errors allows for sustainable captioning of any originally uncaptioned lecture while the development of an integrated mobile speech recognition application enables synchronized live verbal contributions from the class to also be captured through captions.

Keywords: speech recognition, recorded lectures, learning.

1   Introduction

This paper explains three new important enhancements to Synote [1] [1], the freely available, award winning, open source, web based application that can make any public web hosted recording easier to access, search, manage, and exploit for learners, teachers and other users. Commercial lecture capture systems (e.g. Panopto[2], Echo360[3] , Tegrity[4], Camtasia[5]) can be expensive and do not easily facilitate educational student interactions. Synote overcomes the problem that while users can easily bookmark, search, link to, or tag the WHOLE of a recording available on the web they cannot easily find, or associate their notes or resources with, PART of that recording [2]. As an analogy, users would clearly find a text book difficult to use if it had no contents page, index or page numbers. Synote can use speech recognition to synchronise audio or video recordings of lectures or pre-recorded teaching material with a transcript, slides and images and student or teacher created notes. Synote won the 2009 EUNIS International E-learning Award[6,7] and 2011

---

[1] www.synote.org
[2] http://www.panopto.com/
[3] http://echo360.com/
[4] http://www.tegrity.com/
[5] http://techsmith.com/Camtasia
[6] http://www.ecs.soton.ac.uk/about/news/2598
[7] http://www.eunis.org/activities/tasks/doerup.html

K. Miesenberger et al. (Eds.): ICCHP 2012, Part I, LNCS 7382, pp. 108–115, 2012.

Times Higher Education Outstanding ICT Initiative of the Year award[8]. The system is unique as it is free to use, automatically or manually creates and synchronises transcriptions, allows teachers and students to create real time synchronised notes or tags and facilitates the capture and replay of recordings stored anywhere on the web in a wide range of media formats and browsers. Synote has been developed and evaluated with the involvement of users and with the support of JISC[9] and Net4Voice[10]. Fig. 1 shows the Synote player interface. The technical aspects of the system, including the Grails Framework and the Hypermedia Model used, have been explained in detail elsewhere [3]. The synchronised bookmarks, containing notes, tags and links are called Synmarks (see Fig. 2). When the recording is replayed the currently spoken words are shown highlighted in the transcript. Selecting a Synmark, transcript word or Slide/Image moves the recording to the corresponding synchronised time. The provision of text captions and images synchronized with audio and video enables all their communication qualities and strengths to be available as appropriate for different contexts, content, tasks, learning styles, learning preferences and learning differences. Text can reduce the memory demands of spoken language; speech can better express subtle emotions; while images can communicate moods, relationships and complex information holistically. Synote's synchronised transcripts enable the recordings to be searched while also helping support non native speakers (e.g. international students) and deaf and hearing impaired students understand the spoken text. The use of text descriptions and annotations of video or images help blind or visually impaired students understand the visually presented information. So that students do not need to retype handwritten notes they had taken in class into Synote after the recording had been uploaded notes taken live in class on mobile phones or laptops using Twitter[11,12] can be automatically uploaded into Synote. Until Microsoft Office 2010 was published with its undocumented changes to its saved PPT format Synote could successfully create synchronized and searchable audio, transcripts and slides (including titles, text and notes) from narrated PowerPoint slides. The ability to import narrated PowerPoint files means that anybody can capture their lectures without requiring institution wide expensive lecture capture systems and section 2 of this paper reports on the development of a new PPTX to Synote xml format converter so that PowerPoint 2010 can be used successfully for recording lectures for Synote. Synote builds on 12 years work on the use of speech recognition for learning in collaboration with IBM, and the international Liberated Learning Consortium [4] [5]. The integration of the speaker independent IBM Hosted Transcription System with Synote has simplified the process of transcription giving word error rates of between 15% - 30% for UK speakers using headset microphones. This compares well with the National Institutes of Standards (NIST) Speech Group reported WER of 28% for individual head mounted microphones in lectures [6]. Commercial rates for manually transcribing and synchronising a lecture recording are typically around £2/minute[13] (rates

---

[8] http://www.ecs.soton.ac.uk/about/news/3874

[9] http://www.jisc.ac.uk

[10] http://spazivirtuali.unibo.it/net4voice/default.aspx

[11] http://twitter.com/synote

[12] http://www.ecs.soton.ac.uk/about/news/2812

[13] http://www.automaticsync.com/caption/

vary dependent on quality and quantity) and for automatic speech recognition to be used sustainably it must therefore cost less than this; including the manual correction of speech recognition transcription errors. A possible sustainable approach to obtaining accurate transcriptions is described in section 3 and involves students in the classes themselves correcting errors they find in the transcript, either voluntarily or through being paid or through being given academic credit. The requirement of using headset microphones to obtain good speech recognition transcription accuracy means that contributions from students in the class are not easily recorded or transcribed. To address this problem Syntalk, a mobile transcription server, has been developed and is described in section 4. Section 5 summarises some evaluations that have been undertaken.

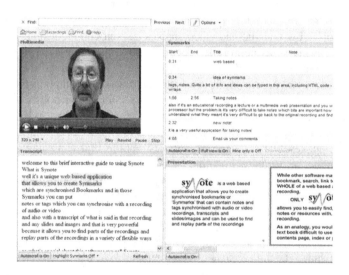

Fig. 1. Synote Player Interface

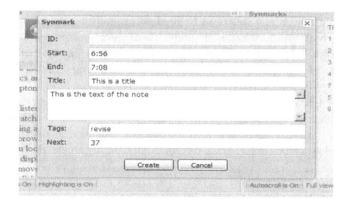

Fig. 2. Synote Synmark Creation

2   PowerPoint PPTX Converter

A narrated PowerPoint file can be used by a teacher to capture their lecture but each student would have to download the PowerPoint file to replay it on their own system. Office 2010 allows the narrated PowerPoint to be converted into a video that could be replayed by students but the video would not be captioned and the slide text would not be readable by a screen reader. The Synote PowerPoint converter enables the user to simply caption the recording using the slide notes and creates screen reader accessible text annotations for the slide images. The original Synote PPT converter was written in Java using the Apache POI9 library[14] (POI-HSLF) which only provides an API for data extraction for Microsoft PowerPoint's original PPT format. There is no Java library available that supports Microsoft's 2010 PPT format file.

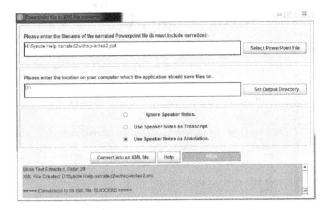

Fig. 3. PowerPoint PPTX to Synote Converter

The new Synote PPTX converter (Fig. 3) changes the extension of the .PPTX file to .zip and extracts the slide text data and timing information and concatenates the audio .wav files that PowerPoint saves for each slide. The user needs to manually save the slide images as .png files. As PowerPoint does not record audio during slide transitions either the lecturer should not use any slide transitions or they should not speak during these transitions. The converter can automatically synchronise any text that the lecturer types into the slide notes with the narration either as a transcript or as an annotation.

3   Crowdsourcing Speech Recognition Transcription Correction

Universal Subtitles[15] is a recent Mozilla Drumbeat project designed to allow users to manually caption web based videos but only allows one person at a time to create or edit the captions. YouTube and Synote both enable automatic speech recognition

---

[14] http://poi.apache.org/
[15] http://www.universalsubtitles.org

captioning of videos but also allowed only one person at a time to correct its captions. Since there is no correct version of the transcript in existence there is no way of knowing whether the person creating or correcting the captions is making errors or not. The approach that we have adopted therefore is to allow many people to edit the captions and then compare their edits.   The newly developed crowdsourcing correction tool shown in Figure 4 stores all the edits of all the users and uses a configurable matching algorithm to compare users' edits to check if they are in agreement.

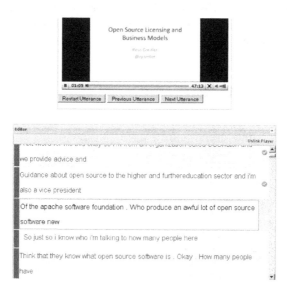

Fig. 4. Crowdsourcing Correction Tool

The tool allows utterances from specified sections of the transcript to be presented for editing to particular users or for users to be given the freedom to correct any utterance. Administrator settings allow for different matching algorithms based on the closeness of a match and the number of users whose corrections must agree before the system accepts the edit as 'correct'. The red bar on the left of the utterance indicates to a user that they are not allowed to edit the utterance and the white on green tick on the right denotes that a successful match has already been achieved and so no further editing of the utterance is required. The green bar on the left of the utterance denotes that the required match for this utterance has yet to be achieved. Users can be awarded points for a matching edit and it is also possible to remove points for corrections that do not match other users' corrections.

4   Captioning Contributions from Students Using Syntalk

Syntalk (Fig. 5) consists of two applications: an Android application which is used by students to capture and transcribe and if required also correct their utterances and a web application (Fig. 6) which is used by lecturers for managing the system. Users can choose to use any of three different free server based speech recognition systems, Google, EML[16] or iSpeech[17] . At the start of a lecture the lecturer makes their lecture 'live' using the Syntalk web application control panel. Users can then select this live lecture on their Syntalk mobile application. When the user talks into their mobile's microphone the Syntalk mobile application sends the speech to the speech recognition server and when the transcribed text is returned by this server to the Syntalk application it is then sent to the Syntalk web server as well as being displayed on the mobile's screen for editing. If the user chooses to edit any speech recognition errors the corrected text is then also sent to the Syntalk server which creates an XML file containing the text captions and timings which can be uploaded into Synote as synchronized annotations.

Fig. 5. Syntalk Android Application

Fig. 6. Syntalk Web Application

---

[16] http://www.eml-development.de
[17] http://www.ispeech.org

If everybody in a class used the Syntalk application on their personal mobile phone it would be possible to transcribe all spoken interactions. The current Syntalk application does not capture the spoken audio for Synote to replay.

5   Classroom Use and Evaluation of Synote

Since 2008 Synote has been used by teachers in universities in the UK, Italy, Germany, Pakistan, Australia, US and Canada with over 1000 recordings publically available on Synote (most with synchronised transcripts) for students to use for their learning. Dr Wald has used Synote with over a hundred recordings of his lectures with synchronised transcripts and slides for his teaching of many hundreds of students on undergraduate and postgraduate Electronics and Computer Science (ECS) modules at The University of Southampton. The provision of a verbatim synchronised transcript enables students to concentrate on learning and take only brief synchronised notes in Synote (e.g. 'revise this section for exam', 'I don't understand this fully' etc.). This feature is of value to all students, not only deaf students who need to lipread or watch a sign language interpreter and so can't take notes or dyslexic students or non-native speakers who find it difficult to take notes. The fact that Synote is used and valued by all students means that non native speakers and disabled students feel more included and do not have to use special technology. Also the quality of recording from a teacher's wireless head worn microphone is significantly better than from small personal digital recorders placed by students at the front of the class to record lectures. Questionnaire results from hundreds of students with a wide range of abilities and disabilities confirms that Synote successfully supports most browsers, is easy to use and improves learning, attention, motivation, efficiency, enjoyment, results and notetaking. Students also want all their lectures to be presented on Synote. The PPTX converter was successfully trialed by 60 MSc students producing publically available accessible narrated captioned online presentations on Synote of their accessibility evaluations of web and software applications. The feedback provided by the users enabled the PPTX converter to be improved with regard to usability and robustness. An evaluation of the Syntalk Android application conducted with 25 users having different levels of computer skills showed that the application was easy to use to capture and transcribe students' contributions. Users preferred Google speech recognition because of its recognition accuracy and transcription speed but users would like the latency/time delay in receiving the captions back from the Server to be reduced. The crowdsourcing editor was trialed with ten undergraduate students who understood the recorded material better as a result of the editing process suggesting that a marks incentive for editing might be justified on educational grounds. Some improvements were also suggested to the system which continues to be further developed.

6   Conclusion and Future Work

Commercial lecture capture systems are expensive and do not easily facilitate educational student interactions. Synote has been shown to provide very well received enhancements to web based teaching and learning from recordings and to integrate well with other applications including PowerPoint, Twitter and Speech Recognition Software. The PPTX to Synote XML converter enables lecturers to easily capture their lectures and replay them accessibly using Synote. Syntalk provides a simple and free way to also capture and accessibly display the rich student interactions that can occur in classrooms. There could be great educational benefits and a huge demand for speech recognition lecture transcription if our crowdsource editing tool makes it sufficiently accurate and affordable. A demonstration and further results of the use of the systems described in this paper will be presented at ICCHP 2012.

References

1. Wald, M., Wills, G., Millard, D., Gilbert, L., Khoja, S., Kajaba, J., Li, Y.: Synchronised Annotation of Multimedia. In: 2009 Ninth IEEE International Conference on Advanced Learning Technologies, pp. 594–596 (2009)
2. Whittaker, S., Hyland, P., Wiley, M.: Filochat handwritten notes provide access to recorded conversations. In: Proceedings of CHI 1994, pp. 271–277 (1994)
3. Li, Y., Wald, M., Wills, G., Khoja, S., Millard, D., Kajaba, J., Singh, P., Gilbert, L.: Synote: development of a Web-based tool for synchronized annotations. New Review of Hypermedia and Multimedia, 1–18 (2011)
4. Leitch, D., MacMillan, T.: Liberated Learning Initiative Innovative Technology and Inclusion: Current Issues and Future Directions for Liberated Learning Research. Saint Mary's University, Nova Scotia (2003), http://www.liberatedlearning.com/
5. Wald, M., Bain, K.: Enhancing the Usability of Real-Time Speech Recognition Captioning through Personalised Displays and Real-Time Multiple Speaker Editing and Annotation. In: Proceedings of HCI International 2007: 12th International Conference on Human-Computer Interaction, Beijing, pp. 446–452 (2007)
6. Fiscus, J., Radde, N., Garofolo, J., Le, A., Ajot, J., Laprun, C.: The Rich Transcription 2005 Spring Meeting Recognition Evaluation. National Institute of Standards and Technology (2005)

Development of New Auditory Testing Media with Invisible 2-Dimensional Codes for Test-Takers with Print Disabilities

Mamoru Fujiyoshi[1], Akio Fujiyoshi[2], Akiko Ohsawa[1], Toshiaki Aomatsu[3], and Haruhiko Sawazaki[4]

[1] National Center for University Entrance Examinations
{fujiyosi,ohsawa}@rd.dnc.ac.jp
[2] Ibaraki University
fujiyosi@mx.ibaraki.ac.jp
[3] National School for the Blind of Tsukuba University
aomatsu@nsfb.tsukuba.ac.jp
[4] Tokyo Metropolitan Kodaira Senior High School
Haruhiko_Sawazaki@member.metro.tokyo.jp

Abstract. Utilizing invisible 2-dimensional codes and digital audio players with a 2-dimensional code scanner, we developed two types of new auditory testing media. The result of experimental evaluation of the new testing media shows that, in addition to existing special accommodations such as large-print-format test and braille-format test, the introduction of the new auditory testing media enables all test-takers with print disabilities, including the newly blind, the severely partially sighted and the dyslexic, to take the National Center Test for University Admissions.

1 Introduction

The National Center Test for University Admissions is the joint first stage achievement test for admissions into all national and local public universities as well as many private universities in Japan. Every year, about 550,000 students take it. As for test-takers with disabilities, special accommodations regarding testing media such as large-print-format test and braille-format test have been administered [1]. However, auditory testing media have not been available yet. In most advanced countries, auditory testing media such as human readers, audio cassettes or computer screen readers are available for test-takers with print disabilities [4,5].

It is necessary to develop new auditory testing media for the National Center Test. It is almost impossible to take the National Center Test with ordinary types of auditory testing media because the documents are very long and the document structure very complicated. Computer screen readers often misread some combinations of Chinese characters in Japanese documents.

For auditory testing media for the National Center Test, the utilization of DAISY (Digital Audio Accessible Information System) and Tablet PC has been

K. Miesenberger et al. (Eds.): ICCHP 2012, Part I, LNCS 7382, pp. 116–123, 2012.

studied [2]. DAISY is a world standard audio system for people with visual disabilities. Test-takers can listen to the document from any point, such as from an underlined or blank part, without delay. They can also use the talk-speed-control function. However, DAISY is not convenient enough for tests which have complicated document structure. On the other hand, tablet PC has been identified as appropriate testing media [2]. However, there are difficulties in administration because security of test administration and prevention of machine trouble cannot be ensured.

Utilizing invisible 2-dimensional codes and digital audio players with a 2-dimensional code scanner, we developed two types of new auditory testing media for test-takers with print disabilities. In 2009, auditory tests of speech sounds on document structure diagrams were developed [3], and, in 2010, multimodal tests of speech sounds on ordinary texts were developed.

Experiments were conducted to evaluate the two types of new auditory testing media. The result shows that, in addition to existing special accommodations such as large-print-format test and braille-format test, the introduction of the new testing media enables all test-takers with print disabilities, including the newly blind, the severe partially sighted and the dyslexic, to take the National Center Test for University Admissions.

2 Two Types of New Auditory Testing Media

Using the two types of new auditory testing media, tests can be administrated only with digital audio players and paper booklets (Fig. 1). The introduction of invisible 2-dimensional codes enable us to develop the new testing media.

We employ 'GridOnput', an invisible 2-dimensional code system developed by Gridmark Solutions Co., Ltd (Fig. 2, left). Dots of GridOnput are arranged at intervals of about 0.25 mm. The size of a code is about 2 mm square. Since the intervals are large enough for the size of dots themselves, dots are almost invisible. If we use invisible ink, which absorbs only infrared light, instead of black ink, dots become totally invisible.

As a reading device for the new auditory testing media, we employ 'Speaking Pen' developed by Gridmark Solutions Co., Ltd (Fig. 2, right). Speaking Pen has a 2-dimensional code scanner at its top. When a 2-dimensional code is scanned with Speaking Pen, the corresponding speech sound is reproduced. We can listen to the sound through a headphone or built-in speaker. The sound volume and speed can be adjusted with its buttons mounted at the front side. The sound data is stored in an SD memory card. 1G byte is enough to store all sound data of 1-year amount of the National Center Test.

2.1 Auditory Tests of Speech Sounds on Document Structure Diagrams

For newly blind test-takers, partially sighted test-takers and dyslexic test-takers who can read neither braille nor printed characters, auditory tests of speech sounds on document structure diagrams were designed [3].

Fig. 1. Test Scene

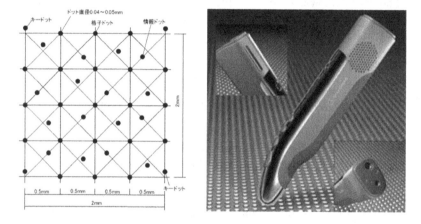

Fig. 2. 2-Dimensional Code (left), and Speaking Pen (right)

Document structure diagrams represent the organization of test documents. Fig. 3 (left) is an example of a document structure diagram in the Japanese language. Each document structure diagram of a problem can be arranged within a sheet of paper. The first line shows the subject name 'Kokugo 1' and the second line the problem number 'Dai 2 Mon'. The upper part shows the document structure of the theme document of the problem. Each line '(1)'-'(3)' corresponds to a paragraph in the theme document. The symbol '—' represents a sentence in a paragraph, and the symbols 'a'-'e' represent underlined parts of the theme document. The lower part shows the document structure of the questions of the problem. Each line 'Toi 1'-'Toi 2' corresponds to a question. The numbers '3'-'4' represent answer items, and the number symbols '1'-'4' represent multiple-choice answers for an answer item.

Document structure diagrams and corresponding invisible 2-dimensional codes are printed on white paper by an LED printer (OKI Data Corporation). Braille characters and braille lines may also be embossed on the same paper

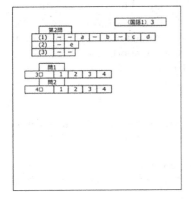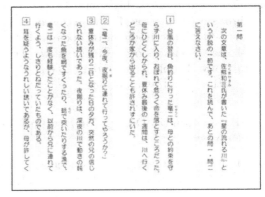

Fig. 3. Document Structure Diagram (left), and Ordinary Text with 2-Dimensinal codes (right)

overlappingly for newly blind test-takers. When any part of a document structure diagram is touched by a digital audio player with a 2-dimensional code scanner, the invisible code is scanned, and the corresponding speech sound is reproduced.

2.2 Multimodal Tests of Speech Sounds on Ordinary Texts

For dyslexic test-takers and partially sighted test-takers who can read some printed characters, multimodal tests of speech sounds on ordinary texts were designed.

In a test-booklet of multimodal tests of speech sounds on ordinary texts, normal characters or large-print characters are printed overlappingly with corresponding invisible 2-dimensional codes. Fig. 3 (right) is an example of a page of a test-booklet.

Similarly to the document structure diagrams, when any part of the texts is touched by a digital audio player, the invisible code is scanned, and the corresponding speech sound is reproduced. Paragraph numbers are prepared so that test-takers can reproduce the speech sound of each paragraph.

3   Evaluation Experiment

3.1 Experimental Design for Partially Sighted Subjects and Dyslexic Subjects

The experimental design is a repeated 3x3 Graeco-Latin square method.

The partially sighted subjects are 9 partially sighted high school students including some fresh graduates. The median of their corrected visual acuity is 0.08. They are divided into three subject groups. The dyslexic subjects are 9 dyslexic adults. Only one of them is a high school student because it was difficult to find dyslexic high school students in Japan. They are also divided into three subject groups. There are three testing media: large-print-format test, auditory test of speech sounds on document structure diagrams, and multimodal test of speech sounds on ordinary texts. The speech sounds are recorded as natural voice. Problems are from three study subjects: Japanese, English, and mathematics. The test procedure is administered without time limits.

3.2   Experimental Design for Braille User Subjects and Nondisabled Subjects

The braille user subjects are 15 students from a high school for the blind. The nondisabled subjects are 21 high school students. Both of them are divided into three subject groups. There are three testing media: braille-format test, auditory test of speech sounds on document structure diagram with recorded human voice, and auditory test of speech sounds on document structure diagram with computer-synthesized voice for the blind subjects. The nondisabled subjects take ordinary text tests instead of braille-format tests. Problems are from the same three study subjects: Japanese, English, and mathematics. The test procedure is administered without time limits.

3.3   Results on Distributions of Score

In Fig. 4 (1), Fig. 4 (2), and Fig. 4 (3), the box-and-whiskers plots of distributions of score of three testing media for each study subject are shown. The box-and-whiskers plots are sorted by the median of score.

The vertical lines on the right-hand side of plots represent the results of Scheffe's method of pair wise multiple comparison. There is no significant difference among box plots tied by a line or significant difference between them not tied by a line.

We can see similar tendencies of the testing media among the three study subjects.

As a result of Scheffe's method of pair wise multiple comparison, there are no significant differences among the distributions of score concerning the testing media for each subject group in each study subject except the distributions of score for nondisabled in English.

As a result of Mann-Whitney's test, we can see that learning achievement levels are almost similar among the four subject groups for Japanese, English and Mathematics because there are no significant difference among distribution of score for braille-format test of the blind group, that for large-print-format test of the partially sighted group, that for large-print-format test of the dyslexic group, and that for ordinary format test of the nondisabled group.

3.4   Results on Distributions of Answering Speed

In Fig. 5 (1), Fig. 5 (2), and Fig. 5 (3), the box-and-whiskers plots of distributions of answering speed of the testing media for each study subject and the results

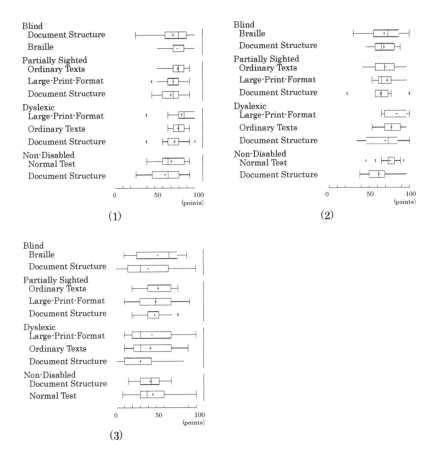

Fig. 4. (1) Distribution of Score of Japanese, (2) Distribution of Score of English, and (3) Distribution of Score of Mathematics

of Scheffe's method of pair wise multiple comparison are shown. The box-and-whiskers plots are sorted by the median of answering speed.

As a result of Scheffe's method of pair wise multiple comparison, the distributions of answering speed of auditory tests of speech sounds on document structure diagram are significantly slower than that of the other testing media for each study subjects.

As a result of Mann-Whitney's test, distribution of answering speed of ordinary format test for the nondisabled group is significantly faster than that of other test media for the print disabled groups in each study subjects.

3.5   Discussion

The result of experimental evaluation of the new testing media shows that, in addition to existing special accommodations such as large-print-format test and

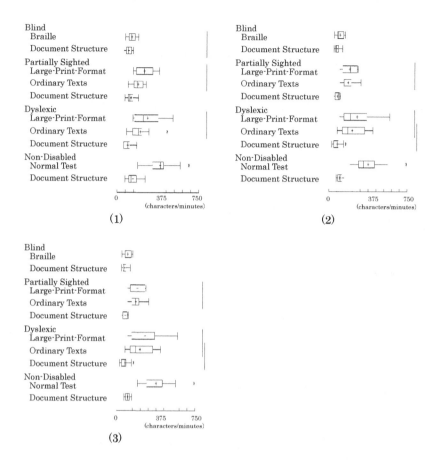

Fig. 5. (1) Distribution of Answering Speed of Japanese, (2) Distribution of Answering Speed of English, and (3) Distribution of Answering Speed of Mathematics

braille-format test, the introduction of the two types of new auditory testing media enables all test-takers with print disabilities to take the National Center Test for University Admissions. Test-takers with print disabilities can get the same score as nondisabled test-takers for Japanese, English and Mathematics if the learning achievement levels of them are the same. Answering speeds of the nondisabled group are significantly faster. However, the disabled and the nondisabled can take a test fairly if we put adequate time limit of a test for each test-taker with print disabilities.

4   Conclusion

Utilizing invisible 2-dimensional codes and digital audio players with a 2-dimensional code scanner, we developed two types of new auditory testing media:

auditory tests of speech sounds on document structure diagrams [3], and multimodal tests of speech sounds on ordinary texts.

The result of the experimental evaluation shows that, in addition to existing special accommodations such as large-print-format test and braille-format test, the introduction of the two new testing media enables almost all test-takers with print disabilities to take the National Center Test for University Admissions.

When auditory tests of speech sounds on document structure diagrams become practical, the newly blind and the severely partially sighted can take the National Center Test. Test-takers do not have to be able to read braille to take auditory tests of speech sounds on document structure diagrams because the shape of the document structure diagrams helps enough to guide the positions of 2-dimensional codes to scan. Actually, such newly blind students can take the test in the experimental evaluation.

With multimodal tests of speech sounds on ordinary texts, the partially sighted and the dyslexic can actively and efficiently read texts taking advantage of the modality characteristics of speech sounds and ordinary texts.

In addition, the easiness of administration and security management of the new testing media is noteworthy. Tests can be administrated only with a digital audio player with 2-dimensional code scanner and paper booklets on which document structure diagrams or ordinary texts and corresponding invisible 2-dimensional codes are printed. When machine trouble happens, tests can be continued with a replacement of a digital audio player. Price of a digital audio player is reasonable (about 30 euro).

As a future work, the authoring system of computer-synthesized speech voices and test-booklet with invisible 2-dimensional codes should be developed. We want to make the two types of new testing media practical within 3 years.

References

1. Fujiyoshi, M., Fujiyoshi, A.: Estimating testing time extension ratios for students with disabilities from item cumulative curves. In: New Developments in Psychometrics: Proceedings of the International Meeting of the Psychometric Society, IMPS 2001, pp. 265–272 (2003)
2. Fujiyoshi, M., Fujiyoshi, A.: A New Audio Testing System for the Newly Blind and the Learning Disabled to Take the National Center Test for University Admissions. In: Miesenberger, K., Klaus, J., Zagler, W., Karshmer, A.I. (eds.) ICCHP 2006. LNCS, vol. 4061, pp. 801–808. Springer, Heidelberg (2006)
3. Fujiyoshi, M., Fujiyoshi, A., Aomatsu, T.: New Testing Method for the Dyslexic and the Newly Blind with a Digital Audio Player and Document Structure Diagrams. In: Miesenberger, K., Klaus, J., Zagler, W., Karshmer, A.I. (eds.) ICCHP 2010. LNCS, vol. 6179, pp. 116–123. Springer, Heidelberg (2010)
4. Mandinach, E.B., Bridgeman, B., Cahalan-Laitusis, C., Trapani, C.: The impact of extended time on SAT test performance, College Board Research Report No. 2005-8, ETS RR-05-20, pp.1–35 (2005)
5. Ragosta, M., Wendler, C.: Eligibility issues and comparable time limits for disabled and nondisabled SAT examinees. ETS Research Report, RR-92-35, pp.1–33 (1992)

More Accessible Math

The LEAN Math Notation

John Gardner and Courtney Christensen

ViewPlus Technologies, Inc, Corvallis, OR 97333, USA
{john.gardner,courtney.christensen}@viewplus.com

Abstract. Blind people generally access written information linearly – through Braille or speech/audio. Math can be written in linear form, e.g. LaTeX, MathML, computer programming languages, or word descriptions. These forms are too verbose to be practical for reading any but the simplest math equations. They are even worse for authoring or "doing pencil and paper math". Braille is more useful, but relatively few blind people are fluent in any of the many special Braille math codes, none of which is robust enough for back-translation to be useful for authoring math. The authors of this paper have developed a very compact notation, which could be the basis of a new math Braille font, but which is useful today for reading / writing using computers with all common speech screen readers. Translators to/from MathML have been written and integrated with Microsoft Word / MathType. Preliminary usability data will be reported.

Keywords: linear math notation, Braille math codes, audio math.

1   Introduction

Until recently it has been necessary for math to be represented in electronic documents as images in order to be displayable in all circumstances. The math markup language MathML [1] has now become preferable for many reasons. One is that MathML equations are font-rendered, and thus simply look better. Equations are searchable, computable, and, most importantly for the present context, accessible in principle. The MathJAX project [2], which cleanly renders MathML in nearly any modern web browser, has stimulated the exponentially-increasing use of MathML. Within a few years, MathML will undoubtedly become the dominant math language of electronic documents.

The only other major modern math language, LaTeX [3], will undoubtedly continue to be used for years by many scientific authors. Transformers [4] are available that will transform LatTeX documents to a format in which math is represented by MathML. The remaining piece of the puzzle for "making math accessible" is the improvement of user-friendly tools by which blind people can read and write math in MathML.

K. Miesenberger et al. (Eds.): ICCHP 2012, Part I, LNCS 7382, pp. 124–129, 2012.

2   Current Technologies for Reading and Writing Math Usable by Blind People

2.1   Braille

There are several computer applications that can transform MathML to a math Braille string. The popular Duxbury Braille [5] application can transform Microsoft Word documents with MathType [6] equations (MS Word + MathType) to Braille. The math equations can be expressed in several different Braille codes. The free liblouis [7] Braille translator can transform an XML document to Braille. Several Braille math code output choices are available, including the most accurate Nemeth Braille translation available today. ViewPlus is a sponsor of the liblouis project, and its TSS [8] application uses liblouis to transform MS Word + MathType documents to Braille. A number of other Braille translators include simple math translation but are not useful for more advanced math.

There are some experimental back-translation applications intended to allow Nemeth math Braille readers to communicate to a sighted audience. We are unaware of any back-translators being written for other math Braille languages. Unfortunately, Braille math codes have structures and inherent ambiguities that make them fragile to back-translation. Small typographic errors can result in bizarre translations, having little relation to what was intended. Standard Braille codes can serve well for personal use, but not as a way to communicate math to others.

2.2   Internet Explorer + MathPlayer Speech Math Reader

[X]HTML web documents with math expressed as MathML can be read in speech using MathPlayer's [6] Internet Explorer plug-in. MathPlayer exposes the equation to screen readers as a paragraph of words. English and several other languages are supported. The limitations of current-day screen readers, however, do not permit showing the equations on Braille displays. Eventually, screen readers will have this capability, and this could be an excellent way to read math on the web. This is, however, not an authoring system.

2.3   Chatty Infty Accessible Scientific Document Reading/Authoring App

The ChattyInfty editor available from the Japanese Infty group permits simple scientific documents to be read and authored in a user-friendly manner [9-10]. ChattyInfty is self-voicing and permits text and equations to be displayed on a status line accessible to braille screen readers. Equations displayed in braille are currently given in LaTeX, but other types of Braille are planned for future versions. ChattyInfty can import documents created by the Infty Reader Math Optical Character Recognition (OCR) application and can export files in several mainstream-accessible formats, including DAISY and XHTML+MathML. English and Japanese versions are available. ChattyInfty is an excellent idea, but funding realities make it difficult for the Infty group to make this a robust product. Consequently, they have little choice but to sell it at a relatively high price. Barring some major investment, it seems destined to remain a specialty item.

2.4   Reading and Writing Math with LaTeX in MS Word+MathType

Microsoft Word documents with MathType equations are accessible to blind readers who know math LaTeX. One can select an equation (or the entire document), press a hotkey, and flip the selected equations to LaTeX. Equations can be reverted back to standard MathType equations with another press of that hotkey.

For users who know LaTeX, equations can be written into the document as plain text, surrounded by the standard Latex math indicator symbols. When the document is selected and the hotkey pressed, those equations are converted to standard MathType. While anyone can use this, it is particularly advantageous for blind users, who may find math authoring tools inadequately accessible. A tutorial is available at http://www.access2science.com/jagqn/WordLatex.html.

This application works well for blind people who can read LaTeX and who can write equations accurately in LaTeX. Its major disadvantages are that the user must know LaTeX and that great care is required when writing long or complicated equations. Formatting is also difficult for blind people to control reliably. And since there are no blind-friendly error-handling capabilities, it is possible to make a small error and end up with a completely unreadable equation.

3   Triangle and Lambda Notations

Triangle is a compact notation system developed twenty years ago at Oregon State University [11] to make reading and writing math easy for blind people. As originally conceived, it was based on LaTeX syntax and largely just a very compact way to write math in LaTeX. It did use a special Triangle symbol set designed for convenience of blind readers. That symbol set included symbols for starting and ending roots, fractions, arrays, etc, along with various separators within those structures. It also had font, subscript, superscript, etc, indicator symbols. A small "cheat sheet" made it possible for any sighted scientist to read or write in Triangle notation, and it was used successfully by a number of blind students. It did not become mainstream however, and some attempts to convert to/from mainstream formats of the day were discontinued when funding ran out.

The European Lambda [12] project is based on content MathML but shares the same basic notational philosophy as Triangle. Lambda is used in a number of European schools and universities but has also been limited in its impact due to lack of adequate funding.

4   The New LEAN Math System

4.1   Overview

We have extended the Triangle/Lambda concepts to a fully Unicode formulation called LEAN (Linear Editing and Authoring Notation). Important linearizing symbols such as fraction, table, and script indicators are single LEAN symbols. LEAN syntax is based on presentation MathML, so anything that can be expressed in the presentation version of MathML 3.0 can be displayed or authored in linear form containing LEAN Math symbols.

4.2   MS Word Integration

The translator scripts to/from LEAN and MathML have been written in Python and can run on any desktop operating system. We have integrated LEAN into Microsoft Word + MathType where it can be used to both read and author math. MathType is a popular and inexpensive math authoring application that works extremely well with Word. We have leveraged the MathType API to allow quick conversion to/from LEAN math notation. With this, the vast majority of blind screen reader users should be able to have a good math reading/authoring system. It will be made available as a free application.

Word+MathType+LEAN Math users can press a hotkey and convert the MathType equations in a Word document into LEAN notation. These will be spoken by any modern screen reader. Another press of that toggle converts back to MathType. One can author in LEAN notation by clicking open an editing dialog that allows the user to compose an equation. It includes some simple error-checking. When the "OK" key is pressed, the equation is inserted at the cursor position in the document. That editor has menus for finding any math Unicode character and a set of hotkeys for power users.

4.3   Display Font and Screen Reader Compatibility

We have added LEAN math characters into the private Unicode section of the Microsoft's screen font Segoe UI Semilight. The characters are simple, text-only representations of a single math function or concept. While this is more verbose than graphical symbols, there is virtually no learning curve.

Blind users can gain equal access by adding LEAN characters to screen reader speech dictionaries. Once complete, the equation can be read linearly by sighted users and blind users alike.

4.4   Distribution

The installation package will install the LEAN Math Word macro, the background translator, and the screen font necessary for viewing the special LEAN private Unicode characters. Pronunciation dictionary updates for popular screen readers will be available so LEAN Math Unicode symbols are spoken as intended.

In principle, one can author any equation expressible in Presentation MathML. LEAN notation is very intuitive, so we expect the learning curve for this application to be quite small. A prototype LEAN notation version will be demonstrated at ICCHP 2012, and preliminary usability data will be presented.

5   LEAN Examples

We present images of LEAN equations and also provide a text representation for blind readers. Non-ASCII Unicode characters are enclosed in square brackets as, for example [plus or minus] below. Letters in brackets are italic but pronounced as, for example b or c, and not italic b or italic c. It is easy enough to determine whether a letter is standard or italic by checking the Unicode position with a standard screen reader hotkey. A big advantage of using italic characters is that they are pronounced individually by a screen reader, for example ab is pronounced as a b, not ab. Pronunciation of Unicode characters is easily user-changeable.

$$x = [_{\text{frac}} -b \pm [_{\text{root}} b^2 - 4ac_{\text{root}}] \,{}^{\text{frac}}_{\text{sep}}\, 2a_{\text{frac}}]$$

Fig. 1. The solution to the quadratic equation in LEAN would be spoken as: "[x] = [fraction][minus][b][plus   or   minus][root][b][squared][minus]4[a][c][end   root][over]2[a][end fraction]"

$$\text{The cubed root of 8, } {}^{\text{root}}_{\text{ndx}} 3[_{\text{root}} 8_{\text{root}}] \text{ is 2.}$$

Fig. 2. This line would read as: "The cubed root of 8, [root index]3[root]8[end root] is 2"

$$\sigma = [_{\text{root}} [_{\text{frac}} 1\,{}^{\text{frac}}_{\text{sep}}\, N_{\text{frac}}] \Sigma\,{}^{\text{under}}_{\text{scrpt}}\, [i=1]\,{}^{\text{over}}_{\text{scrpt}}\, N(x_{\text{sub}} i - \mu)^2{}_{\text{root}}]$$

Fig. 3. The   sample   standard   deviation   in   LEAN   would   read   as: "σ   = [root][fraction]1[over][N][end   fraction]   Σ   [underscript][expression][i]=1[end expression][overscript][N][open paren][x][sub][i][minus]μ[close paren][squared][end root]"

$$\sin\theta = [_{\text{frac}} e^{\text{sup}}[i\theta] - e^{\text{sup}}[-i\theta]\,{}^{\text{frac}}_{\text{sep}}\, 2i_{\text{frac}}]$$

Fig. 4. Euler's, would read as: "sin θ = [fraction][e][superscript][expression][i]θ[end expression][minus][e][superscript][expression][minus][i]θ[end   expression][over]2[i][end fraction]"

$$\int_{\text{sub}} 1^{\text{sup}} \infty [_{\text{frac}} 1\,{}^{\text{frac}}_{\text{sep}}\, x^2{}_{\text{frac}}] dx$$
$$\int\,{}^{\text{under}}_{\text{scrpt}}\, 1\,{}^{\text{over}}_{\text{scrpt}}\, \infty [_{\text{frac}} 1\,{}^{\text{frac}}_{\text{sep}}\, x^2{}_{\text{frac}}] dx$$

Fig. 5. Two ways to write the same integral in LEAN. They would read as: "∫[subscript]1[superscript]∞[fraction]1[over][x][squared][end fraction][d][x]" and "∫[underscript]1[overscript]∞[fraction]1[over][x][squared][end fraction][d][x]", respectively

$$\ln{}^{\text{left}}_{\text{sup}}[111]$$

Fig. 6. LEAN notation for a left-superscript. For example, the radioactive indium isotope with atomic   weight   111   would   be   written   as   above,   and   spoken   as: "ln[left superscript][expression]111[end expression]"

6   Braille Representation of LEAN

The authors have not done so, but one could define Braille cells for all LEAN indicators and Unicode math characters. It would be implemented as a Braille font – not a Braille code – which could be used for authoring math. If 8-dot Braille is used, most equations could be written without needing multiple cell symbols. Back-translation would be robust (and trivial) because of the one-to-one correspondence between the two display methods.

One would still need multiple Braille cells for more advanced characters, and unfortunately, no present-day screen reader can define character descriptions in this manner. Once implemented, however, it would be a straightforward task to extend the LEAN translator to permit authoring with this Braille formulation.

References

1. Mathematical Markup Language (MathML) Version 3.0, `http://www.w3.org/TR/MathML3/`
2. MathJax: beautiful math in all browsers, `http://mathjax.com/`
3. LaTex – a document preparation system, `http://www.latex-project.org/`
4. Whapples, M.: Producing HTML and MathML from LaTeX by using tex4ht, `http://www.access2science.com/latex/tutorial_txht.xhtml`
5. Braille Translation Software from Duxbury Systems, `http://www.duxburysystems.com`
6. MathType and MathPlayer are applications from Design Science, Inc., `http://www.desssci.com`
7. Liblouis, `http://www.liblouis.org/`
8. Tiger Software Suite is a set of Braille applications bundled with ViewPlus embossers, `http://www.viewplus.com/products/software/braille-translator/`
9. The Infty Research Group, `http://www.inftyproject.org/`
10. The ChattyInfty application by the Infty Research Group, `http://www.sciaccess.net/en/ChattyInfty/index.html`
11. The Science Access Project, Department of Physics. Oregon State University, `http://dots.physics.orst.edu`
12. LAMBDA Linear Access to Mathematic for Braille Device and Audio-synthesis, `http://lambdaproject.org/default.asp?sec=1&langid=14`

Accessible Authoring Tool for DAISY Ranging from Mathematics to Others

Katsuhito Yamaguchi[1] and Masakazu Suzuki[2]

[1] Junior College Funabashi Campus, Nihon University
7-24-1 Narashinodai, Funabashi, Chiba 274-8501, Japan
eugene@gaea.jcn.nihon-u.ac.jp
[2] Institute of Systems, Information Technologies and Nanotechnologies (ISIT)
2-1-22 Momochihama, Sawara-ku, Fukuoka 814-0001, Japan
suzuki@isit.or.jp

Abstract. Although DAISY is an excellent solution for various print-disabled people, producing DAISY content is not necessarily accessible works. In particular, it is almost impossible for them to edit technical DAISY content such as mathematics. Here, a new accessible authoring tool to enable both of sighted people and the print disabled to produce/edit easily a DAISY book ranging from mathematics to others is shown. In it, since a new function to control speech output is implemented, all the content is read out in a correct manner with speech synthesis. This approach can be applied also to DAISY content in many languages other than English or Japanese.

Keywords: DAISY, mathematics, authoring tool, speech control.

1 Introduction

As is well known, "The Digital Accessible Information System (DAISY)" [1] is now becoming a standard format of accessible digital books. For instance, "The International Digital Publishing Forum (IDPF)" [2] decided to adopt DAISY XML as a part of EPUB3 standards in 2011. DAISY is an excellent solution for making printed content more accessible to people with various print disabilities. In the previous version, DAISY2, a mathematical expression was treated as an image with an alternative text. Since MathML is officially adopted in the current version, DAISY3, we would become able to produce a text-based mathematical content, in which one could access a mathematical formula character by character, symbol by symbol with speech synthesis. A blind user can read mathematical documents with speech output. A low-vision reader can improve contrast or magnify the displayed content for ease of reading. Visual tracking and synchronized speech allow a dyslexic reader to maintain focus on a document.

However, there remain unsolved problems in DAISY technical content to deserve greater attention. First of all, print-disabled people, themselves, have no good method to produce/edit such content. They are always regarded just as a

K. Miesenberger et al. (Eds.): ICCHP 2012, Part I, LNCS 7382, pp. 130–137, 2012.

reader, not a person who authors a mathematical material. A disabled student can neither draw up a technical report in DAISY nor write a solution into a work sheet directly.

In terms of Japanese, there is an additional problem concerning speech control. In Japanese, four different-character sets are used simultaneously in a document: "Kanji (Chinese characters)," "Hiragana," "Katakana" and alphanumeric letters. Kanji or their compound (with other Kanji or other letters) usually has several ways to pronounce, according to their context. In mathematics or science, they are often read in a different manner from the usual. However, the DAISY standards do not have a manner to assign different aloud-reading to a text part except for embedding an audio file directly.

Although such problems are less numerous in English literal content, they arise more frequently in technical contexts. For instance, if "a" represents a mathematical quantity, then it should be read as "ei." Both one gram and one unit of gravitational acceleration are written as "1g." To control pronunciation properly in those cases, "the W3C Speech Synthesis Markup Language (SSML)" [1] will be adopted in the forthcoming version, DAISY4. However, this approach does not seem to provide a perfect solution since it does not necessarily take into account technical content.

In addition to the Japanese-technical-term issue, many mathematical symbols or formulas have various ways to read. For instance, a mixed fraction such as $2\frac{1}{3}$ has the same form as the product of an integer and a fraction. x^2 is usually used for "x squared"; however, it sometimes represents another quantity such as the second component of a vector. As far as a unit is concerned, m^2 and m^3 are usually read as "square meter" and "cubic meter" instead of "m squared" and "m cubed," respectively. A symbol for "is congruent with," $\equiv$ in geometry should be read as "is equivalent to" in another context such as algebra. They have to be read in an appropriate manner according to their context. Besides technical terms, we also need a method to define how to read those symbols or formulas with speech synthesis. The SSML approach does not seem to meet this demand. It aims at controlling pronunciation; however, in the case of mathematical content, we need to provide a correct word description rather than the correct pronunciation.

Furthermore, as is obvious, in order to understand the content of a spoken mathematical expression easily, we need to control breaks, intonations and stresses properly in speech output. For instance, a short break is usually required at the end of mathematical syntax such as a fraction, a radical and so on. This point is also less serious in English since a speech engine can easily do that. However, in Japanese, it is often difficult for a speech engine to control pronunciation automatically since the word description of a mathematical expression has no explicit breaks except for punctuation marks. In Japanese, all the words are written continuously in a phrase, a clause or a sentence with no punctuation mark. The current DAISY does not have such a manner to control pronunciation for text-based content, either.

In this paper, after discussing those problems briefly, we show a new authoring tool, which is completely accessible. Using it, both of sighted and print-disabled people can produce easily a text-based/multi-media technical/nontechnical content in DAISY. We also give a new approach to control how to read out mathematical content correctly in DAISY with speech Synthesis. Those functions are actually implemented in our authoring tool.

2   Problems in Text-Based Mathematical Content in DAISY

2.1   Problems in DAISY-Authoring/Browsing Tools

There are many DAISY-playback/browsing tools, both of hardware and software, these days [1], which can treat DAISY3. In terms of Windows OS, "AMIS Ver.3" [1] may be most widely used freeware, which allows a user to read not only a DAISY3 audio-based content but also text-based one with a text-to-speech (TTS) engine. Besides, commercial software such as "Dolphin EasyReader" [3] is also available. However, Most of such software including AMIS and EasyReader cannot treat MathML formulas, yet. In it, mathematical expressions must be treated as an image with an alternative text as was in DAISY2. If the text were not embedded, that expression would not be read out with speech synthesis. For the present, "ReadHear?" (the current version of "ghPLAYER") [4] is probably an only solution to treat MathML formulas directly, which can read out them properly with speech synthesis. In terms of Macintosh OS, for instance, "Voice of DAISY" [5] is useful playback software, which can work also on portable devices such as iPad. However, it cannot display MathML expressions, either.

In terms of authoring tools, combining a free utility "Save as DAISY" [1] with Microsoft Word, we can convert a word file into DAISY3 content. Furthermore, by introducing another utility, "MathDAISY" [6] additionally, we can produce a multimedia DAISY mathematical content, in which the audio files of aloud reading with a TTS engine are embedded. However, there is no method to correct reading errors easily when a speech engine reads out literal/mathematical content in a wrong manner. In that case, we have to embed audio files of correct aloud reading into DAISY XML with another DAISY editor. Commercial software, "Dolphin Converter" [3] is another powerful tool to convert a printed content in various formats into DAISY as well. However, it is not necessarily used widely in Japan since it may be rather expensive.

As was pointed out, one of serious problems is that there is no method for the print-disabled people, themselves to author technical DAISY content. For instance, in terms of Save as DAISY, in order to prepare a source Word file for DAISY conversion, they would be required to use an inaccessible mathematical-document editor such as "MathType" [6]. Furthermore, since there is no accessible authoring tool for technical content, they can neither edit a produced DAISY book nor input mathematical formulae into it. In sum, they cannot do mathematics within DAISY. Thus, DAISY is not necessarily useful for mathematics/science education. In order to make DAISY used more widely in such education, we do need a more accessible authoring environment.

On the other hand, our accessible mathematical-document editor "Chatty-Infty" [7–12] allows blind people to access mathematical/scientific documents with speech output. Information displayed in its main window is completely equivalent to that of "InftyEditor" for sighted people. All mathematical expressions are displayed in the ordinary print style. ChattyInfty reads aloud not only text but also mathematical expressions. Blind people just can read, write or edit scientific documents including mathematical expressions with speech output. Hence, people with and without print disabilities can share the same technical content easily. However, since its current version cannot treat DAISY content, one cannot use it as an authoring tool for DAISY.

2.2 Problems in DAISY Speech Control

As was reported in the ICCHP 2010 [9], we made a brief survey on the ambiguity in Japanese aloud-reading of mathematical or mathematics-related technical terms that were listed by Okamoto et al. with the support of the Mathematical Society of Japan [13]. There are 10,199 entries in total. We picked all terms that had the three following characteristics.

(a) A single Kanji or their compound including no hiragana or katakana
(b) A common noun, an adjective, a prefix or a suffix
(c) A word used in education ranging from elementary school to mathematics or mathematics-related courses at university

However, to avoid overlapping, we did not count a compound of multiple words in principle, although some are included in the list since they are always used as one word.

There are 933 words in the intersection of categories (a), (b) and (c). Among these, 517 have no ambiguity of reading since they are manifestly mathematical or mathematics-related, and thus never used in a nontechnical context. The remaining 416 words can appear in both mathematical and nonmathematical contexts. Among these, 73.6% have only one pronunciation, whereas 26.4%, or 110 words, have more than one pronunciation according to context. Therefore, there is a clear need to specify how to read Kanji technical terms properly.

To avoid this ambiguity, a Japanese printed document often includes so-called "Ruby" characters to specify how to pronounce each Kanji or their compound. It is a kind of phonetic description typically written in hiragana or katakana to the side of the original Kanji in a small (Ruby-type) font. However, Ruby characters are not necessarily placed alongside all Kanji. In the case that there are no Ruby characters in the original printed material, the DAISY version does not include them either. It is thus impossible to determine automatically how to read Kanji on the basis of Ruby only. This is a serious problem for producing a Japanese-language school textbook in DAISY because the content needs to be read out as correctly as possible even if there are no Ruby characters.

As was pointed out in the Section 1, besides the matter of Japanese, language, a similar ambiguity occurs in mathematical expressions. We sometimes need to specify how to read characters or formulas locally according to context. We briefly surveyed this ambiguity for all mathematical syntaxes defined in Infty software. For those frequently used in education ranging from elementary school to mathematics or mathematics-related courses at university, the ambiguity seems to be greatest for the three following types of formulas.

(a) Mathematical formula with fractions
(b) Mathematical formula with superscripts or subscripts
(c) Mathematical formula with enclosing symbols

Although it is difficult to evaluate our result quantitatively, if we may say so, we confirmed that such ambiguity often appears in mathematics textbooks. It should be usually difficult for a speech engine to read out them correctly if there were not appropriate indications. Hence, we need a method to specify how to read the formulas properly with speech synthesis according to context as well as the case of Kanji.

In the forthcoming version of DAISY, DAISY4 [1], it seems that a Ruby tag will be adopted officially in DAISY XML to specify the manner of pronunciation when Ruby characters appear explicitly in an original document. However, as was discussed, it is clear that this approach cannot solve the problem completely. If there are Ruby characters, DAISY-playback software/hardware might be able to read the Kanji correctly. If not, all characters would be read out in the same manner throughout the entire document with speech synthesis. In addition, we cannot assign how to read mathematical formulae using this approach since we cannot apply Ruby characters to them.

In terms of the problem of controlling breaks, intonations and stresses properly in aloud reading of mathematical formulae in Japanese, to make the situation clearer, we actually converted some sample mathematics textbooks ranging from elementary school to senior high school in Japan into text-based DAISY content and got DAISY-playback software to read out them with various text-to-speech (TTS) engines. In the result, as was assumed previously, obtained speech output was usually terrible. Furthermore, we realized that each speech-synthesis engine makes errors in their own manner. Even though a voice can read a mathematical expression correctly, the other voices cannot necessarily do the same. The speech control seems to be speech-engine-dependent job.

3   Accessible Authoring Tool for DAISY with Speech Synthesis

As was discussed in the previous section, in text-based DAISY, we need a new way to control how to read out each technical term in Kanji, symbol or mathematical formula locally according to their context. We refer to this new concept of assigning a pronunciation as "Yomi" (a Japanese word that means "a manner of aloud reading"). To realize the Yomi function in DAISY, we tentatively present a method based on DAISY4 Ruby tag. Here, it should be noted that Ruby and Yomi are conceptually different from each other. Although Ruby is included in an original print document, Yomi is not. The reading given with Yomi, therefore, should not appear explicitly in the DAISY version, unlike the case for Ruby. However, Yomi has to control speech output as well as Ruby.

We worked on upgrading ChattyInfty thoroughly so that a recognized result with our mathematics OCR software, "InftyReader," or an edited file with ChattyInfty can be converted into DAISY XML format with the Yomi function. Thus, the new version of ChattyInfty, "ChattyInfty3" becomes an accessible authoring tool for text-based DAISY. It is also useful for people with low vision or dyslexia as well as the blind. In the software, all the technical/non-technical content is read out properly with the Yomi function. Furthermore, since a result recognized by InftyReader can be imported directly, both sighted people and print-disabled can produce a DAISY book easily from a printed or PDF material by making use of Infty software only. However, those DAISY files do not get "a DAISY-index structure" automatically. Users should establish it easily with the "Index menu."

The window of ChattyInfty3 is divided into two parts—an index window and a main window—in a similar way to other popular DAISY browsers. The index window has a tree structure to show a table of contents in a style similar to that of Windows Explorer. This gives a user random access to a document displayed in the main window. Using a shortcut, one can easily switch the active window. Since all functions in ChattyInfty for browsing and editing mathematical expressions are incorporated as a dynamic link library, ChattyInfty3 is completely accessible as same as the previous version. One can not only browse but easily author technical/non-technical DAISY content. In terms of editing Yomi, by pressing Ctrl + Shift + Up Arrow keys after selecting a part of the text or a mathematical formula, a user can access a dialog to assign it correct aloud-reading (word description).

A remaining problem is of controlling breaks, intonations and stresses in speech output. As was pointed out, it is a speech-engine-dependent job. Since April 2011, we have been working on a collaborative project with the team of the Japan Braille Library to develop a special version of ChattyInfty3, in which we can edit/adjust speech behavior freely. In order to realize that, at first, we had to select one high-quality Japanese speech engine. After examining several engines, we chose "AI Talk" [14] to use in our system. It uses sound pieces of a human voice as elements for speech synthesis and realizes very natural speech output. Then, in line with its features, we are developing an interface to edit its speech behavior for a literal /sentence and a spoken mathematical expression. This speech-output editor is incorporated into ChattyInfty3, the AI-Talk version. This task is almost completed, and we are now preparing to release its beta version.

As was mentioned, unfortunately, there is no good DAISY playback/browsing tools that can treat DAISY3 mathML content in Japanese. Furthermore, each speech engine fails at reading text-based content in its own manner while the current DAISY has no universal method to control that. We, therefore, decided to implement a function in ChattyInfty3 to export an edited document as a multimedia DAISY2 content. In it, audio files of aloud reading corresponding to each of literal sentences and mathematical expressions generated by the speech engine are embedded as well as text-based information. All mathematical expressions are treated as images to meet the DAISY2 standards. Since we can produce this file after correcting all errors in the speech output, any DAISY browser/player can play back that content in a proper manner with the embedded voice.

4   Other Features of ChattyInfty3

In ChattyInfty3, editing the index can be done in an intuitive manner. The head line of each page is automatically treated as a top item in index. It appears on the first level of a tree diagram in the index window. Using "Index" menu, a user can perform various commands concerning DAISY index.

Accessibility of tables in technical content becomes remarkably improved as well. In the previous version of ChattyInfty, a table should be authored in a different pop-up window that was not necessarily accessible enough. On the other hand, it can be drawn up or edited directly in the ChattyInfty3 main window.

Finally, we have to refer to capabilities of Infty software for other languages. In terms of DAISY content in other languages, in ChattyInfty3, users can author/change easily not only how to read mathematical content but also captions in menu items and dialogs as they like since those things are all stored in independent definition files. They, therefore, could customize ChattyInfty3 for each local language if necessary. For the present, although only Japanese and English versions are available, we are working on developing French and some other-language versions. Incidentally, the foreign-language versions other than Japanese use Microsoft Speech API, Ver.5 as a speech engine. Users can produce a text-based/multimedia DAISY content (DAISY3), in which all the mathematical expressions are represented in MathML.

ABBYY FineReader [15] is known as one of most powerful OCR software in the world. Recently, we released FineReader plug-in for InftyReader. By combining it with InftyReader, recognition rate for European languages including extended Latin characters becomes remarkably improved.

5   Conclusion

In ChattyInfty3, print-disabled people can author technical/non-technical DAISY content easily for themselves. All such DAISY content can be read out in a correct manner with the Yomi function and speech control. Persons who verse themselves in technical issues probably could understand content according to its context even if some technical terms and formulas were read out in a wrong manner. However, for non-skillful students, it is clear that a textbook should be read aloud as correctly as possible. Our software could give a certain contribution for education. We have actually produced several mathematics textbooks in DAISY with it to provide them to print-disabled students.

Although ChattyInfty3 is designed mainly for technical content, finally, it should be remarked that Infty software is also the powerful tools for non-technical DAISY as well. Producing a DAISY book with InftyReader and ChattyInfty3 does not require much computer skills, time and costs to sighted teachers or assistants. We believe, it could make a substantial contribution for them to convert inaccessible contents into DAISY.

References

1. The DAISY Consortium, http://www.daisy.org/
2. The International Digital Publishing Forum, http://www.idpf.org
3. Dolphin Computer Access Ltd., http://www.yourdolphin.com/
4. gh, LLC, http://www.ghbraille.com/
5. CYPAC, http://www.cypac.co.jp/vodi/index.html
6. Design Science, Inc., http://www.dessci.com/en/
7. Infty Project, http://www.inftyproject.org/en/
8. NPO: Science Accessibility Net, http://www.sciaccess.net/en/
9. Yamaguchi, K., Suzuki, M.: On Necessity of a New Method to Read Out Math Contents Properly in DAISY. In: Miesenberger, K., Klaus, J., Zagler, W., Karshmer, A.I. (eds.) ICCHP 2010. LNCS, vol. 6180, pp. 415–422. Springer, Heidelberg (2010)
10. Yamaguchi, K., Suzuki, M.: How Infty Software Makes Mathematical Formulas and Tables Accessible in DAISY. In: Proc. the 2011 CSUN International Conference on Technology and People with Disabilities, BLV-2014, San Diego (2011)
11. Yamaguchi, K., Suzuki, M.: Problems in Producing Japanese DAISY Mathematical Content and a Solution for Them. In: Proc. The International Workshop on Digitization and E-Inclusion in Mathematics and Science 2012 (DEIMS 2012), Tokyo, pp. 115–120 (2012), http://www.gaea.jcn.nihon-u.ac.jp/deims12/
12. Yamaguchi, K., Kanahori, T., Gardner, J.A.: Solution for PDF-to-DAISY in Mathematics and Science. In: Proc. the 2012 CSUN International Conference on Technology and People with Disabilities, BLV-025, San Diego (2012)
13. Okamoto, K., et al.: Research on Standardization of Mathematical Terms. Grant-in-Aid for Cooperative Research (A), Research No.: 05306001 (1993-1995)
14. AIJ, http://www.ai-j.jp/ (Japanese only)
15. ABBYY, http://www.abbyy.com/

Blind Friendly LaTeX

An Option for Adapting Electronic Documents Containing Mathematical Text

Wanda Gonzúrová and Pavel Hrabák

TEREZA, Centre for Support of Visual Impaired Students at Universities, Department of Mathematics, Faculty of Nuclear Sciences and Physical Engineering, Czech Technical University in Prague, Czech Republic
{go,hrabacet}@tereza.fjfi.cvut.cz

Abstract. This article focuses on the accessibility of study materials containing mathematics to visually impaired students and students with learning disabilities. The electronic editable document (EED) is introduced within the legislative frame of the "Rules for providing support to the public universities" in the Czech Republic. An idea how to fulfil the requirements of EED by creating a document combining structured text in MS Word with mathematics in LaTeX code is presented. For this purposes it is necessary to define strict and simple rules for LaTeX keeping the code translatable. Basic principles of Czech standard for mathematics in Braille are presented as an inspiration.

Keywords: Czech standards for mathematics in Braille, electronic editable document (EED), blind friendly LaTeX.

1 Introduction

The accessibility of mathematics for visually impaired students is a challenging topic and reminds of a long-distance run. Many software projects try to unify splattered ideas all around the world (for summary see e.g. [4-5]). Main tasks are to enable the student to read materials containing mathematical expressions, to communicate with sighted teacher, and to actually "do" mathematics, i.e. to perform calculations. This article concentrates on the first task, i.e. to make study materials accessible.

Particular goals of this contribution are:

1. to introduce the Czech standard for transcribing mathematics, physics and chemistry in the Braille code,
2. to explain the idea of the electronic editable document EED and introduce a way of creating such a document for a text including mathematics,
3. to provoke involved colleagues into a discussion about a tool "Blind Friendly LaTeX"

In this article the Braille characters are presented via number representation of dots 123456 in braces { }.

K. Miesenberger et al. (Eds.): ICCHP 2012, Part I, LNCS 7382, pp. 138–141, 2012.
© Springer-Verlag Berlin Heidelberg 2012

2   First Goal: Introduction to the Czech Standards

Nowadays, the transcription of mathematics, physics and chemistry in the Czech Republic is based on the Handbook for text transcription into the Braille [1], which became the standard for six-dot Braille notation, being used since 1996. The standard was created respecting the national Braille tradition for literary and elementary mathematical text. The code is based on three principles:

1. *Consistency* in the sense that any mathematical formula can be consistently transcribed into the Braille and vice versa. Furthermore, no special prefix for mathematics is needed, i.e. the mathematical and literary text uses the same character set. Operational symbols + - / : . and round brackets ( ) have the same presentation in literary and mathematical 6-dot code. Possible ambiguities occur in the printed text as well; therefore the blind reader obtains the same information as sighted one. Here we note that in the Czech Braille, there is only one symbol for opening and closing quotation mark and two symbols for round brackets. Other mathematical symbols are represented by characters with diacritical mark, which do not appear in mathematical expression (see Figure 1).

⠒	⠤	⠉	⠿	⠳	⠌	⠡	⠣	⠩	⠊	⠑	⠱	⠄	⠠	⠚
+	−	:	"	/	(	)	ě	é	č	ž	á	í	š
+	−	:	=	/	(	)	<	>	√	∫	sub	up	end

Fig. 1. Braille representation of mathematics. Braille character (first line) can have different meaning in literary text (second line) than in mathematical expression (third line).

4. *Completeness* in the sense that any mathematical expression in the printed document can be consistently transcribed into Braille code without loss of any information. This is achieved by strict rule that the Braille code is connected to the mathematical symbol (or symbols) and not to the meaning of it, e.g., {25}{135} (:o) corresponds to → non regarding whether it means right arrow, implication, or reaction symbol in chemistry.

5. *"Space convention"* enabling the previous two, by making the mathematical text more readable and giving the exact meaning to the otherwise multivalent symbols. The most important rules are:

   — Before any operational symbol or (un)equality sign must be space and after it must not be space.
   — Before and after any logical ($\wedge$, $\Rightarrow$) or set relation ($\cap$, $\cup$, $\in$) must be space.

   The space position specifies the meaning of the symbol, e.g. {45}{15} (lower case Greek letter e) stands for ε, but {}{45}{15}{} (space, lower case Greek letter e, space) means $\in$.

For TEREZA centre such obsession to insist on those three basic principles is typical.

3   Second Goal: Universal Document Design for Students with Special Educational Needs

While 20 years ago TEREZA was the only centre for support of visual impaired students at Universities, nowadays, thanks to the effort to guarantee equal access to higher education to all students, many centres at Czech universities has been established. The legislative frame of support for students with special needs, using the service of these centres, provides the Amendment No. 2 to the "Rules for providing support to the public universities by the Ministry of Education, Youth and Sports of the Czech Republic" [3], which came into force this year.

Concerning the accessibility of study materials to university students, the Amendment No. 2 defines the term Electronic Editable Document (EED) specifying the attributes of the digitization and adaptation of printed text for visually impaired students, students with learning disabilities (mainly dyslexia), sign language users, and students with upper extremities disability.

The Amendment No. 2 explicitly distinguishes two types of the EED: a format for adaptation of study materials for the students using the tactile and voice output (EED II) and students using special software for reading electronic documents (EED I). The documents EED I and EED II differ only in expressing mathematical symbols, figures, tables etc.; the plain text is supposed to be identical. Our goal is to create a methodology for universal design of editable electronic document with mathematical formulas, which can be used by the whole scale of students needing this sort of documents as their study support, making the digitization less time consuming.

The common language for expressing mathematical formula is LaTeX. This leads to an idea of MS - Word document combining the structure strictly defined by the Methodology of text adaptation for visually impaired readers [2] with mathematical expressions written in LaTeX code. Using the correspondence of Mathtype product [7] with LaTeX, such document can be easily transformed into a text with mathematical expressions as picture-like Mathtype objects, which fulfils the demands of EED I. If the translating engines from LaTeX to Braille were reliable enough, this document could be transformed to editable document containing mathematics in Braille code. Despite the efforts, this cannot be done yet. Nevertheless, for the majority of students using mathematics, LaTeX becomes the compulsory language for writing their projects. Moreover, many blind university students or teachers prefer the LaTeX code to the Braille code when reading mathematics. Therefore, it is not too daredevil to offer the non translated document containing LaTeX expressions as the EED II available for LaTeX users by Braille display. But...

4   Third Goal: Blind Friendly LaTeX

Looking closely at source codes we find out that LaTeX is a paintbrush in the hands of mathematicians, and therefore it is more difficult to extract the exact meaning from the superfluously flowery code. Furthermore, transcribing engines do not have the sense of art. This fact immediately invites us to establish basic rules for writing in LaTeX making it simple and accessible.

Proposed solution of this problem by using the so called HrTeX (Human Readable TeX), presented by the Johan Kepler University, does not meet our requirements for universal design of EED. We aim not only to reduce the LaTeX code, but preserve the possibility to translate it via Mathtype as well.

We would like to initiate a discussion about strict rules for writing in LaTeX, which could be called Blind Friendly LaTeX. Such rules should bring certain unity in the way, how to use LaTeX, so it can be read by beginners in the LaTeX typography, and making the automatic translation from LaTeX to Braille more accurate.

The main task is to choose one specific option for writing when there are more possibilities. As an example consider a matrix or column vector. Should we use the environment `pmatrix` or the environment array bounded by `\left(` and `\right)` commands? We believe, any LaTeX user can think of similar examples.

Here we note that our goal is not to restrict the developers of LaTeX or authors of study materials. Our effort is to create a handbook or methodology for the digitization, so the output form of EED can be standardized and unified. We aim, of course, to implement the three basic principles for transcription mentioned above to the possible standard for simple and precisely defined rules of LaTeX, which we call Blind Friendly LaTeX.

References

1. Gonzúrová, W.: Handbook for text transcription into Braille, part I, II, III, IV. The Library and Printing Office for the Blind, Prague (1996)
2. Hanousková, M.: Methodology of text adaptation for visually impaired readers, version VII. Masaryk University, Brno (2010)
3. Dodatek č. 2 k Pravidlům pro poskytování příspěvku a dotací veřejným vysokým školám Ministerstvem školství, mládeže a tělovýchovy, č.j. 2 434/2011-33 ze dne 28. ledna 2011, (č.j.: 23 728/2011-30)[1], http://www.msmt.cz/ekonomika-skolstvi/zasady-a-pravidla-financovani-verejnych-vysokych-skol-pro
4. Bernareggi, C., Archambault, D.: Mathematics on the web: emerging opportunities for visually impaired people. In: Proceedings of the 2007 International Cross-disciplinary Conference on Web Accessibility (W4A) (W4A 2007), pp. 108–111. ACM, New York (2007)
5. Archambault, D., Stöger, B., Batusic, M., Fahrengruber, C., Miesenberger, K.: A software model to support collaborative mathematical work between Braille and sighted users. In: Proceedings of the 9th International ACM SIGACCESS Conference on Computers and Accessibility (Assets 2007), pp. 115–122. ACM, New York (2007)
6. http://www.desssci.com/en/products/MathType/
7. http://www.latex-project.org/

---

[1] The Amendment No. 2 to the "Rules for providing support to the public universities by the Ministry of Education, Youth and Sports of the Czech Republic, reference number 2 434/2011-33".

A System for Matching Mathematical Formulas Spoken during a Lecture with Those Displayed on the Screen for Use in Remote Transcription

Yoshinori Takeuchi[1], Hironori Kawaguchi[2], Noboru Ohnishi[2], Daisuke Wakatsuki[3], and Hiroki Minagawa[3]

[1] Department of Information Systems, School of Informatics, Daido University, 10-3 Takiharu-cho, Minami-ku, Nagoya 457-8530 Japan
ytake@daido-it.ac.jp
[2] Graduate School of Information Science, Nagoya University, Furo-cho, Chikusa-ku, Nagoya 464-8603 Japan
{hironori,ohnishi}@ohnishi.m.is.nagoya-u.ac.jp
[3] Tsukuba University of Technology, Japan
{waka,minagawa}@a.tsukuba-tech.ac.jp

Abstract. A system is described for extracting and matching mathematical formulas presented orally during a lecture with those simultaneously displayed on the lecture room screen. Each mathematical formula spoken by the lecturer and displayed on the screen is extracted and shown to the transcriber. Investigation showed that, in a lecture in which many mathematical formulas were presented, about 80% of them were both spoken and pointed to on the screen, meaning that the system can help a transcriber correctly transcribe up to 80% of the formulas presented. A speech recognition system is used to extract the formulas from the lecturer's speech, and a system that analyzes the trajectory of the end of the stick pointer is used to extract the formulas from the projected images. This information is combined and used to match the pointed-to formulas with the spoken ones. In testing using actual lectures, this system extracted and matched 71.4% of the mathematical formulas both spoken and displayed and presented them for transcription with a precision of 89.4%.

1   Introduction

Hearing-impaired students often need complementary technologies, such as sign-language interpretation and PC captioning, to enable them to fully understand lectures at university or college. PC captioning is already being used at several universities, and a system is being developed that will remotely transcribe an instructor's speech. Various groups have done work in this area. For instance, Kato *et al.* investigated the information required by a remote transcriber and ways to display that information on the transcriber's monitor [1]. In the approach they developed, content keywords are displayed on the monitor to aid the transcriber. Miyoshi *et al.* are developing a remote real-time captioning system [2] that sends

K. Miesenberger et al. (Eds.): ICCHP 2012, Part I, LNCS 7382, pp. 142–149, 2012.

audiovisual signals from a classroom to a remote location where captionists type captions in real time. This system uses the "re-speak" method, in which a captionist listens to the instructor and then repeats what the instructor said [3]. The system is trained on the transcriber's speech, so the recognition rate is high in the subsequent automatic speech recognition step. Another technology that has captured much interest is real-time speech recognition. Wald and Bain, for example, proposed an automatic speech recognition system for universal access to communication and learning [4].

An even more difficult task is the transcription of mathematical formulas. Complex mathematical formulas are often presented in a lecture, and a mathematical formula spoken by a lecturer is sometimes ambiguous. A typical example of a spoken formula is "x minus 1 divided by 2." It can be transcribed as either $\frac{x-1}{2}$ or $x - \frac{1}{2}$. Since transcribers generally transcribe simply what they hear, someone reading the transcription cannot distinguish which mathematical formula the lecturer intended.

We are developing a system for matching mathematical formulas presented orally during a lecture with those simultaneously projected on the lecture room screen. The extracted and matched formulas are then shown to the transcriber to help him or her transcribe the formulas correctly.

Previous research on identifying the object to which someone is pointing includes analyzing the relationship between the pointing gesture and the motion of the stick pointer [5] and analyzing the relationships among the location and locus of the pointer end, the type of object, the position and orientation of the pointer, and the pointing gesture using sensors to detect the position and direction of the pointer and the position and orientation of the person doing the pointing [6]. Other research includes the development of a system that identifies the object to which someone is pointing and matches it to the spoken demonstrative words and phrases [7,8]. We have now extended this idea to the matching of spoken and displayed mathematical formulas.

2   Analysis of the Mathematical Formula in the Lecture

2.1   Recorded Audio and Visual Signals

We videotaped an actual lecture twice in order to analyze the relationship between the utterance of a mathematical formula and the use of a stick pointer. We placed a microphone around the lecturer's neck and a high-definition video camera at the back of the lecture room (Fig. 1 illustrates the configuration.) We captured the sound signals with a 16-bit 48-kHz sampling frequency and the video signals with a 1440×1080 pixel size. The frame rate of the video signal was down-sampled at 10 Hz. Figure 2 shows an example recorded scene.

The lecture was on signal processing, and many mathematical formulas were presented. The lecturer used a stick pointer to point to the formulas on the screen.

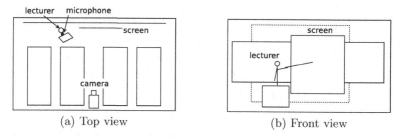

(a) Top view   (b) Front view

Fig. 1. Configuration of the lecture room: (a) top view and (b) front view. Dotted rectangle represents area covered by camera.

Fig. 2. Screenshot of lecture recordings

2.2 Results

We analyzed the recorded video and counted the number of mathematical formulas spoken by the lecturer and the number of those that were pointed to on the screen.

Table 1 shows that about 80% of the mathematical formulas that were spoken were also pointed to on the screen. This suggests that we can extract the spoken mathematical formulas from the projected images by using a system that analyzes the trajectory of the end of the stick pointer.

Table 1. Number of mathematical formulas

Lecture	1	2	Total
Spoken	260	91	351
Spoken and pointed to	205	68	273
Ratio	78.8%	74.7%	77.8%

3 Extracting Mathematical Formulas

3.1 System Overview

An overview of our system for extracting and matching mathematical formulas is shown in Figure 3.

The handouts (e.g., copies of slides, abstract) for the lecture that are typically used for training the language conversion program of the computer used for transcription are also used for training the automatic speech recognition system we use. The mathematical formulas in the handouts are input into the dictionary in the speech recognition engine.

The speech and video signals for the lecture are input to the extraction and matching system in real time. The system extracts the mathematical formula components from the speech signal and the pointing gestures from the video signal. The system then integrates them and matches the mathematical formulas projected on the lecture room screen to those spoken by the lecturer. These extracted and matched formulas are displayed on another monitor for the transcriber to help him or her transcribe the formulas correctly.

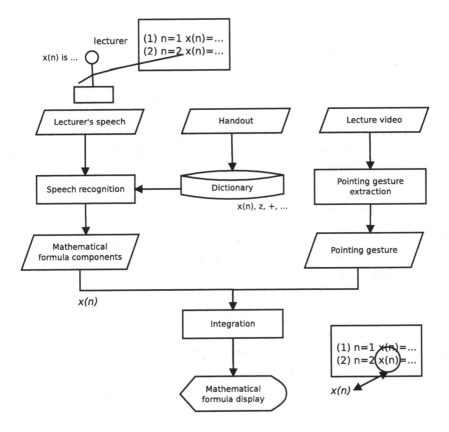

Fig. 3. System overview

3.2   Extracting Mathematical Formulas from Lecturer's Speech

The Julius Speech Recognition Engine (version 3.5) is used to extract the mathematical formulas from the lecturer's speech. A gender-independent triphone model trained with academic presentation speech taken from the Corpus of Spontaneous Japanese is used as the acoustic model in Julius. A word N-gram model is used as the language model. Since mathematical formula components (e.g. $x(n), z$) are not well represented in academic presentation speech, those found in the handouts are added to the dictionary. The probabilities in the language model were adjusted so that more mathematical formula components are obtained from the lecturer's speech. We also tuned three recognition parameters:

– We use larger **beam width** in order to search the word from wider search area.
– A larger **weight for language model** is used in order to obtain better results.
– Since mathematical formula components have small word lengths, a smaller **word insertion penalty** is used in order to divide long words into shorter words more frequently.

Testing following this parameter tuning on actual lecture speech data showed that the recall ratio was about 71% and the precision was about 90%. The recall ratio and the precision was about 36% and 87% respectively without adding the mathematical formula components into the dictionary, and the recall ratio and the precision was about 69% and 89% respectively without recognition parameter tuning. The speech recognition results may not fully agree with the displayed formula. For example, the suffix m is sometimes misrecognized as n because they have similar pronunciation. The system therefore uses the displayed formula in all cases as it is generally correct.

3.3   Extracting Pointing Gestures

The method used for extracting the pointing gestures is the same as that previously used [9]. The pointing gestures are classified as a point, a line, or an ellipse, as shown in Fig.4.

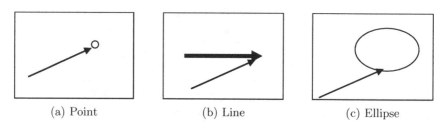

(a) Point   (b) Line   (c) Ellipse

Fig. 4. Classification of pointing gestures: (a) point, (b) line, (c) ellipse

3.4   Matching Pointing Gestures with Utterances

Each pointing gesture is matched with an utterance in order to extract the mathematical formula corresponding to what was spoken by the instructor. The uttered mathematical formulas may be misspoken due to, for example, the omission of a symbol. As consequence, the results of speech recognition may not exactly match the characters and symbols in the formula. Therefore, as mentioned above, the results of speech recognition for a formula are replaced with the formula extracted from the image. This was implemented by carefully investigating the relationship between pointing gestures and mathematical formula utterances. The utterances of mathematical formulas were found to generally occur between two seconds before the start and the end of a pointing gesture. The system combines the pointing gesture with the utterance using

$$t_{gs} - 2.0 < t_{us} < t_{ge}, \tag{1}$$

where t_{gs} and t_{ge} are the start and end times of the gesture, respectively, and t_{us} is the start time of the utterance.

3.5   Extracting Pointed-to Objects Corresponding to Uttered Formulas

The system extracts the object image from the displayed image and draws the trajectory of the pointer on the image. The image is then displayed on the transcriber's second monitor for use in transcribing the formula. Examples of extracted mathematical formulas for the three types of pointing gestures are shown in Figure 5.

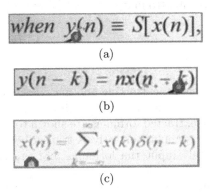

(a)

(b)

(c)

Fig. 5. Examples of extracted mathematical formulas, with tip of stick pointer shown in orange. (a) Lecturer says "y n" and points to "y(n)" using point gesture. (b) Lecturer says "n minus k" and points to "n-k" using line gesture. (c) Lecturer says "x n" and points to "x(n)" using ellipse gesture.

4   Experimental Results and Discussion

We tested our system using the recorded audio-visual signals for two actual lectures. These lectures are the same ones mentioned in section 2.1. As shown in Table 2, the system correctly extracted and matched 195 of the 273 mathematical formulas that were both uttered and displayed.

Table 2. Evaluation results

Lecture	1	2	Total
No. of formulas uttered and displayed	205	68	273
No. of speech recognition result	173	50	223
No. of displayed formulas extracted	170	48	218
No. of utterances correctly matched	150	45	195
No. of utterances incorrectly matched	55	23	78
Recall	73.1%	66.2%	71.4%
Precision	88.2 %	93.8%	89.4%

The system's high performance (recall of 71.4% and precision of 89.4%) is attributed to its ability to match the pointed-to formulas with the uttered formulas. Rather than depending on the speech recognition results, which may have misrecognized components, our system extracts and uses the correct mathematical formula from the displayed image.

From Table 2, it is evident that errors in speech recognition are the major cause of misrecognized components. Some mathematical formulas are too short to be recognized by speech recognition. For example, the suffixes $i, k, and n$ are sometimes recognized as a part of the preceding word including the same pronunciation. The use of the pointed-to mathematical formula eliminates the problem of misrecognition.

5   Conclusion

We have described a system for extracting and matching mathematical formulas presented orally during a lecture with those simultaneously projected on the lecture room screen. The extracted formulas are shown to the transcriber to help him or her transcribe the formulas correctly. A transcriber using this system can more easily and accurately input the formulas and prepare a more complete transcription.

The system combines speech recognition with pointing gesture extraction. Our investigation of the relationship between pointing gestures and mathematical formula utterances showed that the utterance of a mathematical formula generally occurs between two seconds before the start of the gesture and the end time of the gesture. Evaluation of our system using audio-visual signals for two actual lectures showed that it had high performance (recall of 71.4% and precision of 89.4%).

We are now working on reducing the number of miss- and over-detections. This involves improving the speech recognition rate and the accuracy of pointed-to formula extraction. We are also working on improving the method for inputting the extracted formulas into the transcript, which is not an easy task. This involves developing a system for easily copying and pasting the extracted formulas into the transcript. Future work includes extending this system so that it also works with laser pointers.

This research is partly supported by a KAKENHI Grant-in-Aid for Scientific Research(C) (24500642) from the Japan Society for the Promotion of Science (JSPS).

References

1. Kato, N., Kawano, S., Miyoshi, S., Nishioka, T., Murakami, H., Minagawa, H., Wakatsuki, D., Shirasawa, M., Ishihara, Y., Naito, I.: Subjective Evaluation of Displaying Keywords for Speech to Text Service Operators. The Transactions of Human Interface Society 9(2), 195–203 (2007) (in Japanese)
2. Miyoshi, S., Kawano, S., Nishioka, T., Kato, N., Shirasawa, M., Murakami, H., Minagawa, H., Ishihara, Y., Naito, I., Wakatsuki, D., Kuroki, H., Kobayashi, M.: A Basic Study on Supplementary Visual Information for Real-Time Captionists in the Lecture of Information Science. IEICE Transactions on Information and Systems (Japanese Edition) J91-D(9), 2236–2246 (2008)
3. Miyoshi, S., Kuroki, H., Kawano, S., Shirasawa, M., Ishihara, Y., Kobayashi, M.: Support Technique for Real-Time Captionist to Use Speech Recognition Software. In: Miesenberger, K., Klaus, J., Zagler, W., Karshmer, A.I. (eds.) ICCHP 2008. LNCS, vol. 5105, pp. 647–650. Springer, Heidelberg (2008)
4. Wald, M., Bain, K.: Universal access to communication and learning: role of automatic speech recognition. Universal Access in the Information Society 6(4), 435–447 (2007)
5. Sakiyama, T., Mukunoki, M., Katsuo, I.: Detection of the Indicated Area with an Indication Stick. In: Int. Conf. on Multimodal Interfaces, pp. 480–487 (2000)
6. Marutani, T., Nishiguchi, S., Kakusho, K., Minoh, M.: Making a lecture content with deictic information about indicated objects in lecture materials. In: AEARU Workshop on Network Education, pp. 70–75 (2005)
7. Takeuchi, Y., Saito, K., Ito, A., Ohnishi, N., Iizuka, S., Nakajima, S.: Extracting Pointing Object with Demonstrative Speech Phrase for Remote Transcription in Lecture. In: Miesenberger, K., Klaus, J., Zagler, W., Karshmer, A.I. (eds.) ICCHP 2008. LNCS, vol. 5105, pp. 624–631. Springer, Heidelberg (2008)
8. Ito, A., Saito, K., Takeuchi, Y., Ohnishi, N., Iizuka, S., Nakajima, S.: A Study on Demonstrative Words Extraction in Instructor Utterance on Communication Support for Hearing Impaired Persons. In: Miesenberger, K., Klaus, J., Zagler, W., Karshmer, A.I. (eds.) ICCHP 2008. LNCS, vol. 5105, pp. 632–639. Springer, Heidelberg (2008)
9. Takeuchi, Y., Ohta, H., Ohnishi, N., Wakatsuki, D., Minagawa, H.: Extraction of Displayed Objects Corresponding to Demonstrative Words for Use in Remote Transcription. In: Miesenberger, K., Klaus, J., Zagler, W., Karshmer, A.I. (eds.) ICCHP 2010. LNCS, vol. 6180, pp. 152–159. Springer, Heidelberg (2010)

Supporting Braille Learning and Uses by Adapting Transcription to User's Needs

Bruno Mascret, Alain Mille, and Vivien Guillet

Université de Lyon, CNRS
Université Lyon 1, LIRIS, UMR5205
F-69622, France
{bruno.mascret,alain.mille,vivien.guillet}@liris.cnrs.fr

Abstract. This paper focuses on how to improve accessibility for Braille readers on Internet. We criticize actual technologies and show their limits in scientific Braille and Braille personnalization, especially in pedagogical situations. We present NAT Braille, a free software solution designed to respond to pedagogical specific needs. The transcribing process uses a set of customizable XSLT transformations and several XML formats. We detail the design of NAT Braille and the technologies used for transcriptions. Then we explain why NAT Braille improves personnalization in Braille rendering on Internet. We give the example of our Mozilla extension which is able to transcribe web pages including MathML markup, and is set up with adapted transcription rules taking into account the user's preferences. We conclude by raising issues related to our work.

Keywords: Accessibility, Braille, Pedagogy, Web based education.

1 Introduction

New technologies are increasingly making digital data access easier, especially considering the use of Content Management System (CMS), of educational platforms and many other communication tools. The amount of online information grows steadily in all fields -school, industry, business. Therefore, the CMS is a very precious publication tool for many especially for e-learning practices. Inclusive education issues are still very active in a lot of scientific domains : assistive technologies, teaching methods, ergonomics... Concerning visually impaired students, D.Archambault [1] notices the numerous and various papers proposed to the International Council for Education of People with Visual Impairment under the topic "Inclusive Educational Practices". Moreover, he insists on the vocabulary used in English (inclusive education) and French (integration) to underline the difficulties encountered for a real *inclusion* of students into a class. Visual impairement remains a real problem for both teacher and student, because most teachers are not skilled in Braille and only few solutions are designed to teach Braille inside a classroom. In this article, we focus on Braille and give an analysis of what a good automatic transcribing tool should propose to be suitable for inclusive education and for Internet contents.

K. Miesenberger et al. (Eds.): ICCHP 2012, Part I, LNCS 7382, pp. 150–157, 2012.

Transcribing into Braille is not, as one should think, just a plain transcoding of characters. Braille users are mainly blind persons and transcribers. However, a transcriber is not necessarily professional - for example, a teacher with a blind student in his class needs to transcribe his documents into Braille. Conversely, a blind student writing in Braille with his computer is not able to make a transcription than his teacher can understand. Many countries, such as France, tend to integrate most blind students into general courses. Different types of Braille codes are mentioned : the literary code (transcribing each character of the initial document), the abbreviated code (reducing the number of characters thanks to complex contraction rules), the mathematical code (transcribing all scientific notations)[8], the musical code. Each language has its own number of characters (no accents in English but many sorts of accents in other languages). Therefore, each language has its own Braille codes[7], if not each country (British and American codes are different).

We propose to improve Braille support not only by using dedicated softwares in classroom but also by integrating Braille solutions in existing applications such as web browsers for example. In the first section, we propose a critic of the existing solutions and technologies. We argue that pedagogical Braille could be used in a lot of applications, not only educational ones. We claim that using it on Internet could get students and users to improve their Braille reading skills. We show that users need personnalization for Braille according to their skills and needs. Then we introduce NAT Braille[1][10][9], a free software solution designed to respond to pedagogical specific needs. We explain how it works and how it improves personnalization in Braille rendering on Internet. We give the example of our Mozilla extension which is able to transcribe web pages including MathML markup, and is set up with adapted transcription rules taking into account the user's preferences. We conclude by raising issues related to our work.

2   Critics of Actual Technologies for Braille Accessibility

Digital communication tools offer many advantages to most users : time-saving on diffusion, organization, less paper use... But they create new handicap situations to visually impaired persons[6]. The accessibility of these communications media is increasingly better taken into account, thanks to specific software adaptations for visual impairment and to the development of "design for all". However it is mainly based on restoring the structure, contents and conditioning of websites or applications. Reducing the time needed to find a specific piece of information inside a document, especially in a particular context, remains complicated and difficult [3]. Visually-impaired people only have sequential access to information (vocal reading, refreshable Braille display) and therefore cannot directly find the interesting elements, nor consider a document as a whole. The accessibility of digital contents by the document's producer is only rarely considered. Indeed a Braille user needs an adaptation processing to read digital documents containing scientific notations. A vocal synthesizer or a screen reader

---

[1] Downloadable at `http://liris.cnrs.fr/nat`; software under GLP licence.

can give a general idea of the document, but they do not offer an accurate understanding. Besides, they are still unable to transcribe mathematical, musical or graphical notations. Archambault et al. [2] propose a good state of art of the main mathematical solutions. As for text transcribers, there are very few : DuxBurry's DBT² is the only good commercial solution for contracted Braille, Odt2Braille[1] uses the free LibLouisXML library³ for text. BrlTTY[11] and BrlAPI[14] offer refreshable Braille features and a light support for contracted Braille and direct rendering. Even if the transcribing result is good, none of these solutions propose a pedagogical approach for contracted Braille and they offer few possibilities of customization. Moreover, only Odt2braille supports mathematics and text, and none implements chemical or musical notation.

Another criteria to keep in mind is the "time disability"[15]. Very often, visually impaired people waste a lot of time, even with accessible documents : they get lost throughout a document, try to find a precise paragraph, etc. Real time interactions with the document are in fact very limited, and it is up to the user to sort himself out. The communication between visually-impaired and sighted people remains uneasy since they do not share a common working space. This problem is of first importance especially for the inclusion of students into a class. Visually impaired must have the same interacting possibilities as other students during a lesson and their disabilities must be limited to allow them to follow a common pedagogical process[13]. The MaWEN project[2] proposes a tool for mathematics to limit this situation. But for contracted Braille, there is no solution at this time to support the learning process. Moreover, most of the norms have not been revised and new terms (Internet, browser, keyboard...) have no special contractions. Users define their own contraction rules and it is difficult to set up assistive technologies with it. The development of speech synthetizers and screen readers have improved the accessibility of text content. Simple scientific expressions may be accessed. As a result, many students do not wish to learn contracted or mathematical Braille anymore because their screen reader is skilled enough to give them access to content. This general trend becomes a real problem when students have to access to large documents or scientific ones : for complex scientific notation, Braille remains the only good solution. Moreover, at the university, the amount of document to read increases a lot. Contracted Braille may limit the amount of pages to read.

A last important point is the development of E-learning. It is a rising mode of learning, but it increases the time disabilities for visually-impaired students. Investigations on new interacting devices using 2D representations [12], haptic modalities[16] or Braille display have two main disadvantages : they are not able to manage pedagogical Braille and they don't transcribe directly scientific notations like MathML on the web. In the following section we introduce our contribution, NAT Braille[10][9], a free software solution designed to respond to pedagogical specific needs.

---

² http://www.duxburysystems.com/
³ http://code.google.com/p/liblouisxml/

3   NAT Braille, a Transcriber for Personnalization

The NAT Braille project mainly aims at solving the problems previously described, and wishes to produce a solution which could be at the same time accessible to every one, independent from special configurations, highly customizable, and potentially integrated to other systems. The motive is not to compete with transcribing centers -they are far better than any automatic software could ever be- but on the opposite to give them a tool allowing a bigger efficiency and productivity. Furthermore, we have focused on proposing various integrations of NAT Braille in other softwares, like web browsers for example.

3.1   Working Principles

Taking the different constraints into account has led us to a modular organization, based on adaptation to each type of document (format, mixed contents, encodings, etc.). The structure proposes three main modules : conversion, transcription and post-processing. Ideally the user gives the system a file in a given format : the conversion module conforms to the document type and produces an internal XML format file. Then the transcription module transcribes the internal file with chosen XSL filters. Finally the post-processing module manages the presentation, exportation or printing through other XSL filters. The specific role of each component allows the system to be independent during the development process. A new format would only need that a specific converter be associated to it. Transcribing filters are also independent from the initial format.

The transcribing mechanism is original because the different filters and their specialization are interoperable. Their implementation is no longer based on dictionaries but on rules, and therefore gets as close as possible to a human reasoning when using different transcribing processes. Since these filters are interoperable, they allow each document to realize dynamically its own transcribing scenario : using abbreviated or literate Braille code, choosing encodings, choosing Braille code tables, whether transcribe mathematics or not, applying black to Braille or reverse transcription. At the beginning of a transcription, the scenario is written according to many parameters. We will detail the most interesting features in the following section and the technical aspects in section 4. This organization allows us to propose a wide range of customizations.

3.2   Adapting Transcription to Users

NAT is able to propose several kinds of French Braille transcription features : grade 1 or contracted (grade 2) Braille, mathematics and chemistry. Music is still under development. Mathematics and literal Braille codes (contracted or not) can be rendered into black. But each notation contains several possibilities and parameters according to the user's skills. For example, beginners do not use the complementary rules in French grade one, nor specific trigonometric notation in mathematics. Later on they learn contracted Braille and apply these rules too.

Table 1. This table gives several transcriptions of the same expression *"La FONCTION sin(x)"* (The *sin(x)* FUNCTION) according to the user's skill

Possible user	Braille result	Set of rules
Primary school (1st y.)	⠀	basic grade 1
Primary school (adv.)	⠀	advanced g1
College (beginner)	⠀	trigo. & basic g2
College (advanced)	⠀	grade 2

Depending on the user's profile, we have to adapt the transcribing process to take into account the reader's skills. That is why NAT's core does not use any dictionary but is controlled with a large set of rules and parameters. Each of them can be set active or not. Table 1 shows different possible renderings and explains which rules have been involved to produce Braille : basic grade one rules don't make a difference between a full upercase word : *FONCTION* (⠀) and *La* (⠀) use the same simple capital prefix ⠀ ; then complementary grade 1 rules take this difference into account by using the double capital prefix ⠀ for *FONCTION* (⠀) ; "*sin*" (⠀) is represented by ⠀ in specific trigonomic notation ; "la" (the) is one of the first contracted words learnt in French (⠀) ; The contraction of "fonction" (⠀) is learnt afterwards.

Most of the existing solutions propose a set of options to slightly adapt the transcription, but none is able to manage the contraction rules by activating only a subset of them. But most of the time, an inexperienced transcriber is not able to choose which rules have to be activated. Moreover, they are more than 100 signs and locutions, 800 symbols and 75 contraction rules depending on the context or the subset used (signs, symbol, other word...). NAT is able to manage special configurations (pedagogical scenarios) containing steps which activate a set of rules. Scenarios have been made to follow the progression of Braille contraction learning methods like "Étudions l'abrégé"[4]. Each step has been checked by professional transcribers and Braille teachers to validate the quality of the produced Braille and the pedagogical consistence. A user only has to know which step must be activated and may follow a pedagogical sequence given by someone more skilled in Braille. For example, at the beginning of November, students should begin lesson 4 : they go from step 3 to step 4 in the software.

4   Technical Aspects

NAT uses several XML formats to represent the internal format of the document and the rule definitions. The internal format has a fairly simple basis and allows other notation standards (such as MathML) to be integrated[4]. The smallest element is the word or the punctuation mark. All types of contents (mathematical or literary) are organized inside paragraphs which constitute the document. For the time being, the different elements' properties are represented

---

[4] See the dtd at `https://svn.liris.cnrs.fr/nat/trunk/xsl/mmlents/windob.dtd`

through tag attributes, and not as being themselves tags (this is different from HTML). This way the document maintains a simple structure. Including open and standard formats guarantees NAT to be compatible on upfront with all softwares respecting international standards and independent towards specific software distributions.

The XML format for transcription rules is slightly more complicated. It contains the definitions of locutions, signs, symbols and rules on these elements[5]. A rule may contain a simple definition (symbol, sign, locution) or complex rules using regular expressions. Complex rules have a description to allow users to understand the meaning of the rule, and to choose if they want to activate it. This rule file is then parsed by an XSL stylesheet to make sequences, lists and parameters used by the contraction algorithm. The resulting file is an XSL parameters file which will be included by the main xsl stylesheet. We have used the same principle to define the patterns for hyphenation[6].

All Nat Braille's core modules consist of interoperable XSL Stylesheets. The choice of this technology is motivated by its expressiveness for XML transformations. It is also quite easy to set up XSL stylesheets with parameters and to generate custom stylesheets. We have used two kind of XSL stylesheets : system stylesheets, which may receive a set of parameters and may include other system stylesheets; generated stylesheets, which contain the constructed parameters and the main algorithm. Thus the main algorithm is generated and includes the stylesheets it needs, according to the user's preferences. The figure 1 shows the several inclusion possibilities for the transcription.

5   A Mozilla Extension to Render Braille on Web Pages

Classical assistive technologies are not able to manage pedagogical Braille on internet. Moreover, they can't transcribe MathML content on web pages. The modular organization of NAT allowed us to propose conversion and presentation filters dedicated to web rendering. We have developed a Mozilla extension which takes text and MathML contents on web pages, transcribes them into Braille according to the user's preferences, and then displays the result in the browser. The main advantage of this feature is that a web page structure and layout is not changed : only the content is transcribed into Braille. It reduces the time needed to read the page, and provides efficient access to MathML contents. Moreover, users need to set up only one software for Braille transcription : rules used to produce document or web page transcriptions are the same. This functionnality may help Braille learners access a wide range of documents, even on the Web.

The NAT Braille firefox extension is written using the javascript Mozilla extension. When activated, the extension is automatically triggered by mozilla each time a web page has finished downloading. A temporary local file containing the body of the downloaded page is created and its filename is passed as parameter

---

[5] French rule file: https://svn.liris.cnrs.fr/nat/trunk/xsl/dicts/fr-g2.xml
[6] An explanation of the XSL implementation of Liang's algorithm in NAT can be found at http://natbraille.free.fr/xsl/

Generated stylesheets   System stylesheets

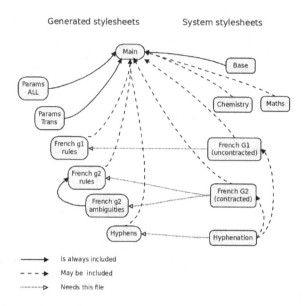

Fig. 1. This figure shows the relationships between the xsl stylesheets involved in Braille transcription

to a NAT wrapper. This wrapper first uses HTML Tidy to clean up the document. This allow to clean up the document for it to be parsable by NAT. The wrapper then uses a local NAT installation for the transcription process, using a command line switch enabling the transcribing process to keep the original markup. The Braille translated document is put in a temporary file. When the wrapper's process ends, the extension replaces the body of the tab by fetching the content of the resulting Braille file. Mozilla refreshes automaticaly the page display which now shows the Braille translation of the document. The writing and reading of temporary files and the execution of the NAT wrapper are done asynchronously by the extension so that the whole browser is not blocked by the translation process.

6   Discussion

We show that NAT Braille is a good solution for inclusive education and web based education. Its modular organization helps to give a web extension able customize the Braille. However it remains a tool and would be advantaged if combined with other assistive solutions. Our transcribing tool is a first step towards developing other assistive tools for Braille learning and transcribing. Some other assistive tools propose interesting features which could be combined or implemented into NAT to improve the understanding of formulas for example. A promising possibility would be to underline the current position in both Braille and black texts like in MaWEN[1]. Pedagogical scenarios could also be further developed thanks to dedicated software[5]. Interaction traces[3] could help their adaptation. Moreover, we are building a web service for NAT Braille to facilitate its integration in web based softwares. Finally we are developing foreign partnerships to propose NAT Braille into other languages and include NAT Braille in publishing chains for producing adaptable documents.

References

1. Archambault, D.: Interaction et usages des modalités non visuelles, accessibilité des contenus complexes. HDR, Faculté d'ingénierie, Université Pierre et Marie Curie-Paris, Paris (2010)
2. Archambault, D., Stöger, B., Batušič, M., Fahrengruber, C., Miesenberger, K.: Mathematical working environments for the blind:what is needed now? In: Proceedings of ICALT Workshop on Advanced Learning Technologies for Disabled and Non-Disabled People, Niigata, Japon (2007)
3. Cordier, A., Mascret, B., Mille, A.: Dynamic Case Based Reasoning for Contextual Reuse of Experience. In: Marling, C. (ed.) Provenance-Awareness in Case-Based Reasoning Workshop. ICCBR 2010, pp. 69–78 (July 2010)
4. Le Reste, J., Perdoux, C.: Étudions l'abrégé. AVH, Paris (2006)
5. Lefèvre, M., Mille, A., Jean-Daubias, S., Guin, N.: A meta-model to acquire relevant knowledge for interactive learning environments personalization. In: Adaptive 2009, Athénes, Gréce (2009)
6. Leporini, B., Buzzi, M.: Learning by e-Learning: Breaking Down Barriers and Creating Opportunities for the Visually-Impaired. In: Stephanidis, C. (ed.) HCI 2007. LNCS, vol. 4556, pp. 687–696. Springer, Heidelberg (2007)
7. Mackenzie, S.C.: World Braille usage: a survey of efforts towards uniformity of Braille notation. In: International Meeting on Braille Uniformity, UNESCO, 1950, Paris (1954)
8. Magna, F.: Le braille mathématique. Revue Bimestrielle du Groupement des Professeurs et Éducateurs d'aveugles et Amblyopes, 183 (2002)
9. Mascret, B., Mille, A.: Supporting the learning process –more than a braille transcription. In: Gelderblom, G.J., Soede, M., Adriaens, L., Miesenberger, K. (eds.) Everyday Technology for Independence and Care - AAATE 2011, Maastricht, The Netherlands, vol. 29. AAATE, IOS Press (September 2011)
10. Mascret, B., Mille, A., Ollier, M.: An ideal braille transcriber? AMSE Journals, Advances in Modelling (December 2008)
11. Nair, N., Pitre, N., Doyon, S., Mielke, D.: Access to the console screen for blind persons using refreshable braille displays. BRLTTY Reference Manual (1995-2011)
12. Rotard, M., Taras, C., Ertl, T.: Tactile web browsing for blind people. Multimedia Tools and Applications 37(1), 53–69 (2008)
13. Thibault, C., Leroux, G.: To optimise the support to young visually impaired persons. In: 12th World Conference on Inclusive Educational Practices, Kuala Lumpur, Malaysia (2006)
14. Thibault, S., Hinderer, S.: Brlapi: Simple, portable, concurrent, application-level control of braille terminals. Arxiv preprint cs/0703044 (2007)
15. Uzan, G.: Temps technologiques, temps individuels, temps sociaux: l'articulation des contraintes temporelles dans l'utilisation de l'informatique par des aveugles. In: Colloque Fisaf (2003)
16. Zeng, L., Weber, G.: Audio-Haptic Browser for a Geographical Information System. In: Miesenberger, K., Klaus, J., Zagler, W., Karshmer, A.I. (eds.) ICCHP 2010. LNCS, vol. 6180, pp. 466–473. Springer, Heidelberg (2010)

A Non-visual Electronic Workspace
for Learning Algebra

Nancy Alajarmeh and Enrico Pontelli

New Mexico State University Department of Computer Science
{nalajarm,epontell}@cs.nmsu.edu

Abstract. In this paper we describe a multi-layer system that is designed to help students who have moderate to severe visual impairments learn algebra while manipulating algebraic equations through an interactive non-visual web-based workspace. The functional algebraic transformation options provided in the interactive system through its various layers, and the carefully provided help associated to each of those domain specific manipulation functions enhanced the overall process by which students who are visually impaired learn and deal with solving equations in the developed non-visual workspace.

1   Introduction

Educational software for teaching, learning, and training is increasingly getting pervasive with growing industry that has already emerged since the 1940's [6]. Recently, reliance on web resources for learning purposes became more apparent; web-based educational platforms have influenced the way students learn and grasp concepts; content is interactively dynamic, updatable, customizable, and available.

The act of learning scientific and mathematical concepts, for example, relies on the active engagement of the students in the discovery process and methodologies like those based on constructivist theory emphasize the importance of guided discovery and self-exploration in the learning process, through problem modeling and practice in the manipulation of mathematical concepts. In particular, the role of constructivism in the teaching of algebra and other forms of mathematics, based on the use of technology and independent problem solving has been widely advocated by the educational community (e.g., [11]). Furthermore, several state testing requirements rely on the acquisition of competency in the practice of algebraic manipulations.

Students who are visually impaired have distinct needs in learning. Learning for that category of learners must be supported by right tools, strategies, and technologies that help overcoming their limited vision [8]. While it takes sighted students a glance to grasp considerable amount of information, the sequential access and processing of the same information require longer for students who are visually impaired [4 - 5].

For reasons related to the subject and the nature of vision disability; students who have impaired vision are more challenged in learning algebra; complexity of algebraic expressions that heavily rely on bi-dimensional representations, abstract algebraic notations that hide a lot of information, disability impacts on a relatively visual topic,

K. Miesenberger et al. (Eds.): ICCHP 2012, Part I, LNCS 7382, pp. 158–165, 2012.

burden associated to and limited capabilities of traditional tools, and lack of technologies that efficiently support mathematics accessibility for students with visual impairments [1], [3]. These challenges became larger within the impact of technology revolution on education that necessitates students to deal with more online resources; curriculum, assignments, assessments, and discussions [8].

Research has shown that performance of students in mathematical problem solving activities is heavily affected by factors like anxiety and lack of comprehensive understanding of the problem structure and components [13]. Thus, it is no surprise that students who are visually impaired tend to under-perform in mathematics compared to their sighted peers, as the lack of fully accessible materials and the lack of mechanisms that allow them to compose the logical steps of a problem solving process exacerbates the level of anxiety and reduces the overall problem comprehension [15].

Students who are visually impaired rely on their teachers at school to learn algebra, and they use Braille writers to apply what they learn in class, with parents help in very rare cases. It is apparent that visually impaired students lack sufficient help and tools in learning algebra. For one reason, teachers cannot be located with their students in the same site all the time, moreover, graphing calculators and other tools that provide final answers do not help students learn, since they tend to remove from students (and perform automatically) critical steps in the problem solving process. On the other hand, Braille writers require the entire work to be entirely redone in case a slight mistake is made by the student; this is tedious, and students receive no help on how to handle the steps in the resolution of algebraic problems. This state of affairs contributes to the lack of adequate mathematical literacy in higher education for students with visual impairments [12].

It is not yet completely possible for students with impaired vision to manipulate mathematics on computers and learn by doing that. Thus, there is a persistent need for a new approach through which students with varying severity levels of visual impairments can manipulate mathematics with minimal effort from their regardless their proficiency level of mathematics [3]. However, in order to gain success and compete as an effective solution, this approach has to exhibit certain behaviors; i.e., the system in [7] provided a good solution, but different severity levels of visual impairments and different algebra mastery levels of were not taken into consideration.

2   A New Framework

In this project, we propose a novel framework, aiming at enabling students who are visually impaired in middle and high school levels to learn algebraic skills while manipulating algebraic equations in an interactive web-based multi-layer system that provides cues and help for algebraic transformations needed to solve equations.

Adding to the features in [8], the "learning by doing" and "trial and error" directions are stressed in the new system. While Braille writer is equivalent to "paper and pencil" in manipulating algebra, the new system offers more than just that single feature; the workspace the system is based gives many options and domain specific functions to select from, it facilitates faster manipulation with minimal editing efforts, and it enables easier recovery and review of the work done so far.

Unlike math editing tools that are not customized to manipulation purpose, do not give special manipulation functions, and require students to entirely edit every single sub-expression (even for sub-expressions that are not involved in the transformation made so far in the very recent action) over and over each time a new step is reached, manipulation in the new framework is easier since students apply manipulation functions over sub-expressions of the equation by selection: the sub-expression of interest is selected, and so is the manipulation function required at certain point.

The previous image of transformation is repeatedly applied on the equation and only some sub-parts of the equation get affected after that type of manipulation is applied on them. Outcome of any transformation is made available through providing the new equation that has undergone some manipulation without having the student re-write the entire previous equation of which large portions remained unchanged. In fact, students in the new system need no editing effort at all; the system responds to their manipulation choices and reflects their preferences on the resulting equation.

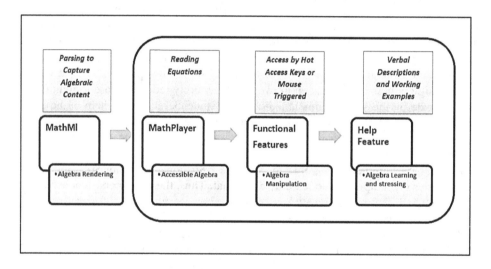

Fig. 1. The framework design: structure and modules

By facilitating the selection of equation sub-expressions, and providing custom manipulation functions for transforming equations accordingly, students proceed faster in a hierarchy of manipulation steps until reaching into a complete solution that is recoverable and reviewable; any step in can be redone and accessed for reviewing the equation that has been reached into at that step, what manipulation it has undergone, and the number of that step in the hierarchy. The equation sub-expressions can be -upon demand- reviewed one at a time in the same way as their parent equation.

Supported by a help feature, each manipulation function can be previewed for grasping its effect and the circumstances at which it can be applied, it is also supported by two different examples that demonstrate how to use that function, what outcomes it results in when applied, and when it is optimally invoked. The help feature can be invoked as many times as students want. There is no limit on how to benefit from this feature, and there is no embarrassing situation students might fall in as if they were at a classroom in front of their peers and asking for help repeatedly, and as a result, students are no longer discouraged to ask for help.

This approach is different from other approaches that solve equations and give instant solutions. The described system is to encourage visually impaired students do the job themselves and build algebraic skills: practice, learn, and master the concepts of the subject by doing algebraic exercises and exploring their building blocks.

3   A Multi-layer System

Authors of [10] proposed USID method that stressed the design issues that have to be taken into account; support of heterogeneous user characteristics, support of adaptive interface, and support for accessibility, and involvement of target user group in the testing phase. In adopting the previous aspects, the non-visual electronic workspace for learning algebra came multi-layered to facilitate learning algebra manipulation by mapping visually impaired students to particular layers in the framework each according to their characteristics; type of visual impairment, severity of the disability accessibility approaches needed, and proficiency level of the subject in accordance to [10,14]. Transition from one layer to another higher one occurs when students exhibit mature performance at that layer, and by then they qualify to switch to more abstract layer that does not require them to perform each little detail of manipulation; as they are assumed to have al-ready built certain skills in previous more basic layers. The support of heterogeneous user characteristics through the framework layers is clear in two aspects:

- Supporting students regardless their proficiency level of mathematics manipulation. Students differ in the pace at which they master mathematical concepts and build skills. Nevertheless, when students advance from one level to another, the behavior of the system has to change relatively; i.e., no need to treat the student as novice in particular aspects of the subject they are supposed to have already built solid background about. The framework gives students three levels of manipulation workspaces; basic, intermediate, and advanced.
- Supporting students who have minor, moderate, or severe impaired vision. The support of distinct characteristics for each category is made through the various approaches that end-users can select from to apply major features of the framework; i.e., magnification, audible rendering, mouse interaction, keyboard interaction, voice commands, and hot access keys.

The interface supports adjusting settings like: font color, font size, background color, and magnification level of the workspace. The framework also supports two modes of interaction: learning mode, and regular mode where no hints given to students when they manipulate algebra. Students were involved in the whole development process, starting from requirements specification phase to explicitly elaborate their needs, within design phase to validate parts of the planned solution, reaching to evaluation and testing for assessing the framework. Think aloud strategy was followed in the evaluation process, in addition to conducting interviews, discussions, and questionnaires.

4   Design and Structure

The design is based on using MathML standard for encoding algebraic equations so that they can be rendered online to support a web-based workspace. In conjunction to embedding MathPlayer plug-in [9], TTS voice feedback, hot access keys, and zooming features (to support students with residual vision), a description and two illustrative examples are contained in a help file associated to each offered algebraic trans-formation option such as: Add, Subtract, Multiply, Divide By, Apply Root, Raise to Power, Cancel, Delete, Combine Like Terms, Insert, and more. Reading equations, going back and forth between steps, cancelling steps, and working on parts of the equation are also included. The basic structure and modules of the system are shown in figure 1.

MathPlayer helps rendering algebraic equations that are encoded in MathML. TTS gives instant or on-demand feedback when applying any of the manipulation functions supported by the system, steps details, contents of dialogue or input boxes, error messages, and more. The system employs hot access keys to invoke and apply manipulation functions, to navigate between sub-expressions, and to invoke any component on the workspace. Hot access keys also help track the student input and interaction with the system. Students with time exhibit easy recall of the hot access keys they need in order to interact with the system. For students to figure out what particular hot access key is set up for a certain function, the system is supported by a help file that contains all shortcuts of hot access keys.

Zooming in and out features are also supported in the system to adjust the display size. The need for zooming features came after interviewing some low vision students who with the help of magnifiers are able to see objects. Some students interviewed worked well with enlarging the display size of the workspace, they used mouse keys for interaction, however, some of the students who had severe visual impairment did not use zooming adjustments and they relied on hot access keys to access the workspace content, they did not use the mouse. Sighted students (not a target end-user) faced no problems working on the workspace either by using the mouse or by hot access keys. The interaction option is left to the student's choice if the level of disability was manageable. However students with severe vision impairment or blindness have no choice in the interaction options.

Figure 2 illustrates the interface of the workspace. On top is the original equation captured from a webpage. Underneath that are the zooming options and "Start" button, that was clicked and the rest of the components in the image appeared as a result. Below zooming options is a caption that details the step number, what has been applied before so that the current equation yielded as a result, in this example no previous steps, so the caption is limited to indicating that it is the starting point of the work. Below the caption is the current equation in the hierarchy. Underneath the recent equation are the sub-expressions resulted from that equation decomposition. Each sub-expression is assigned to a radio button so that they can be selected for manipulation. The buttons at the bottom are the manipulation functions the system provides.

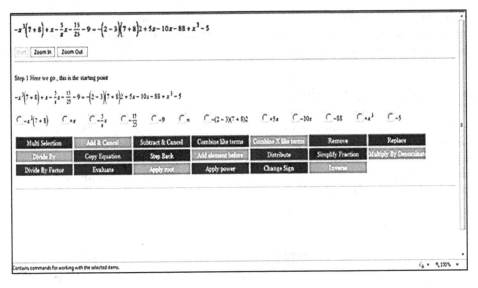

Fig. 2. The workspace of the system

5   Methodology and Testing

Several experiments using a system prototype were conducted evaluating the system. The prototype involved most functional features of the designed workspace: Add, Subtract, Multiply, Divide By, Apply Root, Raise to Power, Cancel, Delete, Combine Like Terms, Insert, and more. A demonstration how to manage the interaction with the workspace components was given to students in advance. The feedback received from the students was collected by observations, interviews, and think-aloud strategy. The goal of the evaluation was to observe to what extent algebraic transformations are easily applied to solve equations via the system compared to the conventional way of doing that. In addition; observing the effectiveness of the system in helping students learn the subject: selecting the right function, the logical order of applying transformations, and the accuracy of final answers. Several experiments were prepared including a prototype of the system with at least four couples of equations covering three degrees of equations: linear, quadratic, and cubic. The levels of equations were simple, average, and slightly hard.

Five participants who have vision impairment were involved in the experiments; two females and three males, aged 13-16 with average academic achievement in algebra, and a disability levels moderate to severe. The participants were asked to perform the "Think Aloud" strategy when they were working on the system. An interview followed the experiments to get the participants feedback and comments. In each of the experiments, participants were asked to solve the given equations by two approaches: the first day through the conventional way they use (CCTV or Braille writer), and the second day through the system after it was fully introduced to them by a demo. Time each student needed to solve the equations, answers reached, mistakes made, were recorded for each participant; in addition to the observations made on how they learnt through the system.

6   Preliminary Results

Most participants made mistakes in solving equations in both approaches; the mistakes were in the priority of applying transformations. Time spent on solving equations was relative to the equation complexity and the student's proficiency of algebra. However, the relative time enhanced after the first two couples of equations especially in the new system as it guided the participants solutions in some way.

Table 1. Comparison between conventional way and new system

Average Experiment	Conventional		New System	
	Time	**Mistakes**	**Time**	**Mistakes**
1	4 min	2	4 min	2
2	5 min	2	4 min	1
3	5.5 min	3	4.5 min	2
4	5 min	2	4.5 min	1

The accuracy of solutions enhanced using our system after invoking the "Help" feature associated with options that the participants were not sure whether they could or not apply at some point. In the "Think aloud" strategy we followed in the experiments, some of the participants were thinking of getting the help of the options provided in the system before applying them, they also were thinking of trying these options and see their effects, they did not bother doing that due to the ease of returning back one step to correct the mistakes they made, in the third experiment most participants avoided trying some of the transformations they already grasped how they perform previously. Results are shown in table 1.

References

1. Archambault, D., Fitzpatrick, D., Gupta, G., Karshmer, A.I., Miesenberger, K., Pontelli, E.: Towards a Universal Maths Conversion Library. In: Miesenberger, K., Klaus, J., Zagler, W., Karshmer, A.I. (eds.) ICCHP 2004. LNCS, vol. 3118, pp. 664–669. Springer, IHeidelberg (2004)
2. Karshmer, A., Pontelli, E., Gupta, G.: Helping visually impaired students in the study of mathematics. In: 29th Annual Frontiers in Education Conference, FIE 1999, vol. 2, pp. 12C4/5–12C410 (1999)

3. Karshmer, A.I., Bledsoe, C.: Access to Mathematics by Blind Students - Introduction to the Special Thematic Session. In: Miesenberger, K., Klaus, J., Zagler, W. (eds.) ICCHP 2002. LNCS, vol. 2398, pp. 471–476. Springer, Heidelberg (2002)
4. Beal, C.R., Shaw, E.: Working memory and math problem solving by blind middle and high school students: implications for universal access. In: Proceedings of the 19th International Conference for Information Technology and Teacher Education (2008)
5. Pontelli, E., Gupta, G., Karshmer, A.: Mathematics Accessibility. In: Universal Access Handbook. CRC Press (2009)
6. Educational software. Wikipedia, The Free Encyclopedia (January 30, 2012), http://en.wikipedia.org/w/index.php?title=Educational_softwa re&oldid=473974948 (retrieved from February 13, 2012)
7. Fayezur Rahman, M.: Hierarchical Manipulation of Mathematical Expressions for Visually Impaired Students. In: Proceedings of the 5th Winona Computer Science Undergraduate Research Symposium, pp. 8–15 (2005), doi:9/01/2011, http://cs.winona.edu/ CSConference/2005conference.pdf (retrieved)
8. Alajarmeh, N., Pontelli, E., Son, T.: From "Reading" Math to "Doing" Math: A New Direction in Non-visual Math Accessibility. In: Stephanidis, C. (ed.) HCII 2011 and UAHCI 2011, Part IV. LNCS, vol. 6768, pp. 501–510. Springer, Heidelberg (2011)
9. Soiffer, N.: Mathplayer: web-based math accessibility. In: ASSETS3905. ACM Press, Baltimore (2005)
10. Nganji, J.T., Nggada, S.H.: Disability-Aware Software Engineering for Improved System Accessibility and Usability. International Journal of Software Engineeering and Its Applications (IJSEIA) 5(3), 47–62 (2011)
11. Selden, J., Selden, A.: Using Technology to Implement a Constructivist Approach to Calculus and Abstract Algebra. In: Annual Conference on Technology in Collegiate Mathematics (1988)
12. Senge, J.: Building a Bridge to College: Success in K-12. In: C-SUN Conference (1998)
13. Osborne, J.W.: Linking Stereotype Thread and Anxiety: Physiological and Cognitive Evidence. Educational Psychology 27 (2007)
14. Gregor, P., Newell, A.F., Zajicek, M.: Designing for dynamic diversity: interfaces for older people. In: Proceedings of the Fifth International ACM Conference on Assistive Technologies (Assets 2002), pp. 151–156. ACM, New York (2002)
15. Dick, Kubiak, E.: Issues and Aids for Teaching Mathematics to the Blind. Mathematics Teacher 90 (1997)

Interaction Design for the Resolution of Linear Equations in a Multimodal Interface

Silvia Fajardo-Flores and Dominique Archambault

EA 4004 – CHArt-THIM
Université Paris 8, France
silvia.fajardo-flores@etud.univ-paris8.fr,
dominique.archambault@univ-paris8.fr

Abstract. This article belongs to the field of Human-Computer Interaction, in the context of the access to Mathematics for people with visual disabilities. In a school scenario, the students with blindness who learn Algebra need to work on mathematical expressions, to collaborate and to communicate with their classmates and teacher. This interaction is not straightforward between students with and without sight, due to the different modalities they use in order to represent mathematical contents and to work with them. The computer presents a great opportunity to promote this type of interaction, because it allows the multimodal representation of mathematical contents. After the conduction of experiments on linear equation solving with students with and without sight, we have modelled their intentions and actions and we present a proposal for the interactions required in a multimodal interface serving this purpose. Lastly, we consider the possibilities and limitations for implementation.

Keywords: visual disability, accessibility, mathematics, HCI.

1 Introduction

The access to mathematics and sciences in general for students with visual disabilities remains a challenge for both educators and researchers. The difficulties are diverse, and they concern the presentation and communication of contents, and the facilitation to perform calculations [1,2]. In a school scenario, students who begin to learn Algebra need to take notes, understand and solve exercises, practise operations related to expressions and solving methods, and communicate with their teacher and peers. This interaction is complicated between students with and without sight, due to the different representation of contents they use. The computer presents a great opportunity to promote interaction between sighted and non-sighted people, because it allows for the multimodal representation of contents and the facilitation of simultaneous access in a common interface. The design of an accessible interface for linear equation solving requires a thorough understanding of the needs of sighted and non-sighted users. In a previous experiment we have identified the user intentions for linear equation solving [3]. The aim of this paper is to present the modelling of those actions,

K. Miesenberger et al. (Eds.): ICCHP 2012, Part I, LNCS 7382, pp. 166–173, 2012.
© Springer-Verlag Berlin Heidelberg 2012

and to propose the interaction features to enable sighted and non-sighted users to work in a synchronised interface.

2   Software Support to Do Mathematics

There exist educational software allowing a complete range of manipulations to work with Algebra at least at a basic level. Examples of this type of software are APLUSIX [4], PIXIE [5] and VP Algebra. A different type of software to do mathematics is the Computer Algebra Systems (CAS), such as MuPAD, Sage, Axiom and Mathematica. These CAS function as symbolic calculators, receiving an expression as input and returning the requested answer with no feedback of the solving process, and therefore they are not recommended for students who begin to learn Algebra. Though they have been used for more advanced calculations, they are suggested to represent an obstacle for the development of algebraic symbolism in students [6,7], due to the finding that in the context of learning with a computer-based environment, the interactions on the machine will play an important role in the student's construction of meaning [8,9]. Following an analysis of the didactical problems related to the functionality of CAS, the Texas Instruments company developed the Symbolic Math Guide (SMG) software for its TI-92 calculator [10]. The SMG allows users to choose the transformations to be applied to the equations and gives feedback on the partial result. All these software applications, though complete in functionality, are not fully accessible for use with screen readers or Braille displays.

The accessibility of mathematical contents for learning has been the subject of several research and software development projects. The Math Genie [11,12] was one of the first efforts to aid students with blindness understand the structure of expressions. Using the keyboard, students are able to browse equations, fold and unfold its subexpressions; the software uses both visual and audio output. The Lambda system [13] is the result of a European project aimed to facilitate the edition and manipulation of expressions for students with blindness. Lambda allows users to write mathematical expressions in a proprietary linear notation, and uses an 8-dot Braille code output in combination with a screen reader. The MaWEn prototypes have been developed for experimenting interaction models. They are based on the synchronous presentation of two views: graphical and Braille, supporting multiple codes; they allow trans-modal pointing and selection of terms or subexpressions [2,14], and include assistants for simplification and manipulation [1,15]. Even though these software and prototypes are accessible and were conceived to facilitate doing mathematics to students with blindness, their possibilities of manipulation are limited.

3   Linear Equation Solving: Understanding Student Goals and Actions

It is suggested that the solution of linear equations belongs to a domain that can be easily characterised and studied [16]. In a study with sighted participants conducted by [17], the solving strategies and actions performed by college students were analysed and organised in three stages:

Attraction. Organisation of occurrences of the unknown in a way that they can be simplified further. e.g. $3x + 1 = x + 2 \rightsquigarrow 3x - x = 2 - 1$

Collection. Addition of common terms in order to reduce the occurrences of the unknown. e.g. $3x - x = 2 - 1 \rightsquigarrow 2x = 1$

Isolation. Elimination of the structure that surrounds the unknown, with the purpose of finding its value. e.g. $2x = 1 \rightsquigarrow x = 1/2$

The results of the study showed that students repeated one or more of these stages depending on their solving strategy, and that the number of repetitions depended on the proficiency of the participant. On the other hand, in our previous study [3] we observed the actions of students with and without sight using an oral protocol, with the aim to compare their needs and look for possible differences in intentions or actions. The exercises included in the experiment required simplifying common terms, multiplying monomials, binomials and polynomials, and solving a linear equation, which were identified in [18] as essential tasks in basic Algebra. It is suggested that equation solving demands the systematic execution of actions depending in the individual strategy, with no regard of visual ability. In terms of interactions, we identified two critical requirements: direct access to specific terms of the equation and minimisation of the user's mental load. These features are considered as fundamental in our proposal.

4   Action Modelling

The actions performed by the participants of our previous study can be categorised in stages, some of which can be matched with those from the study by [17]. These stages represent the intentions of the participants, expressed either explicitly or implicitly.

4.1   Verification

Consists of the analysis of the state of the equation throughout the solving process, beginning by grasping the structure of the equation and the preparation of the solving strategy, continuing by checking the partial result of the applied operation, or searching for other information.

4.2   Simplification: Attraction and Collection

Simplification is the most basic and frequent stage. In our context, it consists in organising and adding common terms. In the frame of the analysis by [17], simplification consists of a combination of the stages of *Attraction* and *Collection*. We will use these terms in our discussion as means to characterise systematically the actions required to carry out a simplification.

4.3 Distribution

Solving a linear equation often requires multiplying monomials, binomials and polynomials. Performing these operations without an adequate external support puts into evidence the limitations of human memory, such as the difficulty of remembering multiple terms and the consequent need to look for them constantly.

4.4 Isolation

This stage consists of removing the surrounding structure of the unknown. It requires the application of transformations on both sides of the equation, which operationally could also be achieved by transposing a term to the opposite member and changing its sign. *Isolation* shares some common actions with *Attraction*.

Table 1 shows the different stages in resolution carried on by two participants. It can be observed that the solving strategies vary, but the actions are similar.

Table 1. Solving strategies of two participants

Equation	Stages/Actions	Equation	Stages/Actions
$x + 2(x + 2(x + 2)) = x + 2$	Attraction Transpose x, $+2$ Change sign	$x + 2(x + 2(x + 2)) = x + 2$	Attraction Add $-x$ on both sides
$-x - 2 + x + 2(x + 2(x + 2)) = 0$	Distribution Multiply $2(x + 2)$	$-x + x + 2(x + 2(x + 2)) = x + 2 - x$	Collection Eliminate instances of x
$-x - 2 + x + 2(x + 2x + 4) = 0$	Collection Add common terms (in parentheses)	$2(x + 2(x + 2)) = 2$	Isolation Divide by 2
$-x - 2 + x + 2(3x + 4) = 0$	Distribution Multiply $2(3x + 4)$	$x + 2(x + 2) = 1$	Attraction Transpose x Change sign
$-x - 2 + x + 6x + 8 = 0$	Verification Find common terms in x Collection Add common terms Verification Find independent terms Arithmetic simplification Add common terms	$2(x + 2) = 1 - x$	Distribution Multiply $2(x + 2)$
$-2 + 6x + 8 = 0$		$2x + 4 = 1 - x$	Attraction Add x on both sides
		$x + 2x + 4 = 1 - x + x$	Collection Add common terms (left member) Add common terms (right member)
		$3x + 4 = 1 - x + x$	Isolation Add -4 on both sides
$6x + 6 = 0$	Isolation Transpose 6 Change sign Divide by 6	$3x + 4 = 1$	Arithmetic simplification Add common terms
$6x = -6$ $x = -1$		$-4 + 3x + 4 = 1 - 4$	Isolation Divide by 3
		$3x = -3$	
		$x = -1$	

5 Interaction Design Proposal

The main objectives of the interface we aim to design are the facilitation of the manipulation tasks involved in learning Algebra, and the communication of contents between sighted and non-sighted students. It is important to clarify that we are not implying that learning Algebra is about manipulating equations. The teaching method must be determined by the teacher, while our interface will enable students to write equations, work with them, and communicate with peers.

The features proposed here aim at facilite access while maintaining automatisation features to a minimum, so that it is the user and not the system that produces the results. Some requirements from other works are implicitly taken into account, such as: navigation within the expression [1,2,11], minimisation of errors caused by memory limitations, and localisation of relevant positions [15]. On the other hand, it is important to consider the allowance for error making, which is inherent to the learning process. In this regard, our proposal allows the possibility to commit execution and arithmetic errors. e.g., Errors resulting from mentally adding coefficients, or from applying an invalid operation such as adding terms of different variables or exponents.

5.1   Use Case Diagrams

The user actions and stages have been organised in use case diagrams. These diagrams, shown in Figure 1, include edition features such as type, delete, copy/paste and select/unselect terms. The use cases that require previous selection are indicated with an asterisk (*).

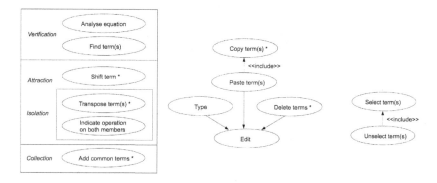

Fig. 1. Use Case Diagrams

5.2   Interaction Features

The use cases can be put into operation by enabling typing, browsing and edition of equations in the interface. Edition involves the use cases for writing and transforming the equation in the stages of *Attraction, Collection* and *Isolation.* Browsing corresponds to the *Analyse equation* use case in the non visual modality, and enables the search for terms needed in most use cases. In addition to the manual work with the equation, our proposal includes auxiliary interactions intended to provide an option to minimise the number of key presses, accelerating the access while maintaining the nature of the task. We do not make a distinction between interactions for sighted and non-sighted users, but the options we propose aim to facilitate access for both. The interactions for each use case are organised and described as follows:

Edition. Users will be able to type, delete and modify terms. Typing will involve the use of numbers, basic operators [+, -, *, /], the usual letters to represent variables, avoiding those that could result ambiguous such as f and d. Up and Down arrows will be used to indicate the beginning and the end of an exponent. Automatic conversion to Presentation MathML will follow each typed character, and will have in turn an audio output. Copy, Paste and Delete commands are considered in edition. Selection is required for many of the use cases: pressing a function key when the cursor is in the position of the desired term will select it. The selection of terms will be kept until the user explicitly indicates end of selection.

Browsing. Equations will be shown on the screen and will also be available in audio on keyboard browsing. Visual and audio output and feedback will be synchronised. Users will be able to navigate: 1) by term or operator, 2) by element within the active term (coefficient, variable, exponent), and c) by line. The unity of navigation by default will be the term. In order to facilitate navigation between lines, we propose to keep the last position of the cursor in each line. Since selection will be persistent, we consider the possibility to alternate the cursor position from the active line to the list of selected terms. This could help minimise the change between lines and probably facilitate the follow-up on distributions.

Auxiliary Interactions. Auxiliary interactions will be available through the use of commands. They include options for finding, writing or reorganising terms faster than if done manually. The proposed auxiliary interactions are: *Find Term [...], Find Common Terms in [...], Transpose, Add term to both sides, Divide by term,* and *Add coefficients.* e.g. A simplification would involve browsing the equation in order to find all terms of a certain exponent, for example x^2, then adding them and writing their sum in the resulting line; by using commands, the operation could be done faster by using either or both commands *Find Common Terms in* $[x^2]$ and *Add coefficients.*

5.3   Implementation Issues and Limitations

The freedom of browsing, writing and manipulation, as well as the allowance for error considered in our proposal, require a high degree of difficulty in implementation. Contrary to literary text, mathematical expressions are bi-dimensional; the current state of technology to display them involves the use of mark-up languages such as Presentation MathML, Content MathML and OpenMath, which allow to display the expressions but do not allow direct browsing and edition. For the implementation of this proposal we have chosen Presentation MathML, because it has a more direct correspondence with human reading and writing than Content MathML, and therefore it allows immediate translation. In addition to that, other software tools have been developed to manipulate Presentation MathML. In order to provide audio feedback, we have considered two possibilities: 1) synchronisation with the user's screen reader, or 2) use of an internal screen reader.

While users are accustomed to browsing and editing by character, which is the default behaviour for text editors, the introduction of default browsing behaviour by term or by subexpression might affect the user's perception of the consequent edition behaviour. Regarding deletion of terms, we have considered a delete-within-current-term protocol as default, and an alternative select-first-then-delete protocol. The replacement of existing terms could imply the introduction of an explicit indication that a change is going to be made to them, in order to avoid errors of unwanted replacement. On the other hand, the introduction of a replacement mode would add complexity for the user.

The feature of persisting selection is particularly subject to observation, since its behaviour differs from text edition where selection is lost on change of cursor position. In the case that this feature would be confusing for the user, an alternative option for marking terms is considered, in order to differentiate it from common selection. All features proposed here are subject to user testing, in order to find out the protocols that suit best each interaction.

5.4   Conclusion

The features desired in a multimodal interface to solve linear equations and the operations related to them could be summarised in: facilitation of direct access to the terms of the equation and minimisation of mental load. After analysis and categorisation of the user actions, we have defined the interactions for the interface, taking into account both visual and non-visual representation. The proposal presented here considers browsing by term and subexpression, which might affect the users' perception on the behaviour of the edition features in relation to text editors. Having considered several alternatives of interaction, we expect this proposal to serve as basis for the development of a prototype which will be subject to user testing, in order to validate its effectiveness from the perspective of students and teachers. By providing a way to facilitate the transformation of equations, and along with an adequate teaching method, this prototype is expected to be useful to facilitate the understanding of algebraic concepts, since it will be the user and not the system who will decide on the transformations and produce the results.

References

1. Miesenberger, K.: Doing mathematics (2008),
   http://www.ascience-thematic.net/en/conferences/paris/Miesenberger
2. Archambault, D.: Non visual access to mathematical contents: State of the art and prospective. In: Proceedings of the WEIMS Conference 2009 (The Workshop on E-Inclusion in Mathematics and Science), pp. 43–52 (2009)
3. Fajardo Flores, S., Archambault, D.: Understanding algebraic manipulation: Analysis of the actions of sighted and non-sighted students. In: Yamaguchi, K., Suzuki, M. (eds.) The International Workshop on Digitization and E-Inclusion in Mathematics and Science 2012 (DEIMS 2012) (2012)

4. Nicaud, J.F.: A general model of algebraic problem solving for the design of interactive learning environments. In: Ponte, J., et al. (eds.) Mathematical Problem Solving and New Information Technologies. NATO ASI Series, vol. 89, pp. 267–285. Springer, Heidelberg (1992)
5. Sleeman, D.H.: Inferring (mal) rules from pupils' protocols. In: Proceedings of the European Conference on Artificial Intelligence, pp. 160–164 (1982)
6. Artigue, M.: Learning mathematics in a cas environment: The genesis of a reflection about instrumentation and the dialectics between technical and conceptual work. International Journal of Computers for Mathematical Learning 7, 245–274 (2002)
7. Monaghan, J.: Computer algebra, instrumentation and the anthropological approach. International Journal for Technology in Mathematics Education 14(2), 63–72 (2007)
8. Balacheff, N.: Artificial intelligence and mathematics education: Expectations and questions. In: Herrington, T. (ed.) Proceedings of the 14th Biennal of the AAMT, pp. 1–24 (1993)
9. Drijvers, P., Gravemeijer, K.: Computer algebra as an instrument: Examples of algebraic schemes. In: Guin, D., Ruthven, K., Trouche, L. (eds.) The Didactical Challenge of Symbolic Calculators: Turning a Computational Device Into a Mathematical Instrument. Springer, Heidelberg (2005)
10. Özgün Koca, A., Edwards, M.T.: Symbolic math guide: An innovative way of teaching and learning algebra using ti-89 and ti-92+ graphing calculators. In: Proceedings of the 2nd International Conference on the Teaching of Mathematics (at the Undergraduate Level). John Wiley & Sons Inc. (2002)
11. Gillan, D.J., Barraza, P., Karshmer, A.I., Pazuchanics, S.: Cognitive Analysis of Equation Reading: Application to the Development of the Math Genie. In: Miesenberger, K., Klaus, J., Zagler, W., Burger, D. (eds.) ICCHP 2004. LNCS, vol. 3118, pp. 630–637. Springer, Heidelberg (2004)
12. Karshmer, A.I., Bledsoe, C., Stanley, P.B.: The Architecture of a Comprehensive Equation Browser for the Print Impaired. In: Miesenberger, K., Klaus, J., Zagler, W., Burger, D. (eds.) ICCHP 2004. LNCS, vol. 3118, pp. 614–619. Springer, Heidelberg (2004)
13. Schweikhardt, W., Bernareggi, C., Jessel, N., Encelle, B., Gut, M.: LAMBDA: A European System to Access Mathematics with Braille and Audio Synthesis. In: Miesenberger, K., Klaus, J., Zagler, W., Karshmer, A.I. (eds.) ICCHP 2006. LNCS, vol. 4061, pp. 1223–1230. Springer, Heidelberg (2006)
14. Archambault, D., Stöger, B., Batusic, M., Fahrengruber, C., Miesenberger, K.: A software model to support collaborative mathematical work between braille and sighted users. In: Ninth International ACM SIGACCESS Conference on Computers and Accessibility (ASSETS 2007) (2007)
15. Stöger, B., Miesenberger, K., Batušić, M.: Mathematical Working Environment for the Blind Motivation and Basic Ideas. In: Miesenberger, K., Klaus, J., Zagler, W.L., Burger, D. (eds.) ICCHP 2004. LNCS, vol. 3118, pp. 656–663. Springer, Heidelberg (2004)
16. Anderson, J.: Human symbol manipulation within an integrated cognitive architecture. Cognitive Science 29, 313–341 (2005)
17. Carry, L., Lewis, C., Bernard, J.: Psychology of equation solving: An information processing study. Technical report, The University of Texas at Austin (1979)
18. Stöger, B., Batušić, M., Miesenberger, K., Haindl, P.: Supporting Blind Students in Navigation and Manipulation of Mathematical Expressions: Basic Requirements and Strategies. In: Miesenberger, K., Klaus, J., Zagler, W., Karshmer, A.I. (eds.) ICCHP 2006. LNCS, vol. 4061, pp. 1235–1242. Springer, Heidelberg (2006)

Development of Software for Automatic Creation of Embossed Graphs

Comparison of Non-visual Data Presentation Methods and Development Up-to-Date

Tetsuya Watanabe[1], Toshimitsu Yamaguchi[2], and Masaki Nakagawa[2]

[1] University of Niigata, Faculty of Engineering, Niigata, Japan
t2.nabe@eng.niigata-u.ac.jp
[2] Graduate School of University of Niigata, Niigata, Japan
{t.yamaguchi@eng,t12c114b@mail.cc}.niigata-u.ac.jp

Abstract. To investigate appropriate representation of numerical data to blind people, a user experiment was conducted. Its results have shown that embossed graphs give quicker and correct access to the data than braille and electronic tables. Based on this observation, we started developing software for creation of embossed graphs which can be operated by blind people. Up until now line graphs can be created with this software.

Keywords: Blind People, Tactile Graphs, Tabular Forms, Braille, Mathematics and Science.

1   Introduction

When numerical data are presented in the form of a graph, the substance of the data (e.g. relative sizes, relative ratios, interpretation of trends, etc.) can be understood instantly. Reading graphs by touch takes longer than by sight, but even then, it should be possible to understand the substance of the data more quickly than when presented in tabular forms. Traditionally, many a graph have been transcribed into their tactile versions by volunteers and braille printing houses and many a research have been done to develop systems to do automatic transcription from the viewpoint of accessibility. But the advantages of tactile graphs over tabular forms have not been shown through experiments. Thus, we conducted an experiment, in which sets of numerical data were presented to blind participants in three ways: tabular forms on braille, tablular forms in electronic data, and embossed graphs and then correct rate and reaction times were compared among these methods.

Supposing tactile graphs have their advantages over tables, however, blind persons do not have any means to create graphs by themselves whereas it is easy for sighted people to create visual graphs using spreadsheet software. This situation prevent blind people who are engaged in intellectual work from dealing with and analyzing numerical data by themselves. Thus, the second objective of our research is to develop a system for automatic creation of tactile graphs from numerical data that can be operated by blind people.

K. Miesenberger et al. (Eds.): ICCHP 2012, Part I, LNCS 7382, pp. 174–181, 2012.

2   Related Work

In Japan, as well as in other countries, a lot of efforts have been devoted to transcribe visual graphs into their tactile counterparts by volunteers and braille printing houses. However, the advantages of tactile graphs over tables have not been proven even in pedagological area for special educational needs.

At the same time, many projects are under way to develop systems designed to make graphs accessible to blind users. These systems are classified as follows, depending on the method of presenting graphs and the method of inputting data.

There are three methods of presenting graphs: (1) conveying data via sound pitch and 2-dimensional acoustics [1-2], (2) vocalizing the form of the graph and individual data [2-3], and (3) making graphs tactile [4-5]. It is difficult to convey data accurately with the acoustic method, and moreover, since acoustics are volatile, information can easily be misheard. There are advantages in the method of vocalizing individual values as long as a screen reader is provided. By combining above two methods - using sound pitch and vocalizing values, drawbacks of those methods are alleviated [2]. To interpret trends in the data, however, the shape of the graph has to be imagined inside the user's head.

Tactile graphs, on the other hand,   have the advantage that the general shape of the graph can be understood by touching it, but hardware is needed to generate tactile charts.

There are two methods of inputting data into graphs: (1) reading an electronic file of numerical data, and (2) scanning a printed graph. Although the former method is easier to use, in many cases only textbooks or other printed materials can be obtained. To address this, the method of scanning a graph, dividing it into text and graphics and re-pasting the braille-converted text into the graphics is being studied [4],[6].

We therefore decided to develop software that would easily allow data to be made tactile. This was based on an assumed situation in which users possess electronic data and make them tactile so that they can read the substance of the data by themselves. Research aimed at the same objective is also under way overseas [5]. There, the user is mainly assumed to be a sighted braille transcriber, and the software has a graphical interface. The output is an SVG-format image file, which is printed on capsule paper and passed through a heater to create a tactile graph.

In Japan, on the other hand, there are many users of embossed diagrams as tactile diagrams [7], and there is a good environment for people working in intellectual professions to use braille embossers in the workplace. Our development target, therefore, was software for automatic creation of embossed graphs operated by CUI (character user interface, which is easy for blind persons to use).

3   Experiment

3.1   Purpose

The purpose of the experiment is to investigate which representation method among braille tables, text files and embossed graphs suits blind people best for grasping the trend of the data quickly and correctly.

3.2   Stimuli

Twelve data sets which were comprised of a title, 20 x values, and 20 y values were prepared as stimuli: Three of them represented linear functions, another three inverse proportions, another three quadratic functions, and the remaining three non-correlated. Nine data sets were first calculated from the function they represented. Then, errors up to 10% of each datum were added to y values in order to imitate observed (not idealistic) data and to prevent the participants from easily calculating y values from the functions. Sizes and plus or minus of errors were determined based on the values calculated by the random function of Microsoft Excel. Non-correlated data were also produced using the random function. All data set had the same scopes of x and y values; $0<x<=10$ and $0<y<120$.

A braille table and an embossed graph used in the experiment are shown in Fig.1.

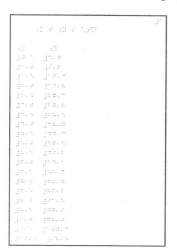 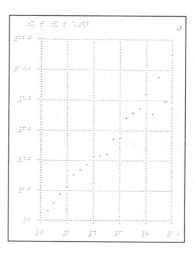

Fig. 1. A braille table (left) and an embossed graph (right) used in the experiment

3.3   Participants

Participants were three blind universty students aging from 19 to 21 who use braille everyday. They have learned mathematics by means of braille textbooks including tactile graphs at a school for the blind. Two of them are majoring mathematics at universities.

3.4   Method

Four data sets representing four functions of the same condition (one of braille table, text file, and embossed graph) were presented to each participant all at once. Participants were then asked to select the function which was best represented by each data set and to explain the selection strategy or the reason for the selection. The experimentor measured the time required for the selection by a stopwatch. Participants were allowed to read the data sets in whichever order and how many times they liked. They were notified in advance that each data set had errors and differed from idealistc values.

There are six permutations to present three data sets. This time, three of them were assigned to three participants. The presenting order is shown in Table 1.

To read an text file, participants used their own personal computers (OS: Windows 7) with various screen readers (VDMW700, JAWS ver. 11, and PC-Talker 7).

Table 1. The order of presenting each condition differed among participants

Participants	A	B	C
First	Embossed graph	Braille table	Text file
Second	Braille table	Text file	Braille table
Third	Text file	Embossed graph	Embossed graph

3.5   Results

Correct Rates: Two out of three participants made perfectly correct answers in all conditions (Table 2). One participant mistook linear and quadratic functions for each other in the braille table and text file conditions. He commneted that these two were hard to distinguish from each other. Nevertheless, he made correct answers in the tactile graph condition in a shorter time.

Reaction Times: All participants carried out the selection with shorter reaction times in the embossed graph condition than in the braille table and text file conditions (Table 3). This phenomenon is observed in all three presenting orders. Between the braille table and text file conditions, participants performed faster in the condition presented later.

Table 2. Correct numbers (numerators) out of questions (denominators)

Participants	A	B	C
Braille table	4/4	2/4	4/4
Text file	4/4	2/4	4/4
Embossed graph	4/4	4/4	4/4

Table 3. Reaction times (minutes:seconds)

Participants	A	B	C
Braille table	4:54	2:45	1:54
Text file	2:01	1:38	8:49
Embossed graph	2:00	0:40	0:26

Selection strategies: Features which were observable or had to be observed (calculated) to distinguish four functions differed in some points between tactile graphs and numerical data (braille table and text file), whereas they are the same between braille table and text file conditions (Table 4).

Table 4. Observed features of each function. Num. and Tac. are abbreviations for numerical data and tactile graph.

Functions	Features	Num.	Tac.
Linear and quadratic functions	General trend: As x grows larger, y grows larger.	*	*
	Ratio of y to x (calculated).	*	
	Changes of y values between neighboring two x values (calculated).	*	
	Plots approach x axis as x values become close to zero (quadratic function).		*
Inverse Proportion	General trend: As x grows larger, y grows smaller.	*	*
	Y values are very large when x values are close to zero.	*	*
	Decreasing rate of y values are very large when x values are close to zero.	*	
	Changes of y values between neighboring two x values (calculated).	*	
	Plots approach x axis as x values become larger.		*
Non-correlated	Changes of y values between neighboring two x values are unstable.	*	
	It felt as if there were multiple grahps or it were a circle.		*

3.6   Comments

- Embossed graphs best suited for grasping the shapes of graphs. It can be achieved instantaneously.
- There was little difference between braille table and text file conditions: It was cumbersome to calculate from numerical data.
- Two participants who are majoring mathematics told that they were willing to use automatic tactile graph creation software when it is available.

3.7   Discussion

The experimental results have shown that tactile graphs are more appropriate for blind people to grasp the relationship between two corresponding variables quickly and correctly than printed or electronic tables. This is due to the difference in understanding strategies: To understand the relationship between x and y written in tables, the ratio of y to x and changes between neighboring y values must be calculated mentally: This calculation is tend to be hindered when the data include errors and deviated from the approximated functions: On the other hand, the shapes of graphs can be understood tactually within a few seconds.

In the future, advantages of tactile graphs should be proven statistically with more participants. Furthermore, disadvantages of them such as tactual limitation on precise reading of quantities should be explored (This would be compensated by using tables.).

4   Development of Software

4.1   System Requirements

After interviewing a researcher with visual impairment who works at a national research institute, we designed the system requirements as follows:

— **Accessibility by Blind Users:** Software should be compatible with screen readers, enabling blind users to operate the system by themselves. CUI will be used in view of its ease of operation by voice. However, if requested by other users, we will also consider adopting GUI.
— **Types of Graphs:** The first development target will be to create bar graphs (including histograms), line graphs and scatter plot graphs.
— **Operating System:** Software should be operated via Linux console. We could consider a Windows environment depending on demand.
— **Braille Embosser:** The targeted embosser is JTR, ESA721 ver.95, which can make embossed diagrams and is widely used in Japan. This model can print three sizes of dots – large (diameter 1.7mm), medium (1.5mm) and small (0.7mm). Plotting accuracy is 0.32mm horizontally and 0.35mm vertically.
— **Graph elements:** Graph elements are images (axes, ticks, grid lines, and graph body) and text (title, axis labels, and unit labels). The user inputs these text elements in *kana* phonetic letters (Japanese alphabet), which are then displayed in braille.
— **Automated Text Control:** Because braille takes up much space, (semi) automated text control functions are necessary. The functions we are planning to implement are showing a message to tell the user to shorten the title when it is too long and overflows the designated space, decreasing the digits of numerical labels, abbreviating the text of labels, and others.

4.2   Tactile Readability

Embossed graphs should be easy to understand by touch, in accordance with guidelines on the creation of tactile graphs and tactile charts in general [8-11]. The main points to bear in mind here are as follows.

Discriminability of Tactile Symbols: We have to use mutually discriminable surface, line and point symbols. Of these, the discriminability of line symbols is particularly important in graphs.

Of the types of dot made by ESA 721 embosser, the small dots are definitely discriminable from the other two sizes, but medium and large dots are harder to discriminate from each other. Therefore, it will only be possible to discriminate two different types with certainty by the type of dot. Changing the intervals between the dots makes various types of lines out of the same size of dots, but only two types can be discriminated with certainty. This will enable us to use four types of lines (two discriminated by different dot sizes and two by different dot intervals).

To make graph lines easily discriminable from grid lines, we intend to use dented dots (embossed from the front of the sheet) and make large enough space (around 3mm) between them by stopping grid lines before graph lines.

Searchability of Tactile Symbols: In line graphs, it has to be easy to search for point symbols from the graph lines. To this end, we either need to use tactually popping-out point symbols, or leave a large enough gap between graph lines and point symbols, or take both of these steps.

4.3   Flow of Operation

The following steps will be followed to create tactile graphs.

1. Read CSV data.
2. Input titles, labels and other text.
3. Set graph display parameters (type of graph, maximum values, minimum values, scale intervals, etc.).
4. Use a braille embosser to print graphs.

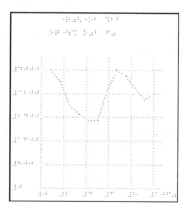

Fig. 2. A line graph created with our system

4.4   Development Up-to-Date

Up until now our system can create line graphs only (Fig. 2). Dented dots for grid lines and automated text control function are not implemented yet.

5   Future Works

Advantages and disadvantages of tactile graphs should be explored thoroughly with more participants.

The development of the software is still under way. When the software is completed, we will conduct experiments to verify its accessibility and tactile readability of graphs. On the accessibility of software, we will verify that blind users can operate the system with a screen reader, and will identify problems in operation. On the tactile readability of graphs, we will verify that lines can be followed and plot searches made accurately.

References

1. Brown, L., Brewster, S., Ramboll, R., Burton, M., Riedel, B.: Design Guidelines for Audio Presentation of Graphs and Tables. In: Proc. of ICAD 2003 (2003)
2. Gardner, J.A.: Access by Blind Students and Professionals to Mainstream Math and Science. In: Miesenberger, K., Klaus, J., Zagler, W. (eds.) ICCHP 2002. LNCS, vol. 2398, pp. 502–509. Springer, Heidelberg (2002)
3. Ferres, L., Verkhogliad, P., Lindgaard, G., Boucher, L., Chretien, A., Lachance, M.: Improving Accessibility to Statistical Graphs: The iGraph-Lite System. In: Proc. of 9th Int. ACM SIGACCESS Conf. Computers and Accessibility, Tempe, pp. 67–74 (2007)
4. Jayant, C., Renzelmann, M., Wen, D., Krisnandi, S., Ladner, R., Comden, D.: Automated Tactile Graphics Translation: In the Field. In: Proc. of 9th Int. ACM SIGACCESS Conf. Computers and Accessibility, Tempe, pp. 75–82 (2007)
5. Goncu, C., Marriott, K.: Tactile Chart Generation Tool. In: Proc. of 10th Int. ACM SIGACCESS Conf. Computers and Accessibility, Halifax, pp. 255–256 (2008)
6. Takagi, N.: Pattern Recognition in Computer-Aided Systems for Transformation of Mathematical Figures into Tactile Graphics. IC-MED J. 3(1), 43–56 (2009)
7. Oouchi, S., Sawada, M., Kaneko, T., Chida, K.: A Survey on Making and Using Tactile Educational Materials in Schools for the Blind. Bulletin Nat. Inst. of Special Education 31, 113–125 (2004) (in Japanese)
8. Edman, P.K.: Tactile Graphics. AFB Press, New York (1992)
9. Eriksson, Y., Strucel, M.: A Guide to the Production of Tactile Graphics on Swellpaper. AB PP Print, Stockholm (1995)
10. Braille Authority of North America, Guidelines and Standard for Tactile Graphics, http://www.brailleauthority.org/tg/index.html
11. Japan Braille Library: An Introduction to Tactile Graphics for Braille Transcription. Japan Braille Library, Tokyo (1986) (in Japanese)

Expression Rules of Directed Graphs for Non-visual Communication

Ryoji Fukuda

Faculty of Engineering Oita University, 700 Dan-noharu Oita 870-1192, Japan
rfukuda@oita-u.ac.jp

Abstract. This paper propose expression rules to describe directed graphs for communication without visual information and corresponding explanation documents. The structures of directed graphs are often complicated especially when they describe visual contents. For the importance of the nodes and edges in these directed graphs, an evaluation method is proposed and this will simplify the structures of the graphs.

1 Introduction

Graphs or figures are prepared to make a target object or objects easily understandable, and many documents contain such elements. However, these elements can prove as barriers for visually impaired persons, even though they are the results of efforts made by sighted persons. These barriers can be overcome, if a suitable equivalent method for capturing the result of these efforts is developed. This study deals with this equivalence and suitability. A significant amount of information can be available at once by using visual information, and this is an important feature of such information. Tactile information is not very capable of conveying a large amount of information and even though auditory information can convey sequential data, a large amount of information can not be captured at once. Thus, when communicating without using visual information, we assume an information unit to be a small packet of information.

Information is often expressed using direct or indirect graphs. Some software tools called idea processors or outline processors have been used to create and arrange ideas or thoughts using graph structures ([1] [2]). In these graphs, units of such thoughts or parameters are represented by nodes and their relations are represented by edges. The units of thoughts and their relations can act as reminders at the time of summarizing the ideas. The convenience provided by these reminders proves the importance of the graphical representation of information. Suppose a geometrical figure, such as a triangle is drawn. One situation may involve the calculation of its area, while another may concentrate only on its three angles. If graphs are suited to each situation, their nodes or their structures may differ each time. Thus, information graphs differ according to the situation, even if they are based on the same figure. Figures may contain different types of information and the corresponding graphs can vary widely. It may be very complicated if all the graphs were to be presented simultaneously. Herein,

K. Miesenberger et al. (Eds.): ICCHP 2012, Part I, LNCS 7382, pp. 182–185, 2012.

we attempt to develop a method to create an optimal graph using a figure, a formula, a table and so on when a description exists. The practical purpose here is the automatic creation of a suitable graph for a given situation. We assume that all the necessary nodes and edges are given and that the situation is described through words. Then our problem is to express the graphs and descriptions, evaluate their nodes and edges, and construct a suitable graph for the situation according to the description. First we define a format to express directed graphs. Next, we decide a format for the descriptions. For the completed information graphs and descriptions expressed using our formats, we estimate values for the nodes and edges in the graph. We can then optimize the graph according to the given description.

2   Expression of Information Graphs

This section explains the format for creating expressions information graphs. The structures of a directed graphs is occasionally closely connected with its usage. In that case, we need to understand conceptual structure of such a graph and develop a method to obtain the graph content.

2.1   Basic Attributes and Data Types

Every attribute has a value type, which could be Char (character), Int (integer), Double (real number), String (character sequence), Name (short character sequence), Vector2 (two-dimensionalvector) and Vector3 (three dimensional vector). The attribute "id" is a running number with which nodes and edges are identified. The attribute "name" can be an identifier in the case where each element has a unique value for "name".

Each XML element corresponds to one data type. The data type is one of the basic attribute value types or a type defined by some class. The word "class" is commonly used in object-oriented programming, and it is a very useful concept in this study. Accordingly we use this word in our expression rules, which are similar to those of C++ language [3]. Every node corresponds to an instance of some class or a basic attribute value. Further, the usage may differ even though the corresponding classes are the same. Fig. 1 is an example of expressions of the definitions.

3   Node Evaluation by Descriptions

3.1   Format of Descriptions

Using the same definitions as for a directted graph, we describe certain properties in this section. The following figure is an example of a description.

```
<DefDesign defName="DgTest2" >
<NodeDef   id="0" name="Node" mess="base node" />
<EdgeDef   id="1" name="Edge" mess="base edge" />
              cccc
<EdgeDef id="005"  fromDefId="002" toDefId="003" name="SpEdge"
                                      mess="special edge" />
</DefDesign>
```

Fig. 1. Example of definition

```
<DgTheorem  name="PythagoreanTheorem">
    <DgPreparation>
        <DgTriangle name="tr" mainTarget="true" />
    </DgPreparation>
    <DgAssumption "right angle">
        . . . . . . .
    </DgAssumption>
    <DgStatement mess="a^2=b^2+c^2">
        <VrbSame>
            <DgObject extCtt="tr.edge1/>
            <DgSubject valType="DgSqSum" >
            <DgReal extCtt="tr.edge2"/>
            <DgReal extCtt="tr.edge3"/>
            </DgSubject>
        </VrbSame>
    </DgStatement>
</EgTheorem>
```

Fig. 2. Example of key event

3.2 Evaluation Rules

The main statement can be categorized into five basic English sentence structures (SV, SVC, SVO, SVOO, and SVOC). This type category is determined by the verb that is described in the common definition. In the above example, the structure of the verb "VrbSame" is SVC. In some elements of a description, there are several objects that correspond to the same classes, which are associated with nodes in a directed graph. Using descriptions with this format, we can estimate the evaluation value of the nodes and edges according to the following rules.

1. The evaluation value of the main target (defined by the attribute "mainTarget") is 100.
2. The evaluation value of a target in "Subject" or "Object" is base value multiplied by 0.7.
3. In an assumption or in a complement, the corresponding base value is multiplied by 0.7.

4. The evaluation value of an edge between the main object and an object in an assumption, a subject, or objects; an object in a subject and objects is similar to the corresponding base value.

The following figure is an example of a simplified information graph.

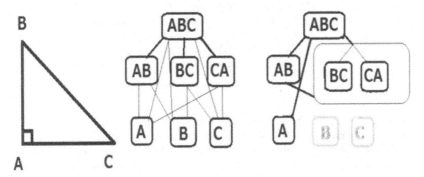

Fig. 3. Simplified Graph

4   Conclusion

Expression formats for directed graphs for visual information, graph editing functions and corresponding descriptions are proposed. Further, evaluation values for nodes and edges in an information graph were obtained, and these values were used to simplify such graphs. However, the proposed rules are not convenient enough unless XML-documents for information graphs and corresponding descriptions are automatically created from some primitive sources of information. This problem will be addressed in our future work.

References

1. Chik, V., Plimmer, B., Hosking, J.: Intelligent Mind-Mapping. In: Proceedings of the 19th Australasian Conference on Computer-Human Interaction: Entertaining User Interfaces. ACM, New York (2007)
2. Midmap editor (web page), http://freemind.sourceforge.net/wiki/index.php/
3. Stroustrup, B.: The C++ Programming Language. Addison-Wesley (1985)

How to Make Unified Modeling Language Diagrams Accessible for Blind Students

Karin Müller

Karlsruhe Institute of Technology
Study Center for the Visually Impaired Students
Engesserstr. 4, 76131 Karlsruhe, Germany
karin.e.mueller@kit.edu
http://www.szs.kit.edu

Abstract. In this paper, we present a survey of the material used in the computer sciences lectures of two blind students showing that they have to deal with a high number and various types of UML diagrams. We also report on different textual representations of UML and present our own solutions. Moreover, we point at a current initiative, BLINDUML, which works at solutions for making UMLs accessible.

Keywords: accessible UML.

1 Introduction

Studying natural sciences, engineering and computer sciences or engineering economics involves knowledge about programming. Many lecturers use the Unified Modeling Language (UML) to teach students object-oriented programming. UMLs are used to make certain aspects of object-oriented programs visible. It is also very common that programmers in companies use UMLs to communicate, design and develop large software systems. Thus, UMLs have become important for programming lectures at universities.

It is a great challenge for blind students to follow those lectures because the different aspects of programming are expressed by visual means. Moreover, the students often have to create UML diagrams themselves. The challenge blind students have to cope with are more complex than for sighted students (especially step (c) & (e)). They need to (a) know the visual shape of the diagrams, (b) understand the semantics of the visual representation, (c) learn an alternative way to design the different aspects of the diagrams, (d) be able to construct the diagrams themselves, (e) communicate with their fellow students and lecturers about the topic and map the descriptions of sighted people to their alternative language for UMLs, (f) learn how to translate the UMLs into programming code.

Usually, it is not possible to skip these lectures and to prove the programming skills with alternative tasks. Moreover, it is an asset to know UML when searching for a qualified job. Thus, the service centers need to know how to make UMLs accessible.

K. Miesenberger et al. (Eds.): ICCHP 2012, Part I, LNCS 7382, pp. 186–190, 2012.

In the past, there were attempts to make UMLs accessible to the blind. The TeDUB system offered a tool that could be used by blind users to read and create UML diagrams [1]. Unfortunately, it does not include revisions of the language. Other attempts developed textual representations of UMLs, e.g. Human-Usable Textual Notation (HUTN) [3] or [4]. However, they only cover few types of diagrams and the first initiative already stopped. We are sure that there are other attempts of service centers to express UMLs textually. A recent approach started to make UML diagrams accessible tactiley with the newly developed HyperBraille display [6].

In the present paper, we present a survey on the study material presented at lectures at two different universities. Section 3 is dedicated to the attempts to make UML diagrams accessible by tactile and textual means. We will discuss the pros and cons of the approaches. Then, we will draw our conclusions.

2   Lectures in Computer Sciences Lectures

In this section, we present a survey on material used at two universities showing the importance to find solutions to make UML diagrams accessible. We supported two blind students during their lectures. One student participated in a basic computer sciences lecture at a university of applied sciences. The second one attended a software engineering lecture at a technical university. The course was based on slides. We analyzed the material of the lectures available for the students. The results are described in Figure 1.

lecture	computer sciences	software engineering
# slides	839	1,361
# graphics	468	425
# UML diagrams	120	313

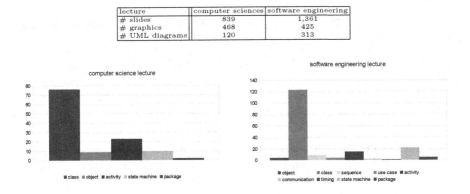

Fig. 1. Number of slides used in the lectures (top), types of UML diagrams at the computer sciences lecture (left) and at the software engineering lecture (right)

The total number of slides for the computer sciences added up to 839 and for the software engineering lecture to 1,361. The number of graphical elements were almost the same, 468 and 425 respectively. Figure 1 shows that at the computer sciences lecture there were 120 (25% of all diagrams) UML diagrams compared to 313 (73%) UML diagrams at the software engineering lecture. The number of diagram types used at the computer sciences lecture was 5 and 9 at the software engineering lecture. Figure 1 reveals that in general, the most frequently used diagram types are class, activity and state machine diagrams. At the computer sciences lecture, class, activity, state machine, object and package diagrams were presented. The most frequently used diagrams at the software engineering lecture were class diagrams followed by state machine, activity, sequence, package, use case, object, communication and timing diagrams. Apart from the high number of slides with UML diagrams, our students had to prepare obligatory exercises. In the software engineering lecture our student had to create object, class, sequence, activity and state diagrams.

3   Attempts to Make UMLs Accessible

We made UMLs accessible in different ways. In a first step, we created all diagram types as tactile graphics. This was necessary to enable our students to follow the lectures and the discussions. Figure 3 (right) displays an example of a sequence diagram pesentend in a lecture. We created a tactile version and printed it with the Emprint of Viewplus. In parallel, we described UML diagrams textually.

class name	shelf
attribute	+take(product:product):void put(product:product):void
methods	

class (multiplicity, role)	type & name of relation, direction	class (multiplicity, role)

Fig. 2. Table describing a class (left), table describing relations between classes (right)

3.1   Textual Solutions

We examined MetaUML, Websequencing and PlantUML and developed our own solutions.

MetaUML allows to create UML diagrams within LaTeX. As most lecturers know LaTeX and our students must learn it as well, we investigated whether MetaUML could be easily used by blind students. However, the code is quite verbose to construct a simple class as a tabular. If a student does not have a visual feedback it is not a suitable method.

Websequencing. There is a web interface which can be used to create sequence diagrams ([5]). It offers a simple description language for a single type of diagrams: sequence diagrams.

PlantUML. When our students attended the lectures, PlantUML only offered two or three types of diagrams and thus, was not an option. However, PlantUML has evolved and now allows seven different types of diagrams (see Fig. 4 (left)).

Our Solutions. For the simpler diagrams such as class, object and state machine diagrams, we developed a table-based approach (see Fig. 2). The table for a class comprises two columns. The first one displays the class name, the attributes and the methods. Relations consist of three columns. More complex diagrams cannot be expressed by tables. A compact list-based language was developed using abbreviations and enumerations (Fig. 4 (right)).

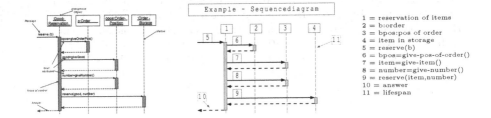

Fig. 3. Original graphic of a sequence diagram (left), tactile graphic (middle) key (right)

```
@startuml                              A -> C: number=giveNumber()
participant ":Good-Reservation" as A   activate C
participant ":o:Order" as B            C - -> A
participant "opos:Order-Position" as C deactivate C
participant ":Order-Storage" as D      A -> D: reserve(good,number)
[-> A: reserve(b)                      activate D
activate A                             D - -> A
A -> B: opos=giveOrderPqs()            deactivate D
activate B                             deactivate A
B - -> A                               ]<- - A
deactivate B                           @enduml
A -> C: good=giveGood
activate C
C - -> A
deactivate C
```

```
participant ":Reserve-Good" as ResGood
participant "o:order" as o
participant "opos:order-position" as opos
participant ":good-storage" as GoodStore

ResGood -> o: opos=giveOrderPos()
o -> ResGood:
ResGood -> opos: item=giveGood()
opos -> ResGood:
ResGood -> opos: number=giveNumber()
opos -> ResGood:
ResGood -> GoodStore: reserve(item, number)
GoodStore -> ResGood:
```

Fig. 4. Same sequence diagrams as in Fig. 3 with PlantUML (left), our solution based on websequencing diagram (right)

4   Discussion and Conclusions

In this paper, we describe the support of two students during their computer sciences and software engineering lectures. We present a survey on their study material. The analysis shows that both students had to deal with a large number UMLs. Tactile graphics helped them to develop a notion of UMLs in the beginning. For more advanced tasks PlantUML can be used. It is an ongoing initiative. Moreover, BLINDUML aims at applying PlantUML for the blind. Thus, it seems to be the most promising approach which might evolve into a standard.

References

1. King, A., Blenkhorn, P., Crombie, D., Dijkstra, S.J., Evans, G., Wood, J.: Presenting UML Software Engineering Diagrams to Blind People. In: Miesenberger, K., Klaus, J., Zagler, W., Burger, D. (eds.) ICCHP 2004. LNCS, vol. 3118, pp. 522–529. Springer, Heidelberg (2004)
2. Rumbaugh, J., Jacobson, I., Booch, G.: The Unified Modeling Language Reference Manual, 2nd edn. Addison-Wesley Professional (2004)
3. Human-Usable Textual Notation (HUTN), http://de.wikipedia.org/wiki/Human-Usable_Textual_Notation (January 31, 2012)

4. Flater, D., Martin, P.A., Crane, M.L.: Rendering UML Activity Diagrams as Human-Readable Text. NISTIR 7469. U.S. Department of Commerce, NIST (2007)
5. Hanov Solutions Inc., Waterloo, Canada http://www.websequencediagrams.com/
6. Loitsch, C., Weber, G.: Viable Haptic UML for Blind People. In: Miesenberger, K., Klaus, J., Zagler, W., Karshmer, A.I. (eds.) ICCHP 2012, Part I. LNCS, vol. 7382, pp. 509–516. Springer, Heidelberg (2012)

AutOMathic Blocks Usability Testing Phase One

Yonatan Breiter, Arthur Karshmer, and Judith Karshmer

University of San Francisco, San Francisco, California, USA
{ygbreiter,akarshmer,jfkarshmer}@usfca.edu

Abstract. The AutOMathic Blocks [1] system has been designed to help young blind students learn arithmetic and beginning algebra through the use of tactile [2, 3] blocks that display their work in two-dimensional space. The traditional method of presenting math problem presentation uses special Braille-like codes that present information in a linear form. It is our hypothesis that learning math via a two-dimensional method will expedite and improve the learning experience for young children. Before upgrading our prototype system, we have chosen to first carry out usability testing experiments testing the advantage of using tactile two-dimensional presentation methods.

Keywords: AutOMathic, Blind, Math.

1   Introduction

The AutOMathic Blocks (see figure 1) system was designed based on the key premise that learning, as well as doing math, would be enhanced through two-dimensional representations of content. Unfortunately, Braille-like math languages can only present math in a linear format with complex embedded notation to help the user in conceptualizing the missing dimensionality inherent in Braille.

Fig. 1. The AutOMathic Blocks Prototype System

K. Miesenberger et al. (Eds.): ICCHP 2012, Part I, LNCS 7382, pp. 191–195, 2012.

2   Test Protocol

Our testing plan is slated for two different testing protocols, 1) basic usability testing, and 2) more advanced cognitive studies. The current paper describes our initial testing concerning the usability of the Braille embossed blocks used in the system.

The protocol is straightforward and only requires equipment that is quite inexpensive. The Braille embossed blocks are stored in a simple plastic "jig" that comes from a commercial version of the Sudoku game. The test grid contains 9 rows by 9 columns.

Figure 2 shows a model of the usability-testing grid, which is used to present arithmetic problems to our subjects. In this case the problem to be solved is: 6687+371 in two-dimensional notation. Figure 3 shows the actual test "jig" as presented to the test subjects.

The top row of the grid has several blocks numbered as 1s and 2s. These blocks have Braille notation on them and are used by the subject to mark a column of the problem space with carry information to aid in problem solution. Below the carry block row is a blank row for placing carry values as appropriate.

Table 1. The Testing Grid Format

Notes	Col 1	Col 2	Col 3	Col 4	Col 5	Col 6	Col 7	Col 8	Col 9
Carry Reservoir	1	1	2	2					
Carry Area									
Upper Test Num					6	6	8	7		
Bottom Test Num					3	7	1			
Solution Space									
Answer Reservoir	0	0	1	1	2	2	3	3	4
Answer Reservoir	4	5	5	6	6	7	7	8	8
Answer Reservoir	9	9							

The next 2 rows are the area in which the problems to be solved are placed. In our early testing we are using only two-dimensional and linear problems with each value being no longer than 4 digits. There is enough space here to present either two-dimensional or linear problems. Directly below the problem values are empty rows for the subject to enter the answer to the problem. Finally, the bottom 3 rows contain a reservoir of blocks from which to choose the correct answer blocks. There are three rows of 2 copies of the digits for 0 to 9. All test problems are computer generated and can be solved by this group of answer blocks (see Figure 4). The numbers above the computer generated problems are for problem identification and are keys to the type of problems presented. For example, the key "4/3 – 7" indicates that the problem contains one 4 digit value and one 3 digit value and is the 7th problem of that type. These codes are useful for record keeping and statistical analysis.

Fig. 2. The Test "jig" composed of visual and Braille labeled blocks

Each block carries a visual representation of its value as well as a transparent Braille representation of the number. Through the use of simple tactile inspection, the student is able to locate numbers in the Answer Reservoir for solving problems. For our first usability testing we are only asking our subjects to solve addition problems, which can require the use of carry information. As the subjects select their numbers, they place them in a Solution Space which is their working space. As the student solves the problems, he/she removes blocks from the Answer Reservoir (see Figure 2) and places them into the appropriate spaces in the Solution Space. All of these activities are totally tactile in nature, except for the sighted population of subjects that worked visually. Each subject is given a series of addition problems with numbers no longer than four digits in length

As the product of each testing period the following data were recovered.

1. Time necessary to solve the problems (quantitative data)
2. The types of problems solved
3. Comments made by the subjects (qualitative data)

4/4-0	4/4-1	4/4-2	4/4-3	4/4-4	4/4-5	4/4-6	4/4-7	4/4-8	4/4-9
4816	4449	4328	3091	1457	1741	6215	4673	1825	2846
5851	2013	6096	9891	3322	1623	8884	4837	1084	4136
10667	6462	10424	12982	4779	3364	15099	9510	2909	6982

4/4-10	4/4-11	4/4-12	4/4-13	4/4-14	4/4-15	4/4-16	4/4-17	4/4-18	4/4-19
6687	3215	3936	5794	2587	6385	8745	2667	327	5867
4371	1203	5845	3815	8132	1939	6108	5703	9821	1409
11058	4418	9781	9609	10719	8324	14853	8370	10148	7276

4/3-0	4/3-1	4/3-2	4/3-3	4/3-4	4/3-5	4/3-6	4/3-7	4/3-8	4/3-9
2855	7118	8789	3976	2107	7015	2863	1860	9485	466
426	354	769	229	972	519	681	635	380	997
3281	7472	9558	4205	3079	7534	3544	2495	9865	1463

4/3-10	4/3-11	4/3-12	4/3-13	4/3-14	4/3-15	4/3-16	4/3-17	4/3-18	4/3-19
6888	9269	1785	1124	5409	4396	6670	2690	2432	5763
901	685	321	624	288	529	187	125	609	632
7789	9954	2106	1748	5697	4925	6857	2815	3041	6395

3/3-0	3/3-1	3/3-2	3/3-3	3/3-4	3/3-5	3/3-6	3/3-7	3/3-8	3/3-9
184	537	196	631	765	854	587	426	153	893
621	345	353	810	961	292	481	659	448	826
805	882	549	1441	1726	1146	1068	1085	601	1719

3/3-10	3/3-11	3/3-12	3/3-13	3/3-14	3/3-15	3/3-16	3/3-17	3/3-18	3/3-19
122	140	455	250	716	822	124	842	952	253
515	295	880	275	102	157	383	891	412	681
637	435	1335	525	818	979	507	1733	1364	934

Fig. 3. The data bank of valid problems

3   Initial Testing

Initial testing was carried out in two distinct locations, San Francisco, California and Verona, Italy. The San Francisco testing was done with sighted subjects from both the University of San Francisco and the local community, while the Verona testing was done with blind lower school and adult students. In total, over 110 tests[1] were conducted.

At first glance, the results were intriguing. While the adult, sighted students took considerably less time to solve their test problems than the non-sighted students in

---

[1] The majority of our subjects were sighted, as it is difficult to locate groups of blind students in our highly „mainstreamed" school system.

Verona, the ratio of time to solve two-dimensional problems versus linear problems was very close. By simply averaging solution time for both groups and creating a ratio of solution times, both groups demonstrated similar ratios. The ratio for the sighted students was 1.9 to 1 while the ratio was 1.6 to 1 for the blind subjects.

Using more sophisticated analysis, it was clear that sighted subjects took considerably less time to solve their test problems than the non-sighted subjects. Mean time to correctly solve the two-dimensional problems was 11.0 for sighted subjects and 111.3 for blind subjects ($p < 0.0001$, $t = 13.04$; df = 46). For the linear problems the mean was 17.5 compared to 209.7 ($p < 0.0001$, $t = 20.15$; df = 53). There was no significant difference in accuracy.

For sighted subjects, it took significantly less time to correctly solve the two-dimensional problems ($\bar{x} = 11.0$) than the linear problems ($\bar{x} = 17.5$), ($p < 0.0001$, $t = 5.96$, df = 43). Although with fewer subjects and at a less significant level, this pattern also held for the blind subjects with the mean time for the two-dimension problems at 111.3 and 209.7 for the linear problems ($p < 0.03$, $t = 4.1288$ df = 3).

Both our qualitative and quantitative tests revealed strong and decisive data in the form of responses by the subjects in both venues. The qualitative evidence from both sites agreed that the two-dimensional representation of arithmetic problems was superior to the linear representation. Overall, the findings suggest that the two dimensional representation of arithmetic problems is superior to the linear representation.

4   Conclusions

Our initial testing, while simple in nature, clearly indicates that two-dimensional presentation in simple arithmetic is far more superior for students with or without vision. Our number of test subjects was heavily weighted toward the sighted subjects – but this is no surprise, as it is more difficult to enroll blind subjects. As we expand our testing to larger populations of blind subjects, our initial findings may change. However, for now, our hypothesis seems to be well supported.

References

1. Karshmer, A.I., Daultani, P., McCaffrey, M.: AutOMathic Blocks, An Automated Systems to Teach Math to K-12 Children with Severe Visual Impairment Allowing Both Physical and Haptic Interaction with An Automated Tutor. In: Proceedings of the Learning with Disabilities Conference, Dayton, Ohio (July 2007)
2. Klatzky, R.L., Lederman, S.J.: The Representation of Objects in Memory: Contrasting Perspectives from Vision and Touch. In: Gruneberg, M.M., Morris, P.E., Sykes, R.N. (eds.) Practical Aspects of Memory: Current Research and Issues. Wiley (1987)
3. Millar, S.: The perception of complex patterns by touch. Perception 14(3), 293–303 (1985)

MathInBraille Online Converter

Klaus Miesenberger, Mario Batusic, Peter Heumader, and Bernhard Stöger

Institut Integriert Studieren,
Altenberger Straße 69, 4040 Linz, Austria
{klaus.miesenberger,mario.batusic,peter.heumader,bernhard.stoeger}@jku.at
http://www.jku.at/iis

Abstract. MathInBraille offers an online portal for converting mathematical formulae and e-Documents with mathematical content into Braille and spoken formats. MathInBraille provides an open conversion service, which can be used for free by anybody what should help to increase access, use and availability of math content for blind people.

1 Introduction and Background

Institut Integriert Studieren [1] as a service centre for students with disabilities at the University of Linz has been working for years on improving access to mathematical content for blind and partially sighted students. MathInBraille complements work and tools developed over the last years in the frame of the International Group on Access to Mathematics (IGUMA) as LaBraDoor [13], UMCL [10,11], etc. MathInBraille offers an easy-to-use web based service to convert mathematical content into Braille or speech formats. By providing easy access to complex conversion services availability and provision of math in Braille and audio should become easier and part of standard (also mainstream) teaching and training activities.

The main target groups for this service are blind and partially sighted people. Other groups like teachers (special and mainstream), parents, peers and co-workers also benefit from this tool when supporting blind people. The service is also useful for editors of math content by providing easy access to a converter without having to know details of special math notations.

2 MathInBraille Converter Portal

The math to Braille converter interface provides a step by step approach to convert math content:

- **Step 1:** Choose the input format. (See figure 1.)
- **Step 2:** Input math content and select the Braille output table as well as the Braille math-notation. Content can be input a) as plain text (MathML or LaTeX), b) with a graphical MathML editor or c) by uploading a file containing math content encoded in MathML or LaTeX. (See figure 2. and 3.)
- **Step 3:** Start conversion and access the converted math content. (See figure 4.)

K. Miesenberger et al. (Eds.): ICCHP 2012, Part I, LNCS 7382, pp. 196–203, 2012.

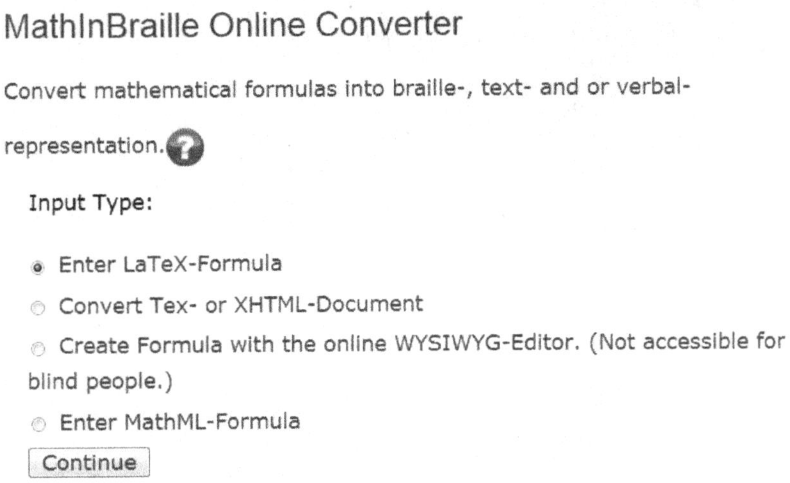

MathInBraille Online Converter

Convert mathematical formulas into braille-, text- and or verbal-

representation.

Input Type:

- Enter LaTeX-Formula
- Convert Tex- or XHTML-Document
- Create Formula with the online WYSIWYG-Editor. (Not accessible for blind people.)
- Enter MathML-Formula

Continue

Fig. 1. Input Form

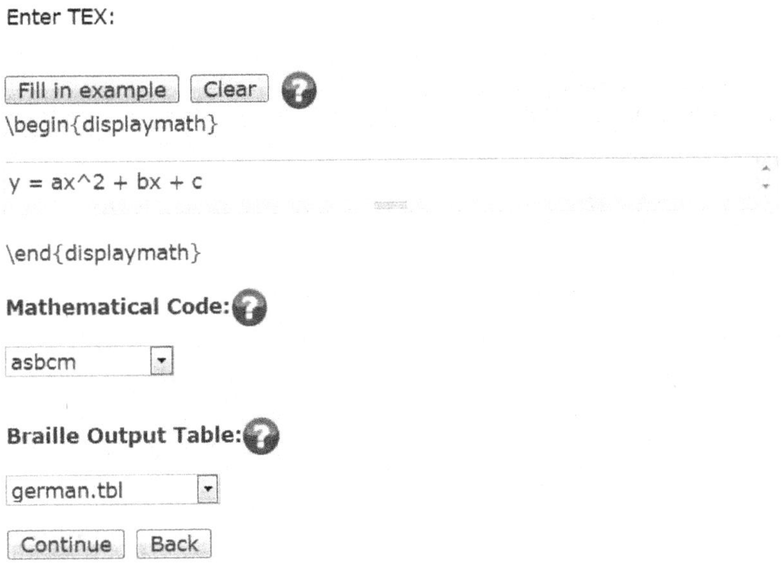

Enter TEX:

Fill in example   Clear

\begin{displaymath}

y = ax^2 + bx + c

\end{displaymath}

Mathematical Code:

asbcm

Braille Output Table:

german.tbl

Continue   Back

Fig. 2. Input plain LaTeX

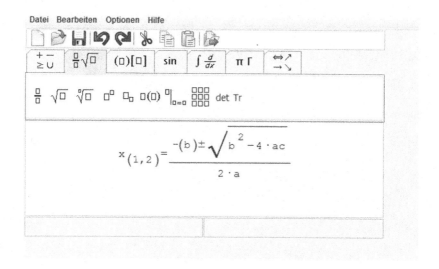

Fig. 3. Input with the online editor

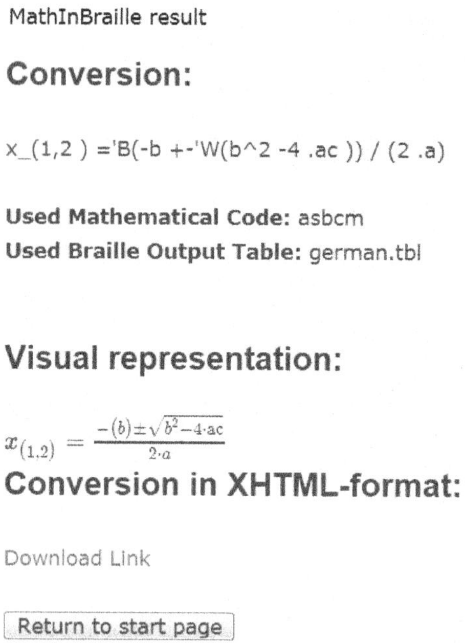

MathInBraille result

Conversion:

x_(1,2) ='B(-b +-'W(b^2 -4 .ac)) / (2 .a)

Used Mathematical Code: asbcm
Used Braille Output Table: german.tbl

Visual representation:

$$x_{(1,2)} = \frac{-(b)\pm\sqrt{b^2-4\cdot ac}}{2\cdot a}$$

Conversion in XHTML-format:

Download Link

Return to start page

Fig. 4. Result of the conversion of the formula created with the online editor

3   Input and Output Options

MathInBraille supports uploading files and online input. The user can choose between different math- or file-formats for input. Currently the UMCL [10,11] conversion library supports three encodings: LaTeX, MathML and XHTML with embedded MathML. UMCL is open source software and allows the implementation of further input modules. UMCL at the moment includes a set of 12 Braille output tables like Marburg Notation (German speaking area) [14], Nemeth Code (North America) [6], several French, Italian and UK notations. All mathematical structures and symbols in traditional Braille codes are defined as one or more Braille cells. Most of them are special symbols: non-letter symbols such as punctuation marks or some seldom used 6-dot-Braille symbols without meaning in a natural language.

Mapping different non-letter Braille symbols to computer character sets can cause difficulties. Most natural languages have their own Braille tables mapping a character set in use to the language specific Braille presentation. In order to obtain the correct Braille presentation of a traditional Braille math notation the user has to select the Braille table which is currently used by the user's screen reader. UMCL covers most of the common Braille tables.

3.1   Two New Output Modules: ASBCM and AVCM

Two new output notations are under development with teachers and experts, one providing optimized output for refreshable Braille displays and Screen Readers, and another one for speech output in German. The Braille output will differ considerably from notations optimized for printing Braille as it avoids context sensitive optimisation of the presentation of formula. This textual math representation also differs for the Braille table in use by the screen reader. [12]

The two new output modules address different purposes:

- **ASBCM:** A Braille math code used by Austrian blind pupils.
- **AVCM:** A textual math code in German language to be used with speech output.

The Braille math code used in Austria, ASBCM, is an adaptation of Human Readable TeX (HRT) [15] - a code developed at the University of Linz. Just like HRT, ASBCM is not meant to be compiled by a TeX program - as will be seen from the examples below, it is only loosely oriented towards the TeX syntax.

Most of the re-definition work was done by teachers at the Federal Institute for the Blind in Vienna [2]. The code is currently being redefined and improved in a subtask of the 'Accessible Schoolbook' project [8].

The Austrian Math Code is actually not a Braille code like, for example, Nemeth Code or Marburg Code. The attempt to use the traditional math-Braille codes in integrated education failed, The basic reason for this is that these notations are no longer known and taught well, and they are not usable on the display screen due to the unavailability of a software solution which would offer two parallel formula renderings: a visual and a Braille one. This issue is not solved sufficiently till up to date. The notation that was defined in this project is a textual, ASCII code that bears a certain resemblance to the regular visual math rendering.

The second module, which is under development at the moment, will render mathematical content in natural German language. This should enable screen reader software to output also mathematical parts of a document through the speech output channel. In contrast to English speaking countries, where plenty of research and some software solutions exist, there is still no definition of spoken math in German language. Again it is planned to do this by setting up an expert group aiming at developing and bringing into discussion a first definition of spoken math in German. This definition then will be implemented as an output module of the MathInBraille Converter Portal.

As an illustration of the new ASBCM code we present two formulae of classical physics - Coulomb's Law and the Relativistic Length Contraction - in ASBCM notation:

Coulomb's Law,

$$F = \frac{1}{4\pi\epsilon_0} \cdot \frac{Q_1 \cdot Q_2}{r^2} \tag{1}$$

is written in ASBCM like this:

```
F ='B(1) / (4'pi 'ep_0) .'B(Q_1 .Q_2) / (r^2)
```

Some explanations:

1. To represent a fraction - e.g., the expression $\frac{1}{4\pi\epsilon_0}$ from the example -, we use the prefix 'B, where the apostrophe ' serves as the escape character [1], and where B stands for the German word "Bruch", which means "fraction". After the 'B prefix, numerator and denominator follow in parentheses, separated by the fraction line, which is represented by a forward slash.
2. The Greek letters - π and ϵ in our example -, are written with the escape character ', followed by the first two letters of their name - in cases where confusion might occur, the first three letters are used.
3. Lower indices - in our case the numbers 0, 1, and 2 - are written using the underscore as a prefix character, just like in TeX. However, contrary to TeX, we use parentheses rather than curly braces for grouping here. For the representation of upper indices - or exponents -, we use the caret, just like in TeX, but again with parentheses instead of braces for grouping - in fact, this method of grouping is used everywhere in ASBCM.

The Relativistic Length Contractin Formula,

$$l = \frac{l_0}{\sqrt{1 - \frac{v^2}{c^2}}} \tag{2}$$

looks like this in ASBCM:

---

[1] This is used as the escape character for special symbols, just like the backslash in TeX. It was chosen because it can be easily reached on a German keyboard.

```
l ='B(1_0) // ('W(1 -'B(v^2) / (c^2)))
```

Again, some explanations:

1. Here we have a double fraction, which is made better visible by doubling the fraction line / in the outer fraction.
2. The square root is prefixed by the string 'W, which consists of the escape character ' and the capital letter W, which stands for the German word "Wurzel", which means "root".

4   Technical Overview

The MathInBraille Online Converter is an HTML user interface for UMCL [10,11] and for the TeX to Hypertext Converter TeX4HT [9]. The portal went online recently and is reachable through the hyperlink www.mathinbraile.at. A LAMP-Server was used to create a stable infrastructure for the portal. LAMP is an acronym for a solution stack of free, open source software based on Linux that provides dynamically generated web content. The letters used in this acronym identify the most important components:

- **Linux:** Operating system of the server
- **Apache:** Open Source Webserver
- **MySQL:** MySQL is a multithreaded, multi-user SQL database management system (DBMS).
- **PHP:** A reflective programming language originally designed for producing dynamic web pages. PHP is used mainly in server-side application software. Perl and Python can be used similarly.

This server hosts Drupal 7[7] which is a free and open-source content management system (CMS) and content management framework. Drupal is coded in PHP and MySQL and therefore allows an easy integration of secure user management, forums, blogs etc. if needed. The functionality of the MathInBraille converter was released as a module for Drupal so the service is easily portable to other platforms also running Drupal 7. As mentioned before, MathInBraille uses the open source libraries UMCL and Tex4HT to convert the input documents into the output documents. The tool is able to convert mathematical content in the following ways:

- **LaTeX/XHTML-file:** The user is able to upload a LaTeX- or XHTML-File which is directly converted by the system.
- **Plain LateX:** A single LaTeX-formula can be used as input. The system wraps this formula into a valid LaTeX-file which is then converted by the system.
- **Plain MathML:** Like plain LaTex a formula can also be entered with plain MathML. Later on the system packs the formula into a valid XHTML-File and converts it.

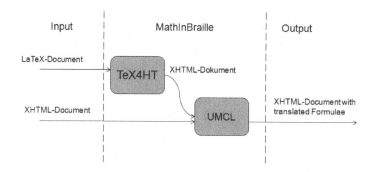

Fig. 5. Functionality of MathInBraille

- **WYSIWYG-Editor:** The WYSIWYG-Editor used in the converter is Drag-Math [3]. This is a free *"drag and drop"* equation editor created at the University of Birmingham by Alex Billingsley under the supervision of Chris Sangwin. The editor runs as a Java applet which can simply run within a web browser on most computers.

As shown in figure 5 the Tex4HT converter is only used when LaTeX is used as input. Tex4HT then translates this input file into a valid XHTML 1.1 plus MathML 2.0. Afterwards UMCL translates all the MathML formulae in this document into the desired braillecode. The final product of MathInBraille is an XHTML file with transladed formulae. This file can be viewed in any browser, providing optimal accessibility for end-users.

5   Future Work

The MathInBraille online service intends to include conversion of math into audio representation as well as extending the number of Braille Notations supported. In cooperation with special teachers and experts in Austria one Braille notation for accessing math content with a Braille display has been implemented and one audio definition for speech rendering is under development. This expert group also works on a notation for German spoken math. Besides that intense user studies and tests are done to refine the converters as well as to improve the quality of the service. In the international network of researchers for access to math partners are invited to include other notations and Braille tables to come to a comprehensive international or global platform for math conversion.

Finally the portal should be extended with (expert) community features facilitating the discussion and further development of existing or new conversion tables supporting harmonisation and sustainable development of software supporting access to math and science.

Acknowledgements MathInBraille is supported by the Internet Foundation Austria [4].

References

1. IIS, Institut Integriert Studieren of the Johannes Kepler University Linz, Austria, http://www.jku.at/iis/
2. Bundes-Blindenerziehungsinstitut Wien - Federal Institute for the Education of the Blind, Vienna (2012), http://www.bbi.at
3. DragMath - a free drag and drop equation editor (2012), http://www.dragmath.bham.ac.uk/
4. IPA, Internet Foundation Austria (2012), http://www.nic.at/ipa/
5. Mathinbraille web page (2012), http://www.mathinbraille.at
6. Nemeth Code - North American Braille Math Code (2012), http://www.dotlessbraille.org/nemethcode.html
7. OSCMSD, Open Source Content Management System Drupal (2012), http://drupal.org/
8. Projekt Schulbuch Barrierefrei (2012), http://schulbuch.accessipedia.info/
9. TeX4ht: LaTeX and TeX for Hypertext on TeX User Group (TUG) (2012), http://www.tug.org/tex4ht/
10. Archambault, D., et al.: Umcl on sourceforge (2012), http://sourceforge.net/projects/umcl/
11. Archambault, D., Batušić, M., Berger, F., Fitzpatrick, D., Miesenberger, K., Moço, V., Stöger, B.: The Universal Maths Conversion Library: an attempt to build an Open Software Library to Convert Mathematical Contents in various Formats. In: Stephanidis, C. (ed.) Proceedings of 3rd International Conference on Universal Access in Human-Computer Interaction (joint with HCI International 2005), Las Vegas, Nevada, USA, 9 pages (July 2005) (proceedings on CD-Rom)
12. Batušić, M., Miesenberger, K.: MathInBraille. In: Gelderbloom, G., Soede, T., Adriaens, L., Miesenberger, K. (eds.) Proceedings of the AAATE 11 Conference on Everyday Technology for Independence and Care. IOS Press, Amsterdam (2011)
13. Batušić, M., Miesenberger, K., Stöger, B.: LABRADOOR, a contribution to making mathematics accessible for the blind. In: Edwards, A., Arato, A., Zagler, W. (eds.) Proc. ICCHP 1998 (6thInternational Conference on Computers Helping People with Special Needs). Oldenbourg, Wien, München (1998)
14. Epheser, H., Pograniczna, D., et al.: Internationale Mathematikschrift für Blinde. Marburg (Lahn), Deutsche Blindenstudienanstalt (1992)
15. Miesenberger, K., Burger, F., Batušić, M., Stöger, B.: Access to mathematics for the blind - Defining HrTEX standard. In: Klaus, J., Auf, E., Kremser, W., Zagler, W. (eds.) 5th International Conference on Interdisciplinary Aspects on Computers Helping People with Special Needs, ICCHP. Oldenbourg, Wien, München (1996)

The Effects of Teaching Mathematics to Students with Disabilities Using Multimedia Computer-Assisted Instruction Coupled with ARCS Model

Chen-Tang Hou[1] and Chu-Lung Wu[2]

[1] National Taichung University of Education, Taichung, Taiwan
hou2@ms3.ntcu.edu.tw
[2] National Taichung University of Education, Taichung, Taiwan
wulongd@gmail.com

Abstract. This study aims to design Multimedia Computer Assisted Instruction(MCAI)coupled with ARCS (Attention, Relevance, Confidence and Satisfaction) model of learning motivation and to investigate the effects of teaching mathematics using MCAI coupled with ARCS model for elementary school students with disabilities. The participants are recruited from the resource room and general classes. The multiple-probe across behavior design is utilized in the study. The independent variable is the strategies of MCAI coupled with ARCS model, and the dependent variables are the performances of learning mathematics. The results indicated that the MCAI program coupled with ARCS model of learning motivation promotes participants' mathematics performance.

Keywords: Multimedia Computer Assisted Instruction (MCAI), Students with Disabilities, ARCS Model, Teaching Mathematics.

1   Introduction

Computer is an educational medium in which a computer delivers instructional content or activities. Computer-Assisted Instruction (CAI), with its ability to incorporate sound, visuals, and interactivity, provides a multimedia and interactive learning environment that enhances the teaching and learning process. The Multimedia Computer-Assisted Instruction (MCAI) uses computer-controlled access in combination with digitized sound, images, and graphics stored on removable media [1]. It allows students to work individually and progress at the students' pace and does not move ahead until they have mastered the skill. Mathematics CAI and MCAI programs demonstrate concepts, instruct, and remediate student errors and misunderstandings for general students.

However, Mathematics CAI or MCAI for students with disabilities faces problems caused by restraints on resources and learning motivation. How to encourage student's motivation and to understand their learning abilities in Mathematics is very important. Educators know the challenge of stimulating and sustaining learner

K. Miesenberger et al. (Eds.): ICCHP 2012, Part I, LNCS 7382, pp. 204–206, 2012.

motivation and the difficulty of finding reliable and valid methods for motivating learners. One approach to meeting this challenge is provided by the ARCS model of motivation. The ARCS model is based on a synthesis of motivational concepts and characteristics into the four categories of attention (A), relevance (R), confidence (C), and satisfaction (S). These four categories represent sets of conditions that are necessary for a person to be fully motivated [2].

Recently, networks based mathematical teaching materials and computerized adaptive testing is growing. The Graduate Institute of Educational Measurement and Statistics at National Taichung University of Education build and applied the Bayesian networks based adaptive test system in practical instruction to diagnose and understand learner's mathematical abilities [3]. Therefore, the study aimed to investigate the effects of Multimedia Computer-Assisted Instruction based on computerized adaptive diagnostic test and ARCS model of learning motivation on promoting mathematics academic performance for students with disabilities. According to the purpose of this study, research questions were addressed as follows: How effectives are the Multimedia Computer-Assisted Instruction based on computerized adaptive diagnostic test and ARCS model on mathematics performance for elementary students with disabilities and special education needs?

1. Does the Multimedia Computer-Assisted Instruction coupled with ARCS model enhance the performances of mathematics for participants?
2. Could the Multimedia Computer-Assisted Instruction coupled with ARCS model maintain the performances of mathematics for participants?

2   Methods

This study designs Multimedia Computer Assisted Instruction (MCAI) based on computerized adaptive diagnostic test and coupled with ARCS model of learning motivation to investigate the effects of teaching mathematics for elementary school students with disabilities. The participants are selected from resource room and general classes in an elementary school. The independent variable is the strategies of MCAI coupled with ARCS model. The program was established according to the content of the textbook, the knowledge structure and computerized adaptive testing. The contents of instruction are three mathematical MCAI units. All sessions of experimental instruction were conducted in a resource room equipped with computers and a variety of items necessary for instruction. The experimental instruction of each unit is offered forty minutes per period, two to three periods per week for round six weeks in each dependent variable as well as lasted for one semester. The dependent variables are the performances of learning mathematics, which mean the correct rates students responded in the teacher-made assessment. The multiple baseline design across behavior of single subject design was employed to examine the effects of the program and the collecting data were presented by graphic method and analyzed by visual analysis as well as time series C statistics. The parents and teacher were considered to be the significant others and answered interview questions about this program, the teaching process, and the participants' performance.

3   Results and Discussion

The results indicated that the lower correct percentage of response on tests during the baseline, and after the intervention was introduced, the higher correct percentage of response on tests was displayed. The results of this study were summarized as follows:

1. Compared to the baseline periods, the percentage of correct response in the treatment periods   being taken by participants on each unit was increased 56.0%, 47.9 %, 65.7%. The results of using C statistic to analysis A+B indicated that there were significantly differences on learning achievement. MCAI coupled with ARCS model can promote the participants' mathematics performance.
2. The accuracy of the evaluation on learning mathematics, being taken by students was became 82.0%, 66.0%, 82.0% in maintenance period. The results of using C statistic to analyze B+C indicated that there were not significantly differences on performance between B and C. The improvements were able to be maintained.

In conclusion, comparing to the baseline periods, the percentage of correct responses of the test on learning mathematics being taken by participants was increased in experimental periods and maintained in maintenance periods. MCAI coupled with ARCS model could promote participants' mathematics performance. In addition, data from interviews with significant individuals indicate a high social validity. The program, the teaching process, and the participants' performance were approved by parents and teachers. The results show that the application of MCAI coupled with ARCS model is effective with children with mild.

References

1. Hou, C.-T., Chang, Y.-H., Chou, T.-H., Chan, Y.-J.: A study of the effects of multimedia computer assisted instruction on the performance of functional mathematic for elementary school students with mental retardation. J. Special Education and Assistive Technology 007, 7–12 (2011)
2. Keller, J.: How to integrate learner motivation planning into lesson planning: The ARCS model approach (2011), http://www.arcsmodel.com/home.html
3. The Graduate Institute of Educational Measurement and Statistics, National Taichung University of Education, http://gsems.ntcu.edu.tw

Information Needs Related
to ICT-Based Assistive Solutions

Renzo Andrich, Valerio Gower, and Sabrina Vincenti

Polo Tecnologico, Fondazione Don Carlo Gnocchi Onlus, Milano Italy
renzo.andrich@siva.it

Abstract. Within the ETNA project – a European Thematic Network aimed at implementing a EU-wide Portal devoted to ICT-based assistive technologies and e-accessibility solution – a study was carried out to detect the information needs of the various stakeholders involved, such as end-users of assistive technologies, professionals in health, social services and education, manufacturers and developers, policy makers and academic/researchers. Thirty "search profiles" were identified, each related to a specific reason why information may be sought in response to a specific information need that people may encounter at given times. In turn, each profile involves a specific body of information. This study provides a detailed insight in the audience's expectations, that is guiding the design of the future Portal. The Portal will stem by the existing Portal of the European Assistive Technology Information Network (EASTIN), enriched by the contributions brought by the ETNA project and its "sister" ATIS4All Thematic Network.

Keywords: Information needs, Information systems, Assistive solutions, e-Accessibility solutions.

1   Introduction

The overall goal of the ETNA thematic network[1] is to establish a European Web Portal able to provide information on assistive products based on ICT (information and communication technologies) and e-accessibility solutions which are available in Europe, and on related organizations and services. The Portal will evolve from the already-existing EASTIN Portal[2] (European Assistive Technology Information Network) [1]; it will be developed in collaboration with ATIS4All[3] (Assistive Technologies and Inclusive Solutions for All) – another Thematic Network.

   The success of the Portal will depend on how far it will meet the various actors' information needs. This calls for a detailed understanding of the specific topics to be covered, as well as of the type, depth and format of the information to be provided. An investigation was carried out leading to the identification of four sub-domains:

---

[1] www.etna-project.eu
[2] www.eastin.eu
[3] www.atis4all.eu

K. Miesenberger et al. (Eds.): ICCHP 2012, Part I, LNCS 7382, pp. 207–214, 2012.

- Stand-alone products
- Non stand-alone products
- Resources for development
- e-Services

Within each sub-domain, a distinction should be made whether mainstream technologies or assistive technologies are considered. The term *assistive* refers to a product/service/technology used by, or aimed at, people with disability to improve functioning in activities that might otherwise be difficult or impossible; while the term *mainstream* refers to products/services/technologies designed for the general public. Assistive, as opposed to mainstream, reflects the concept of *design-for-need* (for meeting specific disability-related problems); while mainstream reflects the concept of *design-for-all* (for everybody, thus including also persons with disabilities and elderly people) [2].

a) Mainstream stand alone product
c) Mainstream non-standalone product
e) Mainstream resource for development
g) Mainstream e-service

b) Assistive stand alone product
d) Assistive non-stand alone product
f) Assistive resource for development
h) Assistive e-service

Fig. 1. Subdomains of the domain "ICT-based assistive solutions"

Fig. 1 shows some visual examples of these perspectives:

- examples of *mainstream stand-alone products* may include a standard mobile phone, or an accessible Automatic Teller Machine (ATM), with built-in accessibility features (a); while examples of *assistive stand-alone products* may include a Voice Output Communication Aid (b);

- examples of **mainstream non stand-alone** products may include a software component – e.g. a speech synthesis engine and screen reader – to be installed on a ICT device to read out the screen contents (c); while examples of **assistive non stand-alone products** may include a switch interface to connect a computer to a head- or a hand-operated switch (d);
- examples of **mainstream resources for development** may include a platform for developing websites compliant with accessibility rules (e.g. WAI/ARIA (e); while examples of **assistive resources for development** may include a software intended to create the layout of a configurable keyboard (f);
- examples of **mainstream e-services** may include an e-commerce rich Internet website with built-in accessibility features (g); while examples of **assistive e-services** may include a on-line service for blind people able to convert a book into a digital recording (h).

2   Method

The work proceeded in four steps.

- First, a literature study was carried out. Academic papers, reports of EU research projects and EU policy documents related to assistive technology and e-accessibility were analyzed. Based on this, a working paper was compiled attempting a first definition of the key terms, of the various sub-domains of the ICT-AT domain, and of the involved stakeholders.
- Second, the working paper was circulated to all Consortium partners. Many remarks and alternative suggestions for the definition of key terms were collected. Enriched with the partners' feedbacks, the document became the core of the *Instrumentum Laboris*, i.e. the preparatory package sent out to all partners.
- Third, the concepts included in the *Instrumentum Laboris* were discussed in depth both in plenary and in parallel sessions during the first ETNA Workshop, held in Milan, Italy, on March 24-25, 2011. Besides providing insight on the various national contexts, on the various technology domains and on the policy framework, the Workshop offered an excellent opportunity for expertise sharing and generated lots of ideas related to the stakeholders' information needs.
- Fourth, the final deliverable was produced through several iterations, in which remarks and contributions were collected and integrated until achieving consensus. The resulting map of information needs is summarized in the following chapter.

3   Results

The prospective audience of the Portal includes a wide variety of stakeholders., whose categorization may be very detailed in terms of roles, professions, background, environment (academy, industry, policy, service provision etc.). However, it is possible to observe some commonalities among certain stakeholders, in terms of "reasons to search in the Portal". Based on these commonalities, a higher level categorization can be done by clustering all stakeholders round *five main target groups*.

End Users. Here the term stands for people actually using assistive solutions, for themselves – people with disabilities, elderly people with reduced functioning, people who experience a temporary disabling situation – or for personal assistance to people with disabilities (family members, caregivers, informal helpers).

Professionals. Here the term stands for professionals working in the provision of services to persons with disabilities and their families. This group includes health care professionals (working in care and rehabilitation services), social services professionals (working in social support services) as well as education professionals (teaching in primary, secondary or higher education). This group includes both persons *occasionally* involved in AT (e.g. occupational therapists carrying out rehabilitation programs; teachers carrying out educational programs with clients who make use of AT) and AT *specialists* (e.g. therapists or rehabilitation engineers assessing clients for recommending appropriate solutions). *Administration officers* involved in AT procurement and financing activities within the service delivery system can be also included in this target group, as they have similar reasons for searching in the Portal.

Manufacturers / Suppliers. The term *manufacturers* refers to companies producing ICT-based products or resources or services, whether mainstream or assistive, that can be part of assistive solutions; *suppliers* refers to companies taking care of their distribution, sale and delivery. Many companies in the ICT area are manufacturers and suppliers at the same time; they may also act as *system integrators*, taking care of integrating different components and products – whether internally produced or bought from third parties – to create assistive solutions.

Researchers / Developers. Here the term indicates people involved in research and development of new ICT products, resources or services. R&D may be carried out in academic institution as well in research Centres, in service-oriented organizations or in industry. Although the distinction between R and D is often blurred, the term *research* mainly refers to discovering new or better solutions to the users' unmet needs, while *development* refers to creating and validating prototypes. This groups also includes *amateur* developers, e.g. people who create freeware or open source software applications and make them available to users or communities of developers.

Policy Makers. Here the term indicates all people having a role in suggesting or deciding on policies related to research, development, provision and funding of assistive solutions. This includes high-level officers of public agencies involved in disability and inclusion policies (e.g. government officers); advocacy bodies such as user organizations (e.g. associations of or for people with disabilities), bringing the user perspective into the public debate; professionals organizations (e.g. Scientific Societies of medical doctors, therapists, teachers etc.), bringing the viewpoint of the various professional stakeholders; industry organizations (e.g. association of AT supplier) bringing the industrial viewpoint.

Table 1. Type of information expected in relation to each search profile

	examples of AT solutions	basic products info	functional details	technical details	Demos	user ratings	price	commercial info	Procurement / financing info	use and maintenance info	possibility to enter ratings	possibility to enter ideas	Professional assessments	Scientific evidence	Case studies	Assessment criteria	Legislation / Regulatory framework	market statistics	third parties components/materials standards	Market actors	construction details	Users' views	possibility to enter product info	Findings of research projects	Funding Opportunities	Possibility to enter R&D products	Resources for development	Possibility to enter info packages
1. Demand develop.	x																											
2. Orienteering	x	x																										
3. Comparing	x	x	x																									
4. Selecting	x	x	x	x	x	x	x																					
5. Buying	x	x	x	x	x	x	x	x																				
6. Paying	x	x	x	x	x	x	x	x	x																			
7. Using	x	x	x	x	x	x	x	x		x																		
8. Rating	x	x	x	x	x	x	x	x		x	x																	
9. Participating	x	x	x	x	x	x	x	x		x	x	x					x					x		x				
10. Informing	x	x	x	x	x	x	x						x															
11. Educating	x	x	x	x	x	x	x						x	x	x													
12. Advising	x	x	x	x	x	x	x						x	x	x	x												
13. Prescribing	x	x	x	x	x	x	x		x				x	x	x	x	x											
14. Training	x	x	x	x	x	x	x			x			x	x	x	x												
15. Outcome assess.	x	x	x	x	x	x	x				x	x	x	x	x	x												
16. Market orient.	x	x	x														x											
17. Positioning	x	x	x	x	x	x	x	x	x	x							x	x										
18. Producing	x	x	x	x	x	x	x	x	x											x	x		x					
19. Supplying									x											x								
20. Delivering																				x								
21. After sales serv.	x	x	x	x	x	x	x			x										x								
22. Advertising																							x					
23. Researching	x	x	x	x	x	x	x						x	x	x					x				x	x			
24. Locating partners	x	x	x	x	x	x	x						x	x	x		x							x	x	x		
25. Developing	x	x	x	x	x	x	x						x	x	x	x				x							x	
26. Benchmarking	x	x	x	x	x	x	x						x	x			x			x		x						
27. Exploiting																										x		
28. Policy developing	x	x															x			x			x					
29. Implementing	x	x			x				x				x				x			x								
30. Awareness raising																												x

Table 2. Details of the information expected in relation to each search profile

	Search reason	Types of information needed
End – users	1. Demand Developing	info useful to clarify one's own need
	2. Orienteering	info on the various solutions that may meet the user need
	3. Comparing	info allowing comparison among the various solutions
	4. Selecting	info helping the choice of the most appropriate solution
	5. Buying	info on where and how to purchase the chosen solution
	6. Paying	info on financial support or public provision opportunities
	7. Using	instructions on usage, maintenance, training opportunities and technical support
	8. Rating	possibility to provide feedback on one's own experience with a product, and learn from other users' experiences
	9. Participating	possibility to provide advice/ideas for solving users' problems, for developing new solutions, for improving existing solutions, for improving policies
Professionals	10.Informing	info useful to keep themselves up-to-date and to instruct their clients about the assistive solutions available in the market
	11.Educating	info useful to increase their overall knowledge on assistive technology and to make their clients aware on how AT may improve their quality of life
	12.Advising	info for recommending the best solution to each individual need, also considering the available resources and the public provision opportunities
	13. Prescribing	info on the regulatory framework, on eligibility for public provision and on the related procedures
	14.Training	info useful for teaching the client to correctly and effectively use the chosen solutions
	15.Outcome assessing	possibility to provide feedback on a product or a category of products – based on research, field evidence or just on one's own experience – and to know about the experience of other professionals and users
Manufacturers and Suppliers	16. Market orienteering	info on the market demand and the users' profiles
	17. Positioning	competing or companion products available in the market
	18.Producing	info on materials, components, production tools and standards that can be useful for the production process
	19.Supplying	market actors that could be part of the selling/service network
	20. Delivering	info on regulations to be followed when delivering the products
	21. After sales servicing	info on technicalities for maintenance and repair
	22. Advertising	possibility of uploading info about their own products
Researchers and developers	23.Researching	info useful to drive the discovery of new solutions e.g. to analyze the market, to better understand the users' unmet needs, to learn from the findings of previous research
	24. Locating partners	info on prospective partners and available funding opportunities for R&D projects
	25.Developing	Info on the available resources and components for development
	26.Benchmarking	info useful for benchmarking the prototypes against other existing solution, in order to detect strengths and weaknesses
	27.Exploiting	disseminating publishable results or contacting possible partners for technology transfer
Policy makers	28. Policy developing	info useful for an overall understanding of the ICT AT environment, of the user needs and the market offer, of ongoing initiatives in the field
	29. Implementing	info on what is happening in the field as a consequence of the enforced policies
	30.Awareness raising	possibility to disseminate info and raise awareness about regulations and opportunities

Having defined the stakeholders, the Study proceeded with identifying 30 different reasons for searching information on assistive technology and e-accessibility solutions. Each "reason to search" brings about a particular "search profile". Tables 1 and 2 summarize these search profiles and the information which each stakeholder expects to find out in relation to each profile.

4   Conclusion and Future Work

The definitions provided in this paper are a useful starting point for the design of the future Portal and of the related search interfaces. The categorization of search profiles is based on the role a person is playing in a given context: for example, a person with disability working in industry may in certain occasions approach the Portal as a user (looking for a solution for him/herself), in other occasions as a developer (realizing the prototype of a new device with built-in accessibility features), in other occasions as a professional (in case the industry supplies AT products, assessing the customer for recommending the most appropriate solution).

A still-open discussion point is the extent to which accessible mainstream products should be considered by the Portal. While *assistive products* can be easily identified as such, in that they have been purposely designed to meet disability-related needs, the extent to which a *mainstream product* can be considered "worth mentioning" is questionable. In an ideal world, all mainstream products should be accessible, thus there would be no need of a specific information system to find them; however, in the real world the border between "accessible" and "inaccessible" is often blurred or depending on the way the product is configured and used. Depending on the accessibility regulations, a product considered "revolutionary good design" in one Country may be considered uninteresting in another which has more advanced regulations and much better products. Today, most existing information resources (e.g. public national databases on disability issues) tend to be very comprehensive in relation to assistive products, and to mention just a few numbers of mainstream products, selected as "best practice examples" of how a product should be designed. This criterion sounds reasonable: however, in case it is going to be followed also in the Thematic Network Portal, indicators of what is meant for "good practice" should be agreed.

The domain of ICT AT and e-Accessibility also poses several other challenges which need to be seriously taken into account in the development of the Portal: the fast ongoing evolution of *social attitudes* towards technology; the growing pervasiveness of ICTs in every aspect of daily life; the different approach of the young "digitally native" generation Vs the "non-digitally-natives"; the taking off of e-Marketing [3].

Rather than being a pure "search engine" or an "integrator of databases and repositories", the Portal should be a "virtual space" that facilitates these processes. Therefore not only data should be available, but also opinions, articles, case studies, ideas, competence Centres that can be contacted, resources that can be directly downloaded, thus offering various opportunities that help the individual to structure his/her own path according to his/her main needs and preferences.

In this sense, mapping the information needs of different users profiles doesn't mean categorizing the stakeholders and their demands in fixed and static groups. Depending on circumstances, whenever accessing the Portal a person will recognize himself/herself in the search profile that is best appropriate in that moment.

Acknowledgements. The ETNA project has been funded by the European Commission's CIP - ICT Policy Support Programme (Grant Agreement n° 270746). The following experts from the ETNA Consortium also contributed to the contents of this paper: Stefania Bocconi, Michela Ott and Marco Tavella from the Institute for Educational Technology, National Research Council, Italy; David Colven and Andrew Lysley from the ACE Centre, UK; Dave Clarke from the Disabled Living Foundation, UK; Alena Galajdova and Dušan Šimsik from Technical University Košiče, Slovakia; Hervé Gauthier from the European Association of Service Providers for Persons with Disabilities, Belgium; Olga Gkaitatzi from CERTH, Greece; María Elena Gómez Martínez from TECHNOSITE, Spain; Anna Evangelinou from Disability Now, Greece; Lindsay Evett from the Nottingham Trent University, UK; John Gill from John Gill Technology, UK; Nils Hanekamp from FTB, Germany; Jeanne Heijkers from Zuyd University, The Netherlands; Evert-Jan Hoogerwerf from the National Spastics Society, Italy; Tuula Hurnasti from the National Institute for Welfare and Health, Finland; Thomas Lyhne from the Danish Centre for Assistive Technology, Denmark; Mats Lundälv from DART, Sweden; Britta Lüssem and Petra Winkelmann from the Institut der deutschen Wirtschaft Koeln, Germany; Klaus Miesenberger from Linz University, Austria; Manuel Montejo Estevez from TECNALIA, Spain; Lucía Perez-Castilla from CEAPAT, Spain; Lucia Pigini from Fondazione Don Carlo Gnocchi Onlus, Italy CNR; Jari Väisänen from the Finnish Association for intellectual and developmental disabilities, Finland.

References

1. Andrich, R.: Towards a global information network: the European Assistive Technology Information Network and the World Alliance of AT Information Providers. In: Gelderblom, G.J., Soede, M., Adriaens, L., Miesenberger, K. (eds.) Everyday Technology for Independence and Care, pp. 190–197. IOS Press (2011)
2. Deloitte & AbilityNet: Internal market for inclusive and assistive ICT, targeted market analysis and legislative aspects. European Commission, Information Society and Media, Bruxelles (2011)
3. i2010 High Level Group: Benchmarking Digital Europe 2011-2015, a conceptual framework. European Commission, Information Society and Media, Bruxelles (2009), http://ec.europa.eu/information_society/eeurope/i2010/docs/be nchmarking/benchmarking_digital_europe_2011-2015.pdf

The European Assistive Technology Information Portal (EASTIN): Improving Usability through Language Technologies

Valerio Gower[1], Renzo Andrich[1], Andrea Agnoletto[1], Petra Winkelmann[2], Thomas Lyhne[3], Roberts Rozis[4], and Gregor Thurmair[5]

[1] Polo Tecnologico, Fondazione Don Carlo Gnocchi Onlus, Milano Italy
{vgower,randrich,aagnoletto}@dongnocchi.it
[2] Institut der deutschen Wirtschaft, Köln, Germany
winkelmann@iwkoeln.de
[3] Hjælpemiddelinstituttet, Taastrup, Denmark
tly@hmi.dk
[4] Tilde, Riga, Latvia
Roberts.Rozis@Tilde.lv
[5] Linguatec GmbH, Munich Germany
g.thurmair@linguatec.de

Abstract. The EASTIN Portal – which aggregates the contents of six national databases and make it searchable in 22 European languages – is currently the major information system on assistive technology available in Europe. Its usability has been recently improved through the use of advanced language technologies, thanks to the EU-funded project EASTIN-CL. The project developed three main components (the *query processing*, the *machine translation*, and the *speech output*) that have been implemented and plugged to the existing EASTIN website.

Keywords: Language technology, AT information, Search query processing.

1 Introduction

The importance of providing accurate information about the opportunities and limitation of Assistive Technologies (AT) to all the stakeholders involved in the AT service delivery systems has been recognized as a key issue by several European studies [1] [2], [3]. In 2006, the UN Convention on the Rights of Persons with Disabilities acknowledged the access to information on AT as a fundamental right (art. 4) that should be ensured by the signing Countries [4].

In 2005, the European Assistive Technology Information Network (EASTIN) was established [5]. The network, that stems from a project founded by the European Commission in 2004-2005 within the eTEN programme, includes the organisations responsible for the major European AT information systems in Denmark, United Kingdom, The Netherlands, Germany, Italy, France and Belgium. National Contacts

K. Miesenberger et al. (Eds.): ICCHP 2012, Part I, LNCS 7382, pp. 215–222, 2012.

Organisations have been recently appointed in Finland, Latvia, Spain, Lithuania, Slovakia, Slovenia, Cyprus, Norway, and Hungary (Fig. 1). The network is now operated by the EASTIN Association, a legal entity based in Italy supported by its partners through their annual membership fees

Fig. 1. Geographic distribution of the partners and national contacts of the EASTIN network

1.1   The EASTIN Portal

The core of the EASTIN network is the web-site www.eastin.eu (Fig. 2). This website provides – in all the official languages of the European Union – information on almost 70.000 products available on the European market and some 20.000 companies (manufacturers/suppliers, retailers); it also includes related material such as fact sheets and suggestions on assistive solutions for daily living.

Fig. 2. The EASTIN Portal homepage

EASTIN is not a database itself: it is an engine. It aggregates the contents of six independent national databases, each running on a different technological platform; it includes a purpose-made search engine able to perform AT product searches across all these databases in all EU languages.

In the EASTIN portal the Assistive Technology (AT) products, and associated information, are classified according to the tasks they are intended for using the ISO

9999:2011 standard "Assistive Products for Persons with Disability – Classification and terminology" [6]. The methods currently available to retrieve information on assistive technology in the EASTIN portal are the following:

- *Guided search* that allows to browse the ISO 9999 classification tree and select the appropriate class (Fig. 3).
- *Search by keyword* that allows to select a keyword from a predefined list alphabetically ordered (e.g. cane, crutches, ...)
- *Search by commercial name or manufacturer name* that allows to specify the name or manufacturer of the product
- *Search by insert date* that allows to search product recently entered in the EASTIN databases
- *Advanced search* that allows to combine the above search methods

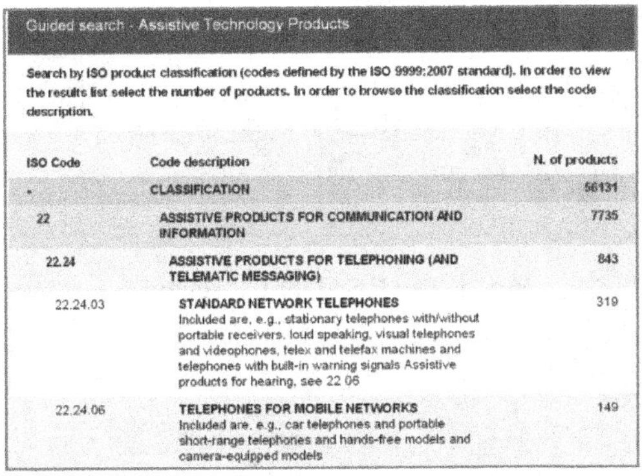
Guided search - Assistive Technology Products

Search by ISO product classification (codes defined by the ISO 9999:2007 standard). In order to view the results list select the number of products. In order to browse the classification select the code description.

ISO Code	Code description	N. of products
-	CLASSIFICATION	56131
22	ASSISTIVE PRODUCTS FOR COMMUNICATION AND INFORMATION	7735
22.24	ASSISTIVE PRODUCTS FOR TELEPHONING (AND TELEMATIC MESSAGING)	843
22.24.03	STANDARD NETWORK TELEPHONES Included are, e.g., stationary telephones with/without portable receivers, loud speaking, visual telephones and videophones, telex and telefax machines and telephones with built-in warning signals Assistive products for hearing, see 22 06	319
22.24.06	TELEPHONES FOR MOBILE NETWORKS Included are, e.g., car telephones and portable short-range telephones and hands-free models and camera-equipped models	149

Fig. 3. Screenshot of the ISO 9999 classification browsing

2 The EASTIN-CL Project

The EASTIN-CL project (`www.eastin-cl.eu`), funded by the European Commission within the ICT policy support programme, worked at improving the usability of the EASTIN portal through the use of advanced language technologies. The project consortium included three partners with expertise in the AT domain (all belonging to the EASTIN Association) and two partners with expertise in language technology: the project co-ordinator Linguatec (DE) and Tilde (LV). The project started in March 2010 and ends in June 2012.

The objective of the project is to facilitate the access to the information provided by the EASTIN portal in three ways:

- by supporting non experts in the AT field: facilitating the query process to retrieve information from the Portal;
- by supporting non-native speakers: providing a machine translation of the information retrieved;
- by offering additional communication channel: through synthetic speech output

3   Design and Implementation

The EASTIN-CL system is made-up of three main components: the *query processing* (QP), the *machine translation* (MT), and the *speech output* (SO). In Fig. 4 the overall scheme of the EASTIN-CL system is depicted.

The QP component allows users to forward a *free text* search request in a "google-like" fashion by entering search terms in their native language. The component analyzes the terms entered and converts the *natural language* query into a *formal query* supported by the EASTIN system (i.e. it identifies the appropriate ISO 9999 classification codes).

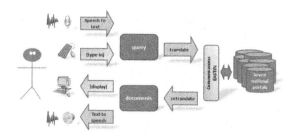

Fig. 4. The EASTIN-CL scheme

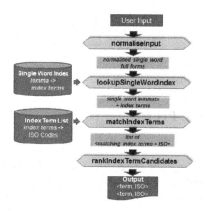

Fig. 5. Overview of Query Processing component steps

The QP is based on a large multilingual vocabulary (or *termlist*) that includes over 12000 terms for each language. In the termlist each term is linked to one or more ISO 9999 codes. The sources that were used to build the English (*master*) version of the termlist were the official ISO 9999 terminology, and the keywords of major AT information systems (such as the US database Abledata [7], the German database Rehadat [8], and the Danish database HMI-Basen [9]).

The processing of the user query is done in several steps (Fig. 5): the user input is split into meaningful single words, decomposed (in case of compound words, quite frequent in German for example), and the canonical forms (*lemmata*) are found. The lemmata are matched against the termlist. In case no match is found the closest candidate is returned (using a slightly modified Levenshtein distance measure). The QP component is therefore able to manage compound words, inflections (e.g. singular/plural, this is quite important for inflected languages like Italian), and spelling errors (e.g. "mobil" instead of "mobile").

A text box has been added on the upper right corner of the homepage (Fig. 6) , when the user enters the search terms (e.g. *mobile phone*) and clicks on the search button four searches are performed in the EASTIN Portal:

1. *Product groups*: retrieves the most relevant group of products according to the terms entered in the textbox;
2. *Products* matching the search terms: retrieves the products whose commercial name (or manufacturer's name) contains the terms entered in the textbox;
3. *Manufacturers* containing the search terms: retrieves information on the manufacturers whose name contains the terms entered in the textbox;
4. *Additional documentation*: allows to search for additional information documentation (fact sheets, FAQ, case studies, ideas, links) on relevant product groups according to the entered terms.

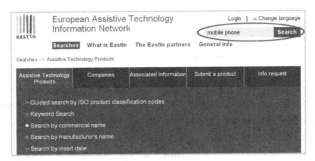

Fig. 6. The search text box in the homepage

The product groups retrieved by the QP component are ordered according to their *relevance*, pictured by a 1 to 5 stars image (Fig. 7), computed with a special algorithm that weights the found keywords. The QP component is available for English, Italian, German, Danish, Latvian, Lithuanian, and Estonian.

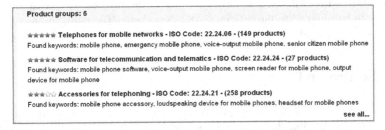

Fig. 7. The search result summary page

By clicking on the number of products a search on the corresponding product group is performed in the EASTIN Portal. In the result page the user can browse the different records and get into the detailed product description.

The machine translation component allows non English speaking users to read the product *free text* description in their native language. If, for example, an Italian user enters the portal and retrieves information on a product stored in the English database, she/he will see all the information in Italian, except for the free text description of the product (Fig. 8 on the left). The EASTIN-CL machine translation component allows the user to translate also the description text into Italian by clicking on the "traduci in Italiano" button. When the button is pressed the text is sent to a translation server, machine translated and then reloaded into the page. The machine translation component is available for Italian, German, Estonian, Latvian and Lithuanian.

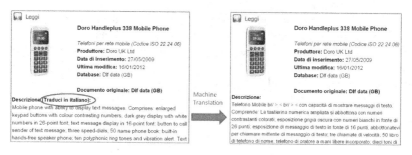

Fig. 8. An example of a product detail page in Italian. On the left the text description is in English while on the right it is translated into Italian.

The speech output system allows to have the product description read by a speech synthesis. When the user clicks on the "read" button on the upper left corner the of the product description (Fig. 8) the text is sent to a server, converted to an mp3 file, and played by a player that pops up in a new window of the browser.

The graphic interface concept was validated by means of a focus group involving 19 professionals working in the AT field (health and social care workers, administration officers, physiotherapists, occupational therapists and rehabilitation engineers). Comments and remarks arisen during the focus group discussion were integrated into the final version of the interface described above.

All the EASTIN-CL components have been plugged a to testing website that replicate the EASTIN portal and functional tests have been done to verify the compliance with the specifications defined at the beginning of the project. The components are now ready to be plugged to the official EASTIN website. The publication is foreseen for the beginning of February 2012.

4   The Testing Phase

In order to test the quality of the QP component, and especially the quality of the termlist that represent the "knowledge basis" of the QP, a special online tool has been developed (Fig. 9). The tool include a sample of 100 images, representative of all the different typology of product included in the ISO 9999 classification, and allows the experts to enter terms that they would use to search for the type of product depicted in each image. The terms entered by expert are then passed to the QP component and the product typology returned by the QP (i.e. the ISO 9999 codes returned) are compared to the product typology represented by each image. This allows to verify whether the term list include the terminology used by AT domain expert when searching for assistive devices, and whether the product typologies returned by the QP component are appropriate.

Fig. 9. The tool to evaluate the quality of the QP

A test plan of the EASTIN-CL components has been designed that foresees both testing of the QP component by domain experts, using the above mentioned tool, and online testing of the overall system by end users (e.g. AT professionals, persons with disabilities and their families, AT manufacturers/suppliers,...). For this purpose a group of validators will be recruited and, after some basic instruction on the system usage, will be asked to perform the *validation exercise* that has been prepared. An online questionnaire[1] has been developed and will be used to collect the validators' opinion on the system. The test phase started in March 2012, soon after (end of May 2012) the components will be plugged to the official ESTIN Portal (www.eastin.eu).

5   Conclusion and Future Work

The EASTIN-CL project developed three components, based on advanced language technology, meant to improve the usability of the EASTIN Portal on two aspects: the retrieval of information and the understandability of the data retrieved. The functional tests prove that the components are reliable and fully respond to the specification defined in the project. The usability test with AT domain experts and end users will represent a valuable information for the fine tuning of the system. In particular data collected from AT domain expert will be used to improve the "knowledge base" of

---

[1] The validation questionnaire, developed with the google documents app, is available at: https://docs.google.com/spreadsheet/viewform?hl=it&formkey=dE dsUlBrZXhUWk1sejgxLUlmV2pPT0E6MQ#gid=0

the QP component, represented by the multilingual termlist. A long term sustainability plan has been prepared: the EASTIN association will be responsible for the maintenance of the AT domain knowledge (basically the termlist) while the language technology components will be hosted by the language technology partners.

Besides being an important tool for AT professionals, end users and everyone interested in the AT field, the EASTIN portal also represents a strategic resource for research and development project. In particular the EASTIN portal will represent the information basis for two European funded research projects: The ETNA thematic network (www.etna-project.eu), aimed at creating the European web portal of ICT-based assistive technology products, accessibility solutions and related services, and the CLOUD4All project (www.cloud4all.info), aimed at developing an infrastructure for the automatic personalization of ICT devices and services on the basis of the individual needs of each person.

Acknowledgements. The EASTIN-CL and ETNA projects are funded by the European Commission's CIP – ICT Policy Support Programme (Grant agreements n° 2504327 and 270746 respectively). The CLOUD4All project is funded by European Commission 7th Framework Programme (Grant agreement n° 289016).

References

1. Deloitte & Touche: Access to Assistive Technology in the European Union. Bruxelles. European Commission, DG Employment (2003)
2. Stack, J., Zarate, L., Pastor, C., Mathiassen, N.E., Barberà, R., Knops, H., Kornsten, H.: Analysing and federating the European assistive technology ICT industry. European Commission Information Society and Media (2009)
3. Deloitte & AbilityNet: Internal market for inclusive and assistive ICT, targeted market analysis and legislative aspects. European Commission, Information Society and Media, Bruxelles (2011)
4. United Nations: The UN Convention on the Rights of People with Disabilities (2007), http://www.un.org/disabilities/
5. Andrich, R.: Towards a global information network: the European Assistive Technology Information Network and the World Alliance of AT Information Providers. In: Gelderblom, G.J., et al. (eds.) Everyday Technology for Independence and Care, pp. 190–197. IOS Press (2011)
6. International standard ISO 9999:2011, Assistive Products for Persons with Disability – Classification and terminology (2011)
7. Lowe, S.W.: AbleData.com's Leap Into the Future. In: Gelderblom, G.J., et al. (eds.) Everyday Technology for Independence and Care, pp. 190–197. IOS Press (2011)
8. Winkelmann, P.: REHADAT: The German information system on assistive devices. In: Gelderblom, G.J., et al. (eds.) Everyday Technology for Independence and Care, pp. 205–213. IOS Press (2011)
9. Lyhne, T.: The Danish National Database on Assistive Technology. In: Gelderblom, G.J., et al. (eds.) Everyday Technology for Independence and Care, pp. 205–213. IOS Press (2011)

Use of Assistive Technology in Workplaces of Employees with Physical and Cognitive Disabilities

Kirsi Jääskeläinen[1] and Nina Nevala[1,2]

[1] Finnish Institute of Occupational Health, Helsinki, Finland
{kirsi.jaaskelainen,nina.nevala}@ttl.fi
[2] University of Jyväskylä, Department of Health Sciences, Jyväskylä, Finland

Abstract. Information technology (IT), especially assistive devices and programs, enable people with disabilities to work. The aim of this study was to determine the knowledge and use of this IT among workers with disabilities in the open labor market. The focus was on the IT accommodation solutions used in workplaces and how these improved the working skills of disabled people. One fourth (27%) of the participants considered their knowledge regarding assistive technology to be very good or good, whereas 39% considered their knowledge to be very poor or poor. Workers with visual disorders were the most aware of assistive technology in computer work. Over half of the respondents indicated that the user interface, display screen, and mouse settings of their computers were not accommodated.

Keywords: Assistive technology, Workplace Accommodation, Disability, Disabled workers, Computer work, Information technology, Employment.

1 Introduction

Assistive Technology (AT) consists of assistive devices and programs that help people with disabilities to be employed at work [1,2].

The most common desktop and web-based email applications appear to contain usability problems that hinder blind users who use screen readers and keyboards to navigate them [3]. Many of these problems could be addressed through relatively minor modifications such as tab order, labeling, terminology, clear confirmation, and the placement of the buttons on an interface. Workers with physical impairments reported that discomfort and pain, limited knowledge of the technology's features, and the complexity of the technology limited their use of it [4]. Among workers with cognitive disabilities, the use of AT demonstrated a higher rate of accuracy and task completion, increased independence and generalization skills [5]. Increasing evidence shows that websites that neglect the guidelines for dyslexic accessibility not only undercut the esteem and success of dyslexic users, but also affect their non-dyslexic counterparts [6].

AT needs to be customized to the individual's specific requirements and preferences if its use is to be optimized, and disabled workers need training in how to use

K. Miesenberger et al. (Eds.): ICCHP 2012, Part I, LNCS 7382, pp. 223–226, 2012.

AT [4]. The barriers that prevent occupational health care and rehabilitation services from using AT can be overcome by reforming policies, laws and delivery systems, and increasing human resources for training and the retention of rehabilitation personnel [7].

2   Material and Methods

2.1   Participants

A total of 205 people aged 16 or over (74% female, 26% male) who received support for a disability from The Social Insurance Institution of Finland and worked in the open labor market took part in the study. The median age of the research group was 50 years. The participants had a physical, visual, or hearing disorder or a communication problem (Table 1).

The largest fields of employment were health care and social services (28%), education (12%), and public administration (12%). Most (81%) of the participants had permanent work, 10% were employed part-time, and 3% worked as entrepreneurs.

2.2   Methods

This was a descriptive cross-sectional study. The research was carried out using the internet-based data collection and feedback management software of Digium Enterprise. The inquiry was first tested on three disabled people who did not belong to the research group, and it was developed according to their opinions. The inquiry was also tested on sighted people to ensure that it is also usable for them.

We inquired about the use of computers through 22 questions which concerned remote work (4 questions), the use of computers (7), the use of assistive devices and programs (8), and user satisfaction of computer accommodation (3). The background material elicited concerned the respondents' age, gender, disability / illness, the use of assistive devices, education, occupation, part-time/full time work, and employment sector.

3   Results

Over half (59%) of the respondents used a computer for over four hours a day. Most (75%) had a desktop computer, and every fifth (22%) had a laptop. Office programs involving word processing, spreadsheets, or presentation graphics were used by 72% of the workers.

Most of the respondents reported that the use and the learning of how to use computer programs was very easy or easy and only 7% considered it very difficult. Workers with communication difficulties and visual impairments found it the most difficult to learn how to use computer programs. However, the difference was not statistically significant.

The workers with visual disorders had the best awareness (p = 0.0003) of the AT used in computer work. One fourth (27%) of the participants considered that they knew AT very well or well, whereas 39% considered that they knew it very poorly or poorly. Workers with physical, communication/learning or other disabilities had the poorest awareness of AT. Men had better knowledge of AT than women (p=0.0126). The differences in awareness of AT between the under 50 and over 50 age groups had no statistical significance.

User interface accommodations had mostly been carried out for the workers with visual disabilities. Only 14% of these reported that no accommodations had been made, whereas the percentage of workers with physical, hearing and learning impairments who did not have accommodated interfaces was around 50%. There was a statistically significant difference (p=0.0052) between the disability groups with user interface accommodations.

Assistive devices and software were used the most by workers with visual impairments. The most typical assistive devices were screen reader software, speech synthesizers, and magnifiers. Among other disability groups the use of AT was rare. The participants seldom used mainstream devices that facilitate computer work. Most of the workers with disabilities (66%) did not use a trackball, ergonomically shaped mice, or mouse trappers.

Participants reported that IT arrangements were mostly organized well at their workplaces. They were also satisfied with IT support, instruction and training. Workers with learning and hearing impairments experienced more dissatisfaction than those belonging to the other groups. The differences between the opinions regarding the IT arrangements of the under 50 and over 50 age groups, or between those of men and women were not statistically significant.

As targets for development, users mentioned that their opinions should be taken into account more in the procurement of assistive devices and programs, and in the personal configurations of computers. In the open answers, respondents indicated that it was sometimes complicated to obtain assistive devices:

"Where to get the devices, who pays for what, giving the client the runaround if he/she is not able to phone the right number in the first place"

"The problems continue, being sent back and forth from one place to another, and the expert or person who understands (the defect and difficulty) is never available! If I'm to stay in work life, I have to pay for a laptop myself, all the necessary applications, and long-term training and support"

4   Discussion

According to this study, computer use is more common among disabled people than among workers in Finland in general. Only one third of the respondents said that they were very familiar with AT, and respondents' knowledge of mainstream technology that supports the use of a computer was rare. The reported ease of use, knowledge and user interface modifications was as a whole best among users with visual impairments. This could be because visually handicapped people have to use adaptive technology while using computers. When the disability is not so obvious, as in the case of learning and reading disabilities, the need for AT is not so apparent. People with learning difficulties, for example, would benefit from the use of screen readers.

Personal assistance should be increased and more accommodations made in computer work for workers with disabilities. Cooperation is essential between occupational health care, information technology management, and computer experts, for example, if disabled workers are to acquire the AT that they need. The acquisition processes used to access AT should also be more consistent and better known by everyone involved.

It is important to increase disabled people's participation in work and to understand that the computer techniques used by disabled people can also serve to help the work of every one of us.

References

1. Chen, H., Liu, Y., Chen, C., Chen, C.: Design and feasibility study of an integrated pointing device apparatus for individuals with spinal cord injury. Appl. Ergon. 38(3), 275–283 (2007)
2. Sauer, A.L., Parks, A., Heyn, P.C.: Assistive technology effects on the em-ployment outcomes for people with cognitive disabilities: a systematic review. Disability and Rehabilitation: Assistive Technology 5(6), 377–391 (2010)
3. Wentz, B., Lanzar, J.: Usability evaluation of Email applications by blind users. Journal of Usability Studies 6, 75–89 (2011)
4. De Jonge, D.M., Rodger, S.A.: Consumer-identified barriers and strategies for optimizing technology use in the workplace. Disabil. Rehabil. Assist. Technol. 1(1-2), 79–88 (2006)
5. Sauer, A.L., Parks, A., Heyn, P.C.: Assistive technology effects on the employment outcomes for people with cognitive disabilities: a systematic review. Disabil. Rehabil. Assist. Technol. 5(6), 377–391 (2010)
6. McCarthy, J., Swierenga, S.: What we know about dyslexia and Web accessibility: a research review. Universal Access in the Information Society 9(2), 147–152 (2010)
7. World report on disability. World Health Organization (2011), http://whqlibdoc.who.int/publications/2011/9789240685215_eng.pdf (accessed February 10, 2012)

Multimodal Guidance System for Improving Manual Skills in Disabled People

Mario Covarrubias, Elia Gatti, Alessandro Mansutti, Monica Bordegoni, and Umberto Cugini

Politecnico di Milano, Dipartimento di Meccanica
Via G. La Masa, 1, 20146 Milano, Italy
{mario.covarrubias,elia.gatti,alessandro.mansutti}@mail.polimi.it,
{monica.bordegoni,umberto.cugini}@polimi.it

Abstract. The paper describes a multimodal guidance system whose aim is to improve manual skills of people with specific disorders, such as Down syndrome, mental retardation, blind, autistic, etc. The multimodal guidance system provides assistance in the execution of 2D tasks as for example: sketching, hatching and cutting operations through haptic and sound interactions. The haptic technology provides the virtual path of 2D shapes through the point-based approach, while sound technology provides some audio feedback inputs about his or her actions while performing a manual task as for example: start and/or finish an sketch; some alarms related to the hand's velocity while sketching and filling or cutting operations. Unskilled people use these interfaces in their educational environment.

Keywords: Haptic Guidance, Unskilled People, Sound Interaction.

1 Introduction

The multimodal system presented in this paper, consisting in a combination of haptic and sound technologies, aims to be a step forward in the field of multimodal devices for supporting unskilled people to improve their skills and in the assessment of manual activities. Sketching, hatching and cutting tasks are assisted through the haptic guidance device. A Magnetic Geometry Effect assist the users hand movement, which is a sort of magnet or spring effect attracting the hand towards the ideal path. The drawn shape can also be physically produced as a piece of polystyrene foam. The cutting operation is performed by using a hot wire tool, which is linked to the haptic device. In addition, several sound metaphors are explored. These sounds are used to give information related to the starting and/or finishing of an activity (e.g. Sound A means, starting to cut while sound B means Stop the cutting activity and Sound C, can be used to indicate that the velocity in the cutting task is the most performing, etc.)

The objective of the multimodal system is to experiment a new tool that allows unskilled people to perform the assessment of manual skills in an intuitive, natural and easy manner. This group of people have demonstrated that with

K. Miesenberger et al. (Eds.): ICCHP 2012, Part I, LNCS 7382, pp. 227–234, 2012.

early intervention programs, their possibilities of having a better life are growing as well. Unfortunately today practice to control the motion control and skill improvements need to be done with continuous assistance given by care assistants, so greatly limiting the possibility to exploit the great potential that those people have. However, there is still much more opportunity for developing tools to help and support them for improving both, their productivity and independence in the workplace. This can be done, by providing tools to employers and employees to assist them to maximize the operational capacity. The multimodal system is designed as a tool that supports manipulation and actions needing a very limited support provided by care assistants, for ensuring the integration and independence in the workforce.

2   Related Work

The research concerning haptic technology has increased rapidly in the last few years, and results have shown the significant role that haptic feedback plays in several fields, including rehabilitation. The interaction is enriched by the use of the sense of touch, so that also visually impaired users can identify virtual objects and perceive their shape and texture. Within the field of virtual reality environments and simulation tools, the sense of touch is provided by haptic interfaces [1]. Haptic interfaces are based on devices that present tactile and force feedback to a human user who is interacting with a simulated object via a computer [2] in order to feel the virtual object properties (i.e., texture, compliance or shape). Examples include devices that provide robotic-assisted repetitive motion [3]. There are, however, very few assisted applications for unskilled people which support them in a specific employment role.

Haptic interface technology can enable individuals who are blind to expand their knowledge by using an artificially made reality built on haptic and audio feedback. Research on the implementation of haptic technologies within Virtual Environments has reported the potential for supporting the development of cognitive models of navigation and spatial knowledge with sighted people [4], [5], [6], [7] and with people who are blind as well [8]. Audio feedbacks have been used coupled to haptic feedback in several fields. In [9] for example have been used to train ophthalmic surgeon on complex optical operation.

We have used the Phantom Desktop device that is available in our laboratory in order to show and prove the concept of the multimodal guidance system. In fact, at the current development stage, the system is a prototype that requires to be engineered in order to built up a very low cost system; a goal that appear very realistic. However, we have planned in the engineering process to integrate the force feedback directly in our guidance system instead of using a commercial phantom device, taking into account several previous work [10], [11] in which the force feedback has been integrated directly into the pantograph mechanism. The guidance haptic device concept has been described in [12]. This paper focuses on the multimodal approach through the sound metaphors and the results of testing the first prototype.

3   System Description

The multimodal guidance system allows the initial definition of a set of geometric shapes that the users will draw, and physically produce thanks to the cutting system in an assisted way. Figure 1 provides a schematic view of the system's architecture. The shapes are initially generated through the use of a generic CAD tool. The shapes are saved in the VRML format, which is a standard file format for representing 3-dimensional interactive vector graphics. This file includes the IndexedFace set list, which represents the 3D shape formed by constructing faces (polygons), and the Coordinate point list, which contains the coordinate of each single node that defines the 3D vertices of the shape. Finally, these data are imported in the H3DAPI software that is used for rendering the haptic guiding path, on the basis of the geometry of the shape.

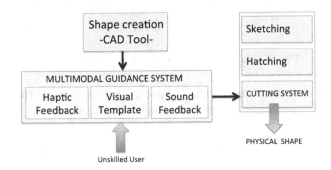

Fig. 1. Multimodal guidance system architecture

This software was chosen because is an open source platform that allows to handle both graphics and haptic data. The software also allows to easily manage the Magnetic Surface constraint, which provides a force on the haptic device based on a given distance from a virtual surface. In this way, a snap constraint is applied allowing to control and vary as needed the stiffness and damping constraints. The snap distance is a parameter that defines the outward distance for the application of the attracting effect.

4   The Concept from the Disabled People Side

Figure 2 provides the isometric view of both, the CAD concept and the real prototype of the multimodal system seen from the users side. The user is sitting in front of the multimodal system as can be seen from Figure 2-a, and then by handling the stylus (3) tries to follow the physical template (1) in order to perform the 2D drafting tasks. This task is driven under the operators movement and assisted by the Magnetic Geometry Effect (MGE). When this option is enabled, a spring force tries to pull the tip of the stylus (3) of the haptic device towards the virtual path. In fact, this effect is used in order to assist the users hand (Figure 2-**b**, Figure 2-**c** and Figure 2-**d**). While user follows the 2D template (1) by using the haptic guidance, the wire tool (6) when activated will cut the polystyrene foam (2). Figure 2-**e** shows the physical prototype and the users hand holding the tool.

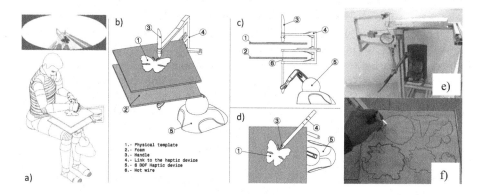

Fig. 2. The concept from the disable people side

The lengths of the links in the Phantom device (1) determine the mechanisms kinematic properties, such as workspace and manipulability.

5   The Concept from the Care Assistants Side

We have designed a Graphic User Interface in order to involve teachers and care assistants during the test phase. In this way, we are also providing some training for the use of the system. Figure 3-**a** shows the teacher while using the GUI interface; Figure 3-**b** shows the first screen asking for the shape selection. We have designed simple and complex shapes, i.e. circle, triangle, hexagon, rectangle, spiral, porcupin, bat, etc. Figure 3-**c** shows the screen that has been selected by the teacher/care assistant in order to have the visual feedback. If the F1 key is pressed, a circle is activated in order to ask the unskilled user to perform the sketch operation, if the F2 key is pressed a triangle is activated and so on. This graphical interface allows the teachers the possibility to switch between different shapes and set the modality task that has to be performed, as sketching, hatching or cutting task.

Figures 3-**d** and 3-**e** show the screen that has been used during the test of the multimodal device. While the unskilled people are the end-users of the technology, it is possible to consider a more person-centered approach to both the evaluation of the multimodal guidance and to the research.

6   Evaluation of the System by the Care Assistants

In our study we have used a qualitative approach to evaluate the ergonomics of the system, and to reach the overall impression from users and their assistant.

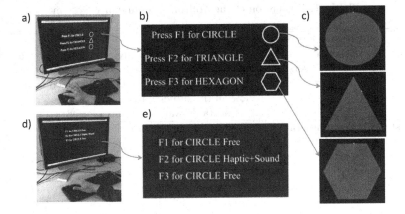

Fig. 3. The concept from the teacher and care assistant side

We decided to interpret data as complementary to the obtained quantitative data. Table 1 shows the qualitative observation of the users.

One of the major problems of the qualitative analysis is the challenging validation of the theories that rise from the recorded impressions. Nevertheless, those kind of information could be an important index regarding the well-functioning of the system and the possible further improvement. The overall impression is positive. The qualitative data have been obtained by two ways. For points 1,4 and 5 reported in Table 1 we directly asked to users or to the educators opinions and suggestions. For the points 2 and 3 we obtained data observing the users behavior. The system helping effect has been found very interesting and rewarding by the users, that have been able to focus their attention on the task.

7   Sound Interaction

The sound feedback of the multimodal haptic device gives the possibility to play metaphoric sounds while the user's interact with the system . These metaphoric sounds provides information to the disable people according to the type of task performed. In fact, once the sound feedback is enabled, the sound feedback gives the following information:

- Metaphoric sound A, if the stylus pen is not located directly on the shape. This sound is a kind of warning alarm and means that the user's pen is located quite far from the haptic shape.
- Metaphoric sound B, is played when the velocity of the stylus pen is higher than an specific value. Also in this case, the sound is rendered as a warning alarm, and is activated when the user's pen goes too fast in the sketching, hatching and cutting tasks.

Table 1. Evaluation of the Multimodal Guidance System

	Main questions	Results
Comfort	Is the system comfortable for the users? They can use it in a comfortable position?	All the participants involved into the evaluation have been able to use the system in a comfortable way; the portability and the reduced dimensions allow all the subjects to set their position in the most comfortable way while they performed the task.
Interest	Is the system able to interest and to focus the user attention on the task?	For all the participants the system has been a great source of interest. In the evaluation phase, all of them have been able to complete the task without distraction.
Usability	Is the system intuitive?	The majority of the subjects started to interact whit the system in a correct way, grasping the stylus and moving it without any instruction.
Utility	Is the system useful in the educators opinion?	For all the educators the system constitutes a valid help to their work, interesting and helping subjects in the drawing and coping task.
System completeness	Provide the system all the cues needed for a good performance of the task?	In the educators opinion more important forces are needed, depending on the user deficit. Moreover, an interactive and funny interface has been suggested in order to involve more the subjects in the task.

8   User Test

The user test has been performed involving 6 subjects (4 males) aged 18 to 40 years. Down syndrome and mental retardation affected all participants. In this experiment a brief familiarization has been offered to the participants and it has been asked to perform a task that involved a combination of visual, haptic and sound feedback in order to design a circle with 100 mm of radius. Figure 4-**a** shows the tracked motion of an spiral shape without haptic and sound feedback, while Figure 4-**b** shows the tracked motion for the same disable people with the haptic and sound feedback. Figure 4-**c** shows the tracked motion of a circle without haptic and sound feedback while Figure 4-**d** shows the tracked circle with the haptic and sound feedback.

In order to systematically assess the contribution of the haptic and sound feedback we computed the error between the radius of two circles as reported from Figures 4-**e** and 4-**f**. Results showed that the error significantly decreases (Wicloxon rank sum test, $p \ll 0.05$) when subjects were guided. For what concerns the evaluation activities related to the developed prototype of the multimodal guidance system, we have decided to evaluate:

1. The applicability of the multimodal guidance system to the learning environment.
2. Gaining feedback on the development, improvement and overall technical assessment of the multimodal guidance device, and suggesting recommendations for functional changes for subsequent prototypes.

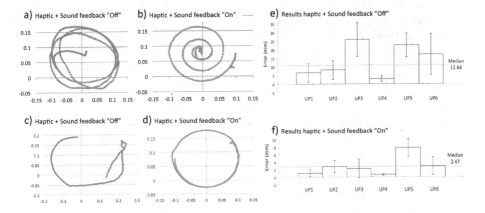

Fig. 4. User's test results

9   Conclusion

The results of our study showed that the multimodal guidance system help people during manual tasks by means of using haptic and sound technology.

The opportunity to create a haptic system that would make real difference in disable peoples life appeared to be a highly motivating factor. We are currently performing an evaluation with unskilled people in order to measure their learning improvements in 2D operations skills. Results show that the effect of using the haptic cutting system increases the accuracy in the tasks operations. We can resume that the system leads to the satisfaction of the following objectives:

- The force feedback enhances the interaction between the user and the physical template.
- The sound feedback as and additional channel information in order to performing the 2D tasks according with the correct velocity required to sketch, hatch and cut the foam.

Acknowledgement. The authors would like to thank all the instructors at Laboratorio Artimedia (Calolziocorte, Italy), Casa Dei Ragazzi Treves De Sanctis O.N.L.U.S., and Centro Diurno Disabili Di Barzan for their support in the preliminary evaluation of the haptic guidance device and for giving us the opportunity to test the system.

References

1. Burdea, G.C., Coiffet, P.: Virtual Reality Technology, 2nd edn. John Wiley and Sons Ltd. (July 2003)
2. Jones, L.A., Lederman, S.J.: Human Hand Function, 1st edn. Oxford University Press, USA (2006) ISBN 0195173155

3. Palsbo, S.E., Marr, D., Streng, T., Bay, B.K., Walter Norblad, A.: Towards a modified consumer haptic device for robotic-assisted fine-motor repetitive motion training. Disability and Rehabilitation: Assistive Technology 6(6), 546–551 (2011)
4. Witmer, B.G., Bailey, J.H., Knerr, B.W., Parsons, K.C.: Virtual spaces and real world places: transfer of route knowledge. International Journal of Human-Computer Studies 45(4), 413–428 (1996)
5. Giess, C., Evers, H., Meinzer, H.P.: Haptic volume rendering in different scenarios of surgical planning. In: The Third PHANToM Users Group Workshop. MIT, Massachusetts (1998)
6. Gorman, P.J., Lieser, J.D., Murray, W.B., Haluck, R.S., Krummel, T.M.: Assessment and validation of force feedback virtual reality based surgical simulator. In: The Third PHANToM Users Group Workshop. MIT, Massachusetts (1998)
7. Darken, R.P., Peterson, B.: Spatial orientation, wayfinding, and representation. In: Handbook of Virtual Environments Design, Implementation and Applications, pp. 493–518. Lawrence Erlbaum Associates, Inc., New Jersey (2002)
8. Colwell, C., Petrie, H., Kornbrot, D.: Haptic virtual reality for blind computer users. In: Assets 1998 Conference, Los Angeles, CA (1998)
9. Boulanger, P., Wu, G., Bischof, W.F., Yang, X.D.: Hapto-audio-visual environments for collaborative training of ophthalmic surgery over optical network. In: HAVE - Haptic Audio Visual Environments and their Applications, Ottawa, Canada (2006)
10. Campion, G., Wang, Q., Hayward, V.: The pantograph mk-ii: a haptic instrument. In: 2005 IEEE/RSJ International Conference on Intelligent Robots and Systems, IROS 2005, pp. 193–198 (August 2005)
11. Avizzano, C.A., Portillo-Rodriguez, O., Bergamasco, M.: Assisting to sketch unskilled people with fixed and interactive virtual templates. In: IEEE International Conference on Robotics and Automation, pp. 4013–4017 (April 2007)
12. Covarrubias, M., Bordegoni, M., Cugini, U.: Sketching Haptic System Based on Point-Based Approach for Assisting People with Down Syndrome. In: Stephanidis, C. (ed.) Posters, HCII 2011, Part I. CCIS, vol. 173, pp. 378–382. Springer, Heidelberg (2011)

Identifying Barriers to Accessibility in Qatar

Erik Zetterström

Mada (Qatar Assistive Technology Center), Doha, Qatar
ezetterstrom@mada.org.qa

Abstract. To identify barriers to accessibility in Qatar a study was conducted by distributing a survey to 211 persons with disabilities and conducting interviews. Lack of awareness, lack of Assistive Technology in Arabic, inaccessible ATM:s and absence of assistive communication services are the largest barriers.

Keywords: statistics, Qatar, accessibility, disabilities.

1   Introduction

Mada, Qatar's Center for Assistive Technology opened on June 1, 2010 as a public private partnership with ictQATAR. Mada is a non-profit organization that strives to empower and enable people with disabilities through Information and Communication Technology (ICT). Mada's mission includes; to provide disabled residents of Qatar with Assistive Technology, provide training on the use of Assistive Technology and best practices in the area of accessibility.

Statistics on disabilities in Qatar and most of the gulf region are limited. Mada's early estimates of the need and barriers to accessibility in Qatar were based on interpolating data from other countries, for example Egypt [1]. However the population structure varies significantly between many countries in the region; Qatar has a very large expatriate population [2] while for example Egypt does not [3]. Statistical data on disabilities as a result of different types of medical conditions (for example Stroke or Diabetes) and accidents are available from medical services in Qatar. This data does not include those previously born in Qatar with a disability, nor those it provide any information on the actual need for assistive technology as a result of for example a stroke.

In order for Mada to deliver the right services to disabled residents of Qatar proper statistics are needed.

2   Scope

The study uses the World Health Organization (WHO) definition of disability [4]. The study has focused on four major areas of disability:

- Visual impairment: People who are blind and those with low vision
- Hearing impairment: People communicating through sign and those using residual hearing

K. Miesenberger et al. (Eds.): ICCHP 2012, Part I, LNCS 7382, pp. 235–242, 2012.

- Physical disabilities: Including wheelchair users, people with upper limb disorders and multiple physical needs
- Learning disabilities: Including those with Dyslexia and those with more profound and complex learning disabilities including AAC users

Analysis at a sub-classification level (e.g. partially blind sub-set within the vision disability category) will be made for specific cases but those results should be seen only as an indication. The aim of the study is to:

- Estimate the total numbers of disabled people within Qatar and the proportion of the disabled population which would benefit from Mada services.
- Identify the key barriers to digital inclusion by people with disability
- Identify key international and regional organizations operating in the area of assistive technology along with organisation's profile and other relevant information
- Establish factbase in Qatar with reference to ICT Accessibility Self-Assessment framework and Digital Accessibility and Inclusion Index
- Develop indicators, design and questionnaire(s) for quantitative data collection
- Assess the level of ICT usage across people with disabilities, their attitude towards Information & Communications Technology and key barriers to ICT uptake through quantitative research

3   Method

To achieve the goals of the study the following key groups of respondents were identified:

- People with disabilities and their families in Qatar
- Schools/Institutes
- Government officials in the departments concerned with formulation, implementation and regulation and monitoring of policies related to the United Nations Convention on the Rights of Persons with Disabilities.
- Current firms/business entities operating as suppliers of Assistive Technology in Qatar
- Legal and Technical experts in the region of Qatar and GCC

In the groups with a large number of individuals a combination of quantitative and qualitative methods were used. Some of the groups of respondents contain a small number of individuals, for these groups only qualitative methods were used.

4   Results

4.1   User Characteristics

A quantitative survey was performed with 211 people with disabilities. In the sample group 71% were Qatari, 12% Arabic speaking expatriates and 17% other expatriates. Of the entire group 67% had been diagnosed with multiple disabilities. The distribution of disabilities can be seen in figure 1 below.

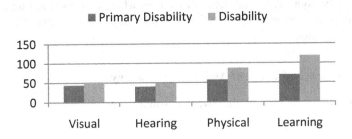

Fig. 1. Disabilities in the sample groups

From the data it is evident that learning disabilities is the most common primary disability and 34% of those with another disability also have a learning disability.

4.2   Lifestyle

How active people with disabilities are is an indication of the accessibility of the society they're living in.

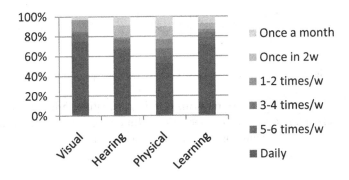

Fig. 2. Frequency of going out per type of disability

The results displayed in figure 2 indicate that people with a physical disability go out less often than people with other types of disability. The likely causes are the lack of accessible venues and transport in Qatar.

4.3   Usage of ICT

The current use of major ICT technologies and Assistive Technology for access to ICT was surveyed across the target groups. 84% of the respondents are using the internet, but only 69% stated that they spent time online. The internet penetration rate for the whole of Qatar is 82% [5]. Usage levels for different kinds of ICT clearly singled out ATMs as inaccessible to people with visual, learning and physical disabilities. The communication needs of the deaf where expressed during interviews, currently they use video telephony for sign language communication but no relay services are available.

4.4   Awareness and Usage of Assistive Technology

For each of the target groups the awareness and usage of assistive technology was measured.

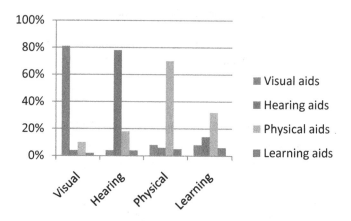

Fig. 3. Awareness of Assistive Technology per type of disability

All target groups expect for people with learning disabilities are aware of Assistive Technology pertaining to their own disability. To find the gaps between the awareness and usage of Assistive Technology the level of usage of Assistive Technology for each disability was measured.

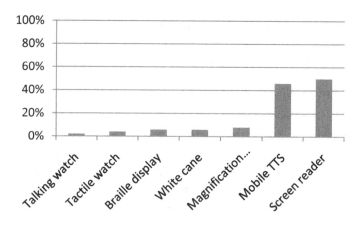

Fig. 4. Usage of Assistive Technology by people with visual impairment

As seen from figure 3 and 4 people with visual impairment have both a high awareness and usage rate of Assistive Technology.

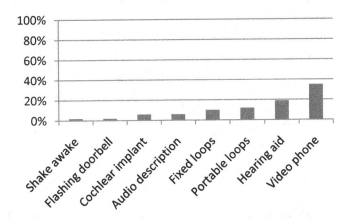

Fig. 5. Usage of Assistive Technology by people with hearing impairment

People with hearing impairments are very aware of available Assistive Technology but the general usage rate is low, as seen in figure 5. However if the hard of hearing and the profoundly deaf are studied separately the usage of Assistive Technology is high in the latter group, for example 79% use video phones.

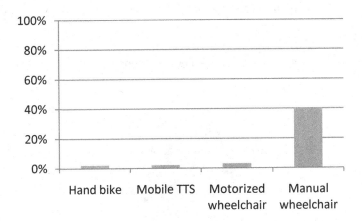

Fig. 6. Usage of Assistive Technology by people with physical disability

People with physical disabilities are aware of available Assistive Technology in general but the usage rate is low. However the detailed data indicates that people with physical disabilities are unaware of Assistive Technology for access to ICT. The awareness and usage (see figure 6) of motorized wheelchairs is low. This is likely due to the lack of a provisioning service for wheelchairs in Qatar.

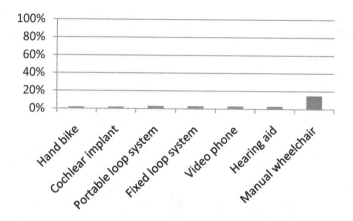

Fig. 7. Usage of Assistive Technology by people with learning disability

People with learning disabilities are not aware of available Assistive Technology and hence the usage rate of Assistive Technology for learning disabilities is non exist-ant, see figure 7. The number of available Assistive Technology solutions in Arabic for people with learning disabilities is also low.

4.5   Cost of Assistive Technology

Most people with disabilities in Qatar get their Assistive technology for free, see figure 8. The 24% of non free Assistive Technologies are likely due to lack of awareness.

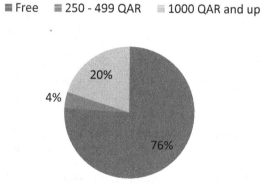

Fig. 8. The cost of Assistive Technology for computers in Qatar

4.6   Reasons for Non-usage of Assistive Technology for ICT

13% of the people with disabilities in the survey do not use Assistive Technology for ICT even though they know it exists and could be of value to them.

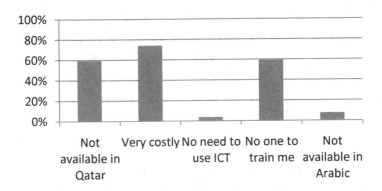

Fig. 9. Reason for not using Assistive Technology for ICT (multiple choices possible) given by people who are aware of available Assistive Technology

As seen in figure 9 most people with disabilities who do not use applicable ICT realize the value of ICT but there main reasons for not using Assistive Technology for ICT is their perception that it is expensive, not available in Qatar or lack of training. This is in most cases a misconception as 76% of all Assistive Technology for ICT in Qatar is free (see figure7). Mada needs to reach this group as Mada can provide all of these things (all the participants in the survey were given information about Mada).

5   Conclusion

The largest barriers to accessibility in Qatar exist for those with a learning disability; this group is not aware of or using Assistive Technology. Lack of localized Assistive Technology for this group is also a major issue. Mada is working continuously with manufacturers of Assistive Technology to facilitate localization of their products.

Inaccessible ATMs is the ICT that causes the most problems for people with disabilities in Qatar. Mada is working with QNB and other banks to bring accessible ATMs to Qatar.

The Deaf community is in dire need of communication services. Currently the lack of relay services makes them an isolated community. A plan for deployment of relay services is being developed. Mada is providing advice to this project.

The lack of accessibility in public transportation and the built environment is likely to have an isolating effect on people with physical disabilities. This is an area for further study. Mada is contacting relevant authorities to raise awareness about this issue.

Mada needs to work on raising awareness about Assistive Technology among people with hearing, physical and learning disabilities as well as communicate Mada's service offering to all people with disabilities.

References

1. Japan International Cooperation Agency: Country Profile on Disability Arab Republic of Egypt, http://siteresources.worldbank.org/DISABILITY/Resources/Regions/MENA/JICA_Egypt.pdf
2. US State Department, Qatar Page, http://www.state.gov/r/pa/ei/bgn/5437.html
3. US State Department, Egypt Page, http://www.state.gov/r/pa/ei/bgn/5309.html
4. World Health Organization: World Report on Disabilities, http://www.who.int/disabilities/world_report/2011/report/en/index.html
5. ictQATAR, Report on Digital Media Landscape in Qatar, http://www.ictqatar.qa/en/news-events/news/ictqatar-publishes-report-digital-media-landscape-qatar

NCBI and Digital Literacy: A Case Study

Denise Leahy and Stuart Lawler

Trinity College Dublin & National Council for the Blind of Ireland

Abstract. The European Commissioner with responsibility for the Digital Agenda has declared that she wants to make "Every European Digital" [1] and it is accepted that knowledge of computing is necessary for everyone in the Information Society [2] The knowledge and skills which are needed are often called "digital literacy". The National Council for the Blind of Ireland (NCBI) has provided training in the use of computers for over 15 years and, in 2010, decided to take part in the European Computer Driving Licence (ECDL) programme and become an authorised ECDL test centre. ECDL is a standard of digital literacy which is accepted in 146 countries and has been taken by over 12 million people. This paper is a case study of the implementation of the ECDL programme in NCBI.

Keywords: Digital literacy, accessibility, ECDL, vision impairment.

1   Introduction

The European Union (EU) has identified digital literacy as vital for all citizens in the Information Society, and says that it is necessary for inclusion, which they define as "eInclusion" or "e-Inclusion" [2]. The National Council for the Blind of Ireland (NCBI) has been providing service and support to people with a vision impairment in Ireland since 1931. Recognising the importance of skills in using technology, the NCBI service has included training in using computers.

NCBI has been involved in digital literacy as a partner in several European projects. They co-operate with the Visually Impaired Computer Society of Ireland (VICS) and have worked with several mainstream computer training providers. While basic computing skills have been part of their training programmes for many years, in 2010 NCBI became a test centre for the European Computer Driving Licence (ECDL). A small group of people with vision impairments have been part of this programme since May 2010. Once a student has achieved certification, his or her place on the training course is taken by another student. By early 2012, eight people had taken part with another five waiting to enter the programme.

This paper examines the experiences of NCBI in this project which tested how the ECDL accessibility adaptations were working in a training centre, seven years after their implementation, and to examine the usefulness or otherwise of the structured approach to digital literacy by users of assistive technology. While this case study comprises a small group of people, the findings could be of value to others researching digital literacy and assistive technology. According to Walsham [3], in case study

K. Miesenberger et al. (Eds.): ICCHP 2012, Part I, LNCS 7382, pp. 243–250, 2012.

research there is no universally acceptable number of cases and such research could be based even on a single case. This is because the validity of the case study has more to do with the "plausibility and cogency of the logical reasoning".

2   The Digital Agenda for Europe

The Digital Agenda is one of seven initiatives in the European Union "EU 2020" growth strategy, which has initiatives grouped into three target areas - "Smart growth", "Sustainable growth" and "Inclusive growth" [4].

The relevant actions for this research are part of Pillar 6 – "enhancing e-skills":-

- Action 57: Make digital literacy and competences a priority for the ESF (European Social Fund)
- Action 59: Make digital literacy and skills a priority of the "New skills for new jobs" Flagship
- Action 63: Systematically evaluate accessibility in all revisions of legislation
- Action 64: Make sure that public sector websites are fully accessible by 2015
- Action 65: Memorandum of Understanding on Digital Access for persons with disabilities
- Action 66: Member States to promote long-term e-skills and digital literacy policies [5]

E-inclusion is a major part of the Digital Agenda [6] and Action 65 was completed by the end of 2011. The aim of the Digital Agenda is to make: "Every European Digital" [1], according to Neelie Kroes, vice-President of the European Commission responsible for the Digital Agenda. Ensuring that all Europeans have e-skills is vital to achieving this objective.

3   The NCBI Project - Addressing the E-Skills Needs

When NCBI became an ECDL Test Centre, it was planned to present structured training according to the ECDL syllabus. This training took place in the Rehabilitation Training Centre at NCBI's head office in Dublin and was based on a determination of each student's needs. Funding for the programme came from the CDVEC (City of Dublin Vocational Education Committee) Adult Literacy section and, since its commencement; this funding has seen a small increase, reflecting the importance that the CDVEC attach to the specific training being offered. There were four students on the first training course, with one teacher and the training centre manager. All six people had a vision impairment. The course ran once per week for three hours in the evening. All participants were in employment and travelled to NCBI from the city centre after work. Students who participated in the initial programme gave a commitment to the weekly three hour classes. Many of them, while being in some way proficient with ICT, had never undertaken any formalised computer training. They all saw ECDL as a way to gain recognised certification, and to increase their future employment and career prospects.

The teacher was a professional IT trainer with a vision impairment. As one course member left, another person was invited to take his or her place. Some of the participants completed the full ECDL certificate and others decided to take an ECDL progress certificate when they had completed some of the modules.

JAWS (Job Access with Speech) and Zoomtext (Screen Magnification software) were the main assistive technologies used by everyone in the class. JAWS is a package which outputs the contents of the computer screen in synthetic speech or refreshable Braille. It can be used with a wide variety of computer software, including the Microsoft Office Suite and a number of internet browsers. JAWS is a wonderful tool, but it presents some hurdles as it takes time to learn and is relatively expensive, usually costing more than the software it can operate with. Zoomtext works by magnifying the on-screen text to the level that is suitable for the low vision user. It can be used in conjunction with speech if desired, in order to minimise fatigue. A free screen reader, Non Visual Desktop Access (NVDA), was introduced to the students during the second year. The experiences of the students using this new screen reader are discussed later in this paper.

4   Initial Findings

A focus group meeting with the team members was held in summer 2011 to discuss their experiences, as they were midway through the initial project. Each member of the team was also interviewed separately to identify particular or individual issues and achievements. While some of the students were happy with the class size, others felt that, in order to give the personal attention needed, it would be preferable to split into two classes of two. All students commented that they were pleased to have been given a place on the course.

All members of the group agreed that a teacher needs knowledge of assistive technology, including knowing, for example, the shortcut keys in the software on which training is to be provided, as well as knowledge of the different versions of software. A major issue identified was the need to understand that there are differences with versions of JAWS, operating systems and application software and it was noted that a different setup of JAWS might be needed for each student.

The personal commitment of the students was high. Two of the students had not been in education for many years and found the testing stressful at the start. "It took a while to get into the learning and testing process" according to one student. All students found that travelling to the course after work and training for three hours was tiring; however, they all acknowledged that it would have been equally difficult to take the course on two evenings. There were some job pressures for the two students who worked in the public service.

The tests – all of the students had some problem with Excel, but on reviewing the issues, it was agreed that this was a problem with mathematics rather than a software problem. Questions which were visual were problematic, but all were overcome. In order to do a test, the student had to get JAWS to read the question and then switch to another document to perform the test. This switching was difficult and time consuming. It was agreed that for certain tests, specifically PowerPoint and Access, the use of a sighted reader would be hugely beneficial.

The experience – all the students enjoyed the experience. The students identified a need for a computer at home with a complete JAWS and Zoomtext set-up to practice. They all agreed that the teacher's notes and support were excellent and were necessary.

Running the tests – The system was run using a manual test system as the available automated test system is not yet accessible. The manual test system administration was quite complex. A practical problem with the administration of the testing was that the printer was on a candidate's desk, this caused distraction when the other students needed to print out test results. The students agreed that during the test, no one should leave the room as this can cause a further distraction for a person who cannot see what is happening.

The comments from the students included:

- *"I needed to be "computer minded" – I needed to change my way of thinking", according to a partially sighted student*
- *One student, who is blind, said, "Personally I can't believe what you can do with a computer" and "this might "open up doors" in work"*
- *Another student said "I learned a huge amount, it is unreal the power of Excel"*
- *"The theory part (Module 1) is very useful in buying a computer – I can understand what the sales people are saying"*

These comments show the effect the use of technology has had on the course participants. They were all in agreement that having the skills to use a computer would help them in work, could help in their normal daily life and they looked forward to being able to communicate with family and friends using technology.

An electronic email forum was also created to support and enhance the learning process. This list also acts as a repository for questions and answers, and provides valuable information for the programme review team.

5   Progress in 2012

The training continued through 2011 and early 2012. In reviewing the project, it was decided to follow up with the participants to get their update on whether the new skills had been beneficial to them. It was also decided to evaluate a new and free screen reader, Non Visual Desktop Access (NVDA). This section describes the results from these activities.

5.1   Update on the Experiences

Interviews with all the people who had taken part in or had been involved in any way were undertaken in April 2012. The objective was to determine:

- The usefulness of the training
- What was of most value
- What was missing from the course or from the certification
- Has it changed the participants' job or promotion prospects

Eight of the participants were interviewed by telephone. They were asked which modules they liked best; four students selected Module 1 - Concepts of Information and Communication Technology, three preferred Module 3 – Word Processing, and one selected Module 2 - Using the Computer and Managing Files. One of the students liked all of the Office-type systems.

With regard to the usefulness of the modules, Word Processing and Web Browsing and Communication were considered to be most useful. The students who were employed said that they found the new skills to be very useful in their work. The students were asked what was missing from the ECDL programme – they suggested modules on (a) assistive technology generally, (b) music and (c) JAWS.

All students felt more confident in using a computer, saying that they were making more use of the Internet, email and other communication on their laptop or home computer. Some comments were:

- *"I am sorry I didn't do this years ago"*
- *"I have purchased the iPhone since starting this course, I wouldn't have done that if I hadn't started this course, it has given me more confidence and made me more aware of what exists"*
- *One student said that he now used the computer .... "especially for writing letters, writing articles for a local newsletter and for looking up timetables"*
- *"Now when I'm going to buy a computer I have a better understanding of what is what."*

The main findings from this small case study confirm the need for considering accessibility early in the development of any user interface, including training and testing. This should include understanding assistive technology and how to interface to such technology. Training is preferable in small groups in order to address individual needs. However, once the systems are in place and the testing is successful, a person who is blind or has a vision impairment can use standard technology and software.

5.2   Non Visual Desktop Access (NVDA)

There are plans to expand on the range of assistive technology used in the NCBI training centre for this digital literacy programme. JAWS is an extremely flexible and feature rich program, but the high cost of the product is a barrier for many users. A free open source screen reading solution, Non Visual Desktop Access (NVDA), is gaining popularity and this software was tested as part of the training programme in the Rehabilitation Training Centre. NVDA offers much of the functionality available from the commercial screen readers [7] and in the testing has proven to be very reliable. The tests were carried out using NVDA 2012.1 release, which is current at the time of writing, and Windows XP, Internet Explorer version 8 and Microsoft Office 2003.

Two modules of ECDL were tested, module 3 and module 7. Six tasks from a test relating to module 3, and six tasks from a test relating to module 7 were selected.

Module 3

1. When opening Microsoft Word with NVDA, the screen reader reported that the application was in focus, and that a new blank document was available to the student. It further announced the line number of the document, something that the students had not seen with JAWS.
2. A question in the test asked the students to delete a sentence. Selecting text using NVDA didn't present any problems and the sentence was quickly deleted.
3. The search and replace function in Microsoft Word worked with no problems.
4. There were difficulties in changing the text colour, identifying the colour selection, as NVDA did not read this dialogue box. JAWS does read this information, so at present, this area of the module would not be accessible to the NVDA user unless the student had a reader for the test.
5. The students moved text from one document to another, inserting the new text at the instructed point in the document with no problem.
6. Finally, the spellcheck function in Microsoft word was tested. The reading of dialogues behaved differently to that of JAWS, but reviewing the appropriate section of the NVDA user manual, which is itself very well written, gave the necessary information to be able to perform this task without any further problems.

Module 7

1. When using Microsoft Outlook 2003 with NVDA everything worked as expected.
2. The students successfully created a new message and attached a document before sending.
3. Reply to, forward and search for a message all worked well.
4. Internet Explorer was used to navigate to a website. The elements list function is similar to that of the links list in Jaws, and students could easily get a snapshot of the hyperlinks on any page.
5. Students were able to easily fill out a web form and submit it. The virtual cursor in NVDA behaves in the same way as JAWS, and, in some cases, it was found to be a lot faster to navigate around web pages.
6. Google was used to perform a web search and it was easy to navigate the search results using the headings shortcut. This behaviour is identical with JAWS.

In summary, out of the tasks above NVDA has worked well. It was found that the experience is very similar to that of JAWS. The screen reader is a little verbose in places, but there was not enough time to thoroughly investigate the manual, so there may be configuration changes which can be made to reduce this extra speech output.

6   Conclusions

Becoming an authorised ECDL test centre and piloting the programme with a small number of people with impaired vision is the first step in NCBI's plan to expand digital literacy training to the regional centres throughout Ireland. The next phase of this development will see this training forming an integral part of the rehabilitative training programme offered to vision impaired people at NCBI's Rehabilitation Training Centre. The Rehabilitation Training course seeks to empower people to acquire new skills and use these skills to move into further training or employment. ECDL is an obvious addition to the programme in this respect and will add to the centre's portfolio of certified courses. By the end of 2012, NCBI hopes to extend digital literacy courses to centres in Dublin, Louth, Westmeath and Wexford, making the certification available to many more people with impaired vision in their locality.

One of the objectives of the European Digital Agenda is to ensure that European society "must be envisioned as a society with better outcomes for all." [8]. In November 2010, the EU announced the "European Disability Strategy" [9] with an accompanying list of actions, entitled "Initial plan to implement the European Disability Strategy 2010 – 2020". Two important action points in this plan are to:

- "Improve e-skills of persons with disabilities" and
- "Monitor recent developments regarding national and/or Europe-wide Curricula for professionals in the built environment, transport and ICT on Design for all to improve their knowledge, skills and competences on accessibility and encourage the development of a European Curriculum".

NCBI recognises that it is important that all people have skills to be part of this new Europe and that it is vital that e-inclusion is ensured. Technology and the internet must not create a greater "digital divide". As Neelie Kroes [10] has said:
"The Internet belongs to all of us".

References

1. Every European Digital, http://blogs.ec.europa.eu/neelie-kroes/every-european-digital/ (accessed October 16, 2011)
2. Digital Literacy: Skills for the Information Society, http://ec.europa.eu/information_society/tl/edutra/skills/index_en.html (accessed January 11, 2011)
3. Walsham, G.: Interpreting Information Systems in Organizations. Wiley, Chichester (1993)
4. Flagship initiatives for EU 2020, http://ec.europa.eu/europe2020/tools/flagship-initiatives/index_en.html (accessed September 22, 2011)
5. European Commission, Information Society, http://ec.europa.eu/information_society/digital-agenda/index_en.html (accessed January 17, 2012)
6. e-Inclusion, http://ec.europa.eu/information_society/policy/accessibility/index_en.html (accessed January 17, 2012)

7. Non Visual Desktop Access, `http://www.nvda-project.org/` (accessed April 18, 2012)
8. A Digital Agenda for Europe, `http://eur-lex.europa.eu/LexUriServ/LexUriServ.do?uri=COM:2010:0245:FIN:EN:PDF` (accessed April 7, 2012)
9. European Disability Strategy, a Renewed Commitment to a Barrier Free Europe, COM (2010) 636 final, SEC (2010) 1342 final, Communication from the Commission to the European Parliament, the Council, the European Economic and Social Committee and the Committee of the Regions
10. Kroes, N.: The internet belongs to all of us, `http://europa.eu/rapid/pressReleasesAction.do?reference=SPEECH/11/285` (accessed April 2, 2012)

A User-Friendly Virtual Guide for Post-Rehabilitation Support Following Stroke

Sascha Sommer, Matthias Bartels, Martina Frießem, and Joachim Zülch

Ruhr-Universität, Bochum, Germany
{sascha.sommer,matthias.bartels,martina.friessem,
joachim.zuelch}@rub.de

Abstract. Post-rehabilitation support aids socio-professional reintegration. Information about options for post-rehabilitation support following stroke is provided by an application based on Wiki-principles and semantic technologies (Virtual Guide). Core feature is a knowledge-management system. Regional health care professionals contribute initial content for the database. User involvement is facilitated by an interface based on internet blog posts describing prototypical situations stroke patients face during post-rehabilitation. On the condition that sufficient users proactively provide regular contributions, the platform will, ideally, develop into a living system representing regional infrastructures for post-rehabilitation support both accurately and up to date.

Keywords: Stroke, semantic technologies, service delivery, socio-professional reintegration, social innovation.

1 Background

In Germany, strokes are the neurological disease most frequently causing chronic functional limitations. Their incidence is increasing even more due to the aging of the German population [1]. However, both people with special needs as well as many German health care professionals themselves lack comprehensive knowledge about options for post-rehabilitation support following stroke. This includes, e.g., information about obtainable health services and products, financing options and contact persons for public assistance. These information gaps are substantial barriers to social participation. The joint project "Post-Rehabilitation-Network" thus establishes a cooperation of health care stakeholders. Network members collect and edit comprehensive information about their local post-rehabilitation infrastructure in order to make it available to patients and other persons involved in the post-rehabilitation process.[1]

The information will be disseminated by a user-friendly internet-based platform ("Virtual Guide"). German approaches to guide patients during post-rehabilitation following stroke currently involve either professional case managers or volunteers of

---

[1] Post-Rehabilitation-Network: Development of Integrative Service Packages for the Vocational and Private Environment (project co-funded by the European Union and the German Federal State of North Rhine – Westphalia).

K. Miesenberger et al. (Eds.): ICCHP 2012, Part I, LNCS 7382, pp. 251–253, 2012.

self-help groups [e.g. 2]. Taking into account increasing economical restrictions in the health care system and decreasing numbers of volunteers to fulfill the demand, certain guiding functions can be taken over by the Virtual Guide as a third, complimentary pillar.

2   User Information Needs and Semantic Organization

Specification of user needs was based on focus interviews with stroke patients and their relatives. Interviewees' case histories were analyzed on the basis of the International Classification of Functioning, Disability and Health [3]. Assistive guiding functions that can be transferred to the Virtual Guide include in particular:

- Information about available measures to facilitate socio-professional reintegration and health service providers like e.g. nursing services, medical supply stores, therapists, pharmacies, architect offices specialized in accessibility etc.
- Information about financing options as well as stakeholders like insurances or public contact persons
- Information about and transfer to local self-help groups and other contact points for further support that cannot be provided by the Virtual Guide (e.g. specific medical advice, issues associated with data privacy etc.)

Core feature of the Virtual Guide is a knowledge-management platform based on Wiki-principles and semantic technologies. It combines the well-known advantages of Wiki-systems like openness and flexibility with the characteristics of structured semantic networks (Fig. 1).

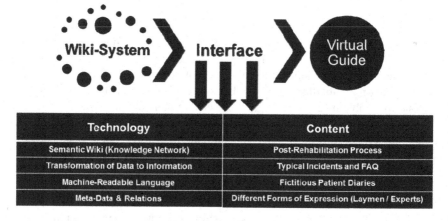

Technology	Content
Semantic Wiki (Knowledge Network)	Post-Rehabilitation Process
Transformation of Data to Information	Typical Incidents and FAQ
Machine-Readable Language	Fictitious Patient Diaries
Meta-Data & Relations	Different Forms of Expression (Laymen / Experts)

Fig. 1. System Architecture

Initial content for the database is provided by local health care professionals. In the next stage, users themselves are invited to contribute actively to the knowledge-management platform. The evolving organization of knowledge elements preserves the advantages of a Wiki-system and enhances it by a dynamic semantic structure [e.g. 4]. On the condition that sufficient users proactively provide regular input, like e.g. about changes in financing regulations or new service providers, the Virtual Guide will, ideally, develop into a living system representing regional infrastructures for post-rehabilitation support both accurately and up to date.

The interface is based upon descriptions of prototypical post-rehabilitation experiences of stroke patients in the form of easily comprehensible internet blogs resembling fictitious patient diaries. E.g., in case of lower limb paretic mobility impairments requiring reductions of barriers in the domestic environment, the user will receive, via the relevant blog post, information about financing options, public contact persons and local architects specialized in accessibility.

3   Conclusions

The Virtual Guide is a cost-free Wiki-based knowledge-management-system for post-rehabilitation support following stroke. It is supervised by a local network of health care stakeholders. About 93% of all experienced German internet users are familiar with Wiki-based systems and 80% use them regularly today [5]. As the Virtual Guide is essentially based on a Web2.0 Wiki-system, no significant usability thresholds should limit active user involvement. First explorative tests of usability and acceptance confirm this expectation.

References

1. Förch, C., Misselwitz, B., Sitzer, M., Steinmetz, H., Neumann-Häfelin, T.: Die Schlaganfallzahlen bis zum Jahr 2050 (The Projected Burden of Stroke in the German Federal State of Hesse up to the Year 2050). Deutsches Ärzteblatt 105(26), 467–473 (2008)
2. Deutsche Schlaganfall-Hilfe (German Stroke-Aid Foundation),
   http://www.schlaganfall-hilfe.de/der-lotse
3. Sommer, S.M., Wiethoff, M., Valjakka, S., Kehagias, D., Tzovaras, D.: Development of a Mobile Tourist Information System for People with Functional Limitations: User Behaviour Concept and Specification of Content Requirements. In: Miesenberger, K., Klaus, J., Zagler, W., Karshmer, A.I. (eds.) ICCHP 2006. LNCS, vol. 4061, pp. 306–313. Springer, Heidelberg (2006)
4. Yu, L.: A Developer's Guide to the Semantic Web. Springer, Heidelberg (2011)
5. Federal Association for Information Technology, Telecommunications and New Media: Wikipedia ist das meistgenutzte Lexikon (Wikipedia is the dictionary most frequently used). Press Release (January 11, 2011)

Musicking Tangibles for Empowerment

Birgitta Cappelen[1] and Anders-Petter Andersson[2]

[1] Institute of Design, Oslo School of Architecture and Design (AHO), Norway
birgitta.cappelen@aho.no
[2] Interactive Sound Design, Kristianstad University (HKR), Sweden
anders@interactivesound.org

Abstract. We present a novel approach towards *understanding* and *design* of *interactive music technology* for people with special needs. The health effects of music are well documented, but little research and interactive music technology has been developed, for Music Therapy and health improvement in everyday situations. Further, the music technology that has been used, exploits little of the potential current computer technology has to offer the Music and Health and Music Therapy fields, because it is designed and used based on a narrow perspective on technology and its potential. We present and argue for a broader understanding of music technology for empowerment and health improvement, building on a multidisciplinary approach with perspectives from Tangible interaction design, *empowerment* and *resource oriented* Music Therapy. We call this approach *Musicking Tangibles*, inspired by Christopher Small's term "musicking". We also present two designed Musicking Tangibles, and argue for their empowering qualities based on user observations.

Keywords: Interaction Design, Empowerment, Tangibles, Music, Health.

1   Introduction

Music and music related activities are important experiences and should be a right [1] in every person's life. The health effect of music, for a number of diseases, has been well documented within biomedical and humanistic health research, over the last 15 years [2] [3]. Currently we know many ways music can improve vitality, empowerment and health [4] [5]. Still very little research has been done and interactive technology been developed, for Music Therapy and health improvement with music in everyday situations [6]. Music instruments, with or without computer technology, represent and offer various cultural and interactional possibilities. Within research related to music technology, for people with special needs, the focus has been on people's ability to control the interface of the instruments [7] [6]. Thereby, in our opinion, great possibilities that computer technology offers music instruments for wellness and health improvement, has been overlooked.

In this paper we present a novel approach towards *understanding* and *design of music technology for people with special needs*. To rethink music technology, we combine perspectives from culture oriented *Tangible interaction design* with

K. Miesenberger et al. (Eds.): ICCHP 2012, Part I, LNCS 7382, pp. 254–261, 2012.

empowerment and *resource oriented Music Therapy* [1] [4]. The paper is structured as follows; In the 2nd section we present the related work we build on in developing our new approach, what we call Musicking Tangibles. In the 3rd section we present the RHYME project, which is the framework for our research, and two Musicking Tangibles prototypes we have developed so far. In the 4th section we present use stories based on video observations [8], in order to argue for the differences between our Musicking Tangible approach and the traditional instrument oriented perspective. In the conclusion, we sum up our contribution to the field of design of interactive music technology, for people with special needs.

2   From Instruments to Musicking Tangibles

Tangible interaction and computational artefacts. Tangible interaction [9] is one of many names concerning design of physical things with computer capabilities. Our focus is on the design and interaction possibilities that lie in the physical, "hybrid" artefact [10], the tangibles, when including computer components, such as sensors, network, hardware and software, into cultural artefacts and everyday objects and things. The computational artefact, the tangibles, embodies cultural interpretation possibilities, which we build on when designing and in using artefacts [9] [11].

Computer based instruments. Music instruments are artefacts, and computer technology has for a long time been used to enrich music instruments. Many computer based instruments can be found in Toy stores and Assistive Technology shops, including software to make any computer into a musical instrument. Some of the most advanced computer based instruments on the market, such as the music game Guitar Hero (guitarhero.com) and Reactable (reactable.com) are results of research within the field. Compared to acoustic music instruments, with material based stimuli-response, computer based music interfaces don't require direct relation between input and output [12] [7]. For people with special needs, music technology therefore offers new and adaptable ways to interact [6] [7]. Potentially, this makes music experiences more accessible for people with special needs, if it is *designed in a thoughtful way*.

Assistive Music Technology. Most music technology used in the Assistive Technology field is MIDI based, containing hard plastic contact switches, such as the pianolike Paletto (kikre.com). Other frequently used electronic instruments have ultrasound sensors like Soundbeam (soundbeam.co.uk) and OptiMusic (optimusic.co.uk). The speaker need not to be located in the same place as the sensor. That most of these instruments are MIDI based, represent an aesthetical limitation of the musical output. Further, most of the instruments are shaped as toys, which express, design vice, what and who they are designed for. We considered them therefore to be aesthetically and socially limited.

Music for health and empowerment. In the humanist health approach we build on, health is an experience of wellbeing rather than cure from illness [3]. Music then becomes a resource for health promotion [5]. The music therapist and researcher Randi Rolvsjord has thoroughly presented and argued for a resource and empowerment oriented perspective in Music Therapy [4]. From this perspective the focus is on the abilities and strengths of the person, not on their diagnosis or weaknesses. The goal is to improve vitality, self-esteem, social relationships and participation, through mutual and equal, positive relation building musical experiences [4] [5]. To design music technology with such goals, the challenges shift from the interface design, to the relation building potentialities of the tangibles. The focus shifts from controlling the interface to motivate social interaction, co-creation and "musicking" [13].

Musicking. The word musicking is developed by the composer and musicologist Christopher Small. With musicking he focuses on the equal, meaning making and relation building activities related to music, such as listen, playing, composing and dancing [13]. When designing for people with different abilities, motivations and activity intensities, we have to offer many possibilities at the same time, in order to make them share the musicking experience, on their own terms. We have to design music technology artefacts, tangibles, that are open to many interpretations, relations and musical actions. Therefore we call them "Musicking Tangibles".

Switch oriented and disempowering. Wendy Magee and Karen Burland [7] are two of few researchers that have focused on use of music technology in Music Therapy. In a study of music therapists' use of MIDI based electronic instruments like Sound-Beam, Magee and Burland [7 p. 132-133] concludes that the client *first* have to understand the *cause and effect of switches*, *before* doing complex musical interactions and music making. But Magee also points out problems with *fatigue* and *decreasing motivation*, caused by too strong focus on trying and failing to master the interface' switches. For us, the limitations of the narrow instrument and interface perspective on music technology in a health improving context, here becomes obvious. To empower the users we instead have to create an arena [8] for positive, mutually shared musicking experiences, not focus on making the user understand how the switch works technically, and potentially demotivating and disempowering him.

Musicking Tangibles for empowerment. Based on a resource oriented and empowerment view, and against Magee and Burland, we argue that music technology should offer a *multitude* of *positive musicking experiences* at once. Musicking Tangibles has to be open to many interpretations, interaction forms and activity levels, where there are no wrong actions. They have to offer many roles to take [12], and be both simple and complex at the same time. The software should build on musical, narrative and communicative principles, to motivate and develop musical competence and musicking experiences, for all users over long time [12]. Musicking Tangibles is our suggested approach for *understanding* and *designing* health improving music technology for people with special needs. So that people with diverse abilities and motivations can experience vitality, mastering, empowerment, participation and co-creation: Musicking. [4]. To achieve these ambitions the Musicking Tangibles should:

1. Evoke interest and positive emotions relevant to diverse people's interpretation of the tangibles and the situation
2. Dynamically offer many roles to take, many musicking actions to make and many ways of self-expression
3. Offer aesthetically consistent response and build relevant cross-media expectations and challenges over time and space, consistent with their character
4. Offer many relations to make to people, things, experiences, events, places

Technically this means that the Musicking Tangibles should be able to respond related to several types of events, to evoke interest and positive emotions. The Musicking Tangibles hold musical and rhetoric knowledge (programmed musical, narrative and communicative rules) and competence, remembering earlier user interactions, in order to respond aesthetically consistent over time and create coherent expectations. It can, physically or wireless, be networked to other actants [10] (people or things) to exchange value and build relations over time. The Musicking Tangibles have physically and musically attractive qualities related to material, shape, texture, character and identity, social and/or cultural. Further on, we will present the project context in which we design, evaluate and discuss Musicking Tangibles.

3   The RHYME Project and the Musicking Tangibles

RHYME. The context for this paper is the RHYME project (RHYME.no), funded by the VERDIKT program and the Research Council of Norway. RHYME is a unique multidisciplinary collaboration between Institute of Design/Oslo School of Architecture and Design, Centre for Music and Health/National Academy of Music and Institute for Informatics/University of Oslo. The project goal is to improve health and life quality for persons with severe disabilities, through use of what we here call Musicking Tangibles. In the project we will develop new generations of Musicking Tangibles every year 2011-2015, focusing on different user situations and user relations.

Method. RHYME is based on a humanistic health approach [5] [3]. The goal is to reduce isolation and passivity through use of Musicking Tangibles. Through multidisciplinary action oriented empirical studies, multidisciplinary discussions and reflections, we develop new generations of Musicking Tangibles and related knowledge. Our design research methodology is user-centred and practice based, where we develop knowledge through design of new generations of Musicking Tangibles. The first empirical study in the RHYME project was of the Musicking Tangibles called ORFI (see Fig. 1). The second was of Wave (see Fig. 2). We observed 5 children, between 7 and 15 years old, with special needs in their school's music room with a close related person, not professional music therapists. We made 4 different actions over a period of 1 month. From one action to the other, we made changes based on the previous action, weekly user surveys, observations and multidisciplinary discussions. All sessions were video recorded from several angels to capture as much as possible. The health aspects of the study have been described and analysed in a separate paper (in press) by researchers and music therapists Karette Stensæth and Even Ruud [8].

3.1   First Generation Musicking Tangibles – ORFI

The first generation of Musicking Tangibles is ORFI (MusicalFieldsForever.com). It consists of 26 soft pyramid shaped tangibles, pillow like modules, in three different sizes, from 30 to 90 centimetres. The modules are made in black textile. Most of the pyramids have orange origami shaped "wings" with bend sensors, and an orange transparent light stick along one side, which gives a high-tech expression. Every module can communicate wirelessly with each other. The modules can be connected together in a Lego-like manner into large interactive landscapes. By interacting with the orange wings (see Fig. 1) the user creates changes in light, dynamic graphics and music.

Fig. 1. Boy interacting with an ORFI-wing, and the whole family musicking in their own manner in front of the wall projection

Some modules contain speakers, so one can experience the vibrations from the sound by sitting, or holding a module in one's lap. ORFI currently offers 8 different music genres to choose between. Two orange pyramids contain microphones, which in the Voxx-genre create live music, based on the users input. ORFI has a full wall projection of dynamic graphics, expressing visually the music genre and the interaction. (see Fig. 1). ORFI is designed to offer as many interpretations, actions and experiences as possible to meet our requirements presented in the 2nd section. More details on the interactive Musicking Tangibles ORFI are presented in earlier papers [14] [12].

3.2   Second Generation Musicking Tangibles – Wave

Wave is the current year's Musicking Tangibles, that we also have designed based on the requirements presented in section 2, but it contains very different technology that we wanted to explore in this generation (RHYME.no). Wave Carpet is a 7-branched, wired, interactive, soft, dark carpet (see Fig. 2), with orange velvet tips that glows, when the user interacts with the arm. One central arm contains a microphone, and two arms contain movement sensors, accelerometer, that changes the recorded sound. Two arms contain bend sensors and create the rhythmical background music. One arm contains a web-camera to play with. Currently Wave contain 5 software programs, offering different music and dynamic graphics to show with the Pico projector embedded in one arm, or on the full wall projection. The carpet contains two robust speakers and a strong vibrator placed as a soft "stomach" in the middle of the carpet. We have also created a glowing soft velvet "bubble field" in the dark carpet of IR-sensors and RGB LED lights, that represent an aesthetically unique input device, that the users already have interacted with in many ways. Design details are documented in a separate paper [15]. With its size, shape, texture and input and output possibilities Wave offers infinite ways to interact and co-create musicking experiences.

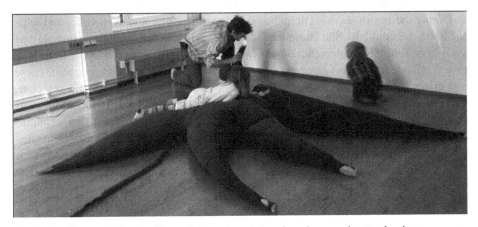

Fig. 2. Family musicking in Wave. Father sings into microphone and gets glowing response. Girl interacts with the "bubble field" and boy dances to the wall projection.

4   Observing and Discussing Musicking Tangibles

In the following we present use stories to argue for a Musicking Tangibles approach.

4.1   Olivia in ORFI

Olivia was 14 years old and liked to sing and play music. She communicated in non-verbal and sign language, and used wheelchair and hearing aid. The first time Olivia entered the room, where ORFI was installed; she sat down on the carpet and leaned against one of the big pyramid modules with speakers. Her companion, Mary, moved an ORFI-module, and Olivia felt the joy and excitement arise, as the music vibrated throughout her body. Mary placed a bunch of small modules within Olivia's reach. Together they moved the small and large modules closer, and created a soft, musical landscape around themselves, as a cozy place to be. Every time they shifted genre, the changing dynamic graphics gave a different colour to their cozy place. The arranging of the modules was part of the creative musicking exploration and relation building and empowering activity. This is in opposition to Magee and Burland's interface oriented view. They advise the therapist to move the switches to handle the clients *fatigue* and *decreased motivation* [7], after repeatedly failing to activate the switches. In our view it could even *disempower* their client. Olivia touched a module and ORFI answered with a new base melody and changed the graphics on the wall. She looked at Mary with a smile, because she was able to create a melody. As opposed to the poor quality of the SoundBeams MIDI-generated sound in Magee's et al studies, Olivia's melodic response from ORFI had good live recorded sound quality and synched to the beat. This created an aesthetically rich shared music experience, for both Olivia and Mary. Olivia became curious of the genre module, gradually understanding that it was the way to shift music genre, and encouraged Mary to change. This created a mutual expectation and shared excitement to experience of what would happen next.

During the fourth session Olivia had developed competency about ORFI and what she liked and could do. She chose the jazz genre, and selected a small module playing saxophone tones. She interacted for two minutes, building a grove, varying from hard to soft sound, from one to many tones. Opposite to Magee's switch oriented, cause and effect response based system that always gave the same poor sound response, every response in ORFI was aesthetically rich and varied musically, according to its character, each time she interacted. This experience increased Olivia's expectations and gave her joy for a long time. She also inspired Mary to contribute as she imitated her by singing and playing. Both Olivia and Mary expressed joy and expanded their relationship with several unique shared aesthetical, musicking experiences. In contrast to Magee and Burland [7], we argue that there is no need to follow a sequence of master cause-and-effect, before being able to create music.

4.2   Wendy in Wave

Wendy was 15 years old and had Down syndrome. She liked to sing, but was shy in others company. The first time Wendy entered the room where Wave Carpet was placed, she spoke carefully into the microphone arm when her companion, Nora, bent it towards her. Wendy said "Hi" and laughed when Wave played back her voice, one octave higher as Nora shook an arm with movement sensor. Still laughing Wendy continued to go through the words she had been practicing with her speech therapist the previous hour: "O", "P, Q, R", "Europe". Wave answered back in a higher pitch. Wendy was happy with her achievement and thought it was fun to listen to the variation. Instead of the same tone, as in Magee's cause-and-effect examples, the pitch shift created an aesthetically rich variation that was motivating to play with over time. Since it was Friday afternoon, Wendy continued to add some of her favorite food, she expected to eat in the weekend: "Say Taco", "Say Pizza", "Can you say ice-cream?" Wendy addressed Wave not merely as tool or piece of technology as in Magee's examples, but as an actor she was friendish with, talked to and begun to develop a relation to, and saying "goodbye" when she left. In the second session Wendy throw herself onto the Wave carpet, recognizing the soft vibrating and glowing creature from last Friday. She didn't behave shy anymore, but at home, safe and excited. She used all of her body to explore and interact with Wave. She co-created together with Nora in several ways. They gathered around the glowing bubble field as if it was a cozy "fireplace", shook their bodies to the beat, kissed and stroke the soft and glowing velvet microphone. They took turns, filming each other and playing with the camera arm. In contrast with Magee, it was not necessary to first focus on the technology, understanding cause-and-effect, *before* being able to create music and play with others. Instead the aesthetically rich cross-media interaction *strengthened* their *ability to act*, at the *same time* as it motivated positive emotions, mutuality, and development of competence over time, with varying musical, graphical and tangible musicking.

5   Conclusion

In this paper we have presented a novel approach for *understanding* and *design* of interactive health improving music technology, what we call Musicking Tangibles, inspired by musicologist Christopher Small's "musicking" term [13]. The Musicking Tangibles approach is an opposition to the traditional instrument, interface and switch oriented music technology perspective, which we consider in many cases to be disempowering. The Musicking Tangibles approach is built on a humanistic, resource and empowerment oriented health approach, and an aesthetic and culture based design approach towards music technology. We have presented 4 qualities the Musicking Tangibles should have to be empowering and health improving: *1) Evoke interest and positive emotions relevant to diverse people's interpretation of the tangibles and the situation, 2) Dynamically offer many roles to take, many musicking actions to make and many ways of self-expression, 3) Offer aesthetically consistent response and build relevant cross-media expectations and challenges over time and space, consistent with their character, 4) Offer many relations to make: to people, things, experiences, events and places.* Further we have presented two examples of Musicking Tangibles, ORFI and Wave, we have designed and tested within the ongoing RHYME project. We have argued for the Musicking Tangibles approach and their qualities in relation to use stories, and against music therapists Magee and Burland's understanding and suggested use of music technology for people with special needs [7].

References

1. Rolvsjord, R.: Therapy as Empowerment. Voices 6 (2006)
2. Bjursell, G., Vahlne Westerhäll, L. (eds.): Culture and Health (in Swedish) Kulturen och Hälsan. Santérus (2008)
3. Blaxter, M.: Health. Polity (2010)
4. Rolvsjord, R.: Resource-Oriented Music Therapy in Mental Health, Barcelona (2010)
5. Ruud, E.: Music Therapy: A Perspective from the Humanities, Barcelona (2010)
6. Magee, W.L.: Music Technology for Health and Well-Being The Bridge Between the Arts and Science. Music and Medicine 3, 131–133 (2011)
7. Magee, W.L., Burland, K.: An Exploratory Study of the Use of Electronic Music Technologies in Clinical Music Therapy. NJMT 17, 124–141 (2008)
8. Stensæth, K., Ruud, E.: Music Furniture or Music Instruments? (in Norwegian) Musikkmøbler eller musikkinstrumenter? Musikkterapi (in press)
9. Dourish, P.: Where the action is. MIT Press (2004)
10. Latour, B.: Pandora's hope. Harvard Univ. Press (1999)
11. Appadurai, A.: The social life of things. Cambridge Univ. Press (1986)
12. Cappelen, B., Andersson, A.-P.: Expanding the role of the instrument. NIME, Oslo (2011)
13. Small, C.: Musicking. Univ. Press of New England (1998)
14. Andersson, A.P., Cappelen, B.: Same But Different. In: AudioMostly 2008 (2008)
15. Cappelen, B., Andersson, A.-P.: Designing Smart Textile for Music and Health. In: Ambience 2011, Borås (2011)

RHYME: Musicking for All

Harald Holone[1] and Jo Herstad[2]

[1] Østfold University College, Halden, Norway
h@hiof.no
[2] University of Oslo, Oslo, Norway
johe@ifi.uio.no

Abstract. This paper describes the RHYME project, aimed at children with multiple disabilities, their families and caregivers. The goal in this cross disciplinary project is to create and evaluate platforms for co-creation through music and physical interaction in order to improve health and well being for the participants. The paper has two main contributions: 1) a review and discussion of Participatory Design in Design for All, and 2) Tangible Interaction and *familiarity* as a basis for the possibility of *musicking for all*, for children, their families and caregivers, on individual terms.

1 Introduction

Musicologist and composer Christopher Small defined *music* as a verb, rather than a noun [23]:

> "To music is to take part in any capacity in a musical performance, and the meaning of musicking lies in the relationships that are established between the participants by the performance"

Small argues that any kind of activity leading up to or being part of a musical performance, can be seen as acts of musicking. This includes composing, performing, and experiencing music. Importantly, it includes activities not requiring any formal musical skills or training, such as reading sheet music or mastering a musical instrument. This inclusion is important as a basis for the views put forward in this paper.

RHYME is a project where the overall goal is to improve health and quality of life for persons with severe disabilities through the use of *co-creative tangibles* [2]. These soft objects in the form of pillows and carpets embed computing and electronic components to enable users to take part in music related activities. This paper presents RHYME from a perspective of Participatory Design in Design for All, and on Tangible Interaction and music, in what we call *Musicking for All*.

The main contributions in this paper is twofold: 1) a review and discussion of Participatory Design in Design for All, and 2) Tangible Interaction and *familiarity* as a basis for the possibility of musicking.

K. Miesenberger et al. (Eds.): ICCHP 2012, Part I, LNCS 7382, pp. 262–269, 2012.

The rest of the paper is organized as follows: First, we give an overview of the RHYME project and the prototypes in Section 2, followed by a review of related work on accessible music, Participatory Design, and Tangible Interaction in Section 3. Section 4 contains a discussion of the role of Participatory Design in Design for All, using RHYME as an example, and further elaborations on Musicking for All. We conclude the paper in Section 5 with an outline of the next steps in the RHYME project.

2   The RHYME Project

We are reporting from the RHYME project, where researchers and designers from the fields of music composition, industrial design, HCI, and music and health take part. The project is a multidisciplinary undertaking with participants from the Centre for Music and Health at the Norwegian Academy of Music, the Institute of Design at Oslo School of Architecture and Design and Institute of Informatics at the University of Oslo.

It is a five year project, where a number of prototypes are developed and tested. The first prototype, ORFI, was tested in the spring of 2011, and testing of the second prototype, WAVE, is taking place in the spring of 2012. We use observation and video recordings of children during their exploration of the prototypes for data gathering, with subsequent iterative coding of the material for analysis.

2.1   ORFI

ORFI is a set of co-creative tangibles created earlier by three of the RHYME participants in MusicalFieldsForever[1]. The ORFI modules, or cushions, communicate wirelessly with each other. They can be freely built, thrown, played in and with as the users like. ORFI responds with changeable graphics, light, and music when the wings of the modules are bent, or the microphone is activated.

ORFI is shaped as a "hybrid between furniture, instrument and toy, in order to motivate different interpretations and forms of interaction. One can sit down in it as in a chair or play on it as on an instrument, with immediate response to interaction. Or one can talk, sing an play with it, as with a friend and co-musician in a communicative way, where ORFI answers vary musically after some time" [3]. The ambiguity [14] of the co-creative tangibles is not only musical, but also on the physical manipulation and use of the pillow; they can be lifted carefully, caressed, supporting your body when lying down or thrown, for example.

From the action oriented, multidisciplinary user study, several weaknesses with ORFI was identified, as well as many desired qualities for a new generation of co-creative tangibles. In particular, the music and health professionals wanted the sound source to be close to the area of interaction, similar to how acoustic instruments work. For interactive objects, this means for example to place the

---

[1] http://musicalfieldsforever.com

Fig. 1. The ORFI prototype

input sensor close to the speaker. This is a complex design challenge involving wireless objects, object sizes and weights, sensor qualities, sound quality and wireless sound transmission. One goal in the RHYME project is to be able to install the co-creative tangibles in families' homes in the future, which represent further design challenges. The desire to explore more sensory stimulation like vibrators and stronger speakers, and creation of more accessible input sensors, integrated microphone, speakers, and camera for new cross-media interaction possibilities were all part of the design input for WAVE, the next RHYME prototype.

2.2   WAVE

The WAVE concept is constantly developed, and currently consists of two different forms of tangibles; the WAVE Carpet and WAVE Orange. WAVE Carpet is a 7-branched carpet, and offers many cross-media possibilities. WAVE Orange is a wireless iOS-based beanbag chair with 2 arms.

The WAVE Carpet includes several input and output devices, including infrared sensors with light response in a bubble shaped field, a microphone with light response in one arm and a camera with light response in another arm. Further, a Pico Projector resides in a third arm, and bend sensors with light are embedded in two separate arms. Accelerometer sensors with light can be found in two separate arms, and a sound vibration element (Visaton), speakers and LEDs are also included.

Arduino hardware and software is used for controlling the input and output, and two amplifiers, a Mini Mac with SuperCollider and Processing is used for sound and graphics.

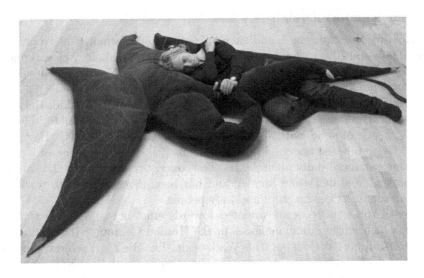

Fig. 2. The WAVE Carpet

3   Related Work

What follows is a review and positioning in three areas relevant to the RHYME project. First, a short review of accessible music is presented, before Participatory Design approaches are introduced. This is followed by a discussion of Tangible Interaction. Involving children and their caregivers is central to the continued development of prototypes in the RHYME project, and Tangible Interaction provides one of the foundations for the communication between users and the musical environment provided by the co-creative tangibles in RHYME.

3.1   Accessible Music

Within the accessibility field, much focus has been on making music *notation* accessible. For instance, special thematic session "Making Music Accessible" at ICCHP 2004 [8] mentions work within Braille Music [28,5], and Spoken Music [7] as central in this domain. The I-maestro project [19] is another example of a project aimed at music education.

Work on accessible music without the focus on musical notation include interactive books for sighted children and blind parents [26], the Benemin [4] and Soundbeam [18]. Some of these projects exploit proximity and movement, however there is little focus on *tangible* interaction in the music experience, as one can find in traditional music instruments used in music therapy [9]. In RHYME, the *co-creative tangibles* of the ORFI and WAVE prototypes [24] are used to investigate how children, caregivers and family members can interact with a computer based music system using tangibles.

3.2 Participatory Design

Participatory Design in the Scandinavian Tradition of informatics has roots back to the 1960's and 70's, with introduction of information technology in workplaces. A core principle in Participatory Design is equal opportunities to influence design for all stakeholders, including designers and different user groups.

Accessibility projects using Participatory Design approaches include the use of cross cultural scenarios for requirement elicitation [22], ATM design for illiterate persons [6], use of agile methods to facilitate Universal Access [20], "Best guess design" for web-based accessible entertainment [25], and the design of a sound and image enhanced daily planner [21]. The concept of *familiarity* [27] can play an important role in Design for All, and has been demonstrated to work well with Participatory Design [10] for elderly people.

Many of these projects are oriented towards efficiency and access to information, which is the dominant focus in the Human Computer Interaction and Computer-Supported Collaborative Work fields. The RHYME project, however, is not about efficiency, it's about creating conditions for the possibilities of *musicking*, and make it available for children, families and caregivers. Its goal is to establish a common ground where users can participate in music related activities on their own terms. This focus aligns well with the third wave of HCI, which is more concerned with experience and meaning making [1,12] than with efficiency.

3.3 Tangible Interaction

A major research direction for HCI has been to explore the interaction that can be facilitated by integrating computer technology with the things and surroundings of our everyday world. This research goes by many names; some examples are Ubiquitous computing [29], Tangible Interaction [16,15], Internet of Things [17], and Embedded Computing [30].

Moving from interaction with mouse, pointers, icons and menus in a desktop environment towards interaction with everyday "things" with embedded computers is a major shift in the HCI field. Since the early prototypes in tangible interaction, numerous prototypes have been made to explore tangible interaction. More recently, Sifteo Cubes, Electronic SCRABBLE Flash, and the Sphero Ball are examples of tangible interaction products available in the marketplace.

Dourish states that "In this world, our primary experience of computation is not with a traditional desktop computer, but rather with a range of computationally-enhanced devices, pieces of paper, pens, walls, books, hammers etc. The opportunity implied by this ubiquitous computing vision is to capitalize on our familiarity, skill and experience in dealing with the everyday world around us" [11]. The use of everyday things, like pillows, carpets, and paper, is characterized by our familiarity with the things and what we can do with them. By focusing on familiarity, we build on users' pre-existing involvement, understanding and relationship of the "everyday" world. Phil Turner references philosophy, and especially Heidegger, in order to explore the phenomenon *familiarity* [27], and proposes familiarity as a basis for Design for All.

Familiarity, as a phenomenon, is subjective in the sense that it involves people's understanding of themselves, the equipmental nexus and the activities in their being-in-the-world. What is observable, from researchers and designers, are the outcomes, such as "easiness, confidence, success, performance, which are all manifestations or signs of familiarity" [15].

4 Discussion

4.1 Participatory Design and Design for All

Fischer uses Communities of Interest [13] to illustrate challenges in cross-disciplinary activities, such as design work. In projects like RHYME, with multiple research traditions and methodologies involved, these challenges are sometimes very obvious. In addition, the children's interaction with the co-creative tangibles must often be interpreted through the caregivers. This form of mediated communication introduces another layer of challenges in Participatory Design processes. However, this also emphasizes the need to work carefully to best understand the different stakeholders, each on their own terms.

4.2 Musicking for All

Tangible Interaction, the manipulation of physical objects as a form of interaction with a computer system, has great potential for enabling Musicking for All. By taking Participatory Design processes seriously, new and promising tangibles can be created to allow for participation in musical activities for multiple users on their own terms. The prototypes ORFI and WAVE are examples of this, where the co-creative tangibles are not simply interfaces to a musical instrument. We have created audio-visual spaces where children and people in their surroundings together can explore the unfamiliar features of carpets and pillows through the familiarity of the same objects. Sometimes the children are also bringing with them familiar objects, such as balls or acoustic guitars to explore. In this way, both the familiarity of these artefacts, together with the familiar design of the co-creative tangibles enables Musicking for All.

Finally, it should be noted that Small's definition of *musicking* [23] applies to a wider range of activities than those directly related to performing music. Further, Small proposes that *musicking* is value-free, that is, it is not necessarily a pleasurable activity. However, in the RHYME project, the setting in which musicking for all takes place is created with well-being in mind.

5 Conclusion and Future Work

We have presented the RHYME project and its prototypes ORFI and WAVE. Further, we have argued that Accessible Music, Participatory Design and Tangible Interaction are fields which create a good foundation for Musicking for All, with examples from the RHYME project. With focus on musicking, rather than accessible music, we hope to contribute with an inclusive approach to music-related activities.

The RHYME project has currently gone through two design iterations, result-ing in the prototypes described in this paper. Future design iterations aims at introducing co-creative tangibles in the homes of the children and their families, to enable musicking at home, and not only in the school setting as is the current case. Further, enabling networked, internet-based co-creation aims at enabling musicking over distance, for instance with friends and family in other locations. These are important steps in the project to truly embrace musicking for all.

Acknowledgements. This research is funded by the Norwegian Research Coun-cil through the Verdikt program. Thanks to Ina Wagner for fine discussions about tangible interaction and Design for All, and to the participants in the RHYME project. We would also like to thank our colleagues at the DESIGN group at the University of Oslo for comments, and Roger Antonsen for inspiration.

References

1. Bødker, S.: When second wave hci meets third wave challenges. In: Proceedings of the 4th Nordic Conference on Human-computer Interaction: Changing Roles, pp. 1–8. ACM (2006)
2. Cappelen, B., Andersson, A.P.: Designing smart textiles for music and health. In: Ambience 2011: Were Art Technology and Design Meet. University of Borås, Borås (2011)
3. Cappelen, B., Andersson, A.P.: Expanding the role of the instrument. In: Pro-ceedings of the International Conference on New Interfaces for Musical Expression (2011)
4. Challis, B.P., Challis, K.: Applications for Proximity Sensors in Music and Sound Performance. In: Miesenberger, K., Klaus, J., Zagler, W., Karshmer, A.I. (eds.) ICCHP 2008. LNCS, vol. 5105, pp. 1220–1227. Springer, Heidelberg (2008)
5. Challis, B.P., Edwards, A.D.N.: Weasel: A system for the non-visual presentation of music notation. In: Proceedings of ICCHP, pp. 113–120. Citeseer (2000)
6. Cremers, A.H.M., de Jong, J.G.M., van Balken, J.S.: User-Centered Design with Illiterate Persons: The Case of the ATM User Interface. In: Miesenberger, K., Klaus, J., Zagler, W., Karshmer, A.I. (eds.) ICCHP 2008. LNCS, vol. 5105, pp. 713–720. Springer, Heidelberg (2008)
7. Crombie, D., Dijkstra, S.J., Schut, E., Lindsay, N.: Spoken Music: Enhancing Ac-cess to Music for the Print Disabled. In: Miesenberger, K., Klaus, J., Zagler, W. (eds.) ICCHP 2002. LNCS, vol. 2398, pp. 667–674. Springer, Heidelberg (2002)
8. Crombie, D., Lenoir, R., McKenzie, N.R., Challis, B.P.: Making Music Accessible. Introduction to the Special Thematic Session. In: Miesenberger, K., Klaus, J., Zagler, W., Burger, D. (eds.) ICCHP 2004. LNCS, vol. 3118, pp. 214–217. Springer, Heidelberg (2004)
9. Darrow, A.-A.: Adaptive instruments for students with physical disabilities. Gen-eral Music Today 25(2), 44–46 (2012)
10. Demirbilek, O., Demirkan, H.: Universal product design involving elderly users: a participatory design model. Applied Ergonomics 35(4), 361–370 (2004)
11. Dourish, P.: What we talk about when we talk about context. Personal and Ubiq-uitous Computing 8(1), 19–30 (2004)

12. Fallman, D.: The new good: exploring the potential of philosophy of technology to contribute to human-computer interaction. In: Proceedings of the 2011 Annual Conference on Human Factors in Computing Systems, pp. 1051–1060. ACM (2011)

13. Fischer, G.: Communities of Interest: Learning through the Interaction of Multiple Knowledge Systems. In: 24th Annual Information Systems Research Seminar In Scandinavia (IRIS 24), Ulvik, Norway, pp. 1–14 (2001)

14. Gaver, W.W., Beaver, J., Benford, S.: Ambiguity as a resource for design. In: Proceedings of the SIGCHI Conference on Human Factors in Computing Systems, pp. 233–240. ACM (2003)

15. Hornecker, E., Buur, J.: Getting a grip on tangible interaction: a framework on physical space and social interaction. In: Proceedings of the SIGCHI Conference on Human Factors in Computing Systems, pp. 437–446. ACM (2006)

16. Ishii, H.: Tangible bits: beyond pixels. In: Proceedings of the 2nd International Conference on Tangible and Embedded Interaction, pp. xv–xxv. ACM (2008)

17. Kortuem, G., Kawsar, F., Fitton, D., Sundramoorthy, V.: Smart objects as building blocks for the internet of things. IEEE Internet Computing 14(1), 44–51 (2010)

18. Magee, W.L., Burland, K.: An exploratory study of the use of electronic music technologies in clinical music therapy. Nordic Journal of Music Therapy 17(2), 124–141 (2008)

19. McKenzie, N.R., Marwick-Johnstone, B.: Making the I-Maestro Music Learning Framework Accessible. In: Miesenberger, K., Klaus, J., Zagler, W., Karshmer, A.I. (eds.) ICCHP 2008. LNCS, vol. 5105, pp. 770–776. Springer, Heidelberg (2008)

20. Memmel, T., Reiterer, H., Holzinger, A.: Agile Methods and Visual Specification in Software Development: A Chance to Ensure Universal Access. In: Stephanidis, C. (ed.) HCI 2007. LNCS, vol. 4554, pp. 453–462. Springer, Heidelberg (2007)

21. Moffatt, K., McGrenere, J., Purves, B., Klawe, M.: The participatory design of a sound and image enhanced daily planner for people with aphasia. In: Proceedings of the SIGCHI Conference on Human Factors in Computing Systems, pp. 407–414. ACM (2004)

22. Okamoto, M., Komatsu, H., Gyobu, I., Ito, K.: Participatory design using scenarios in different cultures. In: Human-Computer Interaction. Interaction Design and Usability, pp. 223–231 (2007)

23. Small, C.: Musicking the meanings of performing and listening. A lecture. Music Education Research 1(1), 9–22 (1999)

24. Stensæth, K., Ruud, E.: Musikkmøbler eller musikkinstrumenter? om forskningsprosjektet rhyme og interaktiv digital helseteknologi i musikkterapien. Musikkterapi (forthcoming, 2012)

25. Tollefsen, M., Flyen, A.: Internet and Accessible Entertainment. In: Miesenberger, K., Klaus, J., Zagler, W., Karshmer, A.I. (eds.) ICCHP 2006. LNCS, vol. 4061, pp. 396–402. Springer, Heidelberg (2006)

26. Tollefsen, M., Flyen, A.: Flexible and Simple User Interfaces in Entertaining Software. In: Miesenberger, K., Klaus, J., Zagler, W., Karshmer, A.I. (eds.) ICCHP 2008. LNCS, vol. 5105, pp. 578–584. Springer, Heidelberg (2008)

27. Turner, P., Walle, G.: Familiarity as a basis for universal design. Gerontechnology 5(3), 150–159 (2006)

28. World Blind Union, Krolick, B.: New international manual of Braille music notation. SVB (1996)

29. Weiser, M.: The computer for the 21st century. Scientific American 265(3), 94–104 (1991)

30. Wolf, W.: What is embedded computing? Computer 35(1), 136–137 (2002)

Enhancing Audio Description: A Value Added Approach

Jack Sade, Komal Naz, and Malgorzata Plaza

Ryerson University, 350 Victoria St., Toronto, Ontario, Canada, M5B 2K3
{ysade,knaz,mplaza}@ryerson.com

Abstract. Audio Description makes films, shows and TV programs accessible to visually impaired audience. It is expensive so wide adoption of this technology is not practical. Canadian Radio-television and Telecommunications Commission requires that broadcaster describes a minimum of four hours of primetime programming a week. Production companies do not see any incentives to move beyond the required minimum. This paper investigates the possibility of making AD profitable by making a described movie, show or program attractive to all kind of audiences including visually impaired. We argue that AD can become a revenue generation product widely adopted by production companies.

Keywords: AD, Business Analysis.

1 Introduction

According to [32], 284 million are visually impaired worldwide. Since a majority of entertainment services lack inclusivity, they fail to cater to that market. The recent legislation imposes video production inclusivity on distributors but is not sufficient. Audio Description (AD) is an access media for blind and low vision viewers, which tries to mimic the viewing experience of the sighted consumer. Due to limited market potential, AD production costs and complications, production companies do not consider AD as an entertainment service but rather an accessibility tool. To that end, the business model for AD consists of only costs without any revenue generating potential. In order to cater to a larger market, AD must evolve and secure an additional revenue stream. This paper argues that AD should become more than just an accessibility tool. By diversifying AD concept to the sighted consumer the production costs can be subsidized with increased revenue potential. This paper presents the alternative production methodology of AD developed at the CLT lab at Ryerson University where the content creators are directly involved in the production of audio description [30]. AD is discussed in Section 2 and its new business model, which makes AD profitable, is presented in Section 3.

2 Literature Review

2.1 Understanding Audio Description

AD describes video elements, which cannot otherwise be grasped by visually impaired and low vision audience. AD describes action, body language, facial

K. Miesenberger et al. (Eds.): ICCHP 2012, Part I, LNCS 7382, pp. 270–277, 2012.

expressions, scenery, and costumes [31]. Viewers select the SAP (secondary audio program) channel in order to hear the regular program audio accompanied by the descriptions [28]. AD can be produced using two methods: Conventional and Alternative, which are on opposites of the production spectrum. The Conventional AD is outsourced to a third party providers while the Alternative AD maintains creative control and production in-house.

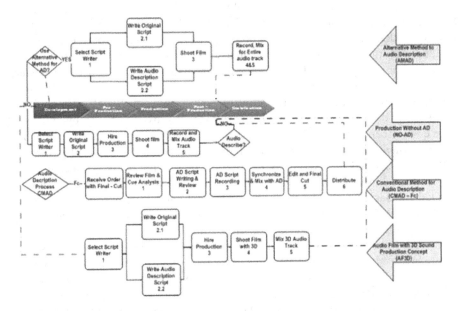

Fig. 1. Conventional, Alternative, and Proposed AD production Schema

Conventional AD uses a third person, covert narrative style that is characterized by neutrality and non-interference in the story [8]. The aim of conventional AD is to provide the end user with a bias free description of the original content. The standard practice for adding AD is for the original production team to send the finished video to an outside service provider, where a process similar to the content production process is used [9]. It is illustrated in Figure 1 as the CMAD-Fc process, in which descriptions are factual and purposely void of emotionally subjective interpretation [17]. CMAD-Fc is a very time consumings expensive and the outcomes are not necessarily optimal [9]. The Alternative method requires the oversight by the creative production team in AD [9] which enables a more intimate and subjective view of the content presented [9]. It enhances the entertainment value in AD and expands the current limited market. The approach is illustrated as AMAD.

[8] studied the impact of AD style on engagement and entertainment factors using one example—an animated situation comedy called Odd Job Jack, produced by Smiley Guy Studios. In the experiment the script writer, director and sound team were all involved in creating and producing the AD. The creative team decided to use a

first - person narrative approach to convey the visual via AD. Unlike conventional [AD], a first - person narration allows the audience to identify with the character and understand the inherent subjectivity of the narrator's version of the story [8]. Although there were various discrepancies in the results with regards to enjoyment of AD, the overall effect of first - person narration proved to be more effective than the conventional third person narration [8].

Following the Alternative Method, film production studio decides very early in the process, ideally in the development phase, whether their creative vision is going to be audio described or not. When a producer works on a vision he/she also shares the idea with the script writers, who include description as part of script writing process. Being cognizant of the AD requirements; scripts writers can introduce pauses, scenarios and emotions in a way that allows the flow of the film to be smoother while offering a more enjoyable experience. Although that approach causes some delays during the production phase, it proves to be on overall much more cost effective than if AD was first introduced at post-production stage. The situation when original and AD scripts are written in parallel is depicted in Figure 1 as Processes 2.1 and 2.2. Adding AD during the production phase is not significantly more time consuming than if the script was created without AD. For example, in the Odd Job Jack case study, it took an additional half of a day to write AD script during the development stage. The entire script for the episode without the description was written in approximately 5 days [9].

AD script can even be considered during pre-production phase, in which case everybody involved (actors, narrators or the directors) would be trained in how to create with universality in mind. If a 1st person narrative approach is then used during Process [3] (Figure 1 AMAD), the actors and narrators voice over the raw shoots, which does not impact the time required to shoot the film or the need to get additional studio time. With effective planning after each scene is "shot" description can be added in-between and/or during next set preparations. As a result, adding AD may cause some delays, but again is not expected to add a significant overhead. In the case of "Odd Job Jack" AD was recorded once the show had been completed and it took an additional ½ day to voice the description.

In the Alternative Method, the AD film and the non-descriptive version can be edited simultaneously during post-production (AMAD 4), improving the show production time. For the production of a 30-minute episode (Odd Job Jack case study), this process is expected to add approximately one more day. Typically, sound mix follows recording and editing (AMAD 5). When Alternative Method is used, regular process timing will take as long as if the Conventional Method was followed.

2.2   Current AD Consumer

In 2008 the home entertainment spending in Canada accounted for \$15.4 billion which is 56% of total consumer spending on culture [14], so the potential market for an expanded AD product is vast. It is estimated that about 65% of all people who are visually impaired are aged 50 and older, while this age group comprises about 20% of the world's population. With an increasing elderly population in many countries, more people will be at risk of age-related visual impairment. It is also estimated that 19 million children are visually impaired [31]. Although in general it may not seem viable to cater to such a vast market internationally, it is evident that major U.S. film studios earn most of their film and home video revenues from sales in foreign markets [11]. In order to propose a suitable business model for the expanded AD, we will review its conventional production method and discuss various potential derivative products which may impact a wider market and enhance the revenue.

3   The New Business Model for AD

3.1   Market Strategy for AD

Business is profitable if the value that it creates is greater than the cost to produce goods or services [24]. In order for AD to be considered a value added service the marginal benefit gained from its production must outweigh the cost. Since AD is considered a cost and not a revenue source [29], the "video creative content" is only described to the extent mandated by the CRTC. Currently the cost of producing AD is not offset in the price, for example, the price of a DVD is the same regardless of whether or not AD is included. The situation is illustrated in Figure 2, where the key issues of the existing AD business model are linked in "vicious circle" of cause-effect dependencies. The problem begins with AD being offered to the limited market, which makes both key players: a Broadcaster and a Production Company, to apply a Cost minimization strategy and respond to the market only when forced by the regulation. As a result, only a very limited effort and time is spent for AD development, which causes it to offer limited entertainment value. AD becomes a simple accessibility tool, which in turn limits the market for it.

We would like to suggest a completely different approach to AD, which should become incredibly appealing to all audiences. To that end, AD must be reengineered to fit somewhere in between two opposite ends of product market spectrum: 1. current concept of AD with expanded market and 2. new product with a new market. Market development could focus on the use of open description, in which AD is a part of the native video for everyone to experience [28]. The concept would promote a description that cannot be turned off [1]. Diversification could result in the derivation of a new product that completely stems away from AD, such as Audio Film introduced by Lopez and Paulette, which enables the visually impaired and sighted listener to experience the audio film in the same way [21 - 22]. The applications of such product can be vast, audio film tracks could become available on a DVD, or as a podcast downloaded via websites such as I-tunes. Audio film would establish grounds for a universally fit product enjoyed by sighted and visually impaired audience equally.

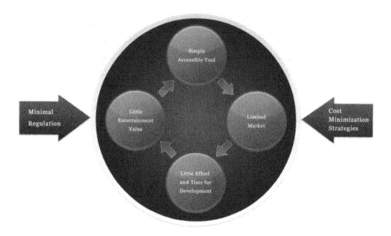

Fig. 2. "Vicious Circle" of the AD business model

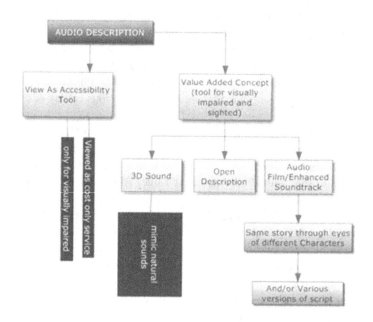

Fig. 3. Exploring the Two approaches to Audio Description – The Accessibility and the Value Added Concept

"Enhanced soundtrack" could also derive multiple soundtracks applicable to a single show and/or film production, which will allow the scriptwriter to create different versions of the script whereby the description of the visual content is portrayed through the eyes of different characters in the story line. Introducing such a feature could also increase the times a show/and or movie is viewed. Theatres could integrate it into their current AD listening devices and the audience could review the same film more than once and listen to all of the different versions of the main story line being described. It may come from the perspective of a character in the story who is a pessimist and give an initial "sad" description of the content, and another character can provide a description where the plot actually may seem funny. This variability in plot audio recording will essentially enhance the production value of a show and/or film.

3.2   Audio Film and 3D Sound Recording

Audio Film is a format of sonic art that eliminates the need for visual elements and of a describer, by providing information solely through sound, sound processing and specialization. It closely resembles the concept of "radio drama"; although it does not use narration but conveys information through surround sound technology. [21 - 22] demonstrated that it is possible to present a clear storyline solely by sound effect, sound processing and surround sound eliminating the need of a narrator.

We propose to use the concept behind audio film with the use of a 3D recording system, which has the ability to position sounds all around a listener. The sounds are created by the loudspeakers (or headphones) but are perceived as coming from arbitrary points in space. 3D works by mimicking the process of natural hearing reproducing the sound localization cues at the ears of the listener. When sound is to the left of the listener, the sound reaches the left ear before the right ear, so the right ear signal is delayed with respect to the left ear signal. We unconsciously use "sound localization cues" such as time delay, amplitude difference and tonal information at each ear to determine the location of the sound [10]. To mimic the process of natural hearing recordings are employed with the use of small microphones [23].

3D recording places the audience in the center of the setting so by using sound effects objects can be conveyed within the surrounding space. The speech description can be limited and the focus can be directed towards content which cannot be portrayed through sound effects such as colors and visual images. Conveying such a reality using the concept behind the Alternative Method for AD is complementary. For example, to portray a character moving through a set, a describer will verbally explain the movement and a little time will be required to describe the actual setting itself. The first person concept can also be reinforced through the sonic sound specialization, which will be portrayed by means of recording and presenting sound stimuli whereby the audience is able to distinguish objects by their interaction within an environment. Research demonstrated that sounds can create a sense of place, although people are not able to precisely recognize a place by only listening to the soundscape [26]. The production concept of audio film is depicted in Figure 1 (AF3D).

4   Conclusions and Further Research

With a wider market reach, evolving the current AD "product" is absolutely necessary. Due to fairly light AD regulations and a current limited market, production companies consider AD a simple accessibility tool and minimize productions costs at the expanse of entertainment value. We reviewed the alternative production method and propose a new direction for AD using 3D sound recording and audio film concepts. Further research needs to be conducted in order to test the potential of Audio film and to identify the actual demographic which may drive the growth of the new product. Further research is also required to determine the true cost of audio description which will allow adapting the production structure of current AD practices.

Acknowledgements. We would like to thank CLIME project and Center for Learning Technologies for supporting us with both funding and research for this paper. We would also like to extend our gratitude to Deborah Fels for her aid in our research.

References

1. Accessible Media Inc. About AMI. Retrieved June 9, 2011, from Accessible Media Inc. (2011), http://www.ami.ca/ami/about_a-m-i.aspx
2. Ansoff, I.H.: Strategies for Diversification. Harvard Business Review (1957)
3. Baxendale, S., Foster, B.P.: Abc Absorption and Direct Costing Income Statements. Cost Management, 5–14 (September/October 2010)
4. Branje, C.: LiveDescribe – Can Amateurs Create Quality Video Description?, Toronto, Ontario, Canada (2006)
5. Canadian Radio-television and Telecommunications Commission. Access to TV for people with visual impairments: audio description and described video (August 5, 2009), http://www.crtc.gc.ca/eng/info_sht/b322.html (retrieved May 4, 2011)
6. CRTC, Broadcasting Public Notice CRTC 2006-6, Ottawa, Ontario (January 19, 2006)
7. CRTC, Broadcasting Policy Monitoring Report 2007, Ottawa, Ontario (July 31, 2007)
8. Fels, D.I., Udo, J.P., Diamond, J.E., Diamond, J.I.: A Comparison of Alternative Narrative Approaches to Video Description for Animated Comedy. Journal of Visual Impairment & Blindness (May 2006)
9. Fels, D.I., Udo, J.P., Ting, P., Diamond, J.E., Diamond, J.I.: Odd job jack described: a universal design approach to described video. Journal Universal Access in the Information Society 5(1) (July 2006)
10. Gardner, W.G.: 3D Audio and Acoustic Environment Modeling, Arlington, Massachusetts, U.S.A. (March 15, 1999)
11. Goeres, J. E., Anoo, S., Rengarajan, S., Surana, R.: Where the true growth lies: The market for digital media (2010), http://www.deloitte.com/assets/Dcom-UnitedStates/Local%20Assets/Documents/TMT_us_tmt/u_tmt_wherethetruegrowthlies_200910.pdf (retrieved May 4, 2011)
12. Grosser, B.: What is Timecode?, Imaging Technology Group (May 23, 1997), http://www.itg.uiuc.edu/help/timecode/ (retrieved September 04, 2010)
13. Hein, G., Jakuska, R.: Podcast Industry. University of Michigan-Dearborn, Center for Innovation Research (2007)
14. Hill, K.: Consumer Spending on Culture in Canada, the Provinces and 12 Metropolitan Areas in 2008. Statistical Insights on the Arts 9(1) (November 2010)
15. IFAC, Evaluating and Improving Costing in Organizations. International Federation of Accountants. PAIB Committee, New York (2009)
16. Kilger, W.: Flexible Plankostenrechnung und Deckungsbeitragsrechnung. Gabler GmbH, Wiesbaden (2002)

17. Konstantinidis, B.M., Price, E., Diamond, J., Fels, D.I.: Described Video Information and animation: A case study of odd Job Jack. International Journal of Social and Humanistic Computting 1(1) (November 1, 2009)
18. Krumwiede, K.: A Closer Look at German Cost Accounting Methods. Management Accounting Quarterly, 37–50 (October 2008)
19. Lawrence, P., Grasso, D.: Are ABC and RCA Accounting Systems Compatible with lean Management. Management Accounting Quarterly 7(1), 12–27 (2005)
20. Li, Z., Duraiswami, R., Gumerov, N.A.: Capture and recreation of higher order 3D sound fields via reciprocity. In: Proceedings of ICAD 2004-Tenth Meeting of the International Conference on Auditory Display, Sydney (2004)
21. Lopez, M.J., Pauletto, S.: The Design of an Audio Film or the Visually Impaired. In: Proceedings of the 15th International Conference on Auditory Display (2009)
22. Lopez, M.J., Pauletto, S.: The Design of an Audio Film: Portraying Story, Action and Interaction through Sound. The Journal of Music and Meaning 8 (2009)
23. Moller, H.: Fundamentals of binaural technolgy. Applied Acoustics 36(3-4), 171–218 (1992)
24. Nguyen, D.-D., Kira, D.S.: Value-Added Systems. The International Encyclopedia of Business and Management 7 (2001)
25. Cooper, R., Kaplan, R.S.: How cost accounting distorts product costs. Management Accountting, 27–36 (1988)
26. Serafin, S.: Sound design to enhance presence in photorealistic virtual reality. In: Proceedings of the 2004 International Conference on Auditory Display, Sidney (2004)
27. Snyder, J.: Audio Description: The Visual Made Verbal. The International Journal of the Arts in Society 2 (2007)
28. Thom, L.: What is Description?, Described and Captioned Media Program (November 2008), http://www.dcmp.org/caai/nadh228.pdf (retrieved May 9, 2011)
29. Udo, J., Fels, D.I.: The rogue poster-children of universal design: closed captioning and AD. Journal of Engineering Design 21(2&3), 207–221 (2009)
30. Whitehead, J.: What is Audio Description. In: Vision 2005 - Proceedings of the International Congress, vol. 1282, pp. 960–963. Elsevier, London (2005)
31. World Health Organization. Visual impairment and blindness. Media centre (April 2011), http://www.who.int/mediacentre/factsheets/fs282/en/ (retrieved May 6, 2011)

Triple Helix – In Action?

Niels Henrik Helms[1] and Susanne Tellerup[2]

[1] University of Southern Denmark
nhh@knowledgelab.sdu.dk
[2] University College Lillebaelt
sute@ucl.dk

Abstract. This paper presents a project i-Space about learning and playful ap-plications, which could also document performance. The target group is mentally impaired citizens. The project is used as reference to a discussion on structures within innovation processes. This discussion leads to a discussion of the user as a sense-making category in multi-disciplinary settings.

Keywords: Innovation, Triple Helix, quadrant model, user categories.

1 Introduction

Innovation is seen as the answer to almost any societal challenge these years. The development of Triple Helix models has been an analytical framework for understanding the new relationship between industries, governance and science. The Triple Helix model offers an understanding and also an overall framework for developing new innovative relations between different domains of society. The question is how the model works in practice, and what are the implications for the Triple Helix model of the growing emphasis on user-driven innovation. Furthermore, the question is how cohesiveness is developed in the temporary settings, which constitute the practical applications of Triple Helix.

2 Triple Helix

The Triple Helix model describes the relationship between the three different systems: Business, Government, and Science. The idea is that the three systems are functional-ly differentiated systems [5] with distinct rationalities. They are not stratified; rather they have the same sociological status. But they can co-function and thereby enable the Triple Helix of innovation.

In order to enable that kind of innovation, different zones of translation and trans-formation are needed. These zones may be thought of as enablers for what is defined as structural couplings. The model thus offers a spiral model for understanding the relationship between these systems. Triple Helix logics are not stable but dynamic, meaning undergoing change [4].

K. Miesenberger et al. (Eds.): ICCHP 2012, Part I, LNCS 7382, pp. 278–283, 2012.

3   Projects in Complex Settings

I-Space is a R&D-project designed and conducted in a partnership of universities, municipalities, private companies and NGO's .The purpose of the project is to develop new technologies, which can enhance learning and motivation of mentally impaired citizens and also document the progress, which hopefully takes place when the target group is using the application. Furthermore, the project should develop educational components, which should secure that professionals use technology on a wider scale in their work within institutions.

The nucleus of the project is combining the technology from Play Alive A/S and Team Online A/S. Play Alive develops and produces intelligent playgrounds. The overall idea of this is to use the fascination of computer gaming to bring kids back to physical play and interaction through an integration of intelligence in different devices in the play-ground such as an outdoor Jungle Gym called the "Octopus".

In the "Octopus", the intelligent part is 18 satellites, touch sensitive, with light and sound which stimulates and motivates children to play and interact. Team Online has produces and develops web-based CMS-solutions to pedagogical and administrative practises within institutions. The basic component is an electronic journal, which includes the logbook, action plans, and calendar. The software features of this sys-tem are not qualitatively different from other systems, but the development process has had the daily practises of the social workers as point of departure rather than the specifications defined by the authorities. This has meant that the system for the social workers has become a pedagogical tool instead of an externally imposed control procedure.

In i-Space, it is the aim that a new combination of the two technologies can enable and motivate for intelligent training and also enable documentation of this training.

Being a Triple Helix project, this project involves a number of different actors, which then again calls for a structured process. This process was structured with the so-called Quadrant-Model. It is a meta-design model, which enables different rationalities to interplay. This again leads a discussion on the notion of user – and finally this enables a further discussion and development of the Triple Helix Model.

4   The Quadrant-Model

The Quadrant-Model has been developed through a number of projects. As a design model the Quadrant-Model showed its strength in combining different traditions within theoretical and practical understandings of user-driven innovation and it turned out to be a generic and comprehensive model.

The model (Figure 1) illustrates four stages in an innovation process. The four stages represent a development in time, knowledge and fulfilment of the projects objectives. At each stage, however iterative processes will and might occur and iterations may also take place across quadrants.

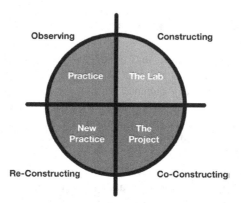

Fig. 1. The Quadrant Model

Quadrant I is characterized by initial observations on the present practice. In this phase, the focus is on understanding the "field". The assumptions related to i-Space could be summarized in the following way: The users would be the users of institutional settings such as men-tally impaired citizens and also the staff (social workers). The work of the ladder would be to enable and develop institutional life which on the hand should enable a life with good life quality and on the other hand ensure that legislative and administrative regulations where fulfilled as well as made meaningful for the users. [6]

In the actual case, we made interviews, short initial workshops and video observations. This quadrant directs attention towards the daily practices including local sense makings and rationalities. This initial description was not "thick" description but rather sketchy [3]. This was a deliberate choice because the description should not be valid from a scientific point of view but rather generate input and inspiration for the initial development of a prototype.

Quadrant II - Constructing: This quadrant delimits the process of actual prototyping of new technologies developed with inspirations from the initial findings in Quadrant I. In *i-Space*, it meant that the participating enterprises made a set up of a mobile physical devise, which was connected with the administrative ICT-system. So, the Jungle Gym was downsized and made more mobile so it could be moved around and be part of a research setup in different contexts.

Quadrant III - Co-Construction: This quadrant involves application of the prototypes and therefore competencies and skills in a new way. The purpose is to use the prototypes to develop new forms of practice and at the same time to generate feedback to the developers for further development of the application.

We took the device back to the institutional settings and tried it together with different user groups. The basic setup was groups with end-users, social workers, and consultants from the participating university of applied science and developers from the participating private companies. The first iterations with users and device generated the following outputs:

- The system should be much more flexible allowing users with a variety of physical and mental disabilities to us it
- The social part of the use was very important – it was important to develop social games and activities
- The game element seemed very motivating also for users with severe disabilities. Game elements and the physical set up such allow for adoption and compensation for disabilities.
- The sound design which in this initial prototype was a rather metallic arcade game type should be maintained for some users but it was scaring for others and even potential harmful for users with tendencies towards epileptic seizure.

Furthermore, we realized that there was a need for a kind of translators between the users and the developers. In the project, we were also asked to develop educational designs, which would secure that results generated within the project should be implemented in basic education for social workers. We decided to combine our observation about "translators" and the goal of developing educational designs in the second iteration of "co-construction". This second iteration was based on a re-developed prototype, which allowed for a much higher degree of flexibility. The satellites were now connected through a wifi local net-work. Each of them had their own power supply. These chances enabled a great number of physical configurations (inside and outside) up to a distance of sixty meters. The satellites were placed in a suitcase were they could be re-loaded with electricity. A magnetic socket was added which provided the option of placing the satellites in different ways - horizontally and vertically. This option of placing satellites in different configurations turned out to be very useful. Some users only used one or two satellites – others participated in set-ups where they made a kind of field courts and also treasure hunts.

Now, at least two results were achieved. Firstly, the technical set up was solid and flexible. Secondly, the set up was easy to use for end-users and staff.

However, we also concluded that there still was a need for more explicit didactic designs and game designs. We had to be more specific in relation to the needs of the concrete user-group: What was useful and beneficial and for whom? The "translators" took up the ladder point. Students from different educational programs were recruited by application to a cross-disciplinary Master Class, given an initial training in research and development work and then working in cross-disciplinary teams together with staff and especially with the end-users. Their findings were then presented to the researchers and developers not as student works but as authentic input and inspiration for the further development process.

Quadrant IV - Re-Construction: This quadrant brings the focus to the implications of sustainable innovation. Whereas, the three first quadrants are somehow outside daily practice with a focus on novelty the focus here is on how this novelty becomes un-novel, how it be-comes part of a daily practice.

In general, this part is about changing processes and structure within practice. So, we will focus on implementation and institutionalization in the institutions for mentally impaired citizens as well as in the educational programs.

The use of a model as the Quadrant-Model could be seen as constraints to innovative processes. Still, the creative process is scaffolded through such constraints [2] and the model has demonstrated that such models are important as a kind of media for participants in innovations projects, which involves different domains. The model becomes a kind of reification of these processes and enables a communication across domains and disciplinary traditions. The model also enables understanding of innovation as a complex process, which involves a spatial-temporary approach where this model affords structured collaboration. This would be a sort of multi-disciplinary rather than cross-disciplinary approach allowing the different approaches and related methodologies to co-exists and co-create.

5   The User

The project demonstrates the complexity in speaking about users and involving users. The end-user would be the mentally impaired citizen. The application should be available for them and it should be fun to use. The availability then introduces two other user categories: The professional staff and authorities. If the professional staff should use and introduce this application, the results from the project seem to emphasize two important features: The application should be easy to use. In general, staff within the field of social work is not very ICT-competent.

Additionally, they are orientated towards what they call human values, and these values are perceived as being incompatible with technology. Therefore, the application should be understood as a pedagogical tool, and not as a technical device. This leads to the second observation in this relation, namely that the application should enable developments and learning for the users. The end-user is not a category. It is an individual and even though we make a rough category such as mentally impaired citizens we have to take into account that within this group we had a very complex variety of social, physical, and social characteristics. Therefore, on the one hand the application should be highly flexible and on the other hand easy and transparent to use, functionalities that very seldom are compliant.

The specific law[1] defines the overall regulations of practices to-wards the mentally impaired citizens. The law reflects a change in the concept of the mentally impaired from client to a full citizen with special needs. The law explicitly says that the intention is "...to promote the individual's ability to take care of him or herself and to ease the daily lives and improve quality of life". The law has changed the life of this group of citizens. They have moved from institutions to their own homes (with special facilities), it has changed the social work from monitoring and caring to enabling and supporting [6]. This changed conception of the mentally impaired is also reflected in the very application we are developing.

The social workers have a dual role. On the one hand, they are representatives of the society as such on the other hand they are enabling and advocating the citizen. The qualified social worker is a professional capable of handling these dilemmas. And

---

[1]   Serviceloven. Retrieved May 29, 2011 from
https://www.retsinformation.dk/forms/R0710.aspx?id=20938

if she should use such applications they mediate these dilemmas. In the case of i-Space, this means that apart from playfulness the application should also offer potentials for physical (and social) progress. The embedded training program reflects this. The operationally is guaranteed by an easy way of distributing the touch sensitive satellites.

6   Concluding

The findings from this project demonstrate that the "user" becomes the media in temporary settings such as a project. The user is the sort of concept that Connolly (2011) defines as 'essentially contested', a concept without a specific core but subject to an ongoing discussion, interpretation of its content, meaning and limitations. Such concepts should not be rejected, they are very important for sense makings in processes of form giving – innovation is a question of giving the latent an accepted form and transforming this form into a new practice. The user becomes the negotiating point of the process and the application becomes its material transformation. The discussions are delegated in the physical devise and thereby the notion of user re-enters the process in an iterative process.

Triple Helix Models are dynamic and in order to stabilize them reifications – and concepts are important. Because we do not have a stable code for the cooperation and interaction, we need an ongoing stabilizer, which continually is under construction. This is generating the cohesiveness of temporary settings.

The Quadrant-Model has scaffolded the process. The model helps the actors in the project delimit different rationalities in different phases of the project. It gives the different groups participating in the project the necessary space for shifting between open and closed processes. Open processes where the participants share knowledge through discussions on findings, prototype and, as mentioned above, user concepts; – and closed processes where they go deeper into the part that is relevant to disciplinary competence.

At least in this case, innovation is a product of multi-disciplinary collaboration where different rationalities and competences become articulated through the process and where the affordances and the constraints of shared models such as the Quadrant-Model scaffold that process.

References

1. Conolly, W.E.: A World of Becoming. Duke University Press, Durham (2011)
2. Elster, J.: Ulysses Unbound: Studies in Rationality, Precommitment, and Constraints. Cambridge University Press, Cambridge (2000)
3. Geertz, C.: Thick Description: Toward an Interpretive Theory of Culture. In: Gertz, C. (ed.) The Interpretation of Cultures: Selected Essays, pp. 3–30. Basic Books, New York (1973)
4. Leydesdorff, L., Meyer, M.: Triple Helix Indicators of Knowledge-Based Innovation Systems: Introduction to the Special Issue. Res. Pol. 10, 1441–1449 (2006)
5. Luhmann, N.: Sociale Systemer. Hans Reitzels Forlag, Copenhagen (2000)
6. Schwartz, I.: Liv med Paedagogerne - om at Saette Maal i Socialpaedagogisk Praksis. Soc. Kri. 120, 80–97 (2009)

Virtual User Models for Designing and Using of Inclusive Products: Introduction to the Special Thematic Session

Yehya Mohamad[1], Manfred Dangelmaier[2], Matthias Peissner[2], Pradipta Biswas[3], and Carlos A. Velasco[1]

[1] Fraunhofer FIT, Schloss Birlinghoven, 53757 Sankt Augustin, Germany
{yehya.mohamad,carlos.velasco}@fit.fraunhofer.de
http://www.fit.fraunhofer.de
[2] Fraunhofer IAO, Nobelstr. 12, 70569 Stuttgart, Germany
{Manfred.Dangelmaier,Matthias.Peissner}@iao.fraunhofer.de
http://www.iao.fraunhofer.de
[3] The University of Cambridge, Department of Engineering,
Trumpington Street, Cambridge, CB2 1PZ United Kingdom
pb400@eng.cam.ac.uk
http://www-edc.eng.cam.ac.uk/

Abstract. This STS on *Virtual User Models for designing and using of inclusive products* is targeted towards generic interoperable user models that describe the relevant characteristics of users, who will interact with products and user interfaces. A user profile is an instantiation of a user model representing either a specific user or a representative of a group of users [1]. With such a model designers can define as many user profiles as needed to address the whole range of requirements from a target population in order to maximize the level of accessibility of products and services according to the selected user profile. The papers in this STS address many of the issues addressed by the VUMS cluster of projects. The cluster is formed by four projects funded by the European Commission under the Theme "FP7-ICT-2009.7.2 Accessible and Assistive ICT"; the projects are VICON, MyUI, GUIDE and VERITAS (http://www.veritas-project.eu/vums/).

1 Introduction

There was a plethora of systems developed during the last three decades that are claimed to be user models. Many of them modelled users for certain applications most notably for online recommendation and e-learning systems. These models in general have two parts a user profile and an inference machine. The user profile section stores details about users relevant for a particular application and an inference machine, which uses this information to personalize the system.

On a different dimension, ergonomics and computer animation follow a different view of user models [3]. Instead of modelling human behaviour in detail, they aim to simulate human anatomy or face which can be used to predict posture, facial expression and so on.

K. Miesenberger et al. (Eds.): ICCHP 2012, Part I, LNCS 7382, pp. 284–287, 2012.

The purpose of this STS is to present papers and approaches in order to facilitate a wider discussion and in particular to establish contacts between researchers involved in relevant activities.

User models can be used to reason about the needs, preferences or future behaviour of a user. One of the main problems is to integrate user profiles supporting different user models in one service/application, or migrating profiles stemming from one application to another. This can be attributed to incompatibilities in user profiles due to differences in scope of modelling, source of modelling information, time sensitivity of the model or update methods (static vs. dynamic model) and so on. In some cases physical (mechanics and control) as well as cognitive processes that underlie the users' actions are relevant in user modelling. User modelling approaches also differ regarding whether they model individual users or whole communities or groups of users. In general one can conclude that user modelling covers many different aspects, including the interaction of the user with interfaces and devices, the analysis of user tasks and the analysis of user characteristics. So it is necessary to put efforts into finding similarities among modelling approaches and making user profiles portable. A common standard with all common characteristics required in different domains for user model interoperability could be an approach to achieve this. This will then support the exchange and sharing of user profiles among different domains.

2   Areas Covered by STS

The Special Thematic Session (STS) attempts to cover the following key areas and topics:

- research and development work on interoperable user models
- prototypes and products utilizing virtual user models
- concepts targeting the evaluation of usability and applicability of user models

In the following a short description of the papers presented in this STS:

Nikolaos Kaklanis (Informatics and Telematics Institute, Centre for Research and Technology Hellas, Thessaloniki) presents a paper with a novel user modelling framework for the detailed description of geometric, kinematic, physical, behavioural and cognitive aspects of users affected by disabilities and elderly. Several aspects of the user's interaction behaviour are examined, while user models are quantified, in terms of their kinematic and dynamic parameters, in tests with disabled users through a multisensory platform, in order to develop accurate and realistic virtual user models. Hierarchical Task and Interaction Models are introduced, in order to describe the user's capabilities in multiple scales of abstraction. The use of alternative ways of a user task's execution, using different modalities and assistive devices, are also supported by the proposed task analysis.

Ana María Navarro (Instituto ITACA, Universidad Politécnica de Valencia) focuses in her paper on the description of the approach used to parameterize the psychological and behavioural user models developed under the FP7 EU Founded project VERITAS. She presents the methodology used to define the relevant psychological and behavioural parameters within the context of VERITAS. Two complementary approaches have been selected: on one hand, the use of existing models of the cognitive architecture Adaptive Control of Thought-Rational (ACT-R) for cognitive simulation purposes; on the other hand, a second approach based on existing metrics coming from medical and human behaviour studies and biomedical models.

Alejandro García (ISOIN) presents a paper discussing software targeted to users with disabilities and elderly. As a matter of fact, the standard WCAG from W3C/WAI has produced some guidelines for helping web designers to create accessible web content. Real-time adaptable graphical user interfaces is a promising solution for designing accessible applications for users with special needs. Essentially, collecting context information and combining it with information about the user can be used to customize the content of the interface itself, and so it allows improving the user experience in his interaction with the application. MyUI an EU-funded project has emerged in the adaptive graphical interfaces domain, addressing important barriers which include the developers' lack of awareness and expertise, time and cost requirements of incorporating accessibility and missing validated approaches and infrastructures of accessible software design. This paper presents the technology used and the experiences collected in the integration process of a regular application into such a framework.

Michael Lawo (University of Bremen) presents a paper elaborating about the development of products that are accessible to the largest possible group of users; this can be regarded as a major challenge for manufacturers of consumer products. It is therefore crucial, that the product development process is supported by practical methods and tools that can help incorporate these essential human factors in early phases of the development process. Ergonomics evaluation and user testing with real users are user centred design methodologies often conducted by companies, but these tasks are not only complex, but can be very time and cost-intensive. As an alternative approach virtual user models (VUM) have been proposed for supporting the early phases of the product development process. The design lifecycle of a product can be segregated into a sketch phase and a design phase. Both phases could profit from a VUM. In the sketch phase a recommendation system, such as a web application could support the designer to design a product for a specified virtual user or set of users. For the design phase a simulation system could be supportive. The purpose of this paper is to outline the technical design of the Virtual User Model and Environment Tools regarding the sketch, design and evaluation phases as a result of the EU funded project VICON.

Ivo Maly (Faculty of Electrical Engineering, Czech Technical University in Prague) presents an approach about model based testing. This includes application testing based on simulations in which the simulation of the usage of the application by means of virtual users is utilized. The model based testing can be used practically in all stages of application development (from the design to evaluation). As in this approach does not employ real users and we can perform significantly more tests to iteratively improve the accessibility of the application. Additionally many types of disabilities and also combinations of disabilities for which real users would be hard to find for testing can be reflected.

3   Future Research Areas

The presented papers are based mainly on conceptualisation and application of user models for a specific domain. For purposes of interoperability and continuity of these efforts standardization of common terms and characteristics is highly required. There are initial efforts in this direction coordinated by the VUMS cluster (see [1][2]), so a list of common terms has been created and an extensible table of user variables and their syntax has been established. An exchange format has been agreed upon and converters between the four projects and the exchange format have been imple-mented. The next steps will include the creation of a public repository, where user profiles and converters/filters will be published. The created model has potential to serve as an application independent user model that can be used to simulate and personalize interaction across a wide variety of digital and non-digital devices and systems. This user model is currently at an intermediate level of maturity; it should be developed further in the next loops of the projects and in the process of disseminating it to international standardization bodies. Individuals, research groups and projects are invited to use it and to contribute to the improvement and dissemination of it.

Acknowledgements. The VUMS cluster projects are funded by the e-Inclusion thread of the European Commission 7th framework IST programme. The authors would like to acknowledge the collective work of the cluster partners in making this session possible.

References

1. VUMS White Paper, http://www.veritas-project.eu/vums/wp-content/uploads/2010/07/White-Paper.pdf
2. VUMS Cluster Glossary of Terms, http://www.veritas-project.eu/vums/wp-content/uploads/2010/07/VUMS-Cluster-Glossary-of-Terms.pdf
3. Duffy, V.G.: Handbook of Digital Human Modeling: Research for Applied Ergonomics and Human Factors Engineering. CRC Press, FL (2008)

Creative Design for Inclusion Using Virtual User Models

Markus Modzelewski[1], Michael Lawo[1], Pierre Kirisci[1], Joshue O. Connor[2],
Antoinette Fennell[2], Yehya Mohamad[3], Svetlana Matiouk[3],
Markus Valle-Klann[3], and Haluk Gökmen[4]

[1] Universität Bremen, Am Fallturm 1, Bremen, 28359, Germany
{modze,mlawo}@tzi.de, kir@biba.uni-bremen.de
[2] National Council for the Blind (NCBI), Whitworth Road, Drumcondra, Dublin 9, Ireland
{joshue.oconnor,antoinette.fennell}@ncbi.ie
[3] Fraunhofer FIT, Schloss Birlinghoven, Sankt Augustin, 53757, Germany
{yehya.mohamad,svetlana.matiouk,markus.klann}@fit.fraunhofer.de
[4] Arcelik A.S. Karaagac, Sutluce Beyoglu Cad No 2-6, Istanbul, 34445, Turkey
haluk.gokmen@arcelik.com

Abstract. The development of products that are accessible to the largest possible group of users can be regarded as a major challenge for manufacturers of consumer products. It is therefore crucial, that the product development process is supported by practical methods and tools that can help incorporate these essential human factors in early phases of the development process. Ergonomics evaluation and user testing with real users are user centred design methodologies often conducted by companies that are not only complex, but can be very time and cost-intensive. As an alternative approach virtual user models (VUM) have been proposed for supporting the early phases of the product development process. In this paper we will present the model-based design approach of the European research project VICON supporting inclusive design of consumer products particularly at the early stages of product development.

1 Introduction

The design lifecycle of a product can be segregated into a sketch phase and a CAD phase. Both phases could profit from a VUM [1]. In the sketch phase a recommendation system, such as a web application could support the designer to design a product for a specified virtual user or set of users. As soon as a first prototypic product model is available within the CAD phase, the framework has the possibility to have a direct impact on specified parameters of the model. Additionally an evaluation framework could help to identify task related problems with the product.

In the following the technical design is outlined of the Virtual User Model and Environment Tools regarding the sketch, design and evaluation phases as a result of the EC funded project VICON (additional information: http://www.vicon-project.eu).

2 Service Oriented Architecture

Fig. 1 shows an overview of VICON services and framework parts [2]. The VICON front end allows the user to test their product by creating a virtual user, an

K. Miesenberger et al. (Eds.): ICCHP 2012, Part I, LNCS 7382, pp. 288–294, 2012.
© Springer-Verlag Berlin Heidelberg 2012

environ-ment as well as a number of tasks, which reflect activities a user can perform with the product. The recommendation system can be accessed in the sketch phase and the simulation system in the CAD phase. The evaluation can then be conducted and reports can be generated. The middleware services deal with all incoming and outgoing connections and provide relevant data to the different applications. Recommendations are marked with a phase attribute. Any recommendation instance consists of a user model-, environment-, task- or component rule, defined as Generic Rule Reasoner Rule Sets (Inference Rule Sets of the Generic Rule Reasoner of Jena, see `http://jena.sourceforge.net/inference/#rules`). The backend services provide the data and the algorithms to implement the functionalities; databases and components comprising the VICON system phases.

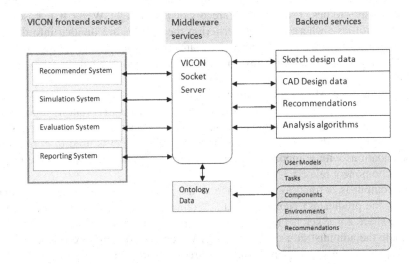

Fig. 1. Overview of VICON Services

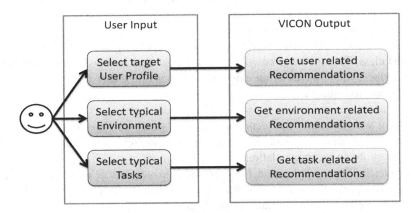

Fig. 2. User's Perspective on the Sketch Phase

Fig. 2 presents the input and output of the system for the sketch phase. Each user input relates to different information about the product and results in different recommendations. Thus each input is used independent as described in the next section.

3   Recommendation System for the Sketch Phase

The data model of the Recommendation System is based on data types and classes of the OWL Ontology. The Virtual User Model (VUM) consists of 5 classes (see Fig. 1):

1. **User Model** class, where all information about a virtual user including physical impairments or limitations are stored. The predicates for this model were achieved through user studies. User models are divided into eight WHO ICF based subgroups (Profiles), where for every criterion the profiles are divided into different levels of impairments. Additionally there are mixed profiles describing the group of elderly people with a mixture of hearing, sight and manual dexterity impairments.

2. The **Component Model** class describes specific constituent parts of the product, called components, and adds specific functionality to appropriate component instances. E.g. a "Button" component consists of the functional attribute of a 2 state switch reflecting that a button can be pressed. This model is used to connect recommendations with components especially in the second phase, where the user input is component related.

3. Every output is defined as an instance in the **Recommendation** class. Each consists of the predicates "Name", "Text", "Summary", Rules, Phases and an Attachment, where e.g. Sketch Phase Template Layers can be stored. In the component attribute the administrator of the ontology is possible to configure rule sets for the CAD phase, if a recommendation can directly adjust specific parameters in the second phase of product development.

4. The **Environment Model** stores all data related to the environment. That includes physical conditions of the environment of the real world, objects and characteristics of the environment etc.

5. Typical Tasks, which can be performed using a product are defined in the Task **Model** class. This model is based on Hierarchical Task Analysis (HTA) providing an interface, where the designer can define actions of the user for the evaluation in the virtual environment.

The system architecture of the recommendation system (see Fig. 3) is divided into a back end, where all data is stored, and a front end, including all client-specific features used to obtain recommendations.

The Sketch Phase Application (recommendation system) deals with user input, where the designer selects a user profile, an environment and a task. These three inputs are not connected to the evaluation application.

In the CAD Phase Application (component related recommendations) specific component or component functionality related recommendations are presented. The designer input of this phase is every input of the CAD software of the product.

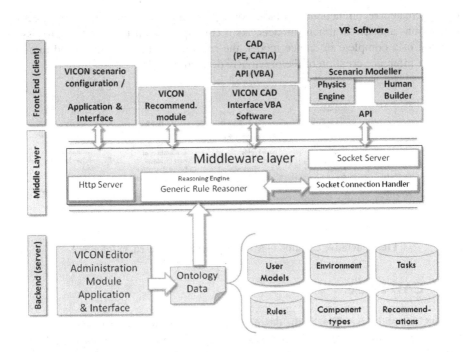

Fig. 3. Architecture of the Recommendation System

The Inference Mode defines user model instances as members of predefined WHO ICF groups. From the viewpoint of these recommendations, the classification of user model instances into specified profiles is necessary, because all recommendations such as components (recommended components) and items (textual recommendations and guidelines) can be specified in each WHO ICF profile. An inference model graph is used to determine new recommendation groups. Within those groups, recommendations are stored through specific rules related to environment and task preferences which are based on the previous inference model.

Fig. 4 illustrates the creation of an Inference Model for the presentation of recommendations. Every step is signed by assigning model-specific forward-chain-logic rules to determine recommendations based on WHO ICF profiles. The rules are used to derive additional RDF (Resource Description Framework) assertions which are inferred from some base RDF - together with any optional ontology information such as the axioms and rules associated with the Generic Rule Reasoner. For every application of rules (user model rules, recommendation rules, environment rules and task rules) this step creates a new inference model that consists of all old and new classes describing the Virtual User Model and the recommendations for every profile. The advantage in the iterative creation of models is that with every step the complexity of rules to determine specified recommendations is growing - so the user gains a larger number of defined predicates. The inference model of task rules for example, is based on the created recommendations based on predicates taken from the User-, Recommendation- and Environment models. As a consequence, in the iterative process of creation of a complete inference model, the rules of the task creation need to come after the inference creation of the previously defined models.

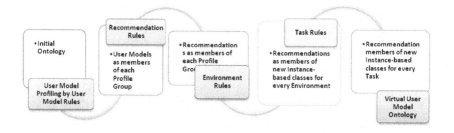

Fig. 4. Iterative Creation of a Virtual User Model based on Inference

4   CAD Phase

In the CAD phase (see Fig. 5) the designer works mainly with a CAD system to create the product design. All functionalities are integrated into a widely-used CAD environment (Siemens NX) as an additional plug-in providing support to:

1. Manually annotate specific components of a product by their functionality and type
2. Describe specific variables in the CAD system directly (e.g. what parameter defines the button height?)
3. Hence apply specific recommendations derived from the Virtual User Model including a component rule to annotated component parameters

These recommendation results, which could not be directly applied to the product's model, can be presented visually to the designer and provided in alternative formats where needed e.g. as textual report.

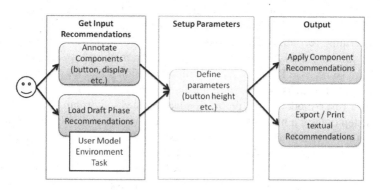

Fig. 5. User's Perspective on the CAD Phase

5   Evaluation Phase

The evaluation of a product design is realised by means of a virtual usage simulation. The simulation is performed in real-time and is visualized in a virtual 3d environment. This enables investigating a range of usability and accessibility questions. In these assessments, environmental aspects such as different lighting conditions and surrounding physical space provide an approximation to the real usage experience.

The evaluation system enables a designer to test his/her 3d product prototype virtually by running a set of different task simulations for a selected user profile and environment. Properties and conditions of the 3d environment and of the virtual user as well as the tasks available for the respective product are coming from VICON's Virtual User Model provided by the Ontology server. While the simulation is running, the designer gets visual and textual feedback on the task progress and its interim success. Subsequent to a task simulation the system presents a report for the task including a binary answer for whether the product can be considered as usable under the given circumstances or not, as well as a differentiated performance assessment. The evaluation results can be stored and used for further iterations within the product design lifecycle.

6   Conclusions and Summary

In this paper a model-based design approach was presented based upon the creation and implementation of a Virtual User Model. It is expected that this design approach is potentially capable of supporting the early product development stage (before developing costly physical prototypes) by providing component and design recommendations as well as virtual experience simulation for a proposed 3d design. The feasibility of the approach has already been demonstrated by implementing a Virtual User Model according to the architecture presented.

The benefits for mainstream manufacturers of consumer products that are easier to use and more inclusive is obvious, as they would be appropriately supported by the Virtual User Model during the entire design process. It would allow for a more efficient solution finding and shorten the entire product development period. It is expected, that the greatest avail get companies who may not be familiar with inclusive design [3].

To proof the validity of the VICON approach all the features of the system will be tested in great detail. We have created plans and specified test cases [4] designed to cover multiple aspects of the application in a similar way to our initial ethnographic studies [6]. The results of the virtual user tests (currently in progress) [5] will be compared with the results of the ethnographic studies [6] in order to ensure the validity of the VICON model as a bona fide tool to facilitate better and more inclusively de-signed products.

References

1. Kirisci, P.T., Thoben, K.-D., Klein, P., Hilbig, M., Modzelewski, M., Lawo, M., Fennell, A., O'Connor, J., Fiddian, T., Mohamad, Y., Klann, M., Bergdahl, T., Gökmen, H., Klen, E.: Supporting Inclusive Design of Mobile Devices with a Context Model. In: Karahoca, A. (ed.) Advances and Applications in Mobile Computing. InTech (2012) ISBN: 978-953-51-0432-2
2. VICON Consortium. Deliverable 3.1 - System Architecture and Interface Specification (2011)
3. Helin, K., Viitaniemi, J., Montonen, J., Aromaa, S., Määttä, T.: Digital Human Model Based Participatory Design Method to Improve Work Tasks and Workplaces. In: Duffy, V.G. (ed.) HCII 2007 and DHM 2007. LNCS, vol. 4561, pp. 847–855. Springer, Heidelberg (2007)
4. VICON Consortium. Deliverable 4.5 – Evaluation Procedure Handbook (2012)
5. VICON Consortium. Deliverable 4.4 – Focus group report (to be published, 2012)
6. VICON Consortium. Deliverable 1.1 – End user and environment field study (2010)

A Methodology for Generating Virtual User Models of Elderly and Disabled for the Accessibility Assessment of New Products

Nikolaos Kaklanis[1,2], Konstantinos Moustakas[1,3], and Dimitrios Tzovaras[1]

[1] Information Technologies Institute, Centre for Research and Technology Hellas, Thessaloniki, Greece
{nkak,moustak,Dimitrios.Tzovaras}@iti.gr
[2] Department of Computing, University of Surrey, Guildford, United Kingdom
[3] Electrical and Computer Engineering Department, University of Patras, Greece

Abstract. The paper presents a highly novel user modeling framework for the detailed description of geometric, kinematic, physical, behavioral and cognitive aspects of users affected by disabilities and elderly. Several aspects of the user's interaction behavior are examined, while user models are quantified, in terms of their kinematics and dynamics parameters, in tests with disabled users through a multisensorial platform, in order to develop accurate and realistic virtual user models. Hierarchical Task and Interaction Models are introduced, in order to describe the user's capabilities in multiple scales of abstraction. The use of alternative ways of a user task's execution, using different modalities and assistive devices, are also supported by the proposed task analysis.

Keywords: User modeling, UsiXML, virtual user, elderly, disabled, simulation, accessibility evaluation, ergonomy evaluation.

1   Introduction

Disability is part of the human condition. Almost everyone will be temporarily or permanently impaired at some point in life. Moreover, aging is strongly connected with difficulties in functioning. People with disabilities often face discrimination and infringement of their rights on a daily basis. Inaccessible products and services create major barriers to participation and inclusion. Even though some environments, products and services are accessible for the majority of the population, including the elderly and disabled, the ergonomy is another factor of great importance that has to be taken into account by the designers. When a product/service is accessible but not ergonomic, although it is usable, the person using the specific product/service faces difficulties in the usage, including great effort, pain, etc.

The incorporation of virtual humans with realistic interaction properties in the design of products and services can play a very crucial role in terms of their accessibility and ergonomy. Simulation can be used to study and compare alternative designs or to troubleshoot existing systems before the real prototype is developed, reducing, thus,

K. Miesenberger et al. (Eds.): ICCHP 2012, Part I, LNCS 7382, pp. 295–302, 2012.

development time and costs. During the last years, the research interest in using digital human modelling for ergonomics purposes has increased significantly. Virtual human modelling reduces the need for the production of real prototypes and can even make it obsolete.

Over the last years, the use of virtual humans and simulation in the automotive industry showed great potential. There are many tools such as JACK [8], RAMSIS [6], SAMMIE [9], HADRIAN [5], SIMTER [4], Safework [1], Santos^{TM}, offering considerable benefits to designers looking to design for all, as they allow the evaluation of a virtual prototype using virtual users with specific abilities. RAMSIS and JACK are the most popular accessibility design software packages, focusing in automotive industry. Both RAMSIS and JACK have anthropometric data sets based on measurements taken from the healthy and the able-bodied groups.

But even if many remarkable researches in this direction can be found in the literature, to the authors' knowledge, a holistic methodology including a formal definition of virtual users with disabilities, a detailed description of user tasks taking into account alternative modalities and the use of assistive devices as well as a set of accessibility and ergonomy metrics, in order to be used in different simulation frameworks, has not yet been proposed. The present paper contributes a holistic methodology for automatic simulated accessibility and ergonomy evaluation of virtual prototypes, based on virtual user models that can sufficiently describe elderly and people with various types of disabilities and on a hierarchical analysis of user tasks.

2   Proposed Methodology

The proposed methodology aims to support the automatic accessibility and ergonomy assessment of virtual prototypes using a novel virtual user model representation framework that is described in the following.

Abstract User Models. The Abstract User Models refer to a high level description of potential user models. An abstract user model includes several disability related parameters like disability description, disability metrics, ICF functional abilities, etc. The Abstract User Models are initially formed by examining the current state-of-the-art, existing standards and guidelines related to several disabilities. Table 1 presents an example of an Abstract User Model.

Table 1. Abstract User Models – Example

Disability category	Disability	Short description	Quantitative disability metrics	Functional limitations (ICF Classification)	Age-related
Motor	Spinal cord injuries (Thoracic injuries)	Spinal cord injuries cause myelopathy or damage to nerve roots or...	**Gait variables:** -Gait Cycle (sec):2.17 (1.05) -Cadence (steps/min): 65.0 (23.1)	S120 Spinal cord and related structures, S1200 Structure of spinal cord, ...	Could be

Generic Virtual User Models. A Generic Virtual User Model (GVUM) refers to a class of virtual users exhibiting one or more specific disabilities. The Generic Virtual User Models describe the tasks affected by the specific disabilities and their associated disability-related parameters. Table 2 presents an indicative example reflecting the main concept of a GVUM. As depicted in the example of Table 2, gait velocity ranges from 0.18 m/sec to 1.03 m/sec and that is because the GVUM refers to a population group not a single user.

Table 2. Generic Virtual User Models – Example

Disability category	Disability	Affected primitive tasks	Affected primitive tasks' parameters
Motor	Hemiplegia	Grasp	The user is able to grasp objects, with size <= *3cm* x *3cm* x *3cm*
		Pull	The user can pull an object with max_Force: 5N
		Walk	Gait velocity ranges from 0.18 to 1.03 m/sec
			Abnormal step rhythm

In order to develop virtual user models that could adequately describe users with disabilities and be used in various simulation platforms performing accessibility and ergonomy assessment, the most common human characteristics affected by various disabilities should be included in a GVUM. Thus, a GVUM includes a large set of anthropometric, kinematic, physical, visual, hearing and speech parameters [3]. Cognitive and behavioral human characteristics are also included.

Instance of a Generic Virtual User Model. An instance of a Generic Virtual User Model (Virtual user, Persona) describes a specific virtual user with specific disability related parameters including disabilities, affected primitive tasks and specific affected primitive tasks' parameters for the specific user. The only difference between a GVUM and an instance of a GVUM is that the first represents a population group, thus, the values of its parameters are ranges, in general, while the second refers to a specific user, thus, the values of its parameters are mainly absolute values.

Primitive Tasks. The primitive tasks define the *primitive human action*s and are related to the disability category. The number of primitive tasks should be limited but also sufficient so as to efficiently model all systematically performed actions in the target application scenarios.

Table 3. Primitive tasks - Example

Primitive task's category	Primitive task
Motor	Grasp
Motor	Walk
Cognitive	Select
Cognitive	Read

The degree of primitiveness that will be adopted may vary and depends on the specific needs of each framework that will be based on the proposed methodology. Table 3 lists some indicative primitive tasks.

Task Models. Task models [2] describe the interaction between the virtual user and the virtual prototype. For each complex task, a Task Model is developed, in order to specify how the complex task can be analyzed into primitive tasks (as they have been defined by the designers/developers, according to the functionality of the proto-types to be tested in terms of accessibility). The Task Models are based on existing relevant state-of-the-art, standards and guidelines but also based on domain knowledge and relevant attributes with respect to the contents of the target application scenarios. Table 4 presents the task analysis performed, in order to define a task model for the complex task "close car door while seated". This complex task is analyzed in four primitive tasks that have to be executed sequentially.

Table 4. Task model example – Close car door while seated

Complex task	Primitive task	Body part	Object
Close car door while seated	Reach	Arm	Door
	Grasp	Hand	Interior door handle
	Pull	Hand	Interior door handle
	Push	Hand	Lock button

Multimodal Interaction Models. A multimodal interaction model describes the alternative ways of a primitive task's execution with respect to the different target user groups, the replacement modalities and the possible use of assistive devices.

Table 5 presents an example of the analysis that has to be performed, in order to develop a Multimodal Interaction Model.

Table 5. Multimodal interaction model example – Pull interior door handle with hand

Task	Body part	Modality	Task object	Disability	Alternative task(s)	Body part	Alternative modality	Alternative task object/ assistive device
Pull	Hand	Motor	Interior door handle	Upper limb impaired	Speak	Mouth	Voice control	Voice activated doors
					Push	Hand/El bow	Motor	Button that closes the door

Simulation Models. A Simulation Model [2] refers to a specific product or service and describes all the functionalities of the product/service as well as the involved interaction with the user. It actually describes the scenario to be followed during the simulation process. In Table 6, the analysis on which the development of a Simulation Model for the automotive sector will be based is presented.

Table 6. Simulation model example – automotive simulation

Scenario	Main tasks	Subtasks
Automotive simulation: *assess the accessibility of the handbrake and the storage compartment*	Use handbrake	Pull handbrake
		Release handbrake
	Use storage compartment	Open storage compartment
		Close storage compartment

A Simulation Model may include three different types of tasks: a) abstract tasks, b) interaction tasks or c) application tasks. An abstract task is a container having two or more children tasks, which are actually executed. An interaction task is a task performed by the virtual user, containing interaction between the virtual user and the virtual prototype. An example of an interaction task could be the door opening. An application task is a task performed automatically by the virtual prototype, without including any interaction with the virtual user. An example of an application task could be the playing of a musical theme when exiting an ICT application. The connection between the tasks within a Simulation Model can be established using a set of temporal operators defining the execution sequence, choice relationships, information passing, etc.

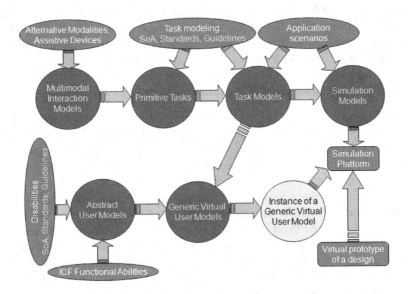

Fig. 1. Architecture of the proposed methodology

The leaves of the hierarchy-tree representing a Simulation Model, which are actually the tasks that will be simulated during the simulation process, may contain complex tasks as well as primitive tasks. In case where a leaf node is a complex task, the information stored in the corresponding Task Model has to be exploited, in order to find out how the specific complex task is analyzed into primitives.

Fig. 1 illustrates an outline of the proposed virtual user modeling methodology and summarizes its most significant properties.

The development of the user models can be performed in four distinct but interrelated steps (Fig. 1):

1. The Abstract User Models are initially formed by examining the current state-of-the-art, existing standards and guidelines related to several disabilities. Moreover, this information is augmented utilizing the WHO ICF functional abilities framework.
2. The Task Models are developed reflecting the actions that are systematically performed by the users in the context of the virtual prototype to be tested. They follow a hierarchical structure from high level tasks to low-level primitive tasks. It is very important to have a limited but sufficient number of primitive tasks, since they will be related to disabilities. Alternative ways of tasks execution are considered, through the development of the Multimodal Interaction Models, in-cluding different modalities and the possible use of assistive devices. The Task Models and the Multimodal Interaction Models are used by the simulation plat-form in conjunction with the Simulation Models, which describe the simulation scenario to be followed during the simulation process with regard to the accessi-bility and ergonomy assessment of the virtual prototype for a specific virtual user.
3. The Generic Virtual User Models refer to a specific category of virtual users and can be comprised from one or more Abstract user models, e.g. a Generic Virtual User Model can include the propanopia and hemiplegia disabilities. They also include description on how the specific disabilities affect the execution of specific tasks (primitive or not) that are described in the task models.
4. Finally, an instance of a Generic Virtual User Model (virtual user, Persona) describes a specific virtual user with specific disability related parameters.

The primitive tasks are the basis of the proposed methodology, as they are the only common reference between the virtual user models, the task models, the multimodal interaction models and the simulation models. The "divide and conquer" approach for task analysis followed by the proposed methodology, which allows the analysis of each complex task into primitives, offers great advantages to the whole simulation process. First of all, within a simulation framework based on the proposed methodology, only the primitive tasks have to be implemented biomechanically. Any possible combination of primitive tasks (constituting a complex task) is then supported without the need of extra implementation effort. Additionally, any possible simulation scenario could be supported for a virtual prototype by simply developing a new simulation model. A simulation model contains primitive tasks or complex tasks, which are analyzed into primitives following the task model hierarchy.

In the context of the VERITAS EC FP7 project, a simulation framework performing automatic simulated accessibility and ergonomy assessment of virtual prototypes has been developed according to the proposed methodology. Experimental results (Fig. 2) that can be found in [2] and [7] show how the proposed methodology can be put into practice and reveal its great potential.

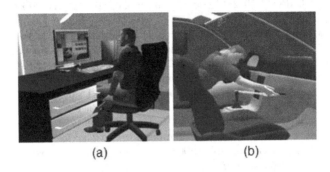

(a)   (b)

Fig. 2. Simulated accessibility and ergonomy assessment. a) Workplace scenario, b) Automotive scenario.

3   Conclusions

In the present paper, a methodology for automatic simulated accessibility and ergonomy testing of virtual prototypes using virtual user models was presented. The proposed virtual user models describe virtual humans with focus on the elderly and people with disabilities. A set of models was introduced, describing the characteristics of the virtual disabled user, how a task of the user can be executed and the simulation scenario to be followed during the simulation process, respectively. The whole methodology is based on the definition of user's primitive tasks, which is the connecting point between all the models. The proposed methodology could be used in various simulation platforms performing accessibility and/or ergonomy assessment of virtual prototypes. Some of the proposed models could be also used in adaptive user interfaces, where the user interface of an application could dynamically change, in order to fulfill user's needs/preferences.

Acknowledgments. This work is supported by the EU co-funded project VERITAS (FP7 – 247765).

References

1. Fortin, C., Gilbert, R., Beuter, A., Laurent, F., Schiettekatte, J., Carrier, R., Dechamplain, B.: SAFEWORK: a microcomputer-aided workstation design and analysis. New advances and future developments. In: Karkowski, W., Genaidy, A.M., Asfour, S.S. (eds.) Computer-Aided Ergonomics, pp. 157–180. Taylor and Francis, London (1990)

2. Kaklanis, N., Moschonas, P., Moustakas, K., Tzovaras, D.: Enforcing accessible design of products and services by enabling automatic accessibility evaluation. In: CONFIDENCE 2010 (2010)
3. Kaklanis, N., Moustakas, K., Tzovaras, D.: An extension of UsiXML enabling the detailed description of users including elderly and disabled. In: Coyette, A., Faure, D., Gonzalez, J.M., Vanderdonckt, J. (eds.) Proc. of 2nd Int. Workshop on User Interface eXtensible Markup Languages USIXML 2012, Lisbon, September 6, pp. 194–201.Thalès Productions, Paris (2011)
4. Lind, S., Krassi, B., Johansson, B., Viitaniemi, J., Heilala, J., Stahre, J., Vatanen, S., Fasth, Å., Berlin, C.: SIMTER: A Production Simulation Tool for Joint Assessment of Ergonomics, Level of Automation and Environmental Impacts. In: The 18th International Conference on Flexible Automation and Intelligent Manufacturing, FAIM (2008)
5. Marshall, R., Case, K., Porter, J.M., Sims, R.E., Gyi, D.E.: Using HADRIAN for Eliciting Virtual User Feedback in 'Design for All'. Journal of Engineering Manufacture; Proceedings of the Institution of Mechanical Engineers, Part B 218(9), 1203–1210 (2004)
6. van der Meulen, P., Seidl, A.: Ramsis – The Leading Cad Tool for Ergonomic Analysis of Vehicles. In: Duffy, V.G. (ed.) HCII 2007 and DHM 2007. LNCS, vol. 4561, pp. 1008–1017. Springer, Heidelberg (2007)
7. Moschonas, P., Kaklanis, N., Tzovaras, D.: Novel human factors for ergonomy evaluation in virtual environments using virtual user models. In: Proceedings of the 10th International Conference on Virtual Reality Continuum and Its Applications in Industry (VRCAI 2011), pp. 31–40. ACM, New York (2011), doi:10.1145/2087756.2087760
8. Phillips, C.B., Badler, N.I.: Jack: A toolkit for manipulating articulated figures. In: Proceedings of the 1st Annual ACM SIGGRAPH Symposium on User Interface Software, pp. 221–229. ACM, New York (1988)
9. Porter, J.M., Marshall, R., Freer, M., Case, K.: SAMMIE: a computer aided ergonomics design tool. In: Delleman, N.J., Haslegrave, C.M., Chaffin, D.B. (eds.) Working Postures and Movements – Tools for Evaluation and Engineering, pp. 454–462. CRC Press LLC, Boca Raton (2004)

VERITAS Approach for Parameterization of Psychological and Behavioral Models

Ana María Navarro, Juan Bautista Mocholí, and Juan Carlos Naranjo

Asociación ITACA Instituto ITACA, Universidad Politécnica de Valencia,
Camino de Vera s/n. 46022, Valencia, Spain
{annacer,juamocag,jcnaranjo}@itaca.upv.es

Abstract. This paper focuses on the description of the approach used to parameterize the psychological and behavioural user models developed under the FP7 EU Founded project VERITAS: Virtual and Augmented Environments and Realistic User Interactions To achieve Embedded Accessibility DesignS. The present paper will focus on the methodology used to define the relevant psychological and behavioural parameters within the context of VERITAS. Two complementary approaches have been selected: on one hand, the use of existing models of the cognitive architecture Adaptive Control of Thought-Rational (ACT-R) for cognitive simulation purposes; on the other hand, a second approach based on existing metrics coming from medical and human behavior studies and biomedical models.

Keywords: Psychological, cognitive models, ACT-R, VERITAS, accessibility, cognitive architectures, cognitive simulation.

1 Introduction

In an aging world with an increased number of people with a disability or with a chronic disease, it is necessary to start developing products and applications with high accessibility and usability standards, in which not only functional physical limitations should be considered, but also behavioral and cognitive aspects should be taken into account.

Having this issue in mind, VERITAS[1] aims to develop, validate and assess tools for built-in accessibility support at all stages of ICT and non-ICT product development. The goal is to introduce simulation-based and virtual reality testing at all stages of the design process in order to ensure that future products and services can be "universally" used, including people with disabilities and elders.

With regards to virtual reality testing, the trend nowadays is to develop virtual user models with a focus on increasing the behaviors realism of the user models, taking into account how emotions and affective states interfere in the interaction with the product.

---

[1] http://veritas-project.eu/about-2/

K. Miesenberger et al. (Eds.): ICCHP 2012, Part I, LNCS 7382, pp. 303–310, 2012.

Currently, a unified psychological modelling theory is still missing. Different theories of human psychological modelling and interaction have been therefore analysed and integrated, focusing on those models that can represent the psychological and behavioural aspects of elderly and disabled people.

In VERITAS, we have focused on how different psychological states affect VERITAS users, elderly and disabled groups. Stress, fatigue, emotions and (de)motivation are amongst the most relevant P&B states that influence elderly and disabled, so we have focused on parameterizing these psychological states, considering qualitative and quantitative metrics and rules of behaviour of these specific P&B states.

2   Study Description and Methodology

The study description will help to understand the context of this study within VERITAS project as well as the used methodology for modeling VERITAS users.

Virtual user modelling is considered as the core research issue in VERITAS. The Psychological and Behavioural (P&B) virtual user models will be generated based on an integration of existing models and studies, based on an analysis of the target groups of users, accessibility issues and cognitive simulation [1].

Virtual user modelling of people under psychological states it is still a very challenging task not yet fully developed, not even at base research level. In order to create these models, the following steps (see Fig.1) have been followed in VERITAS:

1. Creation of P&B Abstract User Models (AUMs): Based on analysis of existing computational models, medical studies, guidelines, methodologies and existing practices, user needs and well known accessibility guidelines and standards, an AUM for representing the different facets of a psychological state was constructed.
2. Appropriate Task models implementation, based on UIML/USIXML language, which can be used to represent specific tasks and interactions. Tasks are subdivided in subtasks, and these composed by primitive tasks.
3. Generation of the P&B Generic Virtual User Models (GVUM), which represents the generic characteristics of users with a psychological state, by merging the Abstract User Model with the affected tasks by psychological state. The P&B GVUM will consist of two different but complementary (in most of the cases) approaches: cognitive modelling with ACT-R and behaviour parameterization. The GVUM will be described with UsiXML language, to represent the users performing specific tasks and interactions.
4. These Generic Virtual User Models (represented in UsiXML) will be instantiated in a second stage of the project in order to generate the Virtual User Models - which represent the characteristics of a specific single user [6]- with simulation purposes.

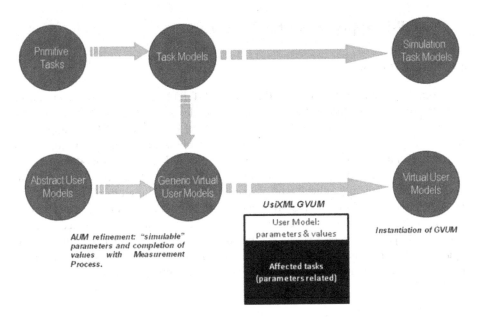

Fig. 1. Representation of VERITAS methodology to develop the virtual user models

In the following sections, the relevant elements result of this methodology will be further detailed.

3   P&B Abstract User Models

In VERITAS, a P&B abstract user model of each psychological state (stress, fatigue, etc.) helps to categorize the representative features of the cognitive and psychological facets of an individual: definitions, types, international standards (ICD, ICF), cognitive functional limitations that may generate, including relevant parameters, measurements and metrics found in both literature and computational modelling approaches.

Under the perspective of VERITAS domains (Automotive, Smart Living Spaces, Workplaces, Infotainment and Healthcare), existing approaches (mainly computational and cognitive architecture models such as ACT-R, GOMS, ACT-Simple, EPIC, ANNs, Fuzzy Logic, etc.) that address and/or model aspects of the cognitive processes were analyzed [2].

A state of art with the strengths and weaknesses of these modeling approaches was performed. This analysis pointed out ACT-R as the most promising and extended modeling approach for psychological simulation, which is consistent with the Abstract User Model intended in VERITAS: an explicit descriptive model of human cognition and behavior that can be afterwards parameterized.

4   ACT-R Approach within VERITAS

4.1   ACT-R Overview

The Adaptive Control of Thought-Rational (ACT-R)2 was the selected cognitive architecture to parameterize the user cognition under a psychological state. ACT-R provides a conceptual framework for the creation of the models of how people will perform a specific task. It reproduces assumptions about the human cognition based on facts resultant from psychology experiments. ACT-R [2] uses a modular organization, which means that the cognition emerges from the interaction of independent modules; each of them is related with a function and specific regions of the brain (Fig. 2). ACT-R is a hybrid cognitive architecture: its symbolic structure is a production system for modeling tasks, whereas the subsymbolic structure is represented by a set of massively parallel processes that can be summarized by a number of mathematical equations, with parameters. ACT-R allows the generalization of new situations, users and domains, which means that allows a wide variation among models.

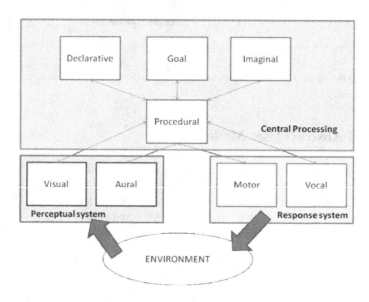

Fig. 2. - ACT-R 6.0. Each ACT-R module is associated with a function

4.2   Behavioural Moderators in ACT-R: P&B States as Overlays

ACT-R parameters are the primary means of configuring the operation of ACT-R both from a usability standpoint and for controlling the performance of a model. So, concerning the development of P&B User Models, specific psychological aspects of a user can be modeled by "overlaying" or tuning these parameters.

---

2 http://act-r.psy.cmu.edu/about/

Overlays are based on popular theories and studies about cognitive and behavioral moderators that can be applied to cognitive architectures [4]. The goal is to specify changes to current mechanisms to simulate the effect of the psychological facets on embodied cognition. These changes will be reflected in the output of the simulation: for instance, if we modify the parameter associated with motor response time, with a mental fatigue overlay (increase time), during the simulation, the movements of the virtual user will be slowed down.

Nevertheless, not all ACT-R parameters are affected by P&B states. A thorough analysis of literature has been performed in order to select the set of relevant ACT-R parameters for modelling P&B states (emotions, fatigue, etc.). In a second step, following the methodology previously described, each parameter has been linked with the affected tasks. In the following table, an example of this analysis can be seen:

Table 1. Analysis of overlays for ACT-R parameter: Visual-attention-latency

ACT-R parameter	Visual-attention-latency [sec]
ACT-R Module	Visual Module
Relevant for P&B states	Yes: emotions, fatigue, stress
Default value	0,085 sec.
Overlays for P&B state	**Acute Stress=0.085 +15%=0,0978** . With stress the latency is increased.
	Negative emotions= Decrease visual attention shift from negative stimuli.(objects) **approx. [-15%].** Shifts faster from disgusting items.
	Positive emotions Positive Stimuli **approx.[+15%]:** shifts slowlier from nice/interesting/surprising items.
	Mental fatigue: Visual_atention_latency >0,085 (increase latency **(+15-+30%)** to model longer shift attention)
Primitive Tasks	Look, See, Focus

The complete collection of these parameters has been included in the final P&B Generic Virtual User Models.

4.3   ACT-R Limit Ations for VERITAS

Despite the fact that ACT-R provides a rigorous framework for simulating (building, running, and testing) computational models of behavior, it presents several limitations that have to be considered for VERITAS project:

- The only motor response well developed is manual and it focuses on computer interaction. Other manual movements are not well (or not at all) developed, whereas other limbs have not been considered, so it won't include all the range needed in VERITAS.

- As for perception processes, only visual perception module is well developed. The other perception systems are limited (aural) or not at all developed.
- There are few quantitative metrics for VERITAS users (elderly and disabled).
- There are very few models of psychological states that have been tested.

Taking into account these limitations, further research has been performed in order to enrich the P&B Generic Virtual User Models.

5   Complementary Approach: Metrics from Medical and Behavioural Studies

P&B states have an impact on different physiological, physical, cognitive and behavioral processes of an individual and "act" as moderators of these processes. The physiological, physical, cognitive and behavioral processes are characterized by several parameters, which have "typical or default values" in neutral situations. We talked about for instance:

- Physiological parameters, i.e.: heart rate, facial expressions, respiration rate;
- Movement parameters, i.e.: kinematics affected by the P&B state;
- Speech parameters, i.e.: pitch, voice intensity, syllable rate;
- Perception parameters, i.e.: visual field;
- Cognitive parameters, i.e.: attention level, reaction time.

Within VERITAS, an extensive research of psychological metrics coming from medical and emotions modeling literature has been performed. Taking into account the previous explanation, the focus has been on how the P&B states "overlay" the different parameters in different domains and contexts. As with ACT-R methodology, by overlay we mean "changes" on the typical values of these processes. There parameters and the different values (either qualitative or quantitative) per type of psychological state will shape the P&B Abstract User Model (AUM). Nevertheless, some of the parameters gathered in the AUM, although relevant for the characterization of P&B states, are not essential for accessibility and/or simulation of models within VERITAS. These parameters have also been included in the P&B Generic Virtual user Model and showed as complementary information to the simulation models.

6   Psychological and Behavioural Generic Virtual User Models for VERITAS

A P&B Generic Virtual User Model (GVUM), as described in this paper, is a parameterized user model that represents a generic user under one of the psychological states selected (stress, fatigue, emotional states). The list of parameters and metrics extracted from both approaches (ACT-R set of parameters and behavior and medical metrics), as well as the link of these parameters with the affected tasks will be included in the models. In Table 1, an example of the view of the Generic Virtual User

Model with ACT-R parameters for users under acute stress can be seen. This table, which represents the GVUM dimensions for the ACT-R models (reduced here for space optimization), includes the Type of P&B state, the International Classification of Diseases corresponding to this P&B state, the functional limitations caused by this P&B state, and the metrics corresponding to the ACT-R model: module, parameter, default value, overlaid metric, and affected primitive tasks.

Table 2. ACT-R GVUM for a user under acute stress

P&B Type	ICD	IC F	ACT-R Computational Model: Parameters and Metrics for Overlays				Affect. PT
			ACT-R Mod.	ACT-R param.	Default	Overlay	
Acute Stress	F. 43	b. 1646	Vision	:visual attention-latency	0,085 sec	0.085 +15%=0,0978	Look See focus
		b. 1648		:visual-finst-span	3.0 sec	Fixation time increases 25%= 3.75.	Look See focus
			Audio	tone-recode-delay	0,285 sec, elderly: (13% in-crease)	20-25% increased by stress.	Hear

Concerning the acute stress metrics extracted from the second approach, an analogous P&B GVUM table (see Table3) has also been produced, including relevant physiological, facial, visual, speech, motor and performance parameters that help to model and categorize this P&B state.

Table 3. GVUM with Complementary Metrics for a user under acute stress

P&B Type	ICD	ICF	Metrics Value for P&B response					Affect. PT
			Type of P&B respons	Param. name	Default	P&B Overlay (Quantitative)	P&B Overlay (Qualitative)	
Acute Stress	F. 43	b. 4100	Physio-logical	Heart rate	Young [60-88], Elderly: [68-90]	typically > 100 bpm	Increases base level with stress level and age	-
		b770 Gait	Motor	Gait cycle	1,09±0,07 sec.	1,01 +-0.09 sec	Decreases cycle	Walk

This second table will be complementary to the ACT-R model parameters gathered in the first table and its structure represents the GVUM dimensions for the Complementary metrics.

7   Conclusions and Next Steps

The current approach provides a complete view of how psychological states moderate users performance with a special focus on accessibility issues and cognitive simulation. A large number of ACT-R models and medical studies have been processed in order to construct a parameterized model of a person under a psychological state. These models will be used in a second stage of VERITAS for simulation purposes in relevant domains for the industry: healthcare, automotive, etc. With this aim, all the P&B GVUM tables are being transformed into UsiXML language, in order to be computed within the Simulation Platform (which uses a XML representation based on Usi-XML standard) together with the simulation tasks and new products developed.

The integration of emotions, stress & fatigue on virtual models will allow creating more human-like models. These models are defined based on real users, on how they feel and behave when confronted to certain positive and negative events. From an application and product development perspective, this knowledge is essential to ensure the acceptability and accessibility of future products and services. Adding these features in virtual models for simulations use opens a large number of possibilities for improving the cycle of product's development.

References

1. VERITAS project (IST- 247765) Annex I- Description of Work (2009)
2. Kolodyazhniy, V., et al.: VERITAS project (IST- 247765) Deliverable D1.4.1 - Abstract Cognitive User Models (2010)
3. Anderson, J., Bothell, D., Byrne, M., Douglass, S., Lebiere, C., Qin, Y.: An integrated theory of the mind. Psychological Review 111(4), 1036–1060 (2004)
4. Ritter, F.E., Reifers, A.L., Klein, A.C., Schoelles, M.J.: Lessons from defining theories of stress. In: Gray, W. (ed.) Integrated Models of Cognitive Systems. Oxford University Press, New York (2006)
5. Jones, G., Ritter, F.E., Wood, D.J.: Using a cognitive architecture to examine what develops. Psychological Science 11(2), 93–100 (2000)
6. Wirsching, H.-J.: VERITAS project (IST- 247765) Deliverable D1.6.1 - Implementation of VERITAS virtual user model platform (2010)
7. Serra, A., et al.: VERITAS project (IST- 247765) Deliverable D1.6.2 - UIML/USIXML task modeling definition (2010)

Integration of a Regular Application into a User Interface Adaptation Engine in the MyUI Project

Alejandro García[1], Jesús Sánchez[1], Víctor Sánchez[1], and José Alberto Hernández[2]

[1] Ingeniería y Soluciones Informáticas del Sur, S.L. (ISOIN), Seville, Spain
{agarcia,jsanchez,vsanchez}@isoin.net
[2] Universidad Carlos III de Madrid, Madrid, Spain
jahgutie@it.uc3m.es

Abstract. Software development is increasingly focusing its design on users suffering from different kinds of disabilities or impairments, as it is the case for the elderly or handicapped people for instance. Real-time adaptable graphical user interfaces is a promising solution for designing accessible applications for users with special needs. Essentially, collecting context information and combining it with information about the user can be used to customize the content of the interface itself, and so it allows improving the user experience in his interaction with the application.

The EU-funded FP7 MyUI project has emerged in the adaptive graphical interfaces domain, addressing important barriers which include the developers' lack of awareness and expertise, time and cost requirements of incorporating accessibility and missing validated approaches and infrastructures of accesible software design. This paper presents the technology used and the experiences collected in the integration process of a regular application into such a framework.

Keywords: Adaptation, user interfaces, accessibility, elderly, disabilities, user profiling.

1 Introduction

The EU-funded FP7 MyUI project combines several elements for building a framework that enables the creation of adaptable user interfaces in a drag-and-drop manner.

The MyUI framework architecture is divided into three essential parts: the user model, the context manager and the adaptation engine. Basically, the adaptation engine uses the information collected by the context manager (which in turn uses the information from the user models) for creating a real-time adaptive interface.

Such an adaptive interface is built up by combining multiple modular "Interaction Patterns", along with an Adaptation Engine which decides which patterns are more suitable for a user, based on the contextual information collected from that particular user. Such interaction patterns translate into HTML code that allows a customized visualization of the application. For instance, if a user suffers from low vision, the adaptaiton Engine may decide to display the context with a larger font-size than for

K. Miesenberger et al. (Eds.): ICCHP 2012, Part I, LNCS 7382, pp. 311–314, 2012.

users without this impairment. Furthermore, if the user suffers from extremely low vision, then the Adaptation Engine may decide to switch to Text-To-Speech and read the contents to the user, rather than displaying it as conventional text.

A number of different patterns for covering all possible aspects of users with special needs are allocated in the so-called Pattern Repository. This approach allows building user interfaces in a modular way, and allows for a rich number of possible user interfaces. The MyUI framework also provides a pattern browser which allows developers to browse through each pattern features so they can choose and select which ones suit their needs.

The Context Manager captures and stores the particular contextual information about the user, including his/her permanent impairments and the current contextual information captured by sensors. Such information feeds the Adaptation Engine to make it decide which Design Patterns are best suited for that user and his context.

An example of a regular application we can think about is an instant messaging (IM) application, in which users can send and receive messages in real time through a server. Next we describe the experiences collected from the IM application development with adapted interfaces.

2   Experiences

This relatively simple IM application provides an interface where a user selects from a contact list the person to whom he is going to send messages. Once the contact is selected, a window prompt lets the user start a new conversation. This window will be displaying the messages as they arrive, below a box allows the users to write the message to be sent to the contact.

The application consists of a server built upon a MySQL database in which the messages are stored. The SQL record for a message stores the sender and receiver IDs, and also a flag that determines whether this message has been read or not.

2.1   CakePHP Modeling

CakePHP has been used as the core framework for MyUI. CakePHP is a PHP framework for building web applications that implements the MVC (model, view, and controller) approach.

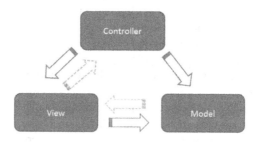

Fig. 1. MVC design pattern

The models of CakePHP have been replaced by the Context Manager, and the views are replaced by the Adaptation Engine. Hence the controller provides the link with the Context Manager and the Adaptation Engine by quering the CM for the user's profile and feeding this information to the adapation engine which generates the appropriate UI dynamically.

2.2   Integration into the Platform

All applications in MyUI (including the Instant Messaging) have been developed as CakePHP plugins, in order to reuse the CM and AE modules for all applications. Hence, the developer does not need to worry about these modules.

This allows reusing the thus allowing other applications to application developed in CakePHP can be integrated into the MyUI platform, but in order to do so it is necessary for the application to be stored as a CakePHP plugin, into the plugins folder following the architecture of the framework. The first step is to download the MyUI platform and put it on our server, this will allow to the developers to see the changes they are making. The structure of this folder is standard for all applications in CakePHP and the controllers, models and views should be stored within the controllers, views and models folders respectively.

The idea is, therefore, that the MyUI framework should have the application developed in CakePHP as a plugin, so the platform can access the application and display it on the menu as an application over the platform.

Doing this step the application would be functional within the MyUI platform, but still not adaptable to the user so far, it is needed the third step.

2.3   Application Adaptation

As aforementioned, the developer does not make decisions about how the application will look like when being displayed on a screen, but he makes the decision about the content to be shown. To do so it is only necessary to use the interaction patterns. These elements will replace our basic html elements for a few items that will be adaptable at the end. Thanks to the adaptation engine the html elements will adapt automatically its visual appearance tailored to the needs of the user.

For using these interaction patterns, the most effective way is to use the MyUI plugin for eclipse. This plugin lets you create a MyUI project which automatically produces the folder structure for integration (first step), in addition to automatically download and configure our application into the platform as a plugin (second step), and finally, the platform will provide to the developers the patterns they need for adapting the application and the patterns browser for exploring the features of them.

3   Conclusions

The resulting experience of using this framework for the creation and integration of an instant messaging application has been proved as a successful and fast way to adapt an application according to the needs of their users, without an extra cost and time in training for developers.

This paper presents MyUI platform not only as web application with adaptable interfaces, but also as a tool that gives developers the capacity to develop accessible applications, without having to worry about how is the adaptation process and what kind of adaptation need a specific user, since the platform itself takes care of adaptations and user disabilities/preferences collection.

Acknowledgments. The authors would like to acknowledge the support of the EU-funded FP7 MyUI project to the development of this work (grant agreement no. FP7-ICT-248606).

References

1. MyUI website, http://www.myui.eu
2. CakePHP framework, http://cakphp.org

Using Annotated Task Models for Accessibility Evaluation

Ivo Malý, Jiří Bittner, and Pavel Slavík

Department of Computer Graphics and Interaction
Faculty of Electrical Engineering, Czech Technical University in Prague
{maly,bittner,slavik}@fel.cvut.cz

Abstract. Evaluation of application accessibility is a challenging task that requires an intensive testing with potential application users. An alternative to user tests is the model based testing using simulations. The simulations provide important feedback about application accessibility particularly when it is hard to involve the target users in the tests which is often the case for users with disabilities. In this paper we propose a methodology of providing the quickly and easily necessary data for the simulations. In particular we show how to annotate task models using application walkthroughs logs that is data obtained by recording the application usage. We create annotated task models, which together with the user models are suitable for simulation of application usage by virtual users with various disabilities. We present tools for recording and processing of the application walkthrough logs and tools for the interactive task model annotation. Finally, we provide actual examples of task model annotation on three scenarios involving the Second Life metaverse.

Keywords: Task Models, Accessibility Evaluation, User Centred Design and User Involvement.

1 Introduction and Motivation

The goal of accessibility testing is to gather specific information on accessibility issues. Traditionally the application testing is performed with well selected target group of users. Specifically when dealing with users with disability it may be very difficult to gather the users for testing and the user based evaluation can become very time consuming and expensive. An alternative to the user based evaluation are expert reviews, which however need not discover some issues of the application for the particular user group. An approach that is expected to receive increasing attention in the future is the model based testing, i.e. application testing based on simulations in which we simulate the usage of the application by means of virtual users [1]. The model based testing can be used practically in all stages of application development (from the design to evaluation). As this approach does not employ real users, we can perform significantly more tests to iteratively improve accessibility of the application. Additionally we can reflect

K. Miesenberger et al. (Eds.): ICCHP 2012, Part I, LNCS 7382, pp. 315–322, 2012.

many types of disabilities and also combinations of disabilities for which real users would be hard to reach and test.

Model based testing methods require detailed specification of the application interface in order to perform the accessibility testing. In other words the task model representing the application needs to be annotated with the actual data values which correspond to particular actions expected to be simulated by the virtual users. These data include for example a specification of a screen area in which a mouse click is expected in a particular simulation step, the key to be pressed and the associated time constrains given by the application. Such information is readily available when evaluating web-based applications since it can be interpreted from the standardized user interface descriptions (such as HTML). When dealing with general applications for which a description of user interface is not available (e.g. third party desktop applications, computer games, etc.) it is not clear how to obtain the actual data representing the user interface for performing the simulations.

In this paper we propose a method which allows to specify the required values for the simulation by recording the interaction with the application, annotating the records and binding the records to the task models. The application records are stored in application walkthrough log files combined with a video stream. These logs represent the expected interaction with the application in the particular task. As the task models are independent of concrete layout and size of user interface they can remain mostly static even if the design of the application interface is updated. Such an approach allows to use highly generic task models that can be reused and we only need to annotate the task model using application walkthrough log for a specific version of the application interface.

2   Related Work

Our work relates to the model based testing of GUI applications. Generally, model based testing works with task models representing tasks and with a model representing the application GUI. Aho et. al [5] use custom GUI driver to extract GUI element representation from the application while walking through the tasks in the tested application. This method is limited to Java based applications and no formal description of tasks is used. The GUITAR project [6] is capable of extraction of GUI element representation from the Windows, Java, Android and iOS applications which exploit the standard widgets of the operating system. Again, the tasks are not defined by means of a formal description.

Bertolini et. al. [7] focus on representation of tasks in formal description and their update for the case of user interface modifications. They use CNL (Controlled Natural Language) notation, which is specific subset of English, for description of the task models (called test cases). These task models are then translated into particular script actions that will perform the interaction with the applications. However, it is not clear how the script derive information about GUI elements. Kaklanis [4] uses UsiXML for description of the task models (called simulation models). Again, there is no connection between the model and the information about particular GUI element.

Paganelli et al. [10] presents tool for extraction of task model from web pages, which is suitable e..g. for model based usability testing of the web page. Using this approach we are able to simulate the user interaction, but it is not possible to add constraints like mark area, where mouse cursor must remain during the movement.

The specification of the interconnection between the model of the user interface and the task model for general applications has not been sufficiently addressed. We propose a combination of task models and application walkthrough logs to achieve this interconnection. Note that a similar approach of the usage of the application walkthrough logs is implemented in the Selenium IDE web browser plug-in [8], but this tool is focused only on HTML pages and does not work with models.

3 User Interaction Simulation with Annotated Task Models

3.1 Model Based Testing

The model based testing approach is based on carefully created user models which reflect the physical and behavioral limitations of real users. The simulation based accessibility evaluation then consist of the following steps:

1. Plan the test - select virtual users for evaluation, create task model
2. **Annotate the task model with actual application data**
3. Perform the simulation for each virtual user
4. Analyze the data from the test and present the test findings
5. If any accessibility issues were discovered, modify the application and continue with step 2
6. Finish accessibility evaluation

Our paper mainly addresses step 2: annotating the task models with actual application data. This step is divided into two sub steps: (1) log file creation and processing and (2) task model annotation.

3.2 Methodology Overview

The task models used for accessibility evaluation usually reflect a particular GUI layout on an abstract level. However for the simulation we need to combine such abstract models with the actual information about the user interface (GUI layout, key bindings) in order to get low level information about the actions expected from the user interaction (mouse movements, key presses). Generally, there are two approaches how to get the required data about the user interface. We can generate these data from the application itself, which either requires that the application conforms to certain standards (e.g. usage of standard GUI library) or it requires the access to the application source code and a possibility to modify the code. An alternative way, which we exploit in our method, is to record a particular series of user actions (application walkthrough log) and using this recording in order to simplify the specification of the required data. While this second approach requires manual intervention its significant advantage is that we can use it for almost any application, even for that in which no modifications are possible at the simulation site.

3.3   Log File Record and Processing

We first record application walkthrough into log files and video streams. These data can then be used to annotate the task model with values needed for the actual simulations. Such integration of the application walkthrough logs and the task models is a key to obtain the actual data describing the user interactions with particular GUI elements and interaction devices. The log files are either created by the application itself or by an external application which we have created that is able to record the interaction of the user interface devices with the operating system [9]. Similarly the video stream is either captured by a dedicated application or hardware.

Before the annotation process begins, we must process the application walkthrough log file, so we can link some of individual low-level interaction into high-level actions, which are more suitable for adding parameters and tasks. This activity is automatically performed by the annotation tool during import of the application walkthrough log file. In our tool we use following high-level actions:

- **Mouse move** consists of several recorded mouse sub-movements. Optionally, it can contain the area in which the mouse cursor must stay during the simulated movement.
- **Mouse click** consists of mouse button press and mouse button release, which are performed at same cursor coordinates. It contains also the information which mouse button was used and the area, in which the mouse click must occur (e.g. bounding box of the button being pressed).
- **Key press** contains information about the key being pressed.
- **Drag and drop** consists of mouse button press, mouse movement and mouse button release. Mouse movement is represented by the vector between start and finish points of the mouse move. It contains information which mouse button was used and it also contains area, in which the mouse click must occur (e.g. bounding box of the button being pressed). Optionally, it can contain keys pressed during the action.

An example of the application walkthrough log file for task *Manipulation with the box* in Second Life metaverse [2] is given in Table 1. In the left part, there are parameters for the low-level actions. In the right part, the high-level actions and their parameters from the annotation process are presented in merged cells. All the parameters added to the high-level action are delegated to the particular low-level actions that constitute the high-level action. Each action, both low-level and high-level, can be part of only one subtask from task model.

Table 1. Excerpt of the processed application walkthrough log file for task *Manipulation with the box* in Second Life metaverse. Annotation data (Task and Click area) are also presented.

Time	Low-level interaction	Coords	Key	High-level interaction	Task	Movement area	Click area	Movement vector
00:04.627	M_MV	392, 601						
...	...	...			Access			
00:05.491	M_MV	624, 326		Mouse move	context			(259,-301)
...	...	...			menu			
00:06.906	M_MV	651, 300						
00:06.906	M_RB_DOWN	651, 300			Access		Rectangle	
00:07.042	M_RB_UP	651, 300		Mouse click	context		(460, 304,	
...	...	...			menu		10, 10)	
00:13.679	K_DOWN		ctrl					
00:13.679	K_DOWN		shift					
00:13.765	M_MV	666, 292						
...	...	...			Select box			
00:14.737	M_MV	678, 310		Mouse move	scaling			(14, 25)
...	...	...			component			
00:16.771	M_MV	680, 317						
00:16.771	M_LB_DOWN	680, 317						
00:16.906	M_MV	680, 317						
...	...	...		Drag and			Rectangle	
00:20.204	M_MV	703, 332		Drop	Scale box		(478, 293,	(30, 17)
...	...	...					9, 5)	
00:26.901	M_MV	710, 334						
00:26.901	M_LB_UP	710, 334						
00:27.513	K_UP		shift					
00:27.513	K_UP		ctrl					

3.4 Task Model Annotation

The goal of the task model annotation is to assign the low-level and high-level actions to the particular task and also add all the parameters (constraints) to low-level and high-level actions so we can simulate and evaluate the task in the simulation. These methods were implemented as several modules of the Integrated Visualization Environment (IVE) [3] (see Fig. 1).

The annotation of the task model is guided by the actions processed form the imported application walkthrough log file. Actions are presented in the form of a timeline or a table and the task model is presented in the form of a tree or a graph, see Fig. 1 – Actions view and Task model view. Actions are added to the task model by the selection of the actions and double clicking at the particular task. For each action we can also specify the area of validity of the mouse click event by interactively marking the associated GUI element in the recorded video stream, see Fig. 1 – Video view. We can select between several shapes of the area: rectangle, ellipse or polygon. The resulting annotated task model can be exported from the application and it can then be used in the simulation process.

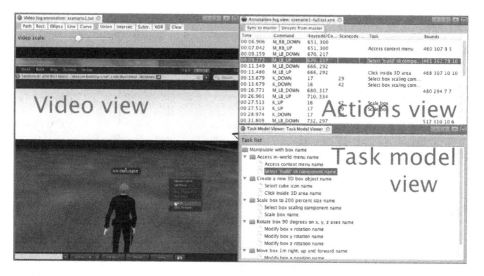

Fig. 1. IVE tool with plug-ins for annotation of task models with application walkthrough log

4   Results

In order to validate the assets of our methodology we have annotated task models describing three scenarios of using the Second Life metaverse viewer [2]. These scenarios are: (1) manipulation with the box in the metaverse, (2) changing avatar outfit, (3) loading an item into avatar inventory.

In Fig. 2 we show an example of the task model which corresponds to the *Change avatar outfit* action in the Second Life viewer. Leaf nodes of the task model in UsiXML format represent user interactions (mouse move, mouse button press, mouse button release) that directly correspond with high-level actions from the application walkthrough log file. The leaf nods can also represent more abstract tasks like in the task model *Manipulation with the box* (see Fig. 3).

In Table 2 are characteristics of the task models and application walkthrough log files and in Table 3 are the results of the annotation process. First, we performed graphical annotation of mouse clicks and drag and drops using the rectangular areas. In average, this annotation took 13 seconds in each scenario, even though the performance may be influenced by the size of the rectangle and its position on the screen due to Fitts' law characteristics of the annotation. Next, we performed assignment of the tasks to actions. There was a difference between the average times in scenario 2 (6 seconds) and the remaining scenarios (about 12 seconds). We believe that the reason may be the low count of annotations.

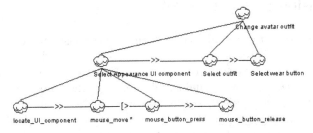

Fig. 2. Task model for the *Change avatar outfit* task in the Second Life metaverse. Inner nodes represent abstract subtasks in Second Life metaverse and leaf nodes represent the most specific tasks, up to the user interaction with particular user interface elements.

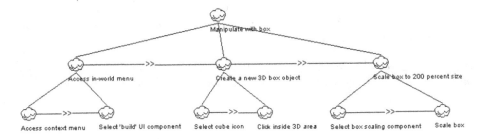

Fig. 3. Excerpt of the task *Manipulation with the box* in the Second Life metaverse

Table 2. Characteristics of the task models

Task model	Leaf sub-tasks	Low-level actions	High-level actions	Actions annotated by geom. parameter (Rectangle tool)	Actions annotated by task model	Application walkthrough log duration [m:s]
Manipulate with the box	62	951	26	10	11	1:24
Change avatar outfit	12	146	8	3	3	0:33
Load item into avatar inventory	36	298	14	5	8	0:29

Table 3. Results of the task model annotation

Task model	Duration of annotation by geom. parameter [m:s]	Time to perform task model annotation [m:s]	Avg. time to perform geom. annotation (Rectangle tool) [m:s]	Avg. time to perform task model annotation [m:s]
Manipulate with the box	2:13	2:10	0:13	0:12
Change avatar outfit	0:40	0:18	0:13	0:06
Load item into avatar inventory	1:12	1:38	0:14	0:12

5   Conclusion and Future Work

This paper proposes a methodology for annotating task models with important data about the user interface. This data is gathered using application walkthrough logs and subsequently used in interactive session to easily specify parameters needed for an actual simulation of application accessibility. This methodology has been applied to the task models describing interaction with the Second Life metaverse viewer. The time and the effort required for the task model annotation was acceptable, depending mainly on the number of high-level actions. Using our method and tools we are able to quickly create models for simulation of the selected application (in our case Second Life metaverse) usage by users with disabilities using Veritas Simulation Platform [1].

In future work we will focus on the actual iterative simulations of the annotated task models within the Veritas project and on the verification of the methodology on more complex models.

Acknowledgments. We want to thank Thanos Tsakiris for fruitful discussions on the topic of task model annotation. This research has been supported by the Veritas project (FP7-ICT-247765).

References

1. The VERITAS project, FP7-247765, http://veritas-project.eu
2. Second Life, http://secondlife.com
3. Maly, I., Mikovec, Z., Vystrcil, J.: Interactive Analytical Tool for Usability Analysis of Mobile Indoor Navigation Application. In: 3rd International Conference on Human System Interaction, Rzeszow, pp. 259–266 (2010)
4. Kaklanis, N., Moschonas, P., Moustakas, K., Tzovaras, D.: A Framework for Automatic Simulated Accessibility Assessment in Virtual Environments. In: Duffy, V.G. (ed.) Digital Human Modeling, HCII 2011. LNCS, vol. 6777, pp. 302–311. Springer, Heidelberg (2011)
5. Aho, P., Menz, N., Raty, T., Schieferdecker, I.: Automated Java GUI Modeling for Model-Based Testing Purposes. In: 8th International Conference on Information Technology, Las Vegas, pp. 268–273 (2011)
6. GUITAR project, http://sourceforge.net/projects/guitar/
7. Bertolini, C., Mota, A.: A Framework for GUI Testing based on Use Case Design. In: 3rd International Conference on Software Testing, Verification, and Validation, Washington, DC, pp. 252–259 (2010)
8. Selenium IDE documentation, http://seleniumhq.org/docs/
9. Malý, I., Hapala, M., Bittner, J., Slavík, P.: On Tools for Game Interaction Analysis. In: 2nd IASTED International Conference on Assistive Technologies (AT 2012), pp. 835–841. ACTA Press, Innsbruck (2012)
10. Paganelli, L., Paterno, F.: Automatic reconstruction of the underlying interaction design of web applications. In: 14th International Conference on Software Engineering and Knowledge Engineering (SEKE 2002), pp. 439–445. ACM, New York (2002)

Web Accessibility in Advanced Technologies

Introduction to the Special Thematic Session

Shadi Abou-Zahra[1], Konstantinos Votis[2], and Karel Van Isacker[3]

[1] W3C Web Accessibility Initiative (WAI)
shadi@w3.org
[2] Informatics and Telematics Institute Centre for Research and Technology Hellas
kvotis@iti.gr
[3] European Platform for Rehabilitation (EPR)
aegis@epr.eu

Abstract. The Web is rapidly evolving and converging with other media and technologies. Today the Web is on mobile devices, televisions, self-service terminals, and computer desktops. It is continuing to be increasingly ubiquitous and indistinguishable from other interfaces and became an ambient part of our daily lives, particularly with the advancement of "the cloud". Thus, there is a need for developers and designers to better understand the relationship and overlap of the existing accessibility methodologies, and introduce Web accessibility in advanced and mainstream technologies for providing accessible products that work better for people who experience difficulties and changes in their abilities due to aging.

Keywords: Web, Accessibility, Ubiquitous Web, Cloud Computing, Digital TV, People with Disabilities, Aging Population.

1   Introduction to This Special Thematic Session (STS)

Given the highly flexible and adaptable nature of the Web, its growth provides a critical potential of increased inclusion and equality for people with disabilities. However, it also raises new challenges for technology, software, and content developers in making their products and services accessible. In particular, the specific accessibility challenges and optimal ways for providing accessibility support are not well understood in all contexts, making it difficult to effectively design and develop accessible mainstream technologies.

This Special Thematic Session (STS) attempts to introduce and discuss experiences with the day-to-day challenges that developers, evaluators, managers, policy makers, and other practitioners observe in implementing web accessibility in advanced technologies for some of the following key applications and areas:

- HTML5 and rich internet applications;
- Websites and applications for mobiles;
- Content Management Systems;

K. Miesenberger et al. (Eds.): ICCHP 2012, Part I, LNCS 7382, pp. 323–324, 2012.

- Digital/IP TV and audio-visual media;
- Web telephony and real-time communication,
- Self-service terminals (e.g. information kiosks, ticketing machines, ATM, etc.),
- Online games and social networks,
- Virtual and augmented environments,
- 3D Web and multi-touch,
- Cloud-based personalized accessible interfaces

2   Areas Covered by This Special Thematic Session (STS)

More specifically, this Special Thematic Session (STS) introduces contributions analyzing good practices, use-cases, end-user requirements, promising accessibility features and solutions, and challenges in applying web accessibility in specific contexts:

- eAccess+ Network: Enhancing the Take-Up of eAccessibility in Europe, with detailed information, use cases and results on eAccessibility by covering areas such as Web Accessibility, Accessible iDTV and convergent Communication and Self-service terminals (SSTs), presented by Klaus Miesenberger;
- Accessibility of Dynamic Adaptive Web TV Applications, presented by Luis Carriço;
- A method for Generating CSS to Improve Web Accessibility for old Users, presented by Jesia Zakraoui;
- Implementing Web Accessibility by introducing the MIPAW Approach, presented by Dominique Burger;
- An Ontology Based Middleware for Ranking and Retrieving Information on Locations Adapted for People with Special Needs, presented by Kevin Alonso;
- Automatic colour improvement of web pages with time limited operators, presented by Sébastien Aupetit;
- Improving web accessibility for dichromat users through contrast preservation presented by Alina Mereuta;
- Sociological Issues of Inclusive Web Design - The German Web 2.0 Accessibility Survey, presented by Michael Pieper;
- Online Shopping Involving Consumers with Visual Impairments - A Qualitative Study of Encountered Challenges, Requirements and Recommendations for Improvement, presented by Christine Strauss;
- Accessibility in Content Management Systems and more specifically by presenting accessibility features on Fabasoft Folio, presented by Mario Batusic.

Acknowledgements. This Special Thematic Session (STS) is jointly organized by the EC-funded WAI-ACT[1], ACCESSIBLE[2] and AEGIS[3] projects.

---

[1] http://www.w3.org/WAI/ACT
[2] http://www.accessible-eu.org/
[3] http://www.aegis-project.eu/

The eAccess+ Network: Enhancing
the Take-Up of eAccessibility in Europe

Klaus Miesenberger[1], Eric Velleman[2], David Crombie[3], Helen Petrie[4],
Jenny S. Darzentas[5], and Carlos A. Velasco[6]

[1] University of Linz, Institute Integriert Studieren, Austria
[2] Stichting Bartimeus Accessibilit, The Netherlands
[3] Stichting Hogeschool voor de Kunsten Utrecht, The Netherlands
[4] University of York, United Kingdom
[5] University of the Aegean, Greece
[6] Fraunhofer Institute for Applied Information Technology FIT, Schloss Birlinghoven, 53757
Sankt Augustin, Germany

Abstract. This short paper introduces the idea, the main tool and the work of the EU-supported **eAccess+** network (www.eaccessplus.eu) for fostering the uptake of eAccessibility in Europe. The rationale for the network starts from the fact that a considerable and elaborated body of knowledge, established in the eAccessibility and Assistive Technology domain, exists but is rarely implemented in mainstream design. There are many reasons for this situation and the network is working to identify and address them and to start processes to remedy the situation.

1   Introduction: Low Take-Up of eAccessibility

Over the last decades the eAcccessibility field has established a solid body of knowledge, including guidelines, methodologies, techniques, training and reference materials and examples how to implement eAccessibility in Information Society products, systems and services (e.g. [1,2]). This consolidated body of knowledge is intended to be applied to mainstream design as an integral part of systems and services in society.

However, eAccessibility seems to stay confined to its domain of origin. This is despite the fact that a) Awareness and acceptance of eAccessibility as a fundamental human right is growing, as can be seen in the UN Convention on the Rights of People with Disabilities [3] and in many EU directives, and in national and international legislation; b) eAccessibility is a key business concern due to the considerable and still growing number of citizens who are dependent on or benefiting from eAccessibility; c) eAccessibility is crucial in dealing with the growing pressure on social systems due to an aging population, correlating with increasing occurrence of disabilities. Finally, the ongoing investment in many initiatives, programmes and projects all demonstrate the need, the feasibility and the viability of eAccessibility.

Yet, although key mainstream players are involved in these programmes, application in day to day practice is scare. Furthermore, the situation even appears worse

K. Miesenberger et al. (Eds.): ICCHP 2012, Part I, LNCS 7382, pp. 325–328, 2012.
© Springer-Verlag Berlin Heidelberg 2012

when we compare these gradual and step by step improvements in the uptake of eAccessibility in the light of the exploding application of ICT in society. This is true for areas which have received much attention over the last years, such as Web Accessibility (e.g. [4]), but it is even worse in other eAccessibiltiy domains [5].

2   eAccess+: Supporting the Implementation of eAccessibility

European institutions reacted to the situation outlined above with actions such as the EC Communication 2008 "Towards an accessible information society" [6] and related feedback such as that from the European Council [7], aiming at improving the situation and calling for related activities. [8]. One of these related activities has been the founding of the **eAccess+** network. **eAccess+** (www.eaccessplus.eu) has established and is systematically developing a cooperative platform for co-ordinating, supporting and improving the implementation of eAccessibility throughout Europe by involving all stakeholder groups in the associated value chains; analysing the present state in order to identify the obstacles or missing links hindering a wider uptake of eAccessibility. The network first **identifies** and **consults** relevant stakeholder groups, **analyses** and discusses with them the state of the art, **supports** stakeholders in adopting eAccessibility and **disseminates** experiences and knowledge all over Europe. Finally a **roadmap** is being drawn up to find appropriate future actions.

Out of the wide range of topics related to eAccessibility, **eAccess+** focuses particularly on fostering the implementation of:

- **Web accessibility.** Here the network focuses on disseminating and increased uptake of the internationally recognized W3C/WAI web accessibility standards, techniques and technical solutions, in particular WCAG 2.0 and Rich Internet Applications, on harmonizing the evaluation methodologies and tools; on web accessibility monitoring; as well as approaches to accessibility statements on a web system.
- **Accessible communication and audio-visual systems and accessible documents:** The switch to digital television and recent technology (ASR, gesture control, smart remote controls and second screens) and applications developments(social media, home care, tele-medicine, etc.) originating either directly from manufacturers or from European research projects alongside standardization activities such as HbbTV (http://www.hbbtv.org/), have greatly facilitated the move towards a truly accessible Web TV experience. eAccess+ supports the relevant stakeholder groups in achieving greater strategic coherence at a technological, economic and political level.
- **Self-service terminals (SSTs) and related devices** for banking and financial services, public transport, tourism and cultural heritage, e-government The proliferation of these services and newer hybrid self service technologies (such as e-boarding cards delivered to smart phones) are capable of making our everyday lives easier. They can offer 24 hour service, consistency in service, greater distribution of services, etc. However some human mediated services are being phased out and replaced with self services. This means that there is no alternative for those who are unable to use SSTs,

due to sensory cognitive, or mobility and dexterity limitations. **eAccess+** is communicating actively with suppliers and deployers of such services to make them more aware of the problems and the need to implement eAccessibility.

eAccess+ is driven by 25 core members, coming from all over Europe. Their main task is outreach to stakeholders, -in particular those who are typically responsible for implementing eAccessibility,- and to expand the network. A clear focus is given to contacting those stakeholders able to act as "ambassadors" or opinion leaders, following the dissemination of innovation theories of Rogers [9]. A web based management system supports this process of involving stakeholders. In addition, **eAccess+** is present at key mainstream events to advocate for eAccessibility.

3   The eAccessibility HUB: Guided Access to eAccessibility

As a core methodology and main tool, **eAccess+** is establishing the "**eAccessibility HUB**" (http://hub.eaccessplus.eu/wiki/Main_Page) which allows guided access to existing resources by adding semantic enrichment and cross-linking (resources are not mirrored). The HUB addresses a very practical problem, namely that people often do not find the right source of information they need in a certain situation. eAccessibility is without doubt a complex issue and the body of knowledge mentioned is vast, diverse and interdisciplinary. Different stakeholders need different "views" to get what they need in practice. **eAccess+** identified the problem of interested parties becoming disoriented -and their difficulties to find the appropriate piece of information; example; method;, tool; and/or competent expertise;- as one of the main issues that discourages stakeholders. Such stakeholders, although interested and motivated, may become hesitant and frustrated and eventually withdraw from efforts to implement Accessibility.

Thus, by systematically analysing the existing body of knowledge, the eAccessibility HUB offers better access and sophisticated search functionalities to support better orientation in the large amount of resources available.

In doing so, the HUB allows for an evidence based discussion of the state of the art and on obstacles to take up. As a media tool, it supports feeding facts; ideas; recommendations; and concepts into appropriate end-user; political; technical; industrial and research channels.

The use of a network as a tool; the creation of the HUB; and the concentration on three implementation areas, all support **eAccess+** to act as a facilitator and coordinator for a better implementation of eAccessibility in practice. In addition, it can be used to plan the future of the next steps at national and European level with regard to standards; policy; guidelines; and tools. Due to the crowd sourcing approach and the involvement of well established networks and associations, we see the eAccessiblity HUB as an approach and a tool that is eminently sustainable.

Acknowledgement. The eAccess+ network is supported the European Commission through its ICT Policy Support Programme.

References

1. Web Accessibility Initiative (WAI) of the World Wide Web Conosrtium (W3C) (April 2012), http://www.w3c.or/wai
2. IBM: Developer Guidelines (April 2012),
   http://www-03.ibm.com/able/guidelines
3. United Nations: Convention on the Rights of Persons with Disabilities (April 2012),
   http://www.un.org/disabilities
4. Goodwin, M.: Towards Automated eGovernment Monitoring, Dissertation submitted to the Faculty of Engineering and Science at Aalborg University, Denmark (2011)
5. Empirica: Measuring Progress of eAccessibility in Europe (MeAC); Assessment of the Status of eAccessibility in Europe (April 2012),
   http://ec.europa.eu/information_society/activities/einclusion/library/studies/meac_study/index_en.html
6. European Commission: EC Communication 2008 "Towards an accessible information society" (April 2012), http://eur-lex.europa.eu/LexUriServ/LexUriServ.do?uri=COM:2008:0804:FIN:EN:PDF
7. Council of the European Union: Council Conclusions on accessible information society (April 2012), http://www.consilium.europa.eu/uedocs/cms_data/docs/pressdata/en/trans/107014.pdf
8. European Commission: EU Disability Action Plan (April 2012),
   http://ec.europa.eu/social/main.jsp?catId=430&langId=en
9. Rogers, E.M.: Diffusion of Innovations. Free Press, New York (1983)

A Method for Generating CSS
to Improve Web Accessibility for Old Users

Jesia Zakraoui and Wolfgang Zagler

Applied Assistive Technologies
Vienna University of Technology
Vienna, Austria
e9827053@student.tuwien.ac.at, zw@fortec.tuwien.ac.at

Abstract. We propose a method to improve Web Accessibility. First, we generate a list of Cascading Style Sheet CSS for Websites depending on user's needs and meaningful contextual information. Second, we rank this list in order to best fit with the current user. In order to provide means for that, formally connected knowledge in user interaction processes are used to support a reasoning unit, which is based on Answer Set Programming (ASP). Finally, visual aspects of user interfaces such as sizes of user interface elements, colours, relative position of the elements or navigation devices are specified. In Web environments, user interface adaptation is needed to tailor user interfaces to older people's needs and impairments while preserving their independence.

Keywords: Ontology, Answer Set Programming, Default knowledge, Web Accessibility, Cascading style sheet, Context, User interaction.

1   Introduction

Currently numerous Websites contain in addition to their standard Cascading Style Sheet (CSS), some different style sheets. These are supposed to cover a wide range of users' preferences and capabilities in the way they perceive Website contents. However, many users are not able to switch to the suitable styles every time they interact with a Website due to many reasons like limited physical/mental capabilities of users. In deed, it is difficult for software designer to create suitable style sheets for all users without knowing the end users. As a consequence, the design of accessible and usable Websites becomes difficult, first due to the variety of users' interests, perceptive capabilities or other meaningful factors and, second due to unavailability of knowledge about users. This difficult task could be facilitated with semantic Web technologies, so that heterogeneous knowledge resources about users could be interconnected and their associations could be made either in design process or at run time.

In deed, physically challenged and old users access many Websites, which are not sufficiently considered as accessible, either because the presented information is not accessible or not usable. Often these users cannot acquire sufficient information without additional effort. To resolve this issue, Web Accessibility,

K. Miesenberger et al. (Eds.): ICCHP 2012, Part I, LNCS 7382, pp. 329–336, 2012.

which means that all users regardless of background (e.g. age, disability, computer experience) can use Websites without difficulty, is important.

One possible solution to this problem is to use a method to detect the type of user of the Website and his/her contextual information related to the interaction process and then adapt its interaction mechanism. The usage of style sheets for providing personalized user interfaces is very beneficial in such environment where users' conditions and time constraints are dynamically changing. In this paper, we show that Cascading Style Sheets (CSS) can automatically be generated according to users' capabilities and to relevant contextual information using a decision mechanism based on Answer Set Programming [6].

Our method consists of two phases. In the first phase, we developed semantically connected ontologies using Distributed Description Logic DDL [1]. In the second phase, these connected ontologies are automatically applied into a reasoning process based on a logical approach. Basically the generation of colours and their contrasts, sizes or position of the different components of the Web interface are considered. As a result, this approach takes away a significant amount of overhead related to manual coding of style sheets in Websites and adapts the user interface in a semi-automatic way. The output of the method is a ranked set of abstract user interfaces suggestions according to user profile and contextual information. In the light of these suggestions the style sheets can be generated and/or adapted on the fly.

In fact, this task is achieved through generation of visual aspects of user interfaces such as sizes of user interface elements, colours, relative position of the elements on navigation devices used. In Web environments, user interface adaptation is needed to tailor user interfaces to older people's needs and impairments while preserving their independence.

2   Related Works

Several approaches to automatic generation of personalised user interfaces can be found in the literature, some of them have been developed with a particular subset of motor-impaired user or only visual-impaired user or both such as [5], however without the consideration of any contextual information.

Other general approaches such as [7] have developed new design methodologies for creating interfaces that can be dynamically adapted by the end-user for their individual needs, however the user may not be able to adjust his/her settings due to disabilities, the user may not know what options exist or how she/he can set them. She/he may have no idea what the best setting is for her/him. A few other interfaces have been created, particularly in the Web domain, but most lack any such adaptation capabilities.

Shuaib et al. introduced the concept Connecting Ontologies [14] with the help of SWRL [15] for providing universal Accessibility. However, due to lack of support for rules or for some concepts like negation as failure, some queries can not be represented concisely and some queries can not be represented at all. In this sense, the use of a rule mechanism such as Answer Set Programming ASP provides a more expressive formalism to represent rules, concepts, constraints, and queries than the rule mechanism used in this approach.

Recently, [12] proposed a method, which is used to achieve Accessibility of Rich Internet Applications (RIAs) using *JavaFX Script* applications. First, source programs of a JavaFX Script application are analyzed, and Accessibility problems are extracted. Then code to apply the Accessibility libraries is generated. Finally, the problematic code is replaced with the generated code. However, in this approach, the end users are explicitly involved in adjusting all components, which could not work if the user is not able to achieve this task. In addition, conflicts between keyboard operations and screen readers are not resolved efficiently.

Unfortunately, current approaches are either not general enough for applying in any information system or do not care about changing environments. For this reason, we propose our method as a powerful tool to build user independent and even device independent Web user interfaces taking constraints in account. Designing a user interface, while taking into account different user groups is an important task toward Web Accessibility for all and is already an extensively explored research domain [13].

Our method as a logical framework derives the user interface characteristics according to the user profile, user's impairments profile and contextual profile. Therefore, the obvious candidates for interaction are the style sheets for use in browsers as well as for integration in some applications adressed to diversities of users.

3 Decision Mechanism for Generating CSS

In order for the information presentation to be fully accessible and usable, it must be shaped based on users' characteristics and their contextual information. This can be achieved by a decision mechanism. The decision mechanism provides ways of adaptation decisions at either level of the user interaction. It comprises the default rules, which refer to static users' characteristics and the run-time rules, which refer to dynamic user characteristics and contextual information. Consequently, a set of these rules has been defined for providing the decision for the selection of appropriate user interaction styles.

Actually, most of the information consists of defaults and the connected Ontologies contain incomplete knowledge motivated us to use a non-monotonic formalism to build a rule layer over them. We might want to express preferences (e.g. aggregate functions) as well as constraints (e.g. integrity constraints) while querying the knowledge stored in Ontologies to be able to discover new knowledge. Answer Set Programming provides with an expressive language to express these knowledge and efficient solvers, like DLV-Hex [3] to reason about it, this motivated us to use ASP as such a non-monotonic formalism. Additionaly, the non-monotonicity is important to allow updates to the user interaction model. First, knowledge about the user, his/her impairment and his/her contextual information which are meaningful in the user interaction process have been modelled in OWL-DL Ontologies [11] and formally interconnected. The connections are developed following a semi-automatic approach using Distributed Description Logics (DDL) [1]. DDL follow the ontology mapping [11] paradigm. It allows to connect multiple DL Knowledge bases with bridge rules [1], a new kind of axioms that represents the mapping. We have chosen DDL since it allows for inter-ontology subsumption [1], a notion that combines well with the vision of Semantic Web [8].

Second, a generic Accessibility rule patterns [16] has been implemented based on ASP, is extendable to cover various scenarios.

3.1 Answer Set Programming ASP

Answer Set Programming (ASP) [6] has emerged as an important tool for declarative knowledge representation and reasoning. This approach is rooted in semantic notions and is based on methods to compute stable models [6]. ASP is one of the most prominent and successful semantics for *non-monotonic* logic programs. The specific treatment of default negation under ASP allows for the generation of multiple models for a single program, which in this respect can be seen as the encoding of a problem specification. With ASP, one can encode a problem as a set of rules and the solutions are found by the stable models (Answer sets) of these rules.

An Answer Set Program consists of rules of the form *head :- body* that can contain variables. The head can be a disjunction or empty and the body is a conjunction or empty. A *term* is either a constant or a variable. An *atom* is defined as $p(t_1, ...t_k)$ where k is called the arity of p and $t_1, ...t_k$ are terms. A *literal* is an atom p or a negated atom $\neg p$, also strong negation (also often referred to as classical negation). A rule without head literal is an *integrity (strong) constraint*. A rule with exactly one head literal is a *normal rule*. If the body of the rule variable-free is empty then this rule is a *fact*.

A *negation as failure literal* (or NAF-literal) is a literal l or a default-negated literal *not l*. Negation as failure is an extension to classical negation, it represents default negation in a program, and infers negation of a fact if it is not provable in a program. Thus, *not l* evaluates to true if it cannot be proven that l is true. This is relevant in our work since we don't have complete information about the user interaction process and we must assume some defaults reasoning until we confirm the reasoner with a new knowledge.

In order to solve a problem in ASP, a logic program should be constructed so that its answer sets correspond to the solutions of the problem. By adding new knowledge, not only new answer sets become possible, but old answer sets are defeated, so that the sets do not grow monotonically. ASP provides us this *non-monotonicity*. An important feature of ASP is that the body of a rule can also contain negation, which is handled as negation as failure, thus allowing methods from non-monotonic reasoning, since additional information might lead to retraction of a previously made inference [4].

In order to compute these answer sets, there exist ASP solvers or engines such as DLV [2], a highly efficient reasoner for ASP which extends the core language with various sophisticated features such as aggregates or weak constraints [9].

3.2 Default Reasoning

In default reasoning one can specify general knowledge for standard cases and modulary add exceptions. When one adds an exception to default, one can not conclude what one could before. In that default reasoning is told non-monotonic.

Static user characteristics represented in the User Profile Ontology UPO have been selected to serve as the basis for the default reasoning. The selection of such meaningful characteristics was made so as to ensure that adequate knowledge exists for the system. Such characteristics have been selected also to serve as the basis for reasoning. These include: user's impairments, familiarity of the user with the Web etc. The dynamic user characteristics and other dynamic contextual information are responsable for the system inference to be triggered. The evaluation of such data can be based on results of specific data aggregation e.g. quality of navigation/user error rate, results of ad-hoc logic rules e.g. user idle time/user response time.

By default, user interface elements in the interface do not have to be adapted if the available knowledge does not trace any anomaly in the way the user could interact with it. Such anomalies are to be specified in a declarative form, by using predicates. When an adaptation is needed, the default mechanism detects an exception to default. Such exceptions allow us to choose the most relevant answer sets in order to allow the user interface characteristics to change dynamically according to this knowledge. This could make improvements of user interaction for all impairments or the combinations of impairments of the users in a generic way instead of focusing only on the stereotypical disabilities.

3.3 Using Constraints

Rules can generate different models. The constraints are used to select only the desired ones among possible models. There are two types of constraints namely strong (integrity) constraints and weak constraints. According to [10], DLV extends the logic programs by the weak constraints. Using weak constraints the answer sets are resulting in a cost ordering. Here, the costs were comprised of the facts that weight the importance of a property, such as the colour contrast in a given scenario and therefore, we can rank the answer sets to the important in user interaction. According to this result, this method may be used in context of the user's personal information management systems as well as in mobile computing systems.

4   Results and Discussion

Preliminary evaluations show that the combination of an ASP-based reasoning component and a semantically connected knowledge base is a good solution for creating an integrated information system in general.

Preliminary scenarios on a few instances showed that answer sets computed by the DLV-Hex [3] solver provide a significant set of user interface styles. These details can also be easily analysed by interface designer, thus supporting them in deriving hints for improving the interface final design.

As an example, an aged person with *central-field vision loss* (seeing only the edges of the visual field) and hand tremor, interacts with a Webbrowser. He/she uses a screen magnifier to help with his/her vision and his/her hand tremor. Moreover, the user has poor experience in using the Web. The goal is to create legible UI elements and use the style sheets to control their layout and their presentation. It is possible for a user who cannot move his/her hands, and also cannot see the central part of the screen well, to use a combination of speech input and speech output, and might therefore need to rely on precise indicators of location and navigation options in a Website for example throuh *ToolTip*. Moreover, screen magnification magnifies a portion of the screen for easier viewing. At the same time screen magnifiers make presentations larger, they also reduce the area of the Website that may be viewed, removing surrounding context. Some screen magnifiers offer two views of the screen: one magnified and one default size for navigation.

Additionally to the visual and motoric convenience of the UI elements, the UI might be sensitive by adapting to user experience level and skills. For this reason, usable help information has been generated to indicate the location of clickable UI elements.

From the generated solutions we can conclude that UI text elements have been generated with a high legibility measure in order to compensate the vision impairment of the aged user. In this case, information perception requires a font size not less than 14pt. That is why, small font sizes have not been suggested at all. From the figure 1, we see that font size 14, 20 and 22 seem to be good candidates for presenting textual information to this user, more precisely, font size 14 and 20 are best candidates in this situation since, the colour contrast ratio for both, is the highest (17) one in the listing allowing for greater legibility of text elements.

Additionaly, other UI elements have been generated with a sufficiently large clickable area so that they can be hit even when the mouse is used with a low precision. Usable help notifications are in this scenario important since the user has a low level of Web experience which has been extracted from his profile. For this reason *ToolTip_Definition* has been generated in order to indicate relevant information to the UI element *CheckBox*.

The most suitable assistive technology to this user, is the *screen magnifier*, however the presentation of Web information in a usable style is more convenient, since using a screen magnifier may remove the surrounding context which make the interaction more difficult. As a consequence, actions can be done such as enlarging the clickable UI elements for a greater usability as well as resizing textual information.

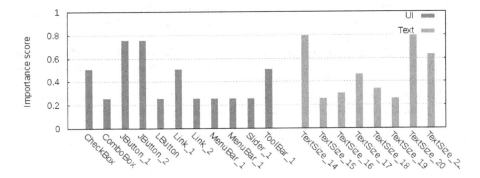

Fig. 1. Suggestion for UI characteristics according to user with mutliple impairments and contextual information

5 Conclusion and Future Work

We have presented a method for generating CSS in order to adapte the UI of Website to users. This method is suitable for generating CSS at run time for a wide range of personal information systems, especially Web interaction. Furthermore, we plan to automatically detect the users intention. In fact, it is foreseen that future work will include a methode to detect and record changes in these characteristics over time, thus causing different adaptations to be effected in the Web interface.

References

1. Borgida, A., Serafini, L.: Distributed Description Logics: Assimilating Information from Peer Sources. In: Spaccapietra, S., March, S., Aberer, K. (eds.) Journal on Data Semantics I. LNCS, vol. 2800, pp. 153–184. Springer, Heidelberg (2003)
2. DLV, http://www.dbai.tuwien.ac.at/proj/dlv/ (last accessed on April 10, 2011)
3. DLV-Hex, http://www.kr.tuwien.ac.at/research/systems/dlvhex/ (last accessed on February 03, 2012)
4. Eiter, T.: Answer Set Programming for the Semantic Web. In: Dahl, V., Niemelä, I. (eds.) ICLP 2007. LNCS, vol. 4670, pp. 23–26. Springer, Heidelberg (2007)
5. Gajos, K.Z., Wobbrock, J.O., Weld, D.S.: Automatically generating user interfaces adapted to users' motor and vision capabilities. In: Proceedings of the 20th Annual ACM Symposium on User Interface Software and Technology, UIST 2007, pp. 231–240. ACM (2007)
6. Gelfond, M., Lifschitz, V.: The stable model semantics for logic programming. In: ICLP/SLP, pp. 1070–1080 (1988)
7. Gregor, P., Newell, A.F.: Designing for dynamic diversity interfaces for older people. In: Proceedings of 5th ACM/SIGAPH Conf. on Assistive Technologies, pp. 151–156. ACM Press (2002)
8. Lee, B.: Weaving the Web. The origial design and ultimate destiny of the Wold Wide Web by its inventor. Harper, San Fransisco (1999)

9. Leone, N., Pfeifer, G., Faber, W., Eiter, T., Gottlob, G., Perri, S., Scarcello, F.: The DLV system for knowledge representation and reasoning. ACM Trans. Comput. Logic 7, 499–562 (2006)
10. Leone, N., Pfeifer, G., Faber, W., Eiter, T., Gottlob, G., Perri, S., Scarcello, F.: The DLV System for Knowledge Representation and Reasoning. ACM Transactions on Computational Logic 7(3), 499–562 (2006)
11. Mcbride, B.: The resource description framework (RDF) and its vocabulary description language RDFS. In: Staab, S., Studer, R. (eds.) Handbook on Ontologies, pp. 51–66. Springer (2004)
12. Shirogane, J., Kato, T., Hashimoto, Y., Tachibana, K., Iwata, H., Fukazawa, Y.: Method to Improve Accessibility of Rich Internet Applications. In: Holzinger, A., Simonic, K.-M. (eds.) USAB 2011. LNCS, vol. 7058, pp. 349–365. Springer, Heidelberg (2011)
13. Shneiderman, B., Plaisant, C.: Designing the User Interface: Strategies for Effective Human-Computer Interaction, 4th edn. Pearson Addison Wesley (2004)
14. Karim, S., Latif, K., Tjoa, A.M.: Providing Universal Accessibility Using Connecting Ontologies: A Holistic Approach. In: Stephanidis, C. (ed.) HCI 2007. LNCS, vol. 4556, pp. 637–646. Springer, Heidelberg (2007)
15. SWRL, http://www.w3.org/Submission/SWRL/ (last accessed on April 09, 2011)
16. Zakraoui, J., Zagler, W.: A Logical Approach to Web User Interface Adaptation. In: Holzinger, A., Simonic, K.-M. (eds.) USAB 2011. LNCS, vol. 7058, pp. 645–656. Springer, Heidelberg (2011)

Implementing Web Accessibility:
The MIPAW Approach

Jean-Pierre Villain[1], Olivier Nourry[1], Dominique Burger[2], and Denis Boulay[2]

[1] Qelios 21, rue de la Guyenne 66100 – Perpignan France
jpvillain@yahoo.fr, olivier.nourry@qelios.fr
[2] BrailleNet/AccessiWeb

Abstract. This paper presents the elaboration of a model for a progressive implementation of WCAG, centered on the notions of access to information and essential users' needs. MIPAW's main goal is to serve as a framework for the elaboration of gradual implementation methodologies, of systems measuring the real level of accessibility, and the setting up of efficient quality assurance management systems. It is based on state of the art, real-world experience, and expertise in accessibility as well as quality assurance. The project aims at providing methodological tools better suited to the constraints of web industrialization, while preserving the deployment of real user-centric accessibility. MIPAW is a project lead as part of the activities of the AccessiWeb GTA (Workgroup on Accessibility), and has received active support from 16 of the most prominent French companies in the area of expertise in digital accessibility.

Keywords: WCAG, AccessiWeb, Accessibility, Progressive Enhancement, User centric, Design for All, Quality Assessments, Access to information, Accessibility Barrier.

1   Introduction

WCAG 2 [1] made it possible for web accessibility to have a mature tool, adapted to modern Web technologies and uses. Although the technical implementation of WCAG, for the basic Web technologies, does not represent an issue anymore, the methodological aspects of it remain to be worked out. The nature of the Web, its industrialization, the diversity of technologies and uses have a direct impact on the management of a Web project, that reveals itself as highly complex to deal with. From that viewpoint, the framework defined by WCAG seems not very operational, and meets only very partly the needs, as expressed by the industry, to benefit from progressive methodologies that favor the handling of objectives defined by WCAG, and measurement systems better suited to the context of continuous production of contents, and more representative of the real level of accessibility. If the latter question is well documented, and is the object of numerous research works [2],[3],[4], the question of implementation methodologies is not very well-researched, and appears to be a theme essentially linked to the state of the art, that approaches these

K. Miesenberger et al. (Eds.): ICCHP 2012, Part I, LNCS 7382, pp. 337–342, 2012.
© Springer-Verlag Berlin Heidelberg 2012

questions only in a factual and partial fashion [5],[6],[7]. After discussing about the characteristics and operational limits of WCAG and the measurement systems on which progressive implementation methodologies could be based, we will present in details the MIPAW model, based on the notion of access to information, user impact and essential needs, then discuss the expected results of the model, before concluding on this project's outlooks.

2   WCAG, Conformity and Measurement

One of the invaluable qualities of WCAG is to approach accessibility under the exclusive angle of contents and technologies. This is one of the keys that made WCAG technically operational. On the other hand, it has had major consequences for the application of WCAG in the context of a Web project. The most characteristic one is that accessibility issues can appear as disconnected from the notion of user experience, which is a central aspect of quality assurance management as applied by Web professionals. If accessibility professionals understand well the notion of user experience, the methodological tools they use, for instance, an assessment audit, are finally only the expression of technical issues; whereas similar areas like ergonomics or usability will consider user-centric notions like the personas [8], for instance, as operational vectors. This area is generally perceived by the project teams as a set of technical constraints to be addressed, making it somehow a "low-level" consideration; whereas it should primarily be a matter of concern for the designers and project managers, on par with other areas of the quality assurance management for instance. The second important consequence is that the favored tool to establish a project methodology is measurement, and more specifically the measurement of conformance. To make a piece of content accessible, in terms of method, consists essentially in ensuring conformance to technical criteria, which tends to make the project stray from satisfying the users' needs and enriching the users experience. These characteristics of WCAG are, from an essential techniques point of view, associated to a prioritization by level (A, AA, AAA) not very readable. This makes it very difficult to answer simple questions like workload increase, prioritization, or even measurement of the improvement of contents quality and the users' needs satisfaction. The question of prioritization is of utter importance because it will very directly affect the project management, for example about the very delicate questions of project resources allocation, and the definition of operational objectives.

3   Accessibility Barriers and the User

To handle these issues, some answers have been proposed, essentially based on the notion of accessibility barrier, using more sophisticated measurement systems, or proposing a rearrangement of the WCAG structure based on users typologies. Two examples allow us to expose briefly these two approaches.

The question of elaborating measurement systems allowing a prioritization of the issues, has been recently approached by R. Hudson [9], who proposes for example a matrix where each issue is assessed through a measure of incidence, associated to a level of severity level, which results in a priority score.

G.Brajnik [10] proposes a rearrangement of WCAG based on a user typology (considered from the viewpoint of impairments) associated to a measure, similar to the previous one, based on impact measurement and the persistence of barriers.

Although these two approaches, briefly exposed here, are very interesting, they address only imperfectly the issues met by Web industrials. Besides, although this kind of prioritization, through the measurement of an incidence ratio, can have very positive effects on the perception of user experience by the project manager, it does not solve the lack of readability for the WCAG levels. The A level remains, because of its incurred workload in particular, seen as an "impassable wall" by most of the project teams.

4   MIPAW, Access to Information and the Essentials Users' Needs

Facing these issues on a daily basis, in our professional activity, we aimed at approaching the issue in a more pragmatic fashion, clearly oriented towards operational goals. We based our study on the Accessiweb reference list, historically the most implemented WCAG-based testing methodology in France. As managers and lead authors of this list, and leaning on the high level of expertise available through the GTA, we were able to use it efficiently to conduct research on the elaboration of a model the gradual handling of the WCAG issues (and their levels) in coherence with the users' needs, at every phase of a project, and specifically at the requirements and design phases. We leant on the notion of access to information, a complex notion, that defines and matches accurately the most essential needs of the user. The first phase of the project was to assess the structuring power of this notion in WCAG (applied to the Accessiweb reference list). For that purpose we set up a panel of experts, involving technical experts as well as expert users, asking them to assess and sort each criterion of the Accessiweb reference list [11], through a notion of access to information that was not defined yet at that stage (each expert was asked to define it on her own terms). Then, in the same time, for each criterion not classified as impacting access to information, to rate its impact on users as either weak or strong. The results of this survey have then been processed statistically. This first survey allowed us to validate some hypotheses:

- The notion of access to information is a very structuring element in WCAG
- The notion of user impact appears to be not correlated to the notion of access to information. This means for instance that a criterion with no impact on access to information can be assessed as having either a weak or a strong impact

Regarding the notion of access to information, one can notice that it impacts the 3 WCAG levels, which confirms the base hypothesis of using this notion as a structure element, in particular linked to the notion of essential need for the user. Besides, its effect is unequal throughout the levels: very structuring for level A, from which it allows the extraction of a basic set of criteria equivalent to 43% of it; but its effect is less perceptible on levels AA and AAA, which confirms that these levels are dedicated to improvements.

5   MIPAW, Model for a Progressive Implementation of Web Accessibility

The MIPAW (an acronym in French for "Modèle d'Implémentation Progressive de l'Accessibilité du Web", translated by "Model for a Progressive Implementation of Web Accessibility") derives from, and adapts the structures revealed during this first phase of the project, to form four sets of criteria. MIPAW is essentially a reformulation of this initial distribution in more operational phases, borrowing from concepts of quality assurance management and ergonomics, which should ease their integration in project management processes.

The first layer of the model consists in the distribution of these sets on a scale of arbitrary values, going from the presence of a device essential to access to information, to the improvement of the user's experience. Seen under this angle, the WCAG have a first turning point where all the issues identified as impacting access to information are adressed. Beyond this turning point, the issues are expressed in terms of user impact. This reformulation of the WCAG structure allows to design phases of gradual approaches of the WCAG levels, with very operational objectives, based on the notion of essential users' needs. They are structured by the notion of access to information which defines the first necessary step, preliminary to the handling of accessibility issues.

On this new structure constituted by four successive phases, the primary structure of WCAG (i.e. the priority levels) is totally preserved.

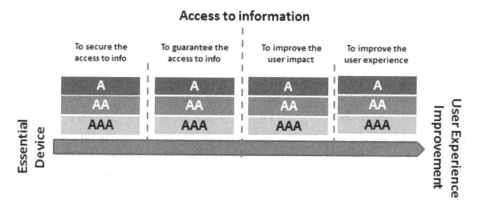

Fig. 1. MIPAW with WCAG priority levels

Actually, this model is an adaptation of the WCAG structure to four successive implementation phases, structured by the notion of access to information, representing the essential users' needs and the notions of user impact and user experience.

The four phases are defined by:

- To secure the access to information: this group is composed of criteria of presence of technical devices or alternative contents, essential for the access to information.
- To guarantee the access to information: This group is composed of criteria of relevance of technical devices or alternative contents, essential for the access to information, partly based on the technical basis implemented at the previous phase.
- To improve the user impact: This group is composed of criteria of presence and relevance of devices or contents having a "strong" impact on the user.
- To improve the user experience: This group is composed of criteria of presence and relevance of devices or contents having a "weak" impact on the user.

This proposition of a model is not a methodology in itself, but it allows the definition of a framework from which methodologies of all kinds can be designed, coherently with the essential needs of the users, defined by the necessity for all to at least access to information.

6   Expected Results and Outlooks

The expected results of the application of this new model on project methodologies appear to be very numerous, and very profitable as well as for the project as for the end users.

On methodologies: a methodological tool based on this model could give to the projects teams a clearer vision of the goals to aim for, a better sense of what to start with, and thus how to better distribute the efforts and project resources.

On measurement systems: they could be more adapted and more representative of the real level of accessibility of the contents. This model does not contradict at all the current researches on issues linked to measurement; on the contrary, it offers them a very favorable ground for expression.

On conformance objectives, since keeping identical WCAG levels allows the elaboration of more subtle strategies, more adapted to users' needs.

And on project management, in particular by favoring a clearer vision of the essential issues, we expect very positive effects on the delicate issues of appropriate allocation of project resources to meet the project's goals.

Finally, we expect from this model that it reinstalls the user at the center of the processes and methodologies, while preserving the extremely valuable qualities of WCAG, of which not one aspect is modified, reinterpreted, or reformulated.

MIPAW is a collaborative project, proposed by the association of Qelios and BrailleNet, editor of the Accessiweb reference list. It is currently in an incubation phase, comprising the setting up of different workgroups and the tools they require. Following implementation in real world projects, first results are expected at the end of the first semester of 2012.

References

1. World Wide Web Consortium (2008) Web Content Accessibility Guidelines (WCAG) 2.0, W3C Recommendation (December 11, 2008), http://www.w3.org/TR/WCAG/
2. Brajnik, G.: A comparative test of web accessibility evaluation methods. In: Proceedings of the 10th International ACM SIGACCESS Conference on Computers and Accessibility (Assets 2008), pp. 113–120. ACM, New York (2008)
3. Vigo, M., Arrue, M., Brajnik, G., Lomuscio, R., Abascal, J.: Quantitative Metrics for Measuring Web Accessibility. In: Proceedings of W4A 2007, Banff, Alberta, Canada, May 7-8, pp. 99–107. ACM Press, New York (2007); Tavel, P.: Modeling and Simulation Design. AK Peters Ltd., Natick (2007)
4. World Wide Web Consortium (2011). Website Accessibility Metrics. Online Symposium (December 5, 2011), http://www.w3.org/WAI/RD/2011/metrics/
5. Groves, K.: Agile & Accessibility (2011), http://www.karlgroves.com/2011/09/28/agile-accessibility/
6. Sloim, E.: L'accessibilité agile (2010),
   http://openweb.eu.org/articles/accessibilite_agile
7. Nourry, O.: Optimiser l'intervention experte dans un projet Web. In: Proceedings of the 5th European eAccessibility Forum, Paris, France (2011),
   http://inova.snv.jussieu.fr/evenements/colloques/colloques/70_article_fr_251.html#contenu
8. Chapman, C.N., Milham, R.: The personas' new clothes. In: Human Factors and Ergonomics Society, HFES 2006, San Francisco, CA (October 2006)
9. Hudson, R.: Accessibility Barrier Scores (2012), http://www.dingoaccess.com/accessibility/accessibility-barrier-scores-2
10. Brajnik, G.: Barrier Walkthrough (2009),
    http://users.dimi.uniud.it/~giorgio.brajnik/projects/bw/bw.html
11. BrailleNet – AccessiWeb reference list 2.1 (2010), http://www.braillenet.org/accessibilite/referentiel-aw21-en/index.php

Accessibility of Dynamic Adaptive Web TV Applications

Daniel Costa, Nádia Fernandes, Carlos Duarte, and Luís Carriço

LaSIGE/University of Lisbon, Portugal
{dancosta,nadiaf,cad,lmc}@di.fc.ul.pt

Abstract. In the last years, TVs have become platforms providing content and entertainment services, such as video on demand, interactive advertising or social networking. Often, these services are Web based applications that run of connected TVs or set-top boxes. Given TV's wide reach, it is paramount TV applications are designed so that information can be perceived by everyone, i.e. should be accessible. These applications increasingly present dynamic aspects, which have been rendering traditional Web evaluation approaches obsolete. Additionally, TV based interaction has specificities that Web based evaluation is unable to cope with. In this paper, we present an automated accessibility evaluation framework to address these challenges. It is based on WCAG 2.0 and Digital TV guidelines. It supports evaluation of the code after browser processing and scanning the whole set of application states. It is capable of evaluating user interface adaptation based on selected user profiles. The paper also presents the evaluation results of three TV based applications according to the proposed framework, which allow a comparison of results of pre and post browser processing as well as pre and post adaptation.

Keywords: Web Accessibility, Web TV applications, Automated Evaluation, Rich Internet Applications.

1 Introduction

The Web is becoming more and more dynamic. User actions and automatically triggered events can alter a Web page's content. The presented content can be substantially different from the initially received by the browser. With the introduction of new technologies, Web sites/pages are becoming complex Web applications [1]. TV follows the same path. Nowadays, it provides extra content and entertainment services such as video on demand, interactive advertising and social networking to mention a few. Moreover, the intrinsic dynamic nature of TV's main content pushes the requirement for further dynamics on all the complementary services. All these are growingly complex Web-based applications running on connected TVs or set-top boxes. More than other, TVs are being used by all types of people, with miscellaneous aptitudes, including those with special needs. Consequently, TV applications must be designed to be perceived by everyone, i.e., be accessible.

Currently, there are several projects regarding accessibility in TV platforms, such as GUIDE [2]. These projects focus on adapting the user interface considering the

K. Miesenberger et al. (Eds.): ICCHP 2012, Part I, LNCS 7382, pp. 343–350, 2012.

skills of elderly or disabled users [3]. However, the resulting adapted user interfaces are not guaranteed to be accessible. First, because the original applications may lack fundamental content, alternative modalities, or simply be built in a way that the adaptation engines are not able to correct. Secondly, because the resulting user interfaces should be validated during the refinement and development of those engines and supporting models. Either way, it is fundamental to find ways to evaluate the TV web applications, and give developers of TV applications and platforms a report of accessibility errors and warnings.

This paper proposes a new type of accessibility evaluation of Web TV applications. First it considers the evaluation of the Web application nearer to what the users actually may perceive, i.e., after browser processing. Then it further addresses the dynamics and complexity of Web and Web TV applications by expanding the initial Web pages to the full state-graph of the application. It also merges Web and selected adequate guidelines for the TV applications word. Finally, it copes with the possible adaptation process by selecting and applying the requested adaptation profiles and evaluating the result considering only the techniques for that profile. The contribution of this paper is thus a framework, methodology and tools, for the evaluation of Web TV adaptive applications, considering dynamic, complexity and user adaptation profiles.

A preliminary experimental evaluation was performed that emphasises the differences between our approach and the classical Web evaluation ones. Furthermore, the adequacy and applicability of our evaluation strategy was demonstrated by its application to a couple of profile adapted applications validated by expert evaluations.

2   Requirements and Related Work

Evaluating accessibility involves two main aspects: the set of guidelines to be applied on the evaluation and the process by which those guidelines are applied.

2.1   Guidelines, TV and Adaptation

The Web Content Accessibility Guidelines (WCAG) 2.0 [5] are the standards to Web accessibility, covering a wide range of recommendations for a large number of disabilities. However, considering Web TV applications, some may be misleading, since it can be different to experience Web application content in a TV instead of a regular computer screen. For instance, TV screens have higher contrast and saturation levels, so developers must be conscious of these characteristics.

There are also Universal Design guidelines for Digital TV services [6], which establish some specific accessibility guidelines for Digital TV. The Global Visual Language, from BBC [7] also proposes a set of design guidelines specific for TV. Google, recently investing in this field, also provides some design considerations which can be helpful to use as well [8]. To maintain the accessibility of TV applications it is important to consider all these types of guidelines. However, a balanced revision and integration should be endeavoured, considering not only the overlapping, the specificity of TV but also the developments and trends in Web technologies. Considering the adaptive strand of some TV frameworks [2], [3], the application of guidelines should not be straightforward. In fact, if the framework transforms the application UI to a specific user profile (say, colour-blind) it makes no sense to evaluate the result considering guidelines targeting another disability (e.g. motor impaired). ACCESSIBLE [13] already provides a harmonized methodology enabling the selection of WCAG guidelines based on disability. Its articulation with the profile selection of the adaptation engines and the merging of specific TV guidelines could provide the necessary means for an adequate accessibility evaluation of the adaptive UIs.

On the original application and UI, however, the evaluation should be able to support the adaptation to a more Universal stance. Nevertheless, evaluation should consider that the adaptation process is able to solve some if not all of the issues pointed by the whole guideline set. For such platforms then, a careful selection of guidelines, which address the fundamental requirements of accessibility that cannot be addressed by UI changes, should be used to weigh the accessibility of the original applications.

2.2   Dynamics and the Evaluation Process

Web Accessibility Evaluation is an assessment procedure to analyse how well the Web can be used by people with different levels of disabilities [12]. Conformance checking [10] with the aid of automated Web accessibility evaluation tools is an important step for the accessibility evaluation. Most of these use WCAG guidelines [9].

However, traditionally, evaluators assess the original Web code as provided by the server. Fernandes et al [4] already performed a study that shows that there are real differences between the accessibility evaluations performed before and after the browser processing. This happens, because a lot of transformations take place during the browser's processing, which significantly alter the HTML document.

Still, the analysis of complex Web applications holds more than just the dynamic assessment of pages after browser processing. These applications include a complex network of states that must be accessed in order to be fully evaluated.

2.3   Subsuming the Challenges

Web TV applications, and particularly those that are handed to and result from an adaptation process, impose different challenges: (1) as rich Web applications, the evaluation should cope with the dynamically introduced code, the complexity of application state transitions and the adequacy and coverage of existing guidelines; (2) as specific TV components, this reassessment should further be refined to cope with TV idiosyncrasies; (3) as inputs of an adaptation process, the evaluation should deal with the assurance of the adaptability of the original TV applications, applying only those guidelines that cannot be automatically solved by the adaptation; and (4) as outputs of that process, the evaluation should consider the specific target users, selecting only those guidelines that apply to the users' profile.

3   The Platform for Accessibility Evaluation of Web TV

The proposed solution is based on the QualWeb evaluator [4]. The evaluator assesses accessibility after browsing processing, thus focussing on the DOM as presented to the user.

To cope with the challenges of the dynamic Web applications we have integrated an Interaction Simulator. This component is responsible for simulating user actions and triggering the interactive elements of the interface. As a result we have access to all the different states (in DOM format) of the Web application [14]. This addresses challenge 1. It is also at the Interaction Simulator level that the new QualWeb will produce the states by simply executing the original Web application or by requesting first an adaptation to a specific user profile. This lays the grounds to fulfil either challenge 3 or 4. The DOMs are then fed to the QualWeb evaluator that cumulatively assesses the quality of the application.

QualWeb currently implements 27 HTML and 17 CSS WCAG 2.0 techniques. From those we selected 25 HTML and 14 CSS that are suited for the TV platform specificities. From the Universal Design guidelines for Digital TV services [6], two guidelines are implemented regarding text size and font family recommendations. Thus, a total of 41 accessibility guidelines were used for the evaluation. The integration of these new techniques was easily supported by the modular approach of Qual-Web. Challenge 2 was addressed by this careful selection of guidelines.

Concerning the adaption nature of the envisioned TV platforms, the QualWeb evaluator was modified to cope with the selective application of techniques. Basically, in this new version it is possible to select a subset of the techniques that will be applied. Predefined subsets were established according to the adaptation profiles. Challenges 3 and 4 are then addressed by this selection in conjunction with the Interaction Simulator option of requesting the previous adaptation of the DOM. Overall, the modifications to the evaluator addressed all the requirements raised in the previous section.

4   Validating the Approach

To validate the approach we devised an experimental study first on an Electronic Programme Guide (EPG), and then on two other TV applications. We have assessed the applications using the proposed platform at three phases of delivery: a) before browser processing, as it would be done by traditional evaluators; b) after browser processing and before the adaptation, considering the whole set of states of the application, to assess the intrinsic quality of the application; and c) after the adaptation, considering two user profiles. The resulting evaluation, in EARL format, was subsequently analysed. Also the application, as perceived by users before and after the adaptation, was inspected by experts.

Fig. 1. EPG adapted for a user with visual impairments

4.1   Results

As a baseline for our experiment, we conducted a pre browser processing evaluation of the accessibility of three TV applications: the EPG, Home Automation (HA) and Video Conferencing (VC). As can be seen on Fig.2, the applications have few Pass results (3 each), some Fails (15 for the EPG, 1 for HA and 3 for VC), and high Warning numbers, with an average of 17. The Warning values are justified as the majority of them are related with CSS techniques, which tend to be less assertive.

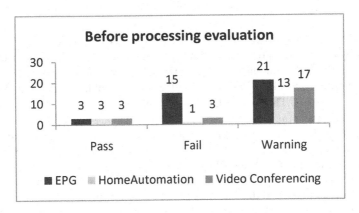

Fig. 2. Results for before processing evaluation

The next step was performing the evaluation on the same three applications, but this time performing it after browser processing and considering all the application states.

In this case we recorded an average increase of the number of elements of about 1200%. This is explained by two arguments: 1) after processing, the scripts are loaded and new elements are injected; and 2) the Interaction Simulator detects a large number of new states as it triggers Javascript functions attached to the many interactive elements of the applications. Regarding the results presented on Fig.3, we can now see a big difference in the numbers when comparing with the previous evaluation.

The Pass results have increased much more relatively to Fails and Warnings in this evaluation, confirming that a post processing evaluation is more adequate when evaluating the accessibility of a Web based application.

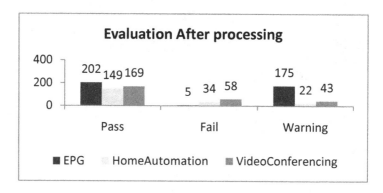

Fig. 3. Results of the evaluation after browser processing

Finally, we performed the evaluation taking in account the user profile of the adapta-tion. Thus the Interaction Simulator has requested a profile to the adaptation engine and only a subset of the accessibility techniques was used on the evaluation process.

Two different user profiles were used, based on real data gathered on user trials conducted by the GUIDE project. The first case accounts a user that has Tritanopia, a specific type of colour blindness. In this case the adaptation engine of GUIDE will render the application taking into account the user's problem, adapting the colour scheme (see Figure 1). The second User Model represents a user that has some visual acuity problems, meaning some adjustments on font size are needed.

The results, depicted on Fig.4, clearly show that when we choose the appropriate techniques for a specific user profile and the corresponding adapted user interface, there is a decrease on the Fails and Warnings scores. For instance, for the colour blind user profile, we can state a 100% decrease on Warnings and 44% on Fails. On the other hand, we can also see that the adaptation made on the applications is not com-pletely effective, increasing the potential of this proposed evaluation framework on the developing phases of this kind of adaptive frameworks, aiding on perfecting the adaptation engines.

As mentioned before, we made an expert analysis on the three TV based applications. For each application three versions of each application were inspected: the standard version, a version with the interface adapted for color blind persons and a version adapted for users with moderate visual impairments. The expert analysis reported that structure of the applications was consistent, with clear separation between page sections and consistent location of scene objects. The layout supports

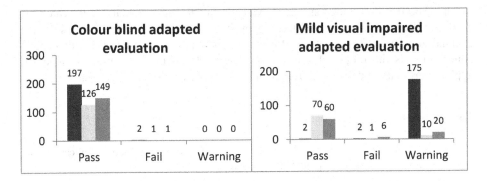

Fig. 4. Evaluation results of the adapted versions

enlargement of screen fonts. The version adapted for colour blind users provides a high contrast alternative, although the initial version was already suitable for most types of colour blindness. The version adapted to visual impaired users offers bigger font size. However, not all the text was increased (only the actionable items), which means moderately impaired users might still have to resort to increasing the font size themselves.

One flaw that all versions of the applications displayed was the lack of pictures and symbols in addition to text in the actionable items. This is most relevant in the calls to action (e.g. the watch channel option in the EPG) that should be supported by clearly understandable icons.

4.2 Discussion

The results demonstrated the differences between the three phases of delivery. It was possible to confirm the inadequacy of pre browser processing evaluation and to notice the differences between the pre and post adaptation versions. The analysis of the EARL and inspection of the applications showed the correctness, yet incompleteness, of the automatic evaluation process and confirmed the need to select the adequate techniques to be applied before and after the adaptation. The experiment also raised a couple of interesting issues on the adaptation itself. In particular it showed some caveats on the adaptation models, by detecting issues on the adapted versions of the UI that should be handled by the engine. That led to the refinement of those models and the engine parameters.

5 Conclusion

This paper provides a solution for automatic evaluation of Web TV applications. It considers the dynamic aspects of these applications and is able to cope with reformulations and refinements of standard accessibility guidelines, as well as the integration of new ones. Besides, it offers the flexibility of filtering the guidelines to be applied thus coping with the adaptation process proposed by some accessibility TV platforms.

The experiment provided an initial evaluation of the approach and highlighted the need for the rationalization of techniques on different rendering contexts of the adaptation process. Besides the tool itself, and the approach it underlies, this paper's contribution is the proposed conceptual framework for the evaluation of Web TV applications that are delivered through and adaptive accessible framework.

References

1. Bhattacharya, P., Neamtiu, I.: Dynamic Updates for Web and Cloud Applications. In: Proc. of the 2010 Workshop on APLWACA (2010)
2. Jung, C., Hahn, V.: GUIDE – Adaptive User Interfaces for Accessible Hybrid TV Applications. In: Second W3C Workshop Web & TV (2011)
3. Duarte, C., Coelho, J., Feiteira, P., Costa, D., Costa, D.F.: Eliciting Interaction Requirements for Adaptive Multimodal TV based Applications. In: Procs. of the 14th HCII (2011)
4. Fernandes, N., Lopes, R., Carriço, L.: On Web Accessibility Evaluation Environments. In: Proc. of the W4A 2011. ACM (2011)
5. Caldwell, B., Cooper, M., Reid, L., Vanderheiden, G.: Web Content Accessibility Guidelines 2.0, W3C Note (December 2008), http://www.w3.org/TR/WCAG20/
6. Universal Design Guidelines for Digital Television Equipment and Services. Draft for public consultation, Centre for Excellence in Universal Design (November 2011), http://www.universaldesign.ie/digitaltv
7. BBC. Future Media Standards and Guidelines - Global Visual Language v2.0, BBC, http://www.bbc.co.uk/guidelines/futuremedia/desed/visual_language.shtml
8. Google Designing for TV (2011), https://developers.google.com/tv/web/docs/design_for_tv
9. Abou-Zahra, S.: Complete List of Web Accessibility Evaluation Tools (March 2006), http://www.w3.org/WAI/ER/tools/complete
10. Abou-Zahra, S.: WAI: Strategies, guidelines, resources to make the Web accessibly to people with disabilities - Conformance Evaluation of Web Sites for Accessibility (2010), http://www.w3.org/WAI/eval/conformance.html
11. Cooper, M., Loretta Guarino Reid, G., Vanderheiden, G., Caldwell, B.: Techniques for WCAG 2.0 - Techniques and Failures for Web Content Accessibility Guidelines 2.0. W3C Note, W3C (October 2010), http://www.w3.org/TR/WCAG-TECHS/
12. Harper, S., Yesilada, Y.: Web Accessibility. Springer (2008)
13. Chalkia, E., et al.: D 3.1 – HAM accessible harmonized methodology. Technical report, ACCESSIBLE, Grant Agreement No 224145 (September 2009)
14. Fernandes, N., Costa, D., Duarte, C., Carriço, L.: Evaluating the accessibility of Rich Internet Applications. In: W4A 2012, Lyon, France, April 16-17. ACM Press (2012)

Ontology Based Middleware for Ranking and Retrieving Information on Locations Adapted for People with Special Needs

Kevin Alonso, Naiara Aginako, Javier Lozano, and Igor G. Olaizola

Vicomtech-IK4
Mikeletegi Pasealekua, 57. Miramon, 20009. Donostia / San Sebastián, Spain
{kalonso,naginako,jlozano,iolaizola}@vicomtech.org

Abstract. Current leisure or touristic services searching tools do not take into account the special needs of large amount of people with functional diversities. However, the combination of different semantic, web and storage technologies make possible the enhancement of such search tools, allowing more personalized searches. This contributes to the provision of better and more suitable results. In this paper we propose an innovative ontology driven solution for personalized tourism directed to people with special needs.

Keywords: information retrieval, ontology, special needs.

1 Related Work

Nowadays a great number of search tasks in complex information systems require the participation of multiple information sources. The information is usually scattered over the web in different sources implemented in different technologies and with different structures [1]. In the last years, there have been many contributions that employ ontology based semantic approaches to improve the access and the integration of heterogeneous information sources. Semantic Web [2] deployment is a slow but constant process, and there are powerful technologies in niche applications (healthcare, finance, publishing among others).

In the touristic domain, the scientific community has provided many relevant works which use ontologies to retrieve information. The REACH project implements an ontology based representation to provide enhanced access to heterogeneous distributed cultural heritage information sources [3]. Another good example can be found in E-Tourism project [4] that develops an ontology based system to improve information creation, maintenance and delivery in the touristic industry by introducing semantic technologies.

Focusing on accessibility, ontologies have been largely used in different domains for the definition of user interface behaviors [5]. But there are other applications, like the PATRAC project, where ontologies are used for the assessment of accessibility in cultural heritage environments [6].

K. Miesenberger et al. (Eds.): ICCHP 2012, Part I, LNCS 7382, pp. 351–354, 2012.
© Springer-Verlag Berlin Heidelberg 2012

2   In Context

Our work is based on the philosophy of PATRAC: not limiting the use of on-tologies to adaptive interfaces, but bringing together tourism and accessibility in the context of restaurant business.

This work has been implemented in a software module that is integrated in an Interactive Community Display (ICD) service, which offers enhanced restaurant business searching capabilities for all kind of users. The proposed system (see Fig. 1), composed by different modules, employs user profiles (Profile Manager) that are adapted with feedback information (Feedback Manager) obtained from user interaction (Interaction Manager). These adaptive profiles store information about user preferences that are the input of the module responsible of accessing, filtering, integrating and ranking of the information requested by the user (Con-tent Manager). The next section describes the Content Managers functionalities and implementation details (see Fig. 2).

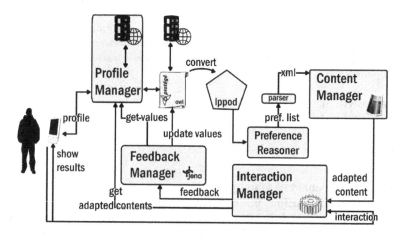

Fig. 1. System architecture

3   Content Manager

The Content Managers input/outputs are based on SOAP web services. The ser-vice request is composed by preferences which can be divided into two categories. The first one is related to the general preferences: actual search parameters and general profile parameters. The second one with the context aware preferences: type of disability (blind, deaf or reduced mobility), gastronomic requirements (vegetarian, diabetic or celiac) and so on.

The Content Manager is formed by three different modules: Ontology and Reasoner Module (Module 1), Repository Module (Module 2) and Ranking and Respond Generation Module (Module 3). Module 1 integrates an ontology with reasoning functionalities. This ontology defines the parsing options for every preference. In the context aware case, these preferences are not always related

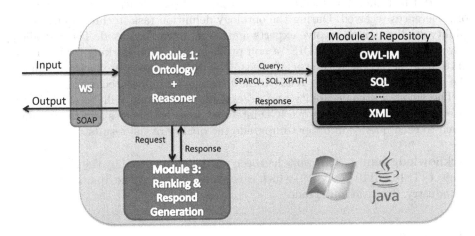

Fig. 2. Content Manager

in a straightforward relationship with the stored information. For that reason, in order to allow the correct matching between the query and the stored information, a parsing process is launched. Due to information source heterogeneity (Module 2), the ontology guides the querying process, selecting the correct repository to send the query and the type of query to be built and its skeleton. This has been validated in three types of scenarios: SPARQL queries for semantic repositories like OWLIM, SQL queries for relational databases like MySQL and XPATH queries for XML repositories.

Module 1 sends several queries taking into account each preference. The outputs of these queries are analyzed and internally stored in a list of results. The rank position of the result will increase for every query accomplished. Finally, Module 3 generates the response, sorting the results according to the ranking that ultimately define the order in which they are displayed to the user.

A use case that sums up the Content Manager functionalities is the case of deaf people searching for a restaurant. Since the system is aware of his/her deafness, it will search restaurants with round tables and with staff who knows sign language. On the one hand, round tables allow deaf to be able to see everyone on the table, so they can read lips in easier way. On the other hand, staff with sign language knowledge offers communication facilities to deaf users. The output of the Content manager will firstly show restaurants that fit best the user preference and needs.

4   Results and Conclusions

The main contribution to the accessibility field is to allow people with disabilities to conduct searches in a system that will internally take into account their special needs. The content manager results have been successfully evaluated and validated by experts. The Content Manager processes based on information sources are performed almost immediately even though it also depends on the number of preferences received. During the ontology definition task, technical and accesibility studies, which involve experts and users, have been used. These studies have been realized by PREDIF[1] a non profit organization working for the integration of the people with special needs. The design of the ontology generalizes the query procedures, being ready to new storage and query technologies.

The whole system usability and accessibility evaluation will be carried out later on. It will help to improve ICD interface, used preferences and the weights given to each queries in order to upgrade the quality of the results.

Acknowledgments. This work has been partially supported by the SEMANTS project (TSI-020110-2009-419) which is partially funded by the Spanish Ministry of Industry, Tourism and Trade.

References

1. Arens, Y., Chee, C.Y., Hsu, C.-N., Knoblock, C.A.: Retrieving and integrating data from multiple information sources. International Journal of Intelligent and Cooperative Information Systems 2, 127–158 (1993)
2. Berners-Lee, T., Hendler, J., Lassila, O.: The semantic web. Scientific American 284(5), 34–43 (2001)
3. Doulaverakis, C., Kompatsiaris, Y., Strintzis, M.: Ontology-based access to multimedia cultural heritage collections - the reach project, vol. 1, pp. 151–154 (November 2005)
4. Sudha Sadasivam, G., Kavitha, C., SaravanaPriya, M.: Ontology based information retrieval for e-tourism. International Journal of Computer Science and Information Security 8, 78–83 (2010)
5. Zakraoui, J., Zagler, W.: An ontology for representing context in user interaction for enhancing web accessibility for all. In: LEAFA 2010 The First International Conference on e-Learning For All (2010)
6. Martín, P., Valverde, B., Muñoz, M., Martínez, M., Finat, J.: A specific ontology and related web services for assessing accessibility issues in cultural heritage environments. In: WebMGS 2010: 1st International Workshop on Pervasive Web Mapping, Geoprocessing and Services, Number XXXVIII-4/W13 (2010)

---

[1] http://www.predif.org

Automatic Color Improvement of Web Pages with Time Limited Operators

Sébastien Aupetit, Alina Mereuţă, and Mohamed Slimane

Université Françlois Rabelais Tours, Laboratoire Informatique (EA6300), France
64, avenue Jean Portalis, 37200 Tours, France
{aupetit,alina.mereuta,slimane}@univ-tours.fr

Abstract. Accessibility is unfortunately not among the main concern when developing web sites. Webmasters create mostly involuntarily numerous obstacles for people with visual impairments. That's why it becomes fundamental to identify the existing barriers and to propose solutions in order to at least diminish their impact to the user. Accessibility guidelines, as WCAG 2.0, indicate that a minimum difference of brightness, tonality and contrast is necessary to reach a minimum level of accessibility. In numerous cases, web designers ignore or just limit their choices to a low level of accessibility. For an user needing a higher level of accessibility than the one offered by the web page, the access to information may be difficult. In this context, we propose to transform the colors of web pages according to user's needs with the help of a client-side HTTP proxy. The requirements for the colors can be expressed as a fitness function. In order to recolor the page to increase accessibility, it's enough to minimize the fitness function.

Trying to find a minimum can be a time consuming task not appropriate for real time recoloring. Finding a minimum can be considered as a search with varying time limits. In this article, our objective is to compare different search methods and their performance under time limit: the search can be interrupted at any time. The studied methods are a random search, different types of pseudo gradient descend and an adaptation of the API metaheuristic. Finally, the different methods are compared.

Keywords: accessibility, assistive technology, recoloring, web, optimization.

1 Introduction

Numerous web sites are not very accessible or have a low usability for visual impaired people (blind, colorblind...). In order to allow universal access to web, associations, lobbies and legislators demand that many principles such as Web Accessibility Guidelines [1,2] be enforced by the web designers. In this context, laws such as [3] were voted. Although all these initiatives are good, they are not enough to allow universal access to all users disregarding of their abilities.

In our previous works, we were interested in developing several tools to allow webmasters to test and correct non-accessible web sites [4,5,6,7]. In order not to

K. Miesenberger et al. (Eds.): ICCHP 2012, Part I, LNCS 7382, pp. 355–362, 2012.

restrict people with visual impairments to a tiny fraction of the web, another approach must be considered. A web site can be very accessible to a person with a certain disability but unaccessible to other persons with other type of disability. A possible solution to the accessibility problem can be to adapt the accessibility requirements to user's needs.

Some improvements concerning accessibility can be done automatically or quasi automatically. Some attempts in this matter were conducted [8,9,10] using a HTTP proxy, but mostly of them remove a large part of the content considered to be unaccesible.

Smart Web Accessibility Proxy (SWAP)[1] is a freely HTTP client proxy designed to transform web pages. When a user access a web page the request passes through proxy which forwards the request to the Internet. Then the response send by the server goes through the proxy which can transform it according to user's needs and send it back to the user. The fact that the document is modified directly on the user's computer has numerous advantages : the privacy is maintained even with secured HTTPS connections, the person's habits while using particular assistive technologies don't change. Hence it becomes possible to adapt the content to user specific needs with almost no human cost. Because it runs client-side, there is no need for a heavy server infrastructure depending on the number of users. This work presented here has been conducted with the SWAP HTTP proxy.

In this article, we are interested in the modification of the colors used for textual information in order to reach a minimum differences of brightness, tonality and contrast but with reduced changes. The minimum thresholds can be the ones defined by [2] or any level considered to be acceptables by the user. The transformation of the colors has to be made while accessing the web page. So, we consider this problem to be a time limited problem: at any time the search for a solution can be stopped and the best found solution becomes the problem's solution. Consequently, more or less solutions can be explored depending on the system load and the user preferences. In the following, we define the problem and the proposed methods. We continue with many experiments and a discussion.

2 Defining the Problem

Let $\mathcal{C} = \{c_1, \ldots, c_{|\mathcal{C}|}\}$ be the set of colors used to represent the textual information of a web page. Let $\mathcal{E}$ be the set of couples (foreground, background) presented in our page and $w_{x,y} \in \mathbb{R}^+$ the associated weights. In our modeling, these weights are the number of characters in the web page that use the couple of color (x, y). Let $c_x^I \in [\![0 : 255]\!]^3$ be the color coordinate $x \in \mathcal{C}$ from the page and $c_x^F \in [\![0 : 255]\!]^3$ the coordinates of the same color after the transformation. Let be $c^I = (c_1^I, \ldots c_{|\mathcal{C}|}^I)$. Since there are interdependencies between colors, a perfect solution for the document does not necessarily exist. In order to allow the comparison of the solutions and to evaluate if they respect or not the defined accessibility constraints, we introduce the functions Φ_{Br}, Φ_{T} and Φ_{Cr}. These

---

[1] https://projectsforge.org/projects/swap

functions take their values in $[0:1]$. The value is zero if the constraint is satisfied and is one (1) in the worst case. For all couples $(m, n) \in [\![0:255]\!]^3 \times [\![0:255]\!]^3$, with $\max^+(x) = \max(0, x)$, we have:

$$\Phi_{\text{Br}}(m, n) = \max^+ \left(\frac{\eta_{\text{Br}} - \Delta\text{Br}(m, n)}{\eta_{\text{Br}}} \right), \tag{1}$$

$$\Phi_{\text{T}}(m, n) = \max^+ \left(\frac{\eta_{\text{T}} - \Delta\text{T}(m, n)}{\eta_{\text{T}}} \right), \tag{2}$$

$$\text{and } \Phi_{\text{Cr}}(m, n) = \max^+ \left(\frac{\eta_{\text{Cr}} - \Delta\text{Cr}(m, n)}{\eta_{\text{Cr}} - 1} \right). \tag{3}$$

Numerous solutions can have an equivalent quality for the three functions (the same evaluations), hence we propose to adjust the colors by inducing the least possible change in their appearance . For so, we introduce the functions $\Phi_{\Delta\text{Eab}}$ and $\Phi_{\Delta\text{EL}}$ as measures for chrominance and luminance in the form of an euclidean distances. These two functions are built by splitting into two parts the classical definition of perceptual distance between colors ΔE. ΔE is a classical reliable measure of the perceived distance between colors by the human eye in CIEL*a*b* color space. For all couple of colors (m, n), we have:

$$\Phi_{\Delta\text{Eab}}(m, n) = \frac{\sqrt{(m^a - n^a)^2 + (m^b - n^b)^2}}{100\sqrt{2}}, \tag{4}$$

$$\Phi_{\Delta\text{EL}}(m, n) = \frac{|m^L - n^L|}{100}. \tag{5}$$

Using the weights to increase the importance of frequent colors, we define:

$$S_w = \sum\nolimits_{(x,y)\in\mathcal{E}} w_{x,y}, \tag{6}$$

$$S_{\text{Br}} = S_w^{-1} \sum\nolimits_{(x,y)\in\mathcal{E}} w_{x,y} \Phi_{\text{Br}}(c_x^F, c_y^F), \tag{7}$$

$$S_{\text{T}} = S_w^{-1} \sum\nolimits_{(x,y)\in\mathcal{E}} w_{x,y} \Phi_{\text{T}}(c_x^F, c_y^F), \tag{8}$$

$$S_{\text{Cr}} = S_w^{-1} \sum\nolimits_{(x,y)\in\mathcal{E}} w_{x,y} \Phi_{\text{Cr}}(c_x^F, c_y^F), \tag{9}$$

$$S_{\Delta\text{Eab}} = S_w^{-1} \sum\nolimits_{(x,y)\in\mathcal{E}} w_{x,y} (\Phi_{\Delta\text{Eab}}(c_x^I, c_x^F) + \Phi_{\Delta\text{Eab}}(c_y^I, c_y^F)), \tag{10}$$

$$S_{\Delta\text{EL}} = S_w^{-1} \sum\nolimits_{(x,y)\in\mathcal{E}} w_{x,y} (\Phi_{\Delta\text{EL}}(c_x^I, c_x^F) + \Phi_{\Delta\text{EL}}(c_y^I, c_y^F)), \tag{11}$$

$$F = \left\lceil 10000 \frac{\epsilon_{\text{Br}} S_{\text{Br}} + \epsilon_{\text{T}} S_{\text{T}} + \epsilon_{\text{Cr}} S_{\text{Cr}}}{\epsilon_{\text{Br}} + \epsilon_{\text{T}} + \epsilon_{\text{Cr}}} \right\rceil + \frac{\epsilon_{\Delta\text{Eab}} S_{\Delta\text{Eab}} + \epsilon_{\Delta\text{EL}} S_{\Delta\text{EL}}}{\epsilon_{\Delta\text{Eab}} + \epsilon_{\Delta\text{EL}}}. \tag{12}$$

with ϵ_{Br}, ϵ_{T}, ϵ_{Cr}, $\epsilon_{\Delta\text{Eab}}$ and $\epsilon_{\Delta\text{EL}}$ being a real positive number, allowing the user to indicate the priorities in the fitness function. The integer part of the function F evaluates the constraints of accessibility, while the fractional part evaluates the changes made in the colors. Clearly, the priority is given to the satisfaction of the constraints but two solutions which may be equivalent regarding the constraints are differentiated by the amount of change. For all $x \in C$, we search for the coordinates $c_x^F \in [\![0:255]\!]$ that minimize F.

The colors change has to be accomplished on-the-fly. In consequence, we cannot spend a lot of time searching for a solution that minimizes F. The available time for the search may vary greatly from one client proxy to another depending, among other, of the computer's performance, other transformations to be performed and the web. That's why the user specifies a maximum time limit to the proxy in order to improve accessibility when accessing a web page. This time is shared between all the proxy transformation processes. The purpose of the transformations is then to make the best changes in the time limit provided.

Likely, the time will be insufficient to achieve optimal transformations. For the recoloring problem, we propose to use several optimisation techniques, to asses their convergence toward the minimum and to consider the ones that can be interrupted at any time: the best solution found will be used to transform the colors. Concerning this work, the transformations of colors are done by inserting in the HTML document the new CSS styles that overwrite the existing styles.

3   Methods for Minimizing F

The algorithms described below have similar computing costs. This can be expressed in terms of number of evaluation of the set of colors with the help of the F function. In order to simplify the writing, we consider that regardless of the number of occurrence of the function F, for the same configuration, the value is computed just once and reused when necessary.

3.1   Random Search (R)

The random search consists in generating uniformly the color coordinates on $[\![0:255]\!]$. The best solution ever found is memorized.

3.2   Line Search (LS)

The line search is not itself a viable method to search for the minimum of F: it will be used together with other two following neighborhood methods. Let $x \in [\![0:255]\!]^{3|\mathcal{C}|}$ be a configuration of colors and $v \in [\![-255:255]\!]^{3|\mathcal{C}|}$ a direction in the space which was followed to attain x. Let $M = ||v||_{\max} > 0$. Let $(y_t)_{t \in \mathbb{N}^+}$ be such that $y_t = x + (t/M)v$. By construction, we have $||y_t - y_{t+1}||_{\max} = 1$. The line search's result is y_T such that $\forall t = 1..T - 1$, $F(y_t) \geq F(y_{t+1})$ and $F(y_T) < F(y_{T+1})$.

3.3   Pseudo Descent on the Basis of the Space (PDB)

The pseudo descent on the basis of the space (PDB) consists in trying to successively change the solution in a direction of the basis. Thus, from a solution

x, we construct a solution y such that for all $i \neq k$, $x_i = y_i$ and $|x_k - y_k| = 1$. Let $\mathcal{V}(x)$ be the set of solutions which we can build starting from x. We have $|\mathcal{V}(v)| = 6|\mathcal{C}|$. For each solution y of $\mathcal{V}(x)$, it is possible to apply the line search in the direction $y - x$. The solutions of $\mathcal{V}(x)$ are chosen in a random order to avoid bias. The search process is applied iteratively until convergence.

3.4 Stochastic Pseudo Descent in the Neighborhood (*PDS*)

The stochastic pseudo descent in the neighborhood (PDS) assume a similar strategy as the pseudo descent on the basis of the space, with the difference that the neighborhood $\mathcal{V}(x)$ is larger and only few solutions of the neighborhood are explored. We consider $\mathcal{V}(x)$ as being the set of solutions at a maximal distance from $D_{\max}$ meaning that for every $y \in \mathcal{V}(x)$, we have $||x - y||_{\max} \leq D_{\max}$. At each exploration of the neighborhood, $\alpha|\mathcal{V}(x)|$ solutions are uniformly chosen and evaluated. The linear search can be used with the direction $y - x$. The algorithm is identical to the previous one with the exception of neighborhood.

3.5 API Metaheuristic (*API*)

The last exploration method that we have considered is an adaptation of the simplified form of the API metaheuristic. The API metaheuristic is an optimization metaheuristic [11], inspired by the foraging strategy of *Pachycondyla apicalis* ants [12,13]. In this paper, we introduce only a shorten description of the algorithm. More details can be found in [11,14,15,16].

Let $a_1, \ldots, a_n$ be a population of n ants which constitutes the colony. Each ant is associated with a position in the solution space and tries to minimize a function F. The metaheuristic behaviour is determined by two operators, $\mathcal{O}_{\text{init}}$ and $\mathcal{O}_{\text{explo}}$, that define the foraging strategy of the ants. $\mathcal{O}_{\text{init}}$ defines the initial position of the nest in the solution space. In our adaptation, $\mathcal{O}_{\text{init}} = c^I$. $\mathcal{O}_{\text{explo}}$ generates a solution y in the neighborhood $\mathcal{V}_i(x)$ of a solution x. This neighborhood depends in general on x and on an amplitude of exploration $\mathcal{A}_i \in]0 : 1]$, specific to the ant a_i. In our adaptation, y is a configuration of colors such that $||x - y||_{\max} \leq \lfloor \mathcal{A}_i * 255 \rfloor$. Let v be an uniformly randomly generated movement on $[\![-\lfloor \mathcal{A}_i * 255 \rfloor : \lfloor \mathcal{A}_i * 255 \rfloor]\!]^{|\mathcal{C}|}$. The generated solution is then $x + v$, where the coordinate are truncated in $[\![0 : 255]\!]$.

The API metaheuristic proceeds as follows. At the beginning the nest position $\mathcal{N}$ is defined with the use of the operator $\mathcal{O}_{\text{init}}$. At every iteration of the algorithm, all the ants move at the same time. The nest $\mathcal{N}$ is moved when each has moved $\mathcal{T}_{\text{move}}$ times. Each time an ant a_i needs to choose a hunting site, it leaves the nest and choose a hunting site in the neighborhood of the nest with the help of the $\mathcal{O}_{\text{explo}}$ operator using the amplitude $\mathcal{A}_i^{\text{site}}$. When an ant a_i needs to explore the neighborhood of the hunting site s_i, it computes the position p of the neighborhood s_i using the operator $\mathcal{O}_{\text{explo}}$ and the amplitude $\mathcal{A}_i^{\text{local}}$. A local exploration is known to be successful if it conducts to a better value of F *i.e.* $F(p) < F(s_i)$. In case of a successful exploration, the ant replaces its hunting site with the new position p. On the contrary, the hunting site is preserved. If a hunting site s_i was explored more than P_i^{local} consecutive times without success, then the hunting site is abandoned and forgotten. The next action of the ant will consist in going out of the nest in search for a new hunting site. Finally, when the nest is moved, the ants forgot all their hunting sites.

For the experiments, we have: $\mathcal{A}_i^{site} = 1 + (0.01 - 1)\frac{i-n}{1-n}$, $\mathcal{A}_i^{local} = \mathcal{A}_i^{site}/10$, $\mathcal{T}_{move} = 20$, $P_i^{local} = 10$ and $n = 10$.

4   Experiments

For the experiments, we considered the AAA accessibility thresholds ($\eta_{Br} = 125$, $\eta_T = 500$ and $\eta_{Cr} = 7$) and the weights $\epsilon_{Br} = \epsilon_T = \epsilon_{Cr} = \epsilon_{\Delta Eab} = \epsilon_{\Delta EL} = 1$. The experiments were conducted on 84 randomly selected web pages. None of these pages do verify completely the accessibility criteria $i.e.$ $F(p) \neq 0$. Each algorithm was run 100 times and up to 20000 evaluations were done. Let $F_a^p(t) \in \mathbb{R}^+$ be the average value of the function F after 100 runs for the algorithm $a \in \mathbb{A}$ for the page $p \in \mathbb{P}$ after t evaluations of configurations of colors have been done. In order to compare the algorithms, we have normalized the average fitness function on $[0:1]$. Let m^p and M^p be the maximum and the minimum evaluation achieved by $F_a^p(t)$ for the algorithms on the page p and $f_a(t)$ the normalized performance for the algorithm a. We have :

$$m^p = \min_{a,t} F_a^p(t) \, , \tag{13}$$

$$M^p = \max_{a,t} F_a^p(t) \, , \tag{14}$$

$$f_a(t) = \frac{1}{|\mathbb{P}|} \sum_{p \in \mathbb{P}} \frac{F_a^p(t) - m^p}{M^p - m^p} \, . \tag{15}$$

The considered algorithm are the random search (R), the pseudo descent on the basis of the space(PDB), the pseudo descent on the basis of the space with a line search (PDB+LS), the stochastic pseudo descent in the neighborhood (PDS(D_{max}, α)), the stochastic pseudo descent in the neighborhood with a line search (PDS(D_{max}, α)+LS) and the API metaheuristic (API), with $D_{max} \in \{1, 2, 3\}$ and $\alpha \in \{10\%, 30\%, 50\%\}$. The experiments show that the algorithms PDS(D_{max}, α) converged around 60%. We notice that the larger the search area D_{max} is, the less effective the search becomes. The best search is achieved with PDS(1,10%). The experiments also showed that the all PDS(D_{max}, α)+LS algorithms performs similarly. The line search provide a significant improvement to PDS. Moreover, we can notice that PDS(1,10%)+LS achieves the same final performance but converges faster on first evaluations than other PDS+LS. The experiments show that the PDB+LS algorithm is a lot more effective than PDB. Again, the line search provides an effective boosting. We can conclude that the line search can be an interesting way to improve the search process to minimize F. If we compare the performance of PDS(1,10%)+LS and PDB+LS with R and API (see Fig. 1), we observe that only two methods are detaching from the

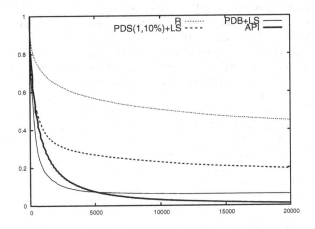

Fig. 1. Normalized performances

others : PDB+LS and API. The first converge to less than 10% and the last to 0% (best final evaluation). PDB+LS has the advantage of a faster convergence but it often gets stuck in a local minimum, while the API metaheuristic converge more slowly but after about 5000 evaluations it continues to find solutions decreasing F. At 5000 evaluations, both algorithms attain about 10% of the best solutions.

5 Conclusion

The experiments show that a line search can greatly improve the convergence speed. Moreover, with relatively few solutions evaluated (about 5000), it is possible to significantly increase the accessibility of colors. 5000 evaluations are enough to reduce in average the fitness to 10% of the best solutions that can be obtained with 20000 evaluations. The pseudo descent gradient combined with a line search and the API metaheuristic offers two viable solutions to the problem of real time minimization of F. Further work is required to explore the possibility of a switching strategy between the two viable methods but also the possibility of hybridization of the metaheuristic API with a line search or the PDB+LS algorithm. Finally, we also plan to take into account the possibilities offered by the API algorithm in terms of parallel computing by considering that recent machines incorporate multi-core technologies.

References

1. W3C Web Accessibility Initiative. Web content accessibility guideline 1.0 (May 1999)
2. W3C Web Accessibility Initiative. Web content accessibility guideline 2.0 (December 2008)

3. République Française. Loi n° 2005-102 du 11 février 2005 pour l'égalité des droits et des chances, la participation et la citoyenneté des personnes handicapées. JO n° 36 du 12 février 2005, p. 2353 (2005)
4. Colas, S., Monmarché, N., Gaucher, P., Slimane, M.: Accessibility of french publics web sites: a new tool and methodology to reach accessibility compliance. In: International Conference on Human-Machine iNteraction (HuMaN 2007), pp. 55–60 (2007)
5. Colas, S., Monmarché, N., Burger, D., Mohamed, S.: A web site migration support tool to reach european accessibility standards. In: 9th European Conference for the Advancement of Assistive Technology in Europe (AAATE 2007), San Sebastian, Spain. Assistive Technology Research Series, vol. 20, pp. 907–911 (October 2007)
6. Colas, S., Bulucua, J., Monmarché, N., Slimane, M.: Accessibilité des informations pertinentes des sites web accrue pour les personnes déffcientes visuelles par extraction d'informations. In: 11éme Colloque Internationale sur le Document Electronique (CIDE 11), Rouen, France, October 28-31 (2008)
7. Colas, S., Monmarché, N., Slimane, M.: Correcteur automatique ou assistance au webmestre pour obtenir un web accessible. In: Vigouroux, N., Gorce, P. (eds.) Handicap 2008, France, Paris, Juin 10-12, pp. 122–127, Cépadués éditions (2008)
8. Hanson, V.L., Richards, J.T.: A web accessibility service: update and findings. In: Proceedings of the 6th International ACM SIGACCESS Conference on Computers and Accessibility, Atlanta, GA, USA, October 18-20, pp. 169–176 (2004)
9. Parmanto, B., Ferrydiansyah, R., Zeng, X., Saptono, A., Sugiantara, I.W.: Accessibility transformation gateway. In: HICSS:Proceedings of the 38th Annual Hawaii International Conference on System Sciences, Big Island. IEEE Computer Society (2005)
10. Takagi, H., Kawanaka, S., Kobayashi, M., Sato, D., Asakawa, C.: Collaborative web accessibility improvement: challenges and possibilities. In: Proceedings of the 11th International ACM SIGACCESS Conference on Computers and Accessibility, Pittsburgh, Pennsylvania, USA, October 25-28, pp. 195–202 (2009)
11. Monmarché, N.: Algorithmes de fourmis artificielles: applications à la classification et à l'optimisation. Thèse de doctorat, Laboratoire d'Informatique de l'Université François Rabelais Tours (December 20, 2000)
12. Fresneau, D.: Individual foraging and path fidelity in a ponerine ant. Insectes Sociaux, Paris 32(2), 109–116 (1985)
13. Fresneau, D.: Biologie et comportement social d'une fourmi ponérine néotropicale (Pachycondyla apicalis). Thèse d'état, Université de Paris XIII, Laboratoire d'Ethologie Expérimentale et Comparée, France (1994)
14. Aupetit, S., Monmarché, N., Slimane, M.: Apprentissage des modéles de Markov cachés par l'algorithme API. In: Fourmis artificielles, des bases algorithmiques aux concepts et réalisations avancés, Traité IC2, vol. 1. Hermes-Lavoisier (2009)
15. Aupetit, S., Monmarché, N., Slimane, M.: Training hidden Markov models using the API ant algorithm. In: Artificials Ants: From Collective Intelligence to Real-Life Optimization and Beyond. ISTE, Wiley (2010)
16. Aupetit, S.: Contributions aux modèles de Markov cachés: métaheuristiques d'apprentissage, nouveaux modèles et visualisation de dissimilarité. Thèse de doctorat, Laboratoire d'Informatique de l'Université François Rabelais Tours, Tours, France (November 30, 2005)

Improving Web Accessibility for Dichromat Users through Contrast Preservation

Alina Mereuţă, Sébastien Aupetit, and Mohamed Slimane

Université François Rabelais Tours, Laboratoire Informatique (EA6300), France
64, avenue Jean Portalis, 37200 Tours, France
{alina.mereuta,aupetit,slimane}@univ-tours.fr

Abstract. Unfortunately, accessibility is not one of designers priorities while developing web sites, resulting in barriers for numerous disabled users. In this context, it is fundamental to identify the difficulties they may experience while surfing web and to propose solutions in order to remove them or diminish their impact. The choice of colors is far from being a random process but often a way to transmit or emphase information. This is particulary true for textual information contained in a web page. The perception of colors by a dichromat user is different. This results in a loss of the information conveyed by color. In our study, we show that there is a significant loss of contrast for a dichromat user resulting in information loss. We propose a method based on a mass-spring simulation to modify the colors with aim to enforce similar contrast for dichromat users. Tests on several websites allow us to conclude that our method significantly reduce the loss of contrast for both protanope and deuteranope users.

Keywords: assistive technology, accessibility, dichromacy, web sites, contrast preservation.

1 Introduction

Web accessibility means that people, disregarding of their abilities can access the Web. For so, it is neccessary that its essential components (contents, user agents, developers, assistive technologies, authoring and evaluation tools [1] work together. The weakness of any component makes websites less accessible or even inaccessible to some users, such as users with disabilities, making their web experience very unpleasant and frustrating. Unfortunatly most websites are created ignoring accessibility guidelines such as the ones proposed by the Web Accessibility Initiative (WAI).In order to remove or diminish some of the difficulties that disabled people may experience while surfing web, numerous transformation and evaluating tools were proposed: (1) evaluation tools which assist the designer in his effort to create accessible web sites [2,3]; (2) server-side tools which transform the pages on the servers [4,5,6,7]; (3) client-side tools which transform the content before browsing [8,9,10,11], or at browser level [12]; and (4) assistive technologies [13].

K. Miesenberger et al. (Eds.): ICCHP 2012, Part I, LNCS 7382, pp. 363–370, 2012.
© Springer-Verlag Berlin Heidelberg 2012

We are focusing our study on a proxy server that runs client-side (the client side proxy part of the SWAP project). Such tools ensure confidentiality, are highly custmomizable to user needs and do not change the way the user uses assistive technologies. Studies [14,15] show that proxy-like transformations tools improve disabled user web experience but also for a standard user. The biggest limit of these tools consists in removing a large part from the web page content believed to be unaccessible resulting in a loss of information. In this paper, we are interested in reducing the information loss that dichromats users may experience. The colors chosen by the author in a web page are usually additional means to present and enhance the message that he wants to transmit. Then, the loss of contrast can be interpreted also as a loss of information. We introduce a method that aims to preserve the same level of contrast for both standard and dichromat users. In the followings , we introduce the SWAP project, which is used to perform our analysis,the dichromacy deficiencies and existing recolorization techniques. After we introduce the problem and our method, many graphical and statistical analysis are conducted to support our approach.

2   Smart Web Accessibility Proxy

This work was carried out using tools from the Smart Web Accessibility Proxy (SWAP) project[1]. The SWAP project has for objective to propose a open source set of tools to implement a modular and extensible client-side transformation proxy to improve accessibility and usability. The proxy can be used by any HTTP client like a web browser or a specialized assistive technology. The one and only requirement is that it must be configured to access the web through the proxy. By being an intermediary between the web and the HTTP client, it allows to do any kind of transformation on the content, even on secured contents (HTTPs) can be done.

SWAP is a web proxy designed to facilitate access to information for users with or without disabilities. One of the goal of the project is to identify the issues arising when both disabled and standard user access the web and to propose methods and tools that better respond to user needs and demandings.

3   Dichromacy

Color is a visual sensation which is produced by the interaction of the light spectrum on the photoreceptors (cones cells) in the retina of the eye. It is commonly accepted that human color perception is a tri-stilumus phenomenon [16] based on three types of cones: S, M and L. The S, M and L cones react respectively to short wavelength (420nm, blue), medium wavelength (534nm, green) and long wavelength (564nm, red). Color deficiency is the diminished ability or the inability to perceive certain colors. Among the color deficiencies are : (1) Achromatopsia - the total lack of cones - the individuals are completely colorblind - they

---

[1] https://projectsforge.org/projects/swap

perceive only black, white and different shades of gray, (2) Anomalous trichromacy (Protanomaly, Deuteranomaly, Tritanomaly) - the individuals have the 3 types of cones, but they do not function properly (3) Dichromacy - the individual has only two types of cones. People suffering from Dichromacy are called : (1) Protanope - (sever) red-green deficiency due to the lack of the L-cones, (2) Deuterope - (sever) red-green deficiency due to the absence of the M-cones and (3) Protanope - (sever) blue-yellow deficiency - S cone missing. About 7% of people have a form of Anomalous trichromacy, and around 2.4 % have a form of Dichromacy [17]. To simulate dichromacy a serie of algorithms [18,19,20] and simulating tools [21] were proposed. In the following sections, we focus our study on the Dichromacy.

4   Related Works

Many attempts were conducted in order to diminish the loss of information for dichromats. Thoses works are focused either on :

- images/maps recoloring in order to preserve details [20,22,23,24,25] using different methods such as linear scalling and substitution of colors;
- document recoloring in order to maintain a level of contrast according to user's needs [26] using simulating annealing ;
- web page recoloring to enhance contrast [27,28] using genetic algorithms or confusion lines;

In order to emphase our problem interest, we have build graphics in Figure 1 using 256^3 colors in the sRGB space. For each pair of colors, we have drawn a scatterplot having as abscissa the contrast value for a standard user and as ordinate the contrast as perceived by a dichromat user. The graphics allow us to conclude that the loss of contrast can be significant for all three types of dichromacy considered.

Fig. 1. Relationship between the standard and simulated constrasts over the sRGB space. The white line ($y = x$) represents the absence of loss of contrast. Abcissa is for the initial contrast and the ordinate is the simulated contrast for dichromacy.

5   Recoloring Module

5.1   General

In order to make the web more accessible to people with disabilities, W3C's Web Accessibility Initiative (WAI) published a series of web accessibility guidelines called WCAG. They are organized using three priority levels (from A to AAA). The WCAG 1.0 guideline 2, checkpoint 2.2 states that "Ensure that foreground and background color combinations provide sufficient contrast when viewed by someone having color deficits or when viewed on a black and white screen".

Beyond the problem of ensuring minimum contrast, we can notice that colors and especially the contrast variations due to the choice of colors help significantly to convey the information provided by the author of the page. We have already seen that the perceived contrast can be changed significantly. Consequently some of the information provided can not be perceived correctly due to an unintentionally variation of contrast. Our work attempts to provide a solution to the possible loss of contrast (and information) induced by the different perception. We solve this problem in two phases: (1) modeling the textual information contained in the web page as a set of entities caracterized by foreground and background colors and (2) optimizing the set of colors by simulating a mass spring system in order to maintain the initial contrast.

5.2   Mass-Spring System

A mass-spring system is defined as a set of objects (masses) connected by springs. At each moment $t \in \mathbb{R}^+$, every object i is defined by a mass m_i and a position $p_i(t)$. Each spring, that connects two objects i and j, is defined by its elasticity $k_{i,j}$ which we consider to be 1 in the following, the rest length $l_{i,j}^0$ and its current length $l_{i,j}(t)$ at each moment $t \in \mathbb{R}^+$. Let $\mathcal{A}_i$ be the set containing the number of objects connected by a spring with the object i. Then, the equation of motion for the mass-spring system is:

$$\frac{d^2 p_i(t)}{dt^2} = \frac{1}{m_i} \sum_{j \in \mathcal{A}_i} k_{ij} \left(1 - \frac{l_{i,j}^0}{l_{i,j}(t)} \right) (p_j(t) - p_i(t)) . \tag{1}$$

A mass-spring system can have one or more equilibrium configurations. To obtain one of them, it is enough to integrate numerically the motion equation using Euler, Verlet or Runge-Kutta method [29]. In the following experiments the integration is done using the Verlet method.

5.3   Modeling and Solving the Problem Using a Mass-Spring System

In the following, we consider the colors as being sRGB colors, represented in $[\![0 : 255]\!]^3$. The positions of the mass-spring system are represented in $\mathbb{R}^3$. When appropriate, the position's coordinates are truncated in $[0 : 255]^3$ and their values are rounded to the closest integer in order to obtain sRGB colors. Let

$\mathcal{C} = \{c_1, \ldots, c_{|\mathcal{C}|}\}$ be the set of colors used to represent the textual information in a web page. Let $\mathcal{E}$ be the set of color couples (foreground, background) from the web page and $w_{a,b} \in \mathbb{R}^+$ the associated weights to the couple $(a, b) \in \mathcal{E}$. In our modeling, these weights correspond to the number of characters from the page that use this couple of colors. For each color $a \in \mathcal{C}$, we define c_a^I the object representing the actual color found on the web page (initial color). We define by $p_{c_a^I}(0) \in \mathbb{R}^3$ the point coresponding to the color a in the sRGB color space and $m_{c_a^I} = +\infty$. In this case, $p_{c_a^I}(t)$ is constant and $p_{c_a^I}(t) = p_{c_a^I}(0)$. c_a^I can be seen as an anchor in the color space. For each color $a \in \mathcal{C}$, we define c_a^F as the object representing the color a after the modification in the space sRGB. At first, no modification is done, hence $p_{c_a^F}(0) = p_{c_a^I}(0)$. The mass of the object is defined as being heavy if the color is often used in the page. Hence an unfrequent color will have a small mass. The objects' mass is given by:

$$m_{c_a^F} = \frac{\sum_{(a,b)\in\mathcal{E}} w_{a,b} + \sum_{(b,a)\in\mathcal{E}} w_{a,b}}{\sum_{(x,y)\in\mathcal{E}} w_{x,y}} . \tag{2}$$

Let $\epsilon > 0$ (0.03 in our experiments) and d_{CIELab} be the Euclidian distance between two colors in CIEL*a*b* color space. Let $\Gamma(x, y) \in [1 : 21]$ be a contrast measure between two colors x and y represented in sRGB space. Let $D(x) \in [\![0 : 255]\!]^3$ be the simulation function for protanope, deuteranope or tritanope. For all couples of colors $(a, b) \in \mathcal{E}$ we define $\Gamma_{a,b}^I$ and $\Gamma_{a,b}^{F,D}$ the initial contrast for a standard user and the final contrast for a dichromat user. We have:

$$\Gamma_{a,b}^I = \Gamma(p_{c_a^I}(0), p_{c_b^I}(0)) , \tag{3}$$

$$\Gamma_{a,b}^{F,D}(t) = \Gamma(D(p_{c_a^F}(t)), D(p_{c_b^F}(t))) , \tag{4}$$

$$\Gamma_{a,b}^{F,D} = \lim_{t\to\infty} \Gamma_{a,b}^{F,D}(t) . \tag{5}$$

To guarantee that the colors will not change too much during the adaptation process, a spring is attached between c_a^I and c_a^F for each color $a \in \mathcal{C}$, in order to reduce the difference of colors' perception. We define for each couple $(a, b) \in \mathcal{E}$:

$$l_{c_a^I,c_a^F}^0 = \epsilon , \tag{6}$$

$$l_{c_a^I,c_a^F}(t) = \epsilon + d_{CIELAB}(p_{c_a^I}(t), p_{c_a^F}(t)) . \tag{7}$$

To ensure that the contrast for a dichromat user $(\Gamma_{a,b}^{F,D})$ is at the level of a standard user $(\Gamma_{a,b}^I)$, we add a spring for all couples $(a, b) \in \mathcal{E}$ such that

$$l_{c_a^F,c_b^F}^0 = \epsilon , \tag{8}$$

$$l_{c_a^F,c_b^F}(t) = \epsilon + \max(\Gamma_{a,b}^I - \Gamma_{a,b}^{F,D}, 0) . \tag{9}$$

When the system converge to a stable configuration, it tends, without necessarily achieving to satisfy the following constraints: (1) $d_{CIELAB}(p_{c_a^I}(t), p_{c_a^F}(t)) = 0$ (maintain the same perceptual distance between the initial and final colors);

(2) $\max(\Gamma_{a,b}^{I} - \Gamma_{a,b}^{F,D}, 0) = 0$ meaning $\Gamma_{a,b}^{F,D} > \Gamma_{a,b}^{I}$ (contrast enhancement) or $\Gamma_{a,b}^{I} = \Gamma_{a,b}^{F,D}$ (compensation of contrast loss). Of course, there is a possibility that the equilibrium positions of the system to be nothing more than a compromise. But, this compromise respects at best the previous conditions for the imposed constraints. In any case, we can consider that the equilibrium configuration gives a solution to the preservation contrast problem by reducing in the same time the change of colors. Moreover, considering $p_{c_a^F}(0) = p_{c_a^I}(0)$, we allow the system to converge towards an equilibrium close to the initial colors. Given these conditions, the mass-spring system and the searching of its equilibrium constitute a deterministic algorithm providing the same solution for the same dataset. This could be problematic at first sight but actually has a good impact on the user because the web page doesn't change its aspect at each visit.

6   Experiments and Discussion

We conduct our experiments on 87 randomly selected web pages. The text and the associated colors were extracted from the web pages through HTML and CSS analysis. The foreground and the background colors were differentiated. The set of colors $\mathcal{C}$ is constituted by the distinct set of colors that define the foreground and the background. For each couple of colors, the associated weight is the number of characters that use the couple in the web page.

The Γ function, for contrast measuring, uses the formulae suggested in the WCAG 2.0. The D function for dichromacy simulation uses the algorithm proposed by Kuhn et al [20]. The average contrast $\bar{\Gamma}^I$, the average weighted contrast $\bar{\Gamma}^{I,W}$ and their equivalents $\bar{\Gamma}_D^I$ and $\bar{\Gamma}_D^{I,W}$ after the dichromacy simulation are given by:

$$\bar{\Gamma}^I = \sum_{(a,b)\in\mathcal{E}} \Gamma(p_{c_a^I}, p_{c_b^I}), \tag{10}$$

$$\bar{\Gamma}^{I,W} = \frac{\sum\limits_{(a,b)\in\mathcal{E}} w_{a,b} * \Gamma(p_{c_a^I}, p_{c_b^I})}{\sum\limits_{(a,b)\in\mathcal{E}} w_{a,b}}, \tag{11}$$

$$\bar{\Gamma}_D^I = \sum_{(a,b)\in\mathcal{E}} \Gamma(D(p_{c_a^I}), D(p_{c_b^I})), \tag{12}$$

$$\bar{\Gamma}_D^{I,W} = \frac{\sum\limits_{(a,b)\in\mathcal{E}} w_{a,b} * \Gamma(D(p_{c_a^I}), D(p_{c_b^I}))}{\sum\limits_{(a,b)\in\mathcal{E}} w_{a,b}}. \tag{13}$$

The equivalent contrast measures on the colors obtained after the mass-spring converged are $\bar{\Gamma}^F$, $\bar{\Gamma}^{F,W}$, $\bar{\Gamma}_D^F$ and $\bar{\Gamma}_D^{F,W}$. The weighted version allows us to consider the frequency of apparition of the colors by favoring the frequent contrasts.

Several statistic tests were made in order to achieve the following conclusions:

- $\bar{\Gamma}^I > \bar{\Gamma}_D^I$: there is an average contrast loss perceived by a dichromat user;
- $\bar{\Gamma}^{I,W} > \bar{\Gamma}_D^{I,W}$: there is an average weighted contrast loss perceived by a dichromat user;

- $\Delta \bar{\Gamma}^I > \Delta \bar{\Gamma}_D^F$: the proposed method allows to compensate the average contrast loss percieved by both protanope and deuteranope users.
- $\Delta \bar{\Gamma}^{I,W} > \Delta \bar{\Gamma}_D^{F,W}$: the proposed method allows to compensate the average weighted contrast loss percieved by both protanope and deuteranope users.

By construction (the same starting configuration), our method is deterministic. From experiments, we observe that the mass-spring considered allows to compensate the contrast loss for both deuteranope and protanope users. On the opposite for the tritanope user our method doesn't compensate the loss. This may be caused by (1) the fact that we try to enforce the same perceptual distance ($l^0_{c_a^I, C_a^F}$) or (2) the initial position $p_{c_a^F}(0)$ leads towards a local minimum. Future work is required to investigate these posibilities and to build new starting configuration with the cost of losing the deterministic aspect of the method.

7   Conclusion

In this paper we were interested in the contrast loss which can be observed by a dichromat user (protanope, deuteranope, tritanope) regarding the textual information contained in a web page. We showed that the loss can be significant for all three types of dichromacy. Contrast itself is often a mean of conveying information. In consequence, a contrast loss results in a potential handicap in understanding the author intent on the webpage.

We have proposed a new method that helps to compensate the loss by modifying the set of colors used to represent textual information in a web page. The principles of the mass-spring system are the baseline of our method. The first experiments on randomly selected data are encouraging, our method succeeds in compensating the loss for both protanope and deutaranope. In our future work, we plan to extend the recoloring to images.

References

1. W3C (October 2011), http://www.w3.org/WAI/intro/components.php
2. A-checker (October 2011), http://achecker.ca/checker/index.php
3. Acc (October 2011), http://appro.mit.jyu.fi/tools/acc/
4. Betsie (October 2011), http://www.bbc.co.uk/education/betsie
5. Brown, S., Robinson, P.: A world wide web mediator for users with low vision. In: Proceedings of Conference on Human Factors in Computing Systems, CHI (2001)
6. Colajanni, M., Grieco, R., Malandrino, D., Mazzoni, F., Scarano, V.: A Scalable Framework for the Support of Advanced Edge Services. In: Yang, L.T., Rana, O.F., Di Martino, B., Dongarra, J. (eds.) HPCC 2005. LNCS, vol. 3726, pp. 1033–1042. Springer, Heidelberg (2005)
7. mod_accessibility (January 2012), http://apache.webthing.com/mod_accessibility/
8. Parmanto, B., Ferrydiansyah, R., Zeng, X., Saptono, A., Sugiantara, I.W.: Accessibility transformation gateway. In: 38th Hawaii International Conference on System Sciences (2005)

9. Han, R., Bhagwat, P., Lamaire, R., Perret, V., Rubas, J.: Dynamic adaptation in an image transcoding proxy for mobile web browsing. IEEE Personal Communications (December 1998)
10. Gupta, S., Kaiser, G.: Extracting content from accessible web pages. In: International Cross-Disciplinary Workshop on Web Accessibility (2005)
11. Gupta, S., Kaiser; G., et al.: Automating content extraction of HTML documents. In: World Wide Web (2005)
12. Hermsdorf, D., Gappa, H., Pieper, M.: A prototype of a www-browser with new special needs adaptations. In: International Conference on Computers Helping People with Special Needs, ICCHP (1998)
13. Dolphin lunar (October 2011), http://www.yourdolphin.com/
14. Brajnik, G., Cancila, D., Nicoli, D., Pignatelli, M.: Do text transcoders improve usability for disabled users? In: WWW (2005)
15. Brajnik, G., et al.: Do dynamic text–only web pages improve usability for pda users? In: Usability Symposium (2005)
16. Levkowitz, H.: Color theory and modelling for computer graphics, visualisation and multimedia applications. Kluwer Academic Publisher (1997)
17. How do people get colorblindness and how many people have it? (November 2011), http://www.webexhibits.org/causesofcolor/2C.html
18. Brettel, H., Vienot, F., Mollon, J.D.: Computerized simulation of color appearance or dichromats. Journal of Optical Society of America (1997)
19. Brettel, H., Vienot, F., Mollon, J.D.: Digital video colourmaps for checking the legibility of displays by dichromats. In: Color Research and Application (1999)
20. Kuhn, G.R., Oliveira, M.M., Fernandes, L.A.F.: An efficient naturalness-preserving image-recoloring method for dichromats. In: IEEE Visualization and Computer Graphics (2008)
21. Vischeck (October 2011), http://www.vischeck.com/
22. Ruminski, J., Wtorek, J., Ruminska, J., et al.: Color transformation methods for dichromats. In: Human System Interactions, HSI (2010)
23. Machado, G.M., Oliveira, M.M.: Real-time temporal-coherent color contrast enhancement for dichromats. IEEE (2010)
24. Rodríguez-Pardo, C.E., Sharma, G.: Adaptive color visualization for dichromats using a customized hierarchical palette. In: Color Imaging XVI: Displaying, Processing, Hardcopy, and Applications (2011)
25. Park, J., Choi, J., Han, D.: Applying enhanced confusion line color transform using color segmentation for mobile applications. In: Computers, Networks, Systems and Industrial Engineering, CNSI (2011)
26. Wakita, K., Shimamura, K.: Smartcolor: Disambiguation framework for the colorblind. In: ASSETS 2005: The Sixth International ACM Access Conference on Assistive Tehcnologies (2005)
27. Ichikawa, M., Tanaka, K., Kondo, S., Hiroshima, K., Ichikawa, K., Tanabe, S., Fukami, K.: Web-Page Color Modification for Barrier-Free Color Vision with Genetic Algorithm. In: Cantú-Paz, E., Foster, J.A., Deb, K., Davis, L., Roy, R., O'Reilly, U.-M., Beyer, H.-G., Kendall, G., Wilson, S.W., Harman, M., Wegener, J., Dasgupta, D., Potter, M.A., Schultz, A., Dowsland, K.A., Jonoska, N., Miller, J., Standish, R.K. (eds.) GECCO 2003. LNCS, vol. 2724, pp. 2134–2146. Springer, Heidelberg (2003)
28. Iaccarino, G., Malandrino, D., et al.: Efficient edge-services for colorblind users. In: 15th International Conference on World Wide Web (2006)
29. Kopchenova, N.V., Maron, I.A.: Computational Mathematics for Differential Equations. MIR Publishers, Moscow (1975)

Sociological Issues of Inclusive Web Design

The German Web 2.0 Accessibility Survey

Michael Pieper

Fraunhofer Institute for Applied Information Technology – FIT
Schloss Birlinghoven, 53754 Sankt Augustin, Germany
michael.pieper@fit.fhg.de

Abstract. The German BIENE award (Barrierefreies Internet Eröffnet Neue Einsichten / Accessible Internet Provides New Insights), a best practice competition for accessible websites organized by the social association "Aktion Mensch" and the endowment "Digitale Chancen" enters into a new competitive phase. For the 2010 competition 224 web pages have been checked for their barrier free accessibility. Web applications that facilitate interactive sharing of *user generated content* are of particular importance, when it comes to Web 2.0 technologies. In this respect it soon turned out, that Web 2.0 services cannot only be made accessible by applying common design guidelines and ad-hoc adap-tations. In addition to conventional software ergonomic verification procedures, accessibility validation has to rely on sociological reasoning about unique Web 2.0 entities and corresponding usage obstacles. Empirically these considerations have been conceptualized by an online survey amongst 671 respondents with all kinds of different disabilities, carried out by "Aktion Mensch".

Keywords: Accessibility, Usability, Human-Computer Interaction, Web 2.0.

1   Introduction

The German BIENE award (Barrierefreies Internet Eröffnet Neue Einsichten / Accessible Internet Provides New Insights) is a best practice competition for accessible websites organized by the social association "Aktion Mensch" and the endowment "Digitale Chancen". For the last 2010 competition 128 contributions out of originally 224 additionally went through a special ergonomic test procedure of process-oriented interaction with competitors' web pages. Accessibility was analyzed on the basis of on-line transactions like purchase, money-transfer or public authority form-filling dialogues. However, of special importance in this respect are transactions that facili-tate interactive sharing of user generated content, when it comes to Web 2.0 technologies. Special attention has to be paid to the technological evolution step concerning the offer and the accessibility of the World Wide Web to a web with which not any more the pure spreading of information or product sales are in the foreground, but the participation of users and the user-centered generation of other additional use. In this respect it soon turned out, that Web 2.0 services cannot only be

K. Miesenberger et al. (Eds.): ICCHP 2012, Part I, LNCS 7382, pp. 371–377, 2012.
© Springer-Verlag Berlin Heidelberg 2012

made accessible through common methods such as the application of conventional design guidelines and/or ad-hoc adaptations. In addition to more or less software ergonomic verification procedures, accessibility validation has most basically to rely on sociological reasoning about unique Web 2.0 entities and corresponding usage obstacles.

2   Sociological Issues of Inclusive Web 2.0 Design

Inclusive Design is a way of designing products and environments so that they are usable and appealing to everyone regardless of age, ability or circumstance. Amongst other issues it follows the concept of working with users to remove barriers in the social, technical, political and economic obstacles to overcome digital divide. As user participation is at stake inclusive design or Web 2.0 accessibility for all becomes a purely sociological issue. The actualization of topical contents continuously occurs through intensive user participation, so that websites become more dynamic and more adapted to user needs, especially to the needs of disabled end users. On account of the immediate participation of the users it is often spoken also of the "democratization" of the net, because the contents of the web are no longer influenced any more by only the operators of the websites, but by the users as well. "We see through a range of already very well-known websites (...), that networks are taking shared responsibility for the construction of vast accumulations of knowledge about themselves, each other, and the world. These are dynamic matrices of information through which people observe others, expand the network, make new 'friends', edit and update content, blog, remix, post, respond, share files, exhibit, tag and so on. This has been described as an online 'participatory culture' [1] where users are increasingly involved in creating web content as well as consuming it" [2]. The (social) role of website operators has changed in web 2.0 in this respect, as that they are responsible, primarily, for the supply of a properly designed platform suitable for interactive and collaborative use as well as for its administration. Finally, the success of a platform provided by the operator or better designer appears in the intensity of its use which generally correlates with the quality of the contents in terms of "customer use" ("Usefulness"). Only in this respect, quality of contents correlates secondarily with the highest possible absence of usage barriers ("usability") [3], [4]. Avoidance of usage barriers in turn depends on a specific execution of certain (social) roles of website developers in general. As Web 2.0 is primarily associated with the term "user generated content" the crucial questions thus arises, in how far end user content generation coincides with low or barely existent usage barriers. Equally the question has to be answered in which way website developers support end users to generate barrier-free content.

2.1   Social Roles of Website Developers and Barrier-Free User Content

Four types of usage obstacles can be distinguished with respect to (social) roles of website developers. These roles can be derived from certain areas of responsibility for website operability, i.e. the responsibility to minimize or remove defined barriers [5].

1. techno-functional barriers:
   o relate to insufficiently applied software technologies or programming and hard- and software restrictions by assistive technologies
   o examples are CAPTCHAS (non machine-readable graphics code)[1], accessibility of Flash-players, missing form identifications etc.
   o area of responsibility: Web programmer and service provider
2. editorial and content barriers:
   o relate to insufficient editorial or structural preparation and implementation of content (poor CMS)
   o examples are difficult language, missing text-structure (e.g. CSS), missing desc. txt etc.
   o area of responsibility: Web editors
3. user interface design barriers
   o relate to insufficient software ergonomic design
   o examples are low contrast, confusing background pictures, non readable fonts etc.
   o area of responsibility: Web designer
4. organizational barriers
   o related to insufficient organizational circumstances and environment
   o examples are missing budget or missing demands for alternative website re-generation and assistive technologies (e.g. speech output for the blind, font size and contrast modification for the vision impaired etc.)
   o area of responsibility: Customers

Due to not always clearly defined areas of responsibility overlapping between these four usage barriers is possible. Such as the responsibility for an adequate web appearance of pictures or Wiki applications in principle lies with the editor, it may partially as well lie with the designer or even with the programmer, when declarative programming statements are needed.

In a two factorial design different role responsibilities of web programmers, service providers, editors, designers and customers interfere with distinguishable content generating and content perceiving usage patterns of end users, thus revealing further refined insights into Web 2.0 usage obstacles. Three kinds of usage patterns can be distinguished:

1. simple form-based usage (e.g. user registration, processing of user profiles, commenting, reading in Wiki-applications and Weblogs)
2. extended form- or editor-based usage (e.g. writing in Wiki-applications and Weblogs)
3. media-intensive usage (e.g. uploading and viewing of pictures, videos, hearing of podcasts)

---

[1] Which cannot be processed by screen readers and is thus not accessible for vision impaired or blind end users.

Table 1. Accessibility problems by type of usage barrier and usage pattern

Usage Barrier / Usage Pattern	Techno-functional barriers	Editorial and content barriers	User interface design barriers
Simple form-based usage	Captchas, indications for form-fillings and buttons, accessibility of Flash-players...	Intelligibility of explanation texts, expected input and error messages...	Design of forms...
Extended form or editor based usage	Graphic editors, font sizes in editors, problems with Java script, accessibility of Flash-players		Design of forms, Perceptibility of editor functionality...
Media-intensive usage	Media upload/download	Quality (Resolution), size and contrast of media, sign-language videos, Podcasts, desc. txt	Controllability of players, Quality (Resolution), size and contrast of media

3   Empirical Findings and Recommendations

Empirically these considerations have been conceptualized by an online survey amongst 671 respondents with all kinds of different disabilities, carried out by "Aktion Mensch" [5]. Respondents' age was between 14 and above 70, amongst them 293 female and 378 male respondents.

Table 2. Barriers by Disability (5)

Barriers / Disability	Visually impaired (n=133)	Blind (n=124)	Hard of hearing (n=96)	Deaf (n=260)	Motor impaired (n=75)	Dyslexia/ reading disability (n=41)	Cognitive / learning disability (n=46)
Barriers total[2]	48%	82%	21%	26%	34%	23%	44%
Non-specified barriers in general	13%	42%	5%	8%	8%	3%	9%
Missing tags / Captchas	5%	39%	1%	-	-	-	3%
Orientation problems	15%	8%	-	2%	6%	10%	12%
Information overload	9%	9%	3%	3%	8%	10%	9%
Missing subtitles and gesture language	2%	-	5%	10%	-	-	-
Understanding problems	2%	1%	5%	6%	6%	-	3%
Problems with Flash	3%	8%	3%	-	3%	-	3%

---

[2] Because multiple barriers have been taken into account for single barrier values, they do not sum up to total barrier value.

The online survey itself was realized free of barriers. Participants with most different impediments were moved with the help of different aids into the position to perceive the survey and to navigate and understand the forms. According to the results of previous BIENE test procedures, all survey contents have been processed accessible for screen readers, by sign language videos and in simple language. The "Aktion Mensch" thus conducted the first truly accessible online survey among people with disabilities. Five complexes of unique Web 2.0 usage obstacles and corresponding recommendations to eliminate these barriers could be attributed to the results of this survey:

3.1   Elimination of Barriers to the Use of Wiki-Applications

To increase the accessibility of Wiki-applications, especially the content has verbally to be elaborated. Comprehension problems caused by complicated language stand in the foreground. The online survey revealed that about one-third of affected end users with limitations in the understanding of written language - amongst them users with reading disability and dyslexia, learning and cognitive disabilities, and deaf end users - had problems in reading Wiki pages. Missing videos in sign language impeded comprehension for deaf end users. Motor-impaired respondents indicated problems in navigating and controlling search fields by speech recognition. Missing values in writing or commenting Wikis indicate that none of the respondents experienced problems caused by their disability. Most of the barriers lie therefore, on the one hand, in the intelligibility and orientation on the GUI of Wikis and to the other in applying the mostly graphic editors and forms to write and annotate content. For the blind, the flow of text for screen readers is partly disrupted due to the large number of links, since these are always especially announced.

3.2   Elimination of Barriers to User Registration and Editing of User Profiles

Most problems appear in the perceptibility, controllability and orientation during user registration or editing user profiles. In many Web 2.0 offerings user registration is the prerequisite for the productive use of the services. It should therefore be very thor-oughly examined and adapted in terms of accessibility. Particularly critical in this respect is the programming of forms and captchas. Improvement should also be carried out concerning the intelligibility of explanations, expected inputs and in particular of error messages. Programming of error messages should as well be checked for compatibility with different assistive input and output devices. In particular, visually impaired and blind end users have massive problems with user registration. Nearly half of the blind end users are able to carry out a user registration independently. The most frequent problems in this respect originate on the basis of security and spam defensive measures from Captchas which are discernible neither from screen readers nor by enlargement software. Unless it is not alternatively offered by audio files this non machine-readable graphics code for access authorization is also hardly accessible for the vision impaired. It can be assumed that roughly two third of the partially sighted and blind end users abort registration processes, leave corresponding applications and are thus excluded from a large variety of Web 2.0 services.

3.3   Elimination of Barriers in Dealing with Pictures (Photos), Videos and Podcasts

Many contents on the Internet are multimedia, which basically leads to disability-caused usage barriers on the side of partially sighted and blind users regarding the visual - and with the hard of hearing and deaf users regarding the auditive share of web offers. Differently than with purely text-based websites screen readers can offer a solution for blind end users only with an appropriate design of multi-media contents (e.g. appropriate 'desc. txt'). To the vision impaired, multimedia web offers are often too small and badly dissolved. Subtitles and sign language videos which could lift the barriers for auditively impaired users do normally not exist with most of the web offers. For uploading and embedding photos and videos, instruction forms are often problematic, since their design is neither clear and concise nor are certain form elements (e.g. buttons) sufficiently distinguished from each other. Additionally, visually impaired end users often get disoriented, because enlargement software limits the view area and complicates thus the allocation of multimedia content. Especially previewing of pictures may no more be recognizable. Even with downloading of podcasts download buttons are often not marked unambiguously. Often Java scripts impede a smooth download of podcasts by assistive technologies (e.g. screen readers). In summary barriers in dealing with multimedia content have therefore to be reduced by improved programming of upload and download forms. For instance, an offer to provide own multimedia content should encourage the user additionally to indicate content descriptions to the media to be uploaded, so that access to all end users can be granted regardless of their perceptive abilities. These additional descriptions can also be recorded by forms and added to the uploaded medium as an appropriate alt attribute. Barriers due to Captchas, Java-script or Flash elements can be minimized by programming alternatives. Inclusion of assistive technologies can thus be simplified.

3.4   Elimination of Barriers to Commenting Functions and Weblogs

Again, using commenting forms and related Captchas is particularly difficult for vision impaired and blind end users of assistive technologies. Input pages are mostly poorly structured and screen readers do not adequately read form fillings in editing fields and therefore do not forward it readably to a braille display. Users with cognitive and learning disabilities experience disability related barriers in dealing with written language by filling out input boxes. End users with dyslexia and reading disability are more likely inhibited by personal self-assessment and public biases in the use of weblogs and commenting functions. In writing web log entries technical as well as linguistic barriers likewise appear. Blind and vision impaired respondents report about problems to completely monitor and control formatting and representation options. Here again usability of editors depends on their controllability by assistive technologies. Thus, the amount of links in a Weblog leads to disorientation and navigation problems, because - if at all - it takes a while for a screen reader to display an entire list of links. As usage of weblogs and commenting functions is mostly form-based, accessibility problems again arise from insufficiently structured form-filling dialogues. To reduce these difficulties, the available elements of the applied descrip-tive language and a logical sequence of end user operations should hence be put into effect.

3.5   Eliminating Barriers in Dealing With Social Networking Sites (SNS)

So far at least between 15% and 29% of differently handicapped survey respondents use SNS. They only mention a few problems, which have partially appeared in the perceptibility and usability of executable functions and the perspicuity of the overall website. Most of the difficulties stem from the multiplicity of functions, information overload and from advertising banners disturbing website access by assistive technologies like screen readers. Also forms, graphic menus and buttons are often not properly designed. Especially for the blind and visually impaired respondents accessibility is a nevertheless particular factor to consider. As 91% of the blind respondents use a screen-reader, compatibility between speech processing software and readability of the web application is of crucial importance to usability. Despite low use of social networks, even the quite low problem values for cognitively and reading impaired survey respondents at least in tendency point out to the fact, that usability apart from raised requirements for media competence is also relevant for this user group. One non neglectable reason for relatively low user rates could also stem from previously indicated barriers of user registration, treatment of user profiles and photos or videos, which are often a precondition for activities in SNS applications.

References

1. Jenkins, H., Clinton, K., Purushotma, R., Robinson, Weigel, A.J.: Confronting the challenges of participatory culture: Media education for the 21st century. MacArthur Foundation (2006), http://www.digitallearning.macfound.org/
2. Beer, D., Burrows, R.: Sociology and, of and in Web 2.0: Some Initial Considerations. Sociological Research Online 12(5), 17 (2007), http://www.socresonline.org.uk/12/5/17.html
3. Davis, F.D., Bagozzi, R.P., Warshaw, P.R.: User acceptance of computer technology: A comparison of two theoretical models. Manag. Sci. 35, 982–1003 (1989)
4. Ma, Q., Liu, L.: The technology acceptance model: A meta-analysis of empirical findings. J. of Organizational and End User Computing 16, 59–72 (2004)
5. Berger, A., Caspers, T., Croll, J., Hoffmann, J., Kubicek, H., Peter, U., Ruth-Janneck, D., Trump, T.: Web 2.0/barrierefrei: Eine Studie zur Nutzung von Web 2.0 Anwendungen durch Menschen mit Behinderungen. Aktion Mensch e.V., POB, 53175 Bonn (2010)

Online Shopping Involving Consumers
with Visual Impairments – A Qualitative Study

Elisabeth Fuchs and Christine Strauss

University of Vienna, Department of Business Studies
Bruenner Str. 72, 1210 Vienna, Austria
{elisabeth.fuchs,christine.strauss}@univie.ac.at

Abstract. Despite the general popularity of online shopping, its usage is not entirely granted to all user groups. In this context, especially consumers with visual impairments are often faced with challenging barriers. To provide a better understanding of their actual needs and to identify experienced difficulties, personal in-depth interviews were conducted with visually impaired users. The obtained results of this empirical qualitative study form a knowledge base of consumer insights, which can be further used as a source for target-group specific improvements and innovations.

Keywords: visual impairment, online shopping, web accessibility, e-inclusion consumer research, qualitative study.

1   Introduction and Subject of Research

Although the enormous expansion of internet services has enriched everyday life of the general public [5], [7] not all user groups are able to profit from this broad diversity. Regarding present online shopping issues, web accessibility is still not granted sufficiently. Consumers with special needs, such as people with visual impairments, are often confronted with massive barriers and challenges during the process of purchasing products online. Therefore, certain individuals are often unable to benefit from the numerous advantages of e-shopping, which results in social discrimination.

To gain an in-depth insight into the current online shopping situation involving consumers with visual impairments, a qualitative study focusing in the individual needs and encountered challenges was conducted. The results were utilized for the identification of dimensions and attributes influencing online shopping processes. A scientific contribution is intended by providing a transfer of know-how, as the obtained knowledge base of consumer insights provides a foundation for future research in this field. Furthermore, the user-centred requirements may be utilized as a source for deriving target group specific innovations and solutions for reducing barriers in online shopping processes. Additionally, organizations operating in the area of e-commerce may profit from these results, in order to support strategy development for e-inclusion. Since it is essential to determine the actual user requirements and preferences of the target group beforehand to set relevant and suitable measures [13], the

K. Miesenberger et al. (Eds.): ICCHP 2012, Part I, LNCS 7382, pp. 378–385, 2012.
© Springer-Verlag Berlin Heidelberg 2012

user centred information provided by this study can be implemented for effective approaches concerning accessible online shops.

2   Background

Despite the social and economic relevance of this issue, there is still a lack of research focusing on the online shopping situation of consumers with visual impairments. Regarding present literature, a remarkable variety of studies analysed the e-commerce behaviour and preferences of the general public (e.g., [8], [14], [18]). Furthermore, there has been some research addressing the shopping behaviour of consumers with impairments in a physical environment (e.g., [1], [2]). Yet, only limited research has been performed on the combination of these two research fields (i.e., an online shopping insight by consumers with visual impairments).

An empirical study focusing on people with visual impairments in the American market has been conducted, which revealed that consumers with special needs gain a high level of personal value if the perceived "normalcy" of the shopping situation is high [1]. However, there is still no sound insight available regarding the European or Austrian market. To fill this research gap, our paper aims to provide a holistic consumer insight in the current online shopping situation experienced by consumers with visual impairments.

3   Research Design

3.1   Research Methodology

A qualitative approach was chosen due to the complexity of this research subject. As suggested by state-of-the-art literature, a qualitative research design is the most suitable method regarding areas of disability studies and in-depth consumer research [16]. An overview of the research model is demonstrated in Figure 1.

To gather relevant knowledge required for the execution of the scientific study and to the development of suitable interview guidelines, a literature research was performed at the initial stage of the research process. At the second research stage the

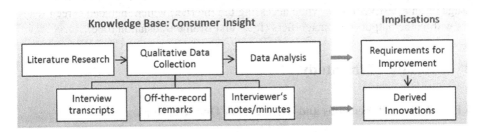

Fig. 1. Research approach: knowledge base and implications

required information concerning online shopping was collected through semi-structured and problem-centred interviews [17] with visually impaired persons, each of them lasting 25 to 75 minutes. Sources of the obtained qualitative data consist of the transcripts of the face-to-face interviews, and impression notes and minutes. Off-the-record remarks were further included to enrich the collected data, since the majority of participants tended to provide additional and more personal insights after the official interview had ended. To encourage a positive interview atmosphere, locations which were familiar to the participants were chosen, such as at home or at work. If participants did not agree on having their interviews recorded, notes were taken during the meeting, and transcribed immediately after the interview in order to prevent information loss.

During the interview the participants were questioned about their individual online shopping behaviour as well as their personal preferences and reasons for the choice of a certain shopping channel. They were further asked to describe experienced situations during the process of online shopping and provide examples for positive and negative incidences as well as the encountered barriers. Additionally, the participants were encouraged to express their individual wishes for improving the personal online shopping situation and identify factors which could encourage and motivate consumers to use online shops more often. The obtained material of the data collection was then processed using an empirical content analysis via the software Atlas.ti in order to provide an initial basis for a knowledge base of consumer insights. Due to the versatile nature of the qualitative approach, a best-practice research framework based on the "Blueprint Providing Guidelines for the Qualitative Analysis Process" [15] was selected. The qualitative data was unitized, categorized and coded during multiple runs using a combined deductive-inductive procedure [15].

3.2 Sample Description

Consumers with visual impairments who have experience with online shopping were selected as interview partners. In total, 15 potential candidates were contacted through an organization for visually impaired persons. Five candidates had never purchased products or services online and thus did not participate in this qualitative study. The final sample of interviewees consisted of six males and four females between 23 and 46 years who live and work in Vienna. The internet was either consumed daily (three participants), frequently (four) or infrequently (three). Each participant mentioned the usage of an assistive device while accessing the internet, which included screen readers with voice output (six), magnifiers (four) and Braille translation (one).

4   Results of the Study

4.1 Derived Dimensions and Attributes of Online Shopping

A broad variety of possible influence factors that had a direct impact the online shopping situation were mentioned by the participants. Those components were categorized into

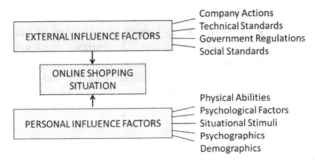

Fig. 2. Dimensions and attributes of influence factors

different key elements of an external or personal dimension, which consisted of attributes of influence on the online shopping quality. This developed model is presented in Figure 2.

Personal influence factors were partly derived from social studies and market segmentation literature [8], and include physical (e.g., impairments) as well as psychological factors (e.g., self-confidence and perception of abilities), situational stimuli (e.g., current demand for a specific product), psychographics (e.g., individual interests and preferences) and demographics (e.g., age, gender, income). Barriers in the online shopping process were perceived as being caused either by different external influences, or by personal factors like the physical as well as the psychological state of the participants.

5   Emotional Consumer Reactions

Regarding the consumer emotion dimension, catchwords which expressed different types of feelings experienced during an online shopping situation were classified and analyzed. The expressed emotions by the users regarding the experienced online shopping incidents varied from positive to negative feelings towards both the external and personal dimension.

Negative emotions may be viewed as an interference factor which had a discouraging effect during the shopping process. On a personal dimension, this was linked to psychological factors and included feelings like frustration with oneself, helplessness and a sense of feeling lost and overstrained due to the complicated setup. Furthermore, users articulated a feeling of being neglected and ignored as a part if the consumer group. Negative emotion expressed towards external influence factors included aggression and aversion towards companies for not taking their needs seriously, but only aiming at the mass market, as well as dissatisfaction and disappointment regarding insufficient government regulations and consequences.

Positive emotions, on the other hand, were experienced during online shopping situations if no barriers were encountered, thus creating a feeling of independence and satisfaction to achieve an activity without requiring help. This created a sense of being regarded as part of the consumer community. Furthermore, users were pleased to experience new possibilities of online services. However, online shopping was generally less regarded as a form of entertainment (only mentioned by two participants), rather than a functional process.

Interviewees who made a self-confident impression were more likely to view external factors as the cause of barriers (e.g., lack of actions taken by companies) rather than their personal features (visual impairment). In contrast, participants who as appeared to be quite shy and less talkative tended to consider themselves as not being able to cope with the complicated process of online shopping, and would therefore see the obstacle within their physical state, which is a severe social issue.

5.1   The Aspect of Independence

Although independence was mentioned as an important aspect by most interviewees, they still appreciated assistance during the shopping process. This was expressed either through help by an acquainted person in the same household or a member of the individual circle of friends, or a professional support such as consumer relationship personnel. The offer and quality of services was generally considered as an important factor of the online shopping process. Nine out of ten users mentioned the weakness of consumer services in online shopping, which was either mentioned as deficits in an assistive service (e.g., consumer hotline if complications arise) or a insufficient after sales support (e.g., if items are returned). Web shops with a high quality level of consumer services were preferred and generally regarded as more trustworthy.

5.2   Overview of Faced Complications

Each participant mentioned that complications were faced when purchasing products online. Barriers potentially arise in different levels of the online shopping process and further lead to complications within a stage, or even to the interruption of the whole activity. As a result, the user was either no longer motivated to continue the shopping process, or is not able to do so although the wish to continue existed. General technical inaccessibility of online shops were pointed out, e.g., if Flash was used which prevented a proper processing by assistive devices. Navigation was often impossible due to drop-down menus or self-refreshing websites. However, even if a site was generally accessible, their lack of usability was often perceived as a key obstacle. This was mainly due to a complicated structure and an unclear product categorization, which influenced the user orientation in a negative way. It was overall criticized by the interviewees that most companies tend to focus very strongly on the optical appearance of a shopping platform without providing an accessible alternative, thus neglecting special needs of consumers with visual impairments. This was mainly the case concerning the information depth of product descriptions, when most of the relevant attributes were solely shown on an image without providing alternative text. Hence it was difficult to determine if a selected product was in fact the one demanded by the consumer. A further key issue mentioned by the users was the arising difficulty of the payment process, which either did not function properly or was regarded as intransparent. Complications further occurred after the actual purchasing process, e.g., if a consumer did not receive an order and had to send a complaint, or wanted to return a product and obtain a monetary refund.

5.3   Product Choice

Since the consumer's shopping behaviour is influenced by a large number of factors, the choice of purchasing products online is a rather complicated process. It can potentially be affected by attributes of both the personal and external dimension. The preferred types of items bought online as well as the decision for specific products was mainly linked to the personal factor of psychographics, which included the consumer's individual tastes and interests. External factors had a rather limited influence on the expressed product choice (e.g., trends in fashion of clothing items mentioned by a female participant, keeping up to date with technology mentioned by three male participants). Situational stimuli (e.g., if a consumer demands a specific product at a certain point of time, such as purchasing a birthday gift) were also mentioned. Personal behavioural elements included multi-channel usage, word-of-mouth-recommendation, as well as a high brand loyalty towards known products. It was observed that a positive association with a brand or a product due to a favourable experience made in the past is a key driver of product choice. Further influence factors included the current demand of the individual consumer, product availability, price, quality and related services.

5.4   Security and Trust Issues

In total, eight out of ten interviewees mentioned security and trust related issues in the context of online shopping. This mainly included the fear of abuse of personal data by third parties, such as credit card details. Security concerns were either directed towards potential hackers which might illegally obtain personalized data, or directly related to the trustworthiness of unknown online companies. Only three participants mentioned the awareness of quality seals and labels of online shops.

6   Conclusion

Users with visual impairments wish to be regarded as an included part of society and actively participate in day-to-day routine. Hence, user requirements for online shopping do not solely include overall basic web accessibility improvements, such as less dynamic elements and a higher focus on function instead of stylish graphical elements. Additionally, the psychological aspect of visually impaired consumers has to be taken into account. Users demand an online shopping experience without discouraging barriers. Furthermore, they wish to be regarded as a part of the economically valuable consumer society. This may be achieved if special consumer needs are taken seriously by companies and proper target group related measures for implementing accessible websites are taken. Regarding the psychological aspects of users, this also coincides with empirical results of previous research on consumer normalcy performed by Baker [1].

Altogether, a diverse range of reasons for and against the usage of online shopping was provided by the interviewees. The purchasing channel selection (online vs. traditional) also greatly varied depending on the product categories as well as the demographic and psychographic factors of the users. However, the key argument for avoiding specific online shops was their inaccessibility as well as the difficulty regarding navigation and orientation. It was discovered that the current online shopping situation was not regarded as favourable by the interviewees due to high degree of encountered barriers. Further critical aspects included security issues, insufficient product descriptions, difficulties during the payment process, lack of consumer services offered and a time consuming process of returning items.

Most of the interviewees mentioned that they would prefer to use online shopping offerings more frequently, if fewer complications were encountered. Hence, it is advisable to encourage the provision of accessible websites, which could potentially be achieved by tightening government regulations in the area of e-commerce, by improving the reward system for companies, or through intensifying social awareness [10], [11], [12]. As a result, users with special needs may enjoy the access to an enormous amount of online offers, whereas companies benefit from a potentially higher profit [4] caused by the high brand loyalty of visually impaired consumers, as well as an improvement of their perceived social image [8] and a more favourable search engine ranking [3]. To overcome severe security and trust concerns, the enhancement of data encryption as well as the emphasis on quality seals might be an effective solution.

The rapid progress in technology leads to a large variety of potential innovation for improving the online shopping experience of users with special needs. Derived from the results of the consumer insights, suggestions for possible innovations as well as extended usage of existing technologies can be developed in the future. This could include for instance the extended integration of technology into day-to-day activities, such as cameras acting as virtual eyes, an improved algorithmic analysis for digital images, intelligent software and product search solutions and an advanced integration of hardware devices such as hyperbraille [8] to enable a smoother navigation process as well as an accessible translation of graphical elements.

However, even if innovative and assistive solutions are enhanced, it is likewise essential that companies design their online shops in an accessible way. The improvement of technical solutions combined with the willingness to offer accessible websites is required to achieve e-inclusion.

References

1. Baker, S.M.: Consumer normalcy: Understanding the value of shopping through narratives of consumers with visual impairments. Journal of Retailing 82(1), 37–50 (2006)
2. Baker, S.M., Holland, J., Kaufman-Scarborough, C.: How consumers with disabilities perceive "welcome" in retail servicescapes: a critical incident study. The Journal of Services Marketing 21(3), 160–173 (2007)
3. Hartjes, R., Strauss, C.: Analyzing Effects of Web Accessibility – A Framework to Determine Changes in Website Traffic and Success. In: Miesenberger, K., Klaus, J., Zagler, W., Karshmer, A. (eds.) ICCHP 2010. LNCS, vol. 6179, pp. 449–455. Springer, Heidelberg (2010)

4. Heerdt, V., Strauss, C.: A Cost-Benefit Approach for Accessible Web Presence. In: Miesenberger, K., Klaus, J., Zagler, W., Burger, D. (eds.) ICCHP 2004. LNCS, vol. 3118, pp. 323–330. Springer, Heidelberg (2004)
5. Heinemann, G.: Multi-Channel-Handel: Erfolgsfaktoren und Best Practices. Gabler Verlag, Wiesbaden (2008)
6. HyperBraille (2012), http://www.hyperbraille.eu (last accessed January 19, 2012)
7. Kaufman-Scarborough, C., Lindquist, J.D.: E-shopping in a multiple channel environment. Journal of Consumer Marketing 19(4), 333–350 (2002)
8. Kotler, P.: Markting Management. Prentice Hall International, New Jersey (2002)
9. Koufaris, M., Kambil, A., LaBarbera, P.A.: Consumer Behavior in Web-Based Commerce: An Empirical Study. International Journal of Electronic Commerce 6(2), 115–138 (2001)
10. Leitner, M.-L., Miesenberger, K., Ortner, D., Strauss, C.: Web Accessibility Conformity Assessment – Implementation Alternatives for a Quality Mark in Austria. In: Miesenberger, K., Klaus, J., Zagler, W., Karshmer, A.I. (eds.) ICCHP 2006. LNCS, vol. 4061, pp. 271–278. Springer, Heidelberg (2006)
11. Leitner, M.-L., Strauss, C.: Exploratory Case Study Research on Web Accessibility. In: Miesenberger, K., Klaus, J., Zagler, W., Karshmer, A.I. (eds.) ICCHP 2008. LNCS, vol. 5105, pp. 490–497. Springer, Heidelberg (2008)
12. Leitner, M.-L., Strauss, C.: Organizational Motivations for Web Accessibility Implementation – A Case Study. In: Miesenberger, K., Klaus, J., Zagler, W., Karshmer, A. (eds.) ICCHP 2010. LNCS, vol. 6179, pp. 392–399. Springer, Heidelberg (2010)
13. Riekhof, H.-C.: Customer Insights: Wissen, wie der Kunde tickt, Mehr Erfolg durch Markt-Wirkungsmodelle. Gabler Verlag, Wiesbaden (2010)
14. Srinivasan, S., Anderson, R., Ponnavolu, K.: Customer loyalty in e-commerce: an exploration of its antecedents and consequences. Journal of Retailing 78(1), 41–50 (2002)
15. Srnka, K., Koeszegi, S.: From words to numbers: how to transform qualitative data into meaningful quantitative results. Schmalenbach Business Review 59, 29–57 (2007)
16. Waldschmidt, A.: Warum Disability Studies? Profil und Aufgaben eines neuen Forschungsfeldes. Presentation at the Conference "Barrierefrei? – Zur Integration der Perspektive der Disability und Gender/Queer Studies". University of Vienna (January 28, 2011)
17. Witzel, A.: Das problemzentrierte Interview. Forum Qualitative Sozialforschung (2000), http://nbn-resolving.de/urn:nbn:de:0114-fqs0001228 (last accessed January 5, 2012)
18. Wolfinbarger, M., Gilly, M.C.: Shopping online for freedom, control, and fun. California Management Review 43(2), 34–55 (2001)

Website Accessibility Metrics:
Introduction to the Special Thematic Session

Shadi Abou-Zahra

W3C Web Accessibility Initiative (WAI)
shadi@w3.org

Abstract. In many situations it is useful to measure the level of accessibility of websites using a more continual scale rather than the rather limited set of four ordinal values (none, A, AA, and AAA) proposed by the W3C/WAI Web Content Accessibility Guidelines (WCAG). For example, a continual scale allows more granular benchmarking of websites to compare them or to help assess improvements made over time. However, finding reliable metrics is a non-trivial challenge for a variety of reasons. This paper introduces a Special Thematic Session to explore this challenge, further to a previously held online symposium of the W3C/WAI Research and Development Working Group (RDWG).

Keywords: Web Accessibility, Accessibility Metrics, Benchmarking, Quality Assurance, Web Content Accessibility Guidelines (WCAG).

1 Introduction to this Special Thematic Session (STS)

On 5 December 2011, the W3C/WAI Research and Development Working Group (RDWG) held an online symposium on Website Accessibility Metrics[1], to explore the current state-of-the-art in the field. 11 extended abstracts were finally accepted and published as part of the symposium proceedings. These published papers include:

- Integration of Web Accessibility Metrics into a Semi-Automatic evaluation process, Naftali M. and Clúa O., University of Buenos Aires;
- Measuring Accessibility Barriers on Large Scale Sets of Pages, Battistelli M., Mirri S., Muratori L.A., and Salomoni P., University of Bologna;
- A Template-Aware Web Accessibility Metric, Fernandes N., Lopes R., and Carriço L., University of Lisbon;
- A Metric to Make Different DTDs Documents Evaluations Comparable, Battistelli M., Mirri S., Muratori L.A., and Salomoni P., University of Bologna;
- Lexical Quality as a Measure for Textual Web Accessibility, Rello L., Universitat Pompeu Fabra and Baeza-Yates R., Yahoo! Research;

---

[1] http://www.w3.org/WAI/RD/2011/metrics/

K. Miesenberger et al. (Eds.): ICCHP 2012, Part I, LNCS 7382, pp. 386–387, 2012.

- Attaining Metric Validity and Reliability with the Web Accessibility Quantitative Metric, Vigo M., University of Manchester, and Abascal J., Aizpurua A., and Arrue M., University of the Basque Country;
- The Case for a WCAG-Based Evaluation Scheme with a Graded Rating Scale, Fischer D., DIAS GmbH, and Wyatt T., feld.wald.wiese;
- A Zero in eChecker Equals a 10 in eXaminator: A Comparison Between Two Metrics by their Scores, Fernandes J., UMIC Knowledge Society Agency - Ministry of Education & Science, and Benavidez C., eXaminator programmer;
- Context-Tailored Web Accessibility Metrics, Vigo M., University of Manchester;
- Web Accessibility Metrics For A Post Digital World, Sloan D., University of Dundee and Kelly B., University of Bath;
- Towards a Score Function for WCAG 2.0 Benchmarking, Nietzio A., Forschungsinstitut Technologie und Behinderung (FTB), and Eibegger M., and Goodwin M., and Snaprud M., Tingtun AS;

This Special Thematic Session (STS) follows the previously held online symposium, to further explore this topic.

2   Areas Covered by this Special Thematic Session (STS)

This Special Thematic Session (STS) includes the following paper contributions:

- Integrating manual and automatic evaluations to measure accessibility barriers, presented by Salomoni P.;
- Following the WCAG 2.0 Techniques: Experiences from designing a WCAG 2.0 checking tool, presented by Nietzio A.;
- Lexical Quality as a Measure for Textual Web Accessibility, presented by Rello L.;
- Assessing the Effort of Repairing the Accessibility of Web Sites, presented by Fernandes N.;
- Accessibility testing of a healthy lifestyles social network, presented by Sik Lányi C.;

Further open research questions and ideas have been identified and are documented in the wiki of the W3C/WAI Research and Development Working Group (RDWG) at: http://w3.org/WAI/RD/wiki/Benchmarking_Web_Accessibility_Metrics. The RDWG welcomes further discussion around this topic and contribution of related resources.

Acknowledgements. This Special Thematic Session (STS) is jointly organized with support from the EC-funded WAI-ACT[2] Project.

---

[2] http://www.w3.org/WAI/ACT/

Integrating Manual and Automatic Evaluations to Measure Accessibility Barriers

Paola Salomoni[1], Silvia Mirri[1], Ludovico A. Muratori[2], and Matteo Battistelli[2]

[1] Computer Science Department, University of Bologna
{paola.salomoni,silvia.mirri}@unibo.it
[2] Polo Scientifico Didattico di Cesena University of Bologna
{matteo.battistelli4,ludovico.muratori3}@unibo.it

Abstract. Explicit syntax and implicit semantics of Web coding are typically addressed as distinct dominions in providing metrics for content accessibility. A more down-to-earth portrait about barriers and their impact on users with disabilities could be obtained whether any quantitative synthesis about number and size of barriers integrated measurements from automatic checks and human assessments. In this work, we present a metric to evaluate accessibility as a unique meas-ure of both syntax correctness and semantic consistence, according to some general assumptions about relationship and dependencies between them. WCAG 2.0 guidelines are used to define boundaries for any single barrier eval-uation, either from a syntactic point of view, or a subjective/human one. In or-der to assess our metric, gathered data form a large scale accessibility monitor has been utilized.

Keywords: Web accessibility metrics, Web accessibility barriers, accessibility evaluation.

1 Introduction

Summing up, national and trans-national regulations about Web accessibility promot-ed and translated guidelines to a set of mandatory constraints, operating rules and evaluation practices (inherited, in case, from the guidelines themselves). Tools and procedures for controlling the respect of the law assumed a key role, due to the very large scale and dynamics of its target. Thousands Web sites, hundreds thousands Web pages must typically be evaluated to be syntactically correct and semantically con-sistent, as regard to the removal (or, at least, to the reduction) of barriers in acquiring Web content by users with disabilities. Automatic tools effectively satisfy the syntac-tic aspect of evaluation, whilst human interventions are needed for the semantic one. In order to provide a suitable, meaningful synthesis of the processes above, metrics about accessibility level have been designed, implemented and investigated. One of the main aspects of such researches is the disjunction between the syntactic dominion and the semantic one in addressing measures.

Starting from an application called AMA (Accessibility Monitoring Application), we designed and implemented to evaluate and collect accessibility status of large sets

K. Miesenberger et al. (Eds.): ICCHP 2012, Part I, LNCS 7382, pp. 388–395, 2012.

of Web sites (according to different guidelines, including WCAG 2.0), we approached the integration of semantic and syntactic measurements to a unique, consistent value. As we will detail in the following, we made some very general assumption about grouping, ordering and relating specific checks (coming from WCAG 2.0) to provide a final formula which is consistent to a realistic evaluation of barriers, both in terms of syntax and in terms of experts' assessments.

The remainder of this paper is organized as follows. Section 2 (Related work) will introduce main related work. Section 3 (The VaMoLà System) will describe the systems which have been exploited in order to gather and report data about Web sites accessibility, by means of automatic and semi-automatic evaluation and monitoring activities. Section 4 (Methodology and approach) will detail our proposed metrics, measuring automatic and manual evaluations and will detail how our metric can be exploited weight an accessibility barriers. Section 5 (Involving experts' assessment) will present an experiment we have assessed with a group of experts. Finally Section 6 (Discussion and conclusions) will close the paper, by showing some final considerations and future work.

2   Related Work

In literature, different metrics to measure Web accessibility barriers have been de-fined and assessed on several works by generally assuming the necessity of a quanti-tative, continuous scale to cover accessibility degrees. They try to go beyond the di-chotomy between an accessible and a not accessible Web content, since binary values might be not meaningful for quality assurance and assessment or they could report misleading values. Some of them are based on specific Web pages sampling methods (often from the same Web site) and they usually include an intense manual control phase too, which can be conducted by experts or users [3], [11], [12], [14]. The metric we present here has been inspired by such previous and related works (in particular by Giorgio Brajnik's Barrier Walkthrough method [2 - 3]), but it has been defined and adapted so as to support an accessibility monitoring activity on a large set of Web sites and to take into account manual evaluations done by different human operators. Brajnik and Lomuscio [3] have defined the Semi-Automatic Method for measuring Barriers of Accessibility (SAMBA), to integrate manual and automatic evaluations on the strength of barriers harshness and of tools errors rate, on the basis of the Barrier Walkthrough method [2]. Through a three phases process a "disability vector" and a "confidence intervals severity matrix" are created, whose values report the probability that each barrier affects a particular disability. Finally, a barrier density factor is com-puted to state the probability that each line of markup may contain a barrier (it is the ratio between the amount of potential barriers and the number of markup lines).

3   The VaMoLà System

VaMoLà is the Italian acronym for "Accessibility Validator and Monitor". It is a sys-tem integrating two applications which respectively provide automatic accessibility checks and periodically monitor accessibility of a wide set of sites. I has been designed and implemented to support surveillance on the Italian Public Administration Web Sites, according to the prescriptions of the Italian Regulation (also known as the Stanca Act [7]).

The tool for accessibility evaluation is based on AChecker [8, 10]. It automatically checks a single URL and allows end-users to specify which requirements (of the Italian Regulation) must be controlled. After the evaluation process, It reports an analysis of actual and potential barriers it has found, as well as some guidelines to the subjective manual evaluation. Details on the VaMoLà Validator design issues and implementation can be found in [1].

The monitoring tool, namely the Vamolà Monitor let the users to provide periodical analysis on a set of Web sites, according to their administrative role inside the Public Administration and the geographical position of their referring institutions. A plethora of parameters can be set up to gather and record specific data about barriers, according to the International Guidelines (WCAG 1.0 and 2.0) and the specific constraints the Italian law imposes. Large scale geo-political approach of monitoring is provided through a suitable Web interface mashing up Google services to localize resources and generating suitable reports (either tabular or graphics). More details about the VaMoLà Monitoring system can be found in [9].

4   Methodology and Approach

The goal of our metric is measuring how far a Web page is from its accessibility version. In other words, it is a quantitative synthesis about how much accessibility barriers affect user's browsing by means of assistive technologies. Hence, the lower is the resulting value and the better is the accessibility level of the evaluated Web page. To associate errors to barriers in the most effective way, we analyzed WCAG 2.0 [13] and their related Techniques [13]. For each error, success criteria and techniques references have been used to identify disabilities/assistive technologies it affects.

A first version of our metric (named Barriers Impact Factor, BIF) is computed on the basis of a barrier-error association table [9]. This table reports, for each error detected in evaluating WCAG 2.0, the list of assistive technologies/disabilities affected by such an error. Barriers have been grouped into 7 sets, which impact in the following assistive technologies and disabilities: screen reader/blindness; screen magnifier/low vision; color blindness; input device in-dependence/movement impairments; deafness; cognitive disabilities; photosensitive epilepsy. For the sake of simplicity, in this version of our metric manually checked controls are not taken into account.

In order to better quantify accessibility barriers within a Web page, thereby providing a more realistic synthesis, we have decided to take into account the whole amount of controls (including manual assessments, once an expert has done his/her evaluation). First of all, we have analyzed the validation checks, comparing them with WCAG 2.0 success criteria [13] and identified relationships among them. When a validation check fails, it means that a certain accessibility error occurs or that a manual control is necessary (to certify the effective presence of an error or not). Success criteria suggest checks on the basis of Techniques and Failures [13]. Some of them are devoted to identify different aspects and shapes of the same accessibility barrier, showing some (necessary) intersections in checks, which have to be manually controlled. In order to avoid overlapping controls on the same accessibility error, we have grouped all the checks into disjoined sets, on the basis of each barrier. Whenever at least one check of a specific group fails, then the related accessibility barrier is actually found in the analyzed Web page. Each barrier is related to one (and only one) success criterion (and so to one level of conformity, A, AA or AAA). We have assumed that, differently from syntactic shortcomings which take binary values, manual evaluations take values on the [0, 1] real numbers interval. In particular, 1 means that an accessibility error occurs, 0 means the absence of accessibility error. Defining our metric, we have taken into account that some barriers should be evaluated both with an automatic parsing and a manual assessment. Each automatic control detects well-known errors, defined by specific syntactic pattern (that in our case are directly referred to WCAG 2.0 techniques [13]). Then the automatic evaluation system outputs 1 for each detected barrier, 0 in case the barrier has been removed. The simplest case to consider is the combination between the `<img>` element and its **alt** attribute:

1. If the ALT attribute is omitted the automatic check outputs 1.
2. If the ALT attribute is present the automatic check outputs 0.

In both cases a manual evaluation could state that:

- there is no lack of information once the images are hidden (this can happen in case 1, if the image is a decorative one);
- there is a lack of information once the image is hidden.

The new BIF value for each barrier is computed as follows:

$$\text{cBIF}(i) = \sum_i \frac{(m(i) * E_m(i) + a(i) * E_a(i))}{m(i) + a(i)} * \frac{weight(i)}{\#check(i)} \qquad (1)$$

where:

- i represents an accessibility barrier by detected errors;
- $cBIF(i)$ is the Barrier Impact Factor referred to i, which takes into account both manual and automatic checks;
- $Ea(i)$ represents the number of detected errors which causes the i barrier and which are automatically controlled;
- $Em(i)$ represents the number of detected errors which causes the i barrier and which are manually controlled by an accessibility expert;
- $weight(i)$ represents the weight which has been assigned to the i barrier;
- $m(i)$ is a parametric weight assigned to the manual evaluation related to i barrier;
- $a(i)$ is a parametric weight assigned to the automatic evaluation related to i barrier;
- $\#check(i)$ represents the number of checks (related to the i barrier) that the system has actually performed (to normalize the number of errors in terms of evaluated checks).

The total cBIF value is computed by summing the cBIF values related to all the barriers faced by the already mentioned seven types of disabilities/assistive technologies. More details about this new version of the metric can be found in [10].

Parameters $m(i)$ and $a(i)$ aim to weight respectively the role of manual and automatic evaluations. Such parameters can be differently assessed for each i barrier and all the cases can be classified as follows:

1. $m(i)=a(i)$: in this case the formula is a mere average between Em(i) and Ea(i);
2. $m(i)>a(i)$: in this case the failure in manual assessment is considered more significant than the automatic one;
3. $m(i)<a(i)$: in this case the failure in automatic assessment is considered more significant than the manual one.

All the values combinations are possible and to mix all the cases in a metric is another issue which has to be addressed. We could assert that the manual assessment is more important than the automatic one (case 2 in the previous list). We could assert that they identically quantify the height of a barrier afflicting the navigation done by the user with disabilities (case 1). Finally, we could say that the automatic assessment is more important than the manual one (case 3). There are many reasons supporting all these points of view and it's out of the scope of this paper discussing this aspect.

5   Involving Experts' Assessments

We have evaluated the accessibility of a set of Web pages, involving a group of experts (composed by 5 people). As Web pages sample, we have chosen the Web sites of the Emilia-Romagna Region Provinces. We have evaluated those pages according to WCAG 2.0 success criterion 1.1.1 [13], by using the automatic validator of the AMA system. Then, we asked to the experts to rate accessibility barriers for the same pages (mainly related to adequateness of image textual alternatives), according to a range over the real numbers interval [0, 1]. During the whole experiment we have assigned 2 to parameter m and 1 to parameter a. The experts have faced different kind of situations and errors in the textual alternatives of images, from too long **alt** text for pure decorative images to the absence of **alt**, **title** or any other textual cue for images used as links. Fig. 1 shows a decorative image which is not used as a link, it is not equipped with a title attribute with an alt text with more than 83 chars. The automatic evaluation system detects an error due to the extreme length of the **alt** content (the related error message is: *"Image Alt text is too long"*). Moreover, the image shows a motorbiker on a provincial road, while the alt text provides information about the winter public service of snow-ploughs, as follows: *"Responsibility for SS45 Road is in charge of ANAS; on Provincial roads more than 100 snowploughs are involved"*. Note that no snowflake or snowplough is shown in the image.

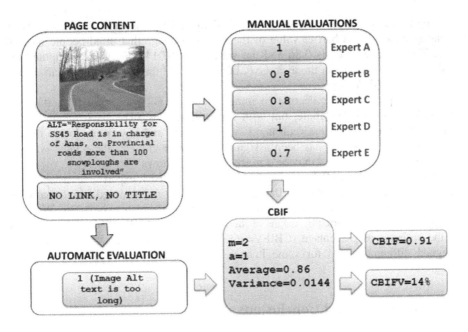

Fig. 1. Manual evaluations of a decorative image textual alternative (with a too long alt text)

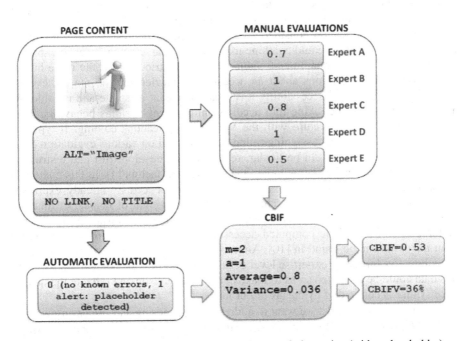

Fig. 2. Manual evaluations of a decorative image textual alternative (with a placeholder)

Experts A and D have assigned 1, experts B and C have assigned 0.8, finally expert E has assigned 0.7 as barrier value of the analyzed image that blind people have to face. The average value is 0.86 and the variance is 0.0144. We have computed the CBIF metrics by means of the average (CBIF=0.91) and the CBIFV as the variance as per-centage (CBIFV=14%).

Fig. 2 depicts another decorative image which is not used as a link, it is not equipped with a title attribute, but with a placeholder as `alt` text (*"Image"*). The automatic evaluation system returns no syntactic error and a warning due to the detected placeholder which has been assigned as the `alt` content (the related warning message is: *"Image Alt text may be a placeholder"*) is shown.

Expert A has assigned 0.7, experts B and D have assigned 1, expert C has assigned 0.8 and finally expert E has assigned 0.5 as barrier value of the analyzed image that blind people have to face. The average value is 0.8 and the variance is 0.036. We have computed the CBIF metrics by means of the average value (CBIF=0.53) and the CBIFV as the variance as percentage (CBIFV=36%). Variance shows that the experts have assigned different values for some images evaluation, thereby expressing that they disagree.

6   Discussion and Conclusions

With this work we faced the problem to portrait accessibility barriers as a suitable arrangement of formal aspects (syntactic correctness) and semantics ones (human judgment). Thus, we designed a metrics taking into account both such aspects.

During this work several considerations have drawing interesting clues for future researches. First of all we could combine many humans' assessment so as to express a more stable and reliable quantitative value from our metric. In fact, the more human operators provide evaluations about an accessibility barrier and the more the value they express (in terms of accessibility level) can be meant as stable and reliable. An interesting idea could be taking into account online rating systems behaviors. They have become a popular feature with the Web 2.0 applications coming. It typically involves a set of reviewers assigning rating scores (based on various evaluation criteria) to a set of objects [8]. In particular, reviewers can develop trust and distrust on rated objects depending on a few rating and trust related factors [4]. In this context, it is worth noting that new reviewers rating can be influenced by already expressed evaluations from other reviewers. This new additional weight of manual evaluations cannot be a mere average of values, because variance must be considered in order to reinforce or not the whole computed accessibility level. Some more considerations about this issue can be found in [10]. Another interesting issue related to such a context is how to express the expertise level of humans who provide manual assessments. This data could be exploited so as to make even more realistic and reliable the quantitative synthesis computing by means of our metric.

Some more future works we want to address are: proposing and discussing weights for the whole WCAG 2.0 set of barriers; (ii) investigate how the number of experts involved in the evaluation, together with the variance, could influence the reliability of the computed values (on the basis of previous results in this field, available in [14]). All these aspects should be been taken into account in improving our metric.

References

1. Battistelli, M., Mirri, S., Muratori, L.A., Salomoni, P., Spagnoli, S.: Making the Tree Fall Sound: Reporting Web Accessibility with the VaMoLà Monitor. Accepted for Publication in Proceedings of the 5th International Conference on Methodologies, Technologies and Tools enabling e-Government, Camerino, Italy, June 30-July 1 (2011)
2. Brajnik, G.: Web Accessibility Testing: When the Method Is the Culprit. In: Miesenberger, K., Klaus, J., Zagler, W.L., Karshmer, A.I. (eds.) ICCHP 2006. LNCS, vol. 4061, pp. 156–163. Springer, Heidelberg (2006)
3. Brajnik, G., Lomuscio, R.: SAMBA: a Semi-Automatic Method for Measuring Barriers of Accessibility. In: Proceedings of the 9th International ACM SIGACCESS Conference on Computers and Accessibility, pp. 43–50 (2007)
4. Chua, F.C.T., Lim, E.: Trust network inference for online rating data using generative models. In: KDD 2010 Proceedings of the 16th ACM SIGKDD International Conference on Knowledge Discovery and Data Mining, Washington, D.C., USA (2010)
5. Gay, G.R., Li, C.: AChecker: Open, Interactive, Customizable, Web Accessibility Checking. In: Proceedings of the 7th ACM International Cross Disciplinary Conference on Web Acces-sibility (W4A 2010), Raleigh, North Carolina, USA. ACM Press, New York (2010)
6. IDRC, Ontario College of Art and Design, AChecker (2012), http://www.atutor.ca/achecker/index.php
7. Italian parliament. Law nr. 4 – 01/09/2004. Official Journal nr. 13 – 01/17/ 2004 (January 2004)
8. Lauw, H.W., Lim, E.: A Multitude of Opinions: Mining Online Rating Data. In: Proceedings of the National Science Foundation Symposium on Next Generation of Data Mining and Cyber-Enabled Discovery for Innovation (NGDM 2007), Baltimore (October 2007)
9. Mirri, S., Muratori, L.A., Salomoni, P.: Monitoring accessibility: large scale evaluations at a geo political level. In: Proceedings of the 13th International ACM SIGACCESS Conference on Computers and Accessibility (ASSETS 2011), Dundee, Scotland, UK (October 2011)
10. Mirri, S., Muratori, L.A., Salomoni, P., Battistelli, M.: Getting one voice: tuning up experts' assessment in measuring accessibility. In: Proceedings of the W4A 2012, Lyon, France, April 16-17. ACM Press, New York (2012)
11. Parmanto, B., Zeng, X.: Metric for Web Accessibility Evaluation. Journal of the American Society for Information Science and Technology 56(13), 1394–1404 (2005)
12. Vigo, M., Arrue, M., Brajnik, G., Lomuscio, R., Abascal, J.: Quantitative Metrics for Measuring Web Accessibility. In: Proceedings of the W4A 2007, Banff, Alberta, Canada, May 7-8, pp. 99–107. ACM Press, New York (2007)
13. World Wide Web Consortium. Web Content Accessibility Guidelines (WCAG) 2.0 (2008), http://www.w3.org/TR/WCAG20/
14. Yesilada, Y., Brajnik, G., Harper, S.: How Much Does Expertise Matter? A Barrier Walkthrough Study with Experts and Non-Experts. In: Proceedings of the Eleventh International ACM SIGACCESS Conference on Computers and Accessibility, ASSESTS 2009 (2009)

Assessing the Effort of Repairing
the Accessibility of Web Sites

Nádia Fernandes and Luís Carriço

LaSIGE/University of Lisbon
Campo Grande, Edifício C6
1749-016 Lisboa, Portugal
{nadiaf,lmc}@di.fc.ul.pt

Abstract. The paper presents a new metric and a framework to assess the effort of repairing the accessibility of a Web site. For that all the HTML elements of all the pages of a site are considered, excluding those that are duplicated. The rationale is that those elements are originated in a reusable construct, such as a template and, therefore, need to be corrected only once. The evaluation then applies the accessibility evaluation techniques on those elements instead of on all the instances that are presented to the user. The reported fails and warnings are then computed in a simple sum metric.

The paper also describes the validation experiment of both metric and framework, providing very important results. These may well contribute to a different perspective from managers and development team leaders about the effort to revamp the accessibility of a site.

Keywords: Web Accessibility, Templates, Automated Evaluation, Metrics.

1 Introduction

Front-end Web development is highly centred on the use of templates to ease implementing and maintaining coherence of Web site structural features. As an estimate 40-50% of the Web content uses templates [1]. However, automatic accessibility evaluations are usually done in Web pages as a whole, i.e., after all templates are composed into the Web page's final form. That happens because templates are usually an incomplete specification that gets filled-in either by the development environment, the delivering platform or, in more dynamic applications by complex coding procedures. As such, it is important to evaluate accessibility as close as possible to what is delivered to the user [2].

The drawback of this Web site evaluation procedure is the possibility of guiding to misleading accessibility results, for the point of view of the developer [3] or of the team manager that tries to assess the effort of repairing a web site. For example, if a template intrinsically contains an accessibility problem, that problem is reported as often as the template is used within the page/site. The same errors and warnings are repeated over and over, which may increase the final reports and, therefore, may confuse developers, concealing fundamental repairing issues.

K. Miesenberger et al. (Eds.): ICCHP 2012, Part I, LNCS 7382, pp. 396–403, 2012.
© Springer-Verlag Berlin Heidelberg 2012

Assessing the repairing complexity, of such a page or site, while using the available metrics, will certainly discourage the development teams from correcting the accessibility issues. A bad result, deriving from a large number of errors in an assessment, may be a consequence of a small number of problems in a frequently used template that can be rapidly corrected. Therefore, common accessibility metrics may be misleading.

This paper presents a measurement solution to more adequately assess the repairing effort of a page or site, and it is part of an automatic Web accessibility evaluation framework. Since it may not have access to the original code, it builds on a simple algorithm for automatic detection of templates that, although approximate, it will still provide a relevant accuracy for the objective at hand.

An experimental study is described that shows the impact of templates' usage in the reported number of accessibility problems of a site. The algorithm is validated trough expert inspection of a sample of the sites assessed in the experiment. The differences between using and not using the template aware approach at the page and intra-page level are clear and sustain the above mentioned arguments.

2   Requirements and Related Work

2.1   Template Detection

Template detection is often used in the fields of Information Retrieval and Web page Clustering. Towards information retrieval, template detection can positively impact performance and resource usage in processes of analysis of HTML pages [5]. Regarding Web page Clustering, templates could help in cluster structurally similar Web pages [4]. Several techniques have been used to detect templates that provide different levels of accuracy [6]. However, for the purpose of estimating effort, a more expedite, possibly less accurate, approach can be used.

Although most of these works are not at the level of accessibility, it was already acknowledged the importance of considering Web page templates in accessibility issues [8] and it was suggested including accessible content templates, in order to preserve the Web page's accessibility [10]. However, the approach hereby proposed is complementary as it is both a means for: i) assessing the effort of repairing a site's accessibility that was originally developed using templates; ii) introducing accessible templates as a form of rapidly repairing a page.

2.2   Metrics

Metrics facilitate the understanding, the observation of experimental studies results and the assessment of the obtained results. There are already some approaches in this matter: UWEM [9] defined as an accessibility metric that uses the failure rate of each Web page to compute a quality value; Lopes et al [7] compute different views (optimistic, conservative and strict) into a final score of accessibility quality; WAQM

[8] calculates the failure rate and the average of the results for each Web page, considering the page weight in the site.

Web Accessibility Metrics allow us to assess the accessibility results. However, none of the studies/approaches/metrics mentioned above directly addresses the developers' efforts to correct the accessibility problems, in relation to the common development process. Templates are a fundamental concept in this process and must be considered.

3   The Accessibility Repairing Effort Metric

The proposed metric to assess the effort of repairing the accessibility of a Web site (AREM) simply considers the sum of the number of fails and warnings reported by accessibility evaluation techniques, towards all the elements of the site, excluding repeated instances. Basically, it only considers once each element of the whole site. So if an element is defined as part of a template (or any other reusable construct), that element is only assessed once, as a fail, warning of pass, for each of the applicable evaluation techniques. We denote those as "primitive elements" in the site, in opposition to its multiple instantiations that are usually considered in metrics. We do not normalize the score since, in the end, this should be converted to an effort unit (e.g. person*hour).

Note that the objective of AREM is to measure the effort to repair the accessibility of a Web site. Commonly, metrics assess the quality of the accessibility of a Web page/site. Although related, these objectives can be at odds. As mentioned before, using any of the currently available metrics, a site, requiring a small effort to repair its accessibility, may report a very large number of fails and warnings. For that to occur, that site may even just be a well-designed one, strongly based on templates and libraries, yet, unfortunately, containing some accessibility issues in just some of those templates.

As a complement, we also propose variations of the normalized metrics in Lopes et al [7]. The choice could as easily fall in several of the other metrics available in the literature. In this case, though, the objective is not to assess effort but quality, as most metrics do. The difference here is that the quality measurement will assess the accessibility of site construction and not the perceived quality of the site towards end-users. Both, of course are relevant.

4   The Platform for Accessibility Evaluation

To compute the metrics we propose a solution is based on QualWeb evaluator [2] and on the Fast Match algorithm [10]. The latter was used to detect templates. It is a simple algorithm to identify common elements amongst the HTML DOM trees. QualWeb was modified to optionally include this algorithm.

4.1   QualWeb Evaluator

QualWeb is a modular accessibility evaluation framework that includes a processing phase unit which obtains the DOM tree of the page to be evaluated. Several alternative units are available to obtain the DOM at the different phases of the delivery process. We will consider the after browser processing phase since it provides the most accurate representation of the page [4], in terms of the correct application of guide-lines.

A tool called Phantom.js[1] is used as a browsing processing simulator. It uses WebKit and can be controlled using Javascript, being consistent with our remainder implementation.

The DOM three is then fed into the evaluator module that selects the accessibility techniques and applies them to the tree nodes as needed. Currently, QualWeb implements most of the WCAG 2.0 evaluation techniques, including HTML and CSS. The results are then passed to the formatter modules. These modules tailor the evaluation results into specific serialisation. EARL [12] is one of the alternatives.

4.2   Considering Templates and Duplicated Nodes

The most important modifications to QualWeb were applied at the processing-phase level. First, a splitting module was build that obtains the set of pages of a site. Then, all pages are processed to get the respective DOM trees. Once all the threes are available, they are systematically compared with each other using the Fast Match algorithm. As a result a structure with all the "primitive" nodes of the site is computed. For each node, the count of the number of pages where they were found is kept as well as the reference to the original DOM.

Primitiveness is established by a comparative function. This function compares elements data to determine an exact match between two elements of them, until all of their descendants are compared. It is based on the Levenshtein Distance [11] between the comparing values. The two thresholds, for depth and proximity, of the Fast Match algorithm were empirically defined, by testing the function on a controlled set of template based web sites.

A second modification was applied at the formatter module level. A new module was derived from the existing ones. It generates reports including the basic EARL data, adding at each item the list of original DOMs (and therefore pages) where it was found. That report is then used by a visualization tool that presents them to the user.

Finally, at the same level, the tool also computes the accessibility repairing effort estimation according to AREM, plus the accessibility quality values for the complementary metrics based on Lopes et al [7], considering primitive and non-primitive elements.

5   Experimental Study

We selected 15 sites to perform an accessibility evaluation: 5 of them heavily based on templates, 5 using very few reusable constructs and the other 5 used templates moderately. To select the sites, we inspected the Alexa Top 100, starting by looking for newspapers and blogs. From those we picked those deeply based on template

---

[1] http://www.phantomjs.org/

usage, and some with moderate use. After that searched for Web pages that have a lower usage of templates, comparing with the other two levels.

Subsequently, we applied the modified QualWeb on all of them, using the after browsing processing unit with the template aware option set. We collected the reports and computed the values for the AREM metric using the element primitiveness criteria (primitive elements) and considering all the element instances (non-primitive), respectively. As a baseline for argumentation we also used the conservative rate metric[7]. As AREM, it accounts for all the errors and warnings, although in a normalized relative way. Warnings have anyway to be checked in corrective action to guarantee the best accessibility quality possible.

5.1   Metrics Results

Figures 1 and 2 show the results obtained from application of the AREM and conservative rate metrics.

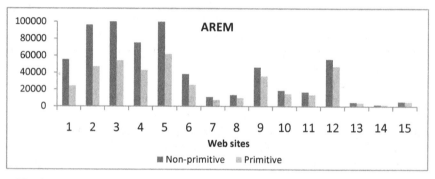

Fig. 1. AREM for non-primitive and primitive elements, for each Web site evaluated

Considering Fig. 1 two cases immediately emerge: a) The AREM for non-primitive elements is higher in Site 1 than in 9, but the AREM of primitive elements in lower than 9; b) the same, with more emphasis, happens between Web sites 1 and 12. Considering both, Site 1 reports the largest amount of errors plus warnings (AREM), when a classic non template aware evaluation is issued (non-primitive). However, it is actually the site that requires less effort to repair, considering the number of elements that must be addressed in a corrective process (primitive).

We can also see that Web site 5 (AREM prim) is the one that requires more effort to repair. However, looking at Fig 2, it has better relative accessibility quality (higher conservative rate - primitive or not) than for example 4, 7 and 11. This shows that the accessibility quality metric does not reflect the real effort of correction of the accessibility problems.

Finally, it is worth noting that comparing the rates for the primitive and non-primitive elements (Figure 2) we can see that the templates can have a positive (as can be seen in sites 1, 6, 7, 8, 10, 12, 13) or negative (in the rest) influence on the accessibility quality of a site, as we suggested in [14].

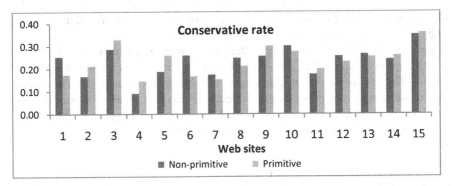

Fig. 2. Conservative rate for non-primitive and primitive elements, for each Web site evaluated.

5.2   Validating the Approach

Using the above reports, we selected 2 sites of each category (heavy, mid, and low template based) and manually inspect the reported fails/warnings/passes in order to assess the adequacy of the template detection algorithm.

Table 1 shows the average percentage of errors of the template detection algorithm, using as basis the error reports of the two higher templates percentage in each rank (heavy, mid or low template based). In average the number of incorrect elements detected by fast match algorithm in less than 10%.

Table 1. Average of errors on the template detection for two Web sites of each rank

Web sites	% template	% errors on template detection
Heavy	56%	14%
template based	51%	8%
Mid	33%	6%
template based	31%	12%
Low	18%	7%
template based	15%	1%

6   Discussion

The results are twofold. First the validation of the template detection method yielded a deviation from the perceived use of templates while inspecting the selected sites, i.e., not all elements considered by the template detection algorithm as being common to more than one page were in fact perceived to be part of a template and vice-versa. Nonetheless the deviation was considered reasonable low especially considering the enormous difference between the reporting using primitive versus non-primitive elements. Besides, for the developer, this could constitute an opportunity to further structure the site. Additionally, it can be observed that the algorithm had more failures in the template detection in sites which use more template based components.

Regarding the AREM metric the difference between the computed values is significant. In fact it reports less that 30% of repairing issues when using the primitive elements. Depending on the sites this value can decrease substantially. These results confirm and support our previous experiment's results [13], where the comparison to find common elements was confined to the home page, i.e. all pages of the site were match with the home page and not among themselves.

7   Conclusion and Future Work

The paper presents a new metric and a framework to assess the effort of repairing the accessibility of a Web site, considering the usage of templates that may simplify the repairing effort for developers.

We performed an experimental showing that: 1) the percentage of templates can be very significant in some Web sites, reducing significantly the effort of correction; and 2) the metric defined can be helpful, since it is a real indicator of the work that have to be done, unlike certain quality metric (e.g. conservative rate) that can be misleading.

To be certain of our results, we performed a validation experiment of both metric and framework and conclude that the template detection algorithm has a high efficacy.

On-going work in being conducted in the following areas; 1) improvements of Fast-Match algorithm to guarantee a higher accuracy level; 2) a large-scale evaluation of the fast match algorithm.

Acknowledgements. This work was funded by Fundação para a Ciência e Tecnologia (FCT) through the QualWeb national research project PTDC/EIA-EIA/105079/2008, the Multiannual Funding Programme, and POSC/EU.

References

1. Gibson, D., Punera, K., Tomkins, A.: The volume and evolution of web page templates. Special Interest Tracks and Posters of the 14th International Conference on World Wide Web. ACM, New York (2005)
2. Fernandes, N., Lopes, R., Carriço, L.: On web accessibility evaluation environments. In: Procs. of the 8th International Cross-Disciplinary Conference on Web Accessibility (W4A). ACM, New York (2011)
3. Law, C., Jacko, J., Edwards, P.: Programmer-focused website accessibility evaluations. In: Procs. of the 7th International ACM SIGACCESS Conference on Computers and Accessibility (ASSETS). ACM, New York (2005)
4. Chakrabarti, D., Mehta, R.: The paths more taken: matching DOM trees to search logs for accurate webpage clustering. In: WWW 2010 Proceedings of the 17th International Conference on World Wide Web. ACM, New York (2010)
5. Vieira, K., Carvalho, A., Berlt, K., Moura, E., Silva, A., Freire, J.: On Finding Templates on Web Collections. World Wide Web 12(2), 171–211 (2009)

6. Bar-Yossef, Z., Rajagopalan, S.: Template detection via data mining and its applications. In: WWW 2002 Proceedings of the 11th International Conference on World Wide Web. ACM, New York (2002)
7. Lopes, R., Gomes, D., Carriço, L.: Web not for all: A large scale study of web accessibility. In: Procs. of the 4thInternational Cross-Disciplinary Conference on Web Accessibility (W4A). ACM, New York (2010)
8. Vigo, M., Arrue, M., Brajnik, G., Lomuscio, R., Abascal, J.: Quantitative metrics for measuring web accessibility. In: Procs. of the 5th ACM International Cross-Disciplinary Conference on Web Accessibility (W4A). ACM, New York (2007)
9. Velleman, E., Meerveld, C., Strobbe, C., Koch, J., Velasco, C.A., Snaprud, M., Nietzio, A.: Unified Web Evaluation Methodology, UWEM 1.2 (2007)
10. Chawathe, S., Rajaraman, A., Garcia-Molina, H., Widom, J.: Change detection in hierarchically structured information. In: SIGMOD 1996 Proceedings of the 1996 ACM SIGMOD International Conference on Management of Data. ACM, New York (1996)
11. Navarro, G.: A guided tour to approximate string matching. ACM Computing Surveys, CSUR (2001)
12. Abou-Zahra, S., Squillace, M.: Evaluation and Report Language (EARL) 1.0 Schema. Last call WD, W3C (2009), http://www.w3.org/TR/2009/WD-EARL10-Schema-20091029/
13. Fernandes, N., Lopes, R., Carriço, L.: A Template-aware Web Accessibility metric. W3C/WAI Research and Development Working Group (RDWG) Website Accessibility Metrics Symposium 2011 (December 5, 2011)
14. Fernandes, N., Carriço, L.: A macroscopic Web accessibility evaluation at different processing phases. In: Procs. of the 9th International Cross-Disciplinary Conference on Web Accessibility (W4A). ACM, New York (2012)

Lexical Quality
as a Measure for Textual Web Accessibility*

Luz Rello[1,2] and Ricardo Baeza-Yates[1,3]

[1] Web Research Group
[2] NLP Research Group,
Dept. of Information and Communication Technologies,
Universitat Pompeu Fabra
[3] Yahoo! Research, Barcelona, Spain

Abstract. We show that a recently introduced lexical quality measure is also valid to measure textual Web accessibility. Our measure estimates the lexical quality of a site based in the occurrence in English Web pages of a set of more than 1,345 words with errors. We then compute the correlation of our measure with Web popularity measures to show that gives independent information. This together with our previous results implies that this measure maps to some of the WCAG principles of accessibility.

1 Introduction

The problem addressed in this paper is the measurement of the lexical quality of a Website, that is, the representational aspect of the textual Web content, and its application to Web accessibility. Lexical quality broadly refers to the quality degree of words in a text (spelling errors, typos, etc.) and it is related to the degree of readability of a website [1]. Although lexical quality is not used as an accessibility metric, we propose that including text quality and correctness in accessibility metrics could be useful, since the quality of words and language impacts the readers understanding. Moreover, lexical quality maps to the WCAG principle of content being "understandable" [2].

Our approach is mainly inspired by the work of Gelman and Barletta [3] that apply a spelling error rate as a metric to indicate the degree of quality of websites. They use a set of ten frequently misspelled words and hit counts of a search engine for this set. While they focus on spelling errors, we have established an original classification of lexical errors in English motivated by their relationship with textual accessibility, such as the errors made by people with dyslexia, and a measure of lexical quality [4].

In this paper we show that our lexical quality measure is related to Web text accessibility and hence could be included as an additional measure in quantitative Web accessibility standards. We have corroborated this through an eye-tracking user study [5].

---

* This work has been partially funded by the HIPERGRAPH project (TIN2009-14560-C03-01) from the Spanish Economy and Competitiveness Ministry.

K. Miesenberger et al. (Eds.): ICCHP 2012, Part I, LNCS 7382, pp. 404–408, 2012.

2   Measuring Lexical Quality

Our error classification for English distinguishes between regular spelling, typographical, non-native speakers, dyslexic and optical character recognition (OCR) errors. Native and non-native misspellings are phonetic errors, typos are behavioral errors, OCR mistakes are visual errors, while dyslexic errors could be phonetic or visual. Detecting different classes of errors provides the possibility of refining the knowledge we have about Web lexical quality [6]. Besides, the fact that dyslexic errors are discriminated from the rest, makes this study valuable to accessible practices for dyslexic Internet users, which is a relatively large group estimated in 10-17% of the USA population [7].

We selected a sample W of 50 target words for English with their corresponding variants with errors, giving us a total of 1,345 different words. Sample W is bigger than previous related work which used ten words [3,4]. For instance, the target word tomorrow has the corresponding errors variants in our sample: *romorrow, *yomorrow, *timorrow, *tpmorrow, *tonorrow, *tomirrow, *tomprrow, *tomoeeow, *tomottow, *tomorriw, *tomorrpw, *tomorroq and *tomorroe (typographical errors); toomorrow (regular spelling error); *tomorow and *tomorou (non-native speakers errors); *torromow (dyslexic error); and *tomorrov, *tamarraw and *tonorrow (OCR errors).

By lexical quality we understand its classic definition taken from the theory of reading acquisition. According to Perfetti [8], a lexical representation has high quality to the extent that (1) it has a fully specified orthographic representation (a spelling) and (2) it has redundant phonological representations (one from spoken language and one recoverable from orthographies-to-phonological mapping).

In this context, a measure of lexical quality for the Web should be independent of the size of the text or the number of pages in a website, to be able to compare this measure across websites or different web segments. One alternative could be to compute the rate of spelling errors, that is, the number of misspellings divided by the total number of words. However, that is hard to compute in the context of the Web. A solution is to use a sample of words and use the rate of spelling errors of those individual words to maintain independence of the text size. However, it is not trivial to find in the Web which are all possible misspells of a word for two reasons: (1) the number of possible variations increases exponentially with the number of errors and (2) there might be more than one correct word at the same distance of errors for a given misspelled word. A possible solution is then to find words that are frequent and that also have a frequent misspell, using that occurrence ratio as a proxy of the exact misspell rate. As the frequency of the most frequent misspell is much less than the correct version,[1] we can approximate the word rate of spelling errors just dividing by the number of correct occurrences instead of the total number of all possible misspells of the word (which as we said earlier is harder to determine).

---

[1] In fact, the distribution many times follows a power law, as the famous Britney Spears example: http://www.google.com/jobs/britney.html.]

Hence, we define our measure of lexical quality as the average rate of the most common misspell for a set of words. That is, given a set of words W, we compute the relative ratio of the most common misspell to the correct spelling averaged over this word sample scaled by 100 to obtain values around 1. That is,

$$LQ = 100 \cdot \text{mean}_{w_i \in W} \left(\frac{df \text{ misspelled } w_i}{df \text{ correct } w_i} \right) , \qquad (1)$$

where df is the document frequency of each word as we will measure lexical quality across web pages and not words. Using the term frequency would be better, but that would imply that computing LQ is much harder as then a standard search engine cannot be used.

Hence, a lower value of LQ (Lexical Quality) implies a larger lexical quality, zero being perfect quality. Notice that LQ is correlated with the rate of lexical errors but it is not the same because is a ratio against the correct words and takes into account the most frequent misspell for each word. To compute LQ, we estimate df by searching each word in the English pages of a major search engine. To measure LQ we first need to select the words in the sample W_M, which is a non-trivial task because different types of errors have to be distinguished without ambiguity. To bound the overall rate of errors in the Web, we have to model the co-occurrence of words in the Web. This is an open problem in general [9], but we can use a simple model that allows to bound the co-occurrences of words.

Although the lexical quality measured will vary with the set of words W_M chosen, the relative order of the measure will hardly change as the size of the set grows. Hence, we believe that LQ is a good estimator of the lexical quality of a website.

3   Comparison with Web Popularity

To show the relevance of LQ as an independent variable we computed the Pearson correlation with the following measures of Web popularity for the top 20 sites in English of Alexa.com in March 2011 and January 2012: Alexa unique visitors, number of pages, number of in-links, and ComScore Unique Visitors. We see that LQ is mildly correlated with the Alexa ranking (see Table 1 and 2) and the size (as expected, more content, more errors). Hence LQ provides independent information about the popularity of a website, which is usually correlated with its quality.

Table 1. Pearson correlation for the top English websites in March 2011

Measure	Alexa	Pages	Links	ComScore
LQ	**0.4451**	0.4167	0.3966	0.2356
Alexa		**0.7659**	0.6897	**0.6589**
Size			**0.8655**	0.3097
Links				0.1319

Table 2. Pearson correlation for the top English websites in January 2012

Measure	Alexa	Pages	Links	ComScore
LQ	**0.8029**	0.7750	0.6780	0.7785
Alexa		**0.8972**	0.7937	0.7904
Pages			**0.8496**	0.6322
Links				**0.4371**

We assess the correlation of lexical and domain quality applying our methodology to several large Web domains and the major English speaking countries. Although there is a correlation between high lexical quality and the content of major websites, some domains that should have high lexical quality do not have it. Among other observations we noticed that the quality of USA and UK universities is similar but the UK government has three times better quality than the USA government. Regarding country domains, the correlation between lexical and domain quality is high and the geographical distribution of lexical quality shows the impact of business Web pages and number of users among English speaking countries. We also computed the lexical quality results in major and social media websites [10]. Many of them have quite good lexical quality in spite of their collaborative nature, like Wikipedia, Flickr and Twitter.

4   Final Remarks

LQ uses a conventionally non-accessibility source and is not an accessibility metric. However, it could be potentially added to traditional metric scores using text quality as a proxy measure for Web text accessibility.

Future work will include improving our technique to study how it converges when the set W_M grows as well as better techniques to bound the overall rate of errors in the Web. We also plan to do larger users studies to see the relation between lexical quality and Web text accessibility.

References

1. Cooper, M., Reid, L.G., Vanderheiden, G., Caldwell, B.: Understanding WCAG 2.0. a guide to understanding and implementing web content accessibility guidelines 2.0 (2010)
2. Caldwell, B., Cooper, M., Reid, L.G., Vanderheiden, G.: Web content accessibility guidelines (WCAG) 2.0. WWW Consortium, W3C (2008)
3. Gelman, I.A., Barletta, A.L.: A "quick and dirty" website data quality indicator. In: The 2nd ACM Workshop on Information Credibility on the Web (WICOW 2008), pp. 43–46 (2008)
4. Baeza-Yates, R., Rello, L.: Estimating dyslexia in the Web. In: International Cross Disciplinary Conference on Web Accessibility (W4A 2011), pp. 1–4. ACM Press, Hyderabad (2011)

5. Rello, L., Baeza-Yates, R.: Lexical quality as a proxy for web text understandability. In: The 21st International World Wide Web Conference (WWW 2012), Lyon, France (April 2012)
6. Baeza-Yates, R., Rello, L.: On measuring the lexical quality of the web. In: The 2nd Joint WICOW/AIRWeb Workshop on Web Quality, Lyon, France (April 2012)
7. McCarthy, J.E., Swierenga, S.J.: What we know about dyslexia and web accessibility: a research review. Universal Access in the Information Society 9, 147–152 (2010)
8. Perfetti, C., Hart, L.: The lexical quality hypothesis. In: Precursors of Functional Literacy, pp. 189–213. John Benjamins, Amsterdam (2002)
9. Baeza-Yates, R., Ribeiro-Neto, B.: Modern Information Retrieval: The Concepts and Technology behind Search, 2nd edn. Addison Wesley, Harlow (2011)
10. Rello, L., Baeza-Yates, R.: Social media is not that bad! the lexical quality of social media. In: The International AAAI Conference on Weblogs and Social Media (ICWSM), Dublin, Ireland (June 2012)

Accessibility Testing
of a Healthy Lifestyles Social Network

Cecília Sík Lányi[1], Eszter Nagy[1], and Gergely Sik[2]

[1] University of Pannonia, Egyetem u. 10.,H-8200 Veszprém, Hungary
lanyi@almos.uni-pannon.hu, nagyeszter6@gmail.com,
[2] Budapest University of Technology and Economics, Műegyetemrkp, 3-9,
H-1111 Budapest, Hungary
sikgeri@gmail.com

Abstract. The current development of the Internet and its growing use makes it necessary to satisfy the needs of all users including those with disabilities having accessibility problems. The healthy lifestyle is increasingly important to people. The number of webpages dealing with healthy lifestyles is growing. "Webstar" healty lifestyle social network was tested by Wave Toolbar, HTML Validator, Web Developer Toolbarand WCAG Contrast Checker.

Keywords: social network, validator, WCAG 2.0.

1 Introduction

There is no doubt that social websites have become one of the greatest inventions of the XXI. century. Maintaining social connections, getting new and new friends, online entertainment: these are the very things we expect a good portal to provide. The concept of the social websites is that upon registration users share a desired amount of personal data with other users and after that they build a so called friend network using their acquaintances as building elements. The more acquaintances are present the more information is accessible during a certain period of time [1]. But the very question arises: are these social sites usable by anyone?

The current development of the internet and its growing use makes it necessary to satisfy the needs of all users including those with disabilities having accessibility problems. Most software engineering companies do not develop products for special users, because they do not see potentiality in this limited market. It is a fact, that 10% of the population worldwide is handicapped.

Due to the growing age of workforce and high accident rates in some countries, the number of handicapped people will increase [2]. In the USA 14% of the population is estimated to suffer from a disability. When we look at people, aged 65 and over, this figure becomes 50%. Disabilities are strongly linked with age. Our societies are facing a growing number of people aged 75 and more, who are likely to have impairments or disabilities. In Europe this group will total up to 14.4% of the population in 2040, compared with 7.5% in 2003: it will almost double [3]. We know very well, the elderly people have several health problems. The number of the elderly

K. Miesenberger et al. (Eds.): ICCHP 2012, Part I, LNCS 7382, pp. 409–416, 2012.

people grows dramatically. A paradigm shift is needed: producers should put these consumers from margin to the mainstream, because the main users will no longer be children and young, or middle aged healthy adults. The now mainstream consumers use the Internet and obviously are members of social sites. They surely would like to continue using these services in their "silver years" in order to maintain their social connections easier. Will they really be able to do so? To do so we have to examine, are those websites barrier free?

Based on our earlier research [1], [5] we tested Webstar (healty lifestyle social network)using Wave Toolbar [6], HTML Validator [7], Web Developer Toolbar [8] and WCAG Contrast Checker [9]. This research was made in the period of September and December in 2011. There are several other validators too. But we have found numerous errors; therefore we didn't tested using that validators. After we used the mentioned validators, we made human test and we developed a questionnaire too. In this report you can find results of our tests.

2   Testing Process

2.1   From the User Perspective: Remarks, Errors, Shortcomings

Before using any validator software, we got acquainted with all the functions of Webstar. We encountered a number of problems from logging in onwards. This chapter contains a short description of these.

- It counts as a general error that it is not possible to mark unread messages read without actually reading them, as well as to mark back read messages unread.
- Tooltips are missing in several places.
- On the front page and in several submenu items the use of mixed language can be seen. Accordingly, some items are in English, others are in Hungarian on the same page while the selected language is Hungarian.
- When a given user is passive, for lack of activity, after a few minutes the user gets logged out. After logging in again, the site is not reloaded in the previously selected (in the present case Hungarian) language. (In this case in German instead.)
- In several places spelling mistakes occur.
- It is not really a significant, but still visible mistake that in the Webshop section not all product names begin with capital letters.
- Due to difficulties with the translation and to missing characters, certain phrases are hardly comprehensible.
- Not all browsers can display the content of the website properly: Mozilla and Chrome the website appeared similarly, however, using the Internet Explorer, the look of the website became disintegrated. Probably it may have occurred due to the non-dynamic screen management. It is very important to bear in mind that screen management should be dynamic so that any browser can display the site properly.
- The virtual environments also have some imperfections. Although it will be noticed by experienced developers only, we also mention that the shadows are not realistic or even missing. What is a much bigger problem is the length of loading time on different platforms.

Since we had experienced several problems on the website, we used the programme Wave Toolbar for software testing first.

2.2   Errors Revealed with the Help of Wave Toolbar

Wave Toolbar is a Firefox add-on, which we preferred to apply as our first validator so that we can determine the deficiencies of the website. This Firefox add-on does not check the accessibility of the website directly, but it helps to eliminate the greater, more general errors, and it is definitely successful in the aspect that a subsequent validation of the already barrier free website can be attained more easily.

- On the front page, after login, according to the validator software, a number of alerts give warning of the unvisible content. The same error occurs on all the pages of the website.
- The so-called link error is also detectable. It manifests itself in the fact that at a button, e.g. „click here", there is a link with the same name, but it links to somewhere else. Similar link errors can be found at the images in the appendix Wave.docx.
- The website indicates the presence of the event handler with a different warning. On a website it is possible to define an event handler corresponding to certain objects. They appear as another attribute in the HTML-definition, the value of which is the JavaScript source code as a character string. If the value of the utterance here is 'false', the function of the object (e.g. submitting the form) will not be activated; in order that everything works (e.g. reconfiguring the status bar), it has to be 'true'. In the case of the present code it is the current object (see: 'this') whose event handler we define. The event handlers are not functions, they cannot be called by JavaScript code, although it is possible to reconfigure them by assignment; in this case, the name of the corresponding function has to be assigned to the field corresponding to the name of the event handler in small letters. This is why we can call it a deficiency of the site tested. It occurs on the website on several further occassions.
- It indicates it as an error that in many places within the site (e.g. on the very first page) the alternative text of the image with a link is missing. This error occurs more than once on a single page.
- Further errors occured.

Fig. 1. Icons of the toolbar (From left, to right: Unvisible content, Link error, Event handler warning, Link missing)

On figure 1 the related icons can be seen.

Figure 2 reveals that the tested website cannot become accessible with so many errors and warnings.

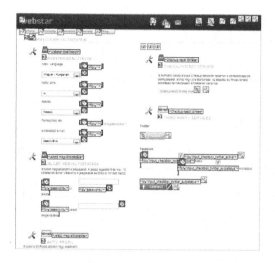

Fig. 2. Testing the settings page with Wave Toolbar

Using Wave Toolbar we found 121 errors and 839 warnings.

2.3   Testing with HTML Validator

The 0.9.1.1 version of HTML is well applicable under Windows and it checks the correctness of HTML/XML coding and if it follows the stardards. The latter is important from our aspect, since if Webstar wants to take a leading position, it is vital that search engines rank it among the first results upon a search.

Errors:

- Attributes are missing in several places
- There are undefined variables
- Resulting from the document type, it uses inadequate elements, or the adequate element is missing
- Tag is not properly closed

Notices:

- Discarding declaration due to unknown properties
- Errors during the interpretation of values
- Other values appear instead of the expected declaration
- Wrong selectors, unknown pseudo-classes

We found 1709 errors and 215 warnings.The testing of Webstart continued with Webdeveloper Toolbar, our findings can be read in the following chapter.

2.4   Testing with Web Developer Toolbar

Web developer toolbars are special browser toolbars for web developers. These toolbars usually provide a combination of tools for debugging, CSS, HTML, DOM, Java Script, and other techniques.

Turning off JavaScript/Java with Web Devloper Toolbar. During the first examination carried out using Web Developer Toolbar we tested the site JavaScript/Java turned off. This test is important because not all users have Java installed on their computers, and the site has to be functional without it. It would also be nice if every function could work even in the lack of JavaScript. It is not a problem if browsing the site is not so convenient from the user's perspective, but all information has to be available. If we take mobile phones, for example, they often fail to handle JavaScript properly.

Once "All JavaScript" function in Web Developer Toolbar is activated, it will be found out which buttons do not function, or block those parts of the site where the font is minimized. Fonts differring from each other very much may cause the webpage to disintegrate. In the following, typically occurring errors will be shown, which arise when Java function is not working.

We fuond several other errors it is written in the expert's report sent to the provider of WebStar.

Checking ALT Texts with Web Developer Toolbar. Why is it practical to test the website for this function as well? It is also useful to check whether ALT texts are defined for the images of the website. These texts are also important because they tell the gist of the image to the visually impaired user. Decorative elements may have blank ALT texts, but in the case of images with links the links have to be in accordance with what can be seen in the image. This function can be especially vital for the visually impaired, who is informed about the content of the page with the help of a reading software. The software will read out what is defined in the ALT text. Lacking this the website is unusable for them.

In the case of Web Developer Toolbar, Alt texts can be displayed activating the Display Alt Attributes in Images menu item.Alt texts are missing even on the front page. A few more similar instances can be found on the website, but fortunately, most of the ALT texts were defined.

2.5   WCAG Contrast Checker

WCAG Contrast checker studies the appearance of websites. The harmony of colours and proportions play an essential role in the appearance. Although many tend to neglect these issues, numerous scientific researches are concerned with this field. All this is based on the colour perception of the eye, which, however unconsciously, may have an influence on buyers' decisions. It does count how relaxing browsing the website is for the eye, or perhaps it is difficult to read the text because of an inappropriate selection of background and font colour (contrast), not to mention the colour-blind. WCAG Contrast checker offers guidance in these matters. It renders it possible to select different areas of the website, and it indicates whether the colours and proportions are properly selected.

In the website we tested relatively few colour- and proportin-related errors can be found. Most elements meet the requirements. In total, the front page of the website is satisfactory.

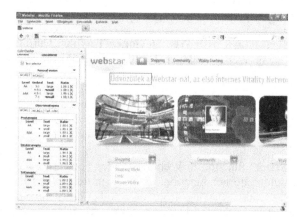

Fig. 3. Assessment of the 'Welcome' tag

Generally speaking, the website meets the contrast standards. The add-on signalled error only with a few smaller tags.

2.6   Validation on a Smart Phone Featuring Android Operating System

The download from the Android Market was flexible and no difficulties were met during the installation process either. We can Register on the appearing page, we can find the Instructional materials. The login process was somewhat lengthy, but we did not encounter any difficulties. From the following page we should be able to have access to the menu items Nutrition, Fitness, MyHome, University, Community and Mission Vitality. However, some of them have not been developed yet. Such are, for example: Nutrition and University, and some parts have not been entirely unfolded.

70% of the functions are available on the Android application, however, some of them cannot be fully utilized. The application was adequate in terms of colours and the pieces of information did not exceed the 7-unit maximum capacity of human short-term memory. It also contained feedback for the users, but it provided informative feedback saying "Please, wait" to no effect, since functions were often downloading even after 5 minutes, which results in the users' impatience, and may easily lead to neglection of the software in the long run. We were also sorry to learn that the application could not be used by visually impaired because such necessary add-ons as changing font size, or sounds for blind users are missing. The parts where the application redirects the user to the main website would also need to be changed in a way that it would not be necessary to go over and enter the page again, because it also hinders its use. But if the operators still want to apply this solution, it would be expedient to create another webpage which loads faster and is easier to understand, where it is not necessary to log in repeatedly and to scroll continuously, as well as to scale up and down. If the developers revise these small errors, an excellent, easy-to-use software may be created which also popularize the main website, as well as the health products, and which helps to maintain our vitality.

2.7 Human Validation with a Questionnaire

Validation was continued with preparing a human questionnaire, which was filled in by users of different age and sex. We consider the number of questionnaires already returned (47) sufficient to draw an approximate conclusion regarding the users' oppinion.

The questions of the questionnaire could be answered with marks 1 (worst) and 5 (best).

- The sex ratio of the respondents was 50-50%.
- Most of them belonged to the age group 14-18, the second most populous age group was that of the 25-34-year-olds.
- There were no respondents younger than18 and older than 64.
- All respondents have at least secondary qualification, and 29% of them are graduates.
- The highest percentage of the respondents were from Western Hungary (80%).
- Most of them had been informed about the website by their acquaintances, and they do not usually visit other websites of the same kind.
- Most people are interested in advice on vitality and in sales (84% altogether), while most of them would not like to receive news letters in these issues.
- Most of them consider that the site renders help to get attuned to healthy lifestyle and that dietary programme planning and online shopping are useful.
- The general image of the site was judged average or good by most questionees.
- However, users found it difficult to find the different menu items. (Daily exercise was the hardest (2.44/5), profile settings was the easiest of them (2.68/5) to find.)
- Nearly all users were unsatisfied with the design of the menu items, meaning that it is difficult to find the different items.
- The transparency of menu items was evaluated somewhat worse than moderate.
- Users find the shopping section the most transparent and coherent, but all agree that the structure is not always logical.
- Finding messaging, registration, ordering, programme planning, dietary adjustments, and the check-up tests were given approximately 2.5 points in a scale of 1 to 5.
- The structure of the site was given 2.36 points in a scale of 1 to 5 by the users.
- Orientation as a new user received the worst assessment.
- Roughly all users were moderately satisfied with the graphics, up-to-dateness, services and the information available.

In general, the users were satisfied with the functionality of the site, however, they missed several things in relation with the structure, they found it difficult to find their bearing, or it was not clear for them where to find what. Thus they found it very difficult to use the site.

We think that, despite a number of difficulties on the users' side, the website is capable of conveying the information and values it is meant to, it does not always opt for the appropriate structure for this purpose, the environment of the information is not always suitable, or some pieces of information is 'impossible to find'. If these imperfection, errors were corrected, it could obtain more users, and also existing users would be more satisfied.

3   Conclusion

In the course of our work, we validated the Webstar portal with the Firefox add-ons HTML Validator and Wave Toolbar first, then with Web Developer Toolbar and WCAG Contrast Checker. After that, we tested it on a smart phone with Android operating system. Beside using various validators, it was not only us to carry out human testing on every page, but we also created an online form to analyze users' opinion. In this way we could get a clearer image of the users' needs and opinions. Our findings were documented, the documents were sent to the "Webstar" service provider.

Webstar in its present state does not conform the standards and recommendations recognized in the technical literature (WCAG 2.0). The Webstar portal is not at all accessible, hence excluding minimum 15-20 % of the European population from the potential users [10], violating the effective regulations of different countries concerning digital accessibility. Since it does not conform with the recommendations and is not accessible.If the developers revise the errors, an excellent, easy-to-use website may be created which helps to maintain our vitality.Our goal of the validation was to contribute to the development of a website which supports healthy lifestyle and renders help with maintaining our vitality by revealing its errors.

References

1. Sik Lányi, C.: Accessibility Testing of Social Websites. In: Furth, B. (ed.) Handbook of Social Network Technologies and Applications, pp. 409–426. Springer (2010)
2. WHO: Situation analysis for health at work and development of the global working life, http://www.who.int/occupational_health/publications/globstrategy/en/index4.html
3. EU Commission: 2010 A Europe Accessible for All, Report from the Group of Experts set up by the European Commission, http://europa.eu.int/comm/employment_social/index/final_report_ega_en.pdf
4. Total Validator, http://www.totalvalidator.com/
5. Czank, N., Sik, A., Sik Lányi, C.: Testing the Accessibility of WEB Sites. International Journal of Knowledge and Web Intelligence (IJKWI) 2(1), 87–98 (2011)
6. Wave Toolbar, http://wave.webaim.org/toolbar
7. HTML Validator, https://addons.mozilla.org/hu/firefox/addon/html-validator/
8. Web Developer Toolbar, https://addons.mozilla.org/en-US/firefox/addon/web-developer/
9. WCAG Contrast Checker, http://www.niquelao.net/wcag_contrast_checker
10. Disabled people worldwide, http://www.realising-potential.org/stakeholder-factbox/disabled-people-worldwide/

Following the WCAG 2.0 Techniques: Experiences from Designing a WCAG 2.0 Checking Tool

Annika Nietzio[1], Mandana Eibegger[2], Morten Goodwin[2],
and Mikael Snaprud[2,3]

[1] Forschungsinstitut Technologie und Behinderung (FTB)
der Evangelischen Stiftung Volmarstein
Grundschötteler Str. 40, 58300 Wetter (Ruhr), Germany
egovmon@ftb-esv.de
http://www.ftb-esv.de
[2] Tingtun AS, PO Box 48, N−4791 Lillesand, Norway
m.eibegger@schoener.at, {morten.goodwin,mikael.snaprud}@tingtun.no
http://www.tingtun.no
[3] University of Agder, PO Box 509, N−4898 Grimstad, Norway

Abstract. This paper presents a conceptual analysis of how the *Web Content Accessibility Guidelines (WCAG) 2.0* and its accompanying documents can be used as a basis for the implementation of an automatic checking tool and the definition of a web accessibility metric. There are two major issues that need to be resolved to derive valid and reliable conclusions from the output of individual tests. First, the relationship of Sufficient Techniques and Common Failures has to be taken into account. Second, the logical combination of the techniques related to a Success Criterion must be represented in the results.

The eGovMon project has a lot of experience in specifying and implementing tools for automatic checking of web accessibility. The project is based on the belief that web accessibility evaluation is not an end in itself. Its purpose is to promote web accessibility and initiate improvements.

1 Web Accessibility Benchmarking with WCAG 2.0

Benchmarking goes beyond the presentation of conformance results such as: "The web content conforms to the guidelines." or "The web content does not conform to the guidelines." If the outcome of the evaluation is represented as numerical value the descriptive power is much higher. It becomes possible to distinguish between web sites which "almost conform" to the guidelines (i.e. sites that have only very few accessibility problems) and web sites that don't meet the guidelines at all. Several metrics have been proposed , such as:

- Failure rate [12]
- Unified Web Evaluation Methodology (UWEM) score [7]
- Web Accessibility Quantitative Metric (WAQM) [5]

K. Miesenberger et al. (Eds.): ICCHP 2012, Part I, LNCS 7382, pp. 417–424, 2012.

– Barrier Impact Factor (BIF) [3]
– Accessibility Score used by WCAG 2.0 Web Assessment Tool (WaaT) [1]

The latter two of the metrics are tailored towards WCAG 2.0 [9] while the others were constructed for WCAG 1.0[8] or can be applied to any kind of accessibility evaluation results. At present, a generally accepted practice for reporting WCAG 2.0 evaluation results does not exist.

On the contrary, the results of tools which claim to check according to WCAG 2.0 often are not comparable. This problem is mainly caused by the varying granularity of tests (Some tools implement several tests per Success Criterion while others only have one test.) and the differences in counting the instances of potential barriers (Some tools count every checked HTML element while others only count each barrier type once.). The tools also differ in how outcomes are grouped into categories like "error", "potential error", or "warning". Some tools only report the absolute numbers for each outcome category, while other tools use some kind of score function. Alonso et al. [2] describe the consequences of this challenge: "This could lead to a situation where different evaluators use different aggregation strategies and thus produce different evaluation results."

In this paper we propose the introduction of aggregation on the level of Success Criteria, as a first step to increase the comparability of the results from different tools. Fortunately, we don't have to re-invent the wheel. As WCAG 2.0 already is constructed to guide and support evaluation of web pages and sites, we can follow the instructions and test procedures in WCAG 2.0 and its supporting documents.

To ensure the validity of our approach, we base the method on WCAG 2.0 and its supporting documents. This contributes to the usefulness of the tool because WCAG 2.0 is widely adopted and much used as a reference for public procurement and quality assurance. Furthermore, it has the additional advantage that the implementation of the tool can keep up with the latest developments in web accessibility by incorporation the regular updates of the WCAG 2.0 Techniques[1] by W3C.

2   Development of the WCAG 2.0 Checker and Score

The score function should be tailored to the structure of the test set (in this case WCAG 2.0). Therefore we start the design of the score function with an analysis of WCAG 2.0, taking also the structural differences between WCAG 1.0 and 2.0 into account.

We also investigate how other implementations of WCAG 2.0 tools address the challenges mentioned above and try to identify potential shortcomings and possible solutions.

---

[1] The development of the eGovMon WCAG 2.0 tool described in this paper is based on the latest version of the *Techniques for WCAG 2.0*, which was published on 3 January 2012.

2.1   Combining Sufficient Techniques and Common Failures

The WCAG 1.0 tests (as defined in UWEM 1.2 and by other tools) are independent: failure of a test also means failure of a WCAG 1.0 Checkpoint. The structure of WCAG 2.0 is different. The techniques with their detailed test procedure provide a natural starting point for the implementation of an evaluation tool. But in the presentation of results the dependencies of the techniques must be taken into account. On the one hand there are Common Failures which directly cause the web content to fail a Success Criterion. On the other hand, conclusions can be drawn from the presence or absence of Sufficient Techniques.

The majority of existing tools implements a strategy that is either based only on Common Failures or only on Sufficient Techniques. While this avoids the problem of reporting the same issue twice, it also misses a number of issues and thus leads to incomplete results.

Some Success Criteria don't define redundant techniques. For instance *3.1.1: Language of Page*, does not have related Common Failures, instead the absence of an implementation of the corresponding Sufficient Techniques is interpreted as failure of the Success Criterion. This case is missed if the evaluation is based solely on Common Failures.

If only the Sufficient Techniques were used, the tool might ignore some specific problems that are only described as Common Failures but can not be derived directly from the Sufficient Techniques. For instance *F3: Failure of Success Criterion 1.1.1 due to using CSS to include images that convey important information* requires the checking of images included via CSS. The Sufficient Techniques for short text alternatives in Success Criterion 1.1.1 target only HTML img elements. Thus a tool that only looks at Sufficient Techniques will miss accessibility barriers caused by CSS background images.

Incorrect results can also occur if the tests for accessibility barriers are derived from negated Sufficient Techniques. This is also described in the *Techniques for WCAG 2.0* document [11]:

> "However, failure of a test procedure for a sufficient technique does not necessarily mean that the success criterion has not been satisfied in some other way, only that this technique has not been successfully implemented and can not be used to claim conformance."

For instance Technique *G134: Validating Web pages* for Success Criterion *4.1.1: Parsing* includes the validation of CSS in its test procedure. However, this does not mean that CSS validation errors cause the web content to fail the Success Criterion. This happens only if none of the other Sufficient Techniques is implemented on the web page either.

An evaluation result can only capture the full image of WCAG 2.0 if both Sufficient Techniques and Common Failures are taken into account. The section *Understanding conformance* of the Understanding WCAG 2.0 document [10] describes the logic required to combine the techniques.

To overcome the problems discussed above, we suggest the following approach to derive an implementation of tests for a Success Criterion (SC):

1. Applicability: Does the web page contain any HTML elements to which the SC is applicable? — No: SC passes. Yes: continue.
2. Does a Common Failure occur? — Yes: SC fails. No: continue.
3. Are the Sufficient Techniques successfully implemented for every element? — Yes: SC passes or SC passes with warning ("human input required"). No: continue.
4. Does the checker provide tests for all techniques related to the SC? — Yes: SC fails with warning ("no Sufficient Technique used"). No: warning ("not checked").

2.2   Combining Results for Techniques

The WCAG 2.0 tool developed by eGovMon specifies simple checks for situations that can easily be captured by a single question. These checks correspond to the WCAG 2.0 Techniques or sometimes even to the individual steps in the test procedures of the technique.

The results of these checks are then combined as described in the Understanding WCAG 2.0 document [10]. The following example illustrates our approach:

Success Criterion 3.3.2 Labels or Instructions. The following individual tests are applied to check that the purpose of a form control can be identified:

H44: Is there is a **label element** that identifies the purpose of the control?
H65: Is there is a **title attribute** that identifies the purpose of the control?
G167: Is there is an **adjacent button** that identifies the purpose of the control?

The report for Success Criterion 3.3.2 is the result of a logical combination:

```
IF ((H44:cause=no_label OR H44:cause=label_empty)
    AND (H65:cause=title_missing OR H65:cause=title_empty)
    AND G167:cause=empty_button_as_label OR G167:not_applicable)
THEN return SC3.3.2 failed
```

The web content fails Success Criterion 3.3.2 only if neither of the related techniques was successfully implemented.

2.3   Aggregation Beyond Success Criterion

Some techniques are used by several Success Criteria. Therefore an interpretation of the results below the level of Success Criteria is not meaningful. This is a major difference from UWEM 1.2 (and other WCAG 1.0 tools), which has an erratic number of tests per WCAG 1.0 Checkpoint. Each test contributes equally to the score result causing Checkpoints with many tests to be over-represented in the result. Using Success Criteria as intermediary aggregation level addresses this shortcoming and also has several other advantages. The influence of Success Criteria with many techniques is balanced. In an automated tool it becomes easy to highlight which Success Criteria need human judgement or were not tested. Disadvantages of the approach are that the number of instances of a specific feature (such as form control) does not influence the score if each Success Criterion gets the same weight. If a tool does not implement all techniques related to a Success Criterion, no valid conclusion can be drawn. However, this limitation does not occur if the tool results can be complemented by expert evaluations.

2.4   eGovMon Score Function

The theoretical considerations given above lead to the following definition of the score function. Let p denote a web page, c a Success Criterion, and C the set of all Success Criteria that are covered by the evaluation, i.e. all Success Criteria for which at least one test has been carried out.

The instances of application of a test for Success Criterion c on page p are denoted by:

$f_c(p)$ = number of instances where tests for c failed
$n_c(p)$ = number of all instances where tests for c were applied

The intermediary result for c on page p is defined as:

$$S_c(p) = 1 - \frac{f_c(p)}{n_c(p)} \tag{1}$$

Page Score. The page score S is calculated from the intermediary results per Success Criterion.

$$S(p) = \frac{1}{|C|} \sum_{c \in C} S_c(p) \tag{2}$$

Site Score. A web site is a set of web pages $s = \{p_1, p_2, \ldots\}$. The simplest way to calculate a score for the web site is to take the average of the page scores.

$$S_{mean}(s) = \frac{1}{|s|} \sum_{p \in s} S(p) \tag{3}$$

This approach gives equal weight to all pages, irrespective of their size. To take the size of pages into account, we define:

$N(p) = \sum_{c \in C} n_c(p)$ = number of all instances within page p
$N(s) = \sum_{p \in s} N(p)$ = number of all instances within site s

Then the page scores can be weighted by the number of instances.

$$S_{weighted}(s) = \sum_{p \in s} \frac{N(p)}{N(s)} S(p) \tag{4}$$

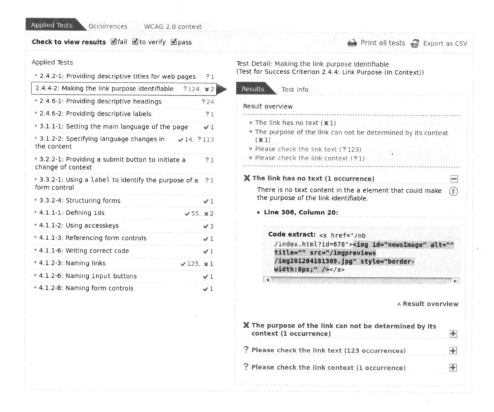

Fig. 1. Screenshot of the detailed results in the eGovMon WCAG 2.0 checker

3   Results and Impact

In the course of the eGovMon project, we were able to gain many insights into how different target groups such as people working in public administration, politicians, accessibility experts, and software developers, use the results from web accessibility evaluation and benchmarking. There are few occasions were the presentation of a single number per web site was used for actual improvements (rather than mere blaming and shaming). Site owners who are really interested in improving their web site need more information.

EGovMon has developed an online interface[2] that presents a detailed report from the accessibility evaluation and explains why the identified issues might cause an accessibility problem and how to fix the issues. It also includes cross-references to the related WCAG 2.0 documents. Figure 1 shows an example of a report related to Common Failure *F89: Failure of Success Criteria 2.4.4,*

---

[2] The eGovMon WCAG 2.0 checker is available at
http://accessibility.egovmon.no/en/pagecheck2.0/. The version of April 2012 provides tests for nine Success Criteria.

2.4.9 and 4.1.2 due to using null alt on an image where the image is the only content in a link. The interface was developed in close collaboration with the eGovMon users – a group of Norwegian municipalities – to ensure its usability and usefulness.

In addition to the detailed results, eGovMon also offers aggregated benchmarking results. So that national authorities in charge of monitoring web accessibility (such as the Agency for Public Management and eGovernment (Difi) in Norway) can make better use of the results.

4 Conclusion and Future Work

The main contribution of this paper is the suggestion to insert a new aggregation layer between individual tests and aggregated accessibility score for a page. This supports the understanding of the different concepts necessary for accessibility for instance "text alternative", "purpose of input elements", and increases the transparency of the evaluation because users of the results can trace how the results are computed. It also supports the validity of the results by establishing a strong link to WCAG 2.0 and its supporting documents.

Furthermore, we have presented some important aspects that have to be considered when building a tool that is consistent with WCAG 2.0. This includes the implicit and explicit definitions of when web content passes or fails a Success Criterion. The implementation of the eGovMon checking tool establishes a proof of concept for the approach.

Our plans for future development include the extension of the suggested framework to the evaluation of complete web sites. This involves addressing the following open questions:

– How can the score calculation accommodate results of tests that are applied on site level?
– How to distinguish Success Criteria that are not applicable from those for which no tests are available ("undocumented techniques")?
– How does the score function deal with conforming alternate versions?

In parallel, the checker user interface will be enhanced. It is our particular interest to add support for user input so that the report about the accessibility of a web page can combine results produced by the checking tool and findings entered by a human expert. The tool will actively prompt the users to enter their judgement for the results that are "to be verified".

Finally, to define a truly unified WCAG 2.0 score and thus achieve actual inter-tool reliability – as demanded by Vigo and Brajnik [6] a dedicated collaboration between tool developers and researches could be envisaged. We feel that credibility of web accessibility tools and metrics is crucial. There are many tools which all present different results for the same web pages. If the users are confused or alienated, the whole purpose of web accessibility evaluations is jeopardised. The users might stop caring about accessibility or they could be tempted to select the tool which gives the best results, and that, of course, is not the right way to improve accessibility.

Acknowledgements. The eGovMon project is co-funded by the Research Council of Norway under the VERDIKT program. Project no.: VERDIKT 183392/S10. The ideas described in this paper were first presented [4] in the *Online Symposium on Website Accessibility Metrics* organised by the W3C/WAI RDWG in December 2011. The feedback received during the Symposium provided us with useful input to the consolidation and elaboration of our approach.

References

1. ACCESSIBLE Project: Web accessibility assessment Tool (WaaT) (2011), http://www.accessible-project.eu/ (retrieved January 30, 2012)
2. Alonso, F., Fuertes, J.L., González, Á.L., Martínez, L.: Evaluating Conformance to WCAG 2.0: Open Challenges. In: Miesenberger, K., Klaus, J., Zagler, W., Karshmer, A. (eds.) ICCHP 2010. LNCS, vol. 6179, pp. 417–424. Springer, Heidelberg (2010)
3. Battistelli, M., Mirri, S., Muratori, L.A., Salomoni, P.: Measuring accessibility barriers on large scale sets of pages. In: Proceedings of W3C Online Symposium on Website Accessibility Metrics (2011)
4. Nietzio, A., Eibegger, M., Goodwin, M., Snaprud, M.: Towards a score function for WCAG 2.0 benchmarking. In: Proceedings of W3C Online Symposium on Website Accessibility Metrics (2011)
5. Vigo, M., Abascal, J., Aizpurua, A., Arrue, M.: Attaining Metric Validity and Reliability with the Web Accessibility Quantitative Metric. In: Proceedings of W3C Online Symposium on Website Accessibility Metrics (2011)
6. Vigo, M., Brajnik, G.: Automatic web accessibility metrics: where we are and where we can go. Interacting with Computers 23(2), 137–155 (2011)
7. Web Accessibility Benchmarking Cluster: Unified Web Evaluation Methodology (UWEM 1.2) (2007), http://www.wabcluster.org/uwem1_2/ (retrieved January 30, 2012)
8. World Wide Web Consortium: Web Content Accessibility Guidelines 1.0. W3C Recommendation (May 5, 1999), http://www.w3.org/TR/WCAG10/ (retrieved April 17, 2012)
9. World Wide Web Consortium: Web Content Accessibility Guidelines 2.0. W3C Recommendation (December 11, 2008), http://www.w3.org/TR/WCAG20/ (retrieved January 30, 2012)
10. World Wide Web Consortium: A guide to understanding and implementing Web Content Accessibility Guidelines 2.0. W3C Working Group Note (January 3, 2012), http://www.w3.org/TR/2012/NOTE-UNDERSTANDING-WCAG20-20120103/ (retrieved January 31, 2012)
11. World Wide Web Consortium: Techniques and Failures for Web Content Accessibility Guidelines 2.0. W3C Working Group Note (January 3, 2012), http://www.w3.org/TR/2012/NOTE-WCAG20-TECHS-20120103/ (retrieved January 31, 2012)
12. Zeng, X.: Evaluation and Enhancement of Web Content Accessibility for Persons with Disabilities. Ph.D. thesis, University of Pittsburgh (2004)

Entertainment Software Accessibility: Introduction to the Special Thematic Session

Dominique Archambault[1] and Roland Ossmann[2]

[1] EA 4004 – CHArt-THIM – Université Paris 8
2 rue de la liberté, 93 526 Saint-Denis cedex, France
dominique.archambault@univ-paris8.fr
[2] Kompetenznetzwerk KI-I,
Altenbergerstraße 69, 4040 Linz, Austria
ro@ki-i.at

The kids of the first generation who grew up with computer games are now in their forties, and younger people have been surrounded by more and more devices allowing to use such games. The descendants of our old game stations which were displaying 2 bars on a black and white TV set to play tennis, are now very close to very powerful computers. Games appeared also on websites and mobile phones, while portable game stations allow some amazing visual features. The budgets of some of the major games have reached the level of motion pictures, and a huge number of small games are developed every year. Computer games are now in the heart of the youngsters culture. At the same time one could observe also that a growing part of the population of other age groups are using computer games. Indeed a lot of software application implementing the games the people of these older groups want to play have been designed and became more and more simple to use, while the people of these groups have been familiarised to computer at their work. Therefore it's not rare to see retired people playing scrabble online or card games.

More than games themselves, game like interfaces are designed on an increasing part of standard applications. We mean here interfaces that does not follow the ordinary scheme : window with a title bar, a menu and a client area under them. Web applications especially have interaction areas spread all over the browser's client area, menus are more and more contextual, etc. Another increasing area is the area of serious games, that can be essential for training or for certain kind of professional activities. In that way computer games are really part of nowadays cultures in most developed countries, and the tendency still is on a growing dynamic.

An important part of people with disabilities are *de facto* excluded from this culture because they simply cannot interact with the interfaces. In order to overcome this inequality, a research community is also growing. It is the sixth time that a session about entertainment software accessibility is presented in the ICCHP conference, and we never had so many paper submitted, and as a consequence so many papers finally in the session.

K. Miesenberger et al. (Eds.): ICCHP 2012, Part I, LNCS 7382, pp. 425–427, 2012.
© Springer-Verlag Berlin Heidelberg 2012

Research topics are of several kinds, that can be categorised in 3 series :

- A first series of works deal with designing specific games for certain groups of people with disabilities. This allow in particular some researches on how to implement specific interactions that are used in computer games with alternative modalities, used by unconventional devices that these groups of people need to use instead of the standard devices. It can be input devices since lots of people cannot use mice, joysticks or game pads, but also output devices. For instance blind people won't be able to access to a screen, which remains the major output device for computer games.
- A second series of researches aim at designing games which can be played by people with specific needs to play as well as by their mainstream peers. The games should be designed according to the principles of design for all. This series can be split in two parts. Indeed this can be achieved in implementation all possible interaction kinds, for all types of alternative devices, in the core of the game. Another solution is to have specific interfaces to these devices, which communicate with the game, in the same way a standard textual application communicates with a screen reader : transferring the information to the assistive software in order to reformat the data into a information that can be displayed in the alternative devices.
- A third series of works appears nowadays which aim at assessing these accessibility of computer games.

The first paper of this session belongs to the last of these categories. Indeed **Mustaquim** presents a work, based on a user survey, on adapting the classical principles of universal design to computer games.

The next two papers are from the first category. They both deal with computer games to help education and development of kids with disabilities. **De Boeck, Daems & Dekelver** present a serious gaming approach to help the education of kids with intellectual disabilities. They propose a set of fun games that are interrupted by didactic content. An administration tool allows to create or edit these didactic content, and to manage settings and to study the results for each user. **Gomez, Cabrera, Ojeda, Garcia, Molina & Rivera** present a project where students of computer science school design specific games for for kids with cerebral palsy. Students are visiting regularly a special school and have contact with the kids and their educators.

Then the biggest group of papers during this session deal with finding alternative ways of accessing mainstream entertainment content, being mainstream computer games, music or comics, which would allow groups of people who are excluded from these content to access them. **Ossmann, Thaller, Nussbaum, Veigl & Weiß** explore the way to use various kind of devices together with a Sony Playstation 3 in order to improve accessibility. Studying of the possibilities of the disabled player allows then for adapting the input device to his particular needs. **Pouris & Fels** present a system creating visualisations of MIDI music which they evaluated with six different kind of music (from metal to classical). **Tessendorf, Derleth, Feilner, Roggen, Stiefmeier & Tröster** introduce a vibrotactile hearing device, allowing to improve the localisation of sounds in computer games. Using the Active Tactile Control technology, the editor for Braille musical notation presented in **Grützmacher** offers auditory feedback when notes are typed in or read. Finally **Ponsard & Dziamski** introduce an OCR in a comics book viewer in order to improve its accessibility.

As mentioned above we have now a large number of papers in the literature dealing with the access to game interaction with alternative devices. We think that the only way to do a substantial step forward now is to create a new accessibility interface allowing communication between games and game-like applications and new specific accessibility interfaces implementing the game interaction with alternative modalities. Like in the case of web content, the games will need to respect some accessibility issues. This important work will need a large international collaboration in order to be accepted. We hope that it will be possible to start this work in a near future.

Assessment of Universal Design Principles
for Analyzing Computer Games' Accessibility

Moyen Mohammad Mustaquim

Department of Informatics and Media, Uppsala University
Box 513, 75120 Uppsala, Sweden
moyen.mustaquim@im.uu.se

Abstract. Universal design is a significant topic of interest in the research of accessibility. However, to date there are no certain verification of these principles on the accessibility issues for computer games. In this paper the existing universal design principles were verified to assess accessibility in computer games. Quantitative analysis of collected data showed that some design principles are not really optimal for assessing computer games' accessibility while other design principles were overlooked. The findings from this study take the argument of alternation of existing universal design principles further ahead and initializes the possibilities of developing accessible games design principles.

Keywords: Accessibility in Games, Universal Design, Design Principles for Accessible Games Design, Inclusive Games Design.

1   Introduction

The idea of universal design is that, it offers a greater extent and possibilities of using product and/or service for the end users. Although the majority tends to consider universal design as a pattern that was strictly initiated and meant to be for people with disabilities and elderly, the attitude towards such thinking has been changing prominently in the last decade [3]. Mainstreaming universal design concept has already extended the boundaries of disability, on which universal design was supposed to be considered to be based on. However, universal design principles can be seen in different perspective and be altered according to the design requirements of some important design concepts, for instance, open innovation and sustainability to initiate effective design [3]. While universal design prioritizes the context of use; both physical and psychological, and the complexity of interactions between products, services and interfaces in specific contexts of use [8], computer games are not an exception to see the impact of universal design for enhancing accessibility in gaming. Considerable amount of research has already been done and are ongoing about game accessibility. However, analyzing universal design principles to see how users tend to act on these design principles, while they are playing computer games is to date not monitored. The focus of this paper's study was therefore, to see how and what were the impacts of universal design principles on game player's act. This thereby can assess game's

K. Miesenberger et al. (Eds.): ICCHP 2012, Part I, LNCS 7382, pp. 428–435, 2012.

accessibility or can be used to come up with better design principles for designing accessible games. The paper is divided into four sections. The background section introduces the present state of games accessibility and universal design principles. The method section describes the methodology of the study performed, followed by the result section which shows the findings and statistical analysis. The paper concludes by a discussions and further research section, describing what research can be initiated from the findings of this paper.

2 Background

2.1 Computer Games and Accessibility

Since computer games have become an important part of our culture, it is being used more by the growing part of the population. Regardless of platform, computer games are therefore an interesting branch of accessibility research. A lot of people are excluded from the computer games because of accessibility issues. Although most gamers play games for entertainment, an inappropriate design of game (in terms of accessibility issues) can lead player's frustrating experiences rather than them to be entertained. Academia and also R&D over the last few years have started to focus on "serious games". "Leading experts speak of "creating a science of games" [1], [5] with the goal of implementing games and game like interfaces of general importance for a growing number of applications and as a general trend in the design of Human-Computer Interfaces (HCI)" [2], [5]. "In addition, general human computer interaction is beginning to use concepts and methods derived from games as they promise an increased level of usability" [5]. Accessibility of games is a more complex problem than any other accessibility issues in information technology, for instance software or web. "The first reason, which seems obvious but is very important, is that: Accessible games must still be games!" [7], [5] "Designing games that work for players with disabilities is quite a challenge: an important research, practical and social issue that has to be carried out now" [5]. Therefore the goal of the present research should be mainstreaming accessibility of games [5]. "Several aspects have to be taken into account: to find out how to handle game interaction situations with alternative devices, to develop models allowing to make mainstream games compatible with these alternative devices, to write according guidelines, methodologies and techniques" [5].

2.2 Universal Design and Its Principles

The concept of universal design is about guaranteeing that surroundings, products, services and interfaces work for people of all ages and abilities [4]. It is a general approach to designing in which designers ensure that their product and services address the needs of the widest possible audience, irrespective of age or ability [9]. The British Standards Institute [6] defines inclusive design as "The design of mainstream products and/or services that are accessible to, and usable by, as many people as reasonably possible ... without the need for special adaptation or specialized design." By meeting the needs of those who are excluded from product use, inclusive design improves product experience across a broad range of users. In a nutshell, universal design aims to produce accessible, usable and desirable products for the whole population.

The original set of universal design principles, described below was developed by a group of U.S. designers and design educators from five organizations in 1997 [4]. The principles are copyrighted to the Center for Universal Design. The principles are used internationally, though with variations in number and specifics analogy [4]. Below we describe the set of universal design principles with a tangible explanation for each of the principle.

- **Equitable Use:** The design does not disadvantage or stigmatize any group of users [9]. It provides the same means of use for all users that is, identical whenever possible, equivalent or not. The goal is not to stigmatize any use and make the design appealing to all users [4]. This principle also make provision for security, safety etc. to be equally available to all users.
- **Flexibility in Use:** The design accommodates a wide range of individual preferences and abilities. Providing choices in methods of use and also providing adaptability to the user's pace is what flexibility promises [9]. User's precision and accuracy facilitating is another objective. Accommodating left and right hand access and use for instance an example of flexibility in use [4].
- **Simple, Intuitive Use:** Use of the design is easy to understand, regardless of the user's experience, knowledge, language skills, or current concentration level [9]. Also information to the user should be arranged so it is consistent according to their importance [9], [4]. Use of different language, wide range of literacy and initiation of effective prompting also commences simplicity and intuitiveness in use.
- **Perceptible Information:** The design communicates necessary information effectively to the user, regardless of ambient conditions or the user's sensory abilities [9] [4]. This principle is important for differentiating elements in ways that can be described, that is, to make it easy for giving instruction or directions.
- **Tolerance for Error:** The design minimizes hazards and the adverse consequences of accidental or unintended actions. Providing awareness and warnings of hazards and error, fail-safe feature promotion are some goal of the principle [9]. The design should also discourage unconscious action in tasks that require vigilance [4].
- **Low Physical Effort:** The design can be used efficiently and comfortably, and with a minimum of fatigue [9]. This principle argues to design in such way so that the user's body position remains natural with reasonable operating force required to perform a task. Also minimizing repetitive action and sustained physical effort is another goal [4].
- **Size and Space for Approach & Use:** Appropriate size and space is provided for approach, reach, manipulation, and use, regardless of the user's body size, posture, or mobility [9]. Providing a clear line of sight is important for the user while they are dealing with several elements on a system.

These principles of universal design give us a general feeling that they are the kind of design principles for creating products or services for a special group of people. And most often this special group of people is identified as physically disabled or elderly population. Sometimes, assistive technology design synonymies with universal design. Although these principles were based on the concept of disabilities during the early stages of concept development for universal design, we believe that these principles have a lot more to offer rather than focusing and be limited to disabilities or similar issues. The reason behind measuring universal design principles in this study is to analyze the principles with the possibility of improving game's accessibility design. It is important to remember and understand that, universal design is not a concept but a design strategy which cannot suddenly be introduced at any phase of design of a system. This means that, if the strategy of universal design is integrated with game's design, the result will only be 'better accessible game'.

3   Methods

"The different types of disability affecting a person's ability to play video games can be broken down into four groups: Visual, Auditory, Mobility and Cognitive and a disabled gamer may span any number of these groups" [3]. We wanted to study how well the existing universal design principles can explain these abilities in terms of computer games playing. Therefore, to find out the impacts of universal design principles towards designing accessible games, has been studied by a quantitative field experiment from 50 participants, who were playing different genres of games. The basis for the analysis was questionnaire responses. The questionnaire items were designed to capture the variables that make up the model. All scales used in the research were prior to the fieldwork tested and optimized for face validity with senior researchers and qualitatively tested with respondents, demographically similar to the final field work respondents. The test bed was set up by allowing a participant play a specific genre of game. Few participants were familiar with playing some of the games but otherwise the participants were unaware of playing the games that they were offered to be played. The participants were requested to play the game for a minimum 30 minutes of time. Then they were requested to answer the questions, which were based on ranking on a scale of 1 to 9. None of the participants had any kind of physical or mental disability that could affect controlling and understanding the games that they were given to play. However, some participants reported to have common key correction problem as limited physical ability. Basic demographic information has been collected. Around 67% participants were male and 33% participants were female with their age ranged from 16 to 24. Most of the participants were university students. The average times spent on playing games per week by the participants were 6.8 hours. The answers from the survey were carefully analyzed by the researcher and coded in to a data sheet in Microsoft Excel. Some participant's data were then eliminated from the spreadsheet since they did not complete the survey. The result from the questionnaires was coded in to SPSS (version 19) and statistical operations were run to come up with results. We first ran exploratory statistical analysis to observe the normality, linearity and outliers in the data. Then we ran factor analysis (with factor loading value 0.40) together with reliability analysis to check which variable's data was not or less reliable. The rejection level was 0.7 for Chronbach's Alpha. The corrected item total value was set to be at least 0.3 for reliability analysis. Finally we conducted regression analysis and ran a correlation matrix analysis to find the relationship between different variables. The rejection level for the analyses was set at $p = 0.05$. The findings are described in the following section.

4   Results

Our result shows that equitability, error tolerance and low physical effort variables from the universal design principles were not observed to be something important by the participants, while they were thinking about accessible computer games. Error tolerance has been noticed to be an important issue by the participants, but we did not find a correlation between error tolerance and any other variables from the universal design. This made error tolerance less significant in game accessibility. However, our finding showed that flexibility, simplicity, perception and low physical effort are in regression (Table 1).

Next we ran a bivariate correlation option from the SPSS to find out the Pearson and Spearman results shown on table 2. Since the p-value for satisfaction is below .05 then we can reject the null hypothesis which means we have a true relationship finding. But p-value of the simple use variable is higher than 0.05 which makes it less confident that, there is a correlation between low physical effort and flexibility variables. Since r-value for satisfaction is higher we get more confident, that there really is correlation. Hence in a regression, satisfaction can work as a dependent variable. We can also say that satisfaction correlates significantly with flexibility, $r (293) =0.548$, $p<=0.5$. Degrees of freedom (df) = n-2, that is, Df = 295-2=293. Also these four factors results a one factor solution in a factor analysis. By the use of this one factor we measured level of accessibility. The scree plot from factor analysis is shown in figure 1.

We came to several conclusions, from where we derive the factors that were making some of the universal design principles less significant. These findings are shown in the form of an evaluation matrix in Table 2. What was most interesting from the finding of this study was that, although the participants were not suffering from any kind of disabilities and the games that they have played were not designed to be inclusive or accessible computer games, the participants still felt the need of some factors to be included in the game design while asked about those by the questionnaires. Adding new factors to universal design principles is thus appropriate for designing appropriate accessible computer games. In a multiple regression with satisfaction as dependent variable and low physical effort, flexibility and simple use as independent variable, 39.4% of the variance in the dependent variable satisfaction is explained by the model. Low physical effort and flexibility variables show some kind of relationship with satisfaction variable. Hence, flexibility and low physical effort variables gave multi-co linearity with satisfaction and they correlate substantially. Low physical effort variable makes the strongest unique contribution for explaining the dependent variable satisfaction, while the variance is explained by all other variables in the model. Flexibility has shown less contribution in the model with lower beta value. However, low physical effort and flexibility variables made significant unique contribution to the prediction of the dependent variable.

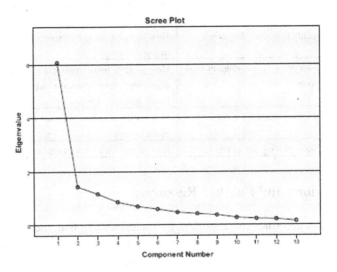

Fig. 1. Scree plot showing tend towards one factor solution

Table 1. Multiple regression

		Satisfaction s1-s5	Low Physical	Flexibility s51+s52	Simple Use
Satisfaction	s1-s5	1		.	.002
n Correlation tailed) N	Pearso Sig. (2-	307	.000	.000	.972
			301	295	297
Low Physical Effort	s39-43	.5	1	.	.609
n Correlation tailed) N	Pearso Sig. (2-	.000	308	.000	.298
		301		300	
Flexibility	s51+s52	.5		1	.315
n Correlation tailed) N	Pearso Sig. (2-	.000	.000	303	294
		295	300		
Simple	Use	.002		-	1
n Correlation tailed) N	Pearso Sig. (2-	.972	.609	.315	305
		297	298	294	

Table 2. An evaluation matrix of universal design principle assessments for computer games

Questions	Resulting Matrix
Can I trust the game to be accessible?	How to make the computer games more trustworthy by giving an equitable feeling to the user?
Is the game easy to learn?	How to improve the learning experience, without too many confusing details?
Can I use multimodality to control the game?	How to make the use of speech, gaze, and gesture in game control?
Will I be able to auto perceive information from my task domain (games)?	How to give more confidence to the users about equitability, error tolerance and low physical effort by the game design?
Is this game design appropriate for me to play?	Explain the benefits, purpose and appropriateness to the users
Can I detect error while playing the game?	How to make the error evaluation ability higher?

5   Discussions and Further Research

The findings from this study are important for understanding that, the existing universal design principles may not be suitable for designing accessible computer games. While mainstreaming accessible games is the slogan of the research, this can be achieved easily if universal design can be mainstreamed. However, improper principles may lead to the kind of accessible design that might not be suitable for large population group with diverse user requirements and disabilities. If design principles are called to be 'universal' then they should return a certain level of satisfaction in terms of universality in design (accessibility in this case), regardless of the platform of the design. This study reflects that using existing universal design principles for designing accessible computer games might result improper accessible games. Re writing universal design principles is therefore needed. Also, writing universal games design principles is another research that is initiated from this study. To date the guidelines or any specific design principles for designing accessible computer games are still missing, as of author's knowledge. It would be nice to follow certain design principles for designing accessible computer games and such design principles is possible to figure out and write from the findings of this study. A game designed followed by those principles can thereby be certified to be universally designed. Finally, the findings from this study can help editing and writing new design principles which will not only be appropriate as general universal design principles, but also will include 'game accessibility problem domain' under the same design principles.

Acknowledgments. The author would like to thank Dr. Kent Norman from the laboratory of automation psychology and decision process, University of Maryland, USA and his student teams, for helping him conducting this study in autumn 2011.

References

1. Zyda, M.: Creating a science of games. ACM Communications 50(7) (July 2007)
2. Kellogg, W., Ellis, J., Thomas, J.: Towards supple enterprises: Learning from N64's Super Mario 64, Wii Bowling, and a Corporate Second Life. In: "Supple Interfaces": Designing and Evaluating for Richer Human Connections and Experiences (September 2007)
3. Bierre, K., Chetwynd, J., Ellis, B., Hinn, M., Ludi, S., Westin, T.: Game not over: Accessibility issues in video games (2005)
4. Center for Accessible Housing. Accessible environments: Toward universal design. North Carolina State University, Raleigh (1995)
5. Archambault, D., Gaudy, T., Miesenberger, K., Natkin, S., Ossmann, R.: Towards Generalised Accessibility of Computer Games. In: Pan, Z., Zhang, X., El Rhalibi, A., Woo, W., Li, Y. (eds.) Edutainment 2008. LNCS, vol. 5093, pp. 518–527. Springer, Heidelberg (2008)
6. British Standard 7000-6:2005. Design management systems - Managing inclusive design – Guide (2005)
7. Archambault, D., Olivier, D., Svensson, H.: Computer games that work for visually impaired children. In: Stephanidis, C. (ed.) Proceedings of HCI International 2005 Conference (11th International Conference on Human-Computer Interaction), Las Vegas, Nevada, 8 pages (July 2005) (proceedings on CD-Rom)
8. Langdon, P., Clarkson, J., Robinson, P.: Designing accessible technology. Universal Access in the Information Society 6(2), 117–118 (2007)
9. Mustaquim, M.: Gaze Interaction – A Challenge for Inclusive Design. In: Pichappan, P., Ahmadi, H., Ariwa, E. (eds.) INCT 2011. CCIS, vol. 241, pp. 244–250. Springer, Heidelberg (2011)

One Way of Bringing Final Year Computer Science Student World to the World of Children with Cerebral Palsy: A Case Study

Isabel M. Gómez[1], Rafael Cabrera[1], Juan Ojeda[1], Pablo García[1], Alberto J. Molina[1], Octavio Rivera[1], and A. Mariano Esteban[2]

[1] Electronic Technology Department, Universidad de Sevilla, Spain
{igomez,almolina}@us.es, {rcabrera,octavio}@dte.us.es,
{juanojeda8,roll_cagesh}@hotmail.com
[2] Guadaltel, S.A. Seville, Spain
amer@guadaltel.es
http://matrix.dte.us.es/grupotais

Abstract. In this paper, a learning project is explained which is being carried out at the school of computer science at the University of Seville. The aim is that students receive knowledge of assistive technologies when in fact there is no this discipline in our curricula. So the best way, it is programming final studies projects in this field. We want to make the projects have a real application and can solve difficulties that children with Cerebral Palsy have in their daily activities in the school.

Keywords: serious games, trainig in assistive technologies, access device.

1   The R & D or Application Idea

In this paper, a learning project is explained which is being carried out at the school of computer science at the University of Seville. The idea is that students who are completing their studies design applications that will contribute to improve the daily school activities of children with motor and cognitive problems. Training and age of these students are good ingredients for achieving this goal. On the one hand technical training in programming and electronics is ideal for application design. On the other hand students are of the generation of video games which they love and have great experience as players. Additionally, this project supplies assistive technologies Knowledge that is lacking in their studies. These applications will be games but there are other possibilities such as interactive stories or learning applications. The student must design them according to a preset goal. The properly access device must also be selected or designed according to the child's physical capabilities.

2   State of the Art

Games can be a very important tool in the lives of children with disabilities. If a high degree of involvement is reached, they can increase children capabilities, improve

K. Miesenberger et al. (Eds.): ICCHP 2012, Part I, LNCS 7382, pp. 436–442, 2012.

motor skills, promote sensory processing, and develop perception, social, emotional and language abilities. It is essential to have appropriate adaptations in all facets of the game use.

New technologies have positively influenced the access of children with great difficulty to games. In many cases helping them overcome their difficulties in a much more optimal way than ordinary rehabilitation therapy. In [1,2] the use of virtual reality systems making child perform exercises in proper way is shown. With these systems, the child shows greater interest, involvement and fun. In [3], virtual reality environments are described simply as a good alternative for leisure time. This will improve self-esteem and help feel the subject more capable. A very thorough assessment of the scope of these games on children with neuromotor impairments is done in [4].

There is a concept called "Serious Game" that is related to the use of games for purposes beyond entertainment. Serious games that are used for learning should have the power to captivate the player for a specific purpose such as acquiring new knowledge or skills [5]. The European Union funded project called Game On Extra Time (GOET), aims to prepare students with sensory and intellectual disabilities for real life situations. A series of serious games are used. The description of such games and their evaluation can be found in [6]. On the other hand [7] is a study of the factors that contribute to literacy for children with cerebral palsy. It is highlighted the importance of educational software to achieve this goal.

The proper choice of access devices helps the user feel comfortable with the application, reducing fatigue and frustration caused by the inability to manipulate a system. Thus the main objectives that are intended: learning, communication and rehabilitation; can be achieved more easily. It is important to consider that solutions and sensors must be adapted to the subjects. The use of switches is very common, but our conclusion after visiting the school analyzing capacities and behavior of children is that accelerometers can be a better alternative. An example of using accelerometers to design an access device can be found in [8]. Another possibility can be sounds acquired through sound card input.

3   The Methodology Used

The aim of the project described in this paper is based on a visit to a school on a normal day, in which interviews were held with staff who care for children. This allows us to establish some working lines related solving of specific needs in different environments: learning in classroom, stories in the library, stimulation in multi sensory classroom and games in the school playground.

A structured system with the aim that all students work with the same pattern is proposed. Different modules that compound the system are independent and thus the system is flexible because modules of the same level can be exchanged and have the possibility to be extended. Figure 1 shows system structure. The acquisition module performs the data reading coming from a user device. This device can be a switch, an accelerometer, a microphone or any hardware adapted to user needs. It is important to discern a voluntary action in data set. The calibration module must be implemented with each user before he starts using the application module. It should be based on classifiers. It is configured to distinguish between the captured data, those used for the application control. Once the user begins using the application, the event detection module detects when the user has generated the control event. Once this detection is produced it will generate a command to the module of the application in order to perform the action corresponding to that event.

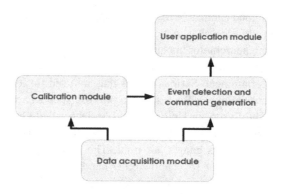

Fig. 1. System Structure

Application module consists of games, interactive stories and learning software. The objective should be to encourage capabilities that this type of user has in a basic level: postural control, action_ reaction, learning curricular materials of different natures and levels. Handling and contents must be designed to respond adequately to a particular user profile. For example, in the case of a person with severe motor difficulties, management will be discrete (on-off), so a single event achieves big changes in application operation. Development should be done in phases and not launch to the next one until the previous one has been assessed by the staff there. Development will be done for both personal computers and mobile devices.

Event detection and command generation module transmits commands to application module in the form of a mouse event. So the interface of applications can only works with this kind of event. This is a constraint in order to make modules designed by different students be interchangeable.

The following programming languages for the realization of this work: C++, C # and Java have been evaluated. Between them C# has been chosen for several reasons: it is easy to use; it has a function library dedicated to game design; it has a framework called XNA Game Studio to facilitate the development of games; games developed for a personal computer can be compiled for XBOX and and make them available on Xbox Live [9].The following section describes how to realize this methodology to a specific case.

4   Case Study: Racing Car Game

In figure 2 main menu of the game entitled CARRERAS US (RACING University of Seville) is shown. This objective of this game is to promote action-reaction capability in children.

Fig. 2. Game Main Menu

Next it describes how different modules of the methodology are implemented. Overall system architecture is shown in figure 3.

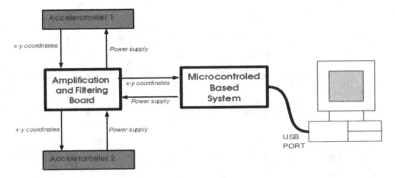

Fig. 3. System Architecture

1. Acquisition module. It is based on accelerometers. Two ADXL322 are used for this purpose. This device is a low cost, low power, complete dual-axis accelerometer with signal conditioned voltage outputs, which is all on a single monolithic IC. The product measures acceleration with a full-scale range of ±2g. Amplification and filtering board is connected to the accelerometer; the aim of this board is to quickly eliminate undesired movements and it allows the system to work with a reduced angle range what increments system usability. The microcontroller-based system reads the accelerometer x-y coordinates and communicates that acceleration to a PC. Another function of this system is to perform digital signal processing. In order to increment the system effectiveness, we have programmed a moving average filter. Arduino has been used for implementing this system. Arduino is an open-source electronics prototyping platform based on flexible, easy-to-use hardware and software [10]. It is based on the Atmel Atmega328 microcontroller.

2. Calibration module. This game has several modes: continuous, discrete, one or two players. In discrete mode, a voluntary movement of the children is selected to generate the event. In the calibration module this is done establishing a threshold in order to distinguish this movement among involuntary ones. This is a simple procedure that will not be valid in all cases, it being necessary to establish more complex classifiers. In continuous mode, users' movements are adjusted to screen dimensions. In this module, user profiles can be considered in order to avoid calibration once it has already been done.

3. Event detection and command generation module. This is once the system calibration is done. If an event is detected, this module translates it to mouse events, cursor movement or click, depending on game mode.

4. Application module. This module has easy graphical interface according to the explanation given by that school psychologist. In figure 4, game screens are shown; a car appears in movement but in determined instant, the situation changes and a reaction is required by the user. If the reaction is good and in time, user wins points, if not, the car crashes. Depending on the game mode, the action required in users is different: in discrete, only the voluntary movement used in calibration time; in continuous, a more precise movement is required being careful not to pass road limits.

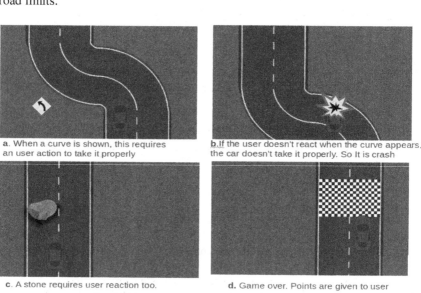

a. When a curve is shown, this requires an user action to take it properly

b. If the user doesn't react when the curve appears, the car doesn't take it properly. So It is crash

c. A stone requires user reaction too.

d. Game over. Points are given to user

Fig. 4. Game Screens

5   Results and Discussion

5.1   Application

This game is for children with low motor and cognitive capabilities. For this reason, several phases have been considered each one with different goals. In a first stage of using the game, it is better one player and one event mode. For this case, we only need an adequate reaction in the user when a stimulus appears in the game screen. In a second stage, when the user has experience, it is possible two events mode, the user must decide between move the car to the left or right. In this case the cognitive capability needed is increased. Two players' mode allows to develop cooperation between children, they learn to respect game turns and work together to obtain the punctuation. Continuous mode allows increasing motor capabilities.

Sound effects like music or car's crash noise have been added in order to stimulate participation and avoid bore. Car speed can be configured too in order to adapt users' needs, expert level and capabilities.

5.2   Access Device

Discrete Mode. It is important distinguish between voluntary and involuntary movements. In this case, it is assumed that involuntary movements are slower which means lower values in accelerometer coordinates. For this reason, the following algorithm is used:

```
μDX= (μDX-1 + x)/2
μDY= (μDY-1 + y)/2
INCX=x-μDX
INCY=y-μDY
INC=SQRT(INCX² + INCY²)
if (INC>THRESHOLD)
VOLUNTARY MOVEMENT DETECTED
```

μ_{DX} and μ_{DY} are the mean values of the coordinate x and y measured with the accelerometer. μ_{D-1} is the previous mean value.

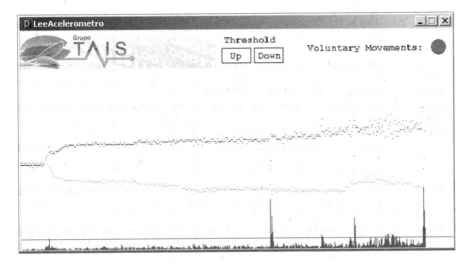

Fig. 5. High part of the image: Accelerometer captured data. Low part: threshold and INC are represented. Threshold can be tuned.

This way of event generation is more flexible and comfortable than using a switch device because it can be adjusted more easily to users' capabilities and preferences.

Continuous Mode. Only needs adjustment to screen resolution according to users' movement

6   Conclusion and Planned Activitities

In this paper an educational experience that takes place in the computer science degree at the University of Seville has been described. The goal is to connect two groups (computer science students and children with disabilities), so that both can broaden their point perspectives and benefit. These are recent happenings so a complete evaluation of it is not yet available. Up to now, students implied in it are motivated and working with interest.

There are several groups of students working on different applications with several aims; one of these has been described. To finish the students' work properly, the school psychologist must evaluated it and finally test it with the children.

Acknowledgments. This project has been carried out within the framework of a research program: (p08-TIC-3631) – Multimodal Wireless interface funded by the Regional Government of Andalusia.

References

1. Bryanton, C., Bossé, J., Brien, M., Mclean, J., Mccormick, A., Sveistrup, H.: Feasibility, Motivation, and Selective Motor Control: Virtual Reality Compared to Conventional Home Exercise in Children with Cerebral Palsy. Cyberpsychology & Behavior 9(2) (2006)
2. Reid, D.T.: Benefits of a Virtual Play Rehabilitation Environment for Children with Cerebral Palsy on Perceptions of Self-Efficacy: a Pilot Study. Pediatric Rehabilitation 5(3), 141–148 (2002)
3. Weiss, P.L., Bialik, P., Kizony, R.: Virtual Reality Provides Leisure Time Opportunities for Young Adults with Physical and Intellectual Disabilities. Cyberpsychology & Behavior 6(3) (2003)
4. Levac, D., Rivard, L., Missiuna, C.: Defining the Active Ingredients of Interactive Computer Play Interventions for Children with Neuromotor Impairments: a Scoping Review. Research in Developmental Disabilities 33 (2012)
5. Susi, T., Johannesson, M., Backlund, P.: Serious Games – An Overview Technical Report HS-IKI-TR-07-001 (Key: citeulike:1137029 (February 5, 2007)
6. Sik Lanyi, C., Brown, D.J., Standen, P., Lewis, J., Butkute, V.: User Interface Evaluation of Serious Games for Students with Intellectual Disability. In: Miesenberger, K., Klaus, J., Zagler, W., Karshmer, A. (eds.) ICCHP 2010, Part I. LNCS, vol. 6179, pp. 227–234. Springer, Heidelberg (2010)
7. Peeters, M., de Moor, J., Verhoeven, L.: Emergent Literacy Activities, Instructional Adaptations and School Absence of Children with Cerebral Palsy in Special Education. Research in Developmental Disabilities 32 (2011)
8. Nakazawa, N., Yamada, K., Matsui, T., Itoh, I.: Development of Welfare Support-Equipment for Personal Computer Operation with Head Tilting and Breathing. In: IECON Thirty-First Annual Conference of the IEEE Industrial Electronics Society (2005)
9. Official webpage XBOX, http://www.xbox.com
10. Arduino, http://www.arduino.cc/

Making the PlayStation 3 Accessible with AsTeRICS

Roland Ossmann[1], David Thaller[1], Gerhard Nussbaum[1], Christoph Veigl[2],
and Christoph Weiß[2]

[1] Kompetenznetzwerk KI-I,
Altenbergerstraße 69, 4040 Linz, Austria
{ro,dt,gn}@ki-i.at
[2] Fachhochschule Technikum Wien
Höchstädtplatz 5, 1200 Vienna, Austria
{veigl,weissch}@technikum-wien.at

Abstract. People with mobility disabilities can hardly play any of the mainstream computer and video games. For most of them, special developed games are the only chance to play games. So, playing together with friends or the family is only possible on a very limited way.

Within the Project AsTeRICS, a flexible and affordable construction set for the implementation of user driven assistive technologies solutions will be developed. This allows the combination of different sensors to process and manipulate the sensor data to control any supported device. This paper will show, how a Sony PlayStation 3 can become the supported device, and how the requirements of a mainstream game can be tailored to the possibilities of a disabled person. Furthermore, possible limitations of this solution will be discussed.

Keywords: Assistive Technology, Games Accessibility, Alternative Game Control.

1 Introduction

The development and usage of accessible games for persons with mobility impairments was mainly limited to special implemented games, using a limited number of switches, controlling them. As a result, several very accessible and enjoyable games had been developed [1, 2]. But this solution has major limitations: each accessible game has to be developed or, with high effort, adapted and the games where mostly games for the PC. Playing mainstream games together with the family or friends is hardly impossible. Also game consoles (Microsoft Xbox, Sony PlayStation, and Nintendo Wii) are inaccessible for many persons with mobility impairments.

One solution for this problem is the development of a special input device or the combination of several special devices. This can be done with the Assistive Technology Rapid Integration and Construction Set (AsTeRICS) [3]. AsTeRICS is a flexible and affordable construction set for the development of user driven assistive technologies solutions with the possibility to combine different sensors, process and

K. Miesenberger et al. (Eds.): ICCHP 2012, Part I, LNCS 7382, pp. 443–450, 2012.

manipulate the sensor data and control any supported device (e.g. also games [4]) with the processed data. This paper will show how a PlayStation 3 (PS3) will become the supported device, using a Human Interface Device (HID) [5] actuator and a special adapted AsTeRICS model.

2   The AsTeRICS Project

AsTeRICS aims to provide a flexible and affordable construction set for building assistive functionalities which can be highly adapted to individual user's needs. The scalable and extensible system allows integration of new functions without major changes. Furthermore, AsTeRICS opens access for people with severe motor disabilities to a standard desktop computer (including Sony PlayStation 3) but also to embedded devices and mobile services, which have not offered highly specialised user interfaces before [6].

The AsTeRICS platform provides a set of components for the realization of assistive technology. Main part is an embedded computing system executing the AsTeRICS Runtime Environment. Sensors and actuators which allow the system to interact with the environment can be connected to the platform (see Fig. 1). [7]

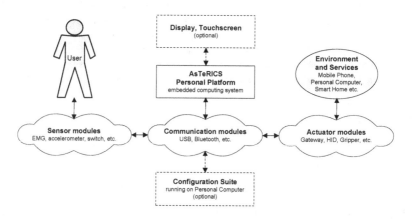

Fig. 1. Schematic concept of AsTeRICS

Beside classic AT-interfaces such as switches, special joysticks, etc. also emerging sensor techniques like Computer Vision and Brain Computer Interfaces (BCI) can be used as sensors. Actuators include digital-to-analogue conversion, simple potential free binary output and also more complex modules like keyboard-, mouse- or joystick emulation, generic infrared remote control, KNX [8] interface to existing building automation systems or mobile phone access.

An optional On-Screen Keyboard displayed on an optional LCD-touchscreen provides selection or adjustment of system parameters via scanning, voice-feedback and touchscreen interaction.

The system can be configured by an application called AsTeRICS configuration suite (ACS), which provides a graphical user interface to combine the different components and therefore to realize AT functionality to the specific needs of the user. [7]

User tests with the AsTeRICS system have shown very good results regarding the usage and control of PC's and control of the environment.

3   Controlling the PS 3

Usually, the PlayStation 3 game console is actuated via the standard "SixAxis"[1] or "DualShock" game controllers, which provide six analogue control axis (two joysticks with x and y-axis and two analogue buttons) and 13 digital buttons. Not every game uses this plethora of input channels – in fact many games can be controlled by just one stick and several buttons, and some games need not more than two or three buttons. However, the existing game controllers represent insuperable barriers for many people with reduced motor capabilities of the hands.

The AsTeRICS project offers a completely new way to control computer games via desired input devices. This allows not only free button remapping but also using desired sensor combinations to completely emulate a game controller. The key element to these functionalities is the Universal HID Actuator module developed in course of the AsTeRICS project.

The Universal HID Actuator module is a USB dongle which acts as mouse-, keyboard- and joystick on a host system (Windows / Linux / Mac computer or game console). The only requirement is that the host system supports standard HID input devices, thus no driver software has to be installed. The control information (for example x/y mouse cursor position and clicking commands) is sent from the AsTeRICS Runtime Environment (ARE) to the HID actuator dongle via a Bluetooth wireless connection or via a USB cable. The ARE can run on the AsTeRICS Personal Platform or on a Laptop/Netbook computer and transforms information of other input devices into the (emulated) game controller actions.

The hardware of the Universal HID Actuator consists of an 8-bit Atmel AVR 90USB1286 microcontroller[2] and a Rayson BTM-222 Bluetooth[3] module with Serial Port Profile support. The AVR microcontroller supports USB 2.0 full speed Device and On-The-Go applications with a dedicated hardware block. The Bluetooth module acts as a cable replacement solution for UART serial data transfers at 115.2 kBaud between the AsTeRICS Personal Platform (or a PC running the AsTeRICS Runtime Environment) and the microcontroller.

The microcontroller firmware builds upon the free LUFA library (Lightweight USB framework for AVRs [9]) and uses 4 of the 6 programmable USB endpoints of the AVR microcontroller to enumerate standard HID devices (mouse, keyboard and joystick) on the host system. This means that the host system cannot distinguish the

---

[1] http://uk.playstation.com/ps3/peripherals/detail/item113530/
DUALSHOCK%C2%AE3-wireless-controller/
[2] http://atmel.com/dyn/resources/prod_documents/7593S.pdf
[3] http://www.rayson.com/product/wireless/BTM-22x.htm

HID actuator from these 3 physical devices after the USB dongle has been attached and enumerated.

By sending a special byte sequence as reply to a device control request in course of the USB device enumeration, the HID actuator mimics the behaviour of the PS3 native controllers and thereby becomes a fully functional replacement for a "sixaxis" gamepad, including the "PS"–button functionality (which is not available when a standard PC-gamepad is attached to the PS 3).

The control information for gamepad emulation (button pressed / release actions, analogue controller-axis orientation) are sent from the AsTeRICS Runtime Environment to the HID actuator via a bi-directional communication protocol. This "CIM-Protocol" [10] specifies commands and features for all functions of the HID devices, in particular of the HID joystick device.

The ARE "RemoteJoystick" actuator plugin transfers signals from other AsTeRICS plugins to the HID actuator via a COM-Port and Bluetooth. The HID actuator prepares and sends according USB reports to the host system. The "RemoteJoystick" Plugin allows the attachment of desired input activities to any button or analogue axis of the controller, so that for example 3 of the 13 buttons can be directly actuated via external switches, the other buttons can be pressed via scanning selection of an On-Screen Keyboard, and the left stick can be controlled by a camera based head tracking. Thus, dedicated system models can be generated to control PS3 games via tailored input configurations. Update rates of 120 Hz and more are possible, which provides a perfect basis for low-latency gaming interfaces.

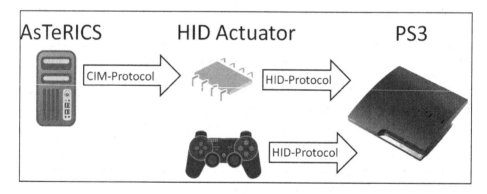

Fig. 2. Schematic drawing: How to control the PS 3

3.1   Other Adaptive PS 3 Controllers

The presented solution is not the first attempt to control the PS3 with special, adaptive devices. Do-it-yourself enthusiastics and professional companies have developed several solutions.

The *PS3IR-1000 Wireless Infra-red Adapter for PlayStation 3* [11] allows the control of the PS3 via an infrared remote control or via an USB connection. With some additional software, it can be used by people with disabilities, controlling the PS3 (as shown in this video: http://www.ablegamers.com/7-gaming-with-a-physical-disability/5648-controlling-ps3-via-pc-using-universal-remote-cont.html).

Another solution is the *PS3-Switch Access Pod* [12], a switch box with seventeen 3.5mm input sockets for the buttons and two connections for the analogue joysticks. Additionally, accessories like analogue and digital joysticks, footswitches, etc. are available for this device.

Comparing these solutions to AsTeRICS, AsTeRICS has the advantage, that more input devices or the combination of several input devices can be used to control the PS3. Furthermore, the input signals can be processed, before sending to the PS3.

4   An Example Game

For the first implementation (as a proof of concept), a pinball game has been adapted. The chosen game was *Marvel Pinball*[4], where only three buttons are needed to control the game. The player needs to trigger the left and right paddle and push one button to insert the ball. These functions were implemented using three push buttons, connected to a General Purpose Input/Output module, which can be positioned according to the requirements of the gamer. In the ACS model (see Fig. 3) these push buttons were mapped to the PS3 buttons, needed to control the game.

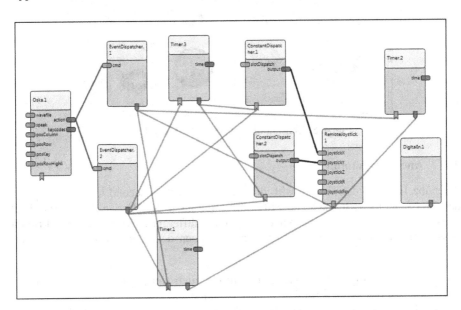

Fig. 3. The ACS model to play Marvel Pinball on the PS3

Additionally the gamer must be able to browse menus, to actually start the game. Therefore he/she needs to move up, down, left, right, select menu items and jump to

---

[4] http://marvelpinball.com/

the previous menu. In the ACS model, *OSKA*[5] (On-Screen Keyboard Application) is used to navigate the menus. A custom developed on screen keyboard layout is shown on the ARE display (see Fig. 4), visualizing the PS3 buttons up, down, left, right, circle (select previous menu), and cross (activate selected menu item). To select a button scanning is used. The actual key press can be activated by different methods like blinking with the eyes, opening the mouth or pressing a push button. Whenever the user presses a button on the screen keyboard, the corresponding PS3 button gets pressed for 250 ms.

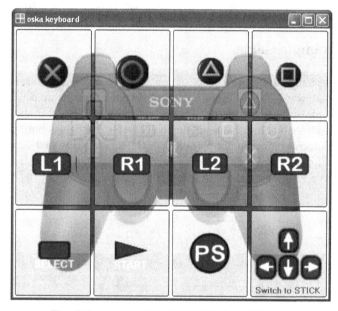

Fig. 4. Screenshot of the OSKA Keyboard Layout

4.1   Another Example

After the first successful tests with the *Marvel Pinball*, a second test case has been developed. To increase the complexity, the racing game *ModNation Racers*[6] has been chosen. For this game, several models with three different input devices and different possibilities for acceleration and breaking had been developed. The used input devices are:

- *Wii Mote* controller of the Nintendo Wii: the pitch value is used to control the direction, the roll value is used for the acceleration and break.
- The *Kinect* of the Microsoft Xbox 360: movements of the hands (like using an imaginary steering wheel) are used to change the steering direction. The distance between the hands and the chest are used for controlling the throttle and brakes, where a higher distance means more throttle.

---

[5] http://www.clarosoftware.com/index.php?cPath=365
[6] http://www.modnation.com/en_gb/index/index.htm

- A standard webcam, where movements of the head are mapped to the steering direction of the car. This means, that the user can steer to the left and right by moving the head slightly in these directions. To control the throttle, the user has to open and close his mouth, where mouth open means accelerate and mouth closed stands for no acceleration.

Beside the already mentioned options for controlling the acceleration and brakes, simple switches, bend sensors, speech recognition or automatic acceleration can be used, by simply changing the AsTeRICS model.

4.2   User Feedback

Two of the three test cases (the webcam model needs some more fine-tuning be-fore testing) had been tested by a small group of people with mobility and/or cognitive impairments. The tests have shown, that people who are having problems with the usage of the standard controller, perform better with the AsTeRICS system. Playing the game was more fun for them, than playing with the standard controller.

The fact, that the new control movements are more related to the real movements of the steering wheel, turns out as a big benefit for people with cognitive disabilities. One test user was twice more fast with the Kinect controlled system than with the standard PS3 controller.

Further tests with a bigger user test group will show, how more functions (like using more buttons) can be used within the different games. This problem might be able to be solved by combining different input devices. One possible addition would be speech input, which is already supported by the Kinect SDK.

5   Further Steps and Outlook

The combination of the different kinds of sensors allows people with very limited mobility the control of games. Tests with a fist user show very promising results. Further user tests will show the usage of AsTeRICS for games in a more detailed way. Nevertheless, this solution has some limitations:

- Each game needs a separate optimized model, where the available (controllable) input devices are mapped to all or at least the main features. In some cases, one input device has to be mapped to several buttons, using timers or on screen keyboards with scanning to select the different buttons.
- Many games require a fast reaction for the gamer. For people with disabilities, this can be a problem. To make more games accessible, the games must provide the possibility to set the game speed and several difficulty levels.

AsTeRICS cannot solve all problems within the area of games accessibility and it cannot make all games accessible to all players with mobility impairments, but it is a big step forward, making many mainstream games accessible to a group of people, which nowadays can only passive watch and not active play these games.

Acknowledgements. The AsTeRICS project is partially funded by the European Commission under the Seventh (FP7 - 2007-2013) Framework Programme for Research and Technological Development, Grant Agreement number 247730.

References

1. Terrestrial Invaders, `http://www.ics.forth.gr/hci/ua-games/index_main.php?l=e&c=579`
2. OneSwitch.org, `http://www.oneswitch.org.uk/4/games/0index.html`
3. The AsTeRICS Project, `http://www.asterics.eu/`
4. Ossmann, et al.: Bring the Users to the Games by the usage of the Assistive Technology Rapid Integration & Construction Set. In: 1st Workshop on Game Accessibility: Xtreme Interaction Design, Bordeaux, France, June 28 (2011)
5. USB Implementers' Forum. Device Class Definition for Human Interface Devices (HID) (2001), `http://www.usb.org/developers/devclass_docs/HID1_11.pdf`
6. Bardram, J.E., Mihailidis, A., Wan, D.: Pervasive Healthcare: Research and Applications of Pervasive Computing in Healthcare. CRC Press (2006)
7. Nussbaum, G., et al.: AsTeRICS - Towards a Rapid Integration Construction Set for Assistive Technologies. In: AAATE Conference 2011, Maastricht, The Netherlands (2011)
8. KNX – the Worldwide Standard for Home and Building Control, `http://www.knx.org`
9. Lightweight USB Framework for AVRs (LUFA) (2011), `http://www.fourwalledcubicle.com/LUFA.php`
10. AsTeRICS. AsTeRICS Developer Manual (2012), `http://www.asterics.eu/index.php`
11. Schmatz: PS3IR-1000 Wireless Infra-red Adapter for PlayStation 3 (2012), `http://www.schmartz.com/PS3IR1000-Wireless-Infrared-Adapter-for-PlayStation/M/B0028S7BZY.html`
12. LEPMIS Game Access Solutions. PS3-Switch Access Pod (2012), `http://shop.lepmis.co.uk/epages/es135457.sf/en_GB/?ObjectPath=/Shops/es135457/Products/PS3-SAP`

Creating an Entertaining and Informative Music Visualization

Michael Pouris and Deborah I. Fels

Ryerson University, Toronto, Ontario, Canada
{mpouris,dfels}@ryerson.ca

Abstract. Auditory music is a universal art form that has spanned millennia. Music provides an insight into the collective culture of a society and acts as a vehicle to transmit shared knowledge that is common to all members of society. People who are deaf, deafened or hard of hearing tend to have a limited access to music and as a result can be excluded from this shared knowledge and cultural experience. A music visualization system, MusicViz, was developed based on a model of audio-visual sensory substitution. An evaluation of six different music genres showed that the visualizations were enjoyable and able to convey some information and emotions to the participants.

1   Introduction

In modern Western culture, music is everywhere: it is heard in restaurants, spas, clubs, concerts, and many other venues. With the advent of technological advancements, individuals carry thousands of songs on MP3 players and phones. Music helps to convey modern culture and provides a shared experience and knowledge space that spans cultural boundaries [1]. Individuals listen to music for entertainment as well as the emotional responses it evokes.

Fourney and Fels [1] state that music, other than recorded music, is often not enjoyed through sound alone; it is accompanied by visuals, such as facial expressions, body language and various special effects in television shows, live concerts and movies in order to reinforce emotional information. Even though visuals provide redundant information, Eldridge and Saltzman [2] show that sensory redundancy increases the robustness of learning and can reinforce conveyed concepts and emotions.

Deaf (D), deafened (DN) and hard of hearing (HOH) individuals have limited access to the emotional experiences, collective culture and shared knowledge that is available to a mainstream hearing culture through music [1]. This is an issue for individuals who desire access to sound-based music. However, this does not mean that deaf culture is devoid of music; deaf communities experience music through a strong bass presence that can be felt by touching or being in close proximity to the sound source or through vibrations in surfaces or the air. Rhythmic gestures can also be performed using sign language creating patterns and music-like structures. Even though the deaf community can make its own form of music, there is also interest by some individuals in that community to have access to sound-based music from the mainstream hearing culture.

K. Miesenberger et al. (Eds.): ICCHP 2012, Part I, LNCS 7382, pp. 451–458, 2012.
© Springer-Verlag Berlin Heidelberg 2012

For HOH individuals, the issues are somewhat different. Individuals who are HOH have some residual hearing (although the extent of this hearing varies extensively). Music is often distorted or missing elements as a result of hearing loss or hearing aids causing it to be a confusing, incomplete or even an unpleasant experience [1].

In this paper we report on a music visualization system, called MusicViz, designed to translate auditory music into pre-attentive visual queues. The translation algorithm is grounded in a psychological model that defines the translation principles (see sections 2 and 3). We also present a preliminary evaluation of the MusicViz system with D/HOH participants.

2   Background

The visualization of music has existed for many years as art installations [3], as well as through commercial music players such as iTunes™ or Windows Media Player™ [1]. Art installations are often created by artists as abstract renditions of their own or other's music [3]. Such endeavors require large amounts of time and effort among production and animation teams for a one time visual interpretation, which is not feasible for every musical piece.

Music players use software algorithms to automatically extract relevant music data such as frequency and time from a digital music file and render that data as visualizations [1]. For the purpose of this paper, music visualization is an automated technique requiring no human intervention and that automatically generates a visual representation of a piece of digital music.

In order to convey the emotional and structural information of music to D or HOH individuals through an automatic visualization, relevant audio information must be translated to appropriate and relevant visual queues. However, there are two main issues to consider. The first issue rests in the method of translating auditory constructs to visual constructs. Physiologically and cognitively, auditory and visual signals are processed differently in the human brain and there is little overlap [4]. This means that there may not be a direct or obvious mapping that conveys the same emotions from music to both systems. There may be no obvious visual equivalent of a specific emotion being conveyed aurally (and vice versa).

The second issue is that the basic models of emotions do not necessarily reflect music. One model categorizes emotion in a discrete set of high-level emotion labels such as anger, fear, sadness, disgust, surprise, anticipation, trust and joy [5]. There is little convention or research that relates music properties such as pitch and beat to these discrete emotions (although people are capable of categorizing songs with discrete emotions).

A second common model of emotion proposed in [6] represents emotion along three different axes: valence (pleasant-unpleasant), arousal (awake-tired) and tension (tense-relaxed). Even though music evokes numerous emotions that differ from song to song, all music is a combination of pitch, tempo and volume [7]. Pitch, tempo and volume are shown in [7] to be the carriers of the three-dimensional model of emotion: valence ratings are affected by volume, tempo and pitch (e.g., fast tempo with lower pitch height is more pleasant); arousal is affected by volume and tempo (high volume and fast tempo is more arousing); and volume, tempo and pitch affect tension (high volume, fast tempo and high pitch has higher tension) [7].

Each of the three dimensions also has visual representations that researchers have found to be pre-attentively understood. First, volume is associated with visual brightness; the louder a sound is the brighter it is [8]. The second affiliation of volume is the psychological reaction to looming objects (the closer an object, the louder it is). Auditory and visual looming queues cause an evolutionary avoidance response to fast approaching danger [9]. Pitch height is associated with colour brightness, object size and vertical height using contour [10]. A higher pitch is psychologically linked with a lighter colour, whereas a lower pitch is linked with a darker colour. A higher pitch is also affiliated with smaller objects, while a lower pitch is linked with larger objects. Faster tempos are shown to intuitively create higher emotional arousal whereas slower tempos trigger calmer emotions [10].

Although the three affective dimensions have been shown to convey pre-attentive emotional information when viewed individually, difficulties arise when they are combined into a single visualization. The issue is that pitch and volume are linked to brightness and size, meaning that pitch and volume cannot both alter these same variables without causing confusion, therefore a decision must be made pertaining to what the variables each alters.

Most music visualizations from conventional digital music player software do not attempt to represent the emotional content but rather provide aesthetic pleasing visualizations only [1]; however, there are some recent efforts to use psychological models as an underlying translation framework. Kunze and Taube [11] propose an algorithm that translates musical notation to blocks along a static timeline. Each block is given a specific colour that is dependent on its pitch. Others [12] describe a method of converting musical notation into 3D space, where each instrument is represented as spheres with colours representing the timbre of instrument. This type of research tends to be focused on a solution that teaches musical constructs and communicates the information of music, not the emotional aspects.

The music visualization solution proposed in this paper is different from the previously described visualizations because its primary goal is not for education or to be aesthetically pleasing but mostly uninformative expression. MusicViz's goal is to combine the informative and entertainment aspects of music visualization for use by HOH or D individuals to understand and enjoy music.

3   Music Visualization System

MusicViz attempts to overcome the problem of combining pitch, volume and tempo into one visualization by exploiting three-dimensional space for these three music elements. The music data for the system is provided through MIDI files as pitch, tempo and volume information is available as separate variables.

A MIDI message is composed of the role, such as note messages or system messages, it plays in the MIDI system and its target channel. The MIDI standard allows for 16 channels where each channel represents a family of similar instruments. For example, a channel can represent string instruments and contain two guitars. The channel setup is unique to each song; however, the 10th channel is always reserved for percussion instruments.

In MusicViz, the MIDI data used are: (1) note on/off messages (channels 1 to 9 and 11 to 16) and (2) percussion messages (channel 10). Note on/off messages are composed of three bytes. The first byte signifies the target channel and whether it is a note on or off signal. The second byte indicates the note (pitch) played and the third byte communicates the volume at which the pitch is played. Volume and pitch are represented by a range of values from 0 to 127. A note on/off message which targets channel 10 is only for percussion.

MusicViz is designed to parse the incoming MIDI messages and translate the data into associated visual representations. MusicViz is designed in Java 6 and uses the 3D graphics technologies of JOGL 2.0 (Java OpenGL).

To represent music in a visual manner, MusicViz presents non-percussive instruments as coloured pipes. The position and size of the pipes are altered as the song changes over time displaying pitch, volume, and tempo changes (see Fig. 1.). Two pipes are assigned to each of the 16 channels, excluding the 10th channel.

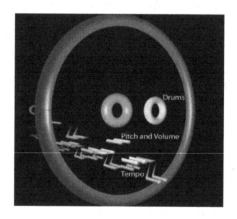

Fig. 1. MusicViz for Rock Example

Table 1. Auditory Mappings into MusicViz

Auditory Construct	MusicViz Translation
Pitch	Pipe's y-axis position
Volume	Pipe size (diameter) and colour brightness (alpha)
Tempo	Pipe's z-axis position
Bass/Drums	Five toroid objects

As described in the previous section, pitch and volume are pre-attentively unders-tood in the visual system when mapped to colour brightness and size; however, the problem is that both musical constructs cannot occupy colour brightness and size concurrently. Our solution to this problem is to use the y-axis to represent pitch height and allow brightness and size to represent volume. Table 1 summarizes the auditory mappings in MusicViz.

4   Methodology

Twelve individuals participated in a study to determine the enjoyability and effective-ness of MusicViz: three H (one male, two female), three (HOH) (two male, one female), six D (three male, three female). An American Sign Language interpreter participated in studies with all of the deaf participants to facilitate discussion. The participants ranged in age from 18 to 64.

Five participants reported listening to music everyday (one D, two HOH, two H), one H participant listened to music "every 2-3 days", three D participants listened to music "once a week", one HOH participant listened to music "once a month" and one D participant never listened to music. There was one D participant who did not an-swer the question.

Seven participants reported enjoying rock music (two H, three HOH, two D), six enjoyed rap/hip-hop/R&B (RHRB) music (two H, two HOH, two D), five enjoyed country music (one H, two HOH, two D), seven enjoyed classical music (two H, two HOH, three D), one D participant enjoyed metal music and six reported enjoying other genres not listed. Seven participants reported listening to music for enjoyment (one D, three HOH, three H), seven reported listening to music for relaxation (three D, two HOH, two H), two reported to listen to music for emotional purposes (one HOH, one D), only one H person reported to listen to music for distraction, and two participants listen to music for other reasons (one D, one H).

Participants were asked to watch six different visualizations of songs approximate-ly one minute long on a 24" LCD display. One song from each of six different genres (classical, country, jazz, pop, RHRB and rock, where each genre contained between 60 and 100 MIDI songs) was randomly selected.

The participants completed a pre-study questionnaire to gather demographic in-formation, such as gender, hearing status, musical preferences, reasons for listening to music and education. During the study, while the participants were watching the visu-alizations, eye-tracking data was collected using FaceLab 5.0 for each of the six songs. After each song, the participants filled out an after-song questionnaire to give feedback on their enjoyment and emotional experience with the visualization. After viewing all six songs, the participants completed a post-study questionnaire to sum-marize what each of the visual constructs meant to the individual. The participants were recorded for the duration of the study such that any spoken or signed comments are cataloged. In this paper, only the data from the six after-song questionnaires are presented.

5   Results and Discussion

5.1   Differences in Level of Enjoyability between Genres

To examine the difference in enjoyability between genres, a repeated measures ANOVA was carried out. Participants rated the level of enjoyment on a 5-point rating scale ranging from "1-Not enjoyable at all" to "5-Enjoyable". The results showed that there was no significant difference in enjoyability between the genres ($p > 0.05$).

Even though there are no statistical differences there are emerging trends in enjoyability. All six genres are rated between "4-Somewhat enjoyable" and "5-Enjoyable" indicating that the visualization is pleasant to view. Rock music is rated the highest for enjoyability (M=4.5, SD=0.85) perhaps because it has the least complex visualizations. It is, however, surprising that RHRB enjoyability ratings are the lowest among the ratings (M=4.0, SD=1.054) and are similar to those of classical music. RHRB type of music is heavily reliant on a strong beat/bass similar to Deaf music and we hypothesized that it would receive a high enjoyability rating. Classical music does not have a strong bass/beat and we hypothesized that the enjoyment rating would be low as a result, however this seems not to be the case (M=4.0, SD=1.247).

5.2   Differences in Levels of Emotion between Genres

Participants rated the levels of valence, arousal and overbearingness using the 9-point self-assessment manikin [13] for each dimension ("1-unhappy" to "9-happy" (happiness) for the valence scale, the second scale ranged from "1-calm" to "9-excited" (arousal) and the third scale ranged from "1-subtle" to "9-overbearing" (overbearingness). To examine the difference in conveyed emotion between genres, a repeated measures ANOVA was carried out. The results show that there is no significant difference in the level of happiness and arousal between genres ($p > 0.05$); however, there is a significant difference in the level of overbearingness [$F(5,55)=2.378$] (assumption of sphericity was met). Paired t-tests show a significant difference between country and pop music ($t(11)=-3.336$, $p < 0.05$) and between pop and RHRB music ($t(11)=2.569$, $p < 0.05$).

Participants appeared to recognize that pop music (M=6.42, SD=1.084) is more overbearing than RHRB (M=4.92, SD=1.564) and country (M=4.25, SD=1.603), which could be explained by the quantity of instruments appearing for each of these genres. Guitars performing with little or no drums often characterize country music, whereas pop music contains more instruments including drums and a prominent bass line that often repeats. Frequently repeating movements were reported by participants to be more energetic, angry and harsh. Even though RHRB contains a strong bass line, it often has stronger voice presence, which is not shown in the visual MIDI representation, and fewer instruments. It would seem that fewer instruments appearing on screen are less overbearing while more instruments, frequently repeating movement and a prominent baseline are considered more overbearing.

In addition to the statistical differences, there are differing trends in the happiness, and overbearingness ratings, which show that even though a genre can be more overbearing, it does not mean it is less happy. For example, pop music has one of the highest overbearing ratings (M=6.42, SD=1.084) and the highest arousal (M=6.08, SD=2.021) and happiness ratings (M= 6.75, SD=2.179).

5.3   Differences in Level of Discrete Emotion Ratings between Genres

A repeated measures ANOVA analysis was carried out in order to examine the difference in participant's ratings of discrete emotions expressed in the songs between genres. Participants rated the levels of emotions expressed in each of the visualizations using four 7-point scales for happiness, sadness, anger and fear where "1" was weak and "7" was strong. There was no significant difference in the happiness, sadness, anger and fear between any of the genres (p>0.05). However, there may be a correlation between the levels of sadness, anger, and happiness but more participants are required to carry out valid correlation statistics.

5.4   Differences in Level of Focus between Genres

Participants were asked to rate their level of focus on the visualization on a five-point Likert scale ranging from "1-My mind wondered a lot" to "5-I was always focused on the visualization". A repeated measures ANOVA analysis was used to determine difference in focus between genres. There was no significant difference in the level of focus on the visualization between the viewed genres (p>0.05).   From the descriptive results, however, participants appeared to pay the most attention to rock (M=4.91, SD=0.302), country (M=4.73, SD=1.206) and jazz (M=4.64, SD=0.505) music visualizations, while paying least attention to pop (M=4.09, SD=1.378) and RHRB (M=4.09, SD=1.578). This is surprising because D and HOH individuals mainly experience music through vibrations from the drums and bass, which are easily identifiable in MusicViz, yet the participants paid the least attention to genres having a dominant percussion line. A possible reason for this result is that D and HOH rely heavily on their visual sense and when the visualizations have changing visual patterns, they capture people's attention. RHRB and pop tend to have repeating percussive and bass elements, which may require less attention.

Participants also rated their level of agreement on a five-point Likert scale pertaining to the likability of the colours. There is no significant difference in the level of agreement (p>0.05), when using a repeated measures ANOVA. However, examining the descriptive data we found that enjoyability of the colours of the pipes was high for all genres (1.6<M<2.4, 0.8<SD<1.6). Considering colours are not meant to elicit emotional responses, it is promising that the colours are pleasant to view regardless of the music genre visualized. The major limitation to the study is the lack of study participants. With additional participants we could examine differences between people with different hearing abilities as well as determine whether the trends observed in the descriptive data could be actual statistical differences.

6   Conclusion

Overall, participants seem to enjoy the visualizations and showed some preferences for rock and pop visualizations. Participants also seemed to enjoy the colours that were used for all genres. Other trends that appeared were that some individuals showed greater preferences to classical music over RHRB. The next step in this research is to increase the number of participants in the study to examine statistical differences and to explore using a true 3D display for the visualizations.

Acknowledgements. We would like to thank NSERC (grant # 184220) and the GRAND NCE for supporting this research through the AESTHVIS project. We also gratefully acknowledge all participants who gave their time and effort in our study.

References

1. Fourney, D.W., Fels, D.I.: Creating Access to Music through Visualization. In: 2009 IEEE Toronto International Conference on Science and Technology for Humanity (TIC-STH), pp. 939–944 (2009)
2. Eldridge, M., Saltzman, E., Lahav, A.: Seeing what You Hear: Visual Feedback Improves Pitch Recognition. European Journal of Cognitive Psychology 22, 1078–1091 (2010)
3. Hiraga, R., Watanabe, F., Fujishiro, I.: Music Learning through Visualization (2002)
4. Bertini, C., Leo, F., Alessio, A., Làdavas, E.: Independent Mechanisms for Ventriloquism and Multisensory Integration as Revealed by Theta-Burst Stimulation. Eur. J. Neurosci. 31, 1791–1799 (2010)
5. Ortony, A., Turner, T.J.: What's Basic about Basic Emotions? Psychol. Rev. 97, 315–331 (1990)
6. Russell, J.A.: A Circumplex Model of Affect. Journal of Personality and Social Psychology 39, 1161–1178 (1980)
7. Ilie, G., Thompson, W.F.: A Comparison of Acoustic Cues in Music and Speech for Three Dimensions of Affect. Music Perception: An Interdisciplinary Journal 23, 319 (2006)
8. Marks, L.E.: On Cross-Modal Similarity: The Perceptual Structure of Pitch, Loudness, and Brightness. Journal of Experimental Psychology: Human Perception and Performance 15, 586–602 (1989)
9. Schiff, W., Caviness, J.A., Gibson, J.J.: Persistent Fear Responses in Rhesus Monkeys to the Optical Stimulus of "Looming". Science 136, 982–983 (1962)
10. Schubert, E.: Modeling Perceived Emotion with Continuous Musical Features. Music Perception 21, 561–561 (2004)
11. Kunze, T., Taube, H.: See: A Structured Event Editor - Visualizaing Compositional Data in Common Music (1996)
12. Smith, S.M., Williams, G.N.: A Visualization of Music. In: Proceedings of Visualization 1997, pp. 499–503 (1997)
13. Bradley, M.M., Lang, P.J.: Measuring Emotion: The Self-Assessment Manikin and the Semantic Differential. J. Behav. Ther. Exp. Psychiatry 25, 49–59 (1994)

Music at Your Fingertips: Stimulating Braille Reading by Association with Sound

Felix Grützmacher

Handy Tech Elektronik GmbH, Brunnenstraße 10
72160 Horb-Nordstetten, Germany
felix.gruetzmacher@handytech.de

Abstract. Driven by the ongoing integration of computers into the daily lives of blind people, the reading experience has been undergoing a significant shift from Braille to synthetic speech. While it is true that speech involves less effort on the part of the reader, the downside is that it creates the illusion of completeness of information while in truth many important elements of layout, punctuation, and spelling are lost. The presentation introduces an application of Active Tactile Control which revolves around the medium of music and is designed in such a way that students can only succeed if they mentally translate auditive impressions into Braille characters.

Keywords: MusikBraille, Learning, Didactic, Active Tactile Control, Braille music notation, software, synaesthesia, auditive feedback, editor.

1   Introduction

Music is perhaps one of the oldest, and certainly the most artistic form of auditory communication among human beings, so any comprehensive approach to literacy for the blind must address musical literacy. The good news is that Louis Braille, in inventing Braille music notation, has opened the door for blind musicians to participate on equal terms in the creation, interchange, and performance of music on all levels of complexity. However, Braille music notation can be shown to have some inherent barriers not found in conventional print music notation.

Section 2 of this paper seeks to identify these inherent barriers of Braille music when compared to print music. Section 3 then goes on to propose solutions and describe the technologies required for their implementation. The author is hoping to demonstrate that all of the required technologies are now in existence and a partial solution to the problems of section 2 has been established. Section 4 concludes by providing an out-line for suggested research.

2   The Barriers

2.1   Maps of Music

Sheet music, in its conventional print form, serves as a particularly good example of a useful map. Its territory is the entirety of musical expression, and its chosen level of

K. Miesenberger et al. (Eds.): ICCHP 2012, Part I, LNCS 7382, pp. 459–462, 2012.

abstraction is pitch over time, or, in other words, when to play what note for how long. Sheet music elegantly models the structure of music in much the same way as a diagram models the structure of a mathematical function. The vertical position of a note signifies its pitch, whereas the horizontal position and extension determine its time characteristics.

Braille music, on the other hand, is strictly linear in that it consists of a one-dimensional string of characters. There is no mapping between pitch and position. Rather, the pitch of a note is entirely determined by its dot pattern and context. Both pitch and length are represented in the dot pattern of a note, greatly increasing the set of possible symbols.

2.2   Demand on Memory

Users of Braille music notation cannot take full advantage of sheet music during practice. While some instruments allow for one-handed playing, leaving the other hand free to peruse the sheet music, blind musicians are usually forced to commit increasing chunks of music to memory and practice them separately.

2.3   Mental Translation Steps

The structure of conventional sheet music enables the reader to visually follow the flow of a melody in space while simultaneously following a mental imprint of the same melody in auditory memory. Over time, the spatial concepts of "up" and "down" become linked to the auditory concepts of "high" and "low," creating in the reader's mind a synaesthesia between the modalities of sight and sound. For Braille music, the link between tactile and auditory impressions has to be established for each note individually.

In addition to dropping the direct link from pitch to position, Braille music notation also omits the time axis. In print notation, rhythm is encoded into the horizontal distribution of notes along a staff, or system. Braille notation does not contain an analogous concept.

3   Bridging the Gap

3.1   Active Tactile Control

The approach presented here is based on a paradigm shift in how Braille displays are used. The traditional role of the Braille display, with the exception of navigation keys and cursor routing, has been that of a passive medium for displaying information to the user. With Active Tactile Control (ATC), the Braille display itself is elevated to the status of an input/output device.

ATC allows a Braille display to detect the position of one or more reading fingers on the Braille cells. From these individual positions the software can deduce with some certainty the current reading position, or focus of attention.

3.2   Associating Tactile and Auditory Stimuli

Section 2 of this paper has developed the idea that the key barrier to learning Braille music notation consists of establishing a mental link between dot patterns and their corresponding notes. The solution proposed here is a software application which runs directly on a Braille display.

The application is currently being developed under the working title of "Musik-Braille," and runs on the Handy Tech ActiveBraille device. Its behaviour can best be described in terms of an editor in which the user can type Braille music using the integrated Braille keyboard. Basic editing operations are provided, such as scrolling, cursor routing, insertion, and deletion. The cursor position is signified by dots 7 and 8, which has the combined advantage of being conventional and not conflicting with 6-dot Braille music.

The key feature of MusikBraille, however, is its ability to provide auditive feedback for both reading and writing operations. Whenever the user enters a valid note, Mu-sikBraille can play that note via the built-in speaker or headphones. Similarly, using ATC, MusikBraille can be configured to play notes as they are being read on the Braille display. The effect is that of the reading position acting as tone arm, or play head, so the dot pattern under the finger is always synchronized with the note being heard. Both reading and typing feedback can be turned off at any time, allowing users to assess their ability to read and write Braille music without audio cues.

Auditory feedback during input of notes is used in a variety of digital audio worksta-tions such as those produced by Cakewalk, Inc. or Sony. However, the Music Braille application described herein is the first to link auditory feedback to reading behavior.

3.3   Time and Performance

With typing and reading feedback, it is impossible to perform a piece of music accurately, as timing depends directly on user input or reading speed rather than on the notation itself. To allow a user to receive an overall impression of the melody, as well as to verify the correctness of note lengths, MusikBraille can play the entire tune from start to finish with exact timing. While the tune is being played, the Braille display scrolls along with the flow of the music, and the cursor is moved over every note in real-time.

4   Suggested Research

The current implementation of MusikBraille is based on the hypothesis that simulta-neous tactile and auditory input, when repeated systematically, can build up mental links, or bidirectional associations, between the two simultaneous stimuli. While this hypothesis holds true during early infancy, making language acquisition possible for blind children, its validity for different age groups and in domains other than natural language remains to be tested. In particular, the author is uncertain whether the audi-tive input might distract from the dot pattern rather than augmenting it. Initial impressions suggest that the method is effective; during presentations of the application, the author observed instances in which blind students, who had never before read or written Braille music, were able to correctly key in simple melodies in a matter of minutes.

The author suggests the following method for further research on the didactic effectiveness of the MusikBraille application and its approach:

1. A method must be developed for measuring the quality and efficiency of the mental link between the Braille notes and their auditory counterparts. In this context, quality refers to the exact means by which the Braille notes are mentally translated into auditory impressions.
2. Using the method developed in the first phase, a group of students who acquired Braille music notation with the aid of the MusikBraille software could be tested against a control group of students who acquired it without any computer-aided approach. Any significant difference may then provide insight into the effectiveness of MusikBraille in its current form, and the results of a questionnaire may hint at ways in which the process could be refined.

Acknowledgments. The author wishes to thank his employer, Handy Tech Elektronik GmbH, for providing the framework of resources and encouragement in which this project could grow. It is a privilege to be working in an area where art and science can unite. May this unity be fruitful to the blind community.

Reference

1. Braille Music Code (April 18, 2012), http://www.brl.org/music/index.html

Improving Game Accessibility
with Vibrotactile-Enhanced Hearing Instruments

Bernd Tessendorf[1], Peter Derleth[2], Manuela Feilner[2], Daniel Roggen[1],
Thomas Stiefmeier[1], and Gerhard Tröster[1]

[1] Wearable Computing Lab., ETH Zurich
Gloriastr. 35, 8092 Zurich, Switzerland
`lastname@ife.ee.ethz.ch`
[2] Phonak AG, Laubisrütistrasse 28, 8712 Stäfa, Switzerland
`firstname.lastname@phonak.com`

Abstract. In this work we present enhanced hearing instruments (HIs) that provide vibrotactile feedback behind the user's ears in parallel to sound. Using an additional feedback modality we display dedicated vibrotactile patterns to support the user in localizing sound sources. In a study with 4 HI users and 5 normal hearing participants we deploy the system in a gaming scenario. The open source availability of the mainstream 3D first person shooter game used in the study allowed us to add code for accessibility. We evaluate the system qualitatively with user questionnaires and quantitatively with performance metrics calculated from statistics within the game. The system was perceived as beneficial and allowed the HI users to achieve gaming performance closer to that of normal hearing participants.

1 Introduction

Hearing impairment affects millions of people with a rising trend, affecting not only the elderly [8]. A major concern for HI and cochlear implant users is lateralization, i.e. locating sound sources in the horizontal plane [10]. We suggest providing bilateral (behind both ears) vibrotactile feedback:

- Vibrotactile feedback does not interfere with ambient sound, so there are no masking effects.
- Tactile reaction time can be faster than to auditory feedback, especially when cognitive load is present [9]. Thus, tactile feedback is particularly appealing for games, because short response times are required.
- Vibrotactile feedback can be integrated into HIs.

We present a newly developed vibrotactile feedback system integrated into HIs. We deploy it in a user study (9 participants, 4 HI users, age 26–45, over 10 hours of gaming data) with a mainstream computer game that we extended for accessibility. We chose to render complex game interaction with an additional modality because:

K. Miesenberger et al. (Eds.): ICCHP 2012, Part I, LNCS 7382, pp. 463–470, 2012.
© Springer-Verlag Berlin Heidelberg 2012

- The game demands quick sound localizing skills from the user. Like in many real-life situations the user is under cognitive load when playing the game.
- A game is a natural environment yet controllable and reproducible for repeatable evaluations. It allows us to collect many relevant events that require lateralization of sound sources in a short time frame.
- Games are a user-friendly technique to familiarize the user with a new assistive technology [4].

We ask the research question "Can HI-integrated bilateral vibrotactile feedback support HI users with lateralization in gaming by compensating lateralization difficulties with sound?" Our concrete contributions in this paper are:

- Integration of vibrotactile feedback into HIs by means of a clip-on device
- Modification of an open source mainstream computer game for accessibility and data collection
- A study that includes HI users to evaluate benefits and user experiences with the system in a gaming scenario.

2   Related Work

A pair of glasses enhanced with 4 vibrators and 3 microphones to locate sound sources for visually and hearing impaired people was presented in [5]. However, the system is based on special goggles rather than bilateral integration into HIs.

In [14] the authors present a device to be placed inside the ear canal to transduce sound intro vibration. The device has two active states with two different vibration intensity levels: one for high and one for low frequency sound.

Research regarding tactile sensitivity measurement revealed that the region behind the ears at the mastoid bone is one of the most sensitive head regions for vibrotactile stimulation [11]. A pedestrian navigation system using vibration of mobile phones is shown in [12]. The running direction is encoded in the length of vibration and the distance in the pause time between two pulses. A cell phone based approach is presented in [3]. The authors investigate to use one vibrator in a mobile-phone device and let the user use it as a vibrating pointing device, e.g. to find a friend in a crowd.

In [7] the computer game Doom is enhanced with closed captioning to improve accessibility by showing textual representations of game sound events.

To the best of our knowledge bilateral vibrotactile feedback to support HI users with lateralization has so far not been considered in the research area of accessible gaming.

3   Enhancement of HIs with Bilateral Vibrotactile Feedback

3.1   Integration of Bilateral Vibrotactile Feedback into Hearing Instruments

We used 3D CAD rapid prototyping to produce a hardware that extends commercial HIs as shown in Fig. 1. It is based on miniaturized coin-shaped vibration

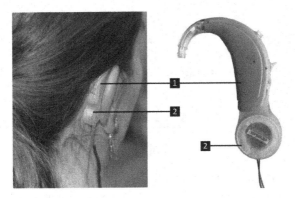

Fig. 1. User wearing the vibrotactile-enhanced HI comprising the commercial HI (1) and the modular extension (2) that holds a vibration motor

motors with a diameter of 10 mm (310-103 Vibration Motor 2.7 mm Button Type from Precision Microdrives) that have been developed for vibrotactile feedback in handheld applications. The user's PC controls the vibration via USB. It weighs 2.7 grams including the motor (one HI alone weighs 4 grams) and has dimensions of 17 mm diameter and 6 mm height. Users can unplug the module from their own HIs when he does not need it. Our device can fit all HIs that support plugging in FM-Receivers, which the majority of available commercial HIs do. The vibration duration was set to 70 ms with unnoticeable delay, and the vibration intensity was set to a level perceived as comfortable by the users.

3.2   Vibrotactile Patterns for Lateralization

In a pre-study with 12 normal hearing participants we evaluated 7 different vibrotactile patterns that support lateralization concerning angular resolution, intuitiveness, user misinterpretation and response time [13]. We identified a trade-off between angular resolution and response time. Based on these results we choose a 4-quadrant encoding scheme as shown in Fig. 2 to meet the requirement of short response times in our application. The front segment is not considered for vibrotactile feedback, because we assume the user's visual sense does not require lateralization assistance for objects in the field of view.

4   Application of the Vibrotactile Feedback System

4.1   Enhancement of a Mainstream Computer Game

Doom is a landmark 1993 first person shooter video game by id Software that is widely recognized for having popularized the first person shooter genre [1]. Despite of its age, it is still very popular and regularly ported to the most recent computer architectures. The player's task is to find the exit of a 3D-world

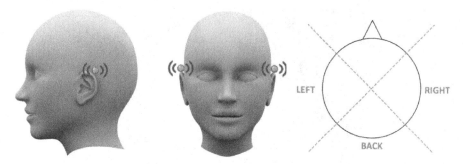

Fig. 2. Bilateral Vibrotactile Feedback is provided behind the user's ears. We divide the horizontal plane into 4 segments for the directions of the sound source to be located: left (vibration on left side), right (vibration on right side), and back (vibration on both sides).

dungeon. Meanwhile enemies attack, e.g. monsters fire rockets from all directions while stereo sound indicates from which direction the rocket was fired. Fig. 3 depicts a screenshot from within the game. As the game is open source [2], we modified it for accessibility and to collect in-game statistics. The original source code has been extended so that the direction and distance of fired rockets and rockets that hit the player are captured from internal data structures. When a rocket is fired at the user its direction (from left, right or back) is displayed to the user with the vibrotactile encoding described in section 3.2. The vibrotactile lateralization support is meant to support the user with detecting a rocket's direction to dodge in time. We use rockets as a first important example, other spatial game sound events could be handled the same way.

Fig. 3. Screenshot of the game showing a monster firing a rocket at the user

4.2   Experimental Procedure

Nine people (4 female, 5 male, age 26–45) participated in the study, none of them played the computer game before, and 4 of them were HI users. The procedure, sound and game settings were the same for all participants. We used a

Lenovo T400 notebook running Linux. We chose not to restrict the user to wear headphones but used the notebook's internal speakers at 100% volume.

Before the main study we performed a pre-experiment. We wanted to better understand how well HI users can decode the game stereo sound to assess if there is actually a need for assistive vibrotactile feedback. Each participant did not play the game yet but judged the perceived rocket direction (rocket fired from left, right, or back) for 36 sound samples. The sounds had been recorded from within the game for two conditions with and without game music. The sound samples were shuffled and then presented to each participant in the same order.

After the pre-experiment the users performed a training phase of about 20 minutes to get familiar with the game and keyboard control. Then the users played the game for about 50 minutes, half the time without and with vibrotactile feedback enabled. The procedure was repeated on another day to mitigate the influence of training effects and form on the day. To judge the HI users' results with vibrotactile feedback we compare to their results without vibrotactile feedback as a baseline performance and to results from normal hearing participants (without vibrotactile feedback) as a reference level to reach. The total procedure per user took about 1.5 hours. In total we recorded more than 10 hours of gaming data in which about 4500 rockets were fired. Finally, we collected subjective feedback on perceived benefit and usability with a questionnaire.

4.3   Evaluation Methodology

Qualitative evaluation is performed using a questionnaire. For quantitative evaluation of the pre-experiment we calculate the accuracy as the ratio of correctly recognized sound samples to the total number of presented sound samples. For quantitative evaluation of the gaming scenario we define the hit rate as how often rockets hit the user (Formula 1):

$$hit\ rate := \frac{\#\ rockets\ that\ hit\ the\ user}{\#\ fired\ rockets} \tag{1}$$

We calculate this measure directly from within the game to describe the user's game performance. A user that can localize fired rockets correctly and dodges them will achieve a lower hit rate.

4.4   Results and Discussion

Pre-experiment. Fig. 4 shows the accuracy for the pre-experiment as a measure of how well the participants can decode the direction of fired rockets solely from stereo sound samples recorded from within the game. HI users show a worse performance in interpreting sound information for lateralization than normal hearing participants, especially when game music is present. This confirms the need to support HI users with lateralization. The accuracy for recognizing sounds when game music is present achieved by HI users corresponds to guessing. This is confirmed by the questionnaire feedback. Without game music it was easier for HI users and normal hearing participants to recognize rocket directions. The performance also depends on the strength of the individual hearing loss. When playing the game, there is cognitive load and the task is even harder than in this pre-experiment where the participants could focus completely on the sound.

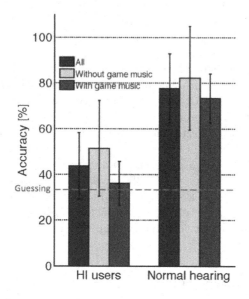

Fig. 4. Results for the pre-experiment: Accuracy for recognizing sound direction solely based on stereo sound samples that were recorded from within the game

Gaming Scenario. Fig. 5 shows the rate of fired rockets that actually hit the user for HI users when there is vibrotactile feedback enabled and not. HI users achieve a lower hit rate with vibrotactile feedback than without. Normal hearing participants without vibrotactile feedback still achieve a lower hit rate than HI users with.

Subjective Feedback by Questionnaire. HI users stated to have problems to localize the direction of a fired rocket based on game sound only. All participants stated that they could in some cases perceive the location information but were not able to react quickly enough to dodge the rocket. We assume, that this effect is the same for all participants. The HI users did not notice the additional weight of the vibrotactile extension. The vibration patterns were perceived as intuitive. Some users suggested implementing a more fine-grained angular resolution and also the distance of the rocket, e.g. by varying the vibration intensity.

5   Conclusion and Outlook

HI users could not benefit from the stereo game sound for localization as good as normal hearing participants. The newly developed HI-integrated vibrotactile

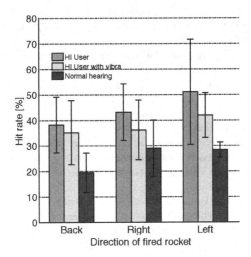

Fig. 5. Hit rate with and without vibrotactile feedback for HI users and without vibrotactile feedback for normal hearing participants. Smaller values indicate a better game performance.

feedback system was found to be useful to help them improve their gaming performance. The promising results from this feasibility study motivate a larger-scale user study. We find open source software, such as the mainstream computer game we used, especially useful for conducting accessibility user studies as it can be modified for accessibility and to collect internal in-game data.

Vibrotactile feedback could be deployed in parallel to closed captioning. A wide range of HIs supports clip-on devices such as the one we presented. We envision that they could optionally be bought in an aftermarket. They can modularly extend HIs for specific applications, e.g. for software applications. This requires support from the software via accessibility APIs or standard interfaces. Recently, the web standard HTML5 has been extended with an API to "programmatically provide tactile feedback in the form of vibration; the API is designed to tackle high-value use cases related to gaming" [6]. Our system could be one way to seamlessly interface with this standard. Similar APIs are available for Java and modern operating systems.

Acknowledgments. This work was part funded by CTI project 10698.1 PFLS-LS "Context Recognition for Hearing Instruments Using Additional Sensor Modalities". The authors gratefully thank all participants of the experiment and the reviewers for their valuable comments.

References

1. Doom, http://en.wikipedia.org/wiki/Doom_(video_game)
2. prboom, http://prboom.sourceforge.net/

3. Ahmaniemi, T., Lantz, V.: Augmented reality target finding based on tactile cues. In: Proceedings of the 2009 International Conference on Multimodal Interfaces, pp. 335–342. ACM (2009)
4. Archambault, D.: Entertainment Software Accessibility: Introduction to the Special Thematic Session. In: Miesenberger, K., Klaus, J., Zagler, W., Karshmer, A. (eds.) ICCHP 2010. LNCS, vol. 6179, pp. 224–226. Springer, Heidelberg (2010)
5. Borg, E., Ronnberg, J., Neovius, L., Lie, T.: Vibratory-coded directional analysis: Evaluation of a three-microphone/four-vibrator DSP system. J. of Rehabilitation Research and Development 38(2) (2001)
6. Consortium, W.: Html5 vibration api, http://www.w3.org/TR/vibration/
7. Kimball, R.B.: Doom closed captioning, http://blog.rbkdesign.com/
8. Kochkin, S.: MarkeTrak VIII: 25-year trends in the hearing health market. Hearing Review 16(11), 12–31 (2009)
9. Mohebbi, R., Gray, R., Tan, H.: Driver reaction time to tactile and auditory rear-end collision warnings while talking on a cell phone. Human Factors: The Journal of the Human Factors and Ergonomics Society 51(1), 102–110 (2009)
10. Mueller, M., Kegel, A., Schimmel, S., Hofbauer, M., Dillier, N.: Localization of virtual sound sources with bilateral hearing aids in realistic acoustical scenes. In: PACS (2011)
11. Myles, K.: Guidelines for Head Tactile Communication. Tech. rep., Army Research Lab Aberdeen Proving Ground Md Human Research And Engineering Directorate (2010)
12. Pielot, M., Poppinga, B., Boll, S.: PocketNavigator: vibro-tactile waypoint navigation for everyday mobile devices. In: Conference on Human Computer Interaction with Mobile Devices and Services (2010)
13. Tessendorf, B., Derleth, P., Feilner, M., Grämer, T., Roggen, D., Spuhler, M., Stiefmeier, T., Tröster, G.: Bilateral vibrotactile feedback patterns for accurate lateralization in hearing instrument body area networks. In: 6th International Conference on Body Area Networks, Bodynets (2011)
14. Weisenberger, J., Heidbreder, A., Miller, J.: Development and preliminary evaluation of an earmold sound-to-tactile aid for the hearing-impaired. J. Rehabil. Res. Dev. 24, 51–66 (1987)

An OCR-Enabled Digital Comic Books Viewer

Christophe Ponsard[1], Ravi Ramdoyal[1], and Daniel Dziamski[2]

[1] CETIC Research Center, Charleroi, Belgium
{christophe.ponsard,ravi.ramdoyal}@cetic.be
[2] University of Mons, Belgium
daniel.dziamsky@gmail.com

Abstract. The generalisation of user-friendly and mobile interfaces like smart phones, eBook readers and tablets has accelerated the transition of comic books to the digital format. Although such user interfaces are not always fit for use by people with special needs, the underlying platform offers a large number of innovative services which opens a wide spectrum of new possibilities for enhancing accessibility.

This paper explores how these new technologies can improve the digital access to comic books. Our main contribution is the inclusion of optical character recognition within text bubble associated to comics characters. The recognised text can then be fed into a text-to-speech engine for an improved experience. We also details performance improvements of other functionalities such as the panel order detection and special backgrounds. Finally, we discuss how these application specific adaptations can be applied to other contexts and which kind of future deployment can be anticipated.

Keywords: comics, accessibility, motor-impaired, low-sighted, mobile users, image processing, cloud, OCR, text-to-speech.

1 Introduction

Comic books [25] are very widespread in many countries and known under different names: Japanese Mangas, French-speaking "BD" (short for "bande dessinée", litterally "drawn strips") and US comics of course.

In previous papers [15,16], we have presented some domain specific adaptations allowing the user to control the navigation throughout digital comics in the most automated way. Our main contribution was a full sequencer able to segment scanned pages and present each panel in the reading order. This work triggered feedback about more advanced processing needs such as intra-bubble text recognition that could be fed into a text to speech engine.

In this paper, we extend our previous work in this direction considering the accessibility features offered by mature Open Source components, but also by Open Source APIs of recent platforms such as Android [11].

The paper is structured as follows: section 2 reminds about our previous work. Based on identified limitations and technological evolutions, section 3 proposes

K. Miesenberger et al. (Eds.): ICCHP 2012, Part I, LNCS 7382, pp. 471–478, 2012.

new features The implementation of those features is described in section 4. Section 5 discusses some related work. Finally, section 6 summarises the achievements, discusses how they can be applied in other kinds of applications and highlights some future directions.

2 State of the Art and Overview of Our Existing Viewer

Our viewer was originally developed in 2008 and was inspired by a number of state of the art comics viewers available then, such as Buoh (Linux)[17], ComicBookLover (MacOS)[21], CBViewer (platform independant) [23], CDisplay (Windows) [4], JOMICS (MacOS)[2]. At that time, little mobile viewers were starting to develop on PDA (e.g. ComicGuru [22]), gaming devices (e.g. ComicDS [5] for Nintendo DS) or mobile phones (e.g. ComicSurfing [7]).

Figure 1 summarises the main innovative feature supported by our tool. Starting from a set of scanned page (left), the viewer :

- extracts the panel locations and sorts them (center of figure), in this process, bubble location within each frame are also identified
- displays them in a specific "box" mode (right of figure) within a page and across pages
- through a simplified user interface providing simple previous/next commands
- available in different modalities: on screen button and remote control.

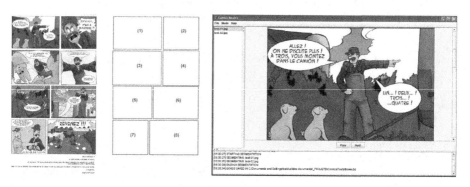

Fig. 1. Existing eComics Application

The prototype is based on ImageJ [1,6] and a watershed plug-in [20]. It is distributed and maintained as Open Source on http://sourceforge.net/projects/ecomics/.

3 New Features in a "Design for All" Spirit

The collected feedback after the validation phase of our previous work pointed out the following user requests of the next major release:

1. recognise text dialogues within bubbles
2. provide more modalities, notably touch screen commands and voice interfaces (integrated with related host platform voice features)
3. improve the performance of-the-box recognition and ordering, which was not always correct in less conventional layouts.

Integrating OCR is useful to improve the accessibility for visually impaired people by displaying them in specific way or feeding them through a text-to-speech engine. It can also benefit to all users, for example by enabling content indexation and search.

With the emergence of tablets, most mobile applications (or "apps") adapted to the larger resolution and interaction capabilities offered by those new devices. Although they offer an experience close to reading a traditional comic with about the same size, the above features remain interesting because people with a lower vision can enjoy a interesting experience on such devices, freeing them from a traditional screen with magnification. In addition, many mobile users will also continue to use lower resolution devices (typically mobile phones) on the move.

All those new features therefore do not specifically address a specific category of user, but enable multiple usage scenarios improving the experience of all users based on their specific profile or usage context. The next section details the implementation of above features.

4   Implementation of the New Features

4.1   Feature#1 - Intra-bubble Text Recognition

A number of Open Source solutions were investigated and evaluated for their OCR performances on a few comics benchmarks: GOCR [10], Ocrad [14], Cuneiform [9], and JavaOCR [8].

Out-of-the-box runs of those tools yielded very poor performance, as they were not capable to manage the specific and very frequent well-named "comic" font used. It was consequently decided to restrict the tested tools to those able to learn the font used in the bubble. This learning phase is not so heavy (about 30 symbols to learn as shown in Figure 2) and it is actually only required in case the default "comic" font is not recognised. Based on these criteria, the JavaOCR library was selected, as it gave the best combined score of maturity, ability to learn and tuning ease.

The OCR extraction algorithm is expressed using high level JavaOCR primitives that can be summarised as follows. The algorithm is illustrated in Figure 3.

1. **Character identification:** sentence boundaries are first identified. Each sentence is broken into words and those words broken into characters.
2. **Character recognition:** characters are matched with the reference character set. A ranking is done with respect to the reference set and the best match is returned. In case the match is too weak, a user interaction can be triggered but this is not a recommended mode for the final user but rather as preparation. The next phase can cope with some recognition errors.

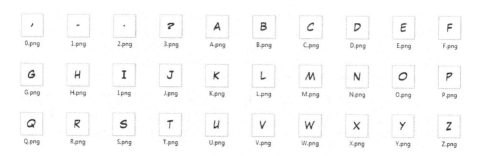

Fig. 2. Training Data Set

3. **Word validation:** in order to validate the text, a semantic check is done on the resulting word. In our case, the OpenOffice.org lexicon was used but more powerful approach are possible, for example using WordNet [24]. The user is prompted in case a word is not recognised, the result can either be a correction or a new word being added to the dictionary if required.

YOU CAN SEE
THE SABAODY
ARCHIPELAGO IF
YOU LOOK FAR FROM
HERE--LUFFY...THIS
IS AS FAR AS WE
CAN TAKE YOU.

Fig. 3. OCR Recognition within Bubbles

4.2 Feature#2 - Port to Android Devices

Porting the application to Android does not require a complete rewrite of the application given Android is based on Java, which conveniently is our implementation language. It essentially requires to adapt the presentation layer with few changes to the processing layer. Third party libraries can also be bundled without major problems. The existing user interface was ported from Swing to the Android User Interface. Actually, the original eComics features were bundled into the Droid Comic Viewer [19] which is an existing comic viewer for Android recently release under the Apache Open Source License.

The target platform is Android Honeycomb (V3.X) which supports tablets. Large touch zones can be provided for controlling the navigation. The voice recognition control and text-to-speech can both be enabled. The experience on recent Honeycomb tablets shows very good performance, enabling "on-the-fly" processing of the comics pages (the results are cached once processed). Figure 4 shows how to enable the automated zoom mode.

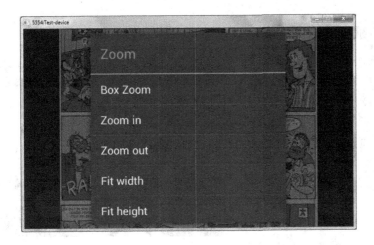

Fig. 4. Box Zoom Feature in Droid Comic Viewer

Then using the right and left touch zones, it is possible to browse the comic books in the right panel order. Figure 5 shows examples of a full page layout (in portrait mode) and of-the-box mode (in landscape mode). The orientation switch is of course automatic when turning the tablet. Touch zones for moving forward/backward depicted by semi-transparent circular zones in the lower right/left corners.

It is worth to be noted that Version 4.X (API level 14) also greatly enhances the accessibility of Android 4.0 for blind or visually impaired users by providing an explore-by-touch mode. Those new features were however not tried yet.

4.3   Feature#3 - Improvements to Box Recognition and Ordering

The panel sorting was improved, using more elaborated comparison algorithm for the bounding box ordering:

- **Case 1 - Top Y coordinates are close** - X order
- **Case 2 - Top Y coordinates are not close**
  - **Case 2.1 - Box1 is disjoined from Box2** - Y order
  - **Case 2.2 - Box1 is including Box2** - Box1 comes first
  - **Case 2.3 - Box2 is including Box1** - Box2 comes first
  - **Case 2.4 - Box1 and Box2 are overlapping** - X order

In case of manga (reversed) order, the X axis is sorted in descending order rather than ascending order. The validation showed a strong reduction in the navigation error rate, most exceptions coming from complex layout where box mode is not adequate. A further improvement was to disable that mode in those cases. Figure 6 shows some complex layouts that are now correctly processed.

Fig. 5. Enhanced viewer in full page (left) and box mode (right)

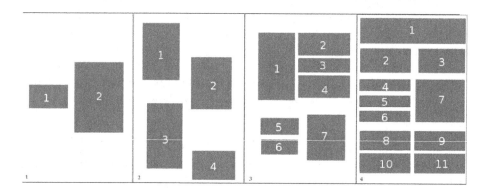

Fig. 6. Complex Box Layouts now supported

5   Related Work

Arai et al have studied the problem of bubble recognition [3]. They propose an automatic and real-time method to detect and extract Japanese characters within a manga comic page. The aim is to manage an online language translation process. Considering the global chain described in our previous paper [16] and this paper, their processing workflow is quite similar to ours: the page is first preprocessed, frames and bubbles are then detected, and finally OCR is applied on the text within the detected bubbles. A notable difference is that content classification is achieved using a contour tracing technique named connected component labeling (CCL) while our work is based on watershed. Both technique result in the identification of the same kind of blobs/regions. More post-processing is applied on the identified blobs, e.g. to qualify them as bubbles. Of course the target character set is also more complex as it is composed of Japanese characters. In this work, the experimental results looks very good: on 15 comic pages used as benchmark, the proposed method has 100% accuracy of flat comic frame extraction and comic balloon detection, and 93.75% accuracy of Japanese character text extraction. However our algorithm seems to perform better for the detection of frameless panels.

Another recent work by Rigaut et al is also relying on connected-component labeling analysis [18]. Again, similar steps are found: preprocessing, identification of regions of interest and their classification. The work was validated on a 42 page comics combining different styles. It is more efficient that Arai et al [3] and also behaves better on frameless panels. A limitation of this work is that he does not describe and assess the final OCR step as we do.

Both works confirm that our general approach is sound. Although not relying on the same algorithms, they share the same global structure and the notion of blob/region of interest. Some additional post-processing steps seem to improve the accuracy with witch regions are classified and could be applied to our own processing chain.

6 Conclusions and Perspectives

This paper presented significant accessibility improvements for digital comic book readers by integrating OCR text recognition for text-to-speech purposes, making the panel sorting more reliable and porting it to Android. In addition to the detailed design presented in this paper, the implementation is available on the eComics forge and is also being contributed back to the Droid Comic Viewer.

In a more general perspective, we believe our contributions can be insightful for the port of other softwares to new generations of user interfaces, especially those developing around Apple and Android ecosystems. Those are about to leave the phone and tablets world to conquer other usage scenarios, for example interactive television (such as GoogleTV [12]) which has a high potential for mobility-impaired and low vision people.

A this point, only partial validation could be achieved with some mobility impaired and comic book fans. Future work will focus on conducting a more controlled validation based on a set of usage scenarios with different user profiles and test sets. These scenarios will also include new technical usage such as "apps-enabled" television, possibly also considering gesture recognition as extra interaction modality. In order to further improve the robustness of specific steps (such as the bubble recognition), more advanced post-processing identified in the related works could also be investigated and adapted to our algorithms.

Acknowledgements. This work was financially supported by the Walloon Region, WIST3 project PIPAS (convention nr. 1017087). The authors also want to thank Dany Isenguerre for authorising the use to reproduce some of their Faldo's adventure strips [13] and Vincent Fries for the preliminary testing phase of the application.

References

1. Abramoff, M., Magelhaes, P., Ram, S.: Image Processing with ImageJ. Biophotonics International 11, 36–42 (2004)
2. Aglassinger, T., als: JOMIC, http://jomic.sourceforge.net
3. Arai, K., Tolle, H.: Method for Real Time Text Extraction of Digital Manga Comic. International Journal of Image Processing (IJIP) 4(6), 669–676 (2011)
4. Ayton, D.: CDisplay Sequential Image Viewer, http://www.geocities.com/davidayton/CDisplay
5. Bonnin, F.: ComicBookDS, http://gnese.free.fr/NDS/ComicBookDS/
6. Burger, W., Burge, M.J.: Digital Image Processing. An Algorithmic Introduction using Java. Springer (2008)
7. Celsis: Comic Surfing, http://www.bonz.co.jp/netnavi
8. Cemer, R.: JavaOCR, http://www.roncemer.com/software-development/java-ocr
9. Cuneiform: Cognitive OpenOCR, http://en.openocr.org
10. GOCR: Open-Source Character Recognition, http://jocr.sourceforge.net
11. Google: Android, http://www.android.com
12. Google: GoogleTV, http://www.google.com/tv
13. Isenguerre, Malroy: Faldo's Adventures (in French), http://www.martinroy.net
14. Ocrad: The GNU OCR, http://www.gnu.org/software/ocrad
15. Ponsard, C., Fries, V.: An Accessible Viewer for Digital Comic Books. In: Miesenberger, K., Klaus, J., Zagler, W.L., Karshmer, A.I. (eds.) ICCHP 2008. LNCS, vol. 5105, pp. 569–577. Springer, Heidelberg (2008)
16. Ponsard, C.: Enhancing the Accessibility for All of Digital Comic Books. e-Minds: International Journal on Human-Computer Interaction 1(5) (2009)
17. Project, C.O.S.: Buoh Online Comic Reader for Gnome, http://buoh.steve-o.org/
18. Rigaud, C., Tsopze, N., Burie, J.C., Ogier, J.M.: Extraction robuste des cases et du texte de bandes dessinées. In: Colloque International Francophone sur lŠEcrit et le Document (CIFED) (March 2012)
19. Robotmedia: Droid Comic Viewer, https://github.com/robotmedia/droid-comic-viewer
20. Sage, D.: Watershed Segmentation. Ecole Polytechnique Fédérale de Lausanne (2008), http://bigwww.epfl.ch/sage/soft/watershed
21. Software, B.: ComicBookLover, http://bitcartel.com/comicbooklover/
22. Solution, R.: Comic GURU, http://www.comicguru.net/
23. Swartout, B.: CBViewer, http://sourceforge.net/projects/cbviewer
24. University, P.: WordNet, a lexical database for English, http://wordnet.princeton.edu
25. Wikipedia: Comic Book, http://en.wikipedia.org/wiki/Comic_book

Spe-Ler: Serious Gaming for Youngsters with Intellectual Disabilities

Joan De Boeck, Jo Daems, and Jan Dekelver

K-Point, K.H. Kempen University College, 2440 Geel, Belgium
{joan.de.boeck,jo.daems,jan.dekelver}@khk.be

Abstract. When working with youngsters with intellectual disabilities, it is often a challenge to teach them 'boring' content (e.g. the 'rules of daily living' in their school or care-center). In this paper we propose a serious gaming approach in order to facilitate the learning process. The novelty in our concept is that we decouple the game and the didactical content, which allows us to transfer the learning to the youngster's leisure time. In our research, we built a framework containing several (fun) games and an administration environment that facilitates the creation of learning content. In a user experiment, measuring the user's joy and motivationwe found that the subjects enjoyed playing the games and were very attentive when the didactical content appeared.

1   Introduction and Problem Statement

Teaching 'boring' content to young people is often a challenge. This is especially true when working with youngsters with intellectual disabilities. The didactical approaches are limited and appear to be too moralising for the target group. On the other hand, a significant group of contemporary youngsters with intellectual disabilities do have a 'natural' interest for computers and computer games. Electronic games are now an everyday part of childhood and adolescence [1]. Exploiting this interest, the idea of offering the didactical content using the concept of serious gaming may be a solution [2]. While the positive results of serious gaming are still under a lot of debate [3][4], literature review also suggests that electronic games present many potential benefits as educational tools for health and physical education [5], and that those games may improve young people's knowledge, skills, attitudes and behaviours in relation to health and physical exercise. This may be true in general, if there were not a huge variety in ICT competences in our target group[6]. Integrating the didactical content directly into a game may sound obvious, however, when the game is too difficult compared to the ICT competences, or simply when the player does not like the game, the entire didactical approach falls off [4].

2   The Concept

For the reason mentioned above, in the Spe-Ler[1] project, we propose and evaluate an alternative approach in which we disconnect the gaming from the learning aspect; an

---

[1] Spe-Ler is an acronym for 'SpelendLeren' which is the Dutch for 'Learn While Playing'.

K. Miesenberger et al. (Eds.): ICCHP 2012, Part I, LNCS 7382, pp. 479–483, 2012.

approach which has been applied in a somewhat less explicit form in the Replay Project [7]. The aim of European Commission funded project REPLAY was to develop a gaming technology platform to provide young people who have become marginalised in society as a result of anti-socialbehaviour with a learning environment to facilitate their reintegration into society.

In the proposed Spe-Ler approach, the key point is that the games are played for fun without any didactical content. The used games are selected based on the success they have among the target group, so that there already is a level of certainty that the users are motivated to play the games. At certain moments (e.g. between two levels, after some time, …), the game is interrupted and the didactical content shows up. The pedagogical team that is interested in offering that specific content to the target group creates this content. This way, the total concept is driven by both end users preferences in relation to games and supporting team. This approach is also suggested in other areas of serious gaming where higher success is expected from a collaborative creation process [8].

The content is offered as a short game interruption by means of a short movie (maximum one or two minutes), as it were a commercial. After the movie we offer one multiple choice question to the user. It is important to note that this question is not a 'knowledge check', but rather offers a 'dilemma' to the player so that he/she is forced to reflect on the offered material. The given answer is stored in a database and is at the coach's disposal for later didactical approaches. After the question has been answered, the game continues. The hypotheses is that the player, being in a good mood while playing the game, is more open to receive the information and messages transmitted during the short interruptions.

3   Technical Implementation

Given this concept, we implemented both a programming framework, as well as an administration tool. As the administration tool is used by people with limited ICT knowledge, creating a 'gaming' session for a particular group or individual must be as easy as possible. Hence, coaches only have to combine games and movies. In a first step, they have to select what games they want to be played (according to the ICT and intellectual skills of the player). Next the coach can select a number of movies that will be shown. All movies, together with the integrated questions are ordered in any desired order, according to the coach's insight.

During the game, the player can freely choose what game to play, but always sees the didactical content in the same order as the coach has decided.

When new content is required, people having a role of 'content provider' add movies. Those content providers have the permission to add extra movies and define a question per movie. Movies are classified by theme, allowing to easily create 'thematic courses'.

Finally, for adding new games, any 'fun' game can be added to the system because the games themselves may not contain learning content. However, to add a new game, the game must be compatible with the framework in order to support the interruptions at regular intervals. To support this in the easiest way, we built a programming framework that allows a programmer to make any computer game compatible by adding only a few lines of code. In our proof of concept, this framework has been build using the DotNet platform, but porting this part of the code to another programming platform (e.g. Java) allows us also to makethose games compatible with the Spe-Ler concept.

4   Case Study

In order to test our approach, we set-up a proof of concept experiment. In the Spe-Ler environment, we imported 6 arcade-games as shown in figure 1. The games were written during a student's project, and adapted afterwards in order to be compatible with our framework. A student in Occupational Therapy, in collaboration with the staff of the MPI[2], created 25 short movies explaining different aspects of the rules of daily living within the centre. All those movies and a multiple-choice question per movie were put into the system. For the experiment, the question was not a dilemma as intended by the Spe-Ler concept, but instead was a simple question that could be answered after understanding the situation in the movie. This gave us a better way to have an impression of how well the movie had been understood.

Fig. 1. Selection screen where the user can choose the game he/she wants to play

Eleven (11) youngsters, 7 boys and 4 girls with an age between 12 and 18, all with mild or moderate intellectual disabilities were asked to participate in our experiment. In the week before, 7 subjects had the opportunity to play the games beforehand, but without didactical interruption.

---

[2] MPI: a multidisciplinary institution for people with mild to severe intellectual disabilities. The MPI has an ambulant, semi-resident as well as a resident department and they accompany/guide /take care of children, youngsters and adults.

Fig. 2. Experimental setup: subject playing game, with coach

In the actual experiment, all participants were asked to come and play the games for half an hour, but they were not told about the didactical content and de interruptions after each level. All subjects, without exception were happy to come and play. For their convenience and their comfort, there was a coach from the centre sitting next to the player, in case they should need any assistance.

A researcher observed the youngsters and scored their behaviour and facial expressions (joy, frustration, concentration, ...) while everything was recorded on video for later reference. After the experiment, one of the coaches shortly asked some subjective questions.

Not any subject showed frustration or disinterest during the interruptions. Some appeared to be amused, others were neutral, but all were well concentrated. From the answers to the questions, we could learn that all subjects tried to answer the questions the best they could.

On the other hand, we found that for those youngsters that had not practiced before, it was difficult to finish a level, so they had not many 'learning' moments. Similarly, we found that for the subjects with moderate intellectual disabilities, understanding the movies was borderline. Hence, special care has to be taken to select games and content at a level perfectly suited to the subject's capabilities.

The subjective questionnaire did not revealed any surprises. All answers were very in line with our observations. Only one of the subjects did not like the games, and wouldn't play again. None of the subjects rejected the interruptions, and all could recall the content of at least one of the movies.

5   Conclusion and Future Work

Based upon a real need of a care centre for people with intellectual disabilities, we proposed a serious gaming approach. Specific to this approach is that the games at itself do not contain any serious content, but instead, the content is provided during short interruptions. This is done using short movies followed by a question. We built an environment that makes it easy for non-ICT people to add content and to create personalised gaming sessions. In a proof of concept experiment, we found that all subjects enjoyed their gaming session and had a positive attitude against the movies. The questions were answered to the subject's best effort.

In a next step, we want to evaluate the net learning effect of our approach, because we realise that the learning periods are short compared to the fun-time. On the other hand, decoupling the game and the didactical content, this approach is one that can be applied during the youngster's leisure time.

We also believe that the Spe-Ler approach can be useful in other domains, such as very young children, as well. This is something that has to be sought-out in the near future, as well.

Acknowledgements. Part of this research has been funded by the Belgian Federal Government (P.O.D. Maatschappelijkeintegratie), combatting the digital divide (project number 2010/020) and has been co-funded by the K.H.Kempen University college.

The authors want to thank Tim Vannuffelen, Mohamed Kadi, Evelien Van Dingenen, GlennCenens en Jeroen Aerts for their effort during the implementation of this project and Lindsay Peters for her help in the creation of the movies.

References

1. Olson, C.K.: Children's motivations for video game play in the context of normal development. Review of General Psychology 14(2), 180–187 (2010)
2. The Next Generation of Educational Engagement I Oblinger I Journal of Interactive Media in Education
3. Johnson, S.: Everything bad is good for you how popular culture is making us smarter. Lane, London (2005)
4. Virvou, M., Katsionis, G., Manos, K.: Combining software games with education: Evaluation of its educational effectiveness. Educ. Technol. Soc. 8(2)
5. Papastergiou, M.: Exploring the potential of computer and video games for health and physical education: A literature review. Computers & Education 53(3), 603–622 (2009)
6. Dekelver, J., Vannuffelen, T., De Boeck, J.: EasyICT: A Framework for Measuring ICT-Skills of People with Cognitive Disabilities. In: Miesenberger, K., Klaus, J., Zagler, W., Karshmer, A. (eds.) ICCHP 2010. LNCS, vol. 6180, pp. 21–24. Springer, Heidelberg (2010)
7. Ibañezen, F., Playfoot, J.: Gaming Technology Platform as a Support Tool for Anti Social Behavior prevention in Young People at Risk to be Marginalized (Replay). In: Proceedings of the 2010 INCLUSO Conference, pp. 29–40. K.U.Leuven, Leuven (2010)
8. Marcosen, A., Zagalo, N.: Instantiating the creation process in digital art for serious games design. Entertainment Computing 2(2), 143–148 (2011)

An Accessibility Checker for LibreOffice and OpenOffice.org Writer

Christophe Strobbe, Bert Frees, and Jan Engelen

Katholieke Universiteit Leuven, Kasteelpark Arenberg 10, B-3001 Heverlee-Leuven, Belgium
c_strobbe-esat@yahoo.co.uk, bertfrees@gmail.com,
jan.engelen@esat.kuleuven.be

Abstract. OpenOffice.org Writer and LibreOffice Writer both implement the OpenDocument Format (ODF) and support output formats such as PDF and XHTML. Through the extensions odt2daisy and odt2braille (developed in the context of the AEGIS project) Writer can also export to DAISY (audio books) and Braille. In order to output usable DAISY or Braille, authors first need to create an accessible source document. The objective of AccessODF, the accessibility checker developed in the context of the European AEGIS project, is to support authors in creating accessible ODF documents and to prepare these documents for conversion to DAISY and/or Braille. The paper discusses the user interface options that were explored, describes how authors can repair errors and warnings, gives examples of automatic and semi-automatic repairs supported by the checker, and describes which errors and warnings are implemented.

Keywords: Accessibility, accessibility evaluation, office documents, OpenOffice.org, LibreOffice, Evaluation and Report Language (EARL).

1 Introduction

Digital accessibility covers many areas. The e-Accessibility Policy Toolkit for Persons with Disabilities developed by the International Telecommunication Union (ITU) and the Global Initiative for Inclusive ICTs (G3ict) to support the implementation of the UN Convention on the Rights of Persons with Disabilities [17] covers the eleven technology areas, one of which is "access to published works" [9]. Access to office formats for word processing, spreadsheets and presentations is a superset of and a precondition for "access to published works".

There are considerably fewer guidelines and tools related to the accessibility of office formats than for web content. However, office formats are often used as a source for web content, for example by exporting word processing files as HTML or PDF. Office formats also need to be accessible in order to be a suitable source for formats aimed at persons with disabilities, notably audio books (typically DAISY books [10]) and Braille. Authors would greatly benefit from guidance for accessible authoring that is integrated into an office suite. The accessibility checker for OpenOffice.org and LibreOffice Writer developed in the framework of the ÆGIS project [4] provides this

K. Miesenberger et al. (Eds.): ICCHP 2012, Part I, LNCS 7382, pp. 484–491, 2012.

kind of guidance. The remainder of this paper describes the background for this tool, how it is implemented and what functionality it offers.

2   Accessibility of Office Formats

2.1   Existing Accessibility Evaluation Tools

Since the publication of the Web Content Accessibility Guidelines (WCAG) 1.0 in 1999 [5], many tools for the evaluation of web content have been developed. The website of the World Wide Web Consortium (W3C) contains a database of Web accessibility evaluation tools that lists a few dozen tools [18]. Compared to this database, the list of accessibility evaluation tools for office formats is very short. A few tools for the evaluation of PDF documents are available (Adobe Acrobat Pro, NetCentric's CommonLook Section 508 for Adobe Acrobat, the freeware PDF Accessibility Checker (PAC) by the Swiss organisation Zugang für Alle/Access for All and the web-based PDF accessibility checker by the eGovMon project in Norway), but these tools cover a final-form output format that cannot be easily edited. Tools that evaluate word processing files are relatively scarce:

- aDesigner is a tool that was originally developed by IBM Tokyo [14] and later donated to the Eclipse Foundation [7]. This tool is a disability simulator for web content that also helps users check the accessibility of OpenDocument Format (ODF) and Flash content.
- The accessibility checker introduced in Microsoft Word 2010, PowerPoint 2010 and Excel 2010, which provides errors, warning and tips [15], is the first evaluation tool that is built into an office suite.
- The "Plug-ins for accessible PDF documents" developed by the ICT-Accessibility Lab of the Zurich University for Applied Sciences for Credit Suisse AG [8]. These plug-ins for Microsoft Word and PowerPoint 2010 help authors remove accessibility issues in word processing documents and presentations that will be made available on the Web as PDF documents.
- The "Save as DAISY" plug-in for Microsoft Word 2003, 2007 and 2010 [6] has a Validate function (under the Accessibility tab in Word 2007 and 2010) that performs a number of accessibility checks. This is not a full accessibility checker, but it is the only plug-in that is compatible with Microsoft Word 2003 and 2007.

aDesigner is the only tool that evaluates the accessibility of ODF content. Other checkers that were developed in the past have been abandoned. The Open Document Format Accessibility Evaluation tool developed by a team of students at the University of Illinois at Urbana-Champaign under the supervision of Dr. Jon Gunderson came online in 2006 [8] but has not been available for several years. The SourceForge project hosting site contains at least 9 ODF accessibility checkers that were started in 2006 as part of the "IBM Accessibility Phase 2 Contest" in Japan. These projects have all been abandoned.

2.2   LibreOffice/OpenOffice.org as a Source for Accessible Formats

Both OpenOffice.org and its recent alternative LibreOffice can be used to create accessible content. Guidance is available in various locations, including the ODF Accessibility Guidelines by the Accessibility subcommittee of the OASIS Open Document Format for Office Applications (OpenDocument) TC [15], the Authoring Techniques for Accessible Office Documents by the Accessible Digital Office Document (ADOD) Project [2] and "OpenOffice.org and Accessibility" by Web Accessibility in Mind (WebAIM) [19]. Thanks to the availability of the open source extensions odt2daisy [13] and odt2braille [12], both developed in the framework of the ÆGIS project, OpenOffice.org and LibreOffice Writer can export OpenDocument Text (ODT) to DAISY books and Braille, respectively. However, in order to create valid and usable DAISY books or Braille documents, the ODT source documents need to fulfil a number of criteria, for example,

- images and other objects need a text alternative, which can be rendered as synthetic speech or Braille,
- headings need to be styled with Heading styles instead of big bold text or other visual characteristics that suggest headings,
- the default language of the document and any language changes inside the document need to be identified in order to select the correct speech synthesis engine or Braille translation table during the conversion process,
- images need to be in JPEG or PNG (Portable Network Graphics) format when exporting to DAISY.

Some accessibility criteria are easy to fulfil, while others are easily overlooked, for example, because they have no visual effect (e.g. adding text alternatives to objects, accidentally creating empty headings). Some criteria are only relevant when exporting to another format, for example, the restriction on image formats in DAISY. It is clear that integrating support for accessible authoring into OpenOffice.org/LibreOffice Writer would make it easier for authors to meet accessibility criteria.

3   The ODT Accessibility Checker

3.1   User Interface

The goal of the accessibility checker is to make users aware of accessibility issues in their content. Ideally, this should be as straightforward as checking the spelling, a feature that is built into several office suites, but accessibility is more complex than spelling. There are several ways in which authors could be alerted to accessibility issues. Several methods were explored in the initial stages of the project.

The **first option** consisted in adding a new layout mode, similar to the Print Layout and Web Layout that can be found in Writer's View menu. This new "Accessibility View" would make authors aware of how assistive technologies (AT) "perceive" the document. For example, where an image has no text alternative, there would be nothing (or just an empty frame). Where headings are faked by means of big bold text instead of the appropriate Heading styles, the content of these headings would be rendered as normal text. However, the Accessibility View would be incomplete without guidance on how to repair the issues. There was also a technical barrier: the accessibility checker is developed as an extension, and extensions cannot create new layout modes. It is possible to work around this by creating a read-only copy of the source document and modifying this copy through the OpenOffice.org API. However, it is not possible to keep this copy synchronised with the source document due to limitations in the OpenOffice.org API.

The **second option** consisted in adding errors and warnings to the source document by means of highlighting and/or some type of comments or notes. When using highlighting, removing the highlighting should be as simple as clicking a button. Unfortunately, adding such highlighting can only be done by modifying the document; the accessibility checker would then need to remove any remaining highlighting when the user closes the document without repairing all the issues (and in this process distinguish between its own highlighting and highlighting added by the user). The same is true for underlining: the type of underlining that is used by the spelling checker cannot be created by an extension, and the type of underlining that can be created by an extension would become part of the document (unlike the wavy underlining for spelling errors). Using OpenOffice.org's built-in comment system to provide information on accessibility issues was judged too technical and insufficiently user-friendly.

The different options were extensively discussed within the ÆGIS project and the developers finally settled on the use of a **taskpanel** to display a list of errors and warnings and all the other required information. The taskpanel is a component that has long been available in Impress (the presentation component of the office suite), where it is used for defining slide layouts, custom animations, slide transitions and other slide features. The taskpanel has been available in Writer only since OpenOffice.org and LibreOffice 3.3.

The taskpanel used by the accessibility checker consists of three parts. The top part displays a list of errors and warnings for issues detected in the document. When the author selects an error or warning, the relevant section of the document is highlighted (in a way similar to the highlighting used by the Except or Reject changes dialog). The middle part displays three types of information for the error or warning currently highlighted in the top part: the name of the issue, a description (which usually explains why something is an accessibility issue) and suggestions for repair. The bottom part contains five buttons: a 'Recheck' button to trigger the accessibility evaluation, a 'Clear' button to clear the list of errors and warnings, a 'Repair' button to repair issues that can be fixed automatically or semi-automatically, an 'Ignore' button that can be used to delete a false positive, and a 'More help' button. The Repair button only becomes active when an issue can be repaired automatically or semi-automatically. Examples of automatic repair include the following:

- When the checker finds an empty heading (i.e. an empty paragraph with a Heading style), activating Repair replaces the Heading style with the Default style.
- When a table allow rows to break across pages and columns, activating Repair unchecks the option "Allow row to break across pages and columns" that authors would otherwise need to find in the Table Format dialog.

Examples of semi-automatic repair include the following:

- When the document has no default language, activating Repair opens the language settings dialog, where authors can set the default language for documents.
- When an image or other object has no text alternative, activating Repair opens the Description dialog, where authors can enter the objects title (which would match HTML's alt attribute) and description.
- When the document's title field is empty, activating Repair opens the document properties dialog, where authors can enter this metadata item. The document title is used by odt2daisy when converting the document to an audio book.

Many repairs cannot be performed automatically or semi-automatically, for example,

- When text is too small, the author needs to modify the applicable style or the direct formatting of the small text.
- When the document contains images in formats not supported by DAISY, the author needs to convert the images to JPEG or PNG outside Writer and re-insert the new image.
- When a table contains merged cells, the author must decide whether to split to cells again or to simplify the table in a different way.

In each of these instances, the repair suggestions explain what the author can do to fix the issue.

3.2   Implemented Issues and Warnings

Web developers and web accessibility advocates can refer to the W3C's Web Content Accessibility Guidelines (WCAG) as the generally accepted reference for web accessibility. Authors of office formats are not so fortunate. They can refer to Accessibility Guidelines Version 1.0 prepared by the ODF Accessibility subcommittee or the Authoring Techniques for Accessible Office Documents by the ADOD project (see above), but these documents don't have a structure based on testable and easily referenceable success criteria that is attractive to evaluation tool developers. The table below provides a mapping between WCAG 2.0 success criteria, the Authoring Techniques for Accessible Office Documents from the ADOD project and the ODF checks that are currently supported. The evaluation tool can perform checks that are applicable only to Braille or to DAISY; these checks can be enabled or disabled in the options dialog. Some checks do not map to any WCAG 2.0 criterion, for example the check for image formats that are not supported by DAISY. Note that the accessibility checker currently only evaluates OpenDocument Text (the word processing format); at the time of writing there is no support for presentations or spreadsheets.

Table 1. Mapping between WCAG 2.0, ADOD and ODF accessibility checks (examples)

WCAG 2.0	ODF Check(s)	Comments
1.1.1 Non-text Content	Error: formula has no text alternative Warning: image has no text alternative; object has no text alternative; special characters or symbols are rendered by means of a special font instead of Unicode.	ADOD Technique 3 Some images may be decorative and therefore not require a text alternative.
1.3.1 Info and Relationships	Warnings: table contains merged cells; table cell contains another table; table has no repeatable heading row(s); table rows break across pages or columns; table is very long; long table has caption below table instead of above; caption is not linked to any image or table; text formatting (e.g. big bold text) suggests that a paragraph should have a Heading style.	ADOD Technique 6 (using named styles instead of direct formatting) ADOD Technique 7.1, 7.2, 7.3, 7.4
1.4.8 Visual Presentation (AAA)	Warnings: text is justified; font size is smaller than 9 points; long span of text in all caps, underlined or italic.	ADOD Technique 9.1 WCAG does not require a minimum font size or prohibit text that is in all caps, underlined or italic.
2.4.5 Multiple Ways (AA)	Warning: Braille edition has no table of contents.	ADOD Technique 7.5, 7.6
2.4.6 Headings and Labels (AA)	Errors: empty Heading style; incorrectly ordered headings; heading inside a frame (DAISY check). Warnings: document contains no Heading styles; document has more than 6 levels of headings (which is not acceptable for a DAISY document).	ADOD Technique 5 Some documents may not require headings, e.g. letters.
3.1.1 Language of Page	Error: document has no default Language	ADOD Technique 2

Note: The above table does not contain all WCAG 2.0 success criteria or all ODF accessibility checks. A full table of checks will be made available at [3].

Some WCAG 2.0 success criteria are not listed in our full list, for example the success criteria for time-based media (audio, video) under Guideline 1.2, which are rarely relevant to word processing documents. Some warnings in AccessODF do not correspond to any success criterion in WCAG 2.0, for example:

- The document contains images in a format not supported by DAISY.
- Material will be omitted in the Braille edition because it is not placed in any volume, supplement or preliminary section.

- In Braille, material is transposed from its original location. This warns the author that lists, text boxes and images inside a table rendered outside the table in the Braille version.
- The document contains 8 dot Braille but the embosser does not support it.

3.3   Evaluation and Report Language

OpenOffice.org and LibreOffice support the use of RDF (Resource Description Framework) for storing metadata inside ODF files. The accessibility checker stores information on errors and warnings as RDF inside the document. The format used for this purpose is the Evaluation and Report Language (EARL)[1], an RDF format for describing test results that is being developed by the World Wide Web Consortium (W3C). In addition to the list of errors and warnings, the metadata also describe which errors and warnings have been repaired or ignored, when the most recent accessibility evaluation was performed, and by which evaluation tool.

4   Conclusions and Future Work

The ODF accessibility checker evaluates many criteria for accessible documents. In addition to repair suggestions, it also supports a few automatic and semi-automatic repair functions. When the accessibility checker becomes available in OpenOffice.org and LibreOffice, it could become part of the Tools menu, below language-related items such as "Spelling and Grammar".

The accessibility checker will probably be released under an open source license, possibly the Lesser General Public License (LGPL) 3, which is also the license for odt2daisy and odt2braille. It could become an extension for Writer or part of the Writer source code.

The accessibility checker currently only evaluates Writer documents. Evaluating presentations and spreadsheets is part of future plans.

Acknowledgements. This work was funded by the EC FP7 project ÆGIS - Open Accessibility Everywhere: Groundwork, Infrastructure, Standards, Grant Agreement No. 224348.

References

1. Shadi, A-Z. (ed.): Evaluation and Report Language (EARL) 1.0 Schema - W3C Working Draft (May10, 2011), http://www.w3.org/TR/2011/WD-EARL10-Schema-20110510/
2. Accessible Digital Office Document (ADOD) Project: Accessibility of Office Documents and Office Applications, http://adod.idrc.ocad.ca/
3. AccessODF, http://sourceforge.net/projects/accessodf/
4. ÆGIS - Open Accessibility Everywhere: Groundwork, Infrastructure, Standards, http://www.aegis-project.eu/

5. Chisholm, W., Vanderheiden, G., Jacobs, I. (eds.): Web Content Accessibility Guidelines 1.0 - W3C Recommendation (May 5, 1999), http://www.w3.org/TR/WCAG10/

6. DAISY Consortium: Save as DAISY - Microsoft Word Add-In (no date), http://www.daisy.org/project/save-as-daisy-microsoft-word-add-in

7. Eclipse Foundation: ACTF aDesigner (no date), http://www.eclipse.org/actf/downloads/tools/aDesigner/index.php

8. ICT-Accessibility Lab, Zurich University for Applied Sciences: Plug-ins for accessible PDF documents (no date), http://www.init.zhaw.ch/en/engineering/institute-of-applied-information-technology/focus-areas/human-information-interaction/plug-ins-for-accessible-pdf-documents.html

9. International Telecommunication Union (ITU) and the Global Initiative for Inclusive ICTs (G3ict): Technology areas (no date), http://www.e-accessibilitytoolkit.org/toolkit/technology_areas

10. National Information Standards Organization (NISO): ANSI/NISO Z39.86-2005. Revision of ANSI/NISO Z39.86-2002. Specifications for the Digital Talking Book, http://www.daisy.org/z3986/2005/Z3986-2005.html

11. Korn, P.: Accessibility test tool for OpenDocument files. Peter Korn's Weblog (December 8 , 2006), http://blogs.oracle.com/korn/entry/automated_testing_of_opendocument_files

12. odt2braille, http://odt2braille.sf.net/

13. odt2daisy, http://odt2daisy.sf.net/

14. International Business Machines Corporation (IBM): BM aDesigner (no date), http://www-03.ibm.com/able/accessibility_services/adesigner.html

15. Microsoft Corporation: Accessibility Checker (no date), http://office2010.microsoft.com/en-us/starter-help/accessibility-checker-HA010369192.aspx

16. OpenDocument - Accessibility SC, http://www.oasis-open.org/committees/tc_home.php?wg_abbrev=office-accessibility

17. United Nations: Convention on the Rights of Persons with Disabilities (2006), http://www.un.org/disabilities/convention/conventionfull.shtml

18. World Wide Web Consortium (W3C): Web Accessibility Evaluation Tools: Overview, http://www.w3.org/WAI/ER/tools/ (last updated March 17, 2006)

19. Web Accessibility in Mind (WebAIM): OpenOffice.org and Accessibility (no date), http://webaim.org/techniques/ooo/

Visualization of Non-verbal Expressions in Voice for Hearing Impaired

Ambient Font and Onomatopoeic Subsystem

Hidetaka Nambo[1], Shuichi Seto[2], Hiroshi Arai[2], Kimikazu Sugimori[2],
Yuko Shimomura[2], and Hiroyuki Kawabe[2]

[1] Kanazawa Univevrsity, Kakuma-machi, Kanazawa, Ishikawa, 920-1192 Japan
nambo@ec.t.kanazawa-u.ac.jp
[2] Kinjo University, 1200 Kasama-machi, Hakusan, Ishikawa, 924-8511 Japan
{seto,arahiro,sugimori,shimo,kawabe}@kinjo.ac.jp

Abstract. Generally, a hearing impaired person is supported by staffs to take a note while hearing a lecture. However, the lecture note cannot express a tone of the teacher's voice. Further, non-verbal information such as a chatting voice in a classroom, speed, loudness and tone of speaker's voice are also difficult to express. As a result, it is difficult for a hearing impaired person to feel the atmosphere in the classroom. In this study, we develop a system to inform atmosphere in the classroom to a hearing impaired person. The system utilizes expression techniques used in Japanese cartoons; they are "Ambient Font", "Balloon & Symbols" and "Onomatopoeic Word". These techniques enable us to inform to the hearing impaired person not only the textual information but also the non-verbal information.

Keywords: Hearing impaired, non-verbal expressions, Onomatopoeia.

1   Introduction

In Japan, there are many impaired students in universities. They are supported on studying in class by volunteer circles or voluntary persons. A note taking is one of the supporting works. It is a task to dictate teacher's speaking in a class, and hearing-impaired person is supported by the work. It needs to volunteers some trainings to dictate speedy and accurately. Therefore some note taking systems using ITC technologies have been proposed recently [1]. However, the dictated text, that is a result of note taking, shows only what the teacher told, but an atmosphere or the teacher's emotion in the classroom cannot be felt from it. In a class, an atmosphere consists of many factors, such as volume, tone, speed of teacher's voice, murmur of students, noises and so on. If these factors are informed to hearing impaired person, they will feel an atmosphere in the classroom and they also can attend to the class as well as normal person, just like being afraid of teacher's angry voice. Furthermore, knowing teacher's emotion will help them studying, because a teacher usually emphasizes keywords or important parts in their class.

K. Miesenberger et al. (Eds.): ICCHP 2012, Part I, LNCS 7382, pp. 492–499, 2012.
© Springer-Verlag Berlin Heidelberg 2012

In this study, we utilize techniques used in Japanese cartoons to inform factors that constitute an atmosphere in a classroom to hearing impaired persons.

2   Cartoon and Cartoon Technique

Japanese cartoons have many characteristics, and their characteristics are different from American or French one. One of the characteristics in Japanese cartoons is using fewer texts and more symbols and figures. Therefore, a lot of techniques to visualize "character's emotion in conversation" or "atmosphere in the field" have been developed. For example, in Fig.1, texts are written by many kinds of size and font sets. For laud voices or hard emotions, big and thick fonts are used. On the other hand, for small voices or soft emotions, small and thin fonts are used. However, readers usually are not aware of these changes. These expressions are regarded as a visual language in Japan, and readers share common images of feeling from the expressions [2].

Fig. 1. An example of Japanese cartoons

Further, other techniques to inform emotions and atmosphere are shapes of balloon, symbols and handwritten expressions of sounds or onomatopoeic words. The shape of balloon represents a speaker's situation or a tone of voice. The symbol is visualization of the emotion and the feeling. The handwritten expression is used to visualize environmental sounds, noises and atmospheres.

Therefore, we think that utilizing these characteristics to dictate texts is effective to inform teacher's emotions and atmospheres in a classroom to hearing impaired persons.

Fig. 2. Balloons and symbols in cartoons

3   Visualizing of Emotion

In this study, we propose a system for hearing impaired person to inform the atmosphere in a classroom. The system consists from three subsystems.

First, we propose "Ambient Font Subsystem", which can express a presence in a classroom. The ambient font reflects speaker's voice parameters such as volume and speed. When the volume is large, the font is enlarged (Fig.3). Moreover, when the speed is fast, the font width is shortened (Fig.4).

Fig. 3. Examples of ambient fonts. (normal, large and small volume)

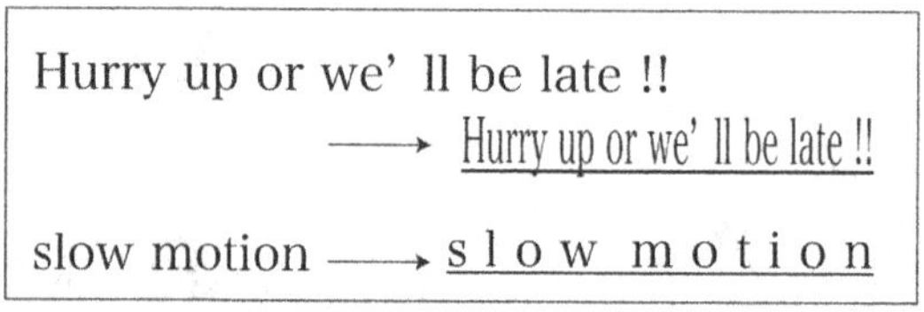

Hurry up or we' ll be late !!
⟶ Hurry up or we' ll be late !!
slow motion ⟶ s l o w   m o t i o n

Fig. 4. Examples of ambient fonts. (normal, fast and slow tone)

Second, we propose "Onomatopoeic Subsystem", which generates and outputs onomatopoeic words. This subsystem infers suitable onomatopoeic words considering environmental sounds in the classroom. Further, the size of the words depends on the volume of sounds. This subsystem helps recognizing the atmosphere such as students' chatting voice and noises in the classroom.

At last, we propose "Balloon and Graphical Symbol Subsystem", which selects and outputs balloons and graphic symbols suitable for properties of speaker's voice. In the balloon, dictated texts of speakers are displayed with Ambient Fonts, and the balloon is decorated by graphic symbols. This subsystem works simultaneously with Ambient Font Subsystem, and it helps to recognize speaker's situation felt from talks of speaker.

The details of our proposed system are described in next chapter.

4   Outline of the Proposed System

4.1   Process Flow of the System

The proposed system consists from three parts, the onomatopoeic subsystem, the ambient font subsystem and the balloon and graphical symbols subsystem (Fig.5). The system requires two audio signals. One is an environmental sound; that is a background sound in the classroom, which contains student's chats or murmurs. The environmental sound is analyzed by the onomatopoeic subsystem, and then onomatopoeic words are extracted from the signal. Another is a teacher's voice signal. This signal is processed by a speech processing system to dictate the teacher's speech. Simultaneously, this signal is used to generate the ambient font, balloons and symbols. Many parameters such as volume, tone and speed are extracted from the signal, and are transferred to the other subsystems. Then, the ambient font subsystem generates the ambient font, and the balloon and symbol subsystem generates balloons and symbols. At last, dictated texts of speech are displayed by using the ambient font with onomatopoeic words, balloons and symbols.

In following sections, details of each subsystem are described.

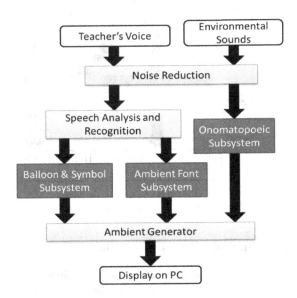

Fig. 5. Process flow of proposed system

4.2   Ambient Font Subsystem

The ambient font subsystem outputs dictated text with the ambient fonts that reflect an ambience of teacher's voice. In first, an input voice is successively sent to Julius that is one of the open source dictation system for Japanese. Julius automatically divides the voice into sentences or phrases and processes the voice recognition. Then, the subsystem obtains alignment information and pitch & volume information from Julius. (We modified Julius to analyze and output pitch and volume information.) The alignment information contains dictated words, start/end time of word and a number of syllables of word (Fig.6). The pitch & volume information contain pitch and volume of each dictated words. The subsystem generates fonts from these information and outputs dictated words using the previously generated fonts. A property of generated font, that is the ambient font, is decides by following factors.

- Size of font: an average volume of voice corresponding to the dictated word
- Expansion rate/Blank of each fonts: a speed that is a ratio of speech time to syllables of word

The size of font is proportion to the volume of voice. Further, a width of font is shortened when the speed of voice is fast, and spaces between each letters are expanded when the speed is slow.

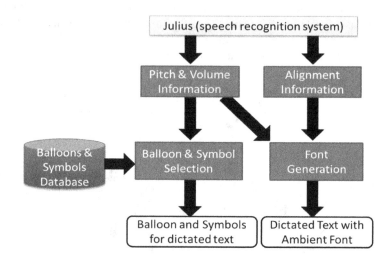

Fig. 6. Process flow of ambient font subsystem and balloon & symbols subsystem

4.3   Balloon and Graphical Symbols Subsystem

The balloon and graphical symbols subsystems outputs balloons or graphical symbols from the pitch and volume of input voice to express the emotion in the voice. The subsystem obtains pitch & volume information from Julius. Then, the emotion in the voice is inferred from them. For example, a laud voice or a big change of pitch means a hard emotion. Finally, the subsystem selects balloons and symbols suitable for the emotion from a pre-registered balloons and symbols database, and outputs them overlaying the ambient fonts. The pre-registered balloons and symbols are decided by advices from experts of cartoons. Figure 7 shows examples of balloons and symbols in the database.

Fig. 7. Examples of balloons and symbols

4.4   Generation and Output of Onomatopoeic Words

The onomatopoeic subsystem outputs onomatopoeic words from the environmental sounds. A process flow of this subsystem is shown in Fig.8. To generate onomatopoeic words, the subsystem learns properties of each onomatopoeic word in advance. Since there are many kinds of sounds and onomatopoeic words, we surveyed onomatopoeic words in a classroom by a questionnaire [3]. We asked about 100 students to vote on onomatopoeic words in a classroom. Table.1 shows a result of the survey. Considering the result, we decided four onomatopoeic words to use in the subsystem; they are "whisper", "sough", "noisy" and "quiet".   First three words correspond to sounds usually generated in a classroom. A last word "quiet" means no sounds.

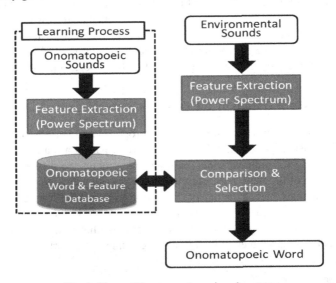

Fig. 8. Flow of the onomatopoeic subsystem

Table 1. The result of the questionnaire about onomatopoeic word in a classroom

Onomatopoeic words(In Japanese)	Number of votes
Raucous (わいわい)	11
Whisper (ひそひそ)	8
Gibber (ぺちゃぺちゃ)	8
Furtive (こそこそ)	6
Sough (ざわざわ)	4
Whim-wham (そわそわ)	4
Chatter (がたがた)	3
Tick tick (カチカチ)	3
Grouchy (カリカリ)	3
Quiet (しーん)	3
Hm-hum (ふむふむ)	3
Chatter (ぺらぺら)	3

Then, to learn a feature of the sound corresponds to an onomatopoeic word, we analyze a sound signal that contains sounds corresponding to the onomatopoeic word. Calculating power spectrums for 1024 sampling points of the sound data, power spectrums between 0~20 KHz are divided into 20 bands, each bandwidth is 1 KHz. Then, the average power set of each band is regarded as a feature of the target onomatopoeic word corresponding to the onomatopoeic sounds. This feature is extracted from each 1024 sampling points of the sound data. Therefore, multiple numbers of feature are extracted from one sound data. We assume these features extracted from the same sound data are similar. Finally, these relations between the onomatopoeic word and these features are registered into the onomatopoeic database.

In generating an onomatopoeic word from environmental sounds, features of an input sound, one of those is the average of powers, are calculated as well as the learning process. Then, the features are compared to those of onomatopoeic words stored in the database. Finally, the system outputs an onomatopoeic word that has the highest similarity of features. The Euclidean distance of features determines the similarity.

4.5   An Example of Output by the Proposed System

Figure 9 shows an example of an output by the proposed system. The output screen of the system is consisted four parts. The lower middle part is a main part, where dictated texts by using the ambient fonts, balloon and symbols are displayed. And at the left and right side of the main part, current onomatopoeic words are displayed. At the upper part of the main part, a history of dictated texts in normal font is displayed. For the reason that the ambient font and decorated texts are hard to read occasionally, and for convenience of checking aforesaid talks, we provide this part. A history of onomatopoeic words is also displayed at the left and right side of the part.

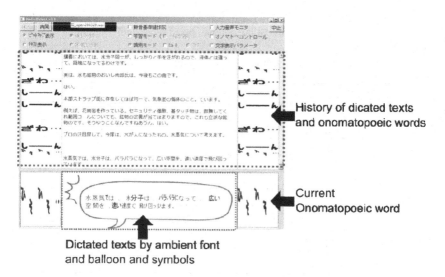

Fig. 9. An example of output by the proposed system

5   System Evaluation

At this time, an evaluation experiment has not conducted. After preparing a prototype system, we will conduct the experiment.

In the experiment, we will conduct a questionnaire survey after using the system. In the survey, we will ask subjects about followings.

- Comprehensibility of the speaker's intention.
- Comprehensibility of the atmosphere in the classroom
- Readability of texts by the ambient font with balloons and symbols

It is important to understand what the speaker said. However, this comprehensibility very depends on the accuracy of the speech recognition system. Therefore, we will exclude this factor from the questionnaire survey.

6   Summary

In this paper, we proposed the system for hearing impaired person, which expresses atmosphere of the classroom. To express the atmosphere, the system utilizes techniques used in the Japanese cartoons such as ambient fonts, balloons, symbols and onomatopoeic words. Using these techniques, many types of atmospheres in the classroom can be expressed by the system. Though we have not conducted the evaluation experiments, we convince that our system contributes to enthusiastic attendances of hearing impaired students to the class and increases conversations with other students.

Acknowledgements. S.S is grateful for a financial support of the Japan Society for the Promotion of Science (JSPS), Grant-in-Aid for Scientific Research (C) (Research No. 22500901).

References

1. Lang, H.G.: Higher Education for Deaf Students: Research Priorities in the New Millennium. Journal of Deaf Studies and Deaf Education 7(4), 267–280 (2002)
2. Seto, S., Arai, H., Sugimori, K., Shimomura, Y., Kawabe, H.: A proposal for a character-based expression technique for conveying a sense of immediacy to people with impaired hearing. In: Human Interface Symposium 2010 (2010)
3. Seto, S., Arai, H., Sugimori, K., Shimomura, Y., Kawabe, H.: Subtitle system visualizing non-verbal expressions in voice for hearing impaired — Ambient Font — In: Proceeding of the 10th Asia-Pacific Industrial Engineering and Management Systems Conference (2010)
4. Seto, S., Arai, H., Sugimori, K., Shimomura, Y., Kawabe, H.: Visualization of Non-verbal Expressions in Voice by using Manga technique -Ambient Font for Hearing Impaired Student-. In: 11th European Conference for the Advancement of Assistive Technology (2011)

XML-Based Formats
and Tools to Produce Braille Documents

Alex Bernier[1] and Dominique Burger[2]

[1] Association BrailleNet
9, quai Saint-Bernard
75252 Paris Cedex 5, France
alex.bernier@upmc.fr
[2] INSERM UMRS_968, Université Pierre et Marie Curie
9, quai Saint-Bernard
75252 Paris Cedex 5, France
dominique.burger@upmc.fr

Abstract. The production of high quality Braille documents is time consuming because it often involves a lot of manual work to be done on the text. To increase the global number of Braille documents available to end-users, special efforts have to be done to automate as most as possible the production processes. At the mean time, the documents quality should not decrease, because Braille is often used in learning situations where errors are harmful for the users. This paper will present recent advances and current developments made in the field of Braille production. Especially, XML-based formats useful to create complex Braille documents will be introduced. Next, some tools operating on these formats will be described, and finally, we will underline the need and the possibility to create fully integrated production workflows based on these tools and formats.

Keywords: accessible publishing, Braille, DAISY, ebooks, EPUB, PEF, print-disabled persons, scientific documents, workflow, XML.

1 Introduction

Even with the emergence of Text-to-Speech (TTS) softwares, Braille remains a valuable way for print-disabled persons to access to knowledge. Braille is often considered by teachers and educators as the best solution for blind people to acquire and to maintain literacy skills. But today, there is still a huge gap between the number of accessible documents for print-disabled users and the number of documents available into the mainstream publishing market. This is explained by the fact that producing high quality accessible Braille documents is time consuming: this task it often involves a lot of manual work to be done on the text. For example, in some languages, Braille codes specify that proper names should not be contracted: also, to produce a conforming document, a transcriber has to manually locate and mark the proper names to make the production software aware of the fact that the corresponding Braille version of these words should not be processed the same way that other segments of the text.

K. Miesenberger et al. (Eds.): ICCHP 2012, Part I, LNCS 7382, pp. 500–506, 2012.

To strongly increase the number of Braille documents available to print-disabled persons, unit production costs should be minimised and consequently, human interventions should be reduced and special efforts have to be done to automate as most as possible the production processes. At the mean time, the documents quality should not decrease, because Braille is often used in learning situations, where errors can be harmful for the pupils or the students.

This paper will present recent advances and current developments made in the field of Braille production. By Braille production, we mean creation of embossed work, but also of electronic Braille documents designed to be rendered on a refreshable Braille display. In section 2, we will describe some formats, all based on XML and we will focus on interesting features of these formats in the context of Braille production. Particularly, we will see that ZedAI, developed by the DAISY consortium, is a well suited format for authoring of highly structured and complex documents, like mathematics books. Next, in section 3, we will introduce tolls operating on these formats, we will mention what they are currently able to do and in which direction developments are necessary to improve them, to take full advantage of the format they rely on. Finally, we will underline the need of workflow which fully integrated these tools and softwares to make Braille production easier and more efficient.

2   Formats

In this section we describe three formats which offer relevant features in a Braille production context.

- ZedAI, an authoring format, semantically rich, from which distribution and embossable formats can be produced. It is designed to be processed by specific authoring and production tools.
- EPUB 3, a distribution format designed to be viewed by an end-user on electronic devices (a Braille display for example).
- PEF, an embossable format used to produce embossed work, or to archive a fixed electronic version of a Braille document.

2.1   ZedAI: A Flexible Authoring Format

ZedAI (Z39.98 Authoring and Interchange [1]) is designed by the DAISY consortium to replace the XML DTBook format defined in the previous DAISY specifications (Z39.86-2005 [2]) [1]. On the DAISY consortium website, ZedAI is presented as "a specification that defines an XML-based framework with which content producers can represent various types of information in an extensible, standards-compliant way, suitable for the transformation into multiple output formats" [3]. The important point here is that ZedAI is not a format defined by a grammar like XML DTBook, but ZedAI is a framework to define grammars.

---

[1] This new format should be approved as a standard by the National Information Standards Organization (NISO) in 2012.

The ZedAI specification describes an *Abstract Document Model* which provides the general framework inside which documents *profiles* can be defined. The model introduces the fact that every document can be decomposed in four distinct layers of decreasing structural granularity:

1. The *section* layer to represent the hierarchical structure of the document (parts, chapters, etc);
2. The *block* layer for containers like lists, tables, headings, figures, etc;
3. The *phrase* layer to contain grammatical and semantically significant segments of the text;
4. The *text* layer which contains character data and formatting information.

This model can be used to design profiles to address general needs: for example, the DAISY consortium has created profiles for books, generic documents and news published on the Web (Newsfeed Aggregator). A profile is a collection of resources (XML Schema files, additional documentation and RDF vocabularies) that define how the targeted content will be marked up. Profiles are divided into different components called *modules*: a module is basically an XML Schema file which describes specific elements of a document. The DAISY consortium has also designed a collection where we can find core modules to describe contents like bibliographies, glossaries, indexes, dialogues, abbreviations, etc. A module is a re-usable component: it can be independently integrated into different profiles (a module is not natively linked to a specific profile).

Thanks to RDF [4] vocabularies, it is also possible in ZedAI to express metadata about document and to semantically inflect the meaning of elements contained in a document. Every ZedAI document is linked to a RDF default vocabulary context. The default ZedAI context includes three vocabularies (the *Instance Metadata*, the *Structural Semantics* and the *Resource Directory Vocabulary*) where definitions are given regarding general concepts like documents types, documents divisions, production notes, lists, proper nouns, etc. Such mechanisms allow for example to assign a property to the "name" element [2] to inflect its meaning (here, to reflect that it contains a personal name): `<name role="personal-name">Arthur Rimbaud</name>`.

ZedAI makes possible to extend existing profiles (creating new modules or adding new definitions in vocabularies) or even to create new ones. So, ZedAI offers a general framework to apply semantic inflection on every segment of text in a document. A processing tool which produces Braille document will have to use a set of rules based on the vocabularies, to determine what kind of processing is appropriate to each definition of the vocabulary.

Such a framework is particularly appropriate to describe complex documents, where the context of an element determines the way it should be processed later during the embossed document production or during the rendering process on a Braille display. For example, in a document containing mathematical equations (ZedAI can embed formulae using MathML) it could be relevant to know that an equation appears inside a theorem, and that the theorem is itself part of a section

---

[2] This element belongs to the "phrase" layer and is used into the "book" profile.

discussing a particular topic [5]. Thus, the presentation of an equation could be adjusted depending of the context where it appears. ZedAI provides the required mechanisms to achieve this goal: it is possible to extend or create new vocabularies to define the theorems, proofs and lemmas concepts; and metadata regarding the topic of the text can be added (to the document level, but even to the section or paragraph level) using the Dublin Core vocabulary. Thanks to such features, the work done in specific formats like OMDoc [6] to represent complex math documents can easily be integrated in ZedAI to produce accessible contents.

2.2 EPUB 3: A Fully Accessible Distribution Format

The final version of EPUB 3 [7] has been published by the International Digital Publishing Forum (IDPF) in October 2011. EPUB 3 is a standard distribution format (i.e. for the end-user of the content) for digital publications and documents. An EPUB 3 document is basically a single compressed file (the container) embedding HTML5 files, CSS, images, metadata and other resources. The accessibility related features (synchronisation mechanisms, skippable and escapable contents) available in DAISY 2005 have been fully integrated into this new version of the EPUB format. So, the DAISY Z39.98 specification will only focus on authoring side (with the ZedAI format described above) and will let the distribution part to EPUB 3.

Like ZedAI, EPUB 3 embeds vocabulary association mechanisms based on RDF. This means that it is possible to transfer semantic inflections of elements from a ZedAI document into EPUB 3 using common concepts shared by ZedAI and EPUB 3 or linking ZedAI-specific vocabularies to the EPUB 3 document when concepts defined in these vocabularies are not already available in EPUB. Next, the reading system will be responsible to correctly interpret these inflections: for example, a Braille device will have to display proper names using the non contracted Braille notation.

2.3 PEF: An Accurate and Unambiguous Embossable Format

PEF [8] is an XML-based format, well suited to archive and emboss Braille documents. A PEF document is an XML file embedding metadata (using Dublin Core), divided into volumes, sections, pages and rows. Braille characters are represented using the Unicode corresponding patterns, which are locale independent an unambiguous (unlike the BRF format, based on the ASCII code, which can not automatically be differentiated from regular ASCII documents).

3 Tools

3.1 BrailleBlaster and LibLouis

BrailleBlaster [9] is an open-source tool under development written in Java. It provides a graphical user interface, accessible to both sighted and blind users.

BrailleBlaster will be able to import files in various XML formats and to export them in BRF and PEF. Its main goal is to provide a WYSIWYG editor including windows to view and modify at the same time the original text of a document and the Braille translated text, allowing users to easily prepare embossed works. Mathematics will be handled using external plugins like MathType or LaTeX conversion tools into MathML.

BrailleBlaster relies on LibLouis [10] to translate text into Braille. LibLouis is written in Python and provides Braille tables for various languages. It is efficient enough to be used as a library by screen-readers (NVDA, Orca) to display Braille dynamically. The translation features of LibLouis are also used in LibLouisXML, a command-line driven tool to transform XML documents into embossalble files (in BRF). LibLouisXML is independent of the input XML formats: it defines a file format (the ".sem" files) to associate semantics (heading, paragraph, etc) to each element of an XML input files and to describe how each element should be presented in Braille (indentation, margins, etc).

3.2   DAISY Pipeline 2

The DAISY Pipeline [11] 2 is an open-source collection of tools developed by the DAISY consortium. It is designed to ensure the connection between ZedAI and other formats (like EPUB 3, previous versions of DAISY and embossable formats).

A Braille Working Group has been set up to provide Braille expertise and to help during the specification and development phases of the tools to automate Braille production. Its main work is to:

- Establish a complete specification of the XML markup required to fully describe Braille documents
- Specify and develop pre-processing tools to automatically annotate and enrich an XML document: for example to detect ISBN, e-mail addresses or telephone numbers using regular expressions, to verify correct balances of parenthesis and quotes using context-free grammars, or to detect proper names and to enhance the XML with hyphenation points using dictionaries, etc.

Currently, the DAISY Pipeline 2 is in a development phase consisting of implementing a prototype for a Braille tool chain. This prototype will be based on LibLouis, but its the design will be modular to allow the integration of different tools during the next phases of the development.

4   A Fully Integrated Production Workflow

The ZedAI and PEF formats, and the tools operating on them (LibLouis and the DAISY Pipeline 2) described above have been designed to be modular and flexible. Because full automation of the Braille document processes seems currently not possible, there will still be a need for interactive softwares integrating these different processing tools to allow transcribers to interact with the document for verifying the results of automated processing and fixing them if required.

Specific tasks required to produce high quality Braille documents mainly consist in marking segments of text to attribute them semantic information. Other tasks that should be manually done to produce accessible documents in general (including audio with TTS and large print) are often of the same nature. So, all the steps required to produce any accessible documents could be done in a general environment able to cover the whole adaptation process allowing the transcriber to:

- Drive OCR softwares like ABBYY FineReader, Nuance Omniqpage or InftyReader [3] and possibly to combine their results;
- Proof-read the text and fix OCR results;
- Structure the text regarding its hierarchical logic, link the notes to their reference, mark specific segments (like non-contractable words, addresses, etc);
- Describe the images;
- Reformat contents like complex tables;
- Export results into a standard formats (ZedAI, PEF or even EPUB for direct delivery)

Some softwares like docWORKS [12] or those developed in the Leibniz project [13] are useful to automate production of accessible documents. But currently, there is no software able to cover the whole adaptation process mentioned above.

5   Conclusion

Formats like ZedAI give solid bases to produce high quality Braille documents. Work is done on open-source tools to reduce production costs and these tools are currently being improved to take advantage of the possibilities provided by this new format. Re-usable pre-processing tools should be developed, to be efficient in different production contexts of Braille documents and to process various languages. In addition to non-interactive tools like LibLouis and the DAISY Pipeline 2, open-source or affordable interactive softwares should also be developed to allow transcribers to easily and efficiently manage the whole production process of an accessible document which possibly embeds complex contents like equations or diagrams.

Extensible formats are necessary to take the variety of representable documents into account. Now that standards are proposed to describe variety and complexity of accessible documents, an important challenge for organisations is to collaborate to establish shared solutions to their needs, to ensure that extensibility will not become an obstacle to interoperability. Using XML-based formats during the whole adaptation process of a document is a good opportunity to achieve this goal because while relying on open and well-documented formats, this approach is the most appropriate to maximise interoperability among various components used to produce accessible contents.

---

[3] These three softwares are able to export OCR results into XML formats.

Acknowledgement. This work is supported by the Agence Nationale de la Recherche (AcceSciTech project). We are grateful to the French Ministry of Culture and Communication and to the Alcatel-Lucent company for their support and cooperation.

References

1. National Information Standards Organization (NISO). ANSI/NISO Z39.98-2012. Authoring and Interchange Framework for Adaptive XML Publishing Specification (Final Draft December 19, 2011),
   http://www.daisy.org/z3998/2012/z3998-2012.html
2. National Information Standards Organization (NISO). ANSI/NISO Z39.86-2005. Revision of ANSI/NISO Z39.86-2002. Specifications for the Digital Talking Book, http://www.daisy.org/z3986/2005/Z3986-2005.html
3. DAISY Consortium: ZedAI Introduction,
   http://www.daisy.org/zw/ZedAIIntroduction
4. W3C. RDF Primer, http://www.w3.org/TR/rdf-primer/
5. Karshmer, A., Gupta, G., Pontelli, E.: Mathematics and Accessibility: a Survey. In: The Universal Access Handbook. CRC Press
6. Kohlhase, M.: OMDOC: Towards an Internet Standard for the Administration, Distribution, and Teaching of Mathematical Knowledge. In: Campbell, J., Roanes-Lozano, E. (eds.) AISC 2000. LNCS (LNAI), vol. 1930, pp. 32–42. Springer, Heidelberg (2001)
7. International Digital Publishing Forum. EPUB 3, http://idpf.org/epub/30
8. Håkansson, J.: PEF 1.0 - Portable Embosser Format, (public draft, revised September 12, 2011), http://files.pef-format.org/specifications/pef-2008-1/pef-specification.html
9. Blaster, B.: Free open source cross-platform braille transcription software,
   http://code.google.com/p/brailleblaster/
10. Liblouis: A Braille translation and back-translation library,
    http://code.google.com/p/liblouis/
11. DAISY Pipeline: A framework for document-related pipelined transformations, for the DAISY Consortium community,
    http://code.google.com/p/daisy-pipeline/
12. Ruemer, R., Miesenberger, K., Kummer, F., Gravenhorst, C.: Improving the Redigitisation Process by Using Software with Automatic Metadata Detection. In: Miesenberger, K., Klaus, J., Zagler, W., Karshmer, A. (eds.) ICCHP 2010. LNCS, vol. 6179, pp. 35–42. Springer, Heidelberg (2010)
13. Leopold, M.: Leibniz - Workflow Tools to Provide Access to Non-fiction Books. In: World Congress Braille21 - Proceedings (septembre 2011)

Japanese Text Presentation System for Pupils with Reading Difficulties

Evaluation in Presentation Styles and Character Sets Changes without Reading Difficulties

Shinjiro Murayama and Kyota Aoki

Utsunomiya University, Graduate school of Engineering, Utsunomiya, Japan
cjc42970@ams.odn.ne.jp, kyota@is.utsunomiya-u.ac.jp

Abstract. There are many pupils with reading difficulty in Japanese schools. The dyslexia is the disability about reading and writing texts. We use Kanji, Hiragana, Katakana characters in Japanese sentences. We propose the Japanese text presentation system that eases the difficulties about reading Japanese texts with or without dyslexia. The kanji is an ideograph. The hiragana and the katakana are phonograms. The reading difficulties include 2 types. One is a difficulty about reading the kanji. Another is the difficulty about tracing the reading sequence. This paper proposes a system that presents the Japanese sentences with suitable presentation method for each pupil with reading difficulties. The main function of the proposed system is 3 levels of highlighting/masking that are independently controlled. The highlighting only is not enough to prevent the error about the reading sequence of character chunks. The 3 level highlighting/masking enables to adapt the presentation to wide varieties of reading difficulties. This paper proposes the design and the experiments of the Japanese text presentation system on the students without reading difficulty.

Keywords: Reading difficulty, Text presentation, Highlighting/Masking, Dyslexia.

1 Introduction

There are many pupils with reading difficulty in Japanese elementary schools. There are many difficulties about learning. The big and first one is the difficulty about reading Japanese texts. Japanese texts are the construction of hiragana (phonetic character), katakana (another type of a phonetic character), kanji (Semantic character) and other characters. The difficulty about reading Japanese texts may have its origin in Dyslexia [1]. However, many pupils have the difficulty about reading Japanese texts without the neurobiological problems. There are many causes of the difficulty about reading Japanese texts. The resulting symptoms are same. This paper proposes the Japanese text presentation system that eases the difficulty about reading Japanese texts.

K. Miesenberger et al. (Eds.): ICCHP 2012, Part I, LNCS 7382, pp. 507–514, 2012.

There are 2 difficulties for reading Japanese sentences. They are the understanding of chunks of characters and the reading kanji characters. Every pupil has those 2 difficulties at first. In the long school life, they studied the skill to conquer those difficulties. Anyway, those 2 difficulties are large barriers for reading and understanding Japanese sentences.

Every infant has no knowledge about the Japanese characters. Every pupil has no knowledge about the huge number of kanji letters at first. Then, they learn hiragana, katakana and kanji characters in a long elementary-school life. The pupils with a learning disability tendency have difficulty about reading Japanese sentences. Off cause, some pupils have difficulty about remembering kanji characters. Most of the pupils remember kanji characters gradually. However, pupils with a learning disability tendency have difficulty with reading Japanese sentences in the case that they can remember the kanji characters. In the case, they may have dyslexia.

There may be many causes of the difficulties on reading Japanese texts. We do not discuss the causes. We only pay attentions to the methods for easing their difficulties. We call their difficulties "reading difficulty" in this paper.

The research about teachers shows that the pupils with ADSH tendency have difficulty about following the characters sequentially and recognizing the grammatical structures [2]. Off cause, there are many types of reading difficulties. There are many causes about the reading difficulties. The resulting reading difficulties show the same symptom that is the difficulty about following the characters sequentially, recognizing grammatical structures and reading kanji characters. This paper proposes the presentation system that eases this reading difficulty with presenting the Japanese texts with a proper method for each pupil. The differences of pupils are ages and disabilities.

For normal non-Japanese students learning Japanese, there are same problems as the Japanese pupils with reading difficulties. They also have difficulties for understanding grammatical structures and reading kanji characters. The proposed system helps the students for reading Japanese texts.

This paper describes the functions and the usage of a visual text presentation system for persons with reading difficulty. First, we discuss about the functions needed in the Japanese text presentation system. Then, we discuss the evaluation of the implemented Japanese text presentation system with the students without reading difficulty. And last, we conclude our work.

2   Presentation System Design

Our goal is to propose the method that helps pupils that have difficulties to read Japanese texts. There are many needs in Japanese elementary schools. However, the proposed system concentrates on the difficulties about reading Japanese texts.

Our goal is the system with it the pupil with reading difficulty can read the Japanese text without the other help. The proposed Japanese text presentation system shows the Japanese text in the way that matches the symptoms at each pupil.

The presentation system has functions for selecting font types, font size, character spacing and line spacing as Notepad has. Some pupils have a difficulty for following a text that is a 1-dimensional sequence of characters. With only proper font and margins, some pupils can read Japanese texts more fluently.

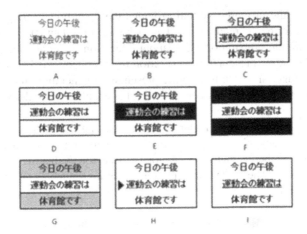

Fig. 1. Highlighting and masking examples

For helping the pupil with ADSH tendency and/or dyslexia tendency, the proposed system has 3 levels highlighting/masking. The pupil may not have ADSH or dyslexia. In elementary schools, the teachers do not make a precise diagnosis. There are the symptoms that the pupils show. Those types of pupils have a difficulty for following a text with a proper font and margins.

For those types of reading difficulties, it is effective at the limitation about the presented information at one time. The DAISY has only the highlighting [3][4]. Figure 1 shows the examples of combinations of highlighting and masking. The B in figure 1 is a normal presentation. The E is an example of DAISY type highlighting. The F is a classical masking. With the masking, there is no information about the masked area. The G is an example of the week masking. With the masking method, we can read the area masked. Figure 2 is an example of 2 levels highlighting of DAISY type. The figure 3 is an example of 3 levels presentation with the combination of a highlighting and a masking. In figure 3, we easily find the sentence, comparing with figure 2. In the 3 levels highlighting, the un-highlighted part is less attractive than the attention part. This type of visual presentation may help to the pupil with ADSH tendency. In special support education schools, the limitation of presented information is effective for the pupils with ADSH tendency.

There are many problems for utilizing the ITC technology in Japanese elementary schools [2]. For solving the problems, the proposed Japanese text presentation system treats only the electronic text. In Japan, a law forces to prepare the electronic readable text of text books [5]. And, there are many documents accessible through the internet. There is no paper document for an input in the proposed system.

The proposed Japanese text presentation system has only 2 functions. For the simplicity, we restrict the functions of the proposed system. The proposed system must have some performance measurements function about pupil. However, performance measurement about pupil is another big theme. The teachers of the pupils with reading difficulties need the objective measurements of the performance about the pupils.

For this purpose, the proposed system provides the operation logging function. The operation logs describe the reading speed at each meaningful chunk of characters.

For decreasing the preparation work about education materials, the proposed system provides the online presentation generation from a plain text. This is the main and most important function. With this online presentation generation, there is no need to prepare the educational materials beforehand. This enables to use the very new materials in a class.

This enables to use one-time materials for measuring the performance of a pupil. Many pupils may remember the full text of the many times used materials as text books. Those remembered materials cannot be used for evaluating the reading performance of a pupil. The online presentation generation enables any new plain text materials at any time.

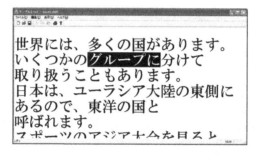

Fig. 2. 1 level highlighting

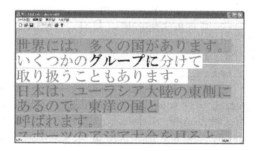

Fig. 3. 1 level highlighting and 1 level masking with background coloring

This online presentation generation enables to adapt the presentation for each pupil with different reading difficulties. DAISY has no function about adaptation for each pupil [3][4].

For adapting the variety of pupils' ages and disability grade, the presentation system has the function to replace the un-studied kanji characters with hiragana characters. The phonic hiragana character is first studied character. There is a little difficulty about reading hiragana.

The operations on the presentation system have the information about a subject. The proposed system logs every operation at the time. This log represents the fluency of the reader.

The presentation system has the highlighting/masking methods. Many presentation systems have highlighting methods for distinguish the point where a reader must look at and pay attention. Some persons with reading difficulty have difficulty following the characters in proper sequence. The highlighting helps to find the place to look, but it does not help to prevent to look at the un-proper place.

The proposed system has rich unified highlighting/masking methods. This enables to help to look at a proper place and not to look at un-proper places.

For controlling the amount of information at each chunk, the proposed system has the function controlling the size of the chunk of characters in semantic senses. Japanese text has no word spacing between semantic chunks of characters. For automatically making proper highlighting/masking, there must be understanding of the semantic structure of the texts. The proposed system uses MeCab for understanding the semantic structure of the texts. MeCab is the free Japanese grammatical parser [2]. With the help of MeCab, the proposed system enables to highlight/masking the text with the proper size of chunks.

The network problem is important in Japanese schools. There is a large limitation about the internet access. As a result, some cloud based implementation cannot work. The proposed system must work without the internet access.

3   Evaluations in Presentation Style Change

We compare the usability on the Notepad and the proposed Japanese text presentation system with normal Japanese sentences with some errors. The errors are typo and the errors in the combination of kanji and hiragana. The subjects are 6 students who are 20s and have a driving license. They have no problem about sight and no difficulties about reading Japanese texts. In the experiment, we don't use the talking function.

3.1   Experiment Japanese Text

We use 2 texts. They describe the PC usage. One is "The examples of convenient keyboard shortcuts for all users". The other is "How to use windows without a mouse". The former is 729 characters and has 8 errors. The latter is 708 characters and has 13 errors.

3.2   Experiment Process

We divided 6 subjects into 2 groups that have 3 subjects. The subjects in the first group read the text-1 with Notepad and the text-2 with the proposed Japanese text presentation system. The subjects in the second group read the text-1 with the presentation system and the text-2 with Notepad.

Each reading session has 2 steps described in the following.

(1) We set up the proposed Japanese text presentation system. The setup controls the font, the size of the character, the colors for highlighting/masking and the length of a highlighted chunk of characters. At the set-up, they use another text for the setup. Each subject selects his favorite presentation design.

(2) The subject reads the experimental text and reports the errors.

3.3   Experimental Results

Table 1 shows the presentation setup at each subject. Overall, they like the condensed representation. They select the long chunk of characters. The favorable presentation design likes Notepad design. There is little difference of error finding ratios between the usages of presentation system and Notepad. A healthy person doesn't need the limitation of presented information. The normal presentation of text is enough for understanding easily. Our former experiments about the pupil with reading difficulty showed that the shorter chunk of characters highlighted helps to understand [7]. The favorable size of a chunk of characters may show the degree of difficulties about reading texts.

In Notepad, the favorable font is MSmincho. The only 1 of 6 subjects selects MSGothic. The persons with reading difficulties like the Gothic. However, healthy persons like the Mincho used widely. The favorable size is about 20 points. It is larger than the standard font size on MS word.

In the presentation system, the font is HGminchoB. This font likes the font in Japanese text books. The 4 subjects in 6 select 30 points. They select larger font than in Notepad.

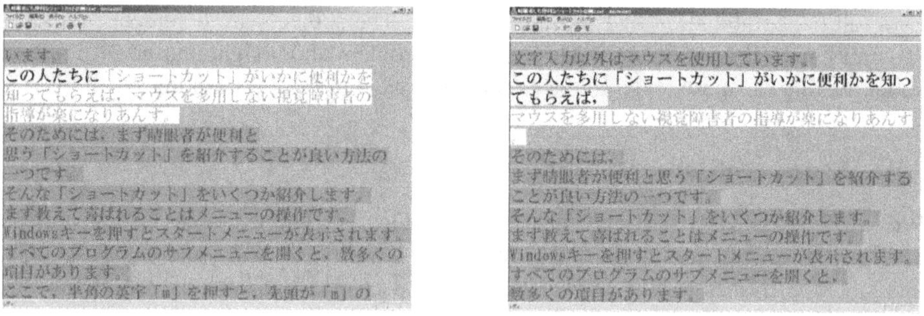

Fig. 4. Change in the length of highlighted chunk of characters

The proposed system has 4 selections in character spacing. They select smallest character spacing.

The proposed system has 4 selections in line spacing. At line spacing, the 3 subjects select the smallest line spacing. The other 3 subjects select next smaller line spacing.

About the length of highlighted chunks of characters, 5 of 6 subjects select punctuation points as the division point. The only 1 subject does "before noun". The length of highlighted chunks of characters is the longest at the division on the punctuation points. The chunk is a whole sentence. Figure 4 shows the change of the length of highlighted chunk of characters. The left one is an example of "before noun". The right one is an example of "punctuation point".

In the experiments on pupils with reading difficulty, the shorter highlighted chunk of characters eases their difficulties. This difference may be the index about the reading difficulty.

At the error finding work, there is no difference between Notepad and the proposed Japanese text presentation system. The average error finding ratio is 74.6%. However, 1 subject marks 95.25%. Other 5 subjects do between 66% and 77%. Some subjects feel easy on the proposed Japanese text presentation system.

Table 1. Selected presentation styles

Subject ID	Line margin	Character margin	Character size	Length of the highlighted chunk	Color
1	Middle	Small	22,5	Punctuation	User
2	Middle	Small	30	Punctuation	User
3	Small	Small	30	Punctuation	User
4	Middle	Small	30	Punctuation	User
5	Small	Small	30	Before noun	Decrease intensity
6	Small	Small	22,5	Punctuation	User

3.4 Problems

They note some problems about the proposed Japanese text presentation system. One is about the scrolling function. The proposed system keeps whole sentence that includes the highlighted chunk on a display. As a result, the highlighted chunk may jump as figure 5. This makes some difficulties about following the texts.

The other is the shortage of the control about character and line margins. The proposed system provides the selections of character and line margins. However, the provided selection is fixed on all font sizes. Therefore, the subjects have difficulty about controlling the margins. Some experiments with low-vision peoples show similar problems. We must refine the proposed Japanese text presentation system at this point.

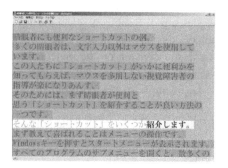 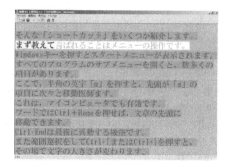

Fig. 5. The jumping of highlighted chunks

4   Conclusion

The proposed Japanese text presentation system makes reading Japanese texts to be easy. We need little preparation works beforehand. The proposed Japanese text presentation system implements all needs of teachers in Japanese elementary schools. The small numbers of experiments show that the presentation system is a helpful tool in elementary-school environments for decreasing the reading difficulties of a pupil and estimating the performance of the reading ability of the pupil.

The preferred presentation styles are different between the pupils with reading difficulty and the normal university students. The preferred presentation style may represent the type and seriousness of the reading difficulty. We need much more experiments on this assumption.

We need the wide distribution of the software. However, this needs not only the software distribution, but also the distribution of the method to use the software effectively.

References

1. Reid Lyon, G., Shaywitz, S.E., Shaywitz, B.A.: A definition of dyslexia. Part I Defining Dyslexia, Comorbidity, Teachers' Knowledge of Language and Reading, Annals of Dyslexia 53(1), 1–14 (2003)
2. Murayama, S., Aoki, K., Morioka, N.: Image processing to make teaching aids for learning disability persons. IEICE-108, IEICE-WIT-488, IEICE (2009)
3. DAISY consortium, DAISY Multimedia, http://www.daisy.org/mutimedia
4. DeMeglio, M., Hakkinen, M.T., Kawamura, H.: Accessible Interface Design: Adaptive Multimedia Information System (AMIS). In: Miesenberger, K., Klaus, J., Zagler, W.L. (eds.) ICCHP 2002. LNCS, vol. 2398, pp. 406–412. Springer, Heidelberg (2002)
5. Japanese Law, http://law.e-gov.go.jp/announce/H20HO081.html
6. Mecab, http://sourceforge.net/projects/mecab/
7. Murayama, S., Aoki, K.: Real Time Image Presentation System for Persons with a Learning-Disabled Tendency. IEICE-ET 109(387), ET2009-96, 25–29 (2010)

Development of a DAISY Player That Utilizes a Braille Display for Document Structure Presentation and Navigation

Kazunori Minatani

National Center for University Entrance Examinations
Komaba 2-19-23, Meguro-ku, Tokyo, 153-8501 Japan
minatani@rd.dnc.ac.jp

Abstract. From the perspective of assistive Technology, the hierarchical document tree structure is particularly relevant to represent a document's logical structure. This research proposes a way of realizing advantages attainable from making use of the logical structure of documents by developing a method of presenting the tree structure information of a document on a braille display. The document browser software developed for this research operates as a DAISY player. Experimentation found that using a user interface of that document browser software improves the efficiency of understanding the document's general structure and finding headings when compared to the user interface of a conventional DAISY player with numeric keypad cursor navigation. Not just the DAISY contents, the proposed user interface can be used for general-purpose applications.

Keywords: Blind person, Multi Modal Interface, Document Structure Presentation and Navigation, Braille Display, DAISY Player.

1 Background

Making use of the logical structure of documents, and especially hierarchical document trees, is important to improving accessibility levels. Information on computers is often handled as structured text. R&D has been conducted into improving information access environments for disabled people, and particularly the blind people, by making use of the logical structure of documents with structured text. Such trials are typical in the field of web accessibility and account for a large percentage of assistive Technology R&D. Similarly, the DAISY format has been heavily influenced by HTML from Version 2 onward, including the use of tags to describe document structures.

Although there are many conceivable ways to represent a document's logical structure, from the perspective of assistive Technology, the hierarchical document tree structure is particularly relevant. Figure 1 illustrates a typical tree structure seen in content formatted as a book. There are three advantages to using a tree structure: (1) able to ascertain the document's entire structure, (2) able to ascertain the positions of each logical element within the tree, and (3) able to ascertain the relative position of

K. Miesenberger et al. (Eds.): ICCHP 2012, Part I, LNCS 7382, pp. 515–522, 2012.

the current segment being browsed within the document. These advantages can be provided to the user if content is implemented with its document structure described in HTML or in the DAISY format. For the user to actually receive the benefits of this practice, however, a browsing environment with the proper assistive Technology (e.g., a web browser, a screen reader, and a DAISY player implemented either hardware or software) is also essential.

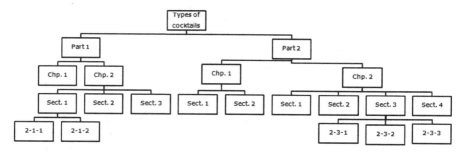

Fig. 1. A typical tree structure seen in content formatted as a book

Unfortunately, the browsing environments for blind people in widespread use today do not fully realize any of the three advantages mentioned above that are attainable from making use of the logical structure of documents. Recent screen readers have functions that report headings and numbers in tables contained in the current web page being browsed. They cannot, however, convey to the user the overall structure of a document with nested headings divided into six hierarchal levels using H tags. Consequently, it is also problematic to inform the user which segment of the structured document is currently being read.

The same holds true for the reading methods of DAISY players on the market. Most DAISY players come with functions that report document information, such as the number of headings contained in the DAISY content or the total length of the recording. A de facto standard content browsing user interface (UI) has also emerged in which the 2, 4, 6, and 8 keys on the numeric keypad are used as navigation cursor e keys, with 2 and 8 moving up and down through the heading hierarchal levels and 4 and 6 moving to the previous or next heading at the current hierarchal level. Despite this, the DAISY player is no different from reading a Web page with a screen reader in that the DAISY player cannot inform the user of the overall structure of a document with hierarchal levels of nested headings and in that it is difficult to tell the user the relative position of the current segment being read in the document.

On the other hand, proposals have been made of implementing more efficient browsing environments for visually impaired users by combining tactile-based navigation with voice-based content reading.[1][2] What is most promising about these proposals is that information having different traits — i.e., the document's content and its structure — is conveyed via different senses — i.e., hearing and touch.

Working from this insight, this research proposes a way of realizing the three advantages attainable from making use of the logical structure of documents by developing a method of presenting the tree structure information of a document on a braille display.

2 Overview of a DAISY Player That Utilizes a Braille Display for Document Structure Presentation and Navigation

2.1 Software Overview

The document browser software developed for this research operates as a DAISY player that displays and reads out content in the DAISY 2.02 format.[3] Because the DAISY 2.02 format can be used to describe structured documents with up to six levels of headings, it was judged that a document browser handling DAISY content was consistent with the research objectives. Another major advantage of DAISY content is that the audio track can be prerecorded instead of being automatically generated from the text, which is prone to misreadings. Also implementing the document browser as a DAISY player enables side-by-side evaluative tests with conventional DAISY players.

The software runs on Apple Computer's Mac OS X operating system. Figure 2 provides a screenshot of the document browser software. The VoiceOver screen reader[4] function built into Mac OS X is used to read out the software's menu options, dialogs, and other basic components.

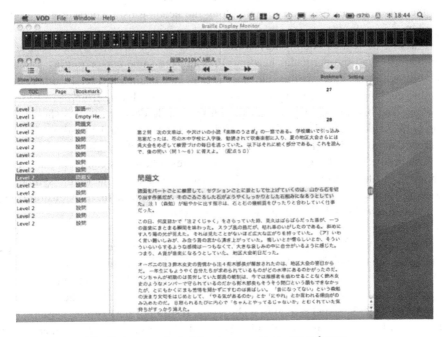

Fig. 2. A screenshot of the document browser software

A braille display (described in detail below) is used as the input-output interface with the user. The document browser software was developed to work primarily with the VarioPro 80 braille display from Baum.[5]

Attention was paid to implementing the same features that conventional DAISY players possess. The speaking rate is adjustable from 0.5 times to 2 times normal speed.

Although with this software the braille display is the primary input-output user interface for indicating the document structure, as an auxiliary input method, it is possible to navigate through the heading hierarchy with buttons equivalent to the cursor keys on a conventional DAISY player. Since the VarioPro 80 does not have buttons equivalent to a numeric keypad, the functions of the 2, 8, 4, 6 keys on a conventional DAISY player were assigned to the buttons at the left and right edges of the braille display.

2.2 The User Interface Using a Braille Display

The software's user interface presents the heading list with braille symbols on the braille display. When DAISY content is loaded into the software, the content's six levels of headings appear on the braille display with one braille symbol per heading. If the content is formatted like a book, the braille display will be equivalent to a table of contents. When the content is played, a cursor using dots 7 and 8 appears under the heading symbol of the section currently being read. As the content is read sequentially, the cursor moves from left to right along the heading list displayed on the braille display.

Pressing the cursor routing key corresponding to any heading symbol causes the software to read the particular heading. Pressing the same cursor routing key again has the software jump to the relevant section and begin playing. In other words, double-clicking on the heading you want to hear begins playing from the start of that section. The braille symbols that appear on the braille display are also shown at the top of the screenshot in Figure 2. It is possible to scroll through the headings list when there are more headings in the content than cells on the braille display.

The braille symbols corresponding to the six level headings can be defined with a preferences file described in XML.[6] It is also possible to set the braille symbols for headings at the same level to indicate the order they appear in. This customization function allows for a diverse range of complex expressions.

Even deeper hierarchal structures can be indicated to the user. For example, we can create a 10-symbol pattern consisting of the letters a to j in one row as our basic pattern in a Louis Braille's braille table, originally created by Louis Braille, the inventor of the braille system. By systematically adding dots to this basic pattern, we can represent four variations. We can create a fifth variation by moving the basic pattern down to dots 2, 3, 5, and 6. Figure 3 shows the resulting Louis Braille's braille table. The Louis Braille's braille table's high regularity has been utilized for other applications as well, such as braille musical notation. When used to indicate a document tree, the table can represent content consisting of five levels with up to 10 elements per level.

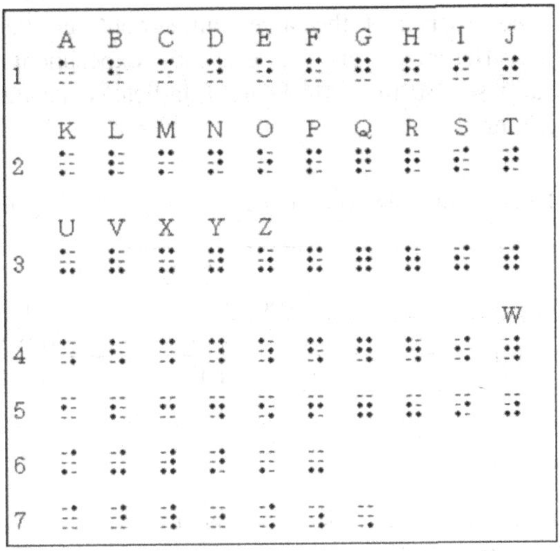

Fig. 3. Louis Braille's braille table

3   Evaluative Testing

3.1   Overview of The Experiment

The experiment evaluated the DAISY player developed for this research project, which utilizes a braille display for document structure presentation and navigation, on its effectiveness in terms of the time needed to understand the document structure and to find headings in the playback content. The developed DAISY player and a conventional DAISY player with numeric keypad cursor navigation were compared to analyze the research's benefits.

Two players were used in the experiment: the DAISY player developed for this research project, which utilizes a braille display for document structure presentation and navigation, and a conventional DAISY player with numeric keypad cursor navigation (Victor Reader Stream from HumanWare[7])

Eight subjects, divided into two groups of four, took part in the experiment. All subjects met the conditions of enrollment in a regular university, able to read braille, and severely visually impaired with at least eight years of braille reading experience.

The playback content used in the experiment had a book format with a maximum of four hierarchal levels of headings, like that shown in Figure 1. The experiment used a task-based procedure without a time limit. The procedure consisted of the following three tasks that required the subjects to ascertain the document structure and find specific headings.

1. Confirmation of the number of headings at the top level
2. Confirmation of whether a given third-level heading indicated by the experiment supervisor has any fourth-level headings or not
3. Play a given fourth-level heading indicated by the experiment supervisor

Due to the nature of the experiment, the same content could not be presented twice to the same subject with different players. Therefore, the experiment design used a two-by-two repetitive Latin square method. Table 1 indicates the design concept used throughout the experiment.

Table 1. Experiment design concept base on a two-by-two Latin square

		Subject Group	
		Group 1	Group 2
Trial order	1	Braille display	Conventional
	2	Conventional	Braille display

3.2   Experiment Results

The following sections discuss the task-speed benefits of the research. The contributions from each of the four test factors — subject group, player, content, and trial order — were investigated, but only the contributions from the players will be detailed here. The level of statistical significance for each of the following results is five percent. Variance analysis was performed in GNU R. [8]

In each of the statistical tests, the normal distribution and homoscedasticity of the population was not negated. In each of the three tasks, the main effects of the subject group factor, the content factor, and the trial order factor on the response speed were all found to be insignificant.

Confirmation of The Number of Headings at The Top Level. The player factor was found to have a significant main effect on the response speed.

A box plot is shown of the response speed distribution per player (Figure 4-1) to compare the distributions of respond speeds between the players. A significant difference was found between the two, with the conventional method (average response time of 9.875 seconds) resulting in slower response speeds than the braille display method (average response time of 3.875 seconds).

Confirmation of Whether a Specified Third-level Heading Has Any Fourth-level Headings or Not. The player factor was found to have a significant main effect on the response speed.

A box plot is shown of the response speed distribution per player (Figure 4-2) to compare the distributions of respond speeds between the players. A significant difference was found between the two, with the conventional method (average response time of 29.375 seconds) resulting in slower response speeds than the braille display method (average response time of 5.875 seconds).

Play a Specified Fourth-level Heading. The player factor was found to have a significant main effect on the response speed.

A box plot is shown of the response speed distribution per player (Figure 4-3) to compare the distributions of respond speeds between the players. A significant difference was found between the two, with the conventional method (average response time of 40.375 seconds) resulting in slower response speeds than the braille display method (average response time of 15.000 seconds).

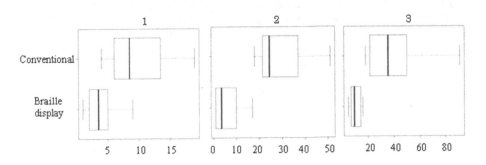

Fig. 4. Box plots of the experiment results

4   Conclusion

In the process of this research, a DAISY player was developed that utilizes a braille display for document structure presentation and navigation. Experimentation found that using a user interface that presents information about the document's tree structure on the DAISY player's braille display improves the efficiency of understanding the document's general structure and finding headings when compared to the user interface of a conventional DAISY player with numeric keypad cursor navigation.

As stated in the opening, the logical structure of a document can be described in a diverse range of content formats, not just the DAISY format, and, thus, the proposed user interface can be used for general-purpose applications. It is hoped that the introduction of user interfaces that present the document tree structure, along with the screen readers and DAISY players in widespread use today, will lead to accessibility and usability improvements.

Acknowledgement. This work was supported by Grants-in-Aid for Scientific Research (KAKENHI 2 2 7 0 0 8 3 5).

References

1. Asakawa, C., et al.: TAJODA: Proposed Tactile and Jog Dial Interface for the Blind. Transaction of IEICE E87-D(6), 1405–1414 (2004)
2. Ifukube, T.: Sound-Based Assistive Technology Supporting 'Seeing', 'Hearing' and 'Speaking' for the Disabled and the Elderly. In: INTERSPEECH 2010, pp. 11–19 (2010), http://www.iscaspeech.org/archive/interspeech_2010/i10_0011.html

3. DAISY 2.02 format, `http://www.daisy.org/z3986/specifications/daisy_202.html`
4. VoiceOver, `http://www.apple.com/accessibility/voiceover/`
5. VarioPro, `http://www.baum.de/cms/en/braille/`
6. XML, `http://www.w3.org/XML/`
7. E Victor Reader Stream, `http://www.humanware.com/en-usa/products/blindness/dtb_players/compact_models/_details/id_81/victor_reader_stream_daisy_mp3_player.html`
8. GNU R, `http://www.r-project.org/about.html`

Acce-Play: Accessibility in Cinemas

Alexandre Paz, Mari Luz Guenaga, and Andoni Eguíluz

DeustoTech Learning, Deusto Foundation, Bilbao, Spain
{alexandre.paz,mlguenaga,andoni.eguiluz}@deusto.es

Abstract. In this paper we present Acce-Play: a system that aims to provide accessible content to all life cycle of films. It is designed to be platform independent and currently allows to play accessible content in cinemas. The content is synchronized with the playing film using audio fingerprinting techniques with the projector audio stream.

Keywords: Accessibility, Cinema, Audio Fingerprinting, Audiovisual Accessibility.

1 Introduction

Accessibility in audiovisual media is a major issue nowadays. Current Spanish laws, like the General Telecommunications Law or the National Accessibility Plan, force that certain percentage of audiovisual production must be adapted to people with sensorial disabilities. However, there are almost no integrated solutions that allow to easily bring accessibility to cinemas. Furthermore, there is the problem of multilingualism: if a cinema wants to play a film in two or more languages, it needs one screen for each language.

All this generates a vicious circle: users don't go to cinema because there is no accessible content and there is no accessible content because there are no consumers.

2 Current Solutions

Currently, accessibility on cinemas is linked to the audio systems. This means that, in fact, there are only two solutions, one from each of the companies that provide those systems: Dolby and DTS.

Dolby ScreenTalk System[1], from Dolby, is practically abandoned even considering that Dolby systems are present in most of Spanish cinemas. This solution allows to show subtitles using another projector, or alternative video devices, and transmitting audio descriptions to a standard audio broadcast station.

DTS Access, from the competitor DTS, is similar to the Dolby ScreenTalk System but has never been installed in Spain. The accessible content is distributed along the audio in CD-ROM and played in a special player that transmits the subtitles to an alternative projector and the audio descriptions to an infra-red broadcast station. An alternative system is provided by MoPix[2], a company that has specialized in selling devices for cinema accessibility using DTS contents.

K. Miesenberger et al. (Eds.): ICCHP 2012, Part I, LNCS 7382, pp. 523–526, 2012.

Both systems have the disadvantage that the accessible content is highly hardware dependent, which means that few films are available. Apart from that, the cost of the rights of projection, up to €3000 each film, may be prohibitive given the size of the target audience.

3   Acce-Play

Acce-Play aims to be an low-cost and integrated solution to provide accessible content to cinemas during all life cycle of films, from the initial exhibition to domestic use. The Acce-Play player is a device designed to play accessible content on cinemas. It has to be installed in the cabin and needs to be connected to the projector audio system, a Dolby solution in most cases. This connection does not affect the audio quality in any way. Once installed, the projectionist just needs to select the title to play and the Acce-Play system will synchronize with the playing film to display the corresponding accessible content, as the figure 1 shows.

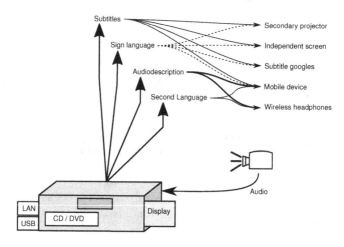

Fig. 1. Acce-Play content processing

3.1   The Synchronization Problem

The main problem for achieving a good integrated audiovisual experience is synchronizing with the film. First, cinemas still use analogical films that need to be cut on multiple coils for easy transport, which removes tenths of seconds randomly. Second, the material they are made of is highly stretchable so that after many playbacks the duration of the film changes. Apart from that, films can be paused and played again and have ads and messages played before. All these problems must be addressed in order to provide an efficient system capable of providing accessible content. Acce-Play achieves synchronization by analyzing the audio stream provided by the projector. It identifies the audio being currently played and locates it in the original audio. Once it gets the actual playing time, the system starts playing the appropriate accessible content.

The localization algorithm is based on a technique called "Audio Fingerprinting". Surveys with more information can be found in [3], [4] and [5]. Our algorithm is based on the technique presented in [6], although some change were made to adapt it to our necessities. Most of audio fingerprinting algorithms are designed to tell apart different recordings, we need to locate a particular fragment inside the whole recording.

The first step we did was splitting the whole film in small fragments, around 200ms each, and then we calculate the fingerprint of each fragment. When the playing starts, the system does the same thing with the projected audio stream, obtaining a new list of fragments. Finally, the list if searched for within the original audio until a section is found where the similarity is maximized.

3.2 Audio Fingerprint

Given an audio fragment, we begin calculating the Fast Fourier Transform (FFT) of the stream, which decomposes the fragment into component of different frequencies. The next steps implies grouping the frequencies into different groups given configurable ranges, for example: 0-500Hz, 500-1000Hz, 1000-1500Hz and 1500-2000Hz (see figure 2). For each range we get the top value among all the frequencies in the range, so we get one value for each range. We use these values as the hash of the fragment and to tell the "likeliness" of two different fragments.

Instead of looking for each hash trough the whole film, we group the hashes in a sequence and the get the film location that maximizes de "likeliness" with the current sequence. With this technique we have achieved synchronization trough most the playing of a film with less than 100ms of difference and being lost for less than a minute in total.

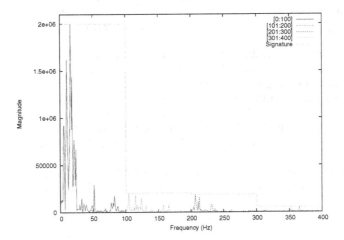

Fig. 2. FFT divided into ranges

3.3   The Complete Solution

Besides the player, the system also includes an editor capable of creating the accessible content used by the player and an on-line distribution system. The editor, like the player, is brought to have the lowest system dependency as possible, accepting most of commonly used audio and video formats and codecs. The distribution system allows to easily deploy the accessible content to cinemas that use the Acce-Play system, on-line or off-line with pen drives.

4   Conclusion

Tests performed by our team show that the system can keep synchronization for over 99.5% of film duration, being the most notable problem the silence many films start with. Apart from that, the difference between the original film and the accessible content stays below 100ms most of the time, which means that the film can be enjoyed as if the extra content was previously synchronized. Future work will include a system to adjust the frequency ranges to specific films to get better synchronization and avoid losing it during the playing.

To conclude, there are some associations, like "Navarra de Cine", that are already preparing accessible content with our system. These organizations are already used to the task of subtitling and preparing audio descriptions and our intention is to design our system to make their job easier.

References

1. Dolby: Dolby screentalk, cinema subtitling and audio description system, http://www.audiomaster.cz/download/katalogy/dolby/do009.pdf   (accessed April 3, 2012)
2. MoPix: Motion picture access, http://ncam.wgbh.org/mopix/ (accessed April 3, 2012)
3. Cano, P., Batlle, E., Kalker, T., Haitsma, J.: A review of algorithms for audio fingerprinting. In: IEEE Workshop on Multimedia Signal Processing, pp. 169–173. IEEE Signal Processing Society (2002)
4. Cowling, M., Sitte, R.: Comparison of techniques for environmental sound recognition. Pattern Recognition Letters 24(15), 2895–2907 (2003)
5. Dannenberg, R.B., Hu, N.: Pattern discovery techniques for music audio. In: In Proc. International Conference on Music Information Retrieval, pp. 63–70 (2002)
6. Haitsma, J., Kalker, T.: A highly robust audio fingerprinting system with an efficient search strategy. Journal of New Music Research 32(2), 211–221 (2003); International Symposium on Music Information Retrieval (ISMIR 2002), Paris, France (2002)

Automatic Simplification of Spanish Text for e-Accessibility

Stefan Bott and Horacio Saggion

Universitat Pompeu Fabra,
Departament of Information and Communication Technologies
C/Tanger 122, 08018 Barcelona, Spain
{stefan.bott,horacio.saggion}@upf.edu

Abstract. In this paper we present an automatic text simplification system for Spanish which intends to make texts more accessible for users with cognitive disabilities. This system aims at reducing the structural complexity of Spanish sentences in that it converts complex sentences in two or more simple sentences and therefore reduces reading difficulty.

Keywords: Automatic Text Simplification, Natural Language Processing, e-Accessibility.

1 Introduction

The United Nations' Convention on the rights of Persons with Disabilities requires that the signing countries promote access to information for persons with disabilities [1]. But the reality is usually different: for people with cognitive disabilities the access to textual information is often hard because texts written for general public are too difficult for them to read. Adapting only the format of the text is not the solution in this case. One possibility to enable access to textual information for people with cognitive problems is to adapt and simplify texts manually. One set of guidelines under the umbrella name of the "easy-to-read" methodology is generally used to adapt already existing textual material or to produce content following the proposed guidelines. There are some organizations which are dedicated to the production of such material, such as the Asociación Facil Lectura [2], but the primary problem is that manual adaptation is very costly in terms of human labour because of the time and knowledge required to produce simplifications. For this reason, making easy-to-read versions of the current volume of textual information (or even a small proportion of it) would be impractical with human efforts alone.

Automatic text simplification is a technology to produce adaptable texts by reducing their syntactic and lexical complexity so that they become readable for a target user group. Automatic text simplification products can be considered a kind of e-Accessibility devices with the potential of helping various user groups including elderly people, second language learners, and inmigrants.

K. Miesenberger et al. (Eds.): ICCHP 2012, Part I, LNCS 7382, pp. 527–534, 2012.

Our research is concerned with the development of an automatic simplification system for Spanish. It forms part of Simplext project[1] which has the aim to provide people with intellectual disabilities access to textual information anytime and anywhere with the help of web and mobile applications. In this paper we report the results of our research so far conducted for the development of the first text simplification system for Spanish. We will briefly describe our efforts to create language resources and a working prototype which is already operative.

2   Text Simplicity and Automatic Simplification

Even if the concept of "easy-to-read" is not universal, it is possible in a number of specific contexts to write a text that will suit the abilities of most people with literacy and comprehension problems. This easy-to-read material is generally characterized by the following features:

- The text is usually shorter than a standard text and redundant content and details which do not contribute to the general understanding of the topic are eliminated.
- Ideally, each sentence should only contain one piece of information. Hence, easy texts are written in fairly short sentences, avoiding subordinate clauses whenever possible.
- Previous knowledge is not taken for granted. Background, difficult words and context are explained but in such a way that it does not disturb the flow of the text.
- Easy-to-read is always easier than standard language. There are differences of level in different texts, all depending on the target group in mind.

While the problem of Automatic text simplification has been studied for some other languages there are no simplification tools for Spanish. Work on automatic text simplification has followed rule-based paradigms where rules were designed following linguistic intuitions [5,6] or statistical machine learning approaches [7] which require a considerable volume of training data. Although automatic text simplification has sometimes been studied without paying attention to the user of the simplification, most research has particular user groups in mind. For example, the PSET project [8] studied simplification for people with aphasia while the PorSimples project [9,10] looked into simplification for people with poor literacy rate. One important issue in text simplification research are the factors making a text more or less readable for a target user group, so research to measure text readability is especially relevant [11,12,13].

One factor that makes the development of automatic simplification tools difficult is a noticeable lack of linguistic resources (parallel corpora and lexical resources). This is especially true for the Spanish language. In the larger context of our research project we are creating a specialized corpus of 200 news texts. Simplified versions are created by human experts and aligned to the original

---

[1] Simplext: An automatic system for text simplification [3]. The idea for creating such a tool for Spanish was born from the Prodis Foundation [4].

texts [14]. The simplified texts have been especially prepared for the target user group, following theoretically motivated guidelines, based on previous studies on readability of Spanish texts [15,16]. The corpus of manual simplifications serves us as a model of texts which are apt for our target users.

In order to determine what kinds of text simplification operations our system would have to cover, we carried out an initial corpus study. The details of this study can be found in [17]. We examined 145 simplified sentences which constituted the first available part of our corpus, contrasting them with the non-simplified versions. In addition to determining the needs of users, we wanted to assess how far the necessary text adjustments could be carried out automatically. In the study we identified different editing operations and evaluated their frequency, together with the possibility to automatize them. We found that many operations human editors perform are either very hard to classify, since they use rather free re-wording instead of clear-cut editing operations, or require complex reasoning on the basis of real-world knowledge. But we also found various editing operations which were regular enough to be automatized.

On the basis of this corpus study we decided to concentrate on the automatic treatment of *lexical simplification, deletion* operations, *sentence split operations*, and the *insertion of definitions*. These four categories are very different in nature and in the resources they require when automatized.

Within our research project we are developing different simplification modules for these different types of simplification operations. At the moment only the module for syntactic simplification (carrying out the *sentence splitting* operations) is in an operational stage. We are aware of the fact that this is only one aspect of text simplification, but we believe it to be an important one. Other modules, namely the modules for *lexical simplification* and *deletions* are under development and will be integrated in our simplification system in the near future.

3   System Components and Evaluation

3.1   The Simplification Grammar

The current version of the prototype concentrates purely on the reduction of structural complexity.[2] The core of the simplification system in its current state consists of a hand-crafted transduction grammar which operates on dependency trees, produced by a dependency parser [18]. The output of the parser is a tree which represents natural language syntax in the form of dependency relations between words. Figure 1 is an example of such a dependency tree and corresponds to example (1a), which we will discuss below. The parser also associates each node in the tree with its morphologic information, such as its part of speech and agreement information.[3]

---

[2] Further details about the system architecture can be found in [17].

[3] Figure 1 is a visualization of the tree produced by the MATE development environment. Morphological information is inherent in the nodes, but it is not shown in the image. A further type of information which is implicit but not shown here is the linear ordering of the words.

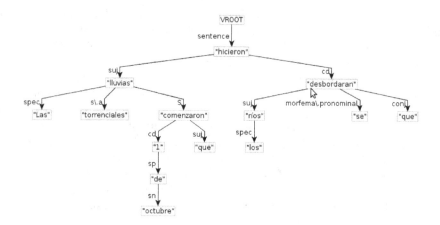

Fig. 1. A target structure containing a relative clause

(1) a. Las lluvias torrenciales, que comenzaron el pasado 1 de octubre (...)
         hicieron que los ríos se desbordaran (...)

         The torrential rains that began on October 1 (...), caused rivers to
         overflow (...)

     b. Las lluvias torrenciales hicieron que los ríos se desbordaran (...)
         Estas lluvias comenzaron el pasado 1 de octubre.

         The torrential rains caused rivers to overflow (...) These rains began
         on October 1.

The grammar itself is being developed within the MATE framework [19]. MATE
is a tree transduction tool which was created with the mapping between different layers of linguistic representation in mind and is especially useful for text
generation. In our context, however, we use MATE as a tool that maps syntactic dependency structures which we detect as requiring simplification onto
simplified versions of these structures.

The simplification grammar typically splits one sentence in two or more
shorter ones. In this process some parts of the syntactic tree may be copied,
deleted or split. Also some reordering operations apply. The process is done in
two steps: first the grammar identifies a target structure which appears to lend
itself to simplification. In a second step the actual simplification is carried out.
This strategy allows for a hybrid approach in which we can let a statistical
classifier decide whether a simplification should be carried out or not after identification. This is particularly important since most of the target structures are
ambiguous in one way or another.

Relative clauses, such as (1a), are a good example of the typical application
of sentence split rules. Relative clauses often express information about a nom-
inal referent which can be expressed in a separate sentence. Such a separation
results in shorter and less complex sentences, especially in cases with multiple
and recursive subordination. Our grammar is able to detect such relative clause

structures and turn them into an output like (1b). In order to manipulate the input text, the grammar first has to identify a matching part of the tree shown in figure 1. More specifically, the grammar looks for a verbal node (in this case *comenzaron/started*) which depends on a noun (*lluvias/rains*) and in turn dominates a relative pronoun (*que/that*). Expressed informally, the rule then cuts the whole subtree dominated by this verb and turns it into a separate sentence which follows the main clause. In order to convert a relative clause into an independent sentence, the relative pronoun has to be replaced by the form of the head noun of the clause (*lluvias/rains*) and an appropriate determiner (in this case *estas/these*) has to be inserted.

Apart from relative clauses, the current version of our grammar is able to simplify gerundive and participle constructions (e.g. (2)), coordinations (e.g.(3), an example of verb phrase coordination) and a special operation which we encountered very often in the corpus and call quote inversion (e.g.(4)). All of these examples are taken from our corpus and the simplified versions have been produced by our grammar.

(2)   a. Los participantes (...) recibirán como obsequio un libro editado por el Ayuntamiento (...)

          The participants (...) will receive a book as a present, edited by the town council (...)

    b. Los participantes (...) recibirán como obsequio un libro. Este libro está editado por el Ayuntamiento (...)

          The participants (...) will receive a book as a present. This book is edited by the town council (...)

(3)   a. (...) los precios se han disparado y mucha gente no puede permitirse el lujo de comprar alimentos.

          (...) the prices have exploded and many people cannot afford the luxury of buying food.

    b. (...) los precios se han disparado. Mucha gente no puede permitirse el lujo de comprar alimentos.

          (...) the prices have exploded. Many people cannot afford the luxury of buying food.

(4)   a. "Se necesita más apoyo que nunca antes", apuntó (...)

          (...) "More support than ever is necessary", he pointed out (...)

    b. Apuntó: "Se necesita más apoyo que nunca antes".

          He pointed out: "More support than ever is necessary".

What these cases have in common is that the sentences resulting from simplification are much shorter and, more importantly, structurally less complex. This corresponds to the idea that, whenever possible, one simplified sentence should not express more than one idea.

Table 1. Precision, recall and frequency of application per rule type

Operation	Precision	Recall	Frequency
Relative Clauses	39.34%	66.07%	20.65%
Gerundive Constructions	63.64%	20.59%	2.48%
Quotation Inversion	78.95%	100%	2.14%
Object coordination	42.03%	58.33%	7.79%
VP and clause coordination	64.81%	50%	6.09%

3.2   Evaluation

An evaluation of the performance of the different simplification operations is given in table 1. This evaluation was carried out over 886 sentences. We counted places where the rule had produced a felicitous output, ignoring minor grammaticality issues which can be solved with further fine-tuning of the grammar rules. The precision here is defined as the percentage of correct applications of each rule. For the calculation of recall we manually annotated 262 sentences for structures which contain a target structure that could be simplified. The frequency of rule application is given as the percentage of sentences affected by a rule.

In interpreting table 1 it is important to note that no statistical filtering has been applied yet in order to resolve structural ambiguities, such as the defining vs non-defining difference for relative clauses. Turning a restrictive clause into an independent sentence leads to an infelicitous output and in Spanish this distinction is usually not reflected in the syntax. Such errors constitute 57% of all errors in the application of this rule. In addition, parse errors are a serious problem and propagate into the simplification module. These constitute a large part of all errors, up to 37% in the category of gerundive constructions. Finally, error analysis showed us that there is still much room for improvement of precision and recall with further grammar engineering.

We have also implemented a series of support vector machine classifiers [20][4] to address specific problems which would be difficult to deal with a rule-based approach alone. The task of the classifier is to help decide whether or not the application of a rule would be correct. We have concentrated on very specific problems such as deciding if a sentence should be split or whether a full sentence should be deleted. For sentence deletions we obtain an F-score of 76.03%, but a simple baseline (deleting the last sentence of each text in the specific text genre) is nearly as accurate (73.00%). In the case of deciding on sentence splitting our classifier can improve significantly over the baseline which only considers sentence length: the classifier yields an F-score of 80.06%, while the baseline only reaches 40.00%. The experiments were only performed on a sample of 40 documents. Although the results are still modest, we believe that with further data and carefully selected features the performance of the classifiers will improve.

---

[4] We used the support vector machine implementation provided in the GATE framework [21,22].

4   Conclusion and Outlook

In this paper we have described the prototype of a text simplification system for Spanish which concentrates on the reduction of syntactic complexity. This prototype is the result of an ongoing research project. The syntactic simplification module is at an operational stage, but we still see much room for improvement. Other components of what we plan to be the final simplification system are still under development and need to be integrated, more specifically a lexical simplification module, a statistic filter for rule application and deletion operations and also a module for the addition of clarifying definitions. The system presented here is part of a software architecture, described in [23], which includes web services, a web browser plugin and mobile phone applications.

In the near future we will carry out an extrinsic evaluation with the help of twenty intellectually disabled persons, in order to compare the reading comprehension of original and simplified texts.

Acknowledgements The research described in this paper arises from a Spanish research project called Simplext: An automatic system for text simplification [3]. Simplext is led by Technosite and partially funded by the Ministry of Industry, Tourism and Trade of the Government of Spain, by means of the National Plan of Scientific Research, Development and Technological Innovation (I+D+i), within strategic Action of Telecommunications and Information Society (Avanza Competitiveness, with file number TSI-020302-2010-84). We are grateful to fellowship RYC-2009-04291 from Programa Ramón y Cajal 2009, Ministerio de Economía y Competitividad, Secretaría de Estado de Investigación, Desarrollo e Innovación, Spain.

References

1. United Nations: Convention on the rights of persons with disabilities, http://www2.ohchr.org/english/law/disabilities-convention.html
2. Asociación Facil Lectura: Social space for research and innovation, http://www.lecturafacil.net
3. Simplext: An automatic system for text simplification, http://www.simplext.es
4. Prodis Foundation: Social space for research and innovation, http://www.fundacionprodis.org/
5. Chandrasekar, R., Doran, C., Srinivas, B.: Motivations and methods for text simplification. In: Proceedings of the International Conference on Computational Linguistics, pp. 1041–1044 (1996)
6. Siddharthan, A.: An architecture for a text simplification system. In: Proceedings of the Language Engineering Conference, pp. 64–71 (2002)
7. Zhu, Z., Bernhard, D., Gurevych, I.: A monolingual tree-based translation model for sentence simplification. In: Proceedings of the International Conference on Computational Linguistics, Beijing, China, pp. 1353–1361 (August 2010)
8. Carroll, J., Minnen, G., Canning, Y., Devlin, S., Tait, J.: Practical simplification of english newspaper text to assist aphasic readers. In: Proceedings of the AAAI 1998 Workshop on Integrating Artificial Intelligence and Assistive Technology, pp. 7–10 (1998)

9. Aluísio, S.M., Specia, L., Pardo, T.A.S., Maziero, E.G., de Mattos Fortes, R.P.: Towards brazilian portuguese automatic text simplification systems. In: ACM Symposium on Document Engineering, pp. 240–248 (2008)

10. Gasperin, C., Maziero, E.G., Aluísio, S.M.: Challenging choices for text simplification. In: The International Conference on Computational Processing of Portuguese, pp. 40–50 (2010)

11. Flesch, R.: A new readability yardstick. Journal of Applied Psychology 32(3), 221–233 (1948)

12. Graesser, A.C., McNamara, D.S., Louwerse, M.M., Cai, Z.: Coh-Metrix: Analysis of text on cohesion and language. Behavior Research Methods, Instruments and Computers 36(2), 193–202 (2004)

13. Feng, L., Jansche, M., Huenerfauth, M., Elhadad, N.: A comparison of features for automatic readability assessment. In: Proceedings of the International Conference on Computational Linguistics (Posters), pp. 276–284 (2010)

14. Bott, S., Saggion, H.: An unsupervised alignment algorithm for text simplification corpus construction. In: ACL Workshop on Monolingual Text-To-Text Generation, Porland, Oregon (2011)

15. Anula, A.: Tipos de textos, complejidad lingüística y facilitación lectora. In: Actas del Sexto Congreso de Hispanistas de Asia, Seúl, pp. 45–61 (2007)

16. Anula, A.: Lecturas adaptadas a la enseñanza del español como L2: variables lingüísticas para la determinación del nivel de legibilidad. In: Cesteros, S.P., Roca, S. (eds.) La evaluación en el aprendizaje y la enseñanza del español como LE/L2, Alicante, pp. 162–170 (2008)

17. Bott, S., Saggion, H.: Text simplification tools for Spanish. In: Proceedings of the International Conference on Language Resources and Evaluation (2012)

18. Bohnet, B.: Efficient parsing of syntactic and semantic dependency structures. In: Proceedings of the Conference on Natural Language Learning (CoNLL), Boulder, Colorado, pp. 67–72. Association for Computational Linguistics (2009)

19. Bohnet, B., Langjahr, A., Wanner, L.: A development environment for MTT-based sentence generators. Revista de la Sociedad Española para el Procesamiento del Lenguaje Natural (2000)

20. Li, Y., Zaragoza, H., Herbrich, R., Shawe-Taylor, J., Kandola, J.: The Perceptron Algorithm with Uneven Margins. In: Proceedings of the 9th International Conference on Machine Learning (ICML 2002), pp. 379–386 (2002)

21. Maynard, D., Tablan, V., Cunningham, H., Ursu, C., Saggion, H., Bontcheva, K., Wilks, Y.: Architectural Elements of Language Engineering Robustness. Journal of Natural Language Engineering – Special Issue on Robust Methods in Analysis of Natural Language Data 8(2/3), 257–274 (2002)

22. GATE: General architecture for text engineering, http://gate.ac.uk

23. Saggion, H., Bott, S., Mille, S., Bourg, L., Figueroa, D., Santos, J., Etayo, E., Madrid-Sánchez, J., Gómez-Martínez, E., Anula, A.: Facilitating information access through automatic text simplification (submitted)

Can Computer Representations of Music Enhance Enjoyment for Individuals Who Are Hard of Hearing?

David Fourney

Department of Mechanical and Industrial Engineering, Ryerson University, Toronto, Canada
dfourney@ryerson.ca

Abstract. Music is an art form present in all cultures and a shared experience. People who are Deaf, Deafened, or Hard of Hearing (D/HOH) do not have full access to the music of the larger hearing cultures in which they live. As a consequence, access to this shared experience and the cultural knowledge it contains is lost. As a result of an increasingly aging global population the number of D/HOH people is growing creating a consumer need for improved access to music information. Challenging the notion that music is only something that can be heard, this paper reviews the state of the art for supporting D/HOH music consumers and describes a study conducted with HOH music consumers to determine how best to support their needs. Results show that HOH people have several difficulties accessing music.

Keywords: Music, Deaf, Hard of Hearing, visualisation.

1   Introduction

Music is a major art form present in all cultures. In Western culture, its presence in one's life is nearly ubiquitous – music is heard in clubs, restaurants, malls, elevators, etc. People may carry music on them wherever they go (e.g., iPods). Music is a shared experience. There is a strong social component to music. People talk to their friends about the music they listen to. People go to concerts to hear music with other people. As a shared experience, music is a shared knowledge space. Some music is so well recognised that people may refer to it by name (e.g., Beethoven's 5th symphony, the Star Wars theme) or simply hum the tune and the reference is instantly recognised by others. We are exploring ways to address the need to represent the emotional, entertainment, and aesthetic elements of music through visualisation of various music information.

2   Background

Hearing loss is considered one of the most common forms of disability around the world. It is estimated that 10% of the global population has a mild or worse hearing loss and 250 million people are thought to have a moderate or worse hearing loss [1]. One estimate suggests that 16% of adult Europeans or about 71 million European

K. Miesenberger et al. (Eds.): ICCHP 2012, Part I, LNCS 7382, pp. 535–542, 2012.

adults aged 18 to 80 years have a hearing loss greater than 25 dB [2]. In North America, hearing loss is the third most chronic disability among older adults and the fastest growing hidden disability. For example, almost 25% of adult Canadians report having some hearing loss. Among Canadians aged 45 to 87, 46% have a hearing loss [3].

As average lifespans gradually increase and the number of people over 60 gets larger, the number of people with age-related hearing loss will grow. According to United Nations global population projections, almost 1 in 10 people are over 60 years old and by 2050, it is estimated that 1 in 5 people will be over 60. Globally, people aged over 60 are expected to outnumber children aged 0-14 by 2050. In developed countries this is expected to occur much sooner, for example, in Canada it is estimated that by 2015 the number of older adults will exceed the number of children [4].

People who are hard of hearing (HOH) tend to have some limited ability to hear music. Depending on degree of hearing loss, whether the loss is mostly high frequency or low frequency, and if the hearing loss is bilateral (i.e., both ears) or one-sided, HOH people experience different barriers when attempting to access the music of the larger hearing culture. Their residual hearing may not allow the individual to hear the full range of tones or perceive sound in stereo.

For example, a one-sided hearing loss has an impact on enjoyment of music. Assuming a person has two working ears, binaural hearing is the ability to use the information provided by the differences between one's two ears [5]. Until one experiences single-sided deafness, "We tend to take our stereo world for granted" [6]. It is the qualities of "rotundity", "spaciousness, voluminousness, richness, [and] resonance" that people who cannot hear in stereo miss [6]. Each of these terms refer to the way that sound can fill a space; its fullness. For example, "richness" refers to sound being full and mellow in tone. From these properties, a listener can sense the depth and distance of music. Without them, music becomes "flat". The ability to hear in stereo provides an avenue of emotional content through the fullness of music and effects such as reverberation[6].

There is scant scholarly literature that makes it clear whether HOH people actively enjoy music. MarkeTrak, a consumer survey which has been used for over 25 years to measure attitudes towards hearing aids (HA) by asking for what activities a given consumer wears their HAs [7], only included "Listening to music" as an item in the year 2000 [8]. One could suppose that, if HOH people are thought to not enjoy music, consumer research in HAs would not include questions regarding music.

HOH people actively try to make use of whatever residual hearing they have [9], unfortunately, HAs are known to distort music [10]. This distortion is a result of HA design. Many HAs have a limiter just after the microphone that is usually set somewhere between 88 and 100 dB. This design decision is based on the logic that since the loudest components of shouted speech are in the range of 85 to 90 dB SPL, any sound above that is considered noise and should be limited. The result is that sounds louder than 90 dB (e.g., rock music can exceed 100 dB SPL) will be cut off.

If HOH people enjoy music, and HAs negatively interfere with their enjoyment of music, will they stop listening to music or stop using HAs? It has been observed that consumer satisfaction of HAs has dropped leading to a high incidence of them being left "in the drawer" [8]. More recent MakeTrak reports show 77% of respondents are satisfied (9% are dissatisfied) with using their HAs while listening to music [11].

Lifestyle choices such as choosing specific genres of music (e.g., songs with deep bass or drums and few vocals) may be among the few available options for HOH music consumers who cannot hear music without HAs and/or are not satisfied with the currently available hearing instruments and/or need additional information to fully enjoy the music experience.

Challenging the notion that music is only something that can be heard, technologies available to support HOH music consumers include visual and tactile representations. One study surveyed several approaches to visualizing music and tested five visualisations in focus groups of D/HOH participants [12]. Their results found that the participants could not see how music was represented in the visualisations.

The Emoti-Chair is a sensory substitution system that presents a high resolution audio-tactile version of music to the back as a means of presenting music to D/HOH consumers. The system uses eight separate audio-tactile channels to deliver sound to the body, and provides an opportunity to experience a broad range of musical elements as physical vibrations [13].

Technologies like the Emoti-chair and music visualisations are meant to be a sensory substitute or sensory supplement to music. As sensory substitutes, the hope is that these technologies will become sufficiently robust to allow D/HOH music consumers to be able to watch the visualisations or feel the vibration without the auditory music and have a similar experience of someone listening to music. As sensory supplements, the hope is that these technologies will become sufficiently robust to allow HOH music consumers to be able to watch the visualisations or feel the vibration together with the auditory music and have more enjoyable experience than listening to the music alone.

Thus, there exist several questions regarding the HOH population that need to be better understood. For example: Do HOH people actively listen to and enjoy music? Do HOH music consumers report issues using their HAs? Do HOH people make specific choices about the music they listen to as a result of their hearing loss?

Technologies such as the Emoti-chair are designed to support music consumers who cannot hear. What, if anything, do HOH music consumers feel they need to better support their experience? Is there a need or expressed desire to represent music in a way that is more accessible for HOH people?

This paper will describe a study conducted with HOH music consumers to determine how best to support their needs.

3   Method

The study took place in two parts: a paper survey and one-on-one interviews.

The 14-item survey used a combination of open and closed questions to collect responses from HOH people on their attitudes towards music, the technologies they use when listening to music, what experiences (good and bad) they have while trying to listen to music and the various strategies they use to improve this experience. The survey also asked what, if anything, participants would want a computer to do to help them better understand or enjoy their music experience. Prior to its use in this study, earlier versions of the survey's questions were tried in a series of small focus groups.

Volunteers were sought among those who had completed the survey to participate in the one-on-one interviews. During the interviews, participants were asked for more detailed information about their hearing loss, their experiences with music, and the strategies they use to access music. In addition, participants were presented with three different visualisations of the same song (participants were not told it was the same song) in randomised order with the audio muted and asked, using a combination of closed survey tools and open interview questions, for their response.

As shown in Figure 1, the three visualisations are: Part Motion, Bars, and Radar.

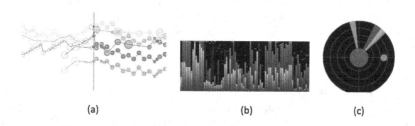

(a)   (b)   (c)

Fig. 1. The visualisations presented in the interviews: (a) Part Motion, (b) Bars, and (c) Radar

The Part Motion or Balls display is a visualisation produced by the Music Animation Machine (MAM) [14]. Notes are represented by circles, the size of which corresponds to the length of the note. The notes of each part (a part is a unique track/channel combination) are connected sequentially by lines. When the note is sounding, the core of each ball detaches from its outline and moves toward the next note in the part. As it moves, the ball shrinks [12].

The Bars visualisation is based on the Spectrum Analyser Plugin for Winamp [15]. Notes are presented in a bar graph format. Each bar rises and falls according to the note's onset, intensity (the louder the note, the higher the bar), and length (the longer the note, the longer the bar continues to be seen).

The Radar visualisation consists of a black circle with lines that span its radius called "blades". While the size of each blade is static, other properties are used to communicate information about the music. The colour of the blade identifies the instrument (or instrument family) being played. The intensity of the colour shows the volume of the note; the louder the note, the more solid the blade appears.

New blades move from the "3 o'clock" position either clockwise or counter-clockwise to show the difference in pitch between instruments in the same family. This provides a sense of the history of the music so far. For example, as the pitch rises higher, the blade rotates counter-clockwise. A new pitch is considered less than the previous pitch, thus the blade rotates counter-clockwise relative to the previous pitch. The speed of a blade's rotation is related to the instrument's own pitch; the higher the pitch, the faster it moves. Like the Bars visualisation, the longer the is note held, the longer the blade is on screen.

4   Results and Discussion

4.1   Survey

The paper survey was conducted at a conference for HOH people. Of the 150 surveys distributed, 36 participants (25 f, 11 m) aged 18 – 65+ completed it. All respondent identified themselves as having a hearing loss with 26 (72.2%) indicating they were HOH, 7 (19.4%) said they have a cochlear implant (CI), 2 (5.6%) identified themselves as deaf, and 1 (2.8%) identified themselves as deafened.

The majority of the respondents (25 or 69.4%) indicated that they always watch television with the captioning decoder turned on. In addition, a number of them (8 or 22.2%) indicated that they sometimes use closed captions while watching television. Only three respondents indicated never using captions. This result suggests that most HOH people use captions where available.

As shown in Table 1, nearly all respondents indicated that they really enjoy (21 or 58.3%) or like (12 or 33.3%) listening to music. Respondents could indicate a neutral response ("I do not like nor dislike music") to which one added the comment, "Can't always hear it properly".

Sixteen (44.4%) respondents indicated listening to music every day. One HOH person wrote that they listen to music not just everyday, but "usually all day". There was a statistically significant association between the frequency with which respondents listened to music and the degree they reported enjoying music X^2 (12) = 64.83, p < .001. Thus, HOH people actively listen to and enjoy music.

Table 1. Frequency of listening to music by Hearing Status / Identity

Hearing Status / Identity	Frequency of listening to music				
	Everyday	Weekly	Sometimes	Rarely	Never
Hard of Hearing	15	4	4	2	1
Deaf	0	1	0	1	0
Deafened	0	1	0	0	0
Cochlear implant	1	2	4	0	0
Total	16	8	8	3	1

Respondents were asked to list the technologies they use when listening to music. There was a range of responses: 18 use the radio, 13 use a home stereo, 12 use a music player such as an iPod, 5 use a computer, and 4 watch music videos (e.g., on a television with captioning).

Respondents were asked to identify the types of solutions they have used to try to access music. There was a range of responses: 26 wear their HAs / CI / FM system (3 indicated they use special cables to directly connect their assistive listening device (ALD) to the stereo/computer playing the music), 25 increase the volume, 18 adjust the settings (e.g., balance, treble, bass, etc.), 16 use earphones / headset, 5 move closer to the speakers, 5 use music playing software with visualisations, 4 only listen to music with a strong beat, 2 have used a balloon, 2 stated they try to memorise the lyrics, 1 indicated trying to cut down as much background noise in their environment as possible, and 1 stated that they have tried putting tape over the microphones of their HA (this may have the effect of fooling the HA into accepting louder input).

When asked if they were satisfied with the solutions they have tried, of 35 respondents who answered this question, 18 (51.4%) indicated they were either satisfied (2 or 5.6%) or somewhat satisfied (16 or 44.4%) while 12 were evenly split between somewhat dissatisfied or dissatisfied (6 each or 16.7%). There was a statistically significant association between the degree of satisfaction with their music listening solutions and the degree respondents reported enjoying music X^2 (12) = 27.9, $p < .01$.

While these results sound like there may not be very many issues for HOH music consumers, many of them still reported frustration with accessing music with and without HAs. For example, one respondent who has a CI and indicated that they really liked music also commented that she "used to" like music and "I would love to like listening to music again. I am happy I can still get the beat of the song but would love to know what song it is." Another commented, "It just does not sound good. I cannot make sense of a song. Old songs are not always recognizable." A HA user said, "Losing more interest. Familiar music does not now sound the same."

Many commented on the special efforts they take to listen to music such as only listening to music they enjoyed before their hearing loss (and thus hopefully remembering how it sounds).

The survey identified significant issues with HAs. Often respondents commented that they can only pick up the beat or some of the music, but not necessarily the lyrics. Some make the effort to memorise lyrics. One CI user said "Wearing my CI, it's either the beat/music or words, but never the clarification of both being blended together. I heard better when I used to wear a hearing aid." Another respondent said, "All my life I have been HOH. I have always listened to music but never for the most part understood words made out through music. I just listen to beats etc."

Respondents were asked to indicate what information, if any, they would most want a computer to help them with. With respect to music information, the survey showed a strong desire (30 responses) for access to lyrics. When asked about access to any other music information (e.g., beat, instrumentation, etc.), song name had 23 responses, artist information had 18, instrument information had 11, and beat had 10. Respondents were asked to indicate three choices from a list, some indicated lyrics to be their first, second, and third choice. While respondents were not asked to rank their choices, in the case of lyrics some specifically noted it was their first choice.

4.2 Interviews

The one-on-one interviews involved eight participants (6 f, 2 m) aged 18 – 65+ who all identified themselves as HOH (this is a cultural label, audiologically some participants were oral deaf, and some were CI users). All but three were born hearing and acquired their hearing loss later in life. In terms of their musical experiences, several participants indicated a reliance on past memory of music to help them enjoy and understand music. A few could no longer hear music at all and were interested in this research as a new way to experience music. As with the survey, all but one participant indicated that they really want access to lyrics.

As shown in Table 2, participants responded well to the Part Motion visualisation indicating that it was the best choice for understanding what instruments were playing and the melody. Participants really enjoyed this visualisation and indicated that it was the one that gave them the best sense of the music.

Table 2. Participant responses to music. (*Items in parenthesis indicate selections made by a single participant who made more than one choice.)

		Visualisation		
	Part Motion	Bars	Radar	None
Best sense of percussion / drums	2(1)	0(1)	3	2
Best sense of Instruments playing	3	2(1)	1(1)	1
Best sense of Melody	5	0	2	1
Best sense of Rhythm	0(1)	3(1)	2	1
Best sense of what was happening in the music	4	1	2	0
Enjoyed most	4	2(1)	1(1)	0

The Bars visualisation was not as well responded to. Participants indicated that this visualisation provided the best sense of the rhythm. Participants responded most poorly to the Radar visualisation. It had several colour palate issues, especially for the older participants.

In trying to understand the images, the participants tended to compare what they were watching to their past experiences, prior knowledge, or to other images. For example, several described the Bars visualisation as looking like a "cityscape".

Some participants quickly saw the music in the visualisation and openly mentioned it without prompting. For example, one said that she thought she saw the song's bridge. When specifically prompted with a question like, "did you see music in that visualisation?", the responses were mixed. Participants with more music experience and music training appeared to respond better to the visualisations than those who did not. Several participants were bothered by the speed of the visualisations.

One participant stated that each visualisation suggested a different genre. This suggests that when designing music visualisations, different visualisations should be used with different music genres (rather than seeking a specific design for all music types).

Participants were asked if they make specific choices about the music they listen to as a result of their hearing loss. All of them, including those who had been hearing for some period in their lives, responded that they had never considered the question. However, those who had lost their hearing all reported listening to music that they knew from before their hearing loss and relying on this past memory of specific music pieces to help them fill the gaps they cannot hear anymore.

5   Conclusion

In a purely auditory presentation, music is not fully accessible to D/HOH audiences. The impact is significant: The music experience is frustrating, the lyrics are difficult to understand, the emotional content is not fully communicated, and the full entertainment experience is lacking. This research challenges the notion that music is only something that can be heard. It raises questions like: What is music exactly? Why do we want to experience music? What benefits does music provide?

The experiments described in this paper show that there are other ways to present music information to D/HOH audiences than audio alone. The surveys and interviews with HOH people reported in this paper showed that there is a significant desire for access to lyrics. How to present a meaningful presentation of lyrics has not been sufficiently researched. For example, captioned videos have been used to explore whether animating the captioned lyrics can help express emotional content. However, the captions were confusing; and not all viewers liked the animation or understood its role [16]. Future research in the area of captioning music lyrics is needed.

References

1. World Health Organisation. Deafness and Hearing Impairment Survey. Report of consultative meeting of principal investigators, WHO Project ICP DPR 001 (2001)
2. Evaluation of the Social and Economic Costs of Hearing Impairment, http://www.hear-it.org/multimedia/Hear_It_Report_October_2006.pdf
3. Canadian Hearing Society Awareness Survey, http://www.canadianhearingsociety.com/survey/
4. World Population Prospects, the 2010 Revision, http://esa.un.org/unpd/wpp/
5. Colburn, H.S., Shinn-Cunningham, B., Kidd Jr., G., Durlach, N.: The perceptual consequences of binaural hearing. Int. J. Audiol. 45(7), 34–44 (2006)
6. Sacks, O.: Musicophilia: Tales of music and the brain. Alfred A. Knopf, New York (2007)
7. Kochkin, S.: MarkeTrak I: Introducing MarkeTrak: The consumer tracking survey of the hearing instruments market. Hear. J. 43(5), 17–27 (1990)
8. Kochkin, S.: Marketrak V: Consumer satisfaction revisited. Hear. J. 53(1), 38–55 (2000)
9. Laszlo, C.: Is there a hard-of-hearing identity? J. Speech-Lang. Path. 18(4), 248–252 (1994)
10. Chasin, M.: Music and hearing aids. Hear. J. 56(7), 36–41 (2003)
11. Kochkin, S.: Customer satisfaction with hearing instruments in the digital age. Hear. J. 58(9), 30–39 (2005)
12. Fourney, D.W., Fels, D.I.: Creating access to music through visualization. In: IEEE Toronto International Conference on Science and Technology for Humanity (TIC-STH), pp. 939–944. IEEE Press, New York (2009)
13. Karam, M., Branje, C., Nespoli, G., Thompson, N., Russo, F.A., Fels, D.I.: The emoti-chair: an interactive tactile music exhibit. In: Proceedings of the 28th of the International Conference Extended Abstracts on Human Factors in Computing Systems (CHI EA 2010), pp. 3069–3074. ACM, New York (2010)
14. Music Animation Machine, http://www.musanim.com
15. Classic Spectrum Analyzer - Accurate, detailed, customizable spectrum analyzer, http://www.winamp.com/visualisation/classic-spectrum-analyzer/165966
16. Vy, Q.V., Mori, J.A., Fourney, D.W., Fels, D.I.: EnACT: A Software Tool for Creating Animated Text Captions. In: Miesenberger, K., Klaus, J., Zagler, W., Karshmer, A.I. (eds.) ICCHP 2008. LNCS, vol. 5105, pp. 609–616. Springer, Heidelberg (2008)

Assistive Photography

Luděk Bártek[1] and Ondřej Lapáček[2]

[1] Faculty of Informatics, Masaryk University, Brno, Czech Republic
bar@fi.muni.cz
[2] Liquid Design s.r.o., Brno, Czech Republic
ondrej.lapacek@gmail.com

Abstract. Many people make photographs of places they visited and when they are browsing the collections they can not often remember the names of buildings on the pictures. There also exist people with visual impairment interested in a photography[1].

This paper deals with the algorithms and methods they can allow people with visual impairment to photograph. They allow to automatically add a semantic description of buildings on a photography and to browse the collection of photographs taken this way even by visually impaired users using the semantic description.

Keywords: visual impairment, photography, geolocation, semantic description.

1 Introduction

Many people are traveling either through their own country or abroad and during these travels a lot of photographs are taken. Even the authors sometimes do not know what is on the picture after a short time. This problem can be partially solved by adding an information about the position where the photo has been taken to the picture. But there still may be problem that we need to know the direction of the camera to be able to locate the object on the picture in cases like similar houses surrounding a square in the city for example. The problems mentioned above are multiplied in the case of a visually impaired photographer.

This paper describes methods allowing to add more precise information about the buildings on the picture to it and methods that can be used to navigate visually impaired photographers to the point of interest. Some results of an experimental evaluation of the proposed methods are included as well.

2 State of the Art

Visually impaired photographers can use several specialized devices and software designed to allow visually impaired users to make a photographs at the present time. The example of such device is Touch Sight[2] camera that displays the picture in the lens using a tactile output.

Another method used to reproduce picture to the visually impaired user is sonification [3]. The sonification assigns a sound characteristic either to a specific color or

K. Miesenberger et al. (Eds.): ICCHP 2012, Part I, LNCS 7382, pp. 543–549, 2012.

to a specific color characteristic, like hue, saturation, value, intensity of some color, etc. The sonification is used in The vOICe program[4] or in a sonification demo at the project GATE[5] website[1]. The disadvantage of the Touch Sight and the sonification based solutions is that the user is not informed what is the name of the object on the picture, he can only guess what exactly is on the picture.

The next application that can be used by visually impaired users to photograph is Assistive Camera[6]. The application tries to get information about objects pointed by camera using the current user position obtained by a built-in GPS receiver and an azimuth obtained by a built-in compass. The position and azimuth are used to get information about buildings at the photo from a map server like OpenStreet Map[2] or Google Maps[3]. The information about buildings on the picture is stored in a separate file and can be used while browsing pictures retrieved by the application (see Fig 1.) using the included photo gallery. The disadvantages of the Assistive Camera are that it does not inform the user about the name of the object that will be photographed. When the user would like to photograph a particular building or static object he must navigate itself to the particular place and there he must select the particular object. It can be a problem not only to a visually impaired user but to the users without impairment as well especially when there are several similar object on the particular place (historical buildings in a center of a city, etc.). Next problem may be processing of near objects only (distant less than 300 meters). The farther objects are not processed.

```
[
 {"religion":"christian",
  "building":"yes",
  "distance":"45",
  "amenity":"place_of_worship",
  "denomination":"orthodox",
  "name":"svaty Vaclav"
 }
]
```

Fig. 1. Sample file with a building description

3   Assistive Photography

To allow to photograph to visually impaired users the following problems during the process has been identified:

1. Location of the object of interest. This task is performed in two steps:
   - getting to the place where is the object located,
   - placing the object in the camera viewfinder – turning to a heading to the object.

---

[1] http://lsd.fi.muni.cz/gate/picture-viewer
[2] www.openstreet.map
[3] maps.google.com

2. Getting information about the objects in the camera viewfinder before the shutter is pressed.
3. Getting information about the objects on the photography.

The last task, obtaining information about objects on the photography is partially solved in the Assistive Camera, that we decided to enhance. The Assistive Camera does not regard to an altitude and to an vertical rotation of the camera. To avoid the objects not in a camera view the following information can be used:

1. Focus distance, current GPS location, the azimuth of the camera, the vertical view angle of the camera and a map server – the focus distance can be used only if the camera supports method to get information about it. Another problem with usage of a focus distance can occur when the object is farther than tens of meters. The camera assumes such a distance to infinity. Therefore this method is usable only for a near objects and this is not the case of buildings.

2. An actual GPS location, an azimuth of the view, a map server with the altitude information, an information about an angle of rotation along the x-axis (see Fig 2.) and a vertical view angle of the camera – the first two information, the location and the azimuth, are available on most of android based devices, the availability of altitude is limited by used map server. The vertical view retrieval must be supported by the smartphone and its platform. When the smartphone platform API does not contain the function returning a vertical view angle, it can be approximately limited to 30 degrees (see [11]) or it can be set manually. The x-axis rotation should be retrievable from the mobile device using its accelerometer. This feature is not available only on the first android based phones (is supported since Android API Level 3 [8]) and almost all today devices (phones and tablets) support it.

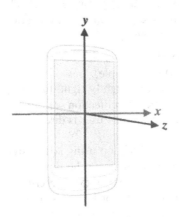

Fig. 2. Mobile device axis [7]

The second task, identification of objects in a camera lens, is almost the same problem as the identification of objects on the photography, therefore the same methods can be used. The only difference is the moment when the information is obtained.

To navigate a photographer to the object of interest existing navigation software can be used but especially the visually impaired users should be aware of some of its limitation while using the voice navigation. The maneuvers like turnings, etc. are announced even tens meters before it should start for example.

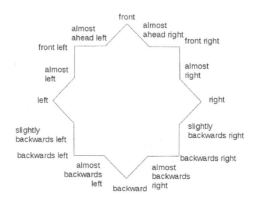

Fig. 3. Specification of an approximate directions

When the user reaches the place where he can take a photography of the requested object, he must turn to the right direction. To find the desired building might be sometimes difficult even for people without any impairment, for example when there are several similar buildings around. To navigate the user to the correct direction can be used the angle between the current horizontal camera orientation and a direction to the building. The camera orientation can be retrieved using a compass that is included in most Android based devices. The desired orientation is calculated using the difference of a current user position and the position of the object of the interest. The resulting angle can be specified following ways:

1. an exact numeric value like turn 45 degrees right or turn 215 degrees right (the same as 145 degrees left) for example,
2. an approximate value like turn slightly right, turn almost backwards to the right, turn right, etc. For the detailed specification see Fig. 3,
3. indicating the direction of rotation – user is directed to turn left/right until he is in a correct direction,
4. signaling the accuracy of a direction using sound signals. Some short tones like DTMF tones [10] are used to indicate the direction (the higher pitch of a tone means a better orientation). The experiment described later in this paper has been performed using the DTMF tone for key 1 as indicator of orientation difference between 90 and 180 degrees, the DTMF tone for key 5 as indicator of orientation difference between 10 and 90 degree and the DTMF tone for key A as indicator of a correct orientation (the difference is less than 10 degrees).

The second, the third and the fourth way seem to be more suitable for most of users. They seem to be enough accurate thanks to the horizontal view angle of the camera (approximately 45 — 55 degrees [11]).

4   Experimental Evaluation

To proof the feasibility and usability of the proposed methods following experiments were planed:

- Feasibility experiments:
  - Test of navigation – users without visual impairment has been instructed to follow the voice navigation on a predefined route and notice the errors. Most of the errors were that the voice navigation announced turn even the displayed information was to turn in 10 — 40 meters. Visually impaired users were not used to perform the test due to their safety.
  - Test of assistive camera – users without visual impairment has been instructed to make pictures of well known buildings in their city. The notes from the users about buildings on the photo and the description created by Assistive Camera has been compared. The discovered problems were especially with distant buildings (farther then approximately 200 meters). Either no description has been generated or the description contained information about nearer buildings on the street. The quality of near buildings description corresponds to the quality of descriptions in the OpenStreetMap database.
- Usability experiments:
  - Experiments using three prototype applications to prove the proposed methods of orientation:
    * user orientation using the approximate angle described in the section Assistive Photography
    * user orientation using the direction of rotation
    * user orientation using a sound signaling of correctness of a direction.
  - Experiments with a prototype application – users have to take a photo of near and distant objects.

The experiments has been performed using a prototype applications implementing the tested methods. Users have evaluated their experience with the methods:

- user friendliness of a particular method
- intuitiveness of a particular method
- usability of a particular method.

The experiments has been performed by users at age from to years. One half has been users with no visual impairment the second half has been users simulating visual impairment using a blindfold.

4.1   Tests of Orientation

The three proposed methods has been evaluated by the same users. The users has rate the method using a number within the range from 1 to 5 (1 – the best evaluation, 5 – the worst one). The users were asked to provide a short feedback with disadvantages of each tested method. The results are shown in Fig. 4. The content of table cells Worst evaluation, Best evaluation and Mean evaluation are triplets containing the values of users-friendliness, intuitiveness and overall usability of the particular method.

The total number of test participants was 12. The users were aged from 7 to 65 years. Three users used the blind fold to simulate visual impairment. The worst evaluation was assigned by the youngest participant who probably did not fully understand the meaning of evaluated criteria.

The comments of users focused to some quality issues of prototype applications used during the tests. Next common comment is to provide some additional information in the case of navigation using the direction of rotation.

The relatively poor evaluation of the orientation using a sound signal may be caused by the used tones. Some users mentioned that the method may be good but it may need some practice. This users often proposed an improvement of a usage of different sounds to indicate different directions of rotation.

Method	Worst evaluation	Best evaluation	Mean evaluation
Approximate value	(3, 4, 3)	(1, 1, 1)	(1.5, 2, 2)
The direction of rotation	(3, 3, 3)	(1, 1, 1)	(2, 1.5, 1.5)
Sound orientation	(1, 1, 1)	(4, 4, 4)	(2, 3, 2)

Fig. 4. Results of experimental evaluation

5   Conclusion and Future Work

The paper described the methods allowing to photograph to visually impaired people. It described methods how to enhance photos with semantic information about buildings on the picture those can be useful when browsing the pictures in the future as well.

There still remains several open tasks to allow the full description of picture like:

- storing photos in a form of annotated SVG pictures [5]
- detection and recognition of people on the photo
- detection of animals, cars, etc. to enhance the semantic description of the picture
- improvement of detection and description of distant buildings
  - experiment how distant buildings can be recognized in a picture,
  - method of selecting the visible distant buildings, etc.

Some of the mentioned tasks are time consuming and may imply the use of computer. The tasks may be performed while post-processing the pictures on a computer or using a server that will process the photo during the process of photographing.

References

1. Beyond Sight Foundation: Blind With Camera (January 2012),
   http://www.blindwithcamera.org/
2. Zhou, L.: Touch Sight – Liqing Zhou (January 2012),
   http://www.liqingzhou.com/touch-sight.html
3. Kopeček, I., Ošlejšek, R.: Hybrid Approach to Sonification of Color Images. In: The 2008 International Conference on Convergence and Hybrid Information Technologies, pp. 722–727. IEEE Computer Society, Los Alamitos (2008) ISBN 978-0-7695-3407-7

4. Meier, P. B. L.: See with your ears! The voice (December 2011),
   http://www.seeingwithsound.com
5. Kopeček, I., Ošlejšek, R.: GATE to Accessibility of Computer Graphics. In: Miesenberger, K., Klaus, J., Zagler, W.L., Karshmer, A.I. (eds.) ICCHP 2008. LNCS, vol. 5105, pp. 295–302. Springer, Heidelberg (2008)
6. Lapáček, O.: Photographing for Visually Impaired, diploma thesis, Faculty of Informatics Masaryk University, (Spring 2012) (in czech)
7. Android Developers Reference – SensorEvent, http://developer.android.com/reference/android/hardware/SensorEvent.html (modification from January 31, 2012)
8. Android Dev Guide – Android API Levels, http://developer.android.com/guide/appendix/api-levels.html (modification from January 31, 2012)
9. Android Developers – Package Index, http://developer.android.com/reference/ http://developer.android.com/reference/packages.htmlpackages.html (modification from January 31, 2012)
10. Schenker, L.: Pushbutton Calling with a Two-Group Voice-Frequency Code. The Bell System Technical Journal 39(1), 253–255 (1960)
11. GeoMark – Calibration, http://geo-mark.com/calibration (modification from January 31, 2012)

The LIA Project – Libri Italiani Accessibili

Cristina Mussinelli

Associazione Italiana Editori
Corso di Porta Romana 108 – 20122 Milan, Italy
Cristina.mussinelli@aie.it

Abstract. The LIA Project – Libri Italiani Accessibili is a biennial project started in 2011. It aims at providing a service to increase availability on the market of digital publications accessible to blind and visually impaired, in full respect of the rights of authors and publishers.

Keywords: Digital publications, e-book, accessible, accessibility, EPUB, mainstream, blind, visually impaired.

1   Introduction

The recent evolution of technology offers visually impaired new opportunities for reading. E-books have the potential to be accessible as they can be read as Braille by interoperability with refreshable Braille displays, as large print thanks to text reflow and magnification and listened to through text to speech or synthetic speech. The LIA Project – Libri Italiani Accessibili aims at providing a service able to increase the availability on the market of digital publications accessible to blind and visually impaired, in full respect of the rights of both authors and publishers.

The LIA Project is coordinated by AIE, the Italian Publishers Association, and managed by its consultancy firm Ediser. The Project is financed by the Italian Ministry for Culture. Funding complies with the "Fund in favour of publishing for blind and visually impaired people". LIA cooperates with UICI, the Italian Blind and Visually Impaired Union, as well as with other stakeholders working in the field of visual impairment, for a wider approach to the issue.

AIE is the only national association of Italian book publishers, representing more than 90% of the publishing market, and belongs to several international networks. Since 2001 AIE, directly or through its consultancy firm Ediser, has been working on the theme of accessibility. The skills achieved thanks to such experience in the field and contacts with the main international networks dealing with accessibility, like Pro Access, eAccess+, the Enabling Technologies Framework of EDItEUR and ETIN, allow AIE with the LIA Project to be up to date on technological innovation going on in production, distribution and fruition of accessible products and to be state-of-the-art in the international scene of accessibility in the publishing sector.

2   State of the Art in the Field

Internationally the issues of accessibility and inclusion have gained momentum and there are several initiatives and projects going on at both corporate and institutional level.

K. Miesenberger et al. (Eds.): ICCHP 2012, Part I, LNCS 7382, pp. 550–553, 2012.

At present production of accessible publications is mostly specifically provided by dedicated facilities that create accessible versions in specific formats (Braille, audiobooks, large print) starting from standard paper books. The existing production process is very slow and expensive and results in a scarce number of publications available in accessible forms, not always in full compliance of copyright rules. Thanks to most recent technological progress, in particular referring to the latest revision of the EPUB standard, the widely adopted format for digital books (e-books), the production of books in accessible formats is increasingly made by scanning texts or elaborating digital files into accessible versions, yet is far from being part of a mainstream flow of production. The situation in Italy is similar to other European countries, so there is a common aim to find the best production system to provide books in accessible version, assuring that the rights of all players are respected: blind and partially sighted people, authors and publishers.

3 Methodology Used

The LIA Project, started in early 2011, is developed in a two-year period and is split in two phases: a pilot phase and a running phase. During the first phase all preliminary studies have been arranged, in order to define every aspect necessary for a proper working structure of the project. More in detail, the following activities have been carried out:

3.1 Survey on Blind and VIP's Reading Habits and Use of Technologies

Thanks to a successful cooperation with UICI (Italian Blind and Visually Impaired Union) and CNUDD (National Conference of University Representatives of Disabilities) a large quantitative survey has been carried out (1,505 telephone interviews to blind and visually impaired people aged from 18 to 65 years) and, in cooperation with the Institute for the Blind of Milan, a qualitative survey as well (3 focus groups including young blind and visually impaired aged from 15 to 28 years and one focus group with two of their experts in visual impairment).
Such survey, carried out by Università degli Studi Milano-Bicocca and Doxa, the leading market research institute in Italy, is by sample broadness and depth of analysis one of the most accurate in the field at international level.

The most significant result emerging from the survey, how much and how frequently blind and visually impaired read, highlights they are keen readers: in a sample totaling 1,505 persons, the average of books read yearly is nine per capita, three times more than the national average of sighted readers.

The Survey also examined the relation between blind and visually impaired and reading and the availability and use by blind and visually impaired of reading digital devices such as tablets, ereaders etc.

3.2   Analysis of Accessible Version Production Formats

Working under the auspices of IDPF (International Digital Publishing Forum), the international organization that manages the EPUB standard, the format presently mostly used by publishers for the production of e-books, LIA identified such format as the most suitable, also considering that in the recent release of the version 3.0 some accessibility features have been integrated. After some preliminary studies, LIA defined the file accessibility features in a specific chart shared with national and international accessibility experts.

3.3   Accessibility Test

To assure a good functionality of the EPUB standard, a test was carried out on how EPUB responds to accessibility needs with assistive technologies and how usable the most common mainstream e-readers and reading software are.

The test's aim was to explore if EPUB files were really accessible with different devices, software and assistive technologies. In the end of this phase, the accessibility of the most important Italian online e-book stores was checked and the accessibility of downloading and buying processes was assessed.

3.4   Analysis of Metadata

Working with EDItEUR, the international group that coordinates the development of the ONIX standard, LIA contributed to the definition of some specific metadata related to accessibility (code list 196), integrated in the new version of ONIX for Books after the EDItEUR Steering Committee Meeting at the 2011 Frankfurt Book Fair and available at large on the EDItEUR website.

3.5   Design of Production, Cataloguing and Distribution of Accessible Versions

After a detailed examination of the situation of distribution of accessible versions at national and international level and the ongoing e-book production, cataloguing and distribution processes, LIA completed the analysis of the production and distribution model of the accessible versions, with the aim to get as much integrated as possible with mainstream distribution channels.

In cooperation with Cefriel, a leading Italian ICT R&D organization, LIA has designed the technological infrastructure architecture necessary to let the LIA platform, where the catalogue of accessible e-books will be located, integrate with the main online libraries where blind and visually impaired will have the possibility to buy LIA titles and with other distribution channels for book lending.

4   Impact

LIA aims to become a reference point for digital publications accessibility for both poles of the publishing world: on the one hand publishers will be provided with practical and state-of-the art guidelines to create e-books in accessible formats in the most efficient and cost-effective way so they can integrate accessibility features in mainstream production; on the other hand end users will have the possibility to enjoy an accessible on-line catalogue of books available in accessible formats, regularly updated. The role of LIA will also be to give support and training to both publishers and readers to let them keep up with the pace of technological evolution.

The catalogue will be available on the LIA website, www.libriitalianiaccessibili.it, a completely accessible site including information on the Project and news from the world of accessibility as well as tips for visually impaired readers for the use of devices, software and technologies for reading accessible e-books.

One aspect that needs to be underlined is that the project is progressing in a really innovative and experimental environment, with many components yet to define, just think of the swift evolution of tablets, ereaders or reading software for digital books. In such a context it is clear that full accessibility does not result solely from the efforts of publishers, indeed all the value chain actors will need to contribute on their turn. For example, tests made on online purchasing procedures showed that both the main online bookstores and credit card payment sections are not presently accessible for blind users. The system related critical elements need to be faced and possibly solved with the broadest collaboration of all the partners and stakeholders involved, as well as of all institutions and organizations playing a role thereto.

5   Conclusion and Planned Activities

The LIA Project aims to create an online catalogue including fiction and non fiction titles of both Italian and foreign authors in accessible version. The process will involve the main Italian publishers, who showed interest in the Project since its early stage. The objective to really grant equal opportunities in book access thanks to a broad catalogue, including new publications, is with no doubt ambitious and makes the Italian Project state of the art at global level. None of the projects going on in other countries can count on such a large participation of stakeholders. The proposed technological infrastructure is unique as to completeness and level of integration.

The running phase of the system, forecast for the whole 2012, aims on the one hand to put into operation the catalogue of accessible books, cooperating with publishers; on the other hand to create the wide technological infrastructure needed for service facilitation and to make accessible publications available online. At the same time LIA intends to gain as much visibility as possible at domestic and international level so as to become a true reference point in the field and to attract funding for its future work.

Inclusion by Accessible Social Media
Introduction to the Special Thematic Session

Harald Holone

Østfold University College, Halden, Norway
h@hiof.no

Abstract. Social Media has great promise for facilitation of inclusion and participation for all. With this Special Topic Session, we wanted to address two perspectives on social media and inclusion: accessibility *to* social media on various device configurations, and inclusion *through use* of and engagement in social media. The papers in this STS falls into two broad categories. Three of four papers mostly look at the accessibility of social media, either with design guidelines, methodological considerations or surveys as central contributions. The fourth paper looks more closely at a case where computers and multimedia is used rehabilitation studies. This introduction provides a short introduction to social media and technology development, the scope of the STS, and a summary of the included papers.

1 Introduction

Social Media as a phenomenon has established itself as a conglomerate of communication platforms over the last few years. With Facebook claiming 850 million users world wide, and Twitter with over 100 million users, there is little doubt that networked communication through social media plays an important role in many peoples lives, and it is likely that this role will continue to increase in the time to come. The common sight of people operating their smart phones to access Facebook, Twitter or WordFeud at the first opportunity in public spaces tells a story of strong social bindings between people, facilitated through the pocket sized, networked multimedia computers we still call phones.

Be it communication between friends, among family members, within interest groups, with public services or broadcasters, social media has established itself with a solid foothold as a go-to solution for keeping in touch. Further, social media can be a powerful way to *identify* those interest groups, find like minded people, and to organize and carry out activities to influence society, or to collect and disseminate information of value to such interest groups.

Technology development is happening fast, and rapid introduction of new features and services is hard to follow, even for the most dedicated users. No wonder then, with the desire to release the next big thing in social media, that accessibility is not always the core concern for developers, despite well-known standards and guidelines, such as W3C's Web Accessibility Initiative (WAI) [2]. There is, however, interesting consequences of the proliferation of mobile devices

K. Miesenberger et al. (Eds.): ICCHP 2012, Part I, LNCS 7382, pp. 554–556, 2012.

into the information ecology. The number of device configurations to support has increased dramatically, often leading to design of simpler, "mobile friendly" web pages. These pages are often implemented with a simpler design, use less Flash, less "Web 2.0 technology" such as AJAX, and subsequently is more compatible with screen readers and other assistive technology used in conjunction with traditional web browsers. Further, the focus on accessibility on mobile phones is increasing, with iOS leading the way and Android and others catching up. Examples here includes automatic speech recognition and text-to-speech implemented at the OS level, as with SIRI, the personal assistant on Apple's iPhone.

2   Areas Covered by the STS

To this STS we invited papers on two different perspectives on inclusion and social media. First, we invited contributions concerning the accessibility of social media. This includes access through well-known web browsers and assistive technology, and the accessibility of social media applications for smart phones, such as iOS and Android based devices. Secondly, we invited papers concerning the value of social media as platforms for inclusion.

With papers ranging from surveys to implementations and standardization work, we wanted to put the spotlight on the current status on e-accessibility to social media, and work in progress to ensure equal opportunities for access to an increasingly important arena for communication in our digital society. Previous work in this category includes for example [5] and [4].

We also wanted to hear about work covering the *use* of social media in the work towards an inclusive society (see for instance [1]). This includes organization of activities, distributed standardization work, use of open API's, and the use of social media to collect and share information about accessible services *and* physical environments, such as route planners (see for example [3]).

3   STS Papers

The first paper is *The use of multimedia to rehabilitate students and release talents* by Luciana Maria Depieri Branco Freire. The paper presents a case study from the city of Olímpia is Brazil, where multimedia capabilities of classroom computers are used as an alternative to traditional school curriculum. Users include children with cerebral palsy, muscle spasticity and Down's syndrome. The study reports positive findings on many levels, from motor control, through cognitive training to self confidence and creativity resulting from the use of computers.

Paper two comes from Spiliotopoulos et al, and is titled *Designing user interfaces for social media driven digital preservation and information retrieval*. The authors present a case where two interfaces for information retrieval are tested in two different application domains. Multimedia content from different social media sources are central in the presented case, and the authors conclude with interface design advice based on their testing.

Third, Dale et al. present *User Testing of Social Media - Methodological Considerations.* They report from the Net Citizen project, and their involvement the development of two social media sites: Braillebook (for Facebook access) and My Education (a social media site for education and training). The authors present results from user tests in these two cases, and provide methodological and practical considerations for testing of social media with accessibility and e-inclusion in mind.

Finally, Fuglerud et al. contributes *Use of Social Media by People with Visual Impairments: Usage Levels, Attitudes and Barriers.* The paper looks at the *use* of social media by people with visual impairments in Norway. The study is based on two surveys, and provides a broad picture of social media usage among people with visual impairments in Norway. The paper also provides a review of previous work in this area, including concerns with the use of typical web 2.0 technologies such as AJAX and CAPCHAs.

4   Conclusion

The papers included in the STS display a variety of approaches and concerns related to the access to and inclusion by social media. From specific case studies on multimedia use, to design recommendations and methodological considerations, the papers combined give a nice overview of the current status of accessible social media, and directions for future research. Continued focus on these issues is paramount to ensure inclusion for all in the digital society, especially with today's rapid development of new technologies and services for interacting socially on the net.

References

1. Asuncion, J.V., Fichten, C.S., Budd, J., Gaulin, C., Amsel, R., Barile, M.: Preliminary findings on social media use and accessibility: A canadian perspective. Presentation at CSUN(California State University, Northridge) Technology and Persons with Disabilities Conference, Los Angeles, California (powerpoint retrieved April 8, 2010)
2. World Wide Web Consortium. Web Accessibility Initiative (WAI) (2011), http://www.w3.org/WAI/ (On-Line; accessed January 12, 2011)
3. Holone, H., Herstad, J.: Social software for accessibility mapping: challenges and opportunities. In: Unitech 2010, Oslo, Norway, Tapir Forlag (2010)
4. Jaeger, P.T., Xie, B.: Developing online community accessibility guidelines for persons with disabilities and older adults. Journal of Disability Policy Studies 20(1), 55–63 (2009)
5. Wentz, B., Lazar, J.: Email Accessibility and Social Networking. In: Ozok, A.A., Zaphiris, P. (eds.) OCSC 2009. LNCS, vol. 5621, pp. 134–140. Springer, Heidelberg (2009)

The Use of Multimedia to Rehabilitate Students and Release Talents

Luciana Maria Depieri Branco Freire

Independent Researcher at Faculty of Medicine - FAMERP of São José do Rio Preto, Brazil
Teacher and Consultant at Secretaria Municipal de Educação of Olímpia, Brazil
luciana-multimidia@hotmail.com

Abstract. The use of new information and communication technologies can improve learning with dynamic, creative strategies. New knowledge will be obtained by exercising the mind, i.e., using the two cerebral hemispheres by neuroplasticity, in a dynamic, intense and active way. It is necessary to show that computer can be used as a means of exercising the mind through different activities and can be also used in pedagogical practices with the purpose of making learning easier. It offers ways that are alternative to those offered by school for students, with or without special necessities, to develop their capacities and potentialities. The computer can be used to develop several activities, which are complex and allow the development of many abilities that help in the solution of problems and make students learn more from their mistakes. These activities will help students develop self-confidence and improve their creative actions and be independent.

Keywords: Education, Inclusive Education, Cerebral Exercise, Multimedia.

1 Introduction

The ICT have been provoking deep reflections due to the world perceptions they make possible to individuals. As the world society tends to computerization, the study and understanding of the language and the possibilities that characterize this process are important in education. Education must seek to establish a connection with reality. Tools and devices help man know and dominate the environment, be it in a concrete (i.e., sensory), abstract (semiotic), spatial or temporal way. This happens through observations, research, development of abilities, use of creativity, awareness and perception of human needs.

Considering these ideas and taking into consideration the work done with children with special needs, some questions are raised: what contributions can technology offer special needs students? How can the teacher use this tool in such a way as to contribute to their education?

This article intends to discuss these issues and emphasize how the computer can be used as a pedagogical tool and offer something that is alternative to school curricula, so that students with and without special needs can develop their abilities and potentialities. More than addressing the possible advantages and gains that technology

K. Miesenberger et al. (Eds.): ICCHP 2012, Part I, LNCS 7382, pp. 557–564, 2012.

can offer, this study intends to seek, in practice, observations, answers and data that will contribute to a wider discussion about this subject and the implementation of this kind of project.

The project that will be mentioned in this article has been implemented in schools run by the government, and also at the Association of Parents and Friends of People with Disabilities (APAE) in the city of Olímpia since 2005. Altogether, 300 children with special needs and 1770 children without special needs from different schools have participated in this project. As for the children with special needs, the participants had conditions such as cerebral palsy, Down Syndrome, moderate, mild and severe levels of intellectual disabilities, hearing, visual and physical impairment, attention deficit and hyperactivity, among others. The softwares used in the computer activities were Microsoft Word, Open Office, Paint, Kolor Paint, besides the internet. The project intended to release talents through different activities, involving, for example, the creation of stories, comic books and drawings in a computer, and was supported by the Town Hall Secretariat of Education. These activities were meant to stimulate intellectual growth, exercise the brain and allow the students to feel there is equality of condition among all classmates and help them conquer appreciation, credibility and respect from society as a whole.

2   Benefits of the Use of Computer in the Classroom: Rehabilitation and the Release of Talents Through Multimedia

In order to begin this discussion, some of authors that address the benefits of the use of computers as a teaching tool will be mentioned. They not only they are part of this reflection on the advantages of this new teaching practice, but they also ground the project applied in Olímpia.

According to Perrenoud (2000, p.125), new information technologies change the way society communicates and that should not be ignored in the classroom.

The use of new information and communication technology should be seen as a way to improve learning with dynamic, creative strategies, allowing the student to create, to think and to argue. Besides, new knowledge will favor brain exercise and affect both cerebral hemispheres, through neuroplasticity, since activities are carried out alternately with the left and with the right hand.

The objective of the project applied in Olímpia was to encourage pedagogical practices involving computing resources, and make students autonomous, creative, intelligent citizens. One clear example of this is the fact that a child with cerebral palsy that was part of the project of Olímpia managed to use the mouse and the keyboard. In other words, the computer proved to be a rich source of stimulus that can help students achieve motor control and cognitive development. In this case, the computer activities promoted a certain level of rehabilitation, making him capable of using the computer in an independent way, drawing, using text editors and using the internet.

According to Vygotsky (apud Galvão Filho, 2003), it is important to human development to appropriate experiences that are part of each person's culture. On the other hand, he adds that limitation tends to become a barrier in the learning process of disabled people. Considering that computing is increasingly becoming part of contemporary culture, offering students activities on the computer both gives them the chance to appropriate an experience that is part of their culture and help them overcome barriers. The idea that this kind of resource can help neutralize barriers is also supported by Galvão Filho (2003, p.42), who adds that social prejudice can be overcome as well when people with disabilities are given tools to interact and learn on equal terms: they get to be treated as different due to their condition and, at the same time, as equals due to the fact that they are able to compete by using the tools that are offered to them, which also helps them get respect.

According to Gouvêa (1999), teachers need to appropriate this new tool and use it in the classroom the same way they did one day in the past with books. In addition to that, Flores (2002) mentions that computing should make the learning process easier and complement school curricula, promoting the full development of students. Thus, technology represents a gain both to teachers and pupils.

Levy (1994) points out that the relation among men, work and intelligence depend on the changes of the communication and information devices, which are becoming more and more sophisticated.

According to Camargo and Bellini (1995, p.10), technology does not improve education just because it exists; it will only offer good results if activities are done by teachers who know what they want. For Santos (2007, p.6), teachers must master not only contents and methods, but also be aware of the possibilities that could facilitate their work in such a way that they can make use of technology, be active and creative, innovate and motivate students (Ábila, 2010).

For Chauí (2004, p.303), through machines, the human brain and the nervous system expand beyond any boundaries. Information technology favors renewal, which can be, for the student, the chance to improve the connections of information and expand knowledge. School can, by diversifying the options of technological learning, help society develop a cultural and scientific environment.

According to Bartoszeck (2007, p.1), the human brain can go through structural and functional changes known as neuroplasticity. One of the most important factors for learning, in neuroplasticity, is experience. So, technologically rich school environments would imply more neural connections and consequently learning more.

The project applied in Olímpia means a new educational paradigm in the present, since the society and the labor market impose the demand for more autonomous, competent citizens. Such paradigm directly influences the process of construction of school knowledge mediated by teachers as far as the use of computer as a didactic resource is concerned.

The project that was applied in Olímpia reinforces, in practice, the improvement of the students under many aspects, such as attention, memorization, motor control, creativity, tranquility, concentration, happiness and satisfaction. These benefits will be noticed by teachers, relatives and friends not only at school, but also at home, especially when children show agility in their activities and intellectual and emotional maturity.

While creating stories, comic books, poems, drawings and other activities, students also develop creativity, patience and critical appraisal and are always encouraged to learn more and outdo themselves. These activities develop motor, cognitive, kinesthetic and affective abilities and enrich the learning environment. They also help solve problems, making the student learn from his mistakes. This will contribute to the development of self-confidence and to the student's progress through creative, independent actions.

3   Pictures

Boy with Severe Cerebral Palsy and Muscle Spasticity. Results and improvement through computer activities using the mouse and the keyboard

Fig. 1. Boy using the keyboard (without an adapter)

Fig. 2. Boy using the mouse

Fig. 3. First contact with the mouse   – random lines/ 2005

In this activity, this boy's progress is clear. In the first picture, he drew random lines. A year later, as can be seen in picture 2, he achieved significant cognitive and motor improvement, since he could draw details in this picture. Besides, the student is happy about his drawings and his results. Nowadays, his drawings are more defined and he uses more varied colors and shapes.

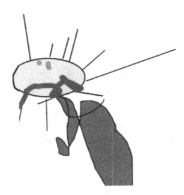

Fig. 4. He drew the sun and some clouds, showing more defined shapes / 2010

The drawings bellow were made by a girl who has Down syndrome. She was initially shy and did not show much interest in school activities. She was usually alone and sad. Through computing, she found out new abilities and became more confident and autonomous in all her activities. Her progress can also be seen in the pictures she drew and in the comic book she created.

Fig. 5. The girl with Down Syndrome is writing a comic book. We can notice a great cognitive advance in the rich details in the progress from one activity to another.

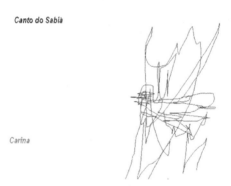

Canto do Sabiá

Carina

Fig. 6. This girl saw the Picture of a bird and tried to reproduce it. She managed to draw a random line, but she did so in an attempt to follow the line of the Picture she observed.

O CANTO DO SÁBIÁ

CARINA FERREIRA DE OLIVEIRA

Fig. 7. Twenty days later, she observed the same picture and managed to draw a bird. She drew details such as the beak, the feet, the tail, besides adding the blue sky.

Fig. 8. Three months later, she was suggested to draw anything she wanted. She then created two drawings in which we can notice her progress and creativity in the many details they contain, such as the sun, the kite, the flower, the grass and the characters.

4   Results

As can be seen in the pictures, computer-based activities have offered meaningful cognitive and social skills improvement to each child, which shows that technology can help the learning process of any child, including those who have special needs, by helping him gain self-control, self-confidence, enthusiasm and self-esteem.

In the first case, there is a great difference between the early drawings and the last ones. The student is more independent, autonomous and self-confident to use the computer and appropriated an experience of his culture.

In the second case, a girl with Down syndrome tried to reproduce the picture of a bird, but only managed to outline the picture and reproduce random lines. After two weeks, she did another reproduction of the same picture, in which she managed to draw details such as the beak, the feet, the tail and she even added a blue sky. In picture 3, which was done 5 months later, she was allowed to draw anything she wanted. She then created drawings that show creativity and richness of detail. She also changed her behavior and became more sociable and communicative, showing an improvement in her interpersonal relationships.

5   Final Considerations

- The use of computer complements school curricula. Some of its advantages are to offer the student with special needs an up-to-date communication and work environment, to make possible for this student to become autonomous and creative, and to promote his social growth, the overcoming of barriers and of prejudice and the participation in a learning environment that is rich in stimulus (Galvão Filho).
- Students showed greater autonomy as for their motor coordination, creativity and choices and overcame not only a disability, but also isolation, achieving greater cognitive and social growth.
- The advantages offered by the use of computers in the classroom should not be left aside, once the activities this tool makes possible interfere in a positive way with the pedagogical, cognitive and social development of the student.
- The results of the project applied in Olímpia have enriched this research and sharing them may help making decisions and even implementing similar projects. Although the results were positive and rewarding, these new teaching practices must be continually studied and its efficacy must be continually checked in order to reflect about the best way to apply them for the benefit of students with and without special needs.
- Finally, the use of technology promotes equality among classmates and the appreciation of each person's work and achievements, two elements that help the student get credibility and respect, which are the basis for a healthy, happy life.

References

1. Ábila, F.: Inovação na Educação. Revista Aprendizagem 2(17), 34–39 (2010)
2. Bartoszeck, A.B.: Relevância de Neurociência na Educação: implicações da pesquisa sobre o cérebro para o ensino [Versão I, Fevereiro 2007]
3. de Camargo, P., Bellini, N.: Computador – o que você precisa aprender para ensinar com ele. São Paulo, Nova Escola, ano X 86, 8–12 (1995)
4. Chaui, M.: Convite à Filosofia, 424 p. Ática, São Paulo (2004)
5. Freire, L.: Apae de, Olímpia: Despertando Talentos. Journal FEAPAES, Batatais (2010)
6. Galvao Filho, T.A., Damasceno, L.L.: Tecnologias Assistivas na Educação Especial. Presença Pedagógica. Dimensão, Belo Horizonte 9(54), 40–47 (2003)
7. Gouvea, S.F.: Os caminhos do professor na Era da Tecnologia. Revista de Educação e Informática, ano 9(13) (April 1999)
8. Levy, P.: As tecnologias da inteligência: o futuro do pensamento na era da informática. Editora 34, São Paulo (1993); Editora 34, Nova Fronteira- RJ (1994)
9. Mendelsohn, P.: Intelligence naturalle et intelligence artificialle, pp. 233–258. PUF, Paris (1993)
10. Perrenoud, P.: 10 Novas Competências para Ensinar. Porto Alegre. Artes Médicas Sul (2000)
11. Valente, J.A. (Org.): O Computador na Sociedade do Conhecimento. UNICAMP/NIED, Campinas (1999)

Use of Social Media by People with Visual Impairments: Usage Levels, Attitudes and Barriers

Kristin Skeide Fuglerud[1], Ingvar Tjøstheim[1],
Birkir Rúnar Gunnarsson[2], and Morten Tollefsen[3]

[1] Norwegian Computing Center, P.O. Box 114, Blindern, NO-0314 Oslo, Norway
{kristin.skeide.fuglerud,ingvar.tjostheim}@nr.no
[2] Blindrafelagid, Icelandic Organization of the Visually Impaired, Hamrahlid 17,
105 Reykjavik, Iceland
Birkir@blind.is
[3] MediaLT, Jerikoveien 22, NO-1067 Oslo, Norway
Morten@Medialt.no

Abstract. Social medias are a central arena for participation, in social life, politics, business and working life. This paper aims to document the social media use among people with visual impairments (VI) in Norway, and to explore some barriers and motivational factors to the use of social media for this group. We present results from two surveys about social media usage among people with VI. One telephone survey was conducted among 150 members of the Norwegian Association of the Blind and Partially Sighted (NABP). This survey contained questions about social media usage. The results from this quantitative survey are discussed in light of results from a web survey with more open-ended questions. The web survey was about how disabled people in Norway use social media, and what accessibility and usability challenges they experience. Through the web survey informants brings to the surface some important accessibility issues and adds nuances to the overall picture. While the telephone survey shows that a high percentage of people with VI participate in social media, the web-based survey indicate they face a variety of problems and typically use the core functionality only. Together, these two surveys give a broad picture of social media usage among people with visual impairments in Norway.

Keywords: universal design, accessibility, visually impaired, social media, social networking sites, assistive technology, security barriers, Captcha, surveys.

1 The State of the Art

ICT is often designed in a way that makes it difficult to use for people with visual impairment (VI) [1-2]. This also applies to the design of social media [3-4]. The research so far has shown that web site compliance with standards and guidelines are a necessity, but do not guarantee Internet services that are usable for all [5-6]. In an empirical study to validate WCAG World Wide Web Consortium (W3C) it was found that only roughly one third of the accessibility problems could have been found through the use of WCAG from the [6]. Thus, existing accessibility guidelines are

K. Miesenberger et al. (Eds.): ICCHP 2012, Part I, LNCS 7382, pp. 565–572, 2012.

criticized for focusing solely on technical accessibility to ensure compliance with assistive technology [5]. New guidelines focusing on a combination of usability and technical accessibility are emerging [5]. The individual ICT skills and competence is another aspect influencing the use of ICT-services. A description of the skills a screen reader user needs in order to work effectively with web interfaces is found in [7].

Several authors have pointed to the need for more accessible web 2.0 [2], [4], [8]. In order to use social media and web 2.0 services, the user often needs to register and authenticate. In connection with this, the use of the Captcha[1] method is identified as a critical accessibility challenge [2], [3], [8-11]. A common use of the method is to make the user read a distorted set of characters from a bitmapped image, and enter those characters into a form. Lately, several services also provide audio Captchas, but severe usability and accessibility problems were found in an evaluation of commonly used audio Captchas [12]. An improved audio Captcha design is also presented in this study. Studies concerning the accessibility of social networking sites have revealed that the dynamic character of such web sites, including the use of AJAX, present accessibility problems for people with VI [3-4], [11], [13-14]. Another question is how user generated content can be made accessible [11].

It is pointed out that there may be a significant overlap between making a web site accessible for a mobile device and for people with disabilities [15]. For example, a user of a mobile device will typically only look at a small portion of a web page at a time, because of the relatively small screen on mobile devices. Similarly, a person using magnifier software with a PC, will only see a small portion of the web page at a time dependent on the degree of magnification. Constraint with regard to navigation is another example. Mobile phone users may have a hard time if a web site requires the use of a mouse, especially if they only have an alphanumeric keypad. Similarly, a blind desktop computer user will have great difficulties in using a web site requiring mouse navigation as the only alternative, because she cannot see where to click. Due to such overlapping requirements it is suggested that mobile computing can draw from traditional web accessibility research [15-16].

In Norway, the newly adopted legislation relating to a prohibition against discrimination on the basis of disability, the Discrimination and Accessibility Act [17], is important because it clearly defines the lack of accessibility as a form of discrimination, and because the principle of universal design is statutory.

In summary, previous research shows that ICT in general and social media in particular, have many accessibility challenges for VI people. Yet, to our knowledge, no representative study exist that document the social media usage of a visually impaired population. In this paper we document the social media usage among VI people in Norway and highlight some factors affecting their social media experience.

2   Methodology

The two surveys addressing social media usage among people with VI (among other things) was conducted in Norway during the last three months of 2010.

---

[1] Completely Automated Public Turing test to Tell Computers and Humans Apart.

The aim of the telephone survey was to investigate the use of mobile phones, mobile Internet, social media and everyday technologies such as ticket machines, vending machines and queuing systems, among people with visual impairments. The questions were developed with input from a focus group meeting, and in collaboration with the Norwegian Association for the Blind and Partially sighted (NABP).

The market research company Synovate was commissioned to do telephone interviews with 150 members of NABP. This organization has about 12000 visually impaired members[2]. Respondents classified themselves into the three categories; being blind; having severe visual impairment or having moderate visual impairment. The national IRB organization with the name NSD approved the project, NABP provided Synovate with membership list and the interviews were carried out in December of 2010. This list contained information about age and whether a member preferred information material in Braille or large print. The survey participants were split into 4 age groups: 15-24 years old, 25-39 years old, 40-59 years old, and 60-75 years old. The reason for splitting into age groups is that the number of people with VI increases significantly with age. A pure random sample based on a membership list will result in a high average age. People with VI are a heterogeneous group. They use a variety of AT depending on the degree of their impairment. About 5% of NABPs members use Braille. In order to get a sufficient number of Braille users for analysis purposes, about 30% Braille users were drawn in each age group. The complete results from the survey are documented in a report [18]. The respondents characterized themselves as blind, severely visually impaired or moderately visually impaired.

As a part of the Norwegian research project NetCitizen[3], a web survey was carried out between October 19th and November 11th 2010. The aim of this survey was to get some answers to what types of challenges people with impairments face when using social media, and also to why people with impairments use social media. A web-based questionnaire was developed and published through e-mailing lists, through Facebook, and on the project webpage. The questionnaire was exploratory with several open questions about social media usage. This web-survey targeted disabled people, but around 70% of the responses were from visually impaired people, and it is these answers that are used in this paper. Among the 101 unique responses, 69 responses were from people with a visual impairment (30 blind and 39 partially sighted). The web survey is further documented in [3].

3   Results

3.1   The Telephone Survey

While nearly all, 99% percentage, of people with VI had a mobile phone, fewer had access to a PC. Distributed by degree of impairment, the percentage of respondents that had access to a PC was as follows; blind 58%, severe visual impairment 73%, and

---

[2] https://www.blindeforbundet.no/internett/english-info
[3] http://www.nr.no/pages/dart/project_flyer_nettborger

moderate visual impairment 77%. According to the Norwegian National Bureau of Statistics (SSB)(www.ssb.no), 93% of the Norwegian population had access to the Internet, and 94% had access to a PC in 2010.

According to the survey the most commonly used assistive technology (AT) among those with access to a PC, was text to speech (TTS) (37%), and followed by magnification (34%) and refreshable Braille display (19%). As expected, respondents commonly make use of a combination of these technologies, especially TTS and either magnification or Braille. By degree of visual impairment, the numbers using respectively Braille, Magnifier and Speech were: among the blind: 62%, 0, and 40%; among the severely visually impaired: 33%, 59% and 52%; and among those with moderate visual impairments: 6%, 31% and 8%.

Among those with access to a PC, the telephone survey documented which social media and web 2.0 services were used. The listed services were included based on a focus group interview. The most popular services were Facebook (90%), Windows messenger (80%), Skype (65%), Twitter (10%), YouTube (10%) and Google docs (50%). Other services, such as blogs were named in an open question section of the survey, but none of these had more than 3-4 percent, at the most. Table 1 shows the use of Facebook distributed on age groups and frequency of use.

Table 1. The use of Facebook

	Daily	Weekly	Monthly	Seldom	Never	Not Rel.
15-24	80%	5%	5%	0%	5%	5%
25-39	38%	19%	15%	4%	20%	5%
40-59	25%	10%	1%	3%	26%	35%
60-75	0%	4%	7%	1%	24%	64%
N=150						

The table shows that 90% of people with VI people between 15-24 years used Facebook at the end of 2011, whereas according to SSB, 96%, among the general Norwegian population between 15-24 years used Facebook in the first months of 2011. Thus, for teenagers and young adults, the Facebook usage among people with VI was high and not far behind that of their sighted peers.

The use of mobile phones was high in all age groups, 99% on average, and the lowest number was 97% in the age group 40-57 years. Among the youngest, those aged 15-24 years, 100% used a mobile phone and 100% used text-messages. The high percentages for text-messages among the young are interesting because this indicate that many used AT with their mobiles. Across all age groups 57% used text-messages.

The use of mobile apps is a relatively new phenomenon. Among the people with VI aged 15-24 years, 45% used mobile apps, and across all age groups 20% used mobile apps. A national survey from TNS Gallup indicated that 21% of the general Norwegian population used mobile apps [19]. Further, 24% of the magnifier users, 28% of the Braille users, and 30% of the TTS users used mobile apps. An explanation of the relatively high usage of mobile apps among users of AT may be that this group need to have advanced phones capable of running AT applications, and thus their phones also have the technical requirements necessary to run mobile apps.

The respondents were also asked about the perceived level of difficulty when using social media, and the perceived level of difficulty associated with logging in to social media services, and their attitudes towards privacy. The figures are 24% easy vs. 20% difficult on use of social media (56% not relevant), and 22% easy vs. 17% difficult on the log in task (61% not relevant). Only 7% answer that they do not carefully consider what kind of personal information they publish on social media. Further, the respondents were asked questions to highlight factors that may motivate them to use social media. In short, the factors were about Emotions, Feedback, Friends, Peers and Real Time. Details can be found in [18]. Preliminary results from the statistical analysis of the survey-data indicate that two of seven factors can be used to predict the value of social media to people with VI. This is "Easy or difficult to use social media" and "Peers", i.e. the importance of having contact with other people with visual impairments". The statistical analysis indicated that two factors, "Friends" and "Peers", contributed to higher scores on self-reported "Quality of life" [20].

In summary, the telephone survey showed that although people with VI still are lagging behind the general population, relatively many people with VI use social media, especially among the young. Moreover, the use of mobile apps seems to be at the same level as the rest of the population. According to this study there are two main factors affecting the overall motivation or value of the use of social media for visually impaired users. The motivation is associated with how easy or difficult it is to use social media and the possibility of interacting with peers and other VI through social media.

3.2   The Web Survey

In the web survey various accessibility and usability barriers were pointed to. The web survey confirms that many VI people find the log on procedure, in particular the Captchas, to be a major accessibility problem. Many of the comments in this survey naturally referred to Facebook since this is the most commonly used service. Most of the pages on Facebook are not navigable pages and they have icons and buttons with images rather than readable texts. Many of these icons and buttons do not have alternative text, making it impossible to know what they are. Emoticons (e.g. smileys, faces etc.) can also be a problem. Some screen readers can recognize them in chat applications, but usually not in web interfaces. Another problem was the integration of apps, computer games and chat functions that are almost or completely inaccessible. Examples of inaccessible user generated content were also given. For example, the lack of alternative text to accompany pictures is a problem, especially when it contains essential information such as who else is logged on. Several of the accessibility problems could have been addressed through conformance to existing accessibility guidelines, e.g. WCAG (W3C).

Accessibility problems associated with use of web 2.0 technology, such as AJAX, that allow reloading of parts of a web page, were identified as another major issue. Several comments were related to the difficulties in working with the frequently changing interfaces of social media. The WAI-ARIA (W3C) guidelines address such issues [11]. Respondents complained that as soon as they had learned to navigate a page, it changed. Another recurring theme in the web survey was the need for more user training and documentation for AT users. It became evident that many people with VI prefer to use the mobile web interface of social medias (such as m.facebook.com) as an alternative to the ordinary web interface because it seemed to be easier and more accessible. However, the functionality in the mobile interfaces is normally limited compared to the web interface.

Not surprisingly, social contact seems to be an important motivational factor for using social media, including getting to know and communicate with other people with VI. The web survey also gave interesting indications that social media gives VI people an added value because they may get information that sighted people more naturally get face to face through visual cues. The following comment from a woman with visual and hearing impairment illustrates this point:

> "...Facebook has become an extremely important arena for me to keep updated. The social aspects of visual or hearing impairments do not matter here. I use what I have learnt on Facebook when I later meet people face to face, and this has made it much easier for me to follow and understand the context of conversations. It has also become much easier to keep in touch with people I otherwise would not have had the resources to keep in contact with. For me, Facebook provides the opportunity for a more active social life out in "real life".

One example that was mentioned was that while seeing people can see whether someone is pregnant, VI people may get such information through Facebook, and then they too are able to start a conversation about this and ask how it is going. Many visually impaired people may also experience limited mobility because they depend on others to travel or move in new places. If they are not present at events they may, to a certain extent, use social media to keep updated on what people in their network do and are interested in. This too can make communication easier when they meet face to face.

4   Discussion

In order to deal effectively with problems of how to make social media more inclusive for people with VI, it is necessary to understand both the nature and the scale of the problems [14]. Although VI people lag behind the general population in social media usage, the social media usage is high, particularly among the youngest age groups. This could be interpreted in different ways. One might conclude that social media is not so difficult for people with VI after all. However both the telephone survey and the web survey documents that people with VI experience many difficulties and accessibility barriers related to the use of social media. In line with other research [11] some of the major accessibility challenges included inaccessible Captchas, and the dynamic changes of page content and layout.

The usage of mobile apps among visually impaired people in Norway seems to be approximately at the same level as the rest of the population. The web survey showed that many people with VI prefer the mobile interface to the web interface. This may also explain the impression from the web-based survey that many people with VI use only the most basic functionality. They read and write status updates on Facebook, but do not seem to use instant messaging, games, invitations to events, and chat. In other words, because the standard web interface is too inaccessible and difficult to use, they use the mobile interface. This is easier because it has less functionality and is more accessible. It may be the case that the mobile interfaces have better accessibility because of partly overlapping requirements between mobile web and accessibility, as indicated in the state of the art section.

People with VI have much of the same motivation as sighted people to use social media, and they want to be present at and participate in the same arenas as others. The surveys indicate that the possibility to have contact with peers and other VI people are important. This is in line with findings in [11]. Additionally, VI people seem to experience an additional value from social media in getting information that their sighted peers gets through direct observation. This may also be an important motivational factor.

5   Conclusion

The objective of this paper has been to document the current state of social media usage among people with VI people in Norway. In summary, many people with VI use social media. Although they experience many accessibility challenges when using social media, their motivation to use these services seems to be high. Many of the challenges are known challenges and could have been addressed by conformance to existing guidelines. It seems clear that reliance on guidelines and National legislation does not ensure accessibility, and the challenges cannot be solved by better accessibility guidelines alone. A user centered and participatory development process, which involves various stakeholders, is needed. These aspects should be highlighted when enforcing universal design as a legal concept, as is done in Norway.

Acknowledgments. The work with this paper has been partly financed by the Research Council of Norway, through the Nettborger (Eng: NetCitizen) project and the e-Me project. Special thanks to all the participants in the two surveys and to the Norwegian Association for the Blind and Partially sighted for their collaboration.

References

1. Lazar, J., Allen, A., Kleinman, J., Malarkey, C.: What Frustrates Screen Reader Users on the Web: A Study of 100 Blind Users. International Journal of Human-Computer Interaction 22, 247–269 (2007)
2. Fuglerud, K.S.: The Barriers to and Benefits of Use of ICT for People with Visual Impairment. In: Stephanidis, C. (ed.) HCII 2011 and UAHCI 2011, Part I. LNCS, vol. 6765, pp. 452–462. Springer, Heidelberg (2011)

3. Tollefsen, T., Dale, Ø., Berg, M., Nordby, R.: Connected! A paper about the disabled and the use of social media. MediaLT (2011)
4. Hailpern, J., Guarino-Reid, L., Boardman, R., Annam, S.: Web 2.0: blind to an accessible new world. In: Proceedings of the 18th International Conference on World Wide Web, pp. 821–830. ACM, Madrid (2009)
5. Leporini, B., Paternò, F.: Increasing usability when interacting through screen readers. Universal Access in the Information Society 3, 57–70 (2004)
6. Rømen, D., Svanæs, D.: Validating WCAG versions 1.0 and 2.0 through usability testing with disabled users. Universal Access in the Information Society, 1–11 (2011)
7. Tollefsen, M., Kalvenes, C., Begnum, M.N.: Demands for screen reader user qualifications 2 (September 2010)
8. Wentz, B., Lazar, J.: Email Accessibility and Social Networking. In: Ozok, A.A., Zaphiris, P. (eds.) OCSC 2009. LNCS, vol. 5621, pp. 134–140. Springer, Heidelberg (2009)
9. Fritsch, L., Fuglerud, K., Solheim, I.: Towards inclusive identity management. Identity in the Information Society 7, 1–24 (October 7, 2010)
10. Sauer, G., Lazar, J., Hochheiser, H., Feng, J.: Towards A Universally Usable Human Interaction Proof. Evaluation of Task Completion Strategies 2, 1–32 (2010)
11. Leahy, D., Broin, U.O.: Social Networking Sites and Equal Opportunity: The Impact of Accessibility. In: 22nd Bled eConference, eEnablement: Facilitating an Open, Effective and Representative eSociety, Bled, Slovenia, pp. 17–31 (2009)
12. Bigham, J.P., Cavender, A.C.: Evaluating existing audio CAPTCHAs and an interface optimized for non-visual use. In: Proceedings of the 27th International Conference on Human Factors in Computing Systems, pp. 1829–1838. ACM, Boston (2009)
13. Gibson, B.: Enabling an accessible web 2.0. In: Proceedings of the 2007 International Cross-disciplinary Conference on Web Accessibility (W4A), pp. 1–6. ACM, Banff (2007)
14. Brown, A., Jay, C., Chen, A., Harper, S.: The uptake of Web 2.0 technologies, and its impact on visually disabled users. Universal Access in the Information Society, 1–15 (2011)
15. Yesilada, Y., Chen, T., Harper, S.: RIAM Framework: Overlaps between Mobile and Accessible Webs. School of Comp. Science, Information Management Group, HCW (2008)
16. W3C: Relationship between Mobile Web Best Practices (MWBP) and Web Content Accessibility Guidelines (WCAG), http://www.w3.org/TR/mwbp-wcag/
17. DTL: Act June 20 2008 No. 42 relating to a prohibition against discrimination on the basis of disability. In: The Ministry of Children, LOV-2008-06-20-42 Lovdata, Norway (2008)
18. Tjøstheim, I., Solheim, I.: The use of social media among blind and visually impaired in Norway 2010. Norsk Regnesentral/ Norwegian Computing Center (2010)
19. Facebook-rekord i Norge (Eng: Facebook-record in Norway), http://www.kampanje.com/medier/article5450029.ece (accessed January 22, 2011)
20. Tjøstheim, I., Solheim, I., Fuglerud, K.S.: The Importance of Peers for Visually Impaired Users of Social Media. In: From Proceeding (746) Internet and Multimedia Systems and Applications/747: Human-Computer Interaction 2011, p. 21 (2011)

User Testing of Social Media – Methodological Considerations

Oystein Dale[1], Therese Drivenes[1], Morten Tollefsen[2], and Arthur Reinertsen[3]

[1] Norsk Regnesentral, P.O. Box 114 Blindern, 0314 Oslo, Norway
{oystein.dale,therese.drivenes}@nr.no
[2] MediaLT AS, Jerikoveien 22, 1067 Oslo, Norway
morten@medialt.no
[3] Karde AS, Pb. 69 Tåsen, 0801 Oslo, Norway
arthur.reinertsen@karde.no

Abstract. The use of social media has in recent years increased dramatically. It is imperative that social media are accessible to all. To ensure this, it is important to conduct user testing as part of an accessibility and usability assessment of social media services. This paper focuses on the methodology applied in such undertakings, and its purpose is to draw attention to important aspects that should guide user testing and user studies of social media services. This is done by sharing the experiences gained in the project Net Citizen. The main target groups for the paper are those planning the implementation of social media services and those who conduct accessibility and usability user testing. Key findings are that cumulative usability issues can be likened to poor accessibility. Further, that web services that are accessible in a strict technical sense, may not necessarily be perceived as accessible by real users.

Keywords: Social media, accessibility, usability, user testing, methodology.

1 Introduction

The use of social media has in recent years increased dramatically since the modest debut of social media like services in the late 1990s. Today, Facebook alone has 800 million users [1]. Despite numerous reports of accessibility issues, many disabled users successfully access social media [7].

To ensure that current and future social media services are accessible to all, it is imperative to conduct user testing to gauge how accessible the services are as experienced by real users in real life conditions. This paper focuses on the methodology applied in such undertakings, and its purpose is to draw attention to important aspects that should guide user testing and user studies of social media services. This is done by sharing the experiences gained in the project Net Citizen.

Net Citizen is a project supported by the Norwegian Research Council and the Norwegian Ministry of Government Administration, Reform and Church Affairs,. It ran from September 2010 through March 2012. Its overall aim was to promote the inclusive design of social media. Some of the major activities include a survey

K. Miesenberger et al. (Eds.): ICCHP 2012, Part I, LNCS 7382, pp. 573–580, 2012.

mapping accessibility issues in social media, assisting in the development and subsequent user testing of two social media demonstrators, and an accessibility evaluation of popular social media smartphone apps. The purpose of the user testing was to detect as many accessibility and usability issues as possible, so that these could be addressed and corrected in subsequent development phases.

The content is extracted from the user testing conducted in Net Citizen, and includes the key findings from these. Further, we will detail some pertinent methodological and practical considerations faced along the way. The key target groups are those planning the implementation of social media services, those who conducts accessibility user testing, and other who takes an interest in accessible web services.

2   State of the Art

There are many ways to evaluate the accessibility of a web page or web service, and a number of tools to assist in such endeavours are available [2]. Although, it may be argued that many accessibility issues can be identified without involving real users [3], ultimately, "the proof of the pudding is in the eating". Thus, user testing and user studies are deemed to be essential to evaluate how accessible a web page or web service is in real life [2].

Despite the fact that numerous reports point out the poor accessibility of social media services [4-8], there are very few publications detailing and describing actual user testing of social media services for accessibility purposes. The reports are either expert evaluations [5], surveys [7], literature reviews [8], or they do not clearly state how the findings came about [6]. Wentz & Lazar [9] have also pointed out a lack of empirical data describing user testing of social media.

Reports of user testing of general web services in an accessibility context are numerous [2], but for reasons of brevity we have chosen to focus on user testing of social media services in this SotA. So far we have located only one published article that details the actual user testing of social media in an accessibility context [9]. It focuses on a comparison between the desktop version and mobile versions of Facebook from a usability perspective for blind users [9]. The mobile version was deemed to be more usable, but lacked a number of features that were included in the desktop version of Facebook.

There are also a number of guidelines detailing how to make accessible web services, such as WCAG 2.0 and WAI-ARIA [10]. There has been suggestions that social media require updated guidelines which further are suited to focus on the multidirectional communication that social media entail [11]. This has been tried absorbed in the more recent guidelines.

3   Methodology

In Net Citizen we have assisted in the development of two social media sites. The first, Braillebook, is a web application that provides access to selected Facebook functionality in an alternative user interface (see Fig. 1). It was specifically designed to cater for the needs of deaf blind screen reader users, and adheres to WCAG 2 level AA. My education (Min utdanning in Norwegian) is a social media inspired site run by Østfold County Council, which provides information on educational and vocational training opportunities (see Fig. 2). The prominent feature of the site is to allow its users to ask questions about educational issues which are answered by counsellors. Both services were comprehensively user tested using the following methodology.

21 users were recruited from relevant user organisations. Four dropped out, so a total of 17 users took part in a total of 19 user tests. The participants had to be 16 years of age and over, and be familiar with using a computer and the Internet. In addition, the users who tested Braillebook had to be Facebook members. We recruited blind and low vision users, users with reading and writing difficulties, users with impaired motor function, and users with dual sensory impairment. Participant characteristics are summarized in Table 1.

Fig. 1. Braillebook (Source: Braillebook, Eikholt National Resource Centre for the Deafblind)

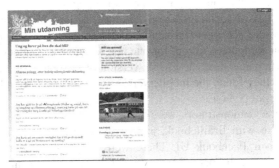

Fig. 2. My education (Source: http://www.minutdanning.origo.no, Østfold CC)

Table 1. User characteristics

Ages:	Disability:	Assistive technology	Self-appraised ICT skills
• 16-63	• Vision impairment 8 (blind 4; low vision 4) • Reading/writing difficulties: 4 • Dual sensory impairment: 2 • Reduced motor function: 3	• Screen reader (SR): 6 • SR on mobile: 3 • Screen magnification: 3 • Roller mouse: 1 • Spelling & writing SW: 2 • Adaptations to OS: 2 • LP keyboard stickers: 1	• Some experience: 1 • Experienced: 10 • Experienced /expert: 4 • Expert: 2

We allocated half of the participants to test Braillebook (9 tests), and the remainder to test My education (10 tests). Two users tested both demonstrators. A testing protocol was designed consisting of a brief interview used for both groups, and demonstrator specific tasks for each. For security and privacy reasons we set up test versions of both demonstrators, and created test Facebook accounts with fictive names and personal details. All tests were conducted on the users' own equipment including assistive technology (AT), and at a location of their choosing. This was usually in their own homes. The tests lasted from one to three hours. The tests were conducted on an one-on-one basis, and in some instances with two researchers present. The sessions were audio recorded, and the participants were encouraged to think aloud, to actively describe what they were doing and to ask questions. The researcher(s) observed and took notes. The content of each session was summarised, categorised and analysed. The cumulative findings were combined in an accessibility and usability report for each demonstrator.

4   Results

4.1   Brief Summary of Key Findings from the User Tests

The main reasons for using social media given by the respondents were to stay in touch with family and friends, and to seek information about their social networks. Some used media for vocational purposes, and some shared photos and music. None stated that they played online games through social media. Anecdotally, we have been told that online games often are inaccessible, and this may help explaining why none played games.

The majority accessed social media on stationary or laptop computers. Many used their mobile phones to access social media, and a couple also used tablets. All tests were conducted on computers, except for one test which was conducted on an iPad. A number of the participants used the mobile version of Facebook, m.facebook.com, on their computers as they found the mobile version more accessible and easier to use as compared to the desktop version.

By and large the demonstrators were well received by the test users. This was particularly the case with Braillebook, and several participants asked if they could start using it as their Facebook UI. There were only some technical accessibility issues in the two demonstrators. There were for instance some minor coding issues like inadequate labelling of a control button, and too many spaces leading to unnecessary navigational key presses on some pages. Further, the contrast for the text input boxes in both demonstrators was deemed to be poor. This meant that for many of the low vision users, they had to search a great deal to locate where to write text. For My education there were also some text size and contrast issues.

It was the usability issues that proved the largest hurdles to overcome for the participants. In other words, although the services were accessible *per se* in a technical sense, the cumulative effect of the usability issues meant that a number of the participants required assistance to complete a number of the tasks, or it took a very long time to conduct them. Some of the usability issues were:

- Inconsistencies and confusing use of terminology, e.g. for My education to ask a question to the counsellors was referred to as "asking a question", "making a contribution" and "writing a message". In Braillebook "a message" could mean three separate things depending on the context.
- Cumbersome procedures, e.g. in My education registering as a new user required many steps to achieve, and if successful one was forwarded to a page with no intuitive way of getting back to the My utdanning service. Similarly, for Braillebook sending a direct message could include unnecessarily many steps.
- Certain procedures in both services include the standard user interface (UI) from other services, i.e. for certain actions in Braillebook standard Facebook UIs appear. This was confusing. Similarly, for My education certain UIs were the ones used by Origo which is the platform on which My education is built. They looked very different to the My education UI.
- Lack of easy to find and clear feedback when actions were performed were requested for both solutions.

There were also usability issues that were applicable only to the individual solutions. My education contained for instance a number of editing choices for writing text which were deemed irrelevant, especially by the screen reader users. The Braillebook test version was very slow, i.e. it could take several seconds from a key was pressed until the solution responded. This seemed to cause irritation with some of the participants.

The cumulative effect of the usability issues can in some instances be likened to poor accessibility, as a number of users were unable to complete some of the tasks without considerable amount of help. There were, however, notable differences between users in terms of the amount of difficulty they encountered. Great effort had been made to make especially Braillebook as accessible as possible, and this was noted by many of the test persons. The fact that some users still encountered problems only goes to show the importance of user testing to further improve such services.

4.2   Methodological and Practical Considerations

Based on our experiences there are a number of methodological and practical considerations when conduction user testing of social media which we would like to convey. These are summarised below. Some of these aspects are universal for all user testing, whereas others are more applicable to the user testing of social media.

Recruitment. When recruiting users, it is very important that they cover a wide variety of design needs. The mix that we were able to recruit proved to be very useful in detecting different accessibility and usability issues some of which we would have omitted if not recruiting so broadly. The downside is that it requires a great deal of effort and resources. It is important to take into attributes such as age, gender, ICT competence, AT requirements and experience with social media. As lower age and exposure to and social media competence often correlate, one should be aware that age may be a cause for bias.

Test Environments and Test User Accounts. Due to the potential security and privacy risks involved with social media, we choose to create test environments and test user accounts. As a result we were able to respect the participant's privacy, but we also experienced that we could not test all the things we wanted to, as there were some technical limitations with the test environments and test user accounts in for instance Braillebook. Further, when interacting with Braillebook the participants did not have access to their real life friends and groups, and as such the tests were somewhat less realistic.

First Time Usage. It was evident that a number of the problematic issues encountered will be less so as one becomes used to using the solution. We chose not to expose the participants to the demonstrators before the tests. In retrospect it may have been better for them having tried them to avoid some of the first time usage issues encountered.

Prior Experience with Social Media. The Braillebook participants needed to be Facebook users to be able to take part. We did, however, not specify this criterion any further, and as a consequence we recruited both expert and novice Facebook users. It was evident that the novice or casual users encountered some usage problems that can be attributed more to their inexperience with the social media platform than to the demonstrator itself. This is a point worth considering when conduction testing on different social media platforms.

Capturing Tools. We opted to only use audio recordings of the sessions. We considered a number of other relevant accessibility and usability tools ranging from eye tracking and the Morae usability suite to use of video. For matters of simplicity and convenience, but chiefly so that the tests could be performed on the users' own equipment without additional elaborate setups. We deemed the most important aspects to be extracted from the sessions to be the users' own words and observing the tasks being conducted. This required no complicated tools.

Selection of Tasks. We opted to test the tasks and functionality we believed to be the most common used by the average users. As such we got a good overview of the whole service. It may be an option to focus on certain aspects that one suspects to be more troublesome than others.

Prior Accessibility Testing. Both services had been tested for accessibility in terms of adherence to recognized web accessibility guidelines prior to the user testing. This is important to do as it may give an indication of which areas to focus the investigation on. Further, any comprehensive accessibility evaluation of a social media service should include both a technical accessibility check using appropriate accessibility guidelines such as WCAG 2.0, as well as user testing.

How to Focus the Interpretation of the Results. To help us in interpreting the results we opted to some extent to try to separate the origin of the different usage problems encountered. We tried to separate the different issues into technical accessibility issues, usability issues and issues pertaining to the user, for instance user competence in general ICT, AT usage etc. This can be a very fruitful exercise as it gives the interpretation of the results more structure. The various attributes pertaining to the user are very important to take into consideration as they play an important role in determining how accessible a particular solution is experienced. In our experience poor ICT skills and/or poor AT mastery may in some instances result in that a service is deemed to be inaccessible or have poor usability, when in fact it is the user´s inadequate skills due to poor training which may be the real issue.

User Generated Content. Social media are naturally overflowing with user-generated content. This content needs of course to be accessible for the users to really be able to enjoy a social media site. We recommend that accessibility assessments of social media sites pay particular attention to the user-generated content, especially where multimedia content is plentiful. As the demonstrators were test sites with sparse content that by and large consisted of text, this was not a big problem for us.

5   Impact or Contributions to the Field

This paper provides some insights into conducting user testing when assessing social media for accessibility. Its findings may be of particular benefit to those who are planning to implement social media services, those who conduct accessibility user testing, and other who takes an interest in accessible web services. It shows that there are a number methodological and practical issues which one needs to heed particular consideration when conducting such tests. Some are overlapping with other user testing contexts, whereas some are unique to the user testing of social media.

The paper further show that although a service may be accessible in a strict technical sense, the accumulation of usability issues may in combination act as an accessibility barrier for many users. This means that a strict focus on assessing for accessibility issues only may not suffice, and it further strengthens the notion that user testing is essential to complement technical accessibility testing.

6   Conclusion and Planned Activities

The special nature of social media warrants a somewhat different approach when conducting user testing and assessing social media for accessibility as compared to user testing of other web services. This pertains to both practical and methodological issues. The experiences with user testing in this project, strengthens the case for involving end-users when conducting accessibility testing. Formalised technical assessments do not suffice to gauge how accessible or not a web service really is – only real people with real accessibility issues can do this. The Net Citizen project is now concluded. Future related activities are being considered.

Acknowledgements. We would like to thank the Norwegian Research Council and the Norwegian Ministry of Government Administration, Reform and Church Affairs for providing funding for the project; all our project partners; and of course – many thanks, to all the informants who generously gave their time to take part.

References

1. Facebook (2012),
   `http://www.facebook.com/press/info.php?statistics`
2. Henry, S.L.: Just Ask: Integrating Accessibility Throughout Design. Lulu.com (2007)
3. EIAO (2012), `http://eiao.net`
4. AbilityNet. State of the eNation web accessibility reports: Social Networking (2008),
   `http://www.abilitynet.org.uk/docs/enation/2008SocialNetworki`
   `ngSites.pdf`
5. Dale, O., et al.: Assistive Technology or Mainstreaming of ICT? Yes, please! In: Emiliani, et al. (ed.) Assistive Technology from Adapted Equipment to Inclusive Environments, pp. 703–707 (2009)
6. Media   Access   Australia.   Social   Media   Accessibility   Review   (2009),
   `http://mediaaccess.org.au/sites/default/files/files/Social%2`
   `0Media%20Accessibility%20Review%20v1_0.pdf`
7. Asuncion, A., et al.: Preliminary Findings on Social Media Use and Accessibility: A Canadian Perspective. In: Presentation at the CSUN 2010, San Diego, March 26 (2010)
8. Taylor, A.: Social Media as a Tool for Inclusion. Social Media as a Tool for Inclusion. Report for Human Resources and Skills Development Canada (2011),
   `http://www.homelesshub.ca/ResourceFiles/Taylor_Social%20Medi`
   `a_feb2011%201_1_2.pdf`
9. Wentz, B., Lazar, J.: Are Separate Interfaces Inherently Unequal? An Evaluation with Blind Users of the Usability of Two Interfaces for a Social Networking Platform. In: Proceedings of the iConference 2011, pp. 91–97 (2011)
10. W3C. Web Accessibility Initiative (2012), `http://www.w3.org/WAI`
11. Jaeger, P.T.: Developing Online Community Accessibility Guidelines for Persons With Disabilities and Older Adults. Journal of Disability Policy Studies 20(1), 55–63 (2009)

Designing User Interfaces for Social Media Driven Digital Preservation and Information Retrieval

Dimitris Spiliotopoulos[1,2], Efstratios Tzoannos[1], Pepi Stavropoulou[2],
Georgios Kouroupetroglou[2], and Alexandros Pino[3]

[1] Athens Technology Centre, Chalandri, Athens, Greece
{d.spiliotopoulos,e.tzoannos}@atc.gr
[2] National and Kapodistrian University of Athens,
Dep. of Informatics and Telecommunications
[3] National and Kapodistrian University of Athens, Accessibility Unit,
Panepistimiopolis, Ilissia, 15784, Athens, Greece
{pepis,koupe,pino}@di.uoa.gr

Abstract. Social Media provide a vast amount of information identifying stories, events, entities that play the crucial role of shaping the community in an everyday heavy user involvement. This work involves the study of social media information in terms of type (multimodal: text, video, sound, picture) and role players (agents, users, opinion leaders) and the potential of designing accessible, usable interfaces that integrate that information. This case examines the design of a user interface that uses an underlying engine for modality components (plain text, sound, image, video) analysis, social media crawling, contextual search fusion and semantic analysis. The interface is the only point of user interaction to the world of knowledge. This work reports on the usability and accessibility methods and concerns for the user requirements phase and the design control and testing. The findings of the pilot user testing and evaluation provide indications on how the semantic analysis of the social media information can be integrated to the design methodologies for user interfaces resulting in maximization of user experience in terms of social information involvement.

Keywords: social media, user interface design, user enablement.

1 Introduction

Social media content is collected from several social media, from users enabled by mobile devices, web pages, smart cameras, etc. Social media are becoming more and more pervasive in all areas of life. The major social media (Twitter, Facebook, Youtube, Flickr and others) are the hubs of the social information, a constant stream of targeted content, enabling people to report, comment, converse while engaged in their everyday activities, like work, study, travel, leisure. The people are enabled to provide content that is highly contextualized, user specific, yet responding to the society events and ideas in a rapid manner [2]. The citizen involvement is now so

K. Miesenberger et al. (Eds.): ICCHP 2012, Part I, LNCS 7382, pp. 581–584, 2012.
© Springer-Verlag Berlin Heidelberg 2012

huge that we have come to the point where the social media information creation and communication now characterizes the information society. It is therefore no surprise that searching the web returns more social media hits than web pages.

As part of the greater approach of the EU ICT ARCOMEM[1] project the design of information retrieval interfaces for the following two domains has been undertaken:

- Socially contextualized Broadcaster/Media archiving
- Socially-aware federated political archiving

The aim of the interfaces is to encourage the user involvement not only on content creation and communication (the purpose of social media) but also on content analysis, preservation and reuse for identifying the major events as they happen, analyze the social input in its content (opinion and sentiment) and re-involve the users in an iterative idea/opinion/evaluation, a socially contextual process [3].

2   Design Considerations

The requirements for both aforementioned domains are similar as a generic concept. The high-level requirements were selected from groups of users from broadcaster organizations and political bodies. The contextual framework for the information retrieval specifications has been identified and described by a list of generic, domain relevant and domain specific terms. The terms include semantic entities/events/topics, sentiment and opinions, social and demographic information, contextual information (actors, influencers) from a range of social media and social media-related sources, such as Blogs, Microblogs, Wikis, Social Networks, Video/Photo/Music/Audio Networks, Discussion groups, Social Bookmarks [1], [4 - 6].

Four social media were selected for this phase of the work, namely Twitter, Flickr, Youtube, Facebook, spanning from text-only heavily opinionated (Twitter) to multimedia oriented ways of integrating the user generated content to the ICT life (Flickr, Youtube). For the pilot design and testing, the socially-aware federated political search and retrieval interface prototype was used.

Accessibility is major concern and it is manifested in the form of universal design that, in our case, dictates that the UI should adhere to principles such as simplicity, flexibility, effort considerations. The integration of opinions, entities, trends, authors and statistics from social networks should be seamless in order to be usable.

Iterative design process from the start to the implementation of the first prototype was followed from the initial design requirements gathering (made via wire-framing) to the mockup user environment, to the online prototype A. Mockups of the tool pages were constructed keeping in mind the three types of information from the functional specifications (Search filtering, Core content, Social content) and the non-functional specifications. The initial experimentation was on the observation of the user perception of processed content (filters, tag clouds, paths), direct content (item descriptions, authors, dates, type of modality) and social content (opinions, trends,

---

[1] ARCOMEM: Archive Communities Memories, www.arcomem.eu, FP7-ICT-270239.

semantics, entities, events). Based on the above, low fidelity mockups were created for the web retrieval interface. Those were subsequently evaluated for the core functionalities (filtering of results, follow-up search, results visualization) as well as usability (user approach to semantic search, information load, user effort, acceptance). An early prototype was build based on the previous feedback and was informally evaluated by usability experts. That intermediate evaluation was a short approach to applying generic accessibility criteria to the early prototype. In our case, universal design principles were applied for the scope of providing a solid basis for extending the interface future versions to multitouch devices (namely iOS) as well as voice interfaces, although the latter is not in the specification. The result of the above approaches was the implementation of the prototype user interface that was evaluated by expert and non-expert users as described in the following section.

3   Experiments

Three distinct experiments based on the initial information derived from the user requirements were set up. The purpose was to refine the state-of-the-art general methods for interface design with social content driven methods of retrieving, navigating, and optimizing information in order to maximize the user engagement and experience.

The first experiment was to evaluate the impact of social media feedback to the search results of the interfaces using guided sorting and filtering per media category. The users have been asked to perform searches based on pre-determined scenarios, and the returned results and dynamic filtering were evaluated for their social media source impact. Between the search results, the users were 3 times more likely to select an item if it had an opinion banner (top-right on the item in Fig. 1). Also, most of the users reported their selections to view specific items were influenced by the trending information (bottom-right in Fig. 1), while the social network source information (bottom-left in Fig. 1) did not influence their selections either positively or negatively.

Fig. 1. Social network source, opinion and trending information

The second experiment investigated how sentiment is transferred from the information content (social media opinion mining) to the target users and how that sentiment (opinion) triggers the follow-up searches (involvement) and the intended results from the user perspective (contextual search validation). The users were asked to randomly perform three initial searches and then follow up their topic of interest. The subjects followed their topics mostly based on entities that carried negative or positive opinions. An important observation was that the subjects' navigation was governed by the amount of opinions about entities or events, while more than 80% of the opinions for the entities were accessed and viewed.

The final experiment was the usability evaluation. One of the main requirements was to measure the impact of the social media derived content (sentiment, modality, topic/event identification) to the user communication and engagement as a parameter for acceptance. Options for facets, filtering of emotions and modality selections were presented to the users and their feedback was measured accordingly. The subjects reported that the connections between the search results and the associated entities (people, places) were on target. The items that did not carry many opinions were quickly passed through by the subjects in order to find items that were very heavily commented upon. The acceptance of the approach was very high, however specific features were requested, mainly timelines for opinion trends. Another conclusion of the logged navigation entries suggests that the ranking of results should be based on amount of opinions associated with them rather than trends or social network sources.

4   Conclusion

Based on the results of the experimenting with fusing and visualizing the social content with semantically driven context sensitive information processing, the classic user interface design methods have been extended to maximize the social impact, encourage user responses and even indicate potential events and associated opinions as very important candidates for policy making. Further work is currently underway for the training of the user groups in setting up and engaging to the socially-aware information retrieval and archiving processes. The results of this work are expected to enhance the design of the user interface to support and sustain a socially driven user involvement into the vast amount of information.

References

1. Agarwal, et al.: Identifying the influential bloggers in a community. In: Proc. of the First International Conference on Web Search and Web Data Mining (WSDM 2008) (2008)
2. Agichtein, et al.: Finding high quality content in social media, with an application to community-based question answering. In: Proc. of ACM WSDM, pp. 183–194. ACM Press, Stanford (2008)
3. Anagnostopoulos, et al.: Influence and correlation in social networks. In: Proc. of the 14th ACM SIGKDD, Int. Conf. on Knowledge Discovery and Data Mining (KDD 2008) (2008)
4. Pang, Lee: Opinion mining and sentiment analysis: Foundations and Trends in Information Retrieval 2(1-2), 1–135 (2008)
5. Weining, et al.: Image retrieval by emotional semantics: A study of emotional space and feature extraction 4, 3534–3539 (2006)
6. Zontone, et al.: Image diversity analysis: Context, opinion and bias. In: The First International Workshop on Living Web: Making Web Diversity a true asset, vol. 515, CEUR-WS (October 2009)

PDF/UA – A New Era for Document Accessibility: Understanding, Managing and Implementing the ISO Standard PDF/UA (Universal Accessibility): Introduction to the Special Thematic Session

Olaf Drümmer[1] and Markus Erle[2]

[1] Callas Software, Berlin, Germany
o.druemmer@callassoftware.com
[2] Wertewerk, Tuebingen, Germany
erle@wertewerk.de

Abstract. Short introduction to the Special Thematic Session about the new ISO standard for PDF accessibility and how PDF/UA changes the game for document software developers, assistive technology vendors, decision-makers, organizations in the public and private sector, accessibility experts, publishers, authors and last but not least the end-users.

Keywords: PDF, WCAG 2.0, PDF/UA, document accessibility, ISO standard, PDF/UA Competence Center.

1 Why PDF Accessibility Matters

The Portable Document Format (PDF) is very widely used for online documents created from different sources. Hence, web accessibility without PDF accessibility is not achievable. Up to now one great obstacle on the way to mainstream PDF accessibility was the lack of clear, understandable and standardized requirements. At this point PDF/UA comes in. [3]

2 What Is PDF/UA?

The new standard for accessible PDF documents PDF/UA – to be published by ISO as «ISO/DIS 14289-1, Document management applications – Electronic document file format enhancement for accessibility – Part 1: Use of ISO 32000-1 (PDF/UA-1)» [1] – will be ratified in summer 2012. PDF/UA aims to achieve for PDF documents what WCAG 2.0 achieves for web pages, and will set a worldwide standard for both PDF documents and PDF authoring as well as assistive technology (AT) aided access to PDF/UA conforming documents.

3 Why Is It Necessary?

PDF/UA regulates how content – graphics, text, multimedia, annotations, form fields – is to be included in a PDF file in order to be considered accessible. While leaving

K. Miesenberger et al. (Eds.): ICCHP 2012, Part I, LNCS 7382, pp. 585–586, 2012.

implementation details – how the content objects are technically incorporated in the PDF file, or how AT takes advantage of accessible content in PDF/UA documents – to solution developers, it provides a clearly defined benchmark: a first in the field of accessible PDF documents. With PDF/UA a new era in document accessibility begins.

4   What Are the Consequences and the Next Steps?

The challenge now lies in:

- understanding PDF/UA and its relation to Web Content Accessibility Guidelines (WCAG) 2.0
- spreading the new ISO Standard to document software developers and assistive technology vendors, decision-makers, organizations in the public and private sector, accessibility experts, publishers, authors and last but not least the end-users
- providing an easy-to-use compliance checker to assure high level PDF accessibility
- implementing PDF/UA in authoring tools – mainstream (Microsoft Office, LibreOffice, Adobe Indesign and others) and specialized solutions
- determining conformance with the PDF/UA standard

As first steps in this special thematic session we deal with:

- how a PDF/UA relates to WCAG 2.0
- how a PDF/UA compliance checker has to be developed
- how PDF/UA conforming PDF documents from Microsoft Word or Adobe Indesign can be created very easily
- what requirements a PDF/UA conforming viewer has to fulfill especially according to the needs of people with low vision, low literacy or cognitive disabilities.

The PDF Association founded the PDF/UA Competence Center [2] which provides resources for developers, marketers and policy makers who need to understand ISO 14289, the International Standard for accessible PDF.

References

1. PDF/UA (Universal Accessibility) / ISO 14289-1, http://pdf.editme.com/PDFUA
2. PDF/UA Competence Center, http://www.pdfa.org/competence-centers/pdfua-competence-center/?lang=en
3. The History of PDF Accessibility - NetCentric President testifies to US Access Board, http://www.commonlook.com/2012-01-pdfua-testimony-us-access-board

PDF/UA (ISO 14289-1) – Applying WCAG 2.0 Principles to the World of PDF Documents

Olaf Drümmer

Callas Software GmbH / Axaio Software GmbH

Abstract. PDF/UA-1 is an upcoming ISO standard defining accessible PDF. It claims to apply principles established by W3C's WCAG 2.0 to the world of PDF documents. This paper discusses a mapping table between WCAG 2.0 Success Criteria and clauses in the PDF/UA-1 standard to point out, how and why PDF/UA-1 can indeed be described as an application of WCAG 2.0 principles to PDF. It is to be expected that this as a consequence will speed up adoption of PDF/UA-1 in the field of accessible electronic content.

Keywords: accessible PDF, tagged PDF, PDF/UA, ISO 14289-1, WCAG 2.0.

1   Introduction

Accessibility of web content has seen significant progress over the last decade, thanks to the development of now widely respected "web content accessibility guidelines" (WCAG). About 13 years after WCAG was originally approved in its first version, and four years after WCAG 2.0 was finalized and published, a similar set of rules addressing PDF documents rather than web content is about to be published as an international standard in summer 2012: ISO 14289-1: Document management applications — Electronic document file format enhancement for accessibility (PDF/UA) — Use of ISO 32000-1 (PDF/UA-1).

When asked about the use of PDF documents, almost all blind people will admit they rather avoid PDF than even trying to access their content. Nevertheless, a substantial amount of relevant content often is only available in PDF format, and in most cases cannot easily be converted into some other readily accessible format like HTML. One of the main reasons that PDF is so widespread goes back to the fact that essentially any program running on a computer can create a printout – and while many programs do not offer a direct export to PDF there are numerous way to convert the print output stream to PDF, whether going through PostScript, PCL, GDI or any of the other print stream languages. So in the field of PDF we are not only confronted with documents specifically designed for print – like books, newspapers, magazines, and so forth – but also with everyday, private or business-related communication from applications for text processing, spreadsheet calculations or presentations which are

K. Miesenberger et al. (Eds.): ICCHP 2012, Part I, LNCS 7382, pp. 587–594, 2012.
© Springer-Verlag Berlin Heidelberg 2012

circulated frequently. As a matter of fact, PDF will most probably be around as long as documents are being created and exchanged – whether in the form of personal letters, invoices, reports or any type of publications.

Instead of forcing creators of "print-minded" documents to always also create a more accessible non-print version of the very same documents (or to forego the creation of such documents altogether) PDF/UA establishes guidelines how to create PDFs that not only serve as printable documents, but that are accessible at the same time – and on the same quality level as for example well crafted web content which conforms to WCAG 2.0.

2   Concept

Work on PDF/UA was started as early as 2004. There is a reason why developing PDF/UA took so many years, and is only about to be approved four years after WCAG 2.0 came out: Typical content structure, usage patterns and technicalities like how content is digitally encoded very often differ substantially between web content and content in PDF documents. Thus while some WCAG 2.0 principles could be mapped to PDF very naturally, others were more difficult to apply to PDFs.

Nevertheless is was obvious to those working on PDF/UA that creating yet another paradigm for accessibility of electronic content just did not make any sense. On one side it would not have been wise to take advantage of the achievements from the WCAG eco-system, on the other side it is important to not unnecessarily introduce conceptual inconsistencies. Where implementers have to develop solutions against more than one standard the cost of implementation increases substantially. Where users have to learn more than one conceptual approach for accessing electronic content, this would just increase the effort needed to master the respective techniques reasonably well.

3   Work

This paper makes use of work currently carried out by the PDF/UA committee within the Association for Information and Image Management (AIIM, www.aiim.org), who tasked themselves to iterate over all WCAG 2.0 checkpoints and describe where and how the PDF/UA standard specifies the same checkpoints. It discusses how WCAG 2.0 principles are mapped to PDF/UA, and aims to achieve two goals:

- Illustrate that a fully conforming PDF/UA document is as accessible as a fully WCAG 2.0 conforming web page or set of web pages.
- Highlight that for equivalent content, PDF/UA follows the very same concepts as established by WCAG 2.0

In addition, the work also discusses areas where content in a PDF document might be of such a different nature from content in a web page that different rules apply.

3.1   PDF/UA Addresses Only PDF Specific Aspects

PDF/UA focuses exclusively on requirements for the PDF file format as such and for tools processing or consuming PDF/UA files. General accessibility principles not specific to the PDF file format are intentionally out of scope for PDF/UA. Thus PDF/UA does not duplicate provisions in WCAG 2.0 or any other set of rules addressing other types or aspects of content, like for example principles for simple language. PDF/UA is also not to be seen as a guideline how to determine WCAG 2.0 conformance for PDF content in the context of a web page or web site.

3.2   Mapping WCAG 2.0 Success Criteria to Provisions in PDF/UA-1

As the overall structure of PDF/UA-1 at least in some parts differs substantially from the way the WCAG 2.0 is organized it is not obvious whether and how a certain criterion in WCAG 2.0 is mirrored by a provision in PDF/UA-1. Thus the WCAG 2.0 – PDF/UA   mapping starts from each WCAG 2.0 Success Criterion, and maps it to the text in PDF/UA-1 that mirrors it, albeit often in a manner specific to the syntax and technicalities of the PDF format.

It is important to understand, that the mapping for a given Success Criterion might not be the only way to meet that criterion, and also the other way around, the PDF/UA-conforming use of a specific feature to which a Success Criterion is mapped, does not necessarily imply conformance with WCAG 2.0.

For example, the WCAG 2.0 Success Criterion 1.2.1 requires that "Either an alternative for time-based media or an audio track is provided that presents equivalent information for prerecorded video-only content."

In comparison, PDF/UA simply requires that media clips (whether content is encoded as video or audio) are accompanied by an alternative representation of the content. Technically this is achieved by requiring a certain entry to be present in the PDF in the context of an embedded media clip, which according to the PDF syntax then makes it necessary to incorporate such alternate representation in the PDF.

PDF/UA does not prescribe in any way exactly how "equivalent information" is to be delivered in PDF files containing such media clips. To comply with Success Criterion 1.2.1 in PDF, therefore, an author or developer must determine either that the alternative representation provided in the PDF file for a media clip constitutes "equivalent information" or that "equivalent information" is provided in some other way. As such, the text: "Design-specific. Authors and developers need to consider this provision and ensure conformance." appears frequently in the mapping table.

3.3   The Role of WCAG 2.0 PDF Techniques

Prior to the development of the PDF/UA-1 standard there was hardly any guidance available about how to make PDF accessible. Based on the fact that web sites frequently offer certain content in the form of PDF documents anybody wishing to make a web site accessible ran into the question, how to achieve accessibility for PDFs offered on that web site for display or download. Honest compliance with WCAG 2.0 of course implied that such PDFs themselves be accessible, unless the same content was also offered in other ways.

The Web Accessibility Initiative complemented the WCAG guidelines by describing techniques that could make PDFs more accessible than they would typically be. Given that it was already difficult to find any tools that could create at least partially accessible PDF or turn existing PDF into more or less accessible PDF, it comes as no surprise that quite a few of the techniques described in the WCAG 2.0 PDF Techniques pretty much come across as band-aid fixes rather than efficient techniques easily adoptable in the real world. Of course WAI is not to be blamed for this – it is rather that developers of creation and fixing tools still have to come up with more adequate implementations. Nevertheless it would be wrong to reposition WCAG 2.0 PDF Techniques as normative descriptions about how to create accessible PDF. The Techniques are an interim solution to be superseded both by better tools as well as by guidelines and techniques to be derived directly from the PDF/UA standard.

3.4   "Accessibility Support Documentation for PDF" (2008) by W3C

The WAI document "Accessibility Support Documentation for PDF" describes the status quo regarding accessible PDF as of 2008, when ISO 32000-1 – the first incarnation of the PDF syntax as an ISO standard – just got published. While useful during the development of PDF/UA-1 it essentially by now is also superseded by PDF/UA-1 itself – which is also based on ISO 32000-1, but goes much further in specifying in detail how the PDF syntax can be used to create accessible PDF documents.

3.5   Linking Success Criteria in WCAG 2.0 to Normative Clauses in PDF/UA-1

There are 61 Success Criteria in WCAG 2.0, each presented as a row in the mapping table. For each Success Criterion, the table points to the relevant subsection of PDF/UA-1.

PDF/UA-1 includes three key sections of requirements:

- section 7 is dedicated to the file-format itself
- section 8 is dedicated to PDF reader software
- section 9 is directed at the assistive technologies (AT) delivering the output of a PDF reader software to the user.

The requirements for the file-format (Section 7) and the reader (Section 8) are provided in separate columns in the mapping table. For additional information, the table includes references to the WCAG 2.0 PDF Techniques and W3C's 2008 report on WCAG 2.0 support in ISO 32000-1.

3.6   Selected Examples: Non-text Content

The entry for "Non-text content" makes it very obvious that there is not necessarily a one to one mapping of a Success Criterion in WCAG 2.0 to a clause in the PDF/UA-1 standard. Rather, for a number of reasons, provisions governing the requirement of text based alternatives to non-text content are stated in four different clauses of the PDF/UA-1 standard. The combination of the provisions in these four clauses though fully covers the WCAG 2.0 criterion.

Table 1. Excerpt from WCAG 2.0 – PDF/UA-1 mapping table: 1.1.1 Non-text Content

WCAG 2.0	ISO 14289-1 (File)	ISO 14289-1 (Reader)	WCAG 2.0 PDF Techniques	W3C "Accessibility Support Documentation for PDF"
1.1.1 Non-text Content. (A) "All non-text content that is presented to the user has a text alternative that serves the equivalent purpose […]."	7.3 addresses content requiring text alternatives. - 7.18.1 paragraph 4 addresses control descriptions. - 7.18.6.2 addresses time- based media alternatives. Test, Sensory and CAPTCHA use-cases are addressed via the technical means employed. - 7.1 paragraph 1 sentence 2 addresses decoration.	8.1	PDF1 PDF4	The PDF specification provides ways to include equivalents for images, as detailed in section 14.9.3 of the ISO 32000-1 PDF specification.

3.7   Selected Examples: Meaningful Sequence

Also in the entry for "Meaningful Sequence" it is necessary to look at several clauses of the PDF/UA-1 standard. Again, the combination of the provisions in these three clauses reflects the WCAG 2.0 criterion adequately.

Table 2. Excerpt from WCAG 2.0 – PDF/UA-1 mapping table: 1.3.2 Meaningful Sequence

WCAG 2.0	ISO 14289-1 (File)	ISO 14289-1 (Reader)	WCAG 2.0 PDF Techniques	W3C "Accessibility Support Documentation for PDF"
1.3.2 Meaningful Sequence (A) "When the sequence in which content is presented affects its meaning, a correct reading sequence can be programmatically determined."	- 7.2 paragraph 2 addresses the meaningful sequence of content. - 7.17 addresses navigation features - 7.18.3 addresses tab order in annotations.	8.2 paragraph 1	PDF3	PDF supports a defined programmatic order to content.

3.8   Selected Examples: Language of Page and Language of Parts

In this example the mapping is very straightforward. In the same way as the (default) language is to be indicated for a whole web page, this can also be done for a PDF document as a whole.

Table 3. Excerpt from WCAG 2.0 – PDF/UA-1 mapping table: 3.1.1 Language of Page

WCAG 2.0	ISO 14289-1 (File)	ISO 14289-1 (Reader)	WCAG 2.0 PDF Techniques	W3C "Accessibility Support Documentation for PDF"
3.1.1 Language of Page (A) "The default human language of each Web page can be programmatically determined."	7.2, paragraph 3	8.2, paragraph 3	PDF16 PDF19	PDF provides support for language identification for documents

3.9   WCAG 2.0 Success Criteria Outside the Scope of PDF/UA

For some of the WCAG 2.0 success criteria it can be said they either do not typically apply to PDF documents in general, or that they are intentionally out of scope for

PDF/UA. This coincides to a high degree with what W3C stated in their document "Accessibility Support Documentation for PDF".

The "Resize text" criterion is one example that by definition can not be addressed as such in PDF, because while any page or part of a page can be resized there is no pre-defined mechanism to selectively resize the text only, as this would imply text reflow, whereas the PDF imaging model is about representation of static two dimensional content. At the same time, this does not stop a PDF reader or assistive technology to derive a representation from essentially any PDF/UA conforming PDF, that displays text as unformatted text, offering text display at any text size, and reflowing the text as needed.

The "Low or No Background Audio" criterion, is another example not easily applicable to PDF, as hardly any PDF file ever created could even achieve background audio. While not 100% impossible – some sophisticated combination between actions or JavaScript and a suitable PDF reader could actually implement background audio in theory – it will probably never be encountered in the real world.

Many timed media provisions – whether for audio or video – are considered out of scope from the point of view of PDF/UA-1. In other words: in cases where audio or video are embedded in a PDF/UA-1 document, provisions for providing alternative access are typically specific to the way the timed media as such is encoded, and what media player is used. Obviously such timed media will have to bring with it the necessary additional or alternate representation of content – like captions for video – but PDF/UA-1 leaves the details of how to do this in a suitable accessible way to other applicable accessibility standards, like WCAG 2.0.

In practice this translates into a duty for a content producer who decides to include audio or video inside a PDF file, to identify the rules applicable to such audio and video, and to make sure the embedded media complies with such rules.

It should be noted that in the real world PDF files with embedded audio or video are the exception, and relatively rarely encountered.

4   Conclusions

For the success of PDF/UA it will be crucial that all relevant stakeholders can easily recognize and acknowledge that PDF/UA does not reinvent the wheel but instead uses the well established and proven conceptual approach of WCAG and applies it to the PDF universe.

This will pave the way for inclusion of the PDF/UA standard in applicable regulations, whether in national legislation like the German BITV or in the pan-European EU Mandate 376. This in turn will increase the likelihood that a healthy market develops – for PDF/UA tools as much as for services around the creation of accessible tagged PDF according to PDF/UA.

In addition, any educational effort will become much easier once it can clearly be seen where and how PDF/UA just directly mirrors the WCAG 2.0 principles, and where there are albeit small differences that should be understood.

Finally, developers implementing tools to help with the creation of accessible content will find it easier to repurpose existing expertise to the world of tagged PDF. This should reduce development cost and increase ease of use.

5   Remarks

The author expects that the PDF/UA committee within AIIM will publish a final document detailing the mapping between WCAG 2.0 and PDF/UA in summer 2012. An almost final version of the document is currently being circulated within the PDF/UA working group within ISO TC 171 SC 2 for review and support.

Work about to be carried out in the PDF/UA working group of the PDF Association, co-chaired by the author, intends to break down the results from the AIIM working group into more easily readable articles, and to use this work to promote adoption of PDF/UA especially by implementers and service providers on the grounds of its proximity to WCAG 2.0 concepts.

Acknowledgements. The author would like to acknowledge that the author himself contributed only in minor ways to the work on the work on the mapping between WCAG 2.0 Success Criteria and PDF/UA-1 clauses. All the thanks go to AIIM's US Committee for PDF/UA, and its chairman Duff Johnson, for sharing the document during its development process. For any errors and shortcomings in this article the author is to be blamed.

References

1. Achieving WCAG 2 with PDF-UA v0.96, by AIIM's PDF/UA committee, http://www.aiim.org
2. DIS/ISO 14289-1.2 — Document management applications — Electronic document file format enhancement for accessibility — Part 1: Use of ISO 32000-1 (PDF/UA-1); International Organization for Standardization (ISO), http://www.iso.org
3. Web Content Accessibility Guidelines (WCAG) 2.0, W3C Recommendation (December 11, 2008), http://www.w3.org/TR/WCAG/
4. Accessibility Support Documentation for PDF, W3C (October 2008), http://www.w3.org/WAI/GL/WCAG20/implementation-report/PDF_accessibility_support_statement
5. Techniques for WCAG 2.0, Techniques and Failures for Web Content Accessibility Guidelines 2.0, W3C, http://www.w3.org/TR/2012/NOTE-WCAG20-TECHS-20120103/
6. PDF/UA, Universal Accessibility, landing page of the PDF/UA within AIIM, http://www.aiim.org/Resources/Standards/Committees/PDFUA

Mainstreaming the Creation of Accessible PDF Documents by a Rule-Based Transformation from Word to PDF

Roberto Bianchetti[2], Markus Erle[1], and Samuel Hofer[2]

[1] Wertewerk, Tuebingen, Germany
erle@wertewerk.de
[2] xyMedia GmbH, Volketswil, Switzerland
{bianchetti,hofer}@xymedia.ch

Abstract. axesPDF for Word is an add-in for Microsoft Word 2007 and Word 2010 allowing to create high quality accessible PDF documents according to guidelines like WCAG 2.0 and standards like PDF/UA. It is characterized by a specific role model, a rule based transformation instead of static conversion and the possibility of n:m-mapping. Even complex documents with elements like footnotes, side notes, captions, references, indices and glossaries can be made accessible without post-processing.

Keywords: PDF, Microsoft Word, WCAG 2.0, PDF/UA, document accessibility.

1 Introduction

A lot of governmental, educational, touristic and medical information in the web is available as PDF documents that are created with Microsoft Word. PDF is the standard format for document exchange in and between organizations. Therefore accessible documents are essential for job integration and inclusion of people with disabilities.

Although there are some mainstream tools and plugins available for the creation of tagged PDF, accessible documents are still an exception. The Swiss Accessibility Study 2011 [6] gives the main reasons:

1. Characteristics: the requirements for accessible PDF documents are not clear.
2. Post-processing and education: the creation of accessible PDF documents is tedious, time-consuming and costly.
3. Tools: there are no reliable programs.

The new ISO standard 14289-1 - PDF/UA-1 (Universal Accessibility) [16] - which is announced for the third quarter of 2012 will solve the first problem. It is based on the PDF specification ISO 32000-1 [9], determines the requirements for accessible PDF documents and specifies the success criteria of the Web Content Accessibility Guidelines (WCAG) 2.0 [18] for the PDF format.

K. Miesenberger et al. (Eds.): ICCHP 2012, Part I, LNCS 7382, pp. 595–601, 2012.

Therefore, we search for a solution which can convert more or less well-structured Word files into accessible PDF documents that

- conform to standards and guidelines available for accessibility (According to PDF: ISO 32000-1 (PDF specification), ISO 14289-1 (PDF/UA – UA stands for Universal Access), Web Content Accessibility Guidelines WCAG 2.0)
- everybody can create without additional education
- contain correct PDF-Tags even for complex elements like footnotes, references, complex tables, images with captions, lists with individual bullets, table of contents, indices.
- do not need post-processing with a PDF editor

We call such PDF files „high quality accessible PDF documents".

2   The State of the Art

There are only a few authoring programs in the field of word processing and office suites, that are able to create tagged PDF files. We looked at the newest versions of available authoring programs – not only Microsoft Word but also the LibreOffice / OpenOffice suite – and at available plugins or published concepts for tools helping authors to create high quality accessible PDF documents. [2-4], [7], [8]

Based on our analysis we could identify 3 trends:

1. Checking the source file for accessibility issues [12], [13]
2. Supporting the author in fixing accessibility problems („guided workflow")[7], [8]
3. Mapping styles to PDF-Tags or remapping PDF-Tags („1:1 mapping")

These 3 trends show the right direction but are not reflected towards a reliable, time- and easy-to-use solution. In conclusion crucial weak points still remain:

- all solutions need extensive accessibility knowledge
- there is still no solution publicly available which enables a configurable 1:1-mapping of Word styles to PDF-Tags
- but even 1:1 mapping of styles to PDF-Tags is very limited according to different document types or nested PDF-Tags
- 1:1-mapping forces the author to adapt himself (or the document) to the program
- there is no authoring tool available which creates PDF files conforming to ISO 32000-1 and to ISO 14289-1
- complex elements like footnotes, side notes, captions, references, indices and glossaries still cannot be made accessible without time-consuming post-processing

3   The Concept

Our proposed concept to eliminate the weak points mentioned above consists of 3 main principles described in the next sections. Our goals were: eliminating the post-processing even for complex elements and enabling even for authors without PDF accessibility knowledge to create high quality accessible PDF documents.

3.1   Role Model

An analysis of the typical workflow for creating accessible PDF documents based on Word documents shows that there are different steps that presuppose different levels of document and accessibility knowledge. Usually in organizations it is not the same person working at the document during the whole process. Based on the 8-step-workflow for creating accessible PDF documents described by Erle [10] we mapped different tasks and specific knowledge to every step. We could identify 3 typical role patterns that we changed to our new role model:

- role 1: the author
- role 2: the creator of the document template and configurator of transformation rules
- role 3: the creator of customized transformation rules

3.2   Rule-Based Transformation Instead of Static Conversion

According to mainstream tools every PDF conversion is static. The specific elements of a source document do not change the conversion process. In order to include different type of documents we selected a data-driven process. This makes sure that the resulting PDF documents contain a semantically and syntactically correct tag hierarchy.

For every identifiable Word element or attribute it is possible to formulate a rule that determines the resulting element in the PDF tag structure. Standard rules can be similar to a 1:1 mapping. Special rules can eliminate typical mistakes like empty paragraphs. Individual rules can help to transform a badly formatted Word document to a well-structured PDF document. Nevertheless: the best source document is a well-structured and correctly formatted Word document.

3.3   A Kind of N:M Mapping

Available tools (e.g. Adobe InDesign CS 5.5 as an authoring tool for professional layouts or the PDF TagRenamer [15] as a post-processing tool for accessible PDF documents) are based on a 1:1 mapping: a Word Style is mapped to a PDF-Tag. But this concept is too limited in order to represent complex tag structures, e.g. nested tags. So we decided to implement a more flexible concept instead similar to n:m mapping. This means that one element to many or many elements to one can be allocated. Additionally the limitation to Word Styles is resolved. In this way a transformation of every identifiable Word-element to PDF-tags is possible. This kind of n:m mapping is fundamental for an flexible and adaptable transformation process.

4   The Result

The described concept was implemented as a Word add-in called „axesPDF for Word"[1]. The add-in consists of 4 components (as shown in graphic 1):

1. The Converter: converts the Word document to an untagged PDF document
2. The Analyzer: analyzes the document structure of the source document and creates a hierarchy – the Word structure. The analyzer also checks for accessibility problems.
3. The Processor: based on the rules that are saved in the Word document template the processor transforms the Word structure to a tag structure.
4. The Tagger: combines the untagged PDF with the tag structure and creates the tagged PDF.

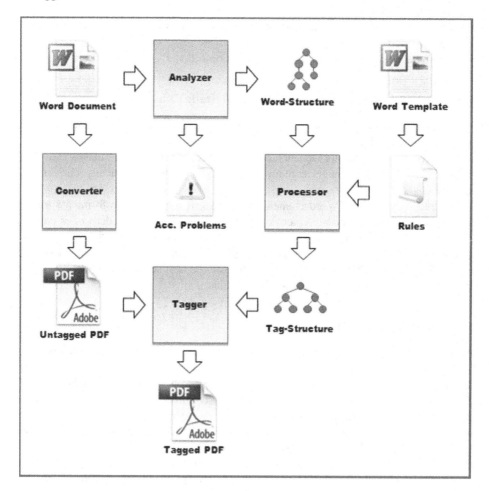

Fig. 1. The 4 components of axesPDF for Word

The add-in runs on Windows XP, Windows Vista and Windows 7 and requires the installation of Microsoft Word 2007 or 2010. At the moment a public beta version of our solution is available.

5   The Evaluation of the Created PDF Documents

High Level PDF accessibility means: conforming to the requirements of the Web Content Accessibility Guidelines (WCAG) 2.0 and the ISO standard for accessible PDF documents PDF/UA (ISO 14289-1). To assure the high level accessibility of the created PDF documents we used 3 steps of evaluation [5]:

1. Checking automatically by using the PDF Accessibility Checker PAC [14] because of the additional checking points in comparison to other common testing tools like the Full Check in Adobe Acrobat X Pro and by using a PDF parser especially developed according to the formal requirements of the PDF specification (PDF 32000-1). Successful parsing of a document is evidence of being a valid PDF. This step deals with the technical and hence with the automatically testable aspects of PDF accessibility.
2. Checking manually by using the PAC preview of the structured document and by using the navigation panels "Tags" and "Content" in Adobe Acrobat X Pro. The PAC preview shows which tags are included in the PDF document and presents the elements in the same way as they would be interpreted by assistive technologies (such as screen readers).This step is very important for evaluating the quality of the logical document structure, the reading order and the semantics of the documents. [11]
3. Checking by users with disabilities using assistive technology like common screen readers with best known PDF support, braille displays or zoom software. During the development we evaluated the usability of solutions according to particular problems (e.g. footnotes, complex tables) by cooperation with the accessibility experts of the foundation "Access for all". This step guarantees the real life accessibility and usability of the created PDF documents for blind and low-vision people.

6   The Impact and Contribution

The axesPDF for Word add-in simplifies the process of creating accessible PDF documents, so that every user of Microsoft Word is capable to produce accessible documents without post-processing. An author can initiate this process without special knowledge. All the special knowledge concerning PDF accessibility is saved as transformation rules into the template. Even for users with disabilities it is possible to create high quality accessible PDF documents as long as they can handle Word.

It is possible to customize the transformation to different document types or workflows. The solution enables to install a reliable workflow. A PDF editor is not necessary any more. Conformity to available accessibility and document standards like WCAG 2.0 and ISO 32000-1 or the future accessible PDF document standard ISO 14289-1 is guaranteed by the transformation itself – only dependent of correct rules.

6.1 Use Cases

Some use cases can exemplify the wide ranges of application for the axesPDF for Word add-in:

- Governmental and educational material: Every employee can create high quality accessible PDF documents by himself if he uses the standard rules fitting to standard document templates or if he can use individual document templates with individual rules that were delivered by power uses with deep accessibility knowledge.
- Third party Documents: Word document output from third party applications like document management systems or medical documentation systems for instance which is only formatted visually can be transformed to accessible PDF documents by using adequate transforming rules.
- Legacy Documents: older publications or archived Word documents that are not formatted properly can be transformed to accessible PDF documents as long as there is a recognizable logical structure that can be translated into transformation rules.

7   Future Work

As next steps after the successful introduction of the final version (1.0) are planned:

- integrated Accessibility Checker that checks accessibility issues during the authoring
- easy-to-use user interface for configuring existing rules or writing individual rules
- support of MathML
- transformation to accessible formats like DAISY and EPUB
- cloud-based application

References

1. axesPDF for Word. project website, http://www.axespdf.com
2. Accessibility Features in Microsoft Office (2010), http://www.microsoft.com/enable/products/office2010/
3. Darvishy, A., Hutter, H.-P., Horvath, A., Dorigo, M.: A Flexible Software Architecture Concept for the Creation of Accessible PDF Documents. In: Miesenberger, K., Klaus, J., Zagler, W., Karshmer, A. (eds.) ICCHP 2010, Part I. LNCS, vol. 6179, pp. 47–52. Springer, Heidelberg (2010)

4. Barrierefreie Dokumente und wie man sie mit Mainstream-Programmen erstellt – Anleitungen, die im Rahmen des Projektes. Digital informiert, im Job integriert." entstanden sind, `http://www.di-ji.de/index.php?option=com_content& view=category&layout=blog&id=28&Itemid=39&lang=de`

5. Bianchetti, R., Erle, M., Riesch, M.: Trau' keinem barrierefreien PDF. Qualitätskriterien für barrierefreie PDF-Dokumente. In: Fachhefte grafische Industrie, German Version is downloadable as accessible PDF, 137 KB, pp.S.13–S.16 (May 2008), `http://www.wertewerk.de/publikationen/Trau%20keinem%20barrie refreien%20PDF_02_2009.pdf`

6. Bianchetti, R., Erle, M.: Barrierefreie PDFs: Die unendliche Geschichte. Die grössten Hürden bei der Prüfung und Erstellung von barrierefreien PDF-Dokumenten. In: Stiftung Zugang für alle: Schweizer Accessibility Studie, German Version is downloadable as accessible PDF, 256 KB, pp. 99–105 (2011), `http://www.access-for-all.ch/ download/Accessibility_Studie_2011_de_099_K09_Barrierefreie_ PDF.pdf`

7. CommonLook Office PAW Panel, `http://www.commonlook.com/commonlook-office-panel`

8. CommonLook Office, `http://www.commonlook.com/docs-commonlook-office`

9. Document management — Portable document format — Part 1: PDF 1.7 1st edn. This document is an ISO approved copy of the ISO 32000-1 Standards document (July 1, 2008), `http://www.adobe.com/content/dam/Adobe/en/devnet/pdf/ pdfs/PDF32000_2008.pdf`

10. Erle, M.: PDF umsetzen und prüfen. In: Hellbusch, J.E., Probiesch, K., Barrierefreiheit verstehen und umsetzen. Webstandards für ein zugängliches und nutzbares Internet, pp.433—516 (2011)

11. Johnson, D.: Review PAC (PDF Accessibility Checker) 1.1, `http://www.appligent.com/talkingpdf-PDFAccessibilityCheckerReview`

12. Learn about the Microsoft Word Accessibility Checker, `http://office.microsoft.com/en-us/word-help/accessibility-checker-HA010369192.aspx`

13. LibreOffice/OpenOffice-Extension AccessODF, `http://extensions.libreoffice.org/extension-center/accessodf`

14. PDF Accessibility Checker PAC, `http://www.access-for-all.ch/en/pdf-lab/pdf-accessibility-checker-pac.html`

15. PDF TagRenamer 1.1, `http://www.xymedia.ch/pdf_tagrenamer.html`

16. PDF/UA (Universal Accessibility) / ISO 14289-1, `http://pdf.editme.com/PDFUA`

17. WCAG 2.0-Techniques for PDF, `http://www.w3.org/WAI/GL/WCAG20-TECHS/pdf.html`

18. Web Content Accessibility Guidelines WCAG 2.0, `http://www.w3.org/TR/WCAG/`

Developing Text Customisation Functionality Requirements of PDF Reader and Other User Agents

Shawn Lawton Henry

shawn@uiAccess.com

Abstract. This paper addresses the text customisation needs of people with low vision, dyslexia, and related conditions that impact reading, including people with declining eyesight due to ageing. It reports on a literature review and an initial study that explores the aspects of text that users customize (e.g., size, colour, leading, linearization/reflow, and more) for reading RTF and PDF documents, in operating system settings, and in web browser settings. It presents the gap between users' needs and PDF user agent (primarily Adobe Reader) functionality. The existing literature and this exploratory study indicate that with the technology currently available, PDF is not sufficiently accessible to many people with low vision, dyslexia, and related conditions that impact reading. This paper aims to encourage additional text customisation functionality in Adobe Reader; and to encourage more rigorous studies to understand, document, and communicate how to better meet users' text customisation needs through mainstream user agents.

Keywords: low vision, dyslexia, readability, adaptability, PDF, Adobe Reader, text customisation, accessibility guidelines, accessibility standards, user agents.

1 Introduction

Communications and interactions are increasingly provided through the Web and electronic media. This offers the opportunity for unprecedented access to information and interaction for people with print disabilities because the accessibility barriers to print can be more easily overcome through technology. Print disabilities encompass people who cannot effectively read "normal" print because of a visual, physical, perceptual, developmental, cognitive, or learning disability [1].

Much of the effort to date in this area has been on providing access for people who are blind [2]; for example, providing screen reader access to PDF (portable document format) documents. However, less effort has been invested to meet the needs of other people with print disabilities, including people with low vision and people with dyslexia. Many user agents (i.e., the tools that people use to interact with electronic information, such as web browsers) do not sufficiently meet the needs of these users. They do not provide adequate text customisation that is necessary for some people to be able to read, understand, and interact with information.

K. Miesenberger et al. (Eds.): ICCHP 2012, Part I, LNCS 7382, pp. 602–609, 2012.
© Springer-Verlag Berlin Heidelberg 2012

Of particular concern is PDF because of the:

- widespread use of PDF as the only way of providing large amounts of essential information, such as tax instructions, scientific papers, educational material, medical information, etc.
- lack of sufficient text customisation functionality available, even for advanced users, in Adobe Reader[1] and other PDF user agents.

Many managers, policy makers, and even accessibility specialists and disability advocates are not aware of the specific PDF accessibility barriers explored in this paper. For many people with print disabilities, there currently is no such thing as "accessible PDF" because they cannot customize the text to be readable.

While electronic media provides an opportunity to increase readability for large groups of people who have difficulty reading and processing text, this opportunity remains unrealized in several areas. Additional research, guidance, and education is needed to encourage user agent developers to provide the text customisation functionality required by people with conditions that impact reading.

This paper reports on one phase of a research project[2] to address these needs. While the project investigates the issue broadly, this paper focuses on PDF.

2   Readability Beyond Legibility

In order to understand the needs of people with low vision, dyslexia, and related conditions that impact reading, it is important understand the distinction between *legibility* and *readability*[3]. [3] *Legibility* is related to perceiving text by distinguishing letters. *Readability* is related to reading and comprehending textual information. Thus text could be somewhat legible to a user, yet not functionally readable; that is, with effort the user could distinguish one letter from another, but could not effectively read sentences because of the text formatting.

Many research studies on text legibility focused on perceiving small amounts of text [4]. Even many studies on readability use work periods as short as one to ten minutes [4]. A study on reading and visual fatigue found little negative effect after six hours of reading; however, these were people without print disabilities [5]. In the study reported in this paper, participants reported that strain, discomfort, and fatigue are significant limiting factors when reading text that is not well formatted for them.

The author assumes that many of the accessibility guidelines for electronic media are also focused on small amounts of text, such as website navigation, forms, and short descriptions. Thus the guidelines may be sufficient for legibility, but not for readability. PDF is often used for providing large amounts of text, where readability is essential. To read large amounts of text, users need to be able to customize more aspects of text formatting.

---

[1] Adobe is a registered trademark and Reader is a trademark of Adobe Systems Incorporated.

[2] TAdER Text Adaptability is Essential for Reading - http://www.tader.info

[3] In his seminal research, Tinker [4] used only the term legibility to avoid confusion with readability formulas for the level of difficulty of the language; however, most literature distinguishes between legibility and readability as used in this paper.

3   User Group

Millions of people cannot read "normal" text, and millions more will not be able to in the coming years as their vision declines due to aging [6-7]. An estimated 15–20% of the population has symptoms of dyslexia [8] and 246 million have low vision (compared to 39 million who are blind) [6].

This project focuses on the largest groups of people with print disabilities: those who can see and can read, but have difficulty reading text in common formats and need to specify different text format in order to read effectively [6-7]; including:

- people with low vision,
- people with declining eyesight due to ageing, and
- people with dyslexia and other reading-related impairments.

The outcomes of this project focus on people who use mainstream technologies and do not regularly use assistive technologies (such as screen magnification) because of cost, complexity, availability, or other factors. It also addresses people who do not use technology much or at all because they have difficulty reading text—that is, for whom readability of text has been a limiting factor to technology adoption.

4   Existing Research Summary

The needs of people who have disabilities and conditions that impact reading have been addressed in a wide range of research studies. Most of the research focuses on one user group, such as older users, and one domain, such as websites. An extensive literature review and analysis is being conducted for this project.

Most research on making text more readable for people with low vision is designed to determine optimum characteristics such as font face and size [9]. There is similar on improving readability of text for people with dyslexia [10]. Many of the results suggest characteristics for readability in print, and more recent literature addresses electronic media. There are some recommendations for online readability, both for older technology and for newer technology such as is available in e-book readers.

There is less research on what users should be able to customize in order to optimize readability for their particular impairment and situation. Work in this area tends focus on a specific user group and situation, such as older users who are new to the Web or adult students with dyslexia. Specialized software has been developed for such users, for example, [11 - 14]. Yet most of this customisation has not been well integrated in mainstream user agents, nor is it sufficiently included in some accessibility standards and support material (such as the Section 508 standards [15]).

Additional research is needed to understand, document, and communicate the needs of users in order to encourage inclusion of additional text customisation functionality in mainstream user agents. [16] says, "…end user customization plays a central role in accessibility considering dyslexia. Nevertheless, only two guidelines where found regarding this subject. Thus, a deeper study on end user customization is an identified gap that needs to be bridged."

5   Approach: Analysing Specific User Needs

The goal of the study is to explore how advanced users customize text when they have a wide range of options available, and to observe their use of PDF documents, which has few options. This paper reports on an initial exploratory study.

Participants included people with low vision from birth, people with declining vision due to ageing, and people with dyslexia, in Europe and the U.S. All are advanced users, recruited through accessibility and disability contacts and mailing lists. Most participants had customized their operating systems settings for text, including colours. Most did not use assistive technology; one used a screen magnifier and a screen reader concurrently.

Participants were first given a rich text file (RTF)[4] and asked to open it in a word processor and change it so that they could read it easily. Then they were asked to read it, aloud or to themselves. Next they were given a PDF file[5] and asked to change it so that they could read it easily. Next they were asked to explain their operating system settings and browser settings. Finally, they were asked to rate the importance of specific aspects of text customisation (listed below) on a scale of 1 to 4.

Participants were encouraged to "think aloud" and share information throughout the sessions. Most voluntarily showed some problems they have with specific websites. Most sessions lasted between one and two hours.

6   Information Gathered

Information was gathered through recorded phone calls and some included viewing and recording the participant's screen.

Data captured included observations on what each user did with each file, which aspects of text they customized with the RTF file and what values (e.g., which font, what leading), and how they handled the PDF file; their system settings for text; and their browser settings related to text. Participants who use custom cascading style sheets (CSS) provided those files. Related information was collected, including screen resolution, monitor size, and details of their impairment.

Participants had different perspectives on the importance of being able to customize specific aspects of text format. The range of responses (with 1 being most important) reported below shows the differences in priority:

- text size – 1
- linearization/reflow, e.g., changing from multiple columns to a single column – 1-2
- text colour and background colour – 1-3
- leading/line spacing – 1-3
- justification – 1-4

---

[4] The RTF was slightly modified from
  http://www.acm.org/sigs/ publications/pubform.doc
[5] The PDF was an excerpt of http://www.adobe.com/accessibility/products/
  indesign/pdf/ accessibledocswithindesignCS4.pdf

- text style, e.g., underlining, italics, all capital letters – 1-4
- other visual characteristics such as borders, margins, indentation – 1-4 (white space / padding to separate the main text from the material around it were mentioned as important by both a participant with low vision and a participant with dyslexia)
- font face/typeface/font family – 2-3
- kerning, letter spacing, and word spacing – 2-4
- line length, i.e., the number of characters per line – 2-4
- hyphenation – 3-4

Text customisation at the element level was not included in the list of aspects participants were asked to rate in this initial study; however, three participants were observed customizing headings different from the main text in the RTF file. Some changed the headings using "Styles" in the word processor. One participant who was having trouble with the Styles, selected all the text and set the text size. He then commented about losing the distinction of the headings.

Two participants pointed out that they set headings smaller than the main text because headings are easier to read because they are short and have space around them. One participant converted both the RTF and the PDF file to HTML and used a custom CSS which has the body text set to 28pt Tahoma, the headings to 0.9em Comic Sans MS, and different coloured text and borders on each heading level. (Markup editing was needed to get the PDF file to work with the participant's CSS.)

7   Outcomes: The Need for Text Customisation

The primary finding from the literature review was that there is not a single text format that will meet most users needs; instead, users need to be able to customize text to meet their particular needs. The need for text customisation was supported by findings from this initial user study.

Research results and published guidelines have different recommendations for many aspects of text format. As just one example, leading/line spacing recommendations for people with low vision, dyslexia, or who are older, range from 1.25 to 2.0 [17-26].

Without customisation, a users' needs can conflict with general best practice. For example, a participant with dyslexia said, "I write and read a lot better in all upper case"; whereas, all guidelines found in the literature review suggest avoiding all caps [e.g., 20-25].

Without customisation, one user's needs can conflict with another user's needs. For example, many people with declining eyesight due to ageing need high contract between text and background colour [24], [26]; whereas many people with dyslexia and other reading impairments need low contrast [14]. The participants in this study used a range of settings, from black text on a brown background to white text on black background. Regarding choosing from pre-defined text and background colour combinations, a participant said: "Someone else's idea [of what I need] is useless."

Not only are there differences between users, but an individual user's needs can change. Participants in this study reported that their needs varied depending on the amount of text to be read, the time of day, fatigue, and complexity of the information.

In summary, the existing literature and the findings from this initial study clearly point to the requirement for users to be able to customize text according to their specific needs at a given time.

8   Gap between Users' Needs and Current Functionality

Most mainstream web browsers provide functionality for users to customize text size, text colour and background colour, font face, and provide zoom functionality. They provide functionality for users to set their own style sheets to additionally customize leading/line spacing (line-height), letter spacing, word spacing, width, text style, justification, and more. (Improving the usability of such functionality is an importance issue, yet outside the scope of this paper.)

In contrast, several aspects of text customisation are not provided by Adobe Reader, even to advanced users. Adobe Reader does provide some functionality: text and background colour customisation, zoom, and reflow that temporarily puts text in a single column. However, there are limitations to the latter two, described below. Additionally, PDF documents cannot be printed when zoomed or reflowed. The importance of printing for people with dyslexia is described in [27].

Adobe says of Reader's reflow limitations: "Text that does not reflow includes forms, comments, digital signature fields, and page artifacts, such as page numbers, headers, and footers. Pages that contain both readable text and form or digital signature fields do not reflow." [28] In reflow mode, the search/find-in-document feature does not work at all.

Documents with some layouts are not functionally readable to some users when zoomed, such as research papers formatted in two columns. When users get to the bottom of a column, they have to scroll up to find the top of the next column and the physical and cognitive effort required can break the flow of reading and understanding substantially. As an example of how significant this is for most users, a participant with dyslexia said about reading text in one column not requiring scrolling: "I struggle with getting to the start of the next line". Getting from the bottom of a column to the top of the next is even more difficult.

Adobe Reader does not provide functionality for users to set font face, text size for specific elements, leading/line spacing, and most other aspects of text formatting. To the authors knowledge, currently no other PDF user agents provide the text customisation that users need. Thus the existing literature and this exploratory study indicate that with the technology currently available, PDF is not sufficiently accessible to many people with low vision, dyslexia, and related conditions that impact reading.

9   Conclusion

To realize the potential of technology to facilitate reading by people with low vision, dyslexia, and related conditions that impact reading, users need to be provided the functionality to customize several aspects of text. The initial work reported in this paper aims to:

- encourage more rigorous studies to understand, document, and communicate the text customisation needs of users with low vision, dyslexia, and related conditions that impact reading; and
- encourage inclusion of specific text customisation functionality in Adobe Reader.

While this paper focuses on PDF, the broader project explores other technologies and user agents. Additional work will further analyze gaps in available knowledge and research, and provide suggestions to fill those gaps. The ultimate goal is to provide specific guidance on text customisation functionality requirements to user agent developers, standards developers, content providers, and policy makers.

References

1. Reading Rights Coalition. The definition of "print disabled",
   http://www.readingrights.org/definition-print-disabled
2. Hanson, V.: The user experience: designs and adaptations. In: Proceedings of the 2004 International Cross-Disciplinary Workshop on Web Accessibility (W4A 2004), pp. 1–11. ACM, New York (2004)
3. Tracy, W.: Letters of Credit: A View of Type Design. Gordon Fraser, London (1986)
4. Tinker, M.: Legibility of Print. Ames. Iowa State University Press, Iowa (1963)
5. Carmichael, L., Dearborn, W.F.: Reading and Visual Fatigue. Houghton Mifflin Co., Boston (1947)
6. World Health Organization. Fact Sheet # 282: Visual Impairment and Blindness. Geneva (2011), http://www.who.int/mediacentre/factsheets/fs282
7. Steinmetz, E.: Americans with disabilities: 2002 U.S. Census Bureau, Washington, DC: (Current Population Reports, P70–107) (2006)
8. International Dyslexia Association. Dyslexia Basics (2008), http://www.interdys.org/ewebeditpro5/upload/BasicsFactSheet.pdf
9. Poole, A.: Which Are More Legible: Serif or Sans Serif Typefaces? (2008), http://alexpoole.info/which-are-more-legible-serif-or-sans-serif-typefaces
10. McCarthy, J., Swierenga, S.: What we know about dyslexia and Web accessibility: a research review. Univers. Access Inf. Soc. 9(2), 147–152 (2010)
11. Hanson, V., Richards, J.: A web accessibility service: update and findings. In: Proceedings of the 6th International ACM SIGACCESS Conference on Computers and Accessibility (Assets 2004), pp. 169–176. ACM, New York (2003)

12. Dickinson, A., Gregor, P., Newell, A.F.: Ongoing investigation of the ways in which some of the problems encountered by some dyslexics can be alleviated using computer techniques. In: Proceedings of the 5fth International ACM Conference on Assistive Technologies, pp. 97–103. ACM Press, Edinburgh (2002)
13. Gregor, P., Dickinson, A., Macaffer, A., Andreasen, P.: SeeWord—a personal word processing environment for dyslexic computer users. British Journal of Educational Technology 34, 341–355 (2003)
14. Gregor, P., Newell, A.: An empirical investigation of ways in which some of the problems encountered by some dyslexics may be alleviated using computer techniques. In: Proceedings of the Fourth International ACM Conference on Assistive Technologies (Assets 2000), pp. 85–91. ACM, New York (2000)
15. US Access Board. Section 508 Homepage: Electronic and Information Technology, http://www.access-board.gov/508.html
16. Santana, V.F., Oliveira, R., Almeida, L.D.A., Baranauskas, M.C.C.: Web Accessibility and People with Dyslexia: A Survey on Techniques and Guidelines. In: Proceedings of the International Cross-Disciplinary Conference on Web Accessibility (W4A 2012). ACM, New York (2012)
17. Calabrèse, A., Bernard, J.B., Hoffart, L., Faure, G., Barouch, F., Conrath, J., Castet, E.: Small effect of interline spacing on maximal reading speed in low-vision patients with central field loss irrespective of scotoma size. Invest. Ophthalmol. Vis. Sci. 51(2), 1247–1254 (2010)
18. Hartley, J.: What does it say? Text design, medical information, and older readers. In: Park, D.C., Morrell, R.W., Shifren, K. (eds.) Processing of Medical Information in Aging Patients, pp. 233–248. Lawrence Erlbaum Associates, Mahwah (1999)
19. Bix, L.: The Elements of Text and Message Design and Their Impact on Message Legibility: A Literature Review. Journal of Design Communication (4) (2002), http://scholar.lib.vt.edu/ejournals/JDC/Spring-2002/bix
20. Kitchel, J.E. APH Guidelines for Print Document Design, http://www.aph.org/edresearch/lpguide.html
21. Arditi, A.: Making Text Legible: Designing for People with Partial Sight. Lighthouse International, New York (1999, 2002)
22. British Dyslexia Association. Dyslexia Style Guide, http://www.bdadyslexia.org.uk/about-dyslexia/further-information/dyslexia-style-guide.html
23. CCLVI. Best Practices and Guidelines for Large Print Documents used by the Low Vision Community, http://www.cclvi.org/large-print-guidelines.html
24. Morrell, R.W., Dailey, S.R., Feldman, C., Mayhorn, C.G., Echt, K.V.: Older adults and information technology: A compendium of scientific research and Web site ac-cessibility guidelines. National Institute on Aging, Bethesda (2002)
25. The Center for the Partially Sighted. Print Guidelines, http://low-vision.org/en/Print_Guidelines
26. Holt, B.: Creating Senior-Friendly Web Sites. Center For Medicare Education Issue Brief 1(4), 1–8 (2000)
27. Rainger, P.: A Dyslexic Perspective on e-Content Accessibility. JISC TechDis. (2003), http://www.jisctechdis.ac.uk/techdis/resources/detail/learnersmatter/Jan03_Dyslexia
28. About Adobe Reader X, http://help.adobe.com/en_US/reader/using/WS4bebcd66a74275c3-7d28390112a81b3ebff-8000.html

Using Layout Applications for Creation of Accessible PDF: Technical and Mental Obstacles When Creating PDF/UA from Adobe Indesign CS 5.5

Olaf Drümmer

Callas Software GmbH / Axaio Software GmbH

Abstract. While substantial progress has been made in widely used applications like Microsoft Word or Adobe Indesign, when it comes to creating accessible PDF documents, a number of problems still exist that make it difficult even for motivated users in a real world production situation to invest additional effort to create decently tagged PDF. Improved features and enhanced user interface in these applications could contribute substantially to increase the likelihood that creators of print-oriented PDF files take the extra work on them to also make these PDF files accessible.

Keywords: tagged PDF, accessible PDF, accessibility, PDF/UA.

1 Introduction

Accessibility for PDF documents has recently seen an increase in interest – Microsoft has been chairing the ISO committee that develops the PDF/UA standard, Adobe has introduced new or extended existing features in Indesign CS 5.5 to make creation of tagged PDF easier for users who are not tagging experts, and the PDF Association has recently launched a PDF/UA Competence Center. The author of this paper sees this as a clear sign that leading software vendors are heavily investing in better accessibility support for PDF.

Nevertheless there is no guarantee that such development efforts necessarily result in a higher number of accessible PDFs being created, or that such accessible PDFs reach a reasonable level of tagging quality. The good news though is that the upcoming international standard for accessible PDF, called PDF/UA-1 (ISO 14289-1, expected to be approved summer 2012) provides a benchmark against which the quality of accessible PDFs can be measured. It also contains requirements for PDF readers and assistive technology claiming to support PDF/UA.

In the field of professional print-oriented layout production, Adobe Indesign CS 5.5 is the first tool that makes creation of a reasonably well tagged PDF a viable option «for the rest of us», both in terms of required specific domain knowledge as well as in extra time spent preparing the document for export to suitably tagged PDF, including a reduction in possibly necessary post-processing.

In addition to that, and building on Indesign's new features, an Indesign plug-in «MadeToTag» by axaio software sets out to fill the knowledge and productivity gaps left still left in Adobe Indesign CS 5.5.

K. Miesenberger et al. (Eds.): ICCHP 2012, Part I, LNCS 7382, pp. 610–616, 2012.
© Springer-Verlag Berlin Heidelberg 2012

2   Concept

The mere fact that a tool set exists does not by itself has an impact on the way people get things done or not. There are several main vectors that impact the usefulness of a tool set, some of which are not necessarily inherent to its core features:

- the degree to which a user understands what the main reasons are why it is worthwhile to achieve a certain result
- the degree to which a user understands how well and how comprehensively the functionality of a tool set correlates with the intended result
- the degree to which guidance is provided how to fully and in a clearly detectable manner achieve an intended result by using the tool set
- the degree to which information is provided to how well and how completely an intended result has been achieved

3   Methodology

Partially based on the master thesis «Barrierefreiheit in PDF-Dokumenten – Welche spezifischen Anforderungen werden an barrierefreie PDFs gestellt, und wie werden sie umgesetzt?» («Accessibility in PDF documents – What specific requirements apply to accessible PDFs, and how are they met?») by Bettina Woock (in progress), and partially based on the beta test of the Indesign plug-in «MadeToTag» carried out by axaio software, this paper discusses technical and mental obstacles that impede creation of suitably tagged PDF in Adobe Indesign CS 5.5, and proposes strategies how to enable the average user in charge of print-oriented layout creation to create accessible PDF documents with as little extra effort as possible without sacrificing tagging quality. The following two aspects are investigated in this project:

- if layout production users are educated in a 30 minute introduction about how users with disabilities may benefit from tagged PDF, how does that impact their willingness to learn tagging techniques, and how does it impact the quality of their tagging results
- if a layout production person is instructed how to judge the effect of a certain aspect of tagging content in the layout application, how does that impact their willingness to learn tagging techniques, and how does it impact the quality of their tagging results

It is to be appointed out that at the time of writing the major portion of the field research of Bettina Woock's Master Thesis is still to be carried out, and the beta test for «MadeToTag» is still continuing, so that this paper can only provide preliminary insights based on initial and mostly heuristic research and feedback from the beta test.

4   Contribution

In the past years, the field of creating tagged PDF has been the domain of a comparably small group of experienced specialists, not to the least due to the fact that adequate and

efficient tools have been rare until today. From numerous discussions with layout production people the author is confident, that the majority of layout production people
would be more than happy to 'go the extra mile' and carry out tasks that allow for
creation of decently tagged PDF. The main obstacles though are so far

- lack of efficient and easy to use tools; this aspect is expected to improve over the
  coming year or two, given the substantial efforts and investments by major as well
  as smaller specialist software vendors in this field
- lack of understanding, most notably why certain steps have to be carried out, how
  to best go about them e.g. by understanding the relative relevance of the various
  aspects of creating tagged PDF, and when to know for sure when a given job can
  be considered completed.

If it can be proven how important it is in the field of creating tagged PDF to make
layout production users understand what to do and why to do it that should help increase suitable awareness among those decision makers who allocate resources for
education and training.

5   Preliminary Results

Mostly during the beta test of the «MadeToTag» plug-in, some preliminary results
could be collected.

5.1   Why Tag, and Which Aspects Are Most Relevant?

The knowledge regarding accessible PDF documents, if present at all, typically boils
down to two aspects

- Content must be tagged with tags for headings or paragraphs
- For images, alternative text must be provided

The main use case is a screen reading situation, but not necessarily in the sense how
for example blind people actually use a screen reader, but rather as a 'read this text
aloud' feature, as provided in Acrobat or on the operating system level of Mac OS X.
   While some knowledge is usually better than no knowledge this level of knowledge is missing main aspects, why and how PDFs should be made accessible. For
example, the only thing a read aloud feature could do with headlines is to read them
slightly differently than other text. The navigational value of headings and heading
levels is not recognized.
   Once users are confronted with the way how a blind person actually does use a
screen reader, they begin to realize important additional information:

- First and foremost, it is important to find out what a document is about - typically
  to be communicated at least minimally through the document title, as opposed to
  just the file name

- The next important aspect for any non-trivial document is, to find your way. The best way to do this is to consult the headings, both by sequentially going through all of them as well as by taking advantage of the structure implied by heading levels.
- Especially for longer documents it is a very welcome option to be able find out about special parts of content, like images, table, lists, links, form fields, etc. as this gives a user relying on AT additional insights about what to expect from the document.

It is amazing to see how a 30 minute demo can open the eyes (pun intended) of layout production people who are not yet familiar with accessibility for electronic documents. This knowledge also makes it possible for creators of PDFs to understand a suitable sequence of steps to be carried out:

- Make sure there are suitable tags for all relevant content
- Headings are especially important as they are the spine of the document
- Where special types of contents are present, tag them accordingly; at the same time while it is understood that tagging lists as lists is a good idea it could happen that smaller lists with just two or three items are not deemed to be very important: in other words, it might be OK to have them as a sequence of regular paragraphs; nevertheless for any longer list it goes without saying they should be tagged as lists

At the same time there are aspects where attendees of a short demonstration really begin to struggle. Examples are topics like footnotes or tables:

- Footnotes, as well as endnotes, are already often not intuitively and flexibly implemented for print-oriented documents, even though such features nominally exist in text processing and layout applications. This implies there is already a tendency to avoid them. The extra challenge introduced by the fact that footnote features are even less intuitively implemented when it comes to creating accessible PDF, increases the tendency to rather avoid footnotes, or their proper formatting and tagging.
- For tables the requirements established by both WCAG 2.0 as well as PDF/UA-1 go far beyond what most users would be ready to consider relevant or applicable to the real world. The main challenge is the fact that the majority of tables in printed material already contradict one or several accessibility principles. In addition, many tables are not even easily accessible for sighted users – so why serve non-sighted users substantially better than sighted users? In this context it is also somehow scary that the excellent e-book «Design and Build Accessible PDF Tables» by Ted Page needs a whopping estimated 75 pages to discuss how to get tables right for an accessible PDF when using tools like Microsoft Word, Adobe Indesign or Adobe Acrobat. For many problems Ted Page's advice is to redesign the tables altogether – not an option that is available in a typical production situation.

5.2   When Am I Done, and Did I Do Well Enough?

One other important aspect in a real world production situation is the question: How do I know when I am done? When have I done enough so that my result can be considered to be finished and of acceptable quality?

It is important to see that in a normal layout production situation there is no time to run elaborate evaluations. Rather it is essential to have a list of criteria to meet, and to have clear indicators, whether a given criterion is met.

Just as an example – users will easily understand why it is relevant to provide alternative text for non-text content. It is less obvious to determine when enough has been done such that all images, graphics etc. are covered, as this is complicated by the fact that there often are also image-like artefacts, for which alternative text is not necessary, and by the lack of features in at least some of the programs to simply inform the user whether any images are left that are still in need of alternative text.

In addition, it is not only challenging to check whether all non-text content has been addressed, it is also cumbersome to carry out quality assurance, in the form of reviewing all alternative text entries in a straightforward way.

As a consequence, tagged PDFs on this background and created by non-expert users who only have received a short training, will typically have alternative text for most images, but some will have been missed, and in addition there are lots of problems with the alternative text – it tends to be phrased inconsistently, the frequency of spelling errors is relatively high, and stupid problems like place holder text are overlooked.

Quality assurance tools like the free PDF Accessibility Checkers can help to compensate for these issues, but as they are used after production, and are not available inside the authoring program and thus during creation of files, they are experienced

- as being an unpleasant extra step,
- fixing something is cumbersome because the export to tagged PDF procedure has to be carried out again
- fixing one problem might create a new problem
- sometimes after export to tagged PDF additional fine tuning has to be carried out before the quality assurance step can be applied; if then a problem is identified, not only has the export to be done again, but also the fine tuning step – which could in itself is a possible source of new errors

While it will always be a good idea to take advantage of a comprehensive quality assurance tool *after* creation of tagged PDF has been completed, it is obvious that at least for all major aspects of tagged content creation, quality assurance features should be available *during* creation.

5.3   Speed, Instant Feedback and Instant Gratification

Several beta testers have changed their mind about the effort required to make a PDF (reasonably) accessible after they have tried out a combination of features in Adobe Indesign CS 5.5 (most notably the Article panel that lets a user arrange page objects in logical reading order without having to change the layout itself) and in MadeToTag (most notably the colorized highlighting feedback for assigned standard tags and a generically formatted preview of an "article", both combined with the option to use keyboard shortcuts). The following factors played the main role:

- Speed
  - when assigning tags to text content
  - because of possibility to use keyboard shortcuts for assigning tags
  - because of possibility to use keyboard shortcuts for creating logical order for articles
- Instant feedback
  - through color coding reflecting assigned tags
  - through generically styled preview of articles
- Instant gratification
  - users felt in control and could continuously track their own progress
  - users were surprised how quickly they could complete the task

It is to be noted that the test material used in these cases were information brochures (four DIN A 4 sized pages) or articles in a magazine (three to eight pages).

5.4   Avoidance of Learning Effort, Decrease of Motivation

In general we observed that users were in principle very open minded towards adding a little bit of extra effort to achieve added accessibility for the documents they were working on. It always very quickly became obvious though that anything that required any of the following would reduce their motivation to almost zero:

- explanation of a single given aspect requires more than a minute or two of explanations; example: showing how to assign tags to style sheets in Indesign and explaining why tags have to be set separately for PDF and EPUB (even though creation of EPUB was not at all a task to be carried out).
- the value added through extra effort is not obvious; example: additional step to be carried out in Acrobat Pro in order to set Tab order to follow Document Structure in the exported PDF
- effort to carry out a necessary task requires a non-trivial sequence of interactions with menus, dialogs and the document; example: selecting images in Indesign and entering or reviewing alternative text
- lack of immediate visual feedback for current state of the document regarding the aspect or task at hand; example: there is no direct mechanism in Indesign that informs a user whether all text has properly assigned tags, and which tag has been assigned to a given portion of text.

These observations make it quite obvious that a number of requirements to learn something complicated go back to limitations in the tools used. Once tools offer features implemented in straightforward ways, the learning curve can be reduced substantially, and users could be freed up to learn what they still may have to learn: basic principles of accessible documents.

6   What's Next

The author uses the findings of this project for the development and ongoing improvement of axaio software's new product «MadeToTag». He believes that adoption of the PDF/UA standard in the real world in general, and the success of this tool, as well as any other such tool or other authoring software, depends on soft factors like suitable mental preparation of users at least as much as on the technical qualities of the software itself. In addition, such tools should ideally be designed in a way to make it easier for users to see the effect of their tagging efforts in an intuitive fashion, and make them understand the direct relationship between a given tagging task and the outcome in the form of respective properties in the resulting tagged PDF.

As an active member of the PDF Association's PDF/UA working group, the author intends to continue to freely share the results of his findings, including publication of articles and sample tutorials, throughout 2012, to help other developers, trainers and users to recognize, how they can make a difference in the world of tagged PDF.

References

1. ISO/DIS 14289-1.2:2011; Document management applications — Electronic document file format enhancement for accessibility — Part 1: Use of ISO 32000-1 (PDF/UA-1), http://www.iso.org
2. Web Content Accessibility Guidelines (WCAG) 2.0; W3C, http://www.w3.org/TR/WCAG/
3. PDF Techniques for WCAG 2.0; W3C, http://www.w3.org/WAI/GL/WCAG20-TECHS/pdf.html
4. Accessibility @ Adobe: Preparing Accessible PDFs with Adobe InDesign CS5.5- Part I/II/III; Adobe TV. Adobe Systems Inc. (December 6, 2011), http://tv.adobe.com/watch/accessibility-adobe/part-1-new-accessibility-features-in-indesign-cs55/
5. Johnson, D., Baker, D., Kassuba, L., Austen, D.: Community Insights: Ensuring Your PDF is Accessible; Webinar (June 1, 2011), http://blogs.adobe.com/acrobat/2011/06/community-insights-ensuring-your-pdf-is-accessible.html
6. Axaio software introduces public beta version of new product – MadeToTag: Much easier, much faster and more reliable preparation of Adobe InDesign files for export to tagged PDF. axaio software GmbH (January 27, 2012), http://www.axaio.com/doku.php/en:news
7. Page, T.: Design and Build Accessible PDF Tables, 1st edn., March 5. BookBaby (2012)

Validity and Semantics – Two Essential Parts of a Backbone for an Automated PDF/UA Compliance Check for PDF Documents

Markus Erle[1] and Samuel Hofer[2]

[1] Wertewerk, Tuebingen, Germany
erle@wertewerk.de
[2] xyMedia GmbH, Volketswil, Switzerland
hofer@xymedia.ch

Abstract. The paper shows why validity and semantics matters for a PDF/UA evaluation concept and how an automated checking tool can address this. In order to translate machine-testable requirements into checking criteria a special query language is developed called PQL (PDF Query Language). PQL will be implemented in PDF Accessibility Checker PAC 2, the first and free PDF/UA compliance checker crowd-funded by the foundation "Access for all".

Keywords: PDF, WCAG 2.0, PDF/UA, document accessibility, validity, semantics, checking, PAC2, PDF accessibility checker, foundation "Access for all".

1   Introduction

The new standard for accessible PDF documents PDF/UA (ISO 14289-1) [8] sets a worldwide standard for both PDF documents and PDF authoring as well as PDF viewers and assistive technology (AT). For a successful implementation and increasing acceptance of PDF/UA automated checking tools and easy-to-use checking workflows are essential. In a first step we identified validity as a prerequisite and semantics as fundamental for a PDF/UA Compliance Check. You can only check a PDF document for PDF/UA conformity if it is a valid PDF. The semantics is built on validity. This paper deals therefore with the following questions? How important is validity for accessible PDF documents? How can the document structure be checked even by users with basic accessibility knowledge? How can the PDF Accessibility Checker (PAC) [6] – the tool with the most advanced validity checking – be improved to a PDF/UA Compliance Check according to validity and semantics?

2   The State of the Art

Available checking tools for accessible PDF documents are not capable to check for PDF/UA Compliance yet. According to the 3 steps of quality assurance for accessible

K. Miesenberger et al. (Eds.): ICCHP 2012, Part I, LNCS 7382, pp. 617–620, 2012.
© Springer-Verlag Berlin Heidelberg 2012

PDF documents described by Erle [2] it is clear, that not every requirement can be checked automatically. But tools can support the evaluator in every step:

- 1. Automated checking
- 2. Manual checking („the visual check")
- 3. User testing

The free available PDF Accessibility Checker (PAC) [6] which is recommended by the W3C [10] is the checking tool with the most advanced validity check and one of its features – the preview – supports evaluators in checking the document structure of a PDF without the need to work with a PDF editing tool or to analyze the PDF tag tree.

3   Our Approach and Results

In a first step we carve out the essential requirements of the new standard PDF/UA and how they can be transferred to automated measurable success criteria. We focus on 2 aspects: validity [1] (correct syntax of the PDF and especially of the PDF tag tree according to ISO 32000-1 [7] and ISO 14289-1 [8]) and correct semantics. In a second step we try to identify the issues that have to be improved in order to develop PAC 2 as a PDF/UA Compliance Checker.

3.1   Is Validity Really Relevant for Accessible PDF Documents?

The new standard PDF/UA emphasizes validity as an essential prerequisite for accessible PDF documents: "Conforming files shall adhere to all requirements of ISO 32000-1:2008 as modified by this part of ISO 14289. A conforming file may include any valid ISO 32000-1:2008 feature that is not explicitly forbidden by this part of ISO 14289."[1]

Sometimes even experts in the field of PDF accessibility pretend, that success criteria 4.1.1 of WCAG 2.0 [11] is not applicable to PDF because PDF is not a markup language. But in order to check conformity automatically validity can help. And guideline 4.1 can be understood in that sense, that a PDF document has to be valid - otherwise it cannot be compatible "with current and future user agents, including assistive technologies". Hence, as a starting point we take the validity check integrated in PAC 1 and identify the issues that have to be improved.

3.2   How to Check the Validity of the Syntax

In order to check the validity of the PDF syntax a special tool is necessary. Therefore we develop a new query language called PQL. PQL stands for PDF Query Language. In some aspects the concept of PQL is similar to XPath [12]. Shortly you can say: what is XPath for XML, that is PQL for PDF.

---

[1]   ISO/DIS 14289-1, 6.2 Conforming files.

The main purpose of PQL is to address parts of a PDF document. PQL enables to select objects from a PDF document by a variety of criteria. It is based on a structural representation of the PDF document, and provides the ability to navigate around the structure.

In a PDF document there are 9 types of objects e.g. dictionaries or arrays which are used to build structures. PQL allows to define checks which validate these structures. Several checks can be bundled to check sets. They in turn can be part of check sets itself. One top level check set will be PDF/UA (universal accessibility), another top level check set can be WCAG (Web Content Accessibility Guidelines) 2.0.

With PQL it is possible to check the validity of the general PDF syntax. The syntax of the semantics is part of that general PDF syntax. The correctness of the semantics itself cannot be checked automatically because of the corresponding content decisions that only can be made by a human.

3.3   How to Evaluate the Semantics or How to Support an Easy Check for Semantics?

Semantics are an essential requirement for accessible PDF documents. [4], [8] PDF/UA declares: "The accessibility of a document is dependent on the inclusion of a variety of semantic information in a document such as (but not limited to) machine-recoverable text presented in a declared language, logical structure of content, and organization of that content in pages, sections, and paragraphs. Semantic information can also contain a variety of descriptive metadata, such as alternative text for images."[2]

The evaluation of the document structure according to correct semantics cannot be performed by automated tools. But a special preview – we call it screen reader preview – can support the evaluator to judge whether a document structure fits to the content of the document. In PAC 1 there is a first implementation of such a preview feature. [5] In a next step we evaluate it and try to identify the issues that have to be improved.

4   The Impact and Future Work

Without validity it is not possible to guarantee that accessible PDF documents can be parsed by standard conforming viewers and assistive technologies. Without correct semantics it is not possible to create high quality accessible PDF documents that are usable for people with disabilities or adaptable and transformable to different presentation modes or formats.

The Foundation "Access for all" with support of the PDF Association initiated a crowd funding for realizing PAC 2 as a free available and easy-to-use PDF/UA Compliance Check.[9] The results of this paper will be incorporated into the development.

---

[2] ISO/DIS 14289-1, Introduction.

References

1. Chisholm, W.: Validity and Accessibility, http://www.w3.org/WAI/GL/2005/06/validity-accessibility.html
2. Erle, M.: PDF umsetzen und prüfen. In: Hellbusch, J.E., Probiesch, K.: Barrierefreiheit verstehen und umsetzen. Webstandards für ein zugängliches und nutzbares Internet, 433–516 (2011)
3. Johnson, D.: Each PDF Page is a Painting, http://www.appligent.com/talkingpdf-eachpdfpageisapainting
4. Johnson, D.: Objects and Semantics, http://www.appligent.com/talkingpdf-objects-and-semantics
5. Johnson, D.: Review PAC (PDF Accessibility Checker) 1.1, http://www.appligent.com/talkingpdf-PDFAccessibilityCheckerReview
6. PDF Accessibility Checker (PAC), http://www.access-for-all.ch/en/pdf-lab/pdf-accessibility-checker-pac.html
7. PDF Reference / ISO 32000-1, http://www.adobe.com/devnet/pdf/pdf_reference.html
8. PDF/UA (Universal Accessibility) / ISO 14289-1, http://pdf.editme.com/PDFUA
9. Foundation "Access for all", a Swiss non-profit organization, and their crowd funding for PDF Accessibility Checker PAC 2, http://www.access-for-all.ch/en/pdf-lab/pdf-accessibility-checker-pac/donation-pac-2.html
10. WCAG 2.0-Techniques for PDF, http://www.w3.org/WAI/GL/WCAG20-TECHS/pdf.html
11. Web Content Accessibility Guidelines WCAG 2.0, http://www.w3.org/TR/WCAG/
12. XML Path Language (XPath) Version 1.0, http://www.w3.org/TR/1999/REC-xpath-19991116/

Two Software Plugins for the Creation
of Fully Accessible PDF Documents
Based on a Flexible Software Architecture

Alireza Darvishy, Thomas Leemann, and Hans-Peter Hutter

ZHAW Zurich University of Applied Sciences
InIT Institute of Applied Information Technology
Winterthur, Switzerland
{alireza.darvishy,thomas.leemann,hans-peter.hutter}@zhaw.ch

Abstract. This paper presents one of two new software plugins for MS PowerPoint and Word documents which allow the analysis of accessibility issues and consequently the generation of fully accessible PDF documents. The document authors using these plugins require no specific accessibility knowledge. This paper introduces the user interface of the Microsoft PowerPoint accessibility plugin. The plugins are based on a flexible software architecture concept that allows the automatic generation of fully accessible PDF documents originating from various authoring tools, such as Adobe InDesign [1], Word and PowerPoint [2], [3]. The accessibility plugin software implemented allows authors to check for accessibility issues while creating their documents and add the additional semantic information needed to generate a fully accessible PDF document.

Keywords: Document accessibility, automatic generation of accessible PDF, screen reader, visual impairment, accessibility, tagged PDF, software architecture, PowerPoint and Word documents.

1 Introduction

There are millions of PDF documents on the internet which are inaccessible to users with visual impairments using screen readers [4]. In many cases, authors use authoring tools, such as Microsoft PowerPoint and Word [2], [3], to create these PDF documents. But all too often the resulting PDFs are not correctly tagged and therefore have to be manually post-processed in order to be turned into accessible PDFs. This is inefficient, very time consuming, and tedious. In addition, a separate solution is needed for each authoring tool because there is no software solution that can be used with different authoring tools. A flexible software architecture was introduced in [6] to overcome these problems. The suggested architecture can be extended to include any authoring tool capable of creating PDF documents. For each authoring tool, a software accessibility plugin must be implemented that analyzes the logical structure of the document and creates an XML representation of it. This XML file is used in combination with an untagged non-accessible PDF to create an accessible PDF version of the document.

K. Miesenberger et al. (Eds.): ICCHP 2012, Part I, LNCS 7382, pp. 621–624, 2012.

As of now, two software accessibility plugins for Microsoft Word and PowerPoint have been implemented based on the suggested architecture.

The typical accessibility issues that arise when creating a PDF document with an authoring tool such as Microsoft PowerPoint or Word are e.g. missing alternative text for images, missing table headers, heading structure and document language, incorrect reading order, etc.

Although newer versions of Microsoft PowerPoint and Word [5] provide facilities to overcome some of the above-mentioned issues, authors still are required to have specific accessibility and authoring tool knowledge in order to fix them.

The implemented plugins for PowerPoint and Word require no special knowledge either of accessibility issues or of fixing them.

2   User Interface

We discuss two important parts of the user interface of the PowerPoint accessibility plugin.

The *Accessibility Tab* (Figure 1) includes the following functions:

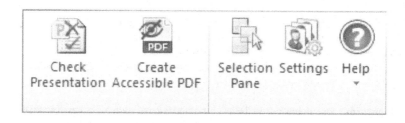

Fig. 1. Accessibility Tab

- *Check Presentation*: This button launches the accessibility check for a presentation. It opens the *Accessibility Issues Pane* (Figure 2).
- *Create Accessible PDF*: This button is used to create an accessible PDF document from the current document. Unlike the PowerPoint function Create PDF/XPS document, here, additional information is added to the PDF document during the creation process to make the document accessible.
- *Selection Pane*: This button opens the Selection and Visibility pane. In this pane you can change the order of the objects on a slide and hide objects.
- *Settings*: This button is used to view the settings for the accessibility checker.

The Accessibility Issues Pane (Fig. 2) appears when the accessibility check has been launched via the Check Presentation button. It shows all accessibility issues found in the current document.

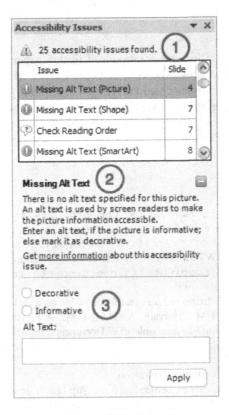

Fig. 2. Accessibility Issues Pane

1. The *List of Accessibility Issues* shows all accessibility issues currently found in the document. It consists of three or four columns: issue status, issue type, item name and slide number.
2. The *Help Descriptions* provide a brief description of the accessibility issue and what needs to be done in order to fix it. For certain issues, hyperlinks ("more information") provide further details on the issue.
3. The A*rea for Fixing the Issue* may look different, depending on the issue category. Where possible, it provides a quick and easy way of taking care of the issue.

3   Using the PowerPoint Plugin

The standard procedure for applying the PowerPoint accessibility plugin is as follows:

1. Create your presentation as usual.
4. Switch to the Accessibility Tab and run an accessibility check by clicking the Check Presentation button.
5. Fix any accessibility issues in whichever order you choose.
6. Create an accessible PDF document (Create Accessible PDF button).

4   Conclusion

The PowerPoint accessibility plugin introduced in this paper is based on a flexible software architecture that allows the same software framework to be used with different authoring tools. The implemented PowerPoint accessibility plugin has been tested by some first users; the results are very positive. The accessibility plugin is available for free in four languages, namely German, English, French and Italian, and can be downloaded from InIT/ZHAW [7].

References

1. Adobe InDesign, http://www.adobe.com/products/indesign/
2. Microsoft Office PowerPoint, http://office.microsoft.com/powerpoint/
3. Microsoft Office Word, http://office.microsoft.com/word/
4. Freedom Scientific JAWS for Windows Screen Reading Software, http://www.freedomscientific.com/products/fs/jaws-product-page.asp
5. Microsoft Office 2010, http://us1.office2010beta.microsoft.com
6. Darvishy, A., Hutter, H.-P., Horvath, A., Dorigo, M.: A Flexible Software Architecture Concept for the Creation of Accessible PDF Documents. In: Miesenberger, K., Klaus, J., Zagler, W., Karshmer, A. (eds.) ICCHP 2010. LNCS, vol. 6179, pp. 47–52. Springer, Heidelberg (2010)
7. PowerPoint Accessibility Plugin Download, http://www.zhaw.ch/fileadmin/user_upload/engineering/_Institute_und_Zentren/INIT/HII/Accessibility/AccessibilityAddins/MSOfficeAccessibilityAddInsSetup.zip

Privacy Preserving Automatic Fall Detection for Elderly Using RGBD Cameras

Chenyang Zhang[1], Yingli Tian[1], and Elizabeth Capezuti[2]

[1] Media Lab, The City University of New York (CUNY), City College
New York, NY USA
{czhang10,ytian}@ccny.cuny.edu
[2] College of Nursing, New York University, New York, NY USA
ec65@nyu.edu

Abstract. In this paper, we propose a new privacy preserving automatic fall detection method to facilitate the independence of older adults living in the community, reduce risks, and enhance the quality of life at home activities of daily living (ADLs) by using RGBD cameras. Our method can recognize 5 activities including standing, fall from standing, fall from chair, sit on chair, and sit on floor. The main analysis is based on the 3D depth information due to the advantages of handling illumination changes and identity protection. If the monitored person is out of the range of a 3D camera, RGB video is employed to continue the activity monitoring. Furthermore, we design a hierarchy classification schema to robustly recognize 5 activities. Experimental results on our database collected under conditions with normal lighting, without lighting, out of depth range demonstrate the effectiveness of the proposal method.

Keywords: Privacy Preserving, Fall Detection, Video Monitoring, Elderly, Activities of Daily Living.

1 Introduction

In 2008, about 39 million Americans were 65 years old or above. This number is likely to increase rapidly as the baby boomer generation ages. The older population increased elevenfold between 1900 and 1994, while the nonelderly increased only threefold, and the oldest old (persons of 85 or older) is the fastest growing segment of the older adult population [1]. The proportion requiring personal assistance with everyday activities increases with age, ranging from 9 percent for those who are 65 to 69 years old to 50 percent for those who are 85 or older. Furthermore, the likelihood of dementia or Alzheimer's disease increases with age over 65 [2]. In 2006, there were 26.6 million sufferers worldwide. These data indicate that the demand for caregivers will reach far beyond the number of individuals able to provide care. One solution to this growing problem is to find ways to enable elders to live independently and safely in their own homes for as long as possible [3]. Recent technology developments in computer vision, digital cameras, radio frequency identification, and computers make it possible to assist the independent living of older adults by developing safety awareness technologies to analyze the activities of elders of daily living (ADLs) at home. Important activities that

K. Miesenberger et al. (Eds.): ICCHP 2012, Part I, LNCS 7382, pp. 625–633, 2012.

effect independence include ADLs (e.g., taking medications, getting into and out of bed, eating, bathing, grooming/hygiene, dressing, socializing, doing laundry, cooking, cleaning). Among these activities, a few are rated as very difficult to monitor, including taking medication, falling and eating [4]. In this paper, we focus on falling detection and recognize it from other similar activities such as sit on floor, *etc.*.

In this paper, we develop a privacy preserving activity analysis framework to recognize five activities related to falling event. Instead of using traditional video surveillance cameras, we utilize Kinect RGBD cameras, which are more easily accepted by older adults and their friends since it is designed for entertainment purposes. Analysis based on depth information has advantages of handling illumination changes and identity protection. If the monitored person is out of the range of 3D camera, RGB video is employed to continue the monitoring. From 3D depth information, kinematic model based features are extracted which consist of two parts: 1) structure similarity and 2) vertical height of the monitored people. In 2D RGB model, we integrate background subtraction and human tracking for activity monitoring and represent actions by quantized histograms of width-height ratios of the monitoring regions. To fulfill the need of privacy protection, only the foreground masks are used for visualization. In the classification phase, we design a hierarchy classification schema to robustly recognize the category of the activities. A comparison with traditional "1-*vs.*-all" classifier structure is performed both theoretically and experimentally. Experimental results demonstrate that our proposed framework is robust and efficient for fall detection.

2   Related Work

Video-based human activity recognition is a hot research area in computer vision to help people with special needs. Nait-Charif *et al.* developed a computer-vision based system to recognize abnormal activity in daily life [5] in a supportive home environment. The system tracked activity of subjects and summarized frequent active regions to learn a model of normal activity. It detected falling events as abnormal activity, which is very important in patient monitoring systems. Unlike using location clues in [5], Wang *et al.* [6] proposed to use gestures by applying a deformable body parts model [7] to detect lying people in a single image, which is a strong cue of falling event.

Different from traditional RGB channel, recognizing activities using depth images has been demonstrated more straightforward and effective in recent years ([9], [10], and [11]), especially after Microsoft released the software development kit (SDK) for Kinect cameras [12]. RGBD images, in fact, are more similar to the visual perception mechanism of human beings since human has two eyes, which enable the depth information. Li *et al.* [10] proposed to use bag of 3D points to represent and recognize human actions which enables 3D silhouette matching. Hidden Markov Model (HMM) is employed with depth images to effectively recognize human activities [11]. In this paper, our goal is to effectively recognize activities related to falling from both 3D depth and 2D appearance information while preserving privacy of subjects.

3   Method of Automatic Fall Detection

3.1   Kinematic Model Based Feature Extraction From Depth Channel

Selecting Joints from Major Body Parts. In Microsoft Kinect SDK [12], there are 20 body joints tracked for each person in each depth frame. Among them, we choose 8 joints on head and torso since other joints (on limbs) introduce more noise than useful information to distinguish whether a person is falling. As shown in Fig. 1 (a), the 8 joints keep a stable structure no matter a person is standing or sitting. However, the coordinates of these joints are no longer reliable when a person falls. Based on this observation, we compute the difference cost $C(\xi)$ of given joints ξ as the first part of our kinematic features.

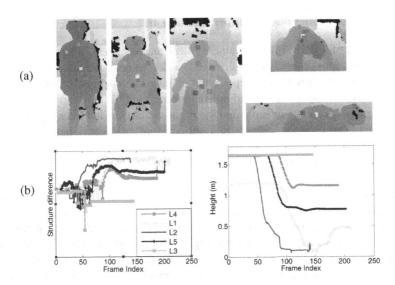

Fig. 1. (a) Structures of selected joints are stable for standing and sitting poses, but unstable for falling. (b) **Left:** logarithm of structure difference in of each event. 2. **Right:** Height sequences in each event. Five activities to be recognized are shown in Table 1.

Table 1. Five activities to be recognized in this work

L_1	fall from chair	L_2	fall from standing	L_3	standing
L_4	sit on chair	L_5	sit on floor		

Computation of Kinematic Features: As shown in Fig. 1 (a), "falling" poses cause much larger deformation on the joint structures than other "non-fall" poses. We define the structure difference cost $C(\xi)$ as following:

$$C(\xi) = \sum_{i=1}^{n} \sum_{j=i+1}^{n} \|\theta(\xi_i, \xi_j) - \theta(\emptyset_i, \emptyset_j)\|, \tag{1}$$

$$\theta(i, j) = \arcsin(\frac{i_x - j_x}{dist(i, j)})/2\pi, \tag{2}$$

where $\theta(\xi_i, \xi_j)$ and $\theta(\emptyset_i, \emptyset_j)$ denote the angles between two joints i and j on two skeletons ξ and $\emptyset$, respectively, the geometry distance between two joints i and j is denoted as $dist(i, j)$.

The structure difference costs (in logarithm) of different activities in video sequences are displayed in Fig. 1 (b) (left graph). Red ("fall from standing") and yellow ("fall from chair") curves indicate significant costs as expected. We calculate the mean μ and variance σ of each activity as the first two feature elements.

Another feature for activity recognition is person height. As shown in the right graph of Fig. 1 (b). We take the highest value h and the minimum value l among person heights in all frame as the last two elements in our feature vector. Finally our kinematic feature vector is denoted as $[\mu, \sigma, h, l]^T$.

3.2   Appearance Model Based Feature Extraction

The depth range of a RGBD Kinect camera is less than 4 meters. When people are out of the range of depth sensor, we employ RGB video to continue human tracking and propose a histogram based feature representation based on background subtraction.

Person tracking by background subtraction: Our background subtraction includes two steps (as shown in Eq. 3 and 4): frame difference and tracking. Frame difference is to obtain changed area where a falling event most likely happens, which is given as follows:

$$D_i := \|I_{i-\tau} - I_i\| \bigcap \|I_{i+\tau} - I_i\|, \tag{3}$$

where D_i denotes the difference mask of the ith frame. I_i denotes the intensity of current frame. $I_{i-\tau}$ and $I_{i+\tau}$ denote predecessor and successor with step τ of I_i. After morphology processing such as median filtering and connected component, a roughly foreground region is obtained as shown in Fig. 2 (a). Since static gestures may result in failure in foreground detection such as lying on the floor, we apply a simple merging strategy to merge current mask and former mask, which is formulated as following:

$$M_i := D_i \frac{1}{1 + e^{-(S-\lambda)}} + M_{i-1} \frac{1}{1 + e^{S-\lambda}}, \tag{4}$$

where S denotes the number of pixels in current foreground mask and λ denotes a parameter we set as a threshold to decide whether to update mask or keep former mask. M_i denotes foreground mask of the ith frame and D_i is the same as in Eq. 3. A sample result of our merging strategy is shown in Fig. 2 (b).

Histogram Represented Features: We observe that the ratio between the width and height of a foreground bounding box can effectively indicator a falling activity. We represent an activity by a histogram of the width-height ratios during a video sequence.

(a)   (b)

Fig. 2. (a) Fragmentary mask due to static legs. (b) Integral mask after merging.

3.3 Hierarchy Classification

Let $\mathbf{L} \equiv \{L_1, L_2, ..., L_k\}$ be the labels of a set of activity categories. If each pair of categories requires one classifier to distinguish as in "1-*vs.*-1" manner, there will be totally $\binom{k}{2}$ classifiers. However, if prior knowledge is available or a clustering process is taken beforehand, a hierarchy binary classifier set can only consist of k-1 classifiers instead of $\binom{k}{2}$ classifiers. Compared with "1-*vs.*-all" manner, which requires k classifiers, hierarchy SVM classifier is more efficient when the number of categories is large. Our experimental result shows that a well-defined hierarchy classifier structure (as shown in Fig. 3) can match "1-*vs.*-all" when features are distinguishable enough for all five labels (kinematic feature) while outperforming it when features are distinguishable between "falling" and "non-falling" labels but not so distinguishable among finer labels (appearance feature).

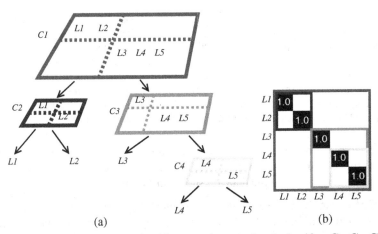

Fig. 3. (a) Structure of our hierarchy classifier set and scope of each classifier. C_1, C_2, C_3 and C_4 denote four classifiers we trained in our model. (b) The mapping relationship from our hierarchy structure to a confusion matrix to clarify the definition of "scope". Labels' meanings are shown in Table 1.

4 Experimental Results

4.1 Dataset

We collect a dataset containing five types of activities performed by five different subjects under three different conditions: 1) subject is *within* the range of depth sensor (< 4 meters distance between the subject and the camera) and *with* normal illumination; 2) subject is *within* the range of depth sensor but *without* enough illumination; and 3) subject is out of the range of depth sensor (> 4 meters distance between the subject and the camera) and *with* normal illumination. There are total of 200 video sequences, including 100 videos for condition 1, 50 videos for condition 2, and 50 videos for condition

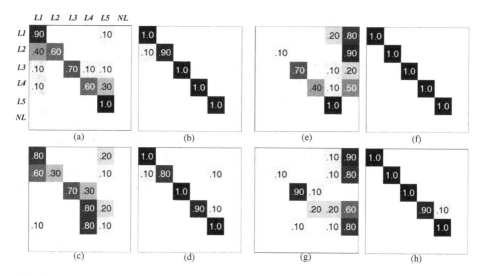

Fig. 4. Performances of proposed methods under different situations. (a)-(d) confusion matrices of activity recognition using hierarchy SVM classifier set. (e)-(h) confusion matrices of activity recognition using "1-*vs.*-all" SVM classifier. (a) and (e) Appearance model in normal case. (b) and (f) Kinematic model in normal case. (c) and (g) Appearance model with sufficient illumination but out of depth range. (d) and (h) Kinematic model with insufficient illumination and within depth range. Meaning of each label is shown in Table 1. *NL* means "no label".

3. Each video contains one activity. In our experiments, we select 50 videos which include all subjects and all types of activities for training. The remaining 150 sequences are used for testing. Some of the data are shown in Fig. 6.

Parameter Setting: In our experiments, parameters in appearance model include background subtraction difference threshold φ, frame step τ, the pixel number threshold λ, maximum acceptable value of width/height ratio m and bin size b in the histogram representation. These parameters remain same throughout all our experiments: $\varphi = 5$, $\tau = 5$ and $\lambda = 0.05$ if a person is in the depth-range and 0.005 for out-range cases; whereas the maximum accepted values and bin widths $\{m, b\}$ in histogram representation for different classifier layers are $\{4, 0.5\}$, $\{2, 0.5\}$, $\{2, 0.1\}$ and $\{2, 0.5\}$ for C_1, C_2, C_3 and C_4, respectively. For kinematic model, there is no manually tuned parameter.

4.2   Performance Analysis

To evaluate the performance of both kinematic model and appearance model under different conditions, we conduct 8 combinations of conditions and classifier structures (2 models times 2 classifier structures times two situations, normal and special). The training set contains 50 videos with normal condition which is used to train both hierarchy and "1-*vs.*-all" classifiers. Performances of two classifier structures as well as models of kinematic and appearance are also compared using corresponding test datasets.

The activity recognition accuracies of the proposed methods are displayed in Fig. 4. As shown in Fig. 4 (a) and (b), appearance features are effective to distinguish activities in a coarse scale between "falling" {fall from chair, fall from standing} and "non-falling" {standing, sit on chair, sit on floor}, and achieve an accuracy rate of 94%. However for activity classification in a finer scale, the appearance model achieves an average accuracy rate at 76% while the kinematic model achieves a much higher accuracy rate of 98% as expected.

As shown in Fig. 4 (c), the accuracy of appearance model based coarse action classes is 92% (C_1), which is comparable to that in Fig. 4 (a). Apparently, recognition accuracy decreases for activity classification in a finer scale, as expected. For kinematic model, as shown in Fig. 4 (b) and (d), we observe that the accuracy of each classifier is high, which demonstrates that our proposed kinematic features are strong for each classifier.

Comparing columns 1 (Fig. 4 (a, c)) and 3 (Fig. 4 (e, g)), the merit of using a hierarchy SVM construction instead of using a "1-*vs.*-all" SVM construction is manifested. Due to the unbalancedness of classifier structure, it tends to classify a test data into negative group when the input features are not strong enough. And when feature is strong enough, kinematic ((b) and (d)) and "1-*vs.*-all" ((f) and (g)) structures reach almost the same performance.

The experiments demonstrate that: 1) the proposed kinematic model is robust in each activity class according to Fig. 4 (b), (d), (f), and (h). 2) Hierarchy based classifier is more robust than "1-*vs.*-all" classifier when using appearance model according to comparison between Fig. 4 (a) (c) and (e) (g).

In feature extraction phase, kinematic approach is much faster than appearance approach. In test phase, kinematic approach takes a little longer (0.0194s) than appearance approach (0.0074s) to answer a query video with 120-220 frames.

Privacy Protection. One of the applications of the proposed models is to monitor a nursing room or a home of elder people. The benefits of the proposed models are twofold. Firstly, it can handle special cases such as when light is turned off (insufficient illumination) or people walk far from the camera (out of depth range) but is still in the view of RGB cameras. Secondly, our models are privacy preserving by only displaying 3D depth information or foreground mask as illustrated in Fig. 5 (a).

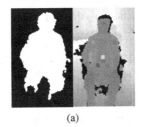

(a)   (b)

Fig. 5. Privacy preserving without reveal person identification. (a) Foreground mask (left) and depth image (right) used in our proposed models for displaying activities, (b) RGB image which reveals personal privacy.

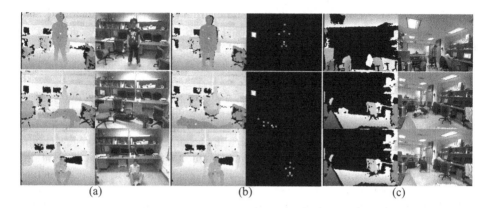

(a)   (b)   (c)

Fig. 6. Examples of actions and extracted features in our dataset. In each image pair, depth image is shown on the left and RGB image is shown on the right. (a) Sufficient illumination within the range of depth sensor. (b) Insufficient illumination within depth range. (c) Sufficient illumination but out of the range of depth sensor.

5 Conclusion

In this paper, we have proposed an effective activity recognition framework based on RGBD cameras. Experiment results have demonstrated that our feature extraction and representation of human activity are robust and efficient. Our future work will focus on integrating RGB and depth information and recognizing more activities, including taking medicines, group activities, and human interactions.

References

1. Hobbs, F.B.:The elderly population. In: U.S. Bureau of the Census,
   http://www.census.gov/population/www/pop-profile/elderpop.html
2. Brookmeyer, R., Gray, S., Kawas, C.: Projections of Alzheimer's disease in the United States and the public health impact of delaying disease onset. American Journal of Public Health 88, 1337 (1998)
3. Lee, H., Kim, Y.T., Jung, J.W., Park, K.H., Kim, D.J., Bang, B., Bien, Z.Z.: A 24-hour health monitoring system in a smart house. Gerontechnology 7, 22–35 (2008)
4. Wilson, D.H., Consolvo, S., Fishkin, K.P., Philipose, M.: Current practices for in-home monitoring of elders' activities of daily living: A study of case managers. Citeseer (2005)
5. Nait-Charif, H., McKenna, S.J.: Activity summarisation and fall detection in a supportive home environment. In: Proc. of International Conference on Pattern Recognition (ICPR), pp. 323–326. IEEE (2004)
6. Wang, S., Zabir, S., Leibe, B.: Lying Pose Recognition for Elderly Fall Detection. In: Proceedings of Robotics: Science and Systems, Los Angeles, CA, USA (2011)
7. Felzenszwalb, P., McAllester, D., Ramanan, D.: A discriminatively trained, multiscale, deformable part model. In: Proc. of IEEE Conference on Computer Vision and Pattern Recognition (CVPR), pp. 1–8. IEEE (2008)

8. Buehler, P., Everingham, M., Huttenlocher, D.P., Zisserman, A.: Upper Body Detection and Tracking in Extended Signing Sequences. International Journal of Computer Vision (IJCV), 1–18 (2011)

9. Zhang, H., Parker, L.E.: 4-dimensional local spatio-temporal features for human activity recognition. In: IEEE/RSJ International Conference on Intelligent Robots and Systems (IROS), pp. 2044–2049. IEEE (2011)

10. Li, W., Zhang, Z., Liu, Z.: Action recognition based on a bag of 3D points. In: IEEE Computer Society Conference on Computer Vision and Pattern Recognition Workshops (CVPRW), pp. 9–14. IEEE (2010)

11. Sung, J., Ponce, C., Selman, B., Saxena, A.: Human activity detection from RGBD images. In: AAAI Workshop on Pattern, Activity and Intent Recognition, PAIRW (2011)

12. Microsoft Research: Windows Kinect SDK Beta from Microsoft Research, Redmond WA

The Proof of Concept of a Shadow Robotic System for Independent Living at Home

Lucia Pigini[1], David Facal[2], Alvaro Garcia[2],
Michael Burmester[3], and Renzo Andrich[1]

[1] Polo Tecnologico, Fondazione Don Carlo Gnocchi Onlus, Milano Italy
{lpigini,randrich}@dongnocchi.it
[2] Fundación Instituto Gerontológico Matia - INGEMA, San Sebastian, Spain
{david.facal,alvaro.garcia}@ingema.es
[3] Stuttgart Media University, Stuttgart, Germany
burmester@hdm-stuttgart.de

Abstract. In the framework of the EU funded SRS (Multi-Role Shadow Robotic System for independent Living) project, an innovative semi autonomous service robot is under development with the aim to support frail elderly people at their home. This paper reports about the user validation of the SRS concept involving 63 potential users of the system coming from Italy, Germany and Spain: in particular they were frail elderly people, their relatives and 24 hour telecare professionals. Results confirmed that monitoring and managing emergency situations as well as helping with reaching, fetching and carrying objects that are too heavy or positioned in unreachable places are the tasks for which a robot is better accepted to address users' needs. To support the scenarios executions and operation modes, the interaction concept should provide three different interaction devices and modalities for each user group.

Keywords: Service robots, tele-operation, elderly people, remote operator, user requirements, user centered design.

1   Introduction

In the framework of the EU funded SRS (Multi-Role Shadow Robotic System for Independent Living) project, an innovative semi – autonomous, remotely controlled and learning service robot is under development with the aim to support frail elderly people at their home [1]. The SRS project follows a user-centered design process [2], therefore, from the beginning of the project, potential users and stakeholders of the system were involved into an iterative design process starting with qualitative focus groups, quantitative questionnaires, and ethnographic analysis aiming at finding the general features of users and stakeholders, their attitude towards new technologies, their needs and expectations from a service robot. The achieved results [2] enabled the researchers to define specific user requirements, to translate them into technical requirements, and to develop a first list of usage scenarios. It is well established that

K. Miesenberger et al. (Eds.): ICCHP 2012, Part I, LNCS 7382, pp. 634–641, 2012.
© Springer-Verlag Berlin Heidelberg 2012

analyzing and understanding old users' perceptions when interacting with technology devices in different scenarios is a key requirement that increases value to assistive technology, providing system developers with meaningful information for further improvements and ensuring that the system addresses to users' needs [3]. Concept and scenario evaluation is an achievable way to study products under development, avoiding being limited to studying those robots now available and autonomously functioning [4].

This paper presents the survey conducted within SRS project regarding analysis and understanding of users' perceptions about achieved requirements with the aim of validating a clear SRS concept allowing the partners involved in the technical tasks to proceed with the development phase.

2   Method

2.1   Participants and Recruitment criteria

Participants in the study were the potential users of the system identified in the first part of the study: the local users (frail elderly people), and the remote operators (their relatives). They were recruited in three countries: Italy, Spain and Germany; In particular they were 30 elderly (64% female) with a mean age of 83 years (75 to 91), 23 family members (60% female), with a mean age of 54 years (29 to 70). Elderly people were recruited according to the criteria of being at least 65 years old, still able to live at home despite some difficulties in performing activities of daily living (e.g., mobility, or sensorial difficulties). Most of them received some form of assistance because of that. A short questionnaire adapted from Barber J.H., et al. 1980, was adopted for the recruitment. Relatives of elderly persons were recruited according to the criteria of being involved in some care-giving task for their relatives. Most of them cared for their parents, but some for grandparents, mothers-in-law, or old aunts. Complementarily, other participants in the study were recruited; in particular:

- Health professionals: people with high levels of experience in the geriatric field, such as geriatric physicians and nurses, physiotherapists, social workers. In particular 5 therapists (mean age 35; 2 physiotherapists and 3 occupational therapists, 3 females, 2 males) were recruited in Italy in order to obtain evaluation of the concept about any safety, ethical, and psychological issues which could arise.
- 24 hour emergency call center employees/experts: the psychological burden and time restrictions of family caregivers who usually work during the week emerged in the first part of the survey. In order to assess the idea of employing a 24-hour professional service center for tele-operation, 5 call centre employees were interviewed in Germany.

2.2   Visual Simulation of the Concept

Visual presentations of the concept were developed with the aim to show through simple visual examples, the hypothesized SRS concept and the selected scenarios.

The presentation consisted of three main parts: the first part about the introduction of the concept of a service robot, its main features, people involved in use and control of the robot and the human interaction modality (figure 1); the second part about selected scenarios, and the last part about the aesthetics of the robot. Before presenting scenarios, personas and situations were introduced and described. Personas also were created on the basis of results achieved in the first user requirement study and in the ethnographic study conducted in parallel. Then four scenarios were presented by showing and explaining sketches to participants. Table 1 reports the main user requirements achieved during the first user survey, the hypothesized SRS concept requirements and an example of the scenario adopted to present requirements to participants through possible realistic usage situations.

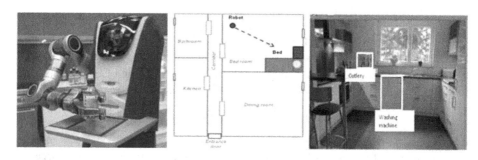

Fig. 1. Examples of images presented to participants: left, the current robotic platform care-o-bot 3 in use in the project (Graf B. t al., 2009) developed by Fraunhofer Institute for Manufacturing Engineering and Automation; center, the possible way to control the robot by navigating it from a remote position using a map of the elderly's apartment; right, the robot ability to recognized already learnt objects.

2.3   Quantitative and Qualitative Questionnaire

A tailored version of quantitative and qualitative questionnaire based on a Likert type scale [1 to 5 range scale, where 5 is the highest degree of acceptance] was developed for each different interviewed group. The questionnaire consisted of 16 to 20 items (depending on the interviewed group) regarding in particular the utility and acceptability of the robot for the particular tasks presented; the acceptance by the proposed people involved in the remote robot control; the possible human-robot interaction devices and interaction modalities and the overall appearance of the robot. After quantitative answers, "why questions" were complementarily presented in order to gather qualitative information for understanding reasons behind a particular rating.

Table 1. From user requirements to concept requirements: an extract of usage scenario derived from user requirements survey

User requirements from first user's survey results	SRS concept requirements, defined from user requirements
• Emergency managing • Fetching and bringing objects Help in standing up • Help in cooking • Low interaction with technology for elderly • Concern for the home environment • Monitoring health of the elderly • Be able to give help at distance • Lowering family assistance charge • Assuring intervention in every case, • Considering privacy and ethics	• Simple and wearable personal device (few large buttons to send an SRS request to a remote operator or to start autonomous robot functions). • Robot Accurate and safe manipulation of objects • SRS on a mobile platform and Autonomous identification of obstacles • Robot' Autonomous functions execution • Portable and ready to use device to tele-operate the robot: navigation through the map of the house, easy teaching of new objects and new procedures to the robot. • Robot automatic recognition of already learned objects and procedures from a database • Call priority chain: first contacting family, then assistance centre. • Telecommunication option and authorization procedure for privacy protection • Professional SRS-workstation to control the robot executing particularly complex maneuvers (manual control of the robotic arm…)

Scenario example- translation of concept requirements into a realistic usage situation

Elisabeth Baker , 84 years old, widow, suffers from high blood pressure; this morning she wakes up and she feels so dizzy that she can't get up to reach the medicine she has to take. She decides to call for the help of the SRS robot using her personal device that she always carries with her. She is not confident with technology so she just sends a call to a remote operator.

The woman's request is sent to her son: The son is at work but seeing a request from the mother on his SRS-portable device starts a remote session from his workplace. So communication is established and he can immediately send the robot to the kitchen ,to take the medicine and a glass of water, then brining them to her mother…

3   Results

3.1   Scenarios Approval

The most popular robotic scenarios were those linked to safety. A robotic solution for **monitoring and managing the emergency** was very well accepted, mostly for intervention in case of emergency, but also just for monitoring the situation at all times. The idea of the robot putting in contact the injured old person and the relative when an emergency happens, providing immediate psychological support and health status information to the remote operator has been considered a good idea by all of the interviewed groups.

A robotic solution for **standing-up assistance** was quite well accepted. However, one of the most meaningful old person's statement looking at the presented scenario was: *"I wish I had something to help me getting up by myself but I wouldn't have enough force to stand up from the ground just grabbing the handle of the robot...the presented solution could be dangerous for me"*. This statement reflects a common conviction shared by all the interviewed people. Most of them liked the idea, but at the same time they have too many concerns about the technical implementation of the robot. Health professionals, experts in Assistive Technologies, especially underlined how difficult it could be for an old person to get up after a fall and so just how dedicated an assistive device of this kind would have to be in order to be effective and safe. So they think that this function should be better implemented into an assistive technology designed just for that purpose and not as one of the functionalities of a service robot.

A robotic solution for help in **fetching and carrying** was quite well accepted, most of all by family members and 24 hours call centre personnel, who consider this robotic function as the more *"feasible"*. Health professionals instead, suggested that the "remotely operated fetching objects function" could better represent an interesting potential solution for visually impaired people, and wheelchair bound people of any age.

Finally, the robotic solution for **preparing food** was not well accepted. Figure 2 shows some extracts of visual simulations used to explain scenarios and mean results and standard errors obtained from the questionnaire section about requirements related to robotic tasks usefulness.

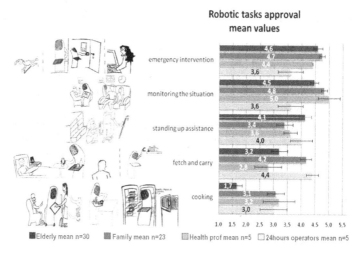

Fig. 2. Approval of the robotic help for the particular task presented [1 to five scale, where 5 is the highest degree of acceptance]. The graph reports mean values and standard error bars of the four groups: 30 frail elderly people, 23 family members, 5 geriatric health professionals and 5 tele-operators. Results are showed using the elderly mean rating scale.

3.2   Remote Operators and Local Operators

Results about the involvement of other possible operators of the SRS system in addition to family members showed the acceptance of an always available external call centre service. Elderly people however, would prefer the help of their relatives or informal caregiver who usually cares for them. However they are not against the idea of a 24 hour service always available, because they are well aware that their relatives could be not available at the time an emergency happens, so a 24 hour service could be very useful, but it should be considered the last option, just in case of relatives' unavailability.

The 24 hour call centre operators interviewed are used to technology. They are often trained as nurses, doctor's assistant or case manager and typically female. They are familiar with a variety of different computer programs and often work with multi-screen setups. Also they are knowledgeable about many different devices used by the elderly (e.g. various types of emergency button systems from various brands, GPS-localization devices, etc.). They are already involved into services that offer help to the elderly and they stated that SRS would be a useful addition; they mentioned for example that it would be helpful to see an elderly person in an emergency situation to assess the severity of the situation (*e.g. "bleeding?, lying on the floor?, epileptic attack?"*). Quantitative results about approval of the introduction of a tele-assistance service are expressed in figure 3.

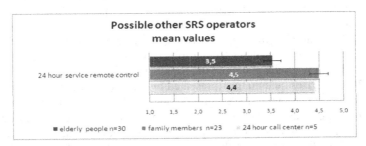

Fig. 3. Approval of the idea of a 24 hour telecare operator as SRS operator. [1 to five scale, where 5 is the highest degree of acceptance]. The graph reports mean values and standard error bars of three groups: 30 frail elderly people, 23 family members, and 5 tele operators at 24 hour call center.

3.3   Human-Robot Interfaces and Interaction Modalities

The elderly liked the idea of using a simple wearable device (mean questionnaire value: 4,6) to control the robot, to contact a remote operator, or to make an emergency call. This is because some of them have already had some experience with wearable alarms or reported cases of other elderly friends who use them.

Most of them also liked the idea of the video call (mean questionnaire value: 3,6), stating that looking at their relatives in the face while talking, could be calming and reassuring or useful in case of an emergency call, to judge the severity of the situation and the eventual need for an intervention.

The 24 hours call center workers however expressed some concerns regarding privacy issues, stating that the elderly may not like the idea of being observed by strangers. However, only a few of the interviewed elderly confirmed these concerns about privacy, mainly because they consider more relevant the need of being in contact with someone that is supposed to help them.

Relatives and the staff of the 24 hour call center were mostly convinced about being able to act as remote operators. Most of them can imagine themselves using some kind of system to remotely control the robot, to teach it how to recognize new objects, and to program the robot so as to execute certain tasks at set times. However family participants would prefer a portable device (mean questionnaire value: 4.6) and expressed some doubts related to how demanding teaching operations could be.

4   Discussion

The overall acceptance of a semi-autonomous, tele-operated, and learning robotic system with the aim to prolong independent living at home was fairly high among all user groups. One of the interviewed stated "I would feel safer having a robot like this at home always with me". This statement is emblematic, because it underlines the main relatives/caregivers' problem of being always available. Even if health professionals mainly stated that human help and contact is better than robotic support, they also recognized that too often the elderly are alone at home and their relatives cannot offer immediate help, causing also potential risks for the elderly individuals. Relatives and health professionals interviewed stated that elderly people "want to act right at that moment, without waiting for help" thus exposing themselves to a risk, because sometimes not aware of their limits. Providing them with a robotic system helping to reach some of their goals without having to wait for someone else doing it for them, actually would allow a safer and more independent condition.

Table 2 summarizes quantitative (presented by the overall mean and standard deviations values of all the interviewed groups) and qualitative results presented in the previous paragraphs about the importance of the tasks the robot should be able to perform. Final validation of the concept expressed in each scenario was considered reached if only light grey couples of quantitative and qualitative results were achieved.

Table 2. Robot usefulness documented in quantitative results (overall mean and standard deviations) and qualitative results. About quantitative results, the light grey color is used when the mean values (rating scale from 1 to 5) is over score 3,5 and dark grey if less then score 3,5. About qualitative results, the light grey background is used when results are mainly positive, and dark grey when they are mainly negative.

Robotic tasks overall approval (Elderly people, Relatives, Health professionals; 24 h service staff)	Quantitative results (mean. n = 63)	Qualitative results "Why questions"
Monitoring the situation	4,6 (0,81)	Providing health status information to the remote operator
Emergency intervention	4,5 (0,80)	Immediate psychological support
Standing up assistance	3,8 (1,29)	Safety concerns arising both for elderly and health professionals
Fetch and carry	3,6 (1,40)	Helping with heavy objects (>1kg) and objects placed too high. Exploitation for other target people possible also.
Preparing food	2,4 (1,43)	Cooking considered an important social function/hobby. Just "heating food in the microwave" considered useless function

Overall results demonstrated also that to support the scenarios and operation modes, along with requirements such as mobility of the elderly and their family, the interaction concept should foresee different interaction devices and modalities for each user group [2]. Feedback from user needs assessment, as well as the analysis of SRS usage scenarios clearly showed the need of a relatively small and mobile "all in one" interaction device for the elderly user and for informal caregivers. However, the professional user works in an office on a fixed workstation in the framework of a 24hrs service center and thus does not need to be mobile. For this last user interface, focus is on maximum of functionality and remote support as the last instance in the support chain. Results provided a clear and shared definition of the SRS concept (figure 4), providing technologists with enough information to proceed with the development phase.

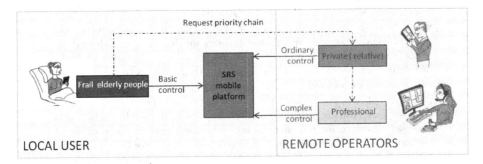

Fig. 4. The developed concept of SRS [2]. The figure shows the users of the systems, the idea of three different devices with increasing complexity that they should use to interact with the robot or with the other stakeholders, and the priority chain of intervention.

References

1. Multi-Role Shadow Robotic System for Independent Living project, http://srs-project.eu/ (accessed January 2012)
2. Mast, M., Burmester, M., Krüger, K., Fatikow, S., Arbeiter, G., Graf, G., Kronreif, G., Pigini, L., Facal, D., Qiu, R.: User-Centered Design of a Dynamic-Autonomy Remote Interaction Concept for Manipulation-Capable Robots to Assist Elderly People in the Home. Journal of Human-Robot Interaction 1(1) (in print, 2012)
3. González, M.F., Facal, D., Navarro, A.B., Geven, A., Tscheligi, M.: Analysis of older users' perceived requests and opportunities with technologies. A scenario-based assessment. International Journal of Ambient Computing and Intelligence (2011) (in press)
4. Cesta, A., Cortellessa, G., Giuliani, V., Pecora, F., Rasconi, R., Scopelliti, M., Tiberio, L.: Proactive Assistive Technology: An Empirical Study. In: Baranauskas, C., Abascal, J., Barbosa, S.D.J. (eds.) INTERACT 2007. LNCS, vol. 4662, pp. 255–268. Springer, Heidelberg (2007)

Task Complexity and User Model Attributes
An Analysis of User Model Attributes for Elderly Drivers

Thomas Grill, Sebastian Osswald, and Manfred Tscheligi

ICT&S Center, University of Salzburg
Salzburg, Austria

Abstract. Modeling users in order to design appropriate interfaces and interactions or to simulate a specific user behavior is an ambitious task. When using user model attributes to design an interface as well as its interactions we focus tasks at different levels of complexity. In our work we address the appropriateness of physical, cognitive, behavioral, and psychological attributes and their relevancy for designing and describing tasks at such levels of complexity. We conducted a study that uses tasks of varying complexity levels that we relate to attributes in terms of the categorization previously described. A driving simulator together with a prototype of in-car controls that allows to perform primitive as well as complex tasks during a driving scenario represent the study context and the user interface for the participants who took part in three different scenarios, where they performed selected tasks that have been identified for the automotive area. Further additional workload tasks were used to induce stress and to investigate in the effect of cognitive, behavioral, and psychological attributes. First results show that the physical parameters address mainly primitive tasks. Regarding cognitive, behavioral and psychological parameters, tasks need to be addressed at a more complex level, which was supported by the results of the study. Concluding the relation of primitive tasks to cognitive, behavioral, and psychological attributes is not viable.

1 Introduction

Research especially in the area of human-computer action focuses on analyzing and describing elderly users to assess requirements for designers and developers. Information about users can be captured through user models while the main effort lies in describing the correct and valid attributes of these models. Different areas of research address this challenge through a variety of techniques like the definition of personas [1], user stories when it comes to an agile development process [2], stereotypes [3] as well as inference methods [4]. When applying models that are described based on user attributes in terms of physical capabilities, the contained values are usually based on measurement studies supporting this approach. Regarding cognitive, behavioral, and psychological aspects the description of attributes focuses on intrinsic attributes of a user that could be used for designing a particular activity. Examples are emotions, stress, or workload.

K. Miesenberger et al. (Eds.): ICCHP 2012, Part I, LNCS 7382, pp. 642–649, 2012.

Another application area of user models is the usage of behavioral attributes to assess and simulate properties of a stereotypical user in terms of physical, behavioral, psychological, and cognitive abilities or disabilities. Regarding physical attributes the applicability of describing primitive tasks already has been investigated. Drumwright et al. elaborate this issue based on motor tasks in the area of human robot interaction and show the applicability of describing primitive tasks by using physical attributes. [5] An example for an applicable attribute is a movement executed to reach a specific object. The particular attribute "field of reach" is used in this case to describe the user's ability to execute the specific task. When it comes to describing specific attributes regarding cognitive as well as behavioral and psychological states of a user, cognitive and psychological abilities influence not only the ability to execute a task but may also influence the potential execution of a particular task. This leads to the assumption that a difference between the relationship of the different types of attributes and the level of task complexity addressed in the user models exists. Levels of task complexity can reach from superficial task descriptions like e.g. driving a car to primitive tasks like e.g. grasping or reaching. Primitive tasks are used to compose more complex tasks. When it comes to filling the defined attributes with data the definition of the particular relationship between a task and an user model attribute is essential. Regarding physical attributes measurement studies are applicable and can be executed also on primitive tasks. When describing cognitive and behavioral and psychological attributes it is common to address them at a higher level of complexity.

In this paper we investigate the possibility to regard to such attributes also on the level of primitive tasks. In order to do this we developed a study setup focusing on this research question. The study elaborated is based in the automotive area and focuses not only on performance values like e.g. task completion times, but also on the relationship described before. With the study we addressed elderly people. As research in cognitive aging is labored recently we conclude that elderly drivers may especially profit from the focus on the effect of workload and stress as a cognitive attribute and on emotions as a psychological attribute. We address this by measuring performance values of physical tasks and investigated the correlations between the cognitive, behavioral, and psychological attributes.

The upcoming sections of the paper are structured as follows. In 2 we elaborate existing work focusing on the different perspectives included in user models. In 3 we present our driving simulator study investigating on user model and task complexity research. Section 4 summarizes our results and describes future work.

2   Related Work

Recently the evaluation, definition and usage of empirical based descriptions of user models gained momentum. In the area of human computer interaction (HCI) the task of defining concrete models of users is addressed mainly during the requirements engineering phase of a user-centered design process. Introduced by Cooper in 1998 [1], personas are proposed as a practical interaction design tool that showed its potential due to its effectiveness and thus rapidly gained popularity. Over time, personas are more often used to create representative models of typical users, as they depict fictitious user representations that are created in order to embody behaviors and motivations that a group of real users might express. Personas aim for emphasizing these factors during a development process to establish a richer picture of the targeted user group. Abstracting the user in this particular way, is reasoned by well documented design practices as elaborated e.g. by Nielsen [6]. According to Pruitt and Grudin [7], personas as user models are often used in research because of their implicit potential and power to predict user behavior based on general knowledge and the human capability to interpret a users mental state.

Regarding the automotive context, Lindgren et al [8] used personas as an interface design tool for advanced driver assistance systems. Based on personas they developed different scenarios and narratives that were used in a workshop to specify user needs and requirements in the interface design process for automotive user interfaces. Another approach to model user characteristics in the automotive context is followed by Islinger et al. [9], who used the General User Model (GUMO) developed by Heckmann [10] to model relevant driver attributes. They addressed psychological attributes like emotion, attention, and drowsiness and elaborated relations to measurable characteristics. Salvucci [11] further proposed an approach that integrates an user model for an interface with an existing driver model that accounts for basic aspects of driver behavior. He argued that during designing and evaluating in-car user interfaces it is possible to predict what effects car interfaces may have on driver behavior and performance.

As these examples show the successful utilization of user models to create behavioral and motivation based representation of future users, the relationship between user models and task complexity is often neglected. Task complexity in general was examined by Wood et al. [12] who proposed a general theoretical model of tasks, in which the three essential components of all tasks are a product and two types of task input required acts and information cues. Campbell [13] on the other hand identified four fundamental task attributes to determine a typology of task complexity. The four classified attributes are: Presence of multiple paths to a desired end-state; presence of multiple desired end-states; presence of conflicting interdependence; presence of uncertainty or probabilistic linkages. The complexity therefore is determined by both, the degree to which a task incorporates individual attributes (like e.g. present or absent, high or low) and by the total number of basic attributes contained in the task. According to the defined attributes, primitive task can be defined by the absence of all complexity attributes. Thus, a task can be considered as primitive/simple.

In the car context the impact of task complexity on driving behavior is an essential research challenge due to its impact on road safety.Tasks complexity therefore need to be evaluated and several studies already defined attributes of task complexity. Osswald et. al [14] evaluated the effect of task complexity on a touch display steering wheel on lane changing behavior to determine driver distraction. They defined the task complexity attributes: task completion time, interaction modalities, interaction steps and interaction variety. Horberry et al. [15] conducted a simulator study that examined the effects of distraction upon driving performance for drivers in three age groups. They concluded that in-vehicle tasks impaired several aspects of driving performance, and that these findings were relatively stable across different driver age groups.

3 Study

To investigate attributes describing the physical, cognitive, behavioral and psychological perspectives on user models and their relationship to specific tasks they address, we conducted a study in the automotive area with elderly people as a target group with an age between 52 and 75 years ($n = 18, \mu = 59, \sigma = 6.55$, 42.11% male and 57.89% female). The study aim was to find out specifics about aging people's in-car interaction during a driving scenario with the goal to investigate in values describing attributes of specific user models.

In our study setup we used a fixed-based driving simulator setup where the CityCar Driving[1] software served as a configurable simulator environment that allowed us to define the driving scenario targeting the evaluation of tasks at different levels (see an example driving task plan in Figure 2). Further we prototyped the hardware for different driving specific tasks that build the basis for the study scenario. These tasks were selected from a list of driving related tasks, identified in an in-depth analysis done within the VERITAS FP7 project[2]. They have been defined in different levels of complexity leading from a general task description to specific actions (called primitive tasks). Figure 1 visualizes a task where the complex task is *accelerating a car*. *Push down the accelerator pedal* is a subtask of lower complexity designed by combining a number of actions called primitive tasks like *stretching the leg*.

In total eight complex tasks have been integrated in the study setup. These tasks were accelerating, activating a direction indicator, braking (slow and emergency brake), changing gear, check surrounding for unsafe situations, maintain lane, and steering. All tasks were analyzed and designed using primitive task descriptions or actions. Such actions are pushing, pulling, grasping, turning an object like a knob, reading, etc. The identified tasks have been integrated in different scenarios and were implemented using interaction devices like a steering wheel, gas and braking pedals, a gear shift, as well as additional buttons. The aim was to abstract a driver's particular in-car interaction like accelerating, braking, changing a radio station, or operating a navigation system.

In the first scenario of the study sessions, the users had to drive a given track (see Figure 2) with the aim to make themselves comfortable with the driving simulator and to alleviate the learning curve of using the simulator. The second scenario required the user to perform the selected tasks. We applied the Wizard of Oz methodology to instruct the participants to do the particular tasks in the same driving situations to achieve comparable results. The third scenario

---

[1] http://www.citycardriving.com
[2] http://veritas-project.eu/

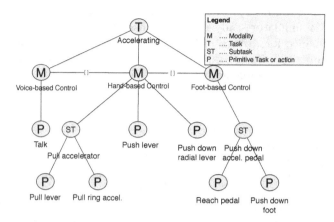

Fig. 1. Task description of an acceleration task including a multi-modal design approach

included a secondary task in addition to the primary driving task in order to raise the participants workload. This secondary task was to count pedestrians that appeared in the simulated traffic. Figure 2 shows a screenshot of the video recordings done during the study. It depicts the prototype of in-car instruments used to allow the drivers to execute the specific tasks. To log the interactions done with the steering wheel we used the HID logging tool USB monitor[3]. We measured the stress level of the participants trough skin conductance (EDA) using Affectiva's QSensor[4]. Additionally, video and audio recordings have been made during the study sessions. After each session the participants filled out a demographic questionnaire, the SSSQ questionnaire to assess a user's stress level and the Nasa TLX questionnaire to assess workload.

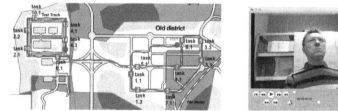

Fig. 2. Predefined track and recording of the study setup

We conducted the study with 24 participants where 6 participants had to abort the study due to simulator sickness problems. The recorded data has been analyzed in terms of reaction time and task completion time based on the physical interaction done during the study sessions. A mapping of these results to the

---

[3] http://www.hhdsoftware.com/usb-monitor
[4] http://www.affectiva.com

cognitive, behavioral and psychologic attributes measured, i.e. stress, workload and emotions, didn't show a normal distribution which implies that a direct correlation between these values and the particular singular tasks is not possible. Thus, a direct correlation between performance values of singular tasks like pressing a button and cognitive attributes is not feasible at the levels of primitive tasks. An explanation for this is that single automated tasks (e.g. braking for an experienced driver) are not influenced by e.g. a participant's cognitive stress level. As depicted in 1 the change of performance regarding the different tasks

Table 1. Change of performance indicators based on the different tasks. The baseline values were measured in a trainings session. A high number indicates lower performance.

No.	Task	Task Performance Scenario 1	Task Performance Scenario 2	diff.
1	Read information	+ 10.5	+ 14.8	+4.3
2	Pull a button	+ 1.3	- 2.6	-3.9
3	Push a button	+ 11	+ 9.6	-1.4
4	Turn a button	+ 32.3	+ 29.4	-2.9
5	Accelerating	+ 16.7	+ 6.2	-10.5
6	Changing gear	+ 8.4	+ 11	+2.6
7	Emergency brake	+ 2.8	- 2.8	-5.6

indicates that for the cognitively demanding tasks (task 1) other driving tasks (task 5,7) and in-car tasks (task 2-4) show an improvement in performance. This can be explained through a higher concentration level during the dual task in scenario 2 in comparison to the pure driving task in scenario 1. The higher value for task 6 can be explained through the usage of a automatic gear box to change the gears which the participants were not familiar with. The QSensor provides measures of the electrodermal activity that can be related to stress values. 3 depicts the comparison of the stress level of 13 users. The lower number of users is due to the fact that the driving simulator scenario aroused sickness with a number of users and we had to ignore additionally five users that have shown first signs of simulator sickness which influenced the EDA measures. The results show that stress is not solely correlated with the workload investigated in the study setup. Indications that the emotional state of the users and whether they perceived the driving scenario as fun or not, influenced the EDA values, were found. This was also confirmed in interviews, could be identified through the questionnaires filled out by the users as well as through an analysis of the recorded videos. This leads to the fact that as can be seen in 3 the data with a focus on correlating the workload induced in the different scenarios compared to the EDA values does not show a normal distribution. One finding identified during the analysis was that participants performed tasks faster when the cognitive demand of the situation increased. This can be explained with the increased

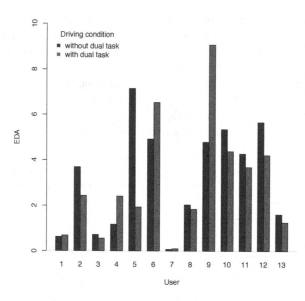

Fig. 3. Evaluation of EDA values shows that the stress does not correlate solely with the workload. See outliers 1,3,7,13

attention during the dual task condition. An analysis of the questionnaires did not result in any correlation of a user's cognitive or emotional attributes to the particular conditions evaluated during the study sessions. Further results of the study showed that primitive tasks are usually tasks executed relatively unconsciously. This leads to the assumption that they are not influenced significantly by a mild cognitive parameter change as e.g. an increase in the workload of a participant. Cognitive load is usually generated through more complex tasks, which are usually a combination of multiple primitive tasks. This statement is supported by the non-normal distribution of the data observed. Audio and video analysis confirm this hypothesis.

4   Conclusion and Future Work

In order to show the dependencies between the different types of attributes of user models, the particular attributes of physical, cognitive and psychological and behavioral user models have been investigated through a user study with elderly users in an automotive context. Specific physical tasks targeting different levels of complexity have been selected and performance values for these tasks has been measured. We conducted a study with elderly people based on three different scenarios, i.e. a training scenario, driving scenario 1, driving scenario with additional workload. The generated workload was measured using questionnaires as well as skin conductance. The results indicate that the difference between physical attributes of user models and cognitive, behavioral and psychological attributes of user models, i.e. stress and emotions, lie in the different level of complexity regarding the tasks they influence. While the physical attributes can be related to primitive tasks based on performance measures this is not possible for cognitive, behavioral and psychological attributes. The results of our study indicate that such a correlation involves multiple cognitive, behavioral and psychological attributes while statistically valid results require focusing on more complex tasks that involve cognitive load. Future work consists in analyzing the relationship between task related interactions and attributes that relate to the different levels of task complexity. Further we want to validate the results also with other user groups, normal people and people having different handicaps with a focus on the user's behavioral and psychological states.

References

1. Cooper, A.: The Inmates Are Running the Asylum: Why High Tech Products Drive Us Crazy and How to Restore the Sanity, 2nd edn. Pearson Higher Education (1998)
2. Cohn, M.: User Stories Applied: For Agile Software Development. The Addison-Wesley Signature Series. Addison-Wesley Professional (2004)
3. Rich, E.: User modeling via stereotypes. Cognitive Science 3(4), 329–354 (1979)
4. Brajnik, G., Tasso, C.: A shell for developing non- monotonic user modelling systems. Int. J. Human Computer Studies 40, 31–62 (1994)
5. Drumwright, E., Ng-Thow-Hing, V.: The task matrix: An extensible framework for creating versatile humanoid robots. In: ICRA 2006, pp. 448–455. IEEE (2006)
6. Nielsen, L.: Constructing the user. In: 10th International Conference on Human–Computer Interaction, HCI International, Crete, Greece (2003)
7. Pruitt, J., Grudin, J.: Personas: Practice and theory (2003), http://research.microsoft.com/users/jgrudin/ (retrieved March 4, 2003)
8. Lindgren, A., Chen, F., Amdahl, P., Chaikiat, P.: Using Personas and Scenarios as an Interface Design Tool for Advanced Driver Assistance Systems. In: Stephanidis, C. (ed.) UAHCI 2007 (Part II). LNCS, vol. 4555, pp. 460–469. Springer, Heidelberg (2007)
9. Islinger, T., Köhler, T., Wolff, C.: Human modeling in a driver analyzing context: challenge and benefit. In: AUI 2011. ACM (2011)
10. Heckmann, D.: Ubiquitous user modeling, vol. 297. IOS Press (2005)
11. Salvucci, D.D.: Predicting the effects of in-car interfaces on driver behavior using a cognitive architecture. In: CHI 2001, pp. 120–127. ACM, NY (2001)
12. Wood, R.E.: Task complexity: Definition of the construct. Organizational Behavior and Human Decision Processes 37(1), 60–82 (1986)
13. Campbell, D.: Task complexity: A review and analysis. Academy of management review, 40–52 (1988)
14. Osswald, S., Meschtscherjakov, A., Wilfinger, D., Tscheligi, M.: Interacting with the Steering Wheel: Potential Reductions in Driver Distraction. In: Keyson, D.V., Maher, M.L., Streitz, N., Cheok, A., Augusto, J.C., Wichert, R., Englebienne, G., Aghajan, H., Kröse, B.J.A. (eds.) AmI 2011. LNCS, vol. 7040, pp. 11–20. Springer, Heidelberg (2011)
15. Horberry, T., Anderson, J., Regan, M.A., Triggs, T.J., Brown, J.: Driver distraction: The effects of concurrent in-vehicle tasks, road environment complexity and age on driving performance. Accident Analysis & Prevention 38(1) (2006)

AALuis, a User Interface Layer That Brings Device Independence to Users of AAL Systems

Christopher Mayer[1], Martin Morandell[1], Matthias Gira[1], Kai Hackbarth[2],
Martin Petzold[2], and Sascha Fagel[3]

[1] AIT Austrian Institute of Technology GmbH, Health & Environment Department,
Biomedical Systems, Muthgasse 11, 1190 Vienna, Austria
christopher.mayer@ait.ac.at
[2] ProSyst Software GmbH, Dürener Str. 405, 50858 Köln, Germany,
[3] Zoobe Message Entertainment GmbH, Kurfürstendamm 226, 10719 Berlin,
Germany

Abstract. Many ICT services older people could derive a benefit from lack of accessibility, adoptability and usability of the user interface concerning arising special needs specific for the target group. AALuis intends to develop an open User Interface Layer that facilitates a dynamically adapted, personalized interaction between an elderly user and any kind of service, with different types of input and output devices and modalities. To achieve this the AALuis User Interface Layer keeps track of changes of a variety of information models to adapt the transformation process from abstract task descriptions to a user interface and to steer the user interaction in a suitable manner. One of the main goals of AALuis is to create and exploit synergies by developing an architecture that allows the easy integration into different established AAL middleware platforms. AALuis aims to significantly contribute to the freedom of choice for end-users of services and users interfaces.

Keywords: AAL, Middleware, User Interaction, User Interfaces.

1 Introduction

The user interface (UI) is the most important feature of interaction between users and (AAL) services. It can be critical to the success or failure of an ICT product or service [1]. In the course of ageing the abilities and special needs of older people change. Many services older people could benefit from lack of accessibility, adoptability and usability of the user interface concerning arising special needs. To comply with the changes in needs of elderly users the exchangeability of user interfaces and thus their standardized integration is of uttermost importance. Furthermore a generality of innovative user interfaces is important to ensure a European wide exploitability and versatility. Thus the focus has to be on these aspects as a step forward in the direction of innovative user interfaces and the easy integration thereof in existing and open middleware systems.

K. Miesenberger et al. (Eds.): ICCHP 2012, Part I, LNCS 7382, pp. 650–657, 2012.

The project AALuis[1] aims at facilitating the exchange of user interfaces and thus the connection of different services to different user interfaces by means of a standardized integration [2]. This will enable future users of AAL systems to use services interacting in their preferred way. Furthermore the solution shall help that (AAL) service developers do not need to bother about accessibility in design, but only requested interactions for the services.

The ideas of AALuis are graphically represented in figure 1 by means of a block diagram. The core of the project is the AALuis Layer that hocks on existing AAL middleware platforms, such as universAAL, UMO, Persona or mPower. AAL services are connected either directly to the middleware or to the middleware via the AALuis Layer. The connection of newly developed AALuis UIs and other user interfaces to the AALuis User Interface Layer is depicted by blocks placed on top of the layer. Possible examples for I/O devices and UIs are multi touch devices, smart phones, avatar based user interfaces and smart TVs. On the right hand side of figure 1 it is indicated that various stakeholders will benefit from the ideas of AALuis.

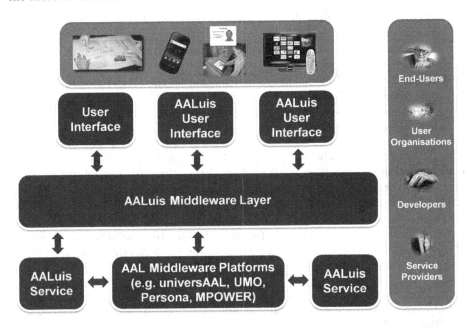

Fig. 1. A rough overview of AALuis

2 User Involvement

To ensure sustainability of project results a user-involved process is followed from the beginning of the project. The project aims at various stakeholder groups as

---

[1] www.aaluis.eu

users, not just older adults. Also carers, service providers and developers are addressed. Stakeholder involvement has started with cultural probes, online questionaires and expert groups. These have revealed requirements for the services, user interfaces and the user interface layer to be developed within the project. In the course of the project two evaluation cycles are planned for the collection of feedback for further improvements of the artefacts and to prove the concept.

3   Methods and Analysis

AALuis intends to develop an open user interface layer that facilitates a dynamically adapted, personalized interaction between an elderly user and any kind of service, with different types of input and output devices, such as smart phones, tablets, TVs or PCs. The AALuis User Interface Layer keeps track of changes of a variety of information models to establish and manipulate user interaction. The models are:

- User Context Model: Holds volatile data like the user's location, and less volatile data like the user's capabilities, preferences, limitations, etc.
- Device Context Model: Contains information about the available devices and their properties.
- Service Context Model: Collects information on the service's state, e.g. lifecycle execution information.
- Environment Context Model: Data about the living space and data outside the before mentioned scopes, e.g. time or room brightness.

The AALuis User Interface Layer uses this information to adapt an internal transformation process from abstract task descriptions to user interfaces. It is also used to steer the user interaction in a suitable manner.

One of the main goals of the AALuis is to create and exploit synergies by developing an architecture that allows the easy integration into different established AAL middleware platforms. To ensure this an analysis of technical results of projects in the AAL domain was carried out by the following criteria, whereas results from some projects are presented in the following:

- Status: What is the current status and impact of the project/technology?
- Openness: Availability of results, conditions, licensing and documentation?
- Richness: Most important and useful functionalities or components for AALuis?
- Communication: Integration possibilities of AALuis into the system?

AMIGO: Aim of this project was the development of a middleware to achieve interoperability between services and devices in heterogeneous systems [3]. The analysis of the project showed a solid approach to dynamic service and device discovery methods based on an OSGi and .NET platform [3]. Besides this AMIGO implemented interoperable service discovery and interaction in its middleware, supporting conversion of incoming and outgoing messages from one protocol to another. Supported technologies include UPnP, Web services and RMI. The conversion of input and output message streams is considered as an essential functionality of the AALuis User Interface Layer.

MonAMI: The main objective of this project was to demonstrate that accessible, useful services for elderly persons and persons with special needs, living at home can be delivered in mainstream systems and platforms [4]. The analysis showed that in the domain of user interaction a communication adapter to the UCH was created [4]. The URC (and by that the UCH) being a standard that promises wide adoption was considered for inclusion into the AALuis User Interface Layer. Since other components of the MonAMI project were project specific, reuse was considered uneconomical.

Universal Remote Console and Universal Control Hub: The URC is an international standard (ISO/IEC 24752) [5] defining a way to control arbitrary electronic devices or services (i.e. hardware or software) with interoperable, pluggable UIs. The UCH [6] realizes the URC standard as a middleware server component providing connection points to existing, non URC compliant entities. Devices targeted by the UCH are discovered and communicated with through UPnP, which is a device communication strategy that is followed by the AALuis User Interface Layer as well.

universAAL: The universAAL project aims to produce an open platform that makes it technically feasible and economically viable to conceive, design and deploy innovative AAL services. The development platform is the synthesis of new developments and a consolidation of existing platforms of former projects [7]. By this the project exhibits to be at the centre of currently ongoing open source AAL middleware platform research and development with first results available. The universAAL reference architecture structures the platform in a loosely layered way with functional groupings of components distributed over networked nodes [8]. While every service is transparently accessible on every node, only a small footprint of the middleware has to be present on each node. This architectural model lends itself to be used with the AALuis User Interface Layer. It could be integrated easily and fully benefit from the distributed system in various fields, e.g. discovery of devices, catering of user interfaces, distribution of services, context information gathering, etc. Analysis showed that the generic platform hosts a hardware abstraction which can be reused. The universAAL middleware employs an openly accessible bus system for location-transparent message exchange. The AALuis User Interface Layer's communication model could take advantage of this as well.

4   Results

As a result of the analysis the following AALuis archictecture has been specified: AALuis will be integrated on top of a preexisting OSGi based AAL middleware and thus itself be based on OSGi. A central point of the analysis and of the idea of placing the AALuis Layer on top of another AAL middleware is the posibility to reuse certain parts. These parts of interest are for example:

- Context information services
- Approach of system distribution
- Communication channels
- Existing OSGi AAL middleware services

Figure 2 sketches the idea of AALuis. Service developers can concentrate on the service interaction on an abstract level and need not to bother about delivery and accessibility of the interaction. They only describe interactions for the services in a defined format, which will be based on the Concurrent Task Trees notation. Based upon this description AALuis synthesises a dynamically adapted and personalized user interaction. AALuis offers the possibility to employ a sensible combination of the input and output channels of the available devices. The AALuis layer can split the interaction into different UI parts, if it makes sense in the current context, e.g. display a graphical input UI on the large TV, but use a tablet for text input. In the following one can find a more

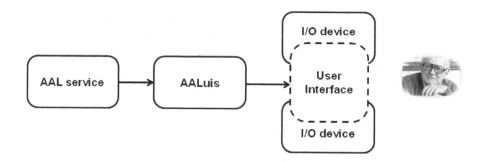

Fig. 2. Rough sketch of AALuis

detailed description of the transformation process planned in AALuis. It explains how the transformation from the task description of a service to a concrete user interface is done. The detailed AALuis architecture is described in figure 3 and consists of the following building blocks:

Services: Services connected to the AALuis platform provide a description of the interaction steps in Concurrent Task Tree (CTT) notation [10] [11]. Additional information on service method bindings has to be provided. These bindings are used by AALuis as instructions for service call-backs. Data on the actual content can also be provided by the services. At the moment this can be either static or dynamic content in textual or pictoral form. In later stages of the project it is planned to allow additional content types, like video, audio streams, etc.

From AALuis's point of view the services reside locally as OSGi bundles. Still the service's business logic could be implemented externally and could be connected by any protocol. In the second implementation iteration a direct mapping from prevailing service technologies, e.g. SOAP web services, is planned. This allows an easier integration of existing services.

Abstract User Interface Creation: Based on the documents an abstract, i.e. modality and device independent, UI description is created. This root document is generated once after service registration. Since this first transformation is static, subsequent user interactions can be based on it. The result is a document based on the MariaXML [9] notation.

Concrete User Interface Creation: Based on the context information and the abstract UI description a modality and device specific UI description is created. Therefor AALuis makes a sensible choice of output and input channels. This is done by applying a modality selection strategy utilising available context information. Depending on the strategy the user's capabilities and preferences can be respected. Due to the flexible architecture the planned strategy based on fuzzy logic may be replaced in the second implementation iteration by a learning algorithm. A set of devices to be used for the interaction can now be easily derived from the selected modalities. If necessary AALuis transforms available content to different output modalities, e.g. text to speech, text to avatar, etc.

Renderable User Interface Creation: Based on the concrete user interface a representation that is directly renderable by an I/O device is created. In a first step this is an HTML5 document that can be displayed directly. Converters to other directly renderable technologies are possible, e.g. VoiceML which can be used by a specialized device.

Device Connector: Via existing protocols (e.g. UPnP) different devices will be connected.

I/O Devices The final UI rendering is done by the devices. Those I/O devices collect the user input and send it back to the AALuis Layer. In the layer these data can be transformed to a suitable representation and be sent to the corresponding service.

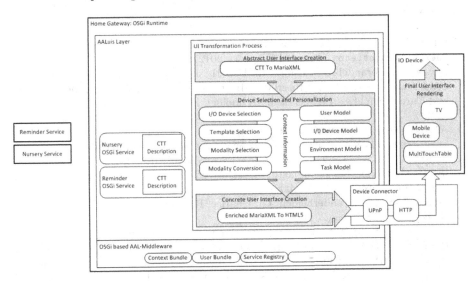

Fig. 3. Architecture of AALuis

Developing AALuis based on this architecture allows to connect different services easily to arbirtary UIs by giving a service description. These assumptions will be evaluated in already mentioned tests in a later stage of the project. The tests will focus on end-users, using the UIs, and on technical users.

5 Conclusion and Further Work

AALuis aims to significantly contribute to the freedom of choice of services and users interfaces for end-users. End-users and end-user organizations really appreciate the idea of being able to select the UI fitting to their preferences and/or special needs. This selection can lead to the feeling of being respected and empowered and will help to support destigmatization of care products and to put them on a selfserve continuum from "Comfort to Care to Cure". AALuis can achieve it by enabling a dynamically adapted, personalized interaction between an elderly user and any kind of service with different types of input and output devices.

The AALuis approach will be further elaborated and implemented in the next months. Besides the layer, AAL services and innovative user interfaces will be developed in an integrated prototype. This prototype will be evaluated with different stakeholders in the course of the project.

Acknowledgments. The project AALuis is cofunded by the AAL Joint Programme (REF. AAL-2010-3-070) and the following National Authorities and R&D programs in Austria, Germany and The Netherlands: bmvit, programm benefit, FFG (AT), BMBF (DE) and ZonMw (NL).

References

1. ETSI User Interfaces, http://www.etsi.org/website/Technologies/UserInterfaces.aspx (accessed February 2012)
2. Mayer, C., Morandell, M., Hanke, S., Bobeth, J., Bosch, T., Fagel, S., et al.: Ambient Assisted Living User Interfaces. In: Everyday Technology for Independence and Care, AAATE 2011. Assistive Technology Research Series, vol. 39. IOS Press (2011)
3. AMIGO Project Consortium (2011), http://www.hitech-projects.com/euprojects/amigo/software.html
4. Steiner, P., et al.: D23.2 Annex MonAMI Architecture description (2011)
5. ISO/IEC Information technology – User interfaces – Universal remote console – Part 1: Framework Geneva (2008)
6. Zimmermann, G., Vanderheiden, G., Charles, R.: Universal Control Hub & Task-Based User Interfaces (2011), http://myurc.org/publications/2006-Univ-Ctrl-Hub.php
7. Hanke, S., Mayer, C., Hoeftberger, O., Boos, H., Wichert, R., Tazari, M.-R., Wolf, P., Furfari, F.: universAAL – An Open and Consolidated AAL Platform. In: Wichert, R., Eberhardt, B. (eds.) Ambient Assisted Living: 4. AAL-Kongress 2011, vol. 63, pp. 127–140. Springer, Heidelberg (2011)

8. Tezari, S., Gema, I.: D1.3-B AAL Reference Architecture (2010)
9. Paterno, F., Santoro, C., Davide Spano, L.: MARIA: A universal, declarative, multiple abstraction-level language for service-oriented applications in ubiquitous environments. ACM Trans. Comput.-Hum. Interact. (2009)
10. Concurrent Task Trees, http://www.cubeos.org/lectures/W/ln_9.pdf (accessed: February 2012)
11. Paterno, F., Mancini, C., Meniconi, S.: ConcurTaskTrees: A Diagrammatic Notation for Specifying Task Models. In: INTERACT 1997 Proceedings of the IFIP TC13 International Conference on Human-Computer Interaction, pp. 362–369. Chapman & Hall (1997)

Comparison between Single-touch and Multi-touch Interaction for Older People

Guillaume Lepicard and Nadine Vigouroux

Université Paul Sabatier, Institut de Recherche en Informatique de Toulouse
F-31062 Toulouse Cedex 9, France
{lepicard,vigourou}@irit.fr

Abstract. This paper describes a study exploring the multi-touch interaction for older adults. The aim of this experiment was to check the relevance of this interaction versus single-touch interaction to realize object manipulation tasks: move, rotate and zoom. For each task, the user had to manipulate a rectangle and superimpose it to a picture frame. Our study shows that adults and principally older adults had more difficulties to realize these tasks for multi-touch interaction than for single-touch interaction.

Keywords: interaction, multi-touch, older people, usability.

1 Introduction

Aging leads to deficiencies. These are the losses of perception, motor skills or cognitive capacities [1]. These deficiencies and more specially the cognitive impairment could explain the advantage of the touch screen interaction versus the mouse interaction for older people [2], [3], [4]. Multi-touch interaction has been used massively since the release of iPhone but is it useful and usable? To compare the single-touch versus multi-touch interaction relevance for older adults, we have developed an experiment platform to study object manipulation tasks: move, rotate and zoom.

2 Method

First, the experimenter explains the test procedure to the subject. Then, the subject is asked to complete an agreement form of informed consent. Once it is filled, the subject is proposed to adjust the height of his/her chair and the distance between him/her and the tablet to ensure good experimental conditions. After that, he/she created alone or with the help of the experimenter a user account where he/she was asked information on sex, guiding hand and birthdate.

This test is divided into three parts: one part for each interaction (single-touch versus multi-touch) and a questionnaire. Interactions based on gestures use one or two fingers of the same hand. The number of necessary fingers depends on the

K. Miesenberger et al. (Eds.): ICCHP 2012, Part I, LNCS 7382, pp. 658–665, 2012.

interaction type. Each interaction session consists of three parts: a learning session, a test and an electronic questionnaire. During the subject learning session, the experimenter explains and illustrates the interaction operating principles for each type of action: move, rotate and zoom. The test purpose is to move an object into a picture frame (see Figure 1). The interaction with one finger uses a 3x3 grid. This number of areas respects the magical number of Miller [5]. Each area has the same size and is associated with one action: the central area allows to move, the border areas to rotate and others to zoom in or zoom out. In the Figure 1, each action is represented by a letter in French (D: Move, T: Rotate, Z: Zoom). For the same test, the interaction with two fingers of the same hand is based on Windows 7 gestures to realize the same three actions (see Figure 2).

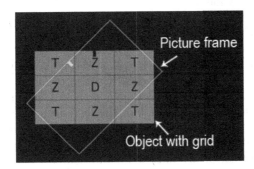

Fig. 1. Single-touch interaction based on a grid representation

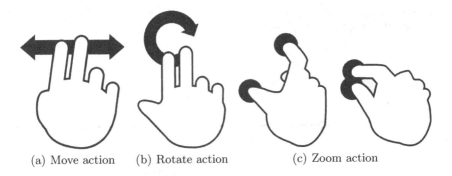

(a) Move action   (b) Rotate action   (c) Zoom action

Fig. 2. Multi-touch interaction [6]

The questionnaire for each interaction asks whether the person has felt motor or visual fatigue; which is easiest, hardest action for him/her and which one is his/her favorite. The post experiment questionnaire consists of two parts: an electronic part that asks the subject to establish the usability grading for the both interactions; and a paper part that contains several specific information on the user and his/her feedback on the experiment.

The experiments were realized on a Dell Tablet PC Latitude XT2, with a 12.1 inch LCD monitor running Microsoft Windows 7 operating system. The screen resolution was 1280 by 800 pixels (124,7dpi). The touch gestures recognition of Windows 7 were disabled. The tablet was set in tactile interaction mode. It was placed on a desk with an inclination of 30 degrees [7].

There are two types of parameters: independent and dependent. We define three independent parameters: the population (younger or older adults), the interaction (single-touch or multi-touch) and the action (move, rotate or zoom); and six dependent parameters:

- Action Completion Time (ACT) is the time to realize the requested action. It is divided into three parts (see Figure 3): Analysis Time, Approach Time and Stabilization Time:
  - Analysis Time (AnT) is the time between the appearance of the new instruction and the first press on the touchscreen;
  - Approach Time (ApT) is the time between the first press on the touchscreen and the time where the user passes over or through the final position;
  - Stabilization Time (ST) is the time between the moment where the user passes over or through the final position and the validation of the instruction.
- Approaching curve is the evolution of the distance to the final position according to the time. This distance is calculated as a percentage to compare the three different actions: ratio between the current measure (distance or angle according the action) and the final measure;
- Error rate. This parameter is not analyzed because all actions were successfully done. Indeed, we realized a pre-experiment that determined the acceptance threshold to validate the action.

In this paper, only three dependent parameters are studied: the Action Completion Time, the Analysis Time and the Approaching curve.

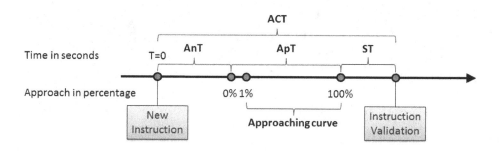

Fig. 3. Decomposition of time for an action

Twelve younger adults aged between 23 and 33 years (mean=28.08 and standard deviation (SD)=3.48) and twelve older adults aged between 63 and 89 years (mean=77.58 and SD=7.89) participated in this study. All subjects had normal or corrected vision, neither cognitive deficiency nor motor impairment.

3   Results

3.1   Qualitative Results

Regardless of the population, most users preferred the single-touch interaction: all older adults preferred the interaction based on the grid, ten younger adults also preferred this interaction.

Regardless of the population, most users find the multi-touch interaction more tiring than single-touch interaction. Two older adults had eyestrain for single-touch interaction while seven ones had motor tiredness and four had eyestrain for multi-touch interaction. Three younger adults had motor tiredness for multi-touch and nobody was tired by the use of single-touch interaction.

3.2   Quantitative Results

Action Completion Time. The three-way ANOVA analysis showed that exist two interactions: between the type of action and the class of population $F(2, 2580) = 11.92$, $p = 7.01^{-6}$; and between the type of interaction and the class of population $F(1, 2580) = 75.56$, $p < 2.2^{-16}$.

The study of interaction between the type of action and the class of population (see Figure 4(a)) shows that older adults are slower to realize each action and that moving action is easier for older people to realize than zooming and rotating actions.

The study of interaction between the type of interaction and the class of population (see Figure 4(b)) shows that multi-touch interaction is worse than single-touch interaction for the two populations. For older population, the difference is more significant than for the younger one.

Analysis Time. The three-way ANOVA analysis showed that exists two interactions: between the type of action and the class of population $F(2, 2580) = 5.44$, $p = 4.37^{-3}$; and between the type of interaction and the class of population $F(1, 2580) = 15.85$, $p = 7.03^{-5}$.

The study of interaction between the type of action and the class of population (see Figure 5(a)) shows that older adults are slower to begin each action. The analysis time of moving action is quicker than analysis times of rotating and zooming action regardless the population. This result seems logical because the moving action requires a cognitive load smaller than the two others. Moreover, younger adults have an analysis time for zooming action longer than zooming action contrary to older adults that have the analysis time for these two actions equal.

The study of interaction between the type of interaction and the class of population (see Figure 5(b)) shows that analysis time of multi-touch is longer than the analysis time of single-touch interaction regardless the population. The analysis time difference between the two interactions is more significant for older adults compare to younger adults. It is possible that the visual reminder of the grid can help to detect more quickly the action to realize. Another explanation is that the motion planning is easier with the use of one finger than the use of two.

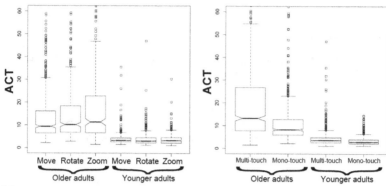

(a) Interaction between the type of action and the class of population

(b) Interaction between the type of interaction and the class of population

Fig. 4. ACT in seconds

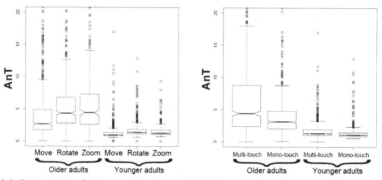

(a) Interaction between the type of action and the class of population

(b) Interaction between the type of interaction and the class of population

Fig. 5. AnT in seconds

Approaching Curve. Figure 6 represents the approaching curve for the moving action. The beginning of the movement is very quick for younger adults. Older adults have a different approach curve, they start slowly to move the object and then they accelerate. The speed of older adults is very irregular for multi-touch interaction. This is due to few drops of the object during the moving action.

For rotating action (see Figure 7), younger adults slow down when the object is close to the final position. They have a similar behavior for the both interactions. With older adults, for the single-touch interaction, the rotating action curve has the same beginning as the moving action curve. Older adults start by rotate the object slowly and then accelerate. Moreover, the end of older adults rotating action curve is similar to this curve of younger adults. For multi-touch interaction, older adults have a constant speed but have more sub-movements and more hesitations.

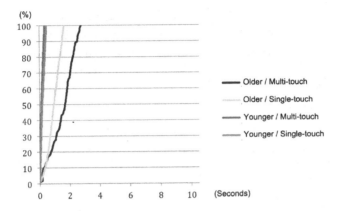

Fig. 6. Approaching curve for moving action of the both classes of population and the both interactions

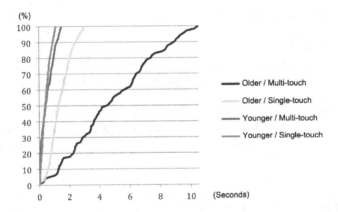

Fig. 7. Approaching curve for rotating action of the both classes of population and the both interactions

For zooming action (see Figure 8), the approaches between two population are quite different. Younger adults have similar approach curve whatever the interaction. Older adults have two distinctive approach curves. The single-touch interaction is much quicker than multi-touch interaction but the both curves have a quite similar aspect. The multi-touch curve for older people is composed of two steps with almost stop near 45% and 95%. These steps are explained by a persistence to spread/gather fingers when it is not physically possible.

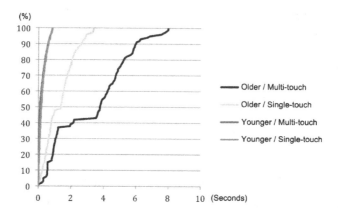

Fig. 8. Approaching curve for zooming action of the both classes of population and the both interactions

4   Discussions and Conclusion

The use of two fingers inevitably leads to a larger surface hidden by the hand. The additional concentration to detect the hidden shape causes more eyestrain. Multi-touch interaction requires greater hand flexibility than single-touch interaction. This leads to a motor tiredness more significant with this interaction.

With approach curves, we can notice that the older adults generally have identical approach behavior whatever the action. They begin the movement with a quite long acceleration phase in order to stabilize their speed. The deceleration phase is also longer than this phase of younger adults. These effects confirm the results of Roy [8].

In summary, single-touch interaction is better than multi-touch interaction. This conclusion is valid for quantitative and qualitative results. We can infer that the multi-touch interaction is not recommended for the older people and it is also the case to a lesser extent of younger people. Rotate and zoom actions lead to difficulties for older people with multi-touch interaction. These results are confirmed by other studies. Piper [4] indicated, for example, that zooming leads to difficulties with the use of two fingers. Moreover, the analyses of our other results show that manipulation task sub-movements are a major cause of the decreasing of performance. Indeed, Morgan [9] explained that older adults realized more sub-movements and had more hesitations for a zigzag pointing task.

The first perspective of this work is to model the performance according to age. To reach this aim, we need a more significant number of users. Moreover, it would be interesting to open the experiment to other population as children.

In this paper, we studied multi-touch interaction with two fingers of the same hand. Previous works have recommended using two fingers of the same hand instead of one finger of each hand for synchronized actions [10]. However, this research is not based on an older population. It would be interesting to observe if this is always the case for older adults. Other perspective of the paper is to study multi-touch interaction with one finger of each hand. Indeed, the advantage of using two hands is that the user gains in mobility. This could solve some problems of the older people agility.

References

1. Carmichael, A.: Style Guide for the Design of Interactive Television Services for Elderly Viewers. In: Independent Television Commission (1999)
2. Tan, D.S., Pausch, R., Stefanucci, J.K., Proffitt, D.R.: Kinesthetic cues aid spatial memory. In: CHI 2002 Extended Abstracts on Human Factors in Computing Systems, pp. 806–807. ACM, New York (2002)
3. Wood, E., Willoughby, T., Rushing, A., Bechtel, L., Gilbert, J.: Use of Computer Input Devices by Older Adults. Journal of Applied Gerontology 24(5), 419–438 (2005)
4. Piper, A.M., Campbell, R., Hollan, J.D.: Exploring the accessibility and appeal of surface computing for older adult health care support. In: Proceedings of the 28th International Conference on Human Factors in Computing Systems, pp. 907–916. ACM, New York (2010)
5. Miller, G.: The Magical Number Seven, Plus or Minus Two: Some Limits on Our Capacity for Processing Information. The Magical Number Seven, Plus or Minus Two. Psychological Review 63(2), 81–97 (1956)
6. Multitouch pictures, http://www.lukew.com/ff/entry.asp?1071
7. Ahlström, B., Lenman, S., Marmolin, T.: Overcoming touchscreen user fatigue by workplace design. In: Posters and Short Talks of the 1992 SIGCHI Conference on Human Factors in Computing Systems, pp. 101–102. ACM, New York (1992)
8. Roy, E.A., Weir, P.L., Leavitt, J.L.: Constraints on prehension: A framework for studying the effects of aging. In: Changes in Sensory Motor Behavior in Aging, pp. 279–314 (1996)
9. Morgan, M., Phillips, J.G., Bradshaw, J.L., Mattingley, J.B., Iansek, R., Bradshaw, J.A.: Age-related motor slowness: simply strategic? Journal of Gerontology 49(3), 133–139 (1994)
10. Moscovich, T., Hughes, J.F.: Indirect mappings of multi-touch input using one and two hands. In: Proceedings of the Twenty-Sixth Annual SIGCHI Conference on Human Factors in Computing Systems, pp. 1275–1284. ACM, New York (2008)

Online Social Networks and Older People

Guillermo Prieto[1] and Denise Leahy[2]

[1] Trinity College Dublin, Computer Science Department, Dublin, Ireland
prietodg@tcd.ie
[2] Trinity College Dublin, Computer Science Department, Dublin, Ireland
denise.leahy@cs.tcd.ie

Abstract. The number of older people is growing significantly and accounts for an ever-increasing percentage of the global population [1]. Online social networks are continuously gaining more relevance and presence in everyday life for communication, work and social interaction. Despite those trends, there is little knowledge on how older people use online social networks, and the benefits derived from it or the possible negative impacts [2], [3]. This paper examines how older people use online social networks and the factors which influence this use.

Keywords: online social networks, older people, design, accessibility, digital divide, adoption.

1 Introduction

This paper examines the area of online social networks (SNs) and older people, focusing on their usage and the perceived challenges and benefits. The influence that factors such as design, accessibility and adoption have on the older person's experience with online social networks is explored.

In order to understand how SNs are impacting older people, some definitions and characteristics must be provided. SNs can be defined as sites that "typically provide users with a profile space, facilities for uploading content (e.g. photos, music), messaging in various forms and the ability to make connections to other people." [4] SNs have changed interactions between users on the World Wide Web from a one-way, consumption model to a multi-way, participation model. This has changed the way people engage in their communication, collaboration and interests [5].

From the demographic perspective, a significant increase over the next decades in the number of older people is expected [1]. In Europe, the number of people aged between 50 and 80 will rise by over 34% by 2050 [6]. Technology has the potential to support older people by improving their quality of life, living independently longer and counteracting the reduced capabilities caused by the ageing process [6]. Social networking can play an important part in this.

2 Accessibility for Older People

Accessibility is a key factor determining the adoption, proliferation and usage of SNs and other ICT among older people. From the physiological point of view, as time

K. Miesenberger et al. (Eds.): ICCHP 2012, Part I, LNCS 7382, pp. 666–672, 2012.

goes by, human beings tend to suffer physical, sensory or cognitive restrictions. Due to this aging process, older people often experience restrictions in an enormous diversity of forms; for example vision decline, hearing loss, motor skill diminishment, and cognitive impairments. As a result of functional limitations, older people are included among the collective of people with disabilities. [7], [8]

The World Wide Web is the main point of access to and use of SNs. Older people face web accessibility barriers due to:

- Poor design and poor coding of websites;
- Complex software and assistive technologies;
- Lack of experience with computers [9].

It must be noted that there are several factors affecting web use: web content, web browsers, media players, assistive technology, user's knowledge and experience, authoring tools and evaluation tools. For a web site to be accessible it is thus crucial that those components are considered [10].

3   Design for Older People

Practical learning in the design of SNs for older people can be gained from AGNES (AGeing in a NEtworked Society), a project funded as part of the European Ambient Assisted Living (AAL) initiative [11].

The aim of the AGNES project was to develop a basic communication and information platform with an easy-to-use SN for individual older persons as its core component. The communication in the platform works in two ways: messages or stories from family members will reach the older person in an ambient form (speech, visual cues) through display devices, and the older person's responses, states and activity reports will be transmitted back [12]. The design principles of the AGNES project may serve as a reference for designers of SNs with older people in mind.

When older people deal with new technologies, they may find themselves in a position that leads to an increase in their sense of frustration and dependency because of barriers (for example related to income, health difficulties, possible disabilities, location and education) [13]. A principle in web design for older people should be to structure the site in a similar manner to the sites that users already know. Online forms on the web can present a difficulty; this is important in e-commerce or e-Government sites. Although they may be confusing for many older people, online forms can benefit users when implemented well [7]. Having too many choices on a web page can confuse people with mild cognitive impairment [7]. An important part of the web is using a search engine. Web designers must be aware of some of the problems encountered by older people when making searches:

- Links which open applications rather than HTML pages;
- Difficulties in entering data in forms;
- Returning to the initial search page;
- Difficulties with scrolling and mouse usage [14].

4   The Digital Divide

The usage patterns of technology amongst older people can be affected by socio-economic and disabilities factors [15]. Another factor contributing to the differences of usage between different age groups is the number of 'younger' people who use ICT at work [15].

Access is vital. It was found in the U.S. that the availability of access to high-speed Internet highly depends on each person's socioeconomic status [16]. In the U.S., it was found that, during 2010, 79% of all adults used the Internet, in comparison with 45% people over 65 [17]. Regarding the use of Social Networks, 61% of all adults connected to the Internet used SNs whereas 34% of people aged between 65 and 73, and 16% of people aged 74 or more did so [17]. In general, the younger the generation, the more they used social networks [17].

The digital divide can be influenced by - public and private initiatives towards IT education and training; investment in science and technology; costs and regulation of telecommunications; cultural attitudes towards using computers; and English language fluency [18].

5   The Research Methodology

An online survey was carried out, during summer 2011, with Irish citizens using SurveyMonkey. Participants were invited to take part by a link on an e-newsletter sent by an organisation working with older people.

The hypotheses to be validated were:

- Older people use SNs differently to the general population;
- Older people's opinions about the benefits and disadvantages of using SNs are different to those of the general population.

The main contribution of this research comes from this online survey. The questions gathered information about the respondents' background and how long they had been using the Internet; their SNs adoption and usage; and the perceived benefits, challenges and negative impacts of using SNs.

In this research, respondents aged 61 or more were considered older persons, while respondents aged less than or 60 were categorised as younger persons. There were 28 older respondents, 17 of them being SNs users. There were 20 younger participants. Therefore the total number of respondents was 48.

Although the online questionnaire was designed with social networks users in mind, non-users could also answer up to five questions, including one which asked why they were not using social networks. Social network users could answer up to twenty-one questions.

6   Findings

The total number of participants in the survey was 48. Of 28 respondents that were aged 61 or more, 17 were SNs users. Asked how long they had been using the Internet, 76.5% of older SNs users and all younger users had been doing so for 5 years or more.

Among older participants who were not using SNs, the main reasons for this were privacy and lack of awareness (27.3% each), followed by the complexity of SNs and friends not using them (18.2% each).

Facebook is the main SN used by older participants (64.7%) and LinkedIn was used by 22.5%. Facebook is also the main SN for younger participants (68.4%). In this age group Twitter was the second most used SN (21.1%). Most of younger users got to know SNs through their friends (68.4%). Older users got to know SNs primarily through family (47.1%) and Internet-based media (29.4%). Friends and traditional media were other sources mentioned as well.

In relation to the length of the average SNs sessions, for most of older users they last between 5 and 19 minutes (35.3%), and 20 to 39 minutes (29.4%). The sessions of the younger users tend to be shorter, lasting between 5 and 19 minutes (68.4%), with less than 5 minutes (15.8%) the next most reported interval. Many older users (41.2%) visit SNs more than once every day and 58% visit SNs a maximum of once a week. Younger users present a heavier use in frequency terms, with 84.2% of participants visiting SNs at least once every day.

Communicating with other members of the SNs (31.3%), and staying in touch with family and friends (18.8%) are the primary reasons for using SNs for older users. The figures for younger users were similar (36.8% and 31.6%). Older SNs users declare less connections (75.1% under 100) and people they communicate with (81.3% under 30) than younger users (73.3% with 100 or more connections, and 44.5% communicating with 30 or more members). In both cases, figures agree with what has been suggested by other studies, i.e. most of users effectively interact with a small subset of contacts [25].

In content creation terms, older and younger users present almost the same ranking of activities, the main ones are writing to other people's web page (62.5% versus 89.5%), commenting on photos or videos (50% versus 89.5%), and uploading photos or videos (50% versus 78.9%). For those and other categories younger users present higher percentages of content creation.

Older users express varied attitudes towards their privacy settings, with a bit more than a half (56.3%) making them more private. Younger users are more worried and conscious about privacy settings, with almost all of them (89.5%) making them more private.

In relation to the perceived benefits from SNs, younger users report more benefits on almost every category, the main ones being improving communication with family and friends (66.7%), and gaining more generic knowledge (50%). The main benefit expressed by older users also was to improve communication with family and friends (46.7%), followed by gaining more specific knowledge about computers and Internet (33.3%).

A similar situation occurs with the perceived negative implications: younger users report more of them in all the categories, the main ones being less time to read (50%), less physical activity (38.9%) and less concentration when doing other activities (38.9%). The majority of older users (73.3%) do not report any negative impact from the use of SNs.

The respondents had an opportunity to comment on their use of social networks and expressed a mixture of opinions:

- "It is brilliant for keeping the mind active and connecting with people in one's life past and present;"
- "I suppose it is nice to be in touch with my grandchildren. It is fast;"
- "If this activity is useful then enjoy it. Avoid giving information that could lead to identity theft;"
- "I deliberately ignore most of the emails that come from social networks. They would waste my time. I am only interested in REAL friends and people with similar hobby/work interests. I don't need to "link" via the Internet; I do not need to retreat into the cyber world;"
- "Many older people are not as aware privacy and security issues as they should be - especially in relation to Facebook e.g. face recognition, tagging, not allowing 'friends of friends' to view your details etc."

7 Discussion

One of the variables influencing whether older people use SNs may be the time respondents have been utilising the Internet. Older SNs users report longer time using the Internet that non-users, but many have been using it for less than 5 years. All younger participants in the survey were using the Internet for 5 years or more. The results obtained in the survey with regards to the benefits, concerns and negative implications could lead to conclude that older users are less literate in SNs terms.

The concept of the digital divide is also very relevant for older people and SNs because usage patterns are not only determined by the age differences among senior citizens, but also socio-economic and disability factors. Although the latter has not been investigated on the online survey, in relation to socio-economic factors older SNs users got to know SNs primarily through family (47.1%), while younger SNs users did so mainly through friends (68.4%).

Today's SNs do not match offline social networks. In the latter, each person clearly identifies strong and weak ties with other people, as well as the group each friend, relative, or acquaintance belongs to. The design of SNs considerably impacts users' behaviours, for example by self censoring themselves in making public comments which they might not do with a known audience [19]. It could be argued that if filters and means to separate communications with different connections and groups were put in place, the adoption and time spent on SNs would significantly increase, particularly among those with more concerns about their privacy and other people's views on their behaviour.

Nowadays, users are increasingly accessing SNs and other web sites through diverse channels. This poses a challenge for providers who increasingly find that this multichannel delivery is more costly to produce and maintain [20]. It is important that SNs designers take this trend into consideration. Allowing switching of input methods according to users' preferences or circumstances can be very beneficial. For instance, when a mobile phone is used either to communicate with other people or as an interface with other devices, it should permit to switch from voice to key input in an environment that becomes noisy [21]. Another example comes from the two proposed types of interfaces: those based on voice commands and natural speech recognition; and those based on gesture recognition [22].

It is important to bear in mind that, like other technologies, ICT will evolve. However, people's social behaviours may remain the same. A useful research approach towards SNs would be to understand people's motivations for using social networks instead of studying the technology behind the SN itself [19]. SNs are a key element in people's empowerment. As such, they have a significant role to play as communication and information channels with growing audiences. The convergence of multimodal technologies and the emergence of smart phones and tablets will reinforce the location features that SNs offer. This may be useful for older people, for instance by making their family and friends aware of their location or by posting and following recommendations that otherwise could be missed or forgotten.

Older people often think that the benefits associated with the use of a computer are outweighed by the necessary effort [23]. Individuals and organisations that interact with older people should promote the value that technology can bring to senior citizens. One of the hardest difficulties in the digital divide is to tackle the group of non-users of ICT which has remained the same since 2001 and accounts for more than 25% of older people [15]. One possible approach to reduce this digital divide could be, instead of beginning with the navigation of random websites or the use of computer applications like Microsoft Office, to encourage senior citizens to use SNs as their initial point of access to computers when they are first introduced to technology.

References

1. The Department of Economic and Social Affairs of the United Nations Secretariat: World Population Ageing. United Nations, New York (2009)
2. Karahasanovic, A., Brandtzæg, P.B., Heim, J., Lüders, M., Vermeir, L., Pierson, J., Lievens, B., Vanattenhoven, J., Jans, G.: Co-creation and user-generated content-elderly people's user requirements. Computers in Human Behavior 25(3), 655–678 (2009)
3. Vasalou, A., Joinson, A., Courvoisier, D.: Cultural differences, experience with social networks and the nature of 'true commitment' in Facebook. International Journal of Human-Computer Studies 68(10), 719–728 (2010)
4. Joinson, A.: Looking at, looking up or keeping up with people?: motives and use of Facebook. In: Proceedings of the Twenty-Sixth Annual SIGCHI Conference on Human Factors in Computing Systems (CHI 2008), pp. 1027–1036. ACM, New York (2008)
5. John, A., Adamic, L., Davis, M., Nack, F., Shamma, D.A., Seligmann, D.D.: The future of online social interactions: what to expect in 2020. In: Proceedings of the 17th International Conference on World Wide Web (WWW 2008), pp. 1255–1256. ACM, New York (2008)
6. European Commission: Digital Agenda for Europe (2010)
7. W3C: Web Accessibility for Older Users: A Literature Review (2008)
8. Abascal, J., Fernández de Castro, I., Lafuente, A.L., Cia, J.M.: Adaptive Interfaces for Supportive Ambient Intelligence Environments. In: Miesenberger, K., Klaus, J., Zagler, W.L., Karshmer, A.I. (eds.) ICCHP 2008. LNCS, vol. 5105, pp. 30–37. Springer, Heidelberg (2008)

9. W3C: Web Accessibility for Older Users Presentation (2010)
10. Web Accessibility Initiative: Essential Components of Web Accessibility (2005)
11. AGNES: Successful Ageing in a Networked Society (2009)
12. Waterworth, J.A., Ballesteros, S., Peter, C., Bieber, G., Kreiner, A., Wiratanaya, A., Poly-menakos, L., Wanche-Politis, S., Capobianco, M., Etxeberria, I., Lundholm, L.: Ageing in a networked society: social inclusion and mental stimulation. In: Proceedings of the 2nd International Conference on Pervasive Technologies Related to Assistive Environments (PETRA 2009). ACM, New York (2009)
13. European Commission: Action Plan on Information and Communication Technologies and Ageing (2007)
14. Aula, A.: User study on older adults' use of the Web and search engines. Universal Access in the Information Society 4(1), 67–81 (2005)
15. European Commission: Seniorwatch 2 - Assessment of the Senior Market for ICT Progress and Developments (2008)
16. Gartner Group: The Gartner Digital Divide and American Society Report. Gartner Group, Stamford (2000)
17. Pew Internet: Change in Internet access by age group (2000-2011). Pew Research Center, Washington (2010)
18. Norris, P.: The Worldwide Digital Divide: Information Poverty, the Internet, and Development. Harvard University, Cambridge (2000)
19. Adams, P.: The Real Life Social Network. Google Research (2010)
20. Chuter, A.: Web Accessible and Mobile: The Relationship between Mobile Web Best Practices and Web Content Accessibility Guidelines. In: Miesenberger, K., Klaus, J., Zagler, W.L., Karshmer, A.I. (eds.) ICCHP 2008. LNCS, vol. 5105, pp. 498–501. Springer, Heidelberg (2008)
21. Yoshida, R., Yasumura, M.: A New Cell Phone Remote Control for People with Visual Impairment. In: Miesenberger, K., Klaus, J., Zagler, W.L., Karshmer, A.I. (eds.) ICCHP 2008. LNCS, vol. 5105, pp. 1145–1152. Springer, Heidelberg (2008)
22. Park, K.-H., Bien, Z., Lee, J.-J., Kim, B.-K., Lim, J.-T., Kim, J.-O., Lee, H., Stefanov, D., Kim, D.-J., Jung, J.-W.: Robotic smart house to assist people with movement disabilities. Autonomous Robots 22(2), 183–198 (2007)
23. Holzinger, A., Searle, G., Kleinberger, T., Seffah, A., Javahery, H.: Investigating Usability Metrics for the Design and Development of Applications for the Elderly. In: Miesenberger, K., Klaus, J., Zagler, W.L., Karshmer, A.I. (eds.) ICCHP 2008. LNCS, vol. 5105, pp. 98–105. Springer, Heidelberg (2008)

"Break the Bricks"
Serious Game for Stroke Patients

Tamás Dömők, Veronika Szűcs, Erika László, and Cecília Sík Lányi

University of Pannonia, Egyetem u. 10.,
H-8200 Veszprém, Hungary
{domoktamas,veronika.szucs01,missaxe}@gmail.com,
lanyi@almos.uni-pannon.hu

Abstract. This study introduces a serious game, "Break the Bricks", which is one of the games planned within the "StrokeBack" project. The aim of this game is to support the rehabilitation process of stroke patients whom have upper limb impairments and damaged psychomotor abilities. In this paper we will present the designing process and the development of the game. We would like to represent the background of serious games, and the planned test methods of "Break the Bricks". We will also delineate future plans and further work with this game.

Keywords: serious game, rehabilitation, stroke patients, locomotor disorder.

1 Introduction

Within the StrokeBack project [1], which is a newly started project partly funded by the EU, we need to increase the speed of the rehabilitation process of stroke patients. A very important criterion is that the patients should stay at home during the therapy, because the closeness of their home has a good effect on them. With the repetition of many small exercises with the arms and shoulders, the damaged psychomotor abilities can be recovered.

The aim of this part of the project is to create games which make the patient do these exercises playfully. One of the planned games is the "Break the Bricks" game. This game is developed for Android operating system, because this platform is frequently and widely used on up-to-date mobile phones and smart phones, so it is easily accessible for the patients or the hospitals.

2 State of the Art

Many applications have been developed all over the world for stroke rehabilitation [2]. One of the most interesting of these researches is the VividGroup's Gesture Xtreme System [3], [4]. It is a unique approach to Virtual Reality (VR), which might have important applications for the rehabilitation of children and adults with physical and/or cognitive impairments [5]. Another way to develop VR applications is to start from existing occupational treatment methods and to develop platforms

K. Miesenberger et al. (Eds.): ICCHP 2012, Part I, LNCS 7382, pp. 673–680, 2012.

for home rehabilitation. In such telemedically controlled systems using low-cost web-based video/audio telemedicine units there is a much higher potential [6]. Connor et al. in San Francisco used a haptic guided error-free learning unit with an active force feedback joystick and computer for rehabilitation of cognitive deficits following a stroke [7].

The project called "Virtual Reality for Brain Injury Rehabilitation" developed at Lund University in Sweden, produced many interesting results. They investigated usability issues of VR technology for people with brain injury, examined the issue of transfer and training, developed different applications of VR for training in daily tasks, such as kitchen work, using an automatic teller machine, finding one's way in a complex environment, using virtual vending and automatic service machines [8], [9]. VR has been used to test executive functioning in patients with focal frontal lesions. It was carried out in a multi-componential VR procedure, the Bungalow Task, and was developed to test strategy formation, rule breaking and prospective memory [10].

In 2006 Lövquist and Dreifaldt presented an application based on an immersive workbench and a haptic device, designed to motivate stroke patients in their rehabilitation of their arm. They developed a virtual labyrinth system. The Labyrinth contributes to an overall pleasant and encouraging exercise experience. The patients see this as a complement to the rehabilitation techniques used today and it gives them alternative exercises that are encouraging, challenging and fun to help ease their recovery [11].

Pictures and real objects have big role in the learning process not only in rehabilitation but in childhood education too. Pictures have big role in learning process of students from families with unfortunate social conditions. Pictures help students recognize their experiences and transfer them into symbolic form [12]. Real objects have big importance for students, who are learning in ICT supported environment. Experience of hands on activity appears when the students work with computers [13].

According to Burke [14], VR games were indeed usable and playable by people with stroke. Furthermore, the games seemed to stimulate a high level of interest and enjoyment by the participants, which may indicate the games are engaging to play.

Considering these results, it is easy to see that rehabilitation of stroke patients aided with games has a reason for existence. This topic has a lot of opportunity, so this is the reason we decided to improve stroke patients' rehabilitation process with developing serious games, including "Break the Bricks". These games will be encouraging and fun to play, so the patients will be motivated to use them more and more. This way, they will practice the rehabilitation exercises more frequently and pleasantly than they would do the traditional therapy. Another advantage is that patients can play anytime they want, without the supervision of a therapist.

3   The Game

"Break the Bricks" is a classic brick-breaker game. The aim of the game is to break all the bricks with a bouncing ball, while keeping the ball from falling down with a block. The user can control the block by moving the phone. These precise arm movements are the rehabilitation exercises, they need concentration, and the game is funny and enjoyable. The patient is also motivated by the levels of the game, which can be defeated, and by the breaking of his or her own highest scores. Also an advantage of the game is that it uses the built-in accelerometer of the phone and relies on the patient's balancing ability, so this capability can also be healed.

3.1   Designing Process

First of all, the requirements of the serious game program had to be identified. The most important ones were the non functional requirements: the application must be easy to use for elderly or disabled people, and it should be available for more platforms. As for the functional requirements, they follow from the use-cases.

The use-case diagram of the "Break the Bricks" game is shown on figure 1. This illustration shows the steps and facilities of the game.

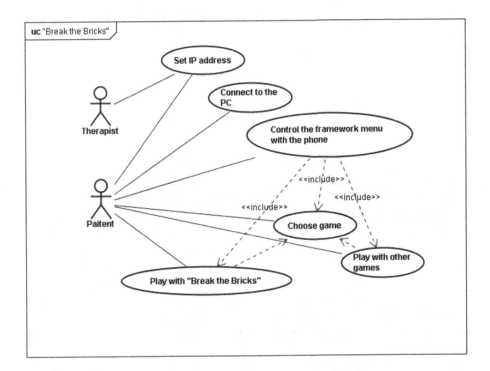

Fig. 1. The use-case diagram of Break the Bricks

As seen on figure 1, there are two actors of the system: the therapist, and the patient, who is the main actor. The therapist only assists the patient if needed with setting up the IP address. In this step, the therapist or the patient has to type in the IP address of the PC which runs the PC Client. After the IP address has been set up, the patient shall connect the mobile phone to the PC to use the program. With the phone connected to the PC, the patient can control the framework and the game. In this menu the patient can choose whether she/he want to set up the program, play with games, or get information about the system. In a submenu, the user can select which game she/he would like to play with. If the patient wants to play with "Break the Bricks", it should be selected in this menu.\

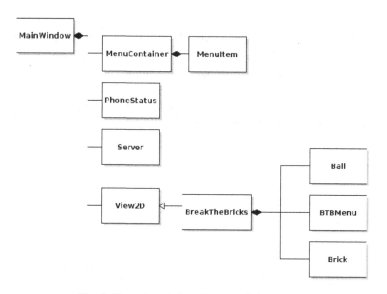

Fig. 2. The reduced class diagram of the system

After the use-cases, the classes and the class hierarchy was designed. A simplified class diagram of the system can be seen on figure 2, which displays only the most important classes. These classes are the ones, responsible for the main functions. For the dynamic menu of the game the *MenuContainer* and the *MenuItem* classes are responsible. These grant that the menu is easily expandable, without writing any source code. The *PhoneStatus* class stores data about the phone's sensors and some calculated values. This information comes from the *Server* class, which is handling the communication of the PC with the mobile phone. The other classes are responsible for the "Break the Bricks" game's functions, managing the bricks, the ball, etc.

The serious game program is using a dummy client, which is connected to a PC client by a TCP connection via WiFi. This topology can be seen on figure 3, the architecture diagram. The PC client is running in the background, it only shows up if a phone is connected.

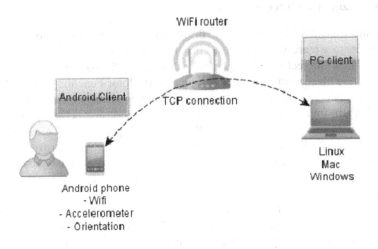

Fig. 3. The architecture diagram of "Break the Bricks" game

The PC client's menu can be controlled with the mobile phone, with flicks. The menu is easily understandable and usable.

The PC client is made with the use of the Qt framework. This is because Qt is a cross-platform, so it can be used irrespectively of the PC's operating system or configuration. The mobile phone's android application is written in Java.

3.2   The Framework

A universal framework is also part of the system, which will include all of the serious game in the "StrokeBack" project. This framework handles the communication of the PCs and the mobile phones, supplies movement data to the games, and provides a main menu for the system.

The most important function of this framework is to support the communication of the games and the mobile phone. The framework manages the connection of the PC and the phone, converts the sensor data received from the phone to the movement data used by the games, and provides this movement data to the games.

Another function provided by the framework is the PC client's main menu. In this menu, the user can reach the "Play games", the "Settings", the "About" and the "Help" submenus, and can quit the program. In the "Play games" menu the games inserted into the framework can be started. With the "Settings" submenu, the user can set some parameters of the PC client. In the "About" menu the user can find information about the authors and the game. The "Help" submenu's goal is to give a hand to the user with showing the controlling and setting up process of the framework.

A big advantage is that the framework can be easily expanded with other games and functions. This way if we design more games on the grounds of the experience we gain from the first games' tests, we can easily add them to the system.

3.3   Analyzing the Outcome Effects

Because the system is not ready yet, the testing with stroke patients hasn't been started. Even so we are working on testing methods to measure the effectiveness of the "StrokeBack" project's serious games, including the "Break the Bricks" game.

One of these planned methods is to use the Wolf Motor Function Test (WMFT) to measure the outcome. The WMFT's purpose is to monitor the physical condition of a patient with arm impairments [15]. The patients will be tested before starting the rehabilitation with serious games, frequently during the process, and after an allotted time period. The WMFT can show if the patient's condition has improved, and it can tell the degree of this advance. As a reference, we would like to make these WMFT's with patients whom are doing the traditional rehabilitation exercises, without playing serious games.

Besides this we would like to ask the users of the system to provide their opinion, using a survey. This questionnaire should include questions about usability, intelligibility, user friendliness. Whether the user finds the system engaging, was it easily understandable and acquirable, was it beneficial and entertaining to play with the "Break the Bricks" game, and with other games of the system. The properties above can be measured with users without arm damages. It is beneficial to test these attributes with more types of users, because the different user groups can have different opinions of the software, and can have different needs. After going over these test results, we can improve our system according to the users' opinions.

We can also compare the results of each game in the system, to see which one is more beneficial for the patients, which could improve the rehabilitation process more.

4   Further Work

As further plans we would like to develop other games, which can be built into the framework. These games will be able to improve other abilities of the patients with movements that aren't practiced with "Break the Bricks", like turning the hand, etc. Some of the games won't only ameliorate the physical capabilities of the patients, but they will improve their power of mind. These games could be memory or logical ones combined with different types of arm movements.

There is another plan, which extends the framework of the system. The "Break the Bricks" game can communicate with the mobile phone using this framework, we would like to expand the services of the framework so that the system could be handled with different types of control devices, for example sensors, mouse, keyboard, etc.

5   Conclusion

This game is a good method for healing stroke patients, because while playing with them the patients will do small, funny, but important exercises, which can advance their recovery. Most of the people like playing games, so the occasionally boring practice can be made funny and pleasurable.

Acknowledgements. The "StrokeBack" research project is supported by the European Commission under the 7th Framework Programme through Call (part) identifier FP7-ICT-2011-7, grant agreement no: 288692.

References

1. StrokeBack project, http://www.strokeback.eu/ (last accessed: April 10, 2012)
2. Sik Lányi, C.: Virtual Reality in Healthcare. In: Ichalkaranje, A., Ichalkaranje, N., Jain, L. (eds.) Intelligent Paradigms for Assistive and Preventive Healthcare. SCI, vol. 19, pp. 87–116. Springer, Heidelberg (2006)
3. Kizony, R., Katz, N., Weingarden, H., Weiss, P.L.: Immersion without encumbrance: adapting a virtual reality system for the rehabilitation of individuals with stroke and spinal cord injury. In: Sharkey, Sik Lányi, Standen (eds.) Proc. 4th Intl Conf. on Disability, Virtual Reality and Assoc. Technologies, Veszprém, Hungary, September 18-20, pp. 55–62 (2002)
4. Kizony, R., Katz, N., Weiss, P.L.: Virtual reality based intervention in rehabilitation: relationship between motor and cognitive abilities and performance within virtual environments for patients with stroke. In: Sharkey, McRindle, Brown (eds.) Proc. 5th Intl Conf. on Disability, Virtual Reality and Assoc. Technologies, Oxford, UK, September 20-22, pp. 19–26 (2004)
5. VividGroup, http://www.vividgroup.com.au (last accessed: April 09, 2012)
6. Broeren, J., Georgsson, M., Rydmark, M., StibrantSunnerhagen, K.: Virtual reality in stroke rehabilitation with the assistance of haptics and telemedicine. In: Sharkey, Sik Lányi, Standen (eds.) Proc. 4th Intl Conf. on Disability, Virtual Reality and Assoc. Technologies, Veszprém, Hungary, September 18-20, pp. 71–76 (2002)
7. Connor, B.B., Wing, A.M., Humphreys, G.W., Bracewell, R.M., Harvey, D.A.: Errorless learning using haptic guidance: research in cognitive rehabilitation following stroke. In: Sharkey, Sik Lányi, Standen (eds.) Proc. 4th Intl Conf. on Disability, Virtual Reality and Assoc. Technologies, Veszprém, Hungary, September 18-20, pp. 77–83 (2002)
8. Davies, R.C., Löfgren, E., Wallergård, M., Lindén, A., Boschian, K., Minör, U., Sonesson, B., Johansson, G.: Three applications of virtual reality for brain injury rehabilitation of daily tasks. In: Sharkey, Sik Lányi, Standen (eds.) Proc. 4th Intl Conf. on Disability, Virtual Reality and Assoc. Technologies, Veszprém, Hungary, September 18-20, pp. 93–100 (2002)
9. Wallergård, M., Cepciansky, M., Lindén, A., Davies, R.C., Boschian, K., Minör, U., Sonesson, B., Johansson, G.: Developing virtual vending and automatic service machines for brain injury rehabilitation. In: Sharkey, Sik Lányi, Standen (eds.) Proc. 4th Intl Conf. on Disability, Virtual Reality and Assoc. Technologies, Veszprém, Hungary, September18-20, pp. 109–114 (2002)
10. Morris, R.G., Kotitsa, M., Bramham, J., Brooks, B., Rose, F.D.: Virtual reality investigation of strategy formation, rule breaking and prospective memory in patients with focal prefrontal neurosurgical lesions. In: Sharkey, Sik Lányi, Standen (eds.) Proc. 4th Intl Conf. on Disability, Virtual Reality and Assoc. Technologies, Veszprém, Hungary, September 18-20, pp. 101–108 (2002)
11. Lövquist, E., Dreifaldt, U.: The design of a hapticexercise for post-stroke arm rehabilitation. In: Sharkey, Brooks, Cobb (eds.) Proc. 6th Intl Conf. on Disability, Virtual Reality and Assoc. Technologies, Esbjerg, Denmark, September 18-20, pp. 309–315 (2006)

12. Munkácsy, K.: Mathematics learning built on pictures. In: The Second International Scientific Colloquium Mathematics and Children, ERIC Database, pp. 37–42, http://www.eric.ed.gov/PDFS/ED517875.pdf
13. Munkácsy, K.: Real Objects and Problem Solving in Mathematics Education. ERIC Database, pp. 180–184 (ED517880), http://www.eric.ed.gov/PDFS/ED517880.pdf
14. Burke, W., McNeill, M.D.J., Charles, D.K., Morrow, P.J., Crosbie, J.H., McDonough, S.M.: Designing engaging, playablegames for rehabilitation. In: Sharkey, Sánchez (eds.) Proc. 8th Intl Conf. on Disability, Virtual Reality and Assoc. Technologies, Viña del Mar/Valparaíso, Chile, August 31-September 2, pp. 195–201 (2010)
15. Rehabilitation measures database, Rehab measures: Wolf Motor Function Test, http://www.rehabmeasures.org/Lists/RehabMeasures/DispForm.aspx?ID=927 (last accessed: April 09, 2012)

Development of a Broadcast Sound Receiver
for Elderly Persons

Tomoyasu Komori[1], Atsushi Imai[2], Nobumasa Seiyama[2], Reiko Takou[2],
Tohru Takagi[1], and Yasuhiro Oikawa[3]

[1] NHK Engineering Service, INC, 1–10–11 Kinuta, Setagaya-ku, Tokyo 157-8540, Japan
{komori.t-bw,takagi.t-fo}@nhk.or.jp
[2] NHK Science and Technical Research Laboratories1-10-11 Kinuta, Setagaya-ku,
Tokyo 157-8510 Japan
{imai.a-dy,seiyama.n-ek,takou.r-go}@nhk.or.jp
[3] Department of Intermedia Art and Science, Waseda University 3-4-1 Ohkubo,
Shinjuku-ku, Tokyo 169-8555, Japan
yoikawa@waseda.jp

Abstract. With the aim of making speech easier to listen to on a TV receiver, a noble method for back-ground-sound suppression processing was proposed, and the results of evaluation tests using broadcast-program sound showed that a prototype device was able to adjust a suitable level of background sound for elderly people. Our proposed method was able to suppress the magnitude of sound components with low correlation by using 2ch stereo signals and perform gain-control only on the speechless intervals. The preparatory evaluation tests confirm that it is possible to suitably reduce program background volume by the proposed method. On the basis of this result, a device for suppressing background sound by decoding the transport stream (TS) of a broadcast program was prototyped. The results of evaluation tests using this device demonstrate that the magnitude of background sound can be adjusted to a suitable level for elderly people.

Keywords: elderly people, phoneme recognition, loudness, stereo correlation, subjective evaluation, background-sound suppression.

1 Introduction

In the case of various kinds of media, it has been reported that the background sound (background music: BGM and sound effects: SE) of broadcast programs is too loud for elderly people. At NHK, investigative research aiming to make it easier for elderly people to hear voices during broadcasts is continuing [1–3]. Up until now, the case that the BGM/SE of broadcast programs is felt to be excessive has been investigated, in a viewing environment close to that of a home, and reported.

Meanwhile, in regard to mixing balance of broadcast-program sounds, a device that takes into consideration "sound masking" and displays the correct balance between narration and background sound has been proposed [4].

K. Miesenberger et al. (Eds.): ICCHP 2012, Part I, LNCS 7382, pp. 681–688, 2012.
© Springer-Verlag Berlin Heidelberg 2012

Aiming to develop a more effective device, the authors previously utilized and analyzed mixing-test results and loudness level [5–6] in developing a device for evaluating the magnitude of program background sound objectively [7]. Furthermore, it was reported that by using narration and background sound before mixing for broadcasting and by independently adjusting the magnitude of background sound in intervals in which narration and background sound are mixed and that in intervals containing background sound only. The adjusting procedure is possible to make listening easier for elderly people [8]. In light of that finding, a method for sequentially estimating speech intervals and speechless intervals from actual broadcast sounds, switching between intervals containing speech and speechless intervals containing BGM/SE only, and controlling volume was proposed. Since this method can control the magnitude of background sound in each interval independently, and can control sound volume without degrading sound quality by simply controlling gain particularly in voiceless intervals, it is effective for reducing sound-quality degradation in the case that the method is applies for a whole program.

In the present study, a device for controlling speech and background sound by operating a "transport stream" (TS)—a kind of actual broadcast signal—as an input signal was prototyped. The result of an experimental evaluation using the control method targeting elderly people confirmed that elderly people can adjust the magnitude of background sound by means of the prototype device.

In the rest of this paper, the background-sound-suppression processing that utilizes estimation results from each of the intervals is described in Section 2. Differences between background-suppression effects due to interval-estimation precision are explained in Section 3, the prototype evaluation device is described in Section 4, and results of evaluation tests using the prototype are presented in Section 5.

2   Proposed Method

Techniques like spectral subtraction are available for suppressing background sound from sound containing a mixture of narration and background sound. It is, however, generally known that in contrast to the case of suppressing steady-state noise (e.g. white noise), in the case of suppressing unsteady-state background sound (e.g. music), sound quality becomes extremely poor. Furthermore, a large proportion of TV broadcasts in Japan are produced in stereo, and in the case of stereo programs, a method that utilizes adaptive filter and suppresses parts with low correlation is effective [9]. With this method, however, degradation of sound quality due to signal processing occurs in the interval containing background sound only. Accordingly, a method that switches suppression processing according to interval is proposed here (see Fig. 1). In addition to its effectiveness in reducing sound-quality degradation, an advantage of this method is that it can independently adjust the optimum magnitude of background sound in the speech intervals and the speechless intervals. Among elderly people, there are a fair number who feel that sounds of programs such as jingles and chimes are too noisy, and there are cases when simply suppressing speechless intervals and improving sound quality is effective for improving transmission of sound to the ear.

Given those circumstances, as a preliminary evaluation experiment, an investigation on "speech-interval estimation methods" was performed. Two methods were used for this interval estimation: one estimates intervals from sound signals only, and one takes intervals displaying closed captions as the assumed speech interval. In Japan, since it is often the case that closed captions pretty much synchronized with the dialog of TV dramas and so on are prepared in advance and presented with the programs, the proposed method can be utilized in that case. However, closed captions are not attached to all programs, and when they are, they are not always in synchronization with the dialog. Comparison of estimated intervals with correct data detected from intervals manually was therefore performed.

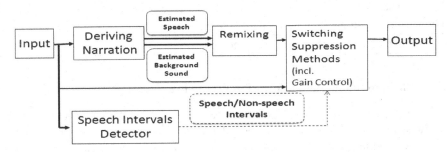

Fig. 1. Proposed method for switching methods for suppressing background sound

2.1　Proposed Voice Activity Detection (VAD)

For estimating speech intervals and speechless intervals, two voice activity detection (VAD) methods are combined: a VAD using phoneme recognition (which utilizes a probabilistic model for feature values such as frequency and power) [10]; and a VAD utilizes amplitude variation of "loudness values," i.e., objectively calculated loudness [6]. Hereafter, this combined method is called "the proposed VAD"

With the VAD by phoneme recognition, sound feature values (e.g. cepstral coefficient) are extracted, a sound model for speech (e.g. narration) and non-speech sound is applied, likelihood values of speech and non-speech (accumulated likelihood) are calculated from the extracted sound feature values, and the existence of a speech interval or a non-speech interval is determined on the basis of those likelihoods.

With the interval-estimation method using amplitude variation of loudness value, in regard to the speech interval, background sound is compared with the speech and typically mixed with a small amount of sound [7], and the amplitude variation of loudness of sounds such as music is very low by the nature of things.　On the other hand, since amplitude variation of loudness of sounds such as speech is big enough even in a period as short as two seconds, an interval in which amplitude varies by more than ±5 phon with respect to an average loudness value over two seconds is estimated to be a speech interval.

In regard to the opening 10 minutes of a TV drama, correct data extracted from speech intervals by hand (interval-extracted data) are prepared, and the precision ratio and recall ratio of the proposed VAD and the closed captions interval estimation method are obtained.

These ratios are listed in Table 1. It is clear from the table that the interval-estimation methods both have high degrees of precision, namely, high precision ratio (the proportion of correct intervals among the estimated intervals) and high recall ratio (the proportion in which estimated intervals are included in correct intervals). The two ratios achieved by both interval-estimation methods are above 87%, thereby confirming that intervals can be estimated at high precision with these methods.

Table 1. Precision ratio and recall ratio of speech-interval estimation method

	Precision ratio	Recall ratio
① Proposed VAD phoneme recognition＋loudness characteristics	87.9%	91.1%
②Closed captions interval estimation method	94.7%	90.6%

2.2   Background-Sound Suppression Processing

After the interval estimation, for background-sound suppression of the intervals estimated as speech intervals, a method that applies adaptive filtering using stereo correlation and adjusts the mixing ratio of estimated speech and background sound is used. The following section describes the principle behind the stereo-correlation method and the problems that arise when only stereo correlation is used.   In addition, as for the switched sections of intervals, applying cross-fade for about one second makes the switching of signal processing smooth.

3   Preliminary Evaluation Experiment

To confirm that program background-sound volume can be correctly reduced by means of the background-sound suppression method (which switches the background-sound suppression processing for each estimated interval), a subjective evaluation test was carried out. Preliminary evaluation experiment, an evaluation test targeting a young person (who is expected to achieve high detection accuracy) was performed first.

3.1   Test Conditions

For the evaluation, 14 scenes of about 30-second duration   are extracted from the TV drama materials used in the interval estimation. In correspondence with each scene, four kinds of materials were prepared: "R" (as the original broadcast-sound), "A" (obtained by using   the proposed VAD), "B" (obtained by using   the closed captions interval estimation method), and "C" (obtained by using   correct data).

To perform pairwise comparison, by taking the six combinations of the four types for every scene and, for each combination, making correct sequences and reverse sequences in benchmark materials and the evaluation materials appear randomly, the ordering effect was taken into consideration. The benchmark materials and the evaluation materials were presented to all the evaluators two times in a row. In the tests, the magnitude of the background sound in relation to the benchmark materials was judged as either "loud" or "soft." The tests were performed in a listening booth.

Video and sound were presented via a DVD player (Panasonic DVD-S75). The video were displayed on a 22-inch LCD TV (SHARP LC-22GD6), and the sound was replayed through compact speakers (Entry-Si by ALR-Jordan) via a professional DA converter (Lucid 88192).

The layout of the evaluation test is shown in Fig. 2.(Left) The evaluators were five young peopple from 21 to 25 years of age (30 dBHL). The estimators were divided into two groups (group one with three people, and group two with two people), and the two groups performed the tests simultaneously. However, in the case of group two, listening-position 3 was left empty. At that time, under the assumed conditions in which elderly people watch TV at home, the sound pressure of the narration was set to a fairly high volume (75 dBA).

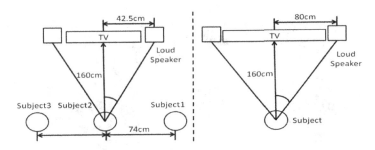

Fig. 2. Layout of evaluation tests (Left: Preliminary test, Right: Prototype device test)

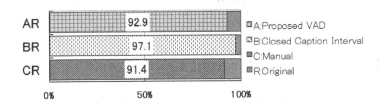

Fig. 3. Subjective evaluation results

3.2   Evaluation Result

The evaluation results concerning the magnitude of the background sound in comparison are plotted in Fig. 3. Comparison with R indicates that all methods sufficiently suppress background sound. However, in the comparison of all the interval-estimation methods, the cases using B (estimation method with closed captions) and C (correct data) are equivalent, but the proportion of estimators who responded that the background sound was "soft" in the case of A (proposed VAD) was high.

From the above-described results, it is confirmed that almost all program background sound can be reduced by our proposed methods.:

4   Prototype evaluation device

It was confirmed by the results presented in Section 3 that the program background sound can be properly suppressed. For the case that the proposed method is used on behalf of elderly people, a suitable magnitude of background sound was targeted, and an evaluation device was prototyped. The device features a TS file for digital broadcasts, a function for delayed playback of video, and a function for extracting speech intervals from delay periods and adjusting the amount of suppression on successive background sounds. An external view of the device is shown in Fig. 4. The magnitude of background sound is adjusted separately for each interval in accordance with the control input of the controller.

Fig. 4. Prototype evaluation device

5   Evaluation Device Targeting Elderly People

The prototype device was utilized in tests for determining the level of program background sound that is pleasant for elderly people to listen to.

5.1   Test Conditions

For the evaluation, 20 scenes (with durations of 30 to 60 seconds) were taken from TV dramas that were pointed out by some listeners to contain background sound with excessive magnitude. In the tests, the participants were instructed to use two controllers to adjust the magnitude of the background sound for each scene to the appropriate level. The controllers can independently adjust the magnitude of background sound in intervals containing mixed sound and speech and in intervals containing background sound only. The tests were performed in a sound booth. The prototype device was used for playing back both video and audio. The video were presented on 40/42-inch flat-screen TV, and the sound was fed via a DA interface for PCs (FirefaceUC by RME) to compact speakers (Entry-Si by ALR-Jordan).

The layout of the evaluation test is shown in Fig. 2.(Right) The presented sound pressure was set to 75 dBA. The evaluators were 11 elderly people in the age range of 62 to 72 years old (40 dBHL). The tests were performed by each person separately, and while adjusting the background sounds, the estimators were allowed to re-playback scenes. However, they were instructed to keep the number of times they replayed scenes to three to five times.

5.2   Test Results

According to a survey given to the evaluators, the evaluators could be split into two groups: those (three people) who preferred a louder background sound, and those (eight people) who preferred a softer background sound. And intervals are classified as those containing mixed speech and background sound and those containing background sound only, and those two interval classification taken together with the two groups concerning likability to make four groups for analysis. In this analysis, the adjustment volume (average value) for each interval for each trial run was taken as the sampled value. The average values and standard deviations of the sampled values are listed Table 2.

In the table, 0 dB expresses the original-broadcast-sound balance, and among the elderly people, the group preferring the smaller background sound differs from the group preferring the larger background sound. In the former case, it was observed that the magnitude of the background sound tends to be adjusted to 2 to 3 dB lower than that of the standard-broadcast background sound.

Table 2. Average values and standard deviation of sampled values (tuning amount)

	Interval for mixed sound (standard deviation)	Interval for BGM/SE only (standard deviation)
Group preferring Louder	1.30 [dB]/ (2.83)	0.46 [dB]/ (1.75)
Group preferring Softer	-2.79 [dB]/ (3.87)	-1.77 [dB]/(3.79)

6   Concluding Remarks

With the aim of making speech easier to listen to on a receiver, a method for background-sound suppression processing was proposed, and evaluation tests using broadcast-program sound were performed. Compared to other methods, the proposed speech-interval estimation method attained high estimation precision. It was confirmed by a preparatory evaluation test that background sound can be appropriately reduced by the proposed method of switching background-sound suppression processing for each estimation region.   Moreover, a device for suppressing background sound by using a broadcast TS was prototyped, and evaluation tests with an adjustment method targeting elderly people were performed. According to the test results, the prototype device can adjust the magnitude of background sound in accordance with the preference of elderly people, and the proposed method will become an elemental technology for adjusting background volume with receivers.

From now onwards, tests on young people will be performed, and the suitable adjustment amount of background sound in accordance with temporal and acoustic variation in programs will be investigated. Furthermore, a speech-enhancement function, for example, will be added to the prototype device, investigations including programs of genres other than TV dramas will be performed, and control parameters than make listening to programs easy will be extracted. By extending the proposed method to become a more useful technology, it is planned to continue developing receiver sets that elderly persons will find easy to listen to.

References

1. Nakamura, H., Sawaguchi, M., Masaoka, K., Watanabe, K., Yamasaki, Y., Miyasaka, E., Yasuoka, M., Seki, H.: Better Audio Balance Broadcasting service for elderly people.- Back Ground Sound Levels of Television Programs for Easy Listening. In: 2003 Proc. Spring Meet. Acoust. Soc. Jpn.,1-5-5, pp. 455–456 (2003) (in Japanese)
2. Komori, T., Takagi, T., Kurozumi, K., Shoda, K., Murakawa, K.: A Device to Evaluate Broadcast Background Sound Balance Using Loudness for Elderly Listeners. In: Miesenberger, K., Klaus, J., Zagler, W., Karshmer, A. (eds.) ICCHP 2010. LNCS, vol. 6180, pp. 560–567. Springer, Heidelberg (2010)
3. Komori, T., Takagi, T.: Subjective evaluation on the background sound of TV program by elderly people in the home environment. In: Proc. Autumn Meet. Acoust. Soc. Jpn., 3-10-14 (September 2009) (in Japanese)
4. Nakayama, Y., Inoue, T., Watanabe, K., Umeda, T., Miyasaka, E.: Perceptual Measurement System for Mixing Balance in Audio Programs. In: Proc. Autumn Meet. Acoust. Soc., pp. 615–616 (September 1997) (in Japanese)
5. Kurozumi, K., Okamoto, N.: Real-time Loudness Level Meter for Broadcasting Stations and Recent Trends of Standardization. Journal of the Institute of Image Information and Television Engineers 60(7), 1012–1017 (2006) (in Japanese)
6. Paulus, E., Zwicker, E.: Computer programs for calculating loudness from 1/3 octave band levels or from critical band levels. Acoustica 27, 253–266 (1972)
7. Komori, T., Komiyama, S., Dan, H., Takagi, T., Shoda, K., Kurozumi, K., Hoshi, H., Murakawa, K.: A Investigation of the Audio Balance Control based on the Loudness Level. IEICE Transactions J92-A(5), 344–352 (2009) (in Japanese)
8. Komori, T., Seiyama, N., Takagi, T.: A Verification on Objective Evaluation Method of Appropriate Broadcasting Sound Balance for Elderly Listeners. In: Proc. Autumn Meet. Acoust. Soc. Jpn., 1-R-2 (September 2010) (in Japanese)
9. Murayama, Y., Hamada, H., Komiyama, S., Kawabata, Y.: Adaptive control for advanced reproduction of narration voice. In: 13th AES Regional Convention, Tokyo (August 2007)
10. Imai, T., Sato, S., Kobayashi, A., Onoe, K., Homma, S.: Online Speech Detection and Dual-Gender Speech Recognition for Captioning Broadcast News. In: Proc. 9th Interspeech Wed1CaP-1, pp. 1–4 (2006)

Complexity versus Page Hierarchy of a GUI for Elderly Homecare Applications

Mustafa Torun[1], Tim van Kasteren[2], Ozlem Durmaz Incel[1], and Cem Ersoy[1]

[1] Department of Computer Engineering, Bogazici University, Bebek 34342 Istanbul/Turkey
[2] AGT Group (R&D) GmbH, Hilbert str. 20a, 64295 Darmstadt, Germany
{ozlem.durmaz,ersoy}@boun.edu.tr,
{mstftrnboun,tim0306}@gmail.com

Abstract. Using computerized devices comes quite natural for many users due to the various graphical user interfaces. However, acceptability of graphical user interfaces by elderly, a rapidly growing group of computer users, is a challenging issue due to different levels of impairments experienced. In the literature, providing simplicity is the main focus of the studies that try to address this challenge. In this paper, we study the acceptance of graphical user interfaces for elderly people with different impairments in the context of in-home healthcare systems. We focus on the relation between two main design parameters of a graphical user interface: page complexity, which is the number of interface elements on each page and the page hierarchy, which is the number of the pages to be traced in order to complete a task. For this purpose, we designed two versions of an interface: one version has a high page complexity and the other version is designed to have a high page hierarchy. We asked 18 experiment-subjects, aged between 65 and 95, to complete three tasks, using both versions. Experiment results are evaluated using both objective and subjective metrics. Results show that the flat version is found to be more acceptable by elderly.

Keywords: Graphical user interface, elderly, acceptance, complexity, hierarchy.

1 Introduction

It is a common observation that the world has become computerized. Today, almost all computerized devices are controlled by graphical user interfaces (GUI). For most people, getting accustomed to computers with the help of those user interfaces comes quite simple, but mainly for elderly, whose population percentage will become about 20% of overall population in 2050 [1], using computerized devices is challenging because they usually have little experience with computers and they have a variety of impairments such as visual, psychomotor, hearing or cognitive impairments [2]. In order to overcome this challenge, computerized systems might be displayed in a proper way regarding those impairments. This will increase the acceptance of computerized devices and systems by elderly people.

In order to be acceptable for elderly, an interface should be "simple" considering their physical and cognitive impairments [3]. In the literature, being simple is mostly

K. Miesenberger et al. (Eds.): ICCHP 2012, Part I, LNCS 7382, pp. 689–696, 2012.
© Springer-Verlag Berlin Heidelberg 2012

considered not to display very complex pages with many interface elements, such as buttons, text and links, at the same time which may cause a cognitive overload [4]. In this paper, we investigate the goal of providing simplicity as the trade-off between the "complexity", which means the level of interface elements such as buttons, text and links on a page, and the "page hierarchy", which means the number of different pages required to complete a task. Based on this trade-off, we define a flat interface as an interface which has several interface elements on each page but having less hierarchy and a deep interface as an interface which has less interface elements on each page but having deeper hierarchy. Consequently, we focus on the following question: "would a flat interface or a deep interface be more acceptable for elderly people?"

For this purpose, we designed two versions of interfaces of a homecare application to be experimented by elderly: the flat version and the deep version. We asked 10 of the test subjects to complete three different tasks on the flat version and repeat one task on the deep version and 8 of them to complete the same tasks on the deep version and repeat one task on the flat version. We recorded five metrics, which are error, time, inter-touch time, clicks and keystrokes, by Recording User Input (RUI) program [5]. By experimenting with these two interfaces, we observe that a flat user interface is more acceptable to elderly compared to a deep user interface.

The rest of the paper is organized as follows: Section 2 is the related work. Section 3 describes our application. Section 4 explains our experimental setup and investigates the results. Finally, we have the conclusion in Section 5.

2   Related Work

There are several projects carried out for elderly people in order to provide them a long-life environment by addressing their needs via pervasive healthcare applications [6, 7]. These needs can be related with the daily life or their cognitive being. In this section, we explain GUI specifications from different aspects, such as color, interactive sentences or the size of buttons, for in-home healthcare applications.

In [8] it is shown that the decline in the lack of registering capability of violet light of eyes results in difficulty for elderly people to distinguish blue, green and violet. It is easier for elderly with less visual sensitivity to see red-yellow tones. Moreover, declined vision and visual field reduction of elderly people put importance on presenting the necessary information in a larger size and displayed close to the center of the screen [9]. As the research shows, other handicaps related to vision can be addressed by manipulating the GUI elements, but the cognitive impairments of elderly have to do with many issues such as the page hierarchy, complexity and the trade-off between them. Accordingly, in this paper we focus on the relation between the page hierarchy and the complexity.

Different interaction types are also experimented by different project groups. It was reported that the use of touchscreen displays for interacting with computerized systems is favorable by the elderly [10]. This motivated us to use a touchscreen device for our experiments.

SOPRANO [11] team dealt with interactive sentences which are used on the buttons in order to make the user accept, confirm or chose a situation. Their experiments implied that using "OK-like" buttons make elderly user confused about what it will mean to push "accept, OK, YES or NO" buttons. Hence it is proposed to use interactive sentences like "I took care of it", "I have done it".

2.1   Two Ways of Presenting an Interface

We define the complexity of a page as the number of interface elements on that page and the page hierarchy as the number of pages that the user interacts in order to complete a task. A designer can provide simplicity in two ways. One is reducing the complexity of each page displayed at a time and the other is decreasing the number of traced pages required to complete a task. Consequently, we call a GUI as flat if it has more complex pages but less page hierarchy with respect to a deep version which has less complex pages but deep page hierarchy.

George A. Miller conducted some experiments about people's cognitive confusion of displayed visual information [12]. He came up with the result that people start to be cognitively overloaded when the number of displayed distinct visual information is seven (Miller's Law). On the other hand, recent research has demonstrated that the correct number is probably around three or four [13].

3   GUI Application: Flat and Deep Versions

The cognitive load of people for holding the visual elements on the working memory allows us to split our GUI's into two categories. For this categorization, we rely on the G. Miller's [12] and Farrington's [13] studies. Although these studies among ordinary people showed that people experience a cognitive overload when more than 7 items are displayed, because of the decline in elderly cognitive capacity with respect to the ordinary people and because of the more recent study of Farrington, we chose 4 as the base number of our calculations. Consequently, we define a deep interface as that the tasks are addressed by more than four steps with that GUI. In contrast, a flat interface means that the user can achieve his goal at most in four steps. Our flat version has 4.14 of complexity index and 3.33 as hierarchy index, whereas our deep version has 2.78 as complexity index and 6.0 as hierarchy index.

Fig. 1. Agenda from the deep version

Fig. 2. Agenda from the flat version

The application has four main functionalities of a pervasive healthcare system for elderly: Agenda, Messaging, Video Calling and Medical Information such as pulse-oximeter readings and medicine intake monitoring. Some information about the day, weather and time is displayed on the homepage. We also display the upcoming reminders, social activities, medical information and visual information about arrived messages on the homepage. Agenda functionality enables a user to set a reminder for his important activities or for some routines. If the user does not respond to a particular reminder for a while, the system informs his relatives or caregivers. The elderly can send messages to their friends, relatives or caregivers, read and compose messages with the help of Messaging functionality. Videoconferencing functionality enables users to call their friends by just touching their picture. The medical activity functionality is for monitoring the daily medical activity of the elderly. On the medical activity page, user can find his weekly or monthly medical routines which are gathered as daily information on homepage. In addition, a user can measure her/his pulse rate and blood oxygen saturation using a wireless pulse-oximeter device. These four functionalities are provided by both flat and deep versions of our application. In Figures 1 and 2, sample pages from both versions for Agenda functionality are shown.

4   Experiments and Results

We carried out our experiments in an elderly rest home in Etiler, Istanbul, with 18 different elderly people, aged between 65 and 95, having different impairments, different educational degrees and occupations such as university lecturer or housekeeper and with different levels of computer experience. Our application interface is displayed on a 23 inch LCD and full HD touchscreen integrated computer with Windows operating system. We chose to use a touchscreen because of usability and adaptability, it allows elderly to easily interact with the system [6].

We used Recording User Input [5] (RUI) program for recording our subjects' inputs during the experiments. RUI is a software tool which records the user input such as mouse clicks, key strokes and mouse movements.

For our experiments, we asked users to complete three different tasks each of which is related to one functionality of our application on two different user interfaces. The tasks we asked to be completed are video-calling a friend, setting a reminder and sending a message with an attachment to a friend. We choose this order in which subjects perform the tasks from the easiest one, which requires less steps of interaction, to the most difficult one.

We have a questionnaire with 11 questions and an interview with 6 questions for getting the test subject's impression and feedbacks about the application and the underlying approach. We choose our objective metrics to be the time for a subject to complete a task, inter-interaction time, which is the time between the user's two subsequent interactions, the number of touches to the screen, the number of keystrokes and the number of errors until finishing the task.

We have two basic approaches corresponding to two experiments. One is the flat approach corresponding to Experiment 1 in which subjects are requested to complete all three tasks on the flat version and repeat one task on the deep version and the other is the deep approach corresponding to Experiment 2 in which subjects are requested to complete all three tasks on the deep version and repeat one task on the flat version. The steps that we go over during the experiments are as follows:

- We provide them a leaflet explaining the task to perform.
- The second step is performing the tasks.
- Immediately after performing three tasks on a specific version, we ask them which of the three tasks was the most difficult for them and want them to repeat it on the other version.
- Then, we provide them a questionnaire to be filled.
- Afterwards, we interview and ask some other subjective questions.

4.1   Results

Questionnaire. Due to page limitations, only four significant questions of the questionnaire and the answers given by elderly are shown graphically in Figure 3.

We have both computer-users and non-users among our subjects and this provides a heterogeneity which makes the experiments more realistic. 50% of the flat version users and 62.5% of the deep version users did not use a computer before, whereas 50% of the flat version users and 37.5% of the deep version users use computer at least once a week.

As shown in Figure 3(a), 70% of the flat version users and 75% of the deep version users find it easy or very easy to complete the tasks. Furthermore, our experiments showed that the choice of using 24 and 36 pixel font size is convenient because 95% of the users said that they found it easy or very easy to read the texts (Figure 3(b)). Only 25% of the deep version users said that it was difficult to find a necessary button or any interface elements to complete a task (Figure 3(c)). This ratio is significantly higher for flat-version users (40%), which is understandable because the flat version interface has more interface elements on an individual page than the deep version. 40% and 50% of the users evaluated the interface as very good in Exp. 1 and 2, respectively (Figure 3(d)). They also said that the application is good with the percentages of 60% and 50% in the Experiment 1 and 2, respectively.

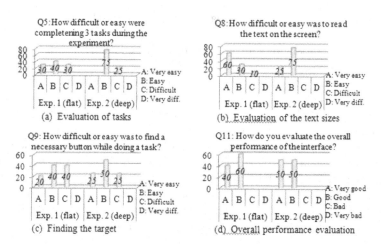

Fig. 3. Questionnaire results

Interview. According to interviews, 61.1% of all subjects, regardless of the version that they used, said that they prefer to use touchscreen rather than keyboard-mouse combination. 27.8% preferred classical keyboard and did not like the touchscreen, mostly because of the difficulty of text inputting. Moreover, all subjects were pleased of the contrast. On the other hand, two subjects did not like the red background. They thought that red, itself, is too flaming and can cause to dazzle their eyes after a while. When we asked about additional functionalities, three of them denoted that having an internet option, chatting and music functionalities will be an improvement for the application. 83.3% did not specify anything as additional functionality. As a negative feedback, one subject wanted us to put individual buttons for the calling and messaging functionality separately at the home page.

Table 1. Objective Metrics Results

		Phone		Agenda		Message		Total	
		Exp. 1	Exp. 2	Exp. 1	Exp. 2	Exp. 1	Exp. 2	Exp. 1	Exp. 2
error	Total Errors	2	6	16	16	7	15	25	37
	Average Error	0.2	0.75	1.6	2	0.7	0.88	2.5	4.63
	Standart Deviation(error)	0	0.5	0.66	1	0.37	0.99	1.20	2.83
	Average Error(per clicks + keys)	0.03	0.09	0.05	0.06	0.02	0.07	0.04	0.07
time	Total Time (sec)	594.6	703	2120	1910	1387.4	1354	4102	3967
	Average Time (sec)	59.46	87.88	212	238.75	138.74	169.25	410.20	495.88
	Standart Deviation(time)	24.59	35.20	78.67	68.61	54.31	69.73	110.64	138.91
	Total Intertouch Time (sec)	109.14	96.89	59.02	65.09	53.23	51.21	73.80	71.06
	Average Intertouch Time(sec)	10.91	12.11	5.90	8.14	5.32	6.40	7.38	8.88
	Standart Deviation(inter-touch time)	5.11	3.53	1.40	1.50	3.08	2.21	2.90	1.93

Objective Metrics. In Table 1, we provide three of our metrics which appeared to be significant according to the ANOVA test. We define an error as touching a wrong button (so, going to a wrong page direction), entering wrong input, not touching a necessary button and skipping a step of the tasks defined on a piece of paper provided for them. According to this definition, flat-version users committed 2.5 errors on average whereas, 4.63 errors are committed by the deep version users (Table 1). The average error implies that the deep interface strains elderly more than the flat version. Moreover, the agenda task appeared to be forcing them to make more errors compared to the other two tasks for both versions.

In order to complete three tasks, flat-version users need 410.2 seconds and deep-version users need about 496 seconds in average (Table 1). The inter-touch time, which means the time past in between two touches of the subject, is also high for the deep version (Table 1). It is convenient to have higher inter-touch time value for the deep version because, for each page, the working memory of the user updates itself. The time between two touches decreases continuously regardless of the task which means that the subjects get familiar when they use the interface (Table 1).

We conducted ANOVA test [14] for our five metrics in order to understand whether there is a significant difference between the results of two versions. The results are given in Table 2. In order to have a significant difference between the variance of two groups, the F-measure value should be greater than 4.49 for 16 degrees of freedom [14]. Thus, according to Table 2, the error, total time and the inter-touch time data indicate the significant difference between two versions of our application.

The inter-touch time also shows a significant difference between two versions for agenda and messaging tasks and a near-significance for the phone task (19.26, 8.15 and 4.27 respectively). Consequently, the inter-touch time metric, in general, reveals a significant dominance of the flat version to the deep version (F-measure: 10.35).

As we mentioned, we asked the subjects to repeat the task which they found to be the most difficult and conducted task repetition test. The majority of the users of both versions found the messaging task as the most difficult one (80% and 87.5% of the flat and the deep-version users, respectively). 50% of the flat version users and 75% of the deep version users found the second version easier. Although the difference of 25% may imply that the flat version is chosen in general, most of subjects who prefer the second version said that this choice was because of the fact that they had become a bit more experienced by using the other version for three tasks.

Table 2. F-Measures (F $_{(0.05, 1, 16)}$)

		Error			Total Time			Inter-touch Time			Number of Clicks			Number of Keystrokes		
		Mean	Std	F-M	Mean	Std	F-M	Mean	Std	F-M	Mean	Std	F-M	Mean	Std	F-M
Phone	Flat	0.25	0.43	2.00	52.64	22.85	5.64	8.98	3.10	4.27	5.68	1.93	4.23			
	Deep	0.75	0.83		87.88	35.12		12.39	3.53		8.75	3.53				
Agenda	Flat	1.38	0.48	2.22	179.88	50.74	3.80	5.40	1.01	19.26	23.25	6.82	0.42	6.25	2.17	0.73
	Deep	2.00	1.00		238.75	68.61		8.10	1.40		25.50	6.14		5.25	2.22	
Message	Flat	0.50	0.50	8.22	115.13	17.84	4.52	4.18	1.00	8.15	15.00	1.73	2.53	9.88	4.48	0.28
	Deep	1.88	1.17		169.25	69.73		5.97	1.43		18.88	6.21		8.63	4.30	
Total	Flat	2.00	0.71	6.5	372.15	85.10	4.62	6.28	1.22	10.35	47.38	9.94	1.02	17.00	3.46	1.26
	Deep	4.63	2.83		495.88	138.91		8.81	1.86		53.13	10.99		13.88	6.49	

5   Conclusion

In this paper, we studied the acceptable user interfaces for elderly from the simplicity point of view in the context of an in-home pervasive healthcare application. Our basic point was the trade-off between the page complexity and the page hierarchy. The results of both subjective and objective metrics revealed that the flat version of our interface is more acceptable compared to the deep version. According to our experiment results, a user interface with pages having a complexity index around 4 and hierarchy index around 3, which can be considered as a flat interface, would not cognitively strain elderly and will be acceptable.

References

1. Kinsella, K., Phillips, D.R.: Global aging: the challenge of success. Population Bulletin 60(1), 15–42 (2005)
2. Kleinberger, T., Becker, M., Ras, E., Holzinger, A., Müller, P.: Ambient Intelligence in Assisted Living: Enable Elderly People to Handle Future Interfaces. In: Stephanidis, C. (ed.) UAHCI 2007, Part II. LNCS, vol. 4555, pp. 103–112. Springer, Heidelberg (2007)
3. Abascal, J., Fernández De Castro, I., Lafuente, A., Cia, J.: Adaptive Interfaces for Supportive Ambient Intelligence Environments. Interface, 30–37 (2008)
4. Lorenz, A., Oppermann, R.: Mobile health monitoring for the elderly: Designing for diversity. Pervasive and Mobile Computing 5(5), 478–495 (2009)
5. Kukreja, U., Stevenson, W.E., Ritter, F.E.: RUI: recording user input from interfaces under Windows and Mac OS X. Behavior Research Methods 38(4), 656–659 (2006)
6. Holzinger, A.: User-Centered Interface Design for Disabled and Elderly People: First Experiences with Designing a Patient Communication System (PACOSY). In: Miesenberger, K., Klaus, J., Zagler, W. (eds.) ICCHP 2002. LNCS, vol. 2398, pp. 33–40. Springer, Heidelberg (2002)
7. Höller, N., Geven, A., Tscheligi, M.: Device and Interface most suitable for the project HERMES. HERMES Public Deliverables (2008), http://www.fp7-hermes.eu
8. Kurniawan, S., King, A., Evans, D., Blenkhorn, P.: Personalising web page presentation for older people. Interacting with Computers 18(3), 457–477 (2006)
9. Cerella, J.: Age-related decline in extrafoveal letter perception. Journal of Gerontology 40(6), 727–736 (1985)
10. Jin, Z.X., Plocher, T., Kiff, L.: Touch Screen User Interfaces for Older Adults: Button Size and Spacing. In: Stephanidis, C. (ed.) UAHCI 2007. LNCS, vol. 4554, pp. 933–941. Springer, Heidelberg (2007)
11. Wolf, P., Schmidt, A., Klein, M.: SOPRANO – An extensible, open AAL platform for elderly people based on semantical contracts 1. In: 18th European Conference on Artificial Intelligence, vol. (8) (2008)
12. Miller, G.: The Magical Number Seven, Plus or Minus Two: Some Limits on Our Capacity for Processing Information. Psychological Review 63(2), 81–97 (1956)
13. Farrington, J.: Seven Plus or Minus Two. Performance Improvement Quarterly 23(4), 113–116 (2011)
14. Christensen, R.: Plane Answers to Complex Questions: The Theory of Linear Models, vol. 84(408), p. 1100. Springer (2002)

Benefits and Hurdles for Older Adults in Intergenerational Online Interactions

Verena Fuchsberger, Wolfgang Sellner, Christiane Moser, and Manfred Tscheligi

HCI & Usability Unit, ICT&S Center, University of Salzburg, Austria
{verena.fuchsberger,wolfgang.sellner,christiane.moser2,
manfred.tscheligi}@sbg.ac.at

Abstract. In order to foster the relationship between geographically distant grandparents and grandchildren, a prototype of an online platform is developed in an Ambient Assisted Living project. After identifying relevant attributes in the requirements analysis together with older adults and experts for children, we conducted two rounds of user studies in a laboratory setting with older adults. In the studies we were not only interested in the usability of the platform and the older participants' computer skills, but especially in the experiences the older users have when interacting with and via the platform. As expected, we found a relation between self-rated computer skills and the usability problems. However, the skills were not decisive for experiencing the interaction regarding curiosity, engagement, social connectedness and social presence. Finally, implications for the design of socially connecting online platforms are presented.

Keywords: Older adults, User-Centered Design, Usability, User Experience.

1 Introduction

In an Ambient Assisted Living project, called FamConnector (funded by the AAL Joint Program, see http://www.mygrandchild.com), an online platform is developed in order to provide meaningful joint online activities for geographically separated grandparents and their 3 to 9 year old grandchildren. Currently two activities are available, i.e. playing games or reading books together. The aim of these activities is to foster the relationship and to facilitate the communication with each other. 2 to 4 additional activities are planned to be integrated in the online platform during the project duration (e.g., painting, learning, or doing handicrafts).

In the project we are focusing on the users by applying user-centered design (UCD). In the requirements analysis we addressed both children and older adults, in the evaluation phase we are focusing on older adults. The research goal is to find out whether the platform is usable for them. Furthermore, we are interested in assessing how they experience the platform. Furthermore, we aim to assess the influence of self-rated computers skills on usability and user experience (UX) aspects. In this paper we present the UCD process, beginning with the requirements analysis including attributes for intergenerational online activities [1], and proceeding with a user study in the laboratory setting. We illustrate the most salient results regarding

K. Miesenberger et al. (Eds.): ICCHP 2012, Part I, LNCS 7382, pp. 697–704, 2012.

usability and user experience and derive implications for technologies, which aim at fostering social online interactions in order to support developers meeting older adults' needs.

2   Related Work

Due to demographic changes towards an aging society, there is currently much research on older adults using computers. This research focuses e.g., on older adults' computer skills (e.g., [2]), usability or accessibility (e.g., web guidelines [3]). Regarding accessibility it is often referred to multiple disabilities of older adults, which might influence their usage (e.g., [4]). Besides usability and accessibility, also the users' experiences are crucial for using the computer, like curiosity [5], engagement [6], social connectedness [7] and social presence [8] in social online interactions.

3   The FamConnector Project

The FamConnector project aims at building an online platform that allows intergenerational interactions between older adults (i.e. grandparents) and young children (i.e. their grandchildren, aged 3 to 9 years) and other geographically distant family members. Grandparents can currently choose from a catalogue of different books and games and invite their grandchildren to participate in the activity. In the 'activity zone', the platform enables to see each other's actions (i.e. cursors). By including video and audio, interaction partners have the possibility to see and hear each other.

3.1   Requirements Analysis

At the beginning of the project we aimed at identifying the users' needs and preferences in terms of their characteristics, the relationship between grandparents and grandchildren as well as joint activities. As we did not want to only rely on usability guidelines for designing an online platform for older adults, we directly involved end users into different studies, i.e. workshops (n = 15), interviews with end users (n = 11) and a survey (n = 301). Furthermore, we conducted 10 expert interviews (with e.g., teachers, psychologists) to assess the children's perspective regarding the relationship to their grandparents (see [9] for a detailed description of the requirements analysis).

3.2   Attributes for Intergenerational Online Activities

From the assessed requirements we were able to derive attributes, which are important to consider when developing intergenerational online activities [1]. These attributes were addressed in the implementation of two activities on the platform, i.e. playing a game together and reading a book together. In order to evaluate whether they were successfully met, the following attributes were considered appropriate to be assessed in the user studies in a laboratory setting.

- **Shortness and Simplicity:** Special user groups, like older adults and children, need special attention in terms of usability and activity design. For example, older adults as well as very young children might not be familiar with computers and web platforms. Additionally, activities should be brief to allow for children's attention spans and not require a too complex handling.
- **Diversity and Balance:** For intergenerational online interactions it is necessary to avoid anxiety or frustration, but to keep them challenging (similar to the concept of flow [10]). Furthermore, the system should provide a balance between activities and communication, i.e. the activities should stimulate the communication, not replace it.
- **Preparation and Initiation:** Offline, grandparents often prepare the activities in advance, by e.g., choosing a book to read. Thus, they need the possibility to do so in an online platform as well. The initiation of the activities needs to be adapted to the computer skills of both involved parties.
- **Social Presence as a User Goal:** The creation of social presence is very important for grandparents when maintaining the relationship to their grandchildren over distance. This can be supported by providing audio and video chats. However, it is important to emphasize the physical meetings in order to avoid the impression that the technology will replace physical meetings, as otherwise older adults are likely to reject it.

The other attributes mentioned in [1] need to be assessed later on in field studies, as they require a natural setting.

3.3   User Studies

In order to evaluate and finally improve the current state of the platform with respect to the mentioned attributes, we conducted user studies in a laboratory setting. The studies focused on the usability (e.g., overall usability, effectiveness, and efficiency) of the platform and especially on the users' experiences (e.g., the users' curiosity and engagement, as well as the potential for experiencing social connectedness and social presence). Therefore, the user studies were not just usability tests, but additionally included the evaluation of the attributes and an assessment of the users' experiences.

Methodological Approach. The FamConnector platform is currently available in English, German and Finnish language. Due to the location of the involved end user organizations, two different studies could be performed in Austria and Finland. The first user studies were conducted in the laboratory of the ICT&S Center at the University of Salzburg (Austria). By using a mobile laboratory, a second round of user studies took place in Tampere (Finland), for which the platform was already improved with regard to main usability issues that appeared in Austria. As the platform targets remote interpersonal interactions between two parties, the grandchild's part was simulated by a wizard (located in a separate room), whose actions were predefined in a detailed guideline.

Within each study a lead, an assistant, a wizard and one participant were involved. At the beginning of the study, the participant filled in a contact sheet, which consisted of sociodemographic questions (e.g., age and occupational status) and a question to rate one's computer skills subjectively (5-point scale form very well to very low). Afterwards, a pre-interview was conducted in order to assess the grandparents' family situation regarding their grandchildren and joint activities. The participants were then asked to perform three predefined tasks, i.e. (1) registering on the platform, (2) inviting the grandchild (wizard) and playing a game together and (3) inviting the grandchild (wizard) and reading a book together. After each task, the participants were asked about the ease of use and the satisfaction with the performance of the platform. At the end of the study, the participants filled in two questionnaires, i.e. the System Usability Scale – SUS [11], and a questionnaire containing self-developed items regarding the participants' curiosity about the platform, and regarding their engagement (items for focused attention and aesthetics, adapted from [6]), among others. Due to the restrictions of the laboratory settings, an extensive evaluation of the user experience factors social connectedness and social presence was hardly possible, as a natural setting (i.e. an interaction with the actual grandchild at home) would have been required. However, in order to assess the grandparents' subjective appraisal of these social factors on the platform, we finally interviewed them at the end of the users studies. In total, a single study took about 1.5 to 2 hours.

Besides those self-reported metrics (e.g., contact data or SUS), we also used issue-based metrics, like the types of usability issues, which were deduced from the think-aloud-protocol and the observer protocol, as well as performance metrics. The performance metrics included the task success (i.e. task completed without help, task completed with help, task not completed), the achieved milestones (i.e. predefined steps for fulfilling the tasks) and the level of assistance (i.e. how many and which assistance hints were necessary to complete the task). Furthermore, the metrics allowed figuring out if the users' experiences were improved from the first round of studies to the second [12].

Sample Description. The participants in Austria (n = 10; 9 female, 1 male) were between 52 and 63 years old ($M = 57.1$, $SD = 3.87$). In Finland (n = 10; 6 female, 4 male) the participants were between 58 and 78 years old ($M = 64.2$, $SD = 6.99$). Regarding the participants' computer skills in Austria 4 participants indicated to have (very) well computer skills, 1 indicated medium and 5 indicated (very) low. In Finland 2 indicated (very) well, 5 indicated medium and 3 indicated (very) low. We did not find a relation between computer skills and age ($r = .063$, p (one-tailed) = .396). All participants had not used the platform before, some of them only heard about the project in general before they participated in the study.

Results Regarding the Usability of the Platform (i.e. SUS, Effectiveness, and Efficiency). The participants experienced many difficulties while using the platform, which were related to usability. In order to quantitatively measure the overall usability of the platform the System Usability Scale (SUS) was applied. The average SUS score in Austria was 47.7 (n = 10, $SD = 25.46$), which means that the users disliked the system [11]. The average SUS score in Finland increased to 64.25 (n = 10, $SD = 18.56$), which means that the users accepted the system [11] after the improvement. Due to the small sample size, the difference was not significant $t(18) = -1.66$, $p = >.05$; however, it did represent a medium-sized effect $r = .33$.

In the first round 99 different usability issues were found in the think-aloud and observer protocols. The major problems referred to (a) the structure of the platform (e.g., overcharging complexity, unstructured texts, unclear steps in order to start an activity), (b) the audio and video setup (e.g., too small window for the settings), and (c) the activity zones (e.g., missing possibility to close the activity besides closing the browser itself). Due to improvements only 44 different issues were identified in the second round of the studies, most of them not related to the already known problems. The additionally found problems addressed e.g., the input fields not allowing special characters (e.g., ä, ö, or ü), which are very important for typing Finnish names. However, only few major problems occurred.

During both studies it became apparent that the task performances (i.e. the usability factor effectiveness) varied strongly between the participants (n = 20) regarding task success, achieved milestones, and required assistant hints. 3 studies had to be terminated, as the participants did not manage to complete the tasks in a predefined time. One of these 3 participants indicated to have medium, one to have rather low and one to have very low computer skills. However, the other 6 participants with (rather) low computer skills managed to complete the tasks. 12 participants only required 3 or less assistant hints (with a slight tendency that older adults with low computer skills needed more help). Overall, the Austrian participants needed almost twice as many assistance hints than the Finnish participants (in total 51 vs. 26 assistance hints).

This finding is consistent with the participants' general impression of the platform. Within the post interview 9 Austrian participants (n = 10) complained about too much complexity (i.e. the usability factor efficiency), like "there is too much text and information on each single page" or "it is too much effort of reading throughout the whole procedure". However, in the second round of user studies in Finland, the participants did not complain about the complexity at all. Thus, the improvements, like reducing texts, including more pictures and bullet points, or simplifying the invitation procedure, were successful. Even for the Finnish participants with rather or very low computer skills the platform was not too complex any more.

Results Regarding the Users' Experiences with the Platform (i.e. Curiosity, Engagement, Social Connectedness and Social Presence). The results revealed that nearly all participants felt curious to explore more features and activities, to actually see, hear and interact with their grandchildren on the platform and to experience how it will work out to play a game, or read a book online with them. Although the Finnish participants indicated to be slightly more curious, the differences were very small (see Fig. 1).

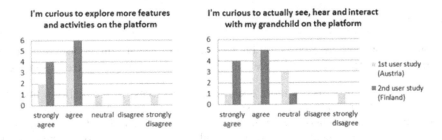

Fig. 1. Participants' curiosity (n = 20; scale indicating number of participants)

Regarding the users' engagement, the aspects aesthetics and focused attention [6] were evaluated. The participants perceived the platform as attractive and appealing (i.e. aesthetics) and also indicated that they would feel strongly involved into the activities when trying them with their actual grandchild (i.e. focused attention) (see Table 1). There were no significant differences between the two rounds or between different levels of computer skills.

Table 1. Items for aesthetics and focused attention (adapted from [6]), n = 20

Items (rated on a 5-point Likert scale from 1 strongly disagree to 5 strongly agree)	**Mean**	**SD**
"The platform is attractive."	3.70	.92
"The platform is aesthetically appealing."	3.75	.91
"I like the graphics and images used on the platform."	2.15	.75
"The platform appeals my visual senses."	3.10	1.12
"The screen layout of this platform is visually appealing."	3.60	.75
"When conducting the same activities on the platform with my grandchild, I would lose myself in the activities."	3.55	1.05
"When conducting the same activities with my grandchild, time would just slip away."	3.95	.76
"When conducting the same activities on the platform with my grandchild, I would feel strongly involved in these activities."	3.90	1.12

Although we could not assess the *quality* of the user experience factors social connectedness and social presence in the laboratory setting, valuable insights were found in the post-interview. The embracing perception of each other (e.g., facial expressions) was appraised as an essential issue for fostering the relationship remotely (i.e. social presence). Furthermore, the participants indicated that the platform could enrich the relationship by keeping up to date about the grandchild's life and to keep themselves in the grandchild's mind (i.e. social connectedness). The participants appraised the platform as a suitable possibility to meet their grandchild and to interact similarly to physical meetings. However, they emphasized the necessity of physical meetings for nurturing the relationship, but if there was no possibility for those meetings (e.g., due to a geographical distance), the platform would be a good alternative. For the user experience aspects curiosity, engagement, social connectedness and social presence, no differences regarding self-rated computer skills were found.

4   Implications and Conclusions

In order to support developers of online platforms, which aim at fostering social interactions, we derived some implications from the gathered insights of the user studies.

• The perceived benefits are more decisive for the success of the platform than the usability. Older adults will find support to overcome usability problems (e.g., family, friends, neighbors, etc.), if they are convinced that the platform will meet their needs regarding social interactions and represent the benefits for them. Thus, foster 'social presence as a user goal'.

- Find out which benefits (e.g., positive experiences) the older adults expect from the platform and focus on them during the evaluation. This might seem obvious, but in usability testing often only formal methods (e.g., task completion time) are used, which do not necessarily assess whether the expected benefits are provided.
- The participants emphasized the importance of perceiving their interaction partner visually and acoustically similar to offline meetings. Thus, correspond to real-world settings as far as possible in order to support the users' experiences.
- The participants demanded simple and short activities. However, simplicity does not mean to have a very reduced interface, but a logical one, which provides small steps to perform at one time. Therefore, consider the attribute 'shortness and simplicity' in the design. By providing a simple entry, the older adults can focus on the activities, which represent the benefit of the platform. Therefore, facilitate 'initiation and preparation' in order to reduce potential hurdles.
- Find a balance between usability and older adults' computer skills. Hurdles for using the computer are often related to its usability and also to the computer skills of older adults. It is important to adapt the ease of the platform to the concrete target group in terms of their skills (i.e. 'balance and diversity'). By using a very simplistic interface, the older adults might not be challenged and/or not feel addressed. Although older adults are often associated with multiple functional limitations (e.g., [4]), this does not apply to every older adult. Instead of treating the users as "being old", the platform needs to be adapted carefully to older users' abilities.

Our evaluation addressed the usability of the online platform, as well as the users' computer skills and especially their experiences while interacting with others on the platform. Furthermore, we assessed selected attributes [1], which were derived from the previous requirements analysis. Unsurprisingly, the results revealed that factors, which are related to functional aspects (e.g., general system usability, efficiency or effectiveness), were appraised more negatively by participants with (very) low self-rated computer skills than by those with (very) high self-rated computer skills. However, the users' experiences regarding curiosity towards the platform, engagement, and the social potential of the platform were not associated with their computer skills. It is crucial to focus on the older users' experiences in order to provide them the benefits, they expect from the platform. Our results showed that older users are open to experience social interactions online, which is promising in terms of future developments of platforms and a virtual inclusion of older adults.

5   Future Work

The next steps in the FamConnector project will be the implementation of two further activities based on the attributes, and their evaluation regarding usability, UX, and the older adults' computer skills. The interplay between age and computer skills has to be investigated in detail regarding the users' experiences when interacting on the platform. The above-mentioned implications will help us to meet older adults' needs best and to focus on their experiences. Besides the benefits of the implications for our own work, we are convinced that they can support other developers addressing older users.

Acknowledgements. This research was enabled by the FamConnector project (funded by AAL JP). Special thanks go to end user organizations (Hilfswerk Salzburg, AT; Kotosalla Foundation, FI; terzStiftung, CH) for the support in conducting the studies.

References

1. Fuchsberger, V., Murer, M., Wilfinger, D., Tscheligi, M.: Attributes of Successful Intergenerational Online Activities. In: Proc. ACE 2011. ACM Press (2011)
2. Wang, F., Burton, J.K.: A Solution for Older Adults' Learning of Computer Skills: The Computer Game-Based Learning Approach. Journal of Research in Education 21(2), 1–9 (2010)
3. Zaphiris, P., Kurniawan, S., Ghiawadwala, M.: A systematic approach to the development of research-based web design guidelines for older people. Univ. Access in the Information Society 6(1), 59–75 (2007)
4. Brajnik, G., Yesilada, Y., Harper, S.: Web accessibility guideline aggregation for older users and its validation. Univ. Access in the Information Society, 1–21 (2011)
5. Väänänen-Vainio-Mattila, K., Wäljas, M., Ojala, J., Segerstahl, K.: Identifying Drivers and Hindrances of Social User Experience in Web Services. In: Proc. CHI 2010, pp. 2499–2502 (2010)
6. O'Brien, H.L., Toms, E.G.: The Development and Evaluation of a Survey to Measure User Engagement. Journal of the American Society for Information Science and Technology 61(1), 50–69 (2010)
7. Van Bel, D.T., Ijsselsteijn, W.A., De Kort, Y.A.: Interpersonal Connectedness: Conceptualization and directions for a measurement instrument. In: Proc. CHI 2008, pp. 3129–3134 (2008)
8. Biocca, F., Harms, C.: Defining and measuring social presence: Contribution to the Networked Minds Theory and Measure. In: Proc. of PRESENCE (2002)
9. Moser, C., Fuchsberger, V., Neureiter, K., Sellner, W., Tscheligi, M.: Older adults' Social Presence supported by ICTs: Investigating User Requirements for Social Presence. In: Proc. 2011 IEEE International on Privacy, Security, Risk and Trust Conf., USA (2011)
10. Csikszentmihalyi, M.: Flow: The psychology of optimal experience (1991)
11. Brooke, J.: SUS: A quick and dirty usability scale. In: Jordan, P.W., Thomas, B., Weerdmeester, B.A., McClelland, A.L. (eds.) Usability Evaluation in Industry. Taylor and Francis, London (1996)
12. Tullis, T., Albert, B.: Measuring the user experience: collecting, analyzing and presenting usability metrics. Morgan Kaufmann, Burlington (2008)

kommTUi:
Designing Communication for Elderly

Wolfgang Spreicer[1], Lisa Ehrenstrasser[2], and Hilda Tellioğlu[1]

[1] Vienna University of Technology
{wolfgang.spreicer,hilda.tellioglu}@tuwien.ac.at
[2] inklusiv Design and Research
design@lisaehren.net

Abstract. Getting older does not mean being merely excluded from digital worlds. Elderly can at least use the current technology to communicate with their friends and family members without toiling, on contrary with joy and easiness. We know this is not true yet. With our research project *kommTUi* we do our part to get closer to this goal. In this paper we present our achievement so far. One of the outcomes is our approach to better design usable and user-sensitive interaction for elderly. We further show how four design workshops, carried out in two years, and tangible user interfaces we developed so far can generate and support playful environments with elderly. We finish our paper with the presentation of the final model of the new devices we are currently developing in our project.

Keywords: User centered design, technology for elderly, participatory design workshops, tangible user interface, interaction design.

1 Introduction

Two of the main reasons why elderly have problems to accept and use current ICT is the usability of the systems and their accessibility. To solve usability barriers user centred approach introduced to design [1]. This involves an early focus on users by empirically capturing users' needs, requirements, and performance, as well as on an iterative and participatory design [2] [3] [4]. The idea is to incorporate user requirements, goals, tasks, and experiences into the design process. Accessibility, on the other hand, is related to the development of HCI. After finishing the first wave of this development in system design which was large-scaled, rule-based, and pre-planned, the focus was on single individuals with different conditions [5]. Even having established pervasive technologies, augmented reality, small interfaces, or tangible interfaces around us, we still do not understand how these technologies change the nature of human-computer interaction [6]. Approaches like user-centred and participatory design help studying and even designing for single individuals – especially with special requirements like elderly – to connect them with others. So, it is about the combination of technology and process design supported by sophisticated approaches. We need grounded design

K. Miesenberger et al. (Eds.): ICCHP 2012, Part I, LNCS 7382, pp. 705–708, 2012.

decisions and ways for involving users from the beginning of the design process. In *kommTUi*, we applied exactly this approach what we present in this paper.

2   Project *kommTUi*

The focus in *kommTUi* is on design workshops to develop an intuitive communication tool for elderly. We conducted an evolutionary design process with participatory workshops, qualitative interviews, and multimodal [7] observation and analysis (Fig. 1).

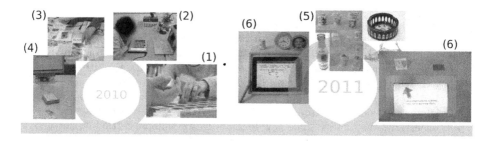

Fig. 1. The timeline of the evolutionary design process in *kommTUi*

In our multimodal workshop [8] series in 2010, we studied basic communication habits of participants and experimented with basic RFID interaction [9]. Our focus was on (Fig. 1): Playful interaction and communication via the popular game "Connect Four": one game equipped with a wooden board triggering multi sensory interactions when played blindfolded (1), one (electronic) game experimenting with playing and communicating remotely supported by a video and audio channel (2); qualitative interviews with each participant using physical artifacts (e.g., photos, personal items, cuddly toys, newspaper clippings, etc.) to unfold the individual communication network and habits (3); experiments with RFID interactions using a technology probe (4): Screen content could be changed by placing tokens on a specially marked device, supported by multi-sensoric feedback. Two use cases have been realized, one feeding a cat and the other making tea.

Based on the results from 2010, we defined the content and probes for the workshops in 2011. This time we focused on tangible interaction with communication devices, i.e., on the design of tokens, the use of personal artifacts as interaction triggers, and on the design of mock-ups. The hands-on set up included the following components: Collaborative design of pre-produced generic tokens (different for calling, sending photos, and sending notes) created by using various design materials and moderated by the research team (5); further definition of the idea of personalized tokens trying to use personal relations to artifacts with a special meaning [10]; each participant was invited to bring personal items to the workshop; these items were photographed and equipped with RFID tags for immediate use as personal tokens during the workshop (5); user interaction with a technology probe (Fig. 2) by triggering events through the previously designed generic tokens and the personal tokens (6); qualitative interviews with each participant during this interaction.

Fig. 2. The technical probe used in the 2011 workshop series

The technical probe presents a communication device based on tangible interactions. On the top of the screen there are two areas on which the users can place their tokens. Each area is equipped with an RFID reader, hidden beneath the wooden case. The left area provides a slot, shaped like the bottom of the generic tokens. The affordance of these tokens inform users where and how to position the token on the probe. With the generic tokens, the user can switch between different functionalities like sending a text note or picture, or starting a Skype call. The personal tokens are placed on the right area, marked with a colored rectangle. Due to differences in shape and size of the personal tokens used in our workshops, we decided to reduce the design of this area to a simple colored marking. The personal tokens both determine the recipient and start the communication. Token interactions are followed by visual and acoustic feedback. Throughout all workshops we had very positive reaction to the interaction with this technical probe. Especially the usage of the generic tokens proved to work without problems.

3   Conclusion

Besides the positive feedback of the users in our workshops, for many participants it is very important to keep the number of electronic devices in their households as small as possible. That is why, we in a next step translate the tangible functionality of the technical probe into a smaller device (Fig. 3), which can be connected to a standard PC or notebook. Additionally, the increasing availability of Near Field Communication technology can be used to interact with personalized tokens. Telephone numbers can be stored in personal objects equipped with RFID tags and than be accessed through reading the tag with the phone (e.g., the cup in Fig. 3). This way we link the *kommTUi* technology with devices that are already present in many households and increase accessibility of ICT for elderly, by using programs or functionalities like web browser, Skype calls, etc. through tangible objects.

Fig. 3. The final model of the new devices in development [11] in *kommTUi*

References

1. Norman, D.A., Draper, S.W.: User Centered System Design; New Perspectives on Human-Computer Interaction. L. Erlbaum Associates Inc., Hillsdale (1986)
2. Gould, J.D., Lewis, C.: Designing for usability: Key principles and what designers think. Communications of the ACM 28, 300–311 (1985)
3. Nielsen, J.: Usability Engineering. Academic Press, Cambridge (1993)
4. Czaja, S.J.: The impact of aging on access to technology. ACM SIGACCESS Accessibility and Computing 83, 7–11 (2005)
5. Hedvall, P.O.: Towards the Era of Mixed Reality: Accessibility Meets Three Waves of HCI. In: Holzinger, A., Miesenberger, K. (eds.) USAB 2009. LNCS, vol. 5889, pp. 264–278. Springer, Heidelberg (2009)
6. Bødker, S.: When second wave HCI meets third wave challenges. In: Proceedings of the 4th Nordic Conference on Human-Computer Interaction: Changing Roles, pp. 1–8. ACM, NY (2006)
7. Ehrenstrasser, L.: Designing Materiality - Unpacking design and development of tangible interfaces. PhD thesis, Vienna University of Technology (in progress)
8. Ehrenstrasser, L., Tellioğlu, H., Spreicer, W.: Multimodal design process: Designing richer interactions for users (submitted)
9. Spreicer, W.: Research Report kommTUi 2010. Technical Report 15, Forschungsarbeiten des Arbeitsbereichs Multidisciplinary Design am Institut für Gestaltungs- und Wirkungsforschung der TU Wien, Vienna (March 2011) ISSN 1021-7363
10. Ehrenstrasser, L., Spreicer, W.: Tokens: Generic or Personal? Basic design decisions for tangible objects. In: Eibl, M., Ritter, M. (eds.) Workshop-Proceedings Mensch & Computer 2011, pp. 25–28. Universitätsverlag Chemnitz, Chemnitz (2011)
11. Spreicer, W.: kommTUi – Object-based, Interactive Communication to Support Social Exchange of Older People. PhD thesis, Vienna University of Technology (in progress)

Reducing the Entry Threshold of AAL Systems: Preliminary Results from *Casa Vecchia*

Gerhard Leitner[1], Anton Josef Fercher[1], Alexander Felfernig[2], and Martin Hitz[1]

[1] Institute of Informatics-Systems
Alpen-Adria Universität Klagenfurt
Universitätsstrasse 65-67, 9020 Klagenfurt, Austria
{gerhard.leitner,antonjosef.fercher,martin.hitz}@aau.at
[2] Institute for Software Technology
Graz University of Technology
Inffeldgasse 16B, 8020 Graz, Austria
alexander.felfernig@ist.tugraz.ac.at

Abstract. Ambient assisted living holds promising solutions to tackle the problems of an overaging society by providing various smart home as well as computing and internet technologies that support independent living of elderly people. However, the acceptance of these technologies by the group of elderly constitutes a crucial precondition for the success of AAL. The paper presents early results from the project Casa Vecchia which explores the feasibility of AAL within a longitudinal field study with 20 participating households. Thereby observed barriers hindering the acceptance of technologies applied in the project are discussed as well as possible solutions to reduce the entry threshold to assistive technology.

Keywords: Ambient Assisted Living, Technology Acceptance, Ethnographic Fieldstudy.

1 Introduction

The majority of studies aimed at identifying the potential drivers and barriers of ambient assisted living (AAL) show that an essential part of the population is reluctant to the usage of technology, especially in the group of elderly, cf. [5,10,18]. Considering the fast approaching problems of the demographic change [16], such as the shortage of qualified personnel or insufficient capacity in nursing institutions, people avoiding technology are in danger of limiting their personal independence and wellbeing. Therefore ways have to be found to convince especially elderly of the benefits of assistive technology. The motivation to address this problem is related to the starting phase of the project Casa Vecchia [4]. For a longitudinal field study, the project is based on, elderly willing to participate for the period of 36 months were addressed. As a benefit the participants are given the possibility to test and evaluate assistive technology without financial investment or further obligations combined with comprehensive support by the project team. Various calls for participation were launched, but although the group of

K. Miesenberger et al. (Eds.): ICCHP 2012, Part I, LNCS 7382, pp. 709–715, 2012.
© Springer-Verlag Berlin Heidelberg 2012

Carinthian elderly (over 65 years) constitutes a population of around 50.000 and channels with a high penetration into the target group where used (e.g. two of the major daily newspapers and a regional radio station), only around one one-thousandth could be motivated to get in touch with Casa Vecchia. Although the reasons are of course manifold, some kind of technosis turned out to be of major importance. People basically interested in the project were not willing to participate anymore when informed that a system supporting aging in place has to be based on computing and Internet technology. Many of them expressed that they would not want to grapple with complicated technology in their retirement. This insight led to the question how technology could be designed to overcome resistance and usage avoidance. After giving a short overview on relevant related work, the subsequent sections describe the basic approaches followed and present some preliminary results or lessons learned, respectively. The paper concludes with an outlook on enhancements of the system either already in development or planned to be implemented in the near future.

2   Related Work

There is a huge amount of research works in the area of ambient assisted living which deserve acknowledgement and are building the basis of the Casa Vecchia project. The focus of the project is to deploy a customized system into more or less arbitrary homes based on the achievements gained by reseachers all over the world. The results the project is build upon range from general works addressing the technological basis of smart homes in general, for an overview see [6], and basic AAL technology in particular, c.f. [1,17]. An overview on related projects the results of which constitute another important pillar for Casa Vecchia is given by [12,2]. Besides the considerations of general aspects, a specific focus is put on interaction aspects [7,15], psychological factors influencing the use of technology [8] and on the deployability and customizability of our basic technology which represents a typical commercial of the shelf (COTS) system.

3   Method

The central goal of Casa Vecchia is to evaluate the deployability of ambient assisted living in rural regions of Carinthia, Austria. The project is based on a longitudinal field study within which 20 households of elderly are equipped with a state-of-the-art smart home system supporting aging in place. The basic functionalities of the system are the provision of health related security and the enhancement of living comfort, functions that are typical for AAL applications [14]. Various approaches were used to reduce the entry threshold to assistive technology as well as to enhance the usability and user experience of the system installed. The system has two major components, a basic radio-based smart home system, similar to other COTS systems available (e.g. meeting the X10 standard) and an embedded PC (as shown in Figure 1) running the Casa Vecchia platform and providing the specific AAL functionality required.

The major insights that could be gained in the project so far and have to be considered in the development of future AAL systems are enumerated as follows:

− *An approach of stepwise installation of components should be followed*

To overcome technosis it does not make sense to overwhelm people with devices. In Casa Vecchia, we have participants who agreed in the necessity of being supported, however, expressed different concerns. For example, one participant mentioned her sensibility to radio waves. Another participant was concerned about installation effort, removability of components and maintenance costs. In both cases only a minimal set of components was installed, and the persons could evaluate the system on the criteria they expressed as being important. Finally, both participants agreed in staying in the project and additional components were installed, in some other cases components were removed again or exchanged by others better fulfilling a certain need.

− *Basic AAL functionality must work autonomously and unobtrusively*

Another concern frequently expressed was the fear of interacting with computing technology because of the probability to go wrong. Our approach was therefore to demonstrate (to those who finally participated) the benefits of assistive technology without the need for active interaction. This was achieved by using a system that can be smoothly integrated even into old building and which is working partly autonomously [3]. Sensors and actuators of the system are connected to devices present in the household without the need to change their original usage. For example, the kitchen stove was equipped with a security function that disconnects it automatically from power when a connected smoke detector is activated. Other sensors such as motion detectors, door contacts or light switches (hidden and connected to existing switches) were used to track activity, again with no need for the person to change his or her habits.

− *Active usage of the system should be facilitated by using alternative interaction concepts*

When the elderly is convinced that the basic technology is useful, interfaces are provided which support and facilitate active interaction. Besides supporting complex functionality on the central unit, the system also provides the possibility to access simple functions such as deactivating the kitchen stove and other potentially dangerous devices when leaving home by simply pressing a wall mount switch, typically placed at the main door (see Fig. 2). The approach followed when designing the more complex functionality on the central unit is focused on overcoming of problems typically occurring in the usage of conventional GUI systems. For example, to be able to write or receive an e-mail with such systems, a certain level of knowledge about the operating system, client applications, network technology etc. has to be acquired. The Casa Vecchia system uses an approach where the components not directly related to the task (such as features of the operating system) are hidden and functions related to the task at hand are emphasized as part of a symbolic metaphor. The basic concept in use is informative art [9] (see Fig. 1).

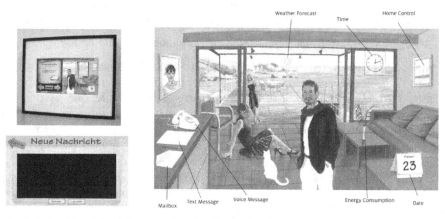

Fig. 1. The Casa Vecchia central unit. Symbolic elements such as a calendar widget on the table, a weather service outside the window or an e-mail client (paper, pencil and envelope) on a side board represent the available functions.

– *The system is adaptable to the needs of the participants to motivate further usage*

With the possibility to test the system on a longitudinal basis, people can develop a better understanding of how the basic technology works, which additional needs can probably be fulfilled and which cannot be supported. It is hoped that the participants develop their own ideas of how to further use the system or how the system could support them in a better way.

– *Positive personal experiences support a positive word of mouth*

Finally, the intention of making available the system for a long period of time in the familiar environment was to motivate people to show it to family and friends,

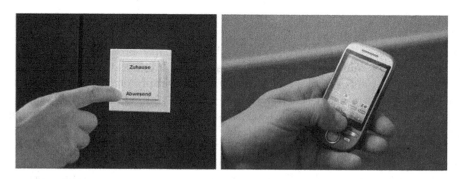

Fig. 2. Additional devices of the Casa Vecchia system. The wall switch on the left is used for simply deactivating critical devices (e.g. stove) when leaving the home. The smartphone for the relative on the right is showing the actual status of the observed elderly.

talk about the drivers and barriers they experience and in this way contribute to reducing technology related fears in their peer group. For example, the information collected by sensors and provided to a person outside the home of the elderly such as a relative or a close friend can support the elderly's perceived security as well as the *peace of mind* of relatives [13], as shown in Figure 2. To peers, representatives of their own demographic group should be more trustworthy than people advertising smart technology such as representatives of health organizations, technicians or researchers.

4   Results

Casa Vecchia has been in operation for about 1,5 years and promising results could be achieved. The approach of smooth integration into existing infrastructure turned out to be successful. With some adaptions we could customize the system to almost every living environment we came across, ranging from a more than two hundred years old farm house to a modern, state-of-the-art low-energy house, inhabited by either single persons or couples. All participants liked the approach of technology that integrates in their environments, giving them additional benefits without the need of changing their habits, not forcing them to actively use devices they do not want to or to carry devices with them. However, they were critical regarding the data transmitted to the outside world (to dedicated relatives and friends). By becoming familiar with the system the interest of using it more intensively was raised. Because of the possibility to evaluate the system in the participants own home it was quite easy to identify additional areas of application. For example, participants wanted the system to inform them about burning lights in the cellar, if someone is at the front door (using a video camera), if a water reservoir is in danger of running out of water etc. Even sceptics were motivated to get more involved, for example, they informed the team when the weather service showed some translation errors or the calendar widget showed a wrong date. A lot of discussions with family and friends were reported by the participants. Some people not involved in the project were concerned about the fact of being sort of surveilled, however, the majority agreed in the usefulness of AAL.

5   Future Work

Based on the positive results achieved so far, the following enhancements of the Casa Vecchia platform are work in progress or planned in the future. On the level of autonomous functionality, the status information provided to the relative is currently computed with default threshold levels corresponding to the colors displayed on the smartphone (e.g. change from green to yellow after one hour). In the enhanced version we are using dynamic thresholds taking into account historical data of the individual household, seasonal deviations, differences between weekdays etc., to enhance the precision. Regarding the interaction recommender technologies are applied to ease the usage of interfaces, especially if they consist of complex interaction sequences. Calculating the transition probability of individual steps in a sequence could support the abbreviation of the sequence. Finally, the concept of informative art also turned out to be useful and the plan is to enhance it with features that allow for keeping the metaphorical approach. For example an alternative method for surveying the participants of Casa Vecchia is developed. This will be based on symbolic elements such as icons or pictures on the basis of which the users should express their current mood and opinion regarding the system. This will be used instead of answering likert scale based questionnaires.

Acknowledgements. We thank the reviewers for their valuable remarks. The Casa Vecchia project is funded by the Austrian Research Promotion Agency within the AAL program benefit (Project.Nr. 825889).

References

1. BMBF/VDE Innovationspartnerschaft, AAL (Hrsg.): Interoperabilität von AAL-Systemkomponenten. Teil 1: Stand der Technik. VDE Verlag, Berlin (2010)
2. BMBF/VDE Innovationspartnerschaft AAL (Hrsg.): Ambient Assisted Living (AAL), Komponenten, Projekte, Services. Eine Bestandsaufnahme. VDE Verlag, Berlin (2011)
3. Das, S.K., Cook, D.J., Bhattacharya, A., Heierman, E.O., Lin, T.Y.: The role of prediction algorithm in the MavHome smart home architecture. IEEE Wireless Commun. 9(6), 77–84 (2002)
4. The Casa Vecchia Project, http://www.casavecchia.at (last access April 20, 2012)
5. Czaja, S.J., Charness, N., Fisk, A.D., Hertzog, C., Nair, S.N., Rogers, W.A., Sharit, J.: Factors predicting the use of technology: Findings from the Center for Research and Education on Aging and Technology Enhancement (CREATE). Psychology and Aging 21, 333–352 (2006)
6. Chan, M., Esteve, D., Escriba, E., Campo, E.: A review of smart homes - Present state and future challenges. Computer Methods and Programs in Biomedicine 91(1), 55–81 (2008)
7. Coughlin, J.F., D'Ambrosio, L.A., Reimer, B., Pratt, M.R.: Older adult perceptions of smart home technologies: Implications for research, policy and market innovations in healthcare. In: IEEE Proceedings of the Engineering in Medicine and Biology Annual Conference, Lyon, France (2007)
8. Dewsbery, G.: The Social and Psychological Aspects of Smart Home Technology within the Care Sector, http://bscw.cs.ncl.ac.uk/pub/bscw.cgi/d55710/Dewsbury-TheSocialandPyschologicalAspectsofSmartHomeTechnology//WithintheCareSector.pdf (last access April 20, 2012)
9. Ferscha, A.: A Matter of Taste. In: Schiele, B., Dey, A.K., Gellersen, H., de Ruyter, B., Tscheligi, M., Wichert, R., Aarts, E., Buchmann, A. (eds.) AmI 2007. LNCS, vol. 4794, pp. 287–304. Springer, Heidelberg (2007)
10. Hernández-Encuentra, E.H., Pousada, M., Gomez-Zuniga, B.: ICT and older people: Beyond usability. Educational Gerontology 35(3), 226–245 (2009)

11. O'Grady, M.J., Muldoon, C., Dragone, M., Tynan, R., O'Hare, G.M.P.: Towards evolutionary ambient assisted living systems. J. Ambient Intelligence and Humanized Computing, 15–29 (2010)
12. Meyer, S., Schulze, E.: Smart Home für ältere Menschen. Handbuch für die Praxis, Stuttgart (2008)
13. Mynatt, E., Rowan, J., Jacobs, A., Craighill, S.: Digital Family Portraits: Supporting Peace of Mind for Extended Family Members. In: Proc. of CHI 2001, pp. 333–340. ACM Press (2001)
14. Kleinberger, T., Becker, M., Ras, E., Holzinger, A., Müller, P.: Ambient Intelligence in Assisted Living: Enable Elderly People to Handle Future Interfaces. In: Stephanidis, C. (ed.) UAHCI 2007, Part II. LNCS, vol. 4555, pp. 103–112. Springer, Heidelberg (2007)
15. Saizmaa, T., Kim, H.C.: A Holistic Understanding of HCI Perspectives on Smart Home. In: Proceedings of the Fourth International Conference on Networked Computing and Advanced Information Management, vol. 2, pp. 59–65 (2008)
16. Steg, H., Strese, H., Loroff, C., Hull, J., Schmidt, S.: Europe is Facing a Demographic Challenge, Ambient assisted Living offers Solutions (2006), http://www.aal-europe.eu/Published/FinalVersion.pdf
17. Sun, H., Florio, V.D., Gui, N., Blondia, C.: Promises and Challenges of Ambient Assisted Living Systems. In: Proceedings of ITNG, pp. 1201–1207 (2009)
18. Ziefle, M., Röcker, C.: Acceptance of Pervasive Healthcare Systems: A comparison of different implementation concepts. In: 4th ICST Conf. on Pervasive Computing Technologies for Healthcare (UCD-PH 2010), pp. 1–6 (2010)

Author Index

Abou-Zahra, Shadi   I-323, I-386
Aginako, Naiara   I-351
Agnoletto, Andrea   I-215
Alabbadi, Reham   II-517
Alajarmeh, Nancy   I-158
Al-Khalifa, Atheer S.   II-560
Al-Khalifa, Hend S.   II-560
Almer, Stefan   II-83
Aloise, Fabio   II-180
Alonso, Kevin   I-351
Anastasiou, Dimitra   II-392
Andersson, Anders-Petter   I-254
Andhavarapu, Abhishek   II-75
Andrášová, Marianna   II-419
Andrich, Renzo   I-207, I-215, I-634
Aoki, Kyota   I-507
Aomatsu, Toshiaki   I-116
Arai, Hiroshi   I-492
Arató, András   II-311, II-599
Archambault, Dominique   I-166, I-425
Ariyasu, Ryohei   II-184
Arredondo Waldmeyer, María Teresa   II-269
Artoni, Silvia   II-137
Aupetit, Sébastien   I-355, I-363

Bäck, Karl   II-361
Baeza-Yates, Ricardo   I-404
Baljko, Melanie   II-315
Ball, Simon   I-33
Bártek, Luděk   I-543
Bartels, Matthias   I-251
Battistelli, Matteo   I-388
Batusic, Mario   I-196
Belotti, Matteo   II-615
Bernareggi, Cristian   II-615
Bernier, Alex   I-500
Bianchetti, Roberto   I-595
Bischof, Werner   II-91
Biswas, Pradipta   I-284
Bittner, Jiří   I-315
Blanchfield, Peter   II-517
Boissière, Philippe   II-451
Bordegoni, Monica   I-227

Borges, José Antonio   I-100
Bott, Stefan   I-527
Boulares, Mehrez   II-52
Boulay, Denis   I-337
Bouzid, Yosra   II-229
Bowden, Richard   II-205
Braffort, Annelies   II-205
Breiter, Yonatan   I-191
Brock, Anke   II-544
Bruckner, Ronald   II-338
Bühler, Christian   II-369
Bujňák, Juraj   II-419
Bumbalek, Zdenek   II-113
Burger, Dominique   I-337, I-500
Burmester, Michael   I-634
Bußwald, Petra   II-225
Buzzi, Maria Claudia   II-137
Buzzi, Marina   II-137

Cabrera, Rafael   I-436
Cabrera-Umpiérrez, María Fernanda   II-269
Camarena, Javier   II-385
Cantón, Paloma   I-65
Capezuti, Elizabeth   I-625
Cappelen, Birgitta   I-254
Carriço, Luís   I-343, I-396
Chen, Cheng-Chien   II-287
Chen, Ming-Chung   II-287, II-483
Chen, Shao-Wun   II-287
Chen, Shizhi   I-1
Chiti, Sarah   II-607
Choi, Saerom   II-275
Choi, Yoonjung   II-48
Christensen, Courtney   I-124
Christensen, Lars Ballieu   I-36, I-77
Chung, Jio   II-117
Chung, Minhwa   II-117
Collet, Christophe   II-205
Connor, Joshue O.   I-288
Constantinescu, Angela   II-566, II-644
Costa, Daniel   I-343
Costa, Ursula   II-180
Coughlan, James M.   II-25, II-41

Covarrubias, Mario   I-227
Crombie, David   I-325
Crowle, Cathryn   II-353
Cugini, Umberto   I-227
Czyzewski, Andrzej   II-133

Daems, Jo   I-479
Dale, Oystein   I-573, II-439
Dangelmaier, Manfred   I-284
Darvishy, Alireza   I-621
Darzentas, Jenny S.   I-325
Debeljak, Mojca   II-153
Debevc, Matjaž   II-213
De Boeck, Joan   I-479
Dekelver, Jan   I-479
de los Ríos Pérez, Silvia   II-269
Derbring, Sandra   II-261, II-303
Derleth, Peter   I-463
Diaz-Orueta, Unai   II-164
Díez, Ibai   II-385, II-623
Dimou, Athanasia-Lida   II-237
Doi, Yasunori   II-596
Dömők, Tamás   I-673
Dornhofer, Markus   II-91
Draffan, E.A.   I-51
Dramas, Florian   II-636
Drivenes, Therese   I-573
Drümmer, Olaf   I-585, I-587, I-610
Duarte, Carlos   I-343
Durmaz Incel, Ozlem   I-689
Dziamski, Daniel   I-471

Ebner, Martin   II-83
Efthimiou, Eleni   II-205, II-237
Eguchi, Kiyoshi   II-184
Eguíluz, Andoni   I-523
Ehrenstrasser, Lisa   I-705
Eibegger, Mandana   I-417
El Ghoul, Oussama   II-229
Engelen, Jan   I-484
Erle, Markus   I-585, I-595, I-617
Ersoy, Cem   I-689
Ertl, Thomas   II-529
Esteban, A. Mariano   I-436
Euler, Craig   II-172

Facal, David   I-634
Fagel, Sascha   I-650
Farcy, René   II-29
Faux, Fern   I-73

Featherstone, Lisa   I-33, I-43, I-73
Feilner, Manuela   I-463
Fajardo-Flores, Silvia   I-166
Felfernig, Alexander   I-709
Fels, Deborah I.   I-451
Felzer, Torsten   II-431
Fenili, Claudia   II-137
Fennell, Antoinette   I-288
Fercher, Anton Josef   I-709
Fernandes, Nádia   I-343, I-396
Fessl, Beate   II-338
Fikejs, Jan   II-200
Finch, David   I-73
Fotinea, Stavroula-Evita   II-205, II-237
Fourney, David   I-535
Frees, Bert   I-484
Freire, Luciana Maria Depieri Branco   I-557
Frießem, Martina   I-251
Fuchs, Elisabeth   I-378
Fuchsberger, Verena   I-697
Fuglerud, Kristin Skeide   I-565
Fujiyoshi, Akio   I-116
Fujiyoshi, Mamoru   I-116, II-505
Fukuda, Ryoji   I-182
Fülber, Heleno   II-459

Galajdová, Alena   II-419
Gansinger, Luzia   II-245
Gappa, Henrike   II-415
García, Alejandro   I-311
Garcia, Alvaro   I-634
García, Pablo   I-436
García-Soler, Alvaro   II-164
Gardner, John   I-124
Gatti, Elia   I-227
Gira, Matthias   I-650
Glauert, John   II-205
Gökmen, Haluk   I-288
Gómez, Isabel   II-331
Gómez, Isabel M.   I-436
González, Ángel L.   I-65
Gonzúrová, Wanda   I-138
Goodwin, Morten   I-417
Gower, Valerio   I-207, I-215
Grill, Thomas   I-642
Grützmacher, Felix   I-459
Guenaga, Mari Luz   I-523
Guger, Christoph   II-180
Guillet, Vivien   I-150

Gunnarsson, Birkir Rúnar   I-565
Gůra, Tomáš   I-18
Guzman, Kevin   II-331
Györkös, Attila   II-529

Hackbarth, Kai   I-650
Hackl, Jürgen   II-225
Häkkinen, Markku   II-552
Hamidi, Foad   II-315
Hanke, Thomas   II-205
Harakawa, Tetsumi   II-672
Hasegawa, Sadao   II-672
Hasuike, Michiko   II-99
Heimonen, Tomi   II-279
Helms, Niels Henrik   I-278
Henry, Shawn Lawton   I-602
Hernáez, Inmaculada   II-385
Hernández, José Alberto   I-311
Herstad, Jo   I-262
Heumader, Peter   I-196, II-157
Hitz, Martin   I-709
Hladík, Petr   I-18
Höckner, Klaus   II-536
Hofer, Samuel   I-595, I-617
Holone, Harald   I-262, I-554, II-1
Holzinger, Andreas   II-213
Hong, Ki-Hyung   II-48, II-275
Hou, Chen-Tang   I-204
Hrabák, Pavel   I-138
Hutter, Hans-Peter   I-621
Hwang, Yumi   II-117

Ikegami, Yuji   II-505
Imai, Atsushi   I-681
Indurkhya, Bipin   II-323
Ioannidis, Georgios   II-59
Iriondo, Pedro   II-623
Isoda, Kyoko   II-99

Jääskeläinen, Kirsi   I-223
Janker, Rebecca   II-338
Jbali, Maher   II-229
Jemni, Mohamed   II-52, II-192, II-229
John, Christopher   II-253
Jouffrais, Christophe   II-521, II-544,
    II-636
Juhasz, Zoltan   II-311, II-599

Kaklanis, Nikolaos   I-295
Kamibayashi, Kiyotaka   II-184
Kammoun, Slim   II-521

Kaneko, Takeshi   II-505
Kankaanranta, Marja   II-552
Karshmer, Arthur   I-191
Karshmer, Judith   I-191
Kauppinen, Sami   II-279
Kawabe, Hiroyuki   I-492
Kawaguchi, Hironori   I-142
Kawamoto, Hiroaki   II-184
Kawano, Sumihiro   II-99
Keegan, Sean J.   I-77
Kencl, Lukas   II-113
Kepski, Michal   II-407
Keskinen, Tuuli   II-279
Khan, Atif   II-588
Khoo, Wai L.   II-573, II-588
Kim, Hoirin   II-447
Kim, Hong Kook   II-475
Kim, Jin   II-117
Kim, Myung Jong   II-447
Kim, Sunhee   II-117
Kipke, Siegfried   II-651
Kirisci, Pierre   I-288
Knudsen, Lars Emil   II-1
Ko, Chien-Chuan   II-287
Kobayashi, Makoto   I-10, II-221
Kobayashi, Masayuki   II-99
Koch, Volker   II-644
Köhlmann, Wiebke   I-84
Kolbitsch, Josef   II-83
Komori, Tomoyasu   I-681
Kong, Byunggoo   II-117
Kosec, Primož   II-213
Kouroupetroglou, Georgios   I-581
Kožuh, Ines   II-213
Krajnc, Elmar   II-91
Kubota, Shigeki   II-184
Kudo, Hiroaki   II-596
Kulyukin, Vladimir   II-75
Kupryjanow, Adam   II-133
Kushalnagar, Poorna   I-59, I-92
Kushalnagar, Raja S.   I-59, I-92
Kutiyanawala, Aliasgar   II-75
Kwiatkowska, Gosia   II-361
Kwolek, Bogdan   II-407

Lapáček, Ondřej   I-543
Lassnig, Markus   II-377
László, Erika   I-673
Lawler, Stuart   I-243
Lawo, Michael   I-288

Layman, Frances   II-353
Leahy, Denise   I-243, I-666
Lechner, Alexander   II-180
Lee, Heeyeon   II-275
Lee, Seung-Yeun   II-117
Leemann, Thomas   I-621
Lefebvre-Albaret, François   II-205
Leitner, Gerhard   I-709
Leitner, Verena   II-338
Lepicard, Guillaume   I-658
Leporini, Barbara   II-137, II-607
Liimatainen, Jukka   II-552
Lin, C.T.   II-172
Loitsch, Claudia   II-509
Lopez, Juan   II-588
Lozano, Héctor   II-385
Lozano, Javier   I-351
Lundälv, Mats   II-261, II-303
Lyhne, Thomas   I-215

Macé, Marc J.-M.   II-521, II-636
Machuca Bautista, Berenice   II-490
MacKenzie, I. Scott   II-423, II-431
Maierhofer, Stefan   II-497
Malik, Szabolcs   II-599
Malý, Ivo   I-315
Mamojka, Branislav   II-659
Manduchi, Roberto   II-9
Manshad, Muhanad S.   II-664
Manshad, Shakir J.   II-664
Mansutti, Alessandro   I-227
Maragos, Petros   II-205
Marano, Daniele   II-536
Mariscal, Gonzalo   I-65
Markus, Norbert   II-311, II-599
Martinez, Manel   II-566
Mascetti, Sergio   II-615
Mascret, Bruno   I-150
Matiouk, Svetlana   I-288
Matsumoto, Tetsuya   II-596
Mayer, Christopher   I-650
McNaught, Alistair   I-43
Medina, Josep   II-180
Mehigan, Tracey J.   II-67
Mekhtarian, Ara   II-172
Mencarini, Simona   II-137
Mereuţă, Alina   I-355, I-363
Merino, Manuel   II-331
Merlin, Bruno   II-459
Miao, Mei   II-59

Miesenberger, Klaus   I-25, I-196, I-325, II-157
Míkovec, Zdeněk   II-467
Mille, Alain   I-150
Minagawa, Hiroki   I-142, II-221
Minatani, Kazunori   I-515, II-630
Mirri, Silvia   I-388
Mittermann, Karin   II-338
Miyoshi, Shigeki   II-99, II-221
Mizumura, Hiroko   II-399
Mocholí, Juan Bautista   I-303
Modzelewski, Markus   I-288
Mohamad, Yehya   I-284, I-288, II-415
Moideen, Febin   II-588
Mojahid, Mustapha   II-451
Molina, Alberto J.   I-436, II-331
Molina, Edgardo   II-33
Montalvá Colomer, Juan Bautista   II-269
Morandell, Martin   I-650
Moser, Christiane   I-697
Moustakas, Konstantinos   I-295
Müller, Karin   I-186
Muratori, Ludovico A.   I-388
Murayama, Shinjiro   I-507
Mussinelli, Cristina   I-550
Mustaquim, Moyen Mohammad   I-428

Nagy, Eszter   I-409
Nagy, Péter   II-295
Nakagawa, Masaki   I-174
Nakata, Yoshio   II-184
Nambo, Hidetaka   I-492
Naranjo, Juan Carlos   I-303
Navarro, Ana María   I-303
Navas, Eva   II-385
Naz, Komal   I-270
Neittaanmäki, Pekka   II-552
Németh, Géza   II-295
Neumüller, Moritz   II-497
Neuschmid, Julia   II-536
Nevala, Nina   I-223
Newman, Russell   I-51
Niederl, Franz   II-225
Nietzio, Annika   I-417, II-369
Nishioka, Tomoyuki   II-221
Nordbrock, Gaby   II-415
Nourry, Olivier   I-337
Nousiainen, Tuula   II-552
Novák, Marek   II-419

Nussbaum, Gerhard   I-443, II-157, II-164

Oberzaucher, Johannes   II-83
Ocepek, Julija   II-153
Ochiai, Naoyuki   II-184
Odya, Piotr   II-133
Ohnishi, Noboru   I-142, II-596
Ohsawa, Akiko   I-116
Ohtsuka, Satoshi   II-672
Oikawa, Yasuhiro   I-681
Ojeda, Juan   I-436
Olaizola, Igor G.   I-351
Oouchi, Susumu   II-505
Opisso, Eloy   II-180
Oriola, Bernard   II-521, II-544
Ortner, Rupert   II-180
Ossmann, Roland   I-425, I-443, II-164
Osswald, Sebastian   I-642
Othman, Achraf   II-192

Padilla Medina, José Alfredo   II-490
Palmer, Frank G.   II-125
Páramo del Castrillo, Miguel   II-269
Park, Ji Hun   II-475
Paz, Alexandre   I-523
Pecyna, Karol   II-164
Peissner, Matthias   I-284
Pelz, Jeffrey B.   I-92
Petridou, Maria   II-517
Petrie, Helen   I-325
Petz, Andrea   I-25, II-377
Petzold, Martin   I-650
Phethean, Chris   I-51
Philipp, Josef   II-225
Picard, Delphine   II-544
Pieper, Michael   I-371
Pigini, Lucia   I-634
Pino, Alexandros   I-581
Pitt, Ian   II-67
Plaza, Malgorzata   I-270
Poláček, Ondřej   II-467
Pons, Christiane   II-338
Ponsard, Christophe   I-471
Pontelli, Enrico   I-158, II-664
Poobrasert, Onintra   II-346
Pouris, Michael   I-451
Prescher, Denise   II-59
Prieto, Guillermo   I-666
Prückl, Robert   II-180

Pullmann, Jaroslav   II-415
Purgathofer, Werner   II-497
Putz, Veronika   II-180
Pyfers, Liesbeth   II-188

Quintian, D. Michael   I-1

Radu, Nicoleta   II-377
Rajaniemi, Juha-Pekka   II-279
Ramdoyal, Ravi   I-471
Rasines, Irati   II-623
Rausch, Michaela   II-338
Ravenscroft, John   II-353
Raynal, Mathieu   II-459
Reichinger, Andreas   II-497
Reichow, Brian   II-105
Reinertsen, Arthur   I-573
Rello, Luz   I-404
Rinderknecht, Stephan   II-431
Rist, Florian   II-497
Ritterbusch, Sebastian   II-644
Rivera, Octavio   I-436
Ro, Tony   II-125
Roggen, Daniel   I-463
Rotovnik, Milan   II-213
Rozis, Roberts   I-215
Ruiz, Carlos   I-65

Sade, Jack   I-270
Saggion, Horacio   I-527
Salomoni, Paola   I-388
Sampath, Harini   II-323
Sánchez, Jesús   I-311
Sánchez, Víctor   I-311
Sánchez Marín, Francisco Javier   II-490
Sankai, Yoshiyuki   II-184
Sasaki, Nobuyuki   II-672
Sawazaki, Haruhiko   I-116
Scharinger, Josef   II-180
Schauerte, Boris   II-566
Scheer, Birgit   II-369
Schettini, Francesca   II-180
Schmitz, Bernhard   II-529
Schrenk, Manfred   II-536
Schulz, Trenton   II-145, II-439
Seidel, Eric L.   II-573
Seiyama, Nobumasa   I-681
Sellner, Wolfgang   I-697
Senette, Caterina   II-137
Seong, Woo Kyeong   II-475

Seto, Shuichi   I-492
Shen, Huiying   II-25, II-41
Shimomura, Yuko   I-492
Shin, Daejin   II-117
Shirasawa, Mayumi   II-99
Sik, Gergely   I-409
Sík Lányi, Cecília   I-409, I-673
Siman, Daniel   II-419
Šimšík, Dušan   II-419
Sivaswamy, Jayanthi   II-323
Skeide Fuglerud, Kristin   II-145
Sklenák, Tomáš   II-200
Skuse, Sebastian   I-51
Slavík, Pavel   I-315
Slimane, Mohamed   I-355, I-363
Snaprud, Mikael   I-417
Sommer, Sascha   I-251
Spiliotopoulos, Dimitris   I-581
Spindler, Martin   II-59
Sporka, Adam J.   II-467
Spreicer, Wolfgang   I-705
Stahl, Christoph   II-392
Stark, Jacqueline   II-338
Stavropoulou, Pepi   I-581
Stevns, Tanja   I-36, I-77
Stiefelhagen, Rainer   II-566
Stiefmeier, Thomas   I-463
Stöger, Bernhard   I-196
Strauss, Christine   I-378
Strobbe, Christophe   I-484
Suchomski, Piotr   II-133
Sugimori, Kimikazu   I-492
Suzuki, Masakazu   I-130
Suzuki, Takuya   I-10
Szűcs, Veronika   I-673

Takagi, Tohru   I-681
Takahashi, Yoshiyuki   II-399
Takeuchi, Yoshinori   I-142, II-596
Takou, Reiko   I-681
Tanaka, Nobuhito   II-596
Tang, Hao   II-581
Tedesco, Robert   II-105
Tellerup, Susanne   I-278
Tellioğlu, Hilda   I-705
Teplický, Peter   II-659
Teshima, Yoshinori   II-505
Tessendorf, Bernd   I-463
Thaller, David   I-443
Thurmair, Gregor   I-215

Tian, Yingli   I-1, I-625, II-17, II-33
Tjøstheim, Ingvar   I-565
Tmar, Zouhour   II-192
Tollefsen, Morten   I-565, I-573
Tomé, Dolores   I-100
Torun, Mustafa   I-689
Tóth, Bálint   II-295
Tröbinger, Thomas   II-361
Tröster, Gerhard   I-463
Truillet, Philippe   II-544
Tschare, Georg   II-225
Tscheligi, Manfred   I-642, I-697
Turunen, Markku   II-279
Tzoannos, Efstratios   I-581
Tzovaras, Dimitrios   I-295

Ulm, Michael   II-91
Umehara, Midori   II-99

Valle-Klann, Markus   I-288
Van Isacker, Karel   I-323
van Kasteren, Tim   I-689
Veigl, Christoph   I-443, II-164
Velasco, Carlos A.   I-284, I-325, II-415
Vella, Frédéric   II-451
Velleman, Eric   I-325
Vigouroux, Nadine   I-658, II-451
Villain, Jean-Pierre   I-337
Vincenti, Sabrina   I-207
Votis, Konstantinos   I-323

Wakatsuki, Daisuke   I-10, I-142
Wald, Mike   I-51, I-108
Wang, Hwa-Pey   II-287
Wang, Po-Jen   II-172
Wang, Shuihua   II-17
Wasserburger, Wolfgang   II-536
Watanabe, Tetsuya   I-174, II-630
Watanabe, Yasunari   II-505
Weber, Gerhard   II-59, II-509
Weber, Michael   II-59
Weiss, Chris   II-164
Weiß, Christoph   I-443
Williams, Benjamin   I-59
Williams, Peter   II-361
Winkelmann, Petra   I-215
Wongteeratana, Alongkorn   II-346
Wu, Chu-Lung   I-204
Wu, Ting-Fang   II-483

Yamaguchi, Katsuhito   I-130
Yamaguchi, Toshimitsu   I-174
Yamawaki, Kanako   II-184
Yamazawa, Kenji   II-505
Yang, Chang-Yeal   II-117

Zagler, Wolfgang   I-329
Zakraoui, Jesia   I-329
Zaman, Tanwir   II-75

Zamfir, Bogdan   II-105
Zegarra, Jesus   II-29
Zelenka, Jan   II-113
Zetterström, Erik   I-235
Zhang, Chenyang   I-625
Zhu, Zhigang   II-33, II-125, II-573,
    II-581, II-588
Zülch, Joachim   I-251
Zupan, Anton   II-153